The 2007 World Book

YEAR BOOK

A REVIEW OF THE EVENTS OF 2006

The Annual
Supplement to
The World Book
Encyclopedia

World Book, Inc.
a Scott Fetzer company
Chicago

www.worldbook.com

World Book, Inc.
233 N. Michigan Ave.
Chicago, IL 60601

ISBN: 978-0-7166-0463-1
ISSN: 0084-1439
Library of Congress Control Number: 62004818

Printed in the United States of America.

Here are your

2007 Year Book Cross-Reference Tabs

For insertion in your WORLD BOOK set

Put these Tabs in the appropriate volumes of your **World Book Encyclopedia** now. Then, when you later look up some topic in **World Book** and find a Tab near the article, you will know that one of your **Year Books** has newer or more detailed information about that topic.

How to use these Tabs

First, remove this page from the **YEAR BOOK**.

Begin with the first Tab, **ARCHITECTURE.** Take the A volume of your **World Book** set and find the **ARCHITECTURE** article in it. Moisten the **ARCHITECTURE** Tab and affix it to that page.

Glue all the other Tabs in the appropriate **World Book** volume.

STAFF

CONTRIBUTORS

Contributors not listed on these pages are members of the editorial staff.

ANDREWS, PETER J., B.A., M.S.; free-lance writer. **[Chemistry]**

BARNHART, BILL, B.A., M.S.T., M.B.A.; financial markets columnist, *Chicago Tribune*. **[Stocks and bonds]**

BARRETT, NORMAN, M.A.; free-lance writer. **[Soccer** Special Report: **The 2006 World Cup; Soccer]**

BECK, STEFAN, B.A.; Associate editor, *The New Criterion* magazine. **[Literature]**

BERGER, ERIC R., B.A, M.A.; science writer, *Houston Chronicle*. **[Houston]**

BOUCHER, GEOFF, B.A.; Staff writer, *Los Angeles Times*. **[Popular music]**

BOYD, JOHN D., B.S.; Economics writer. **[Economics, U.S.; Economics, World; International trade]**

BRADSHER, HENRY S., A.B., B.J.; foreign affairs analyst. **[Asia and Asian country articles]**

BRETT, CARLTON E., B.A., M.S., Ph.D.; Professor of Geology, University of Cincinnati. **[Paleontology]**

CAMPBELL, GEOFFREY A., B.J.; free-lance writer. **[Human rights; U.S. government articles]**

CARDINALE, DIANE P., B.A.; Research Associate, Toy Industry Association, Incorporated. **[Toys and games]**

CASEY, MIKE, B.S., M.A.; Assistant editor, *Kansas City Star*. **[Automobile]**

DEEB, MARIUS K., B.A., Ph.D.; Professor, School of Advanced International Studies, Johns Hopkins University. **[Middle East and Middle Eastern country articles; North African country articles]**

DEEB, MARY-JANE, B.A., Ph.D.; Arab World Area Specialist, Library of Congress. **[Middle East and Middle Eastern country articles; North African country articles]**

DeFRANK, THOMAS M., B.A., M.A.; Washington Bureau Chief, *New York Daily News*. **[Armed forces; Immigration** Special Report: **Immigration Politics 2006]**

DILLON, DAVID, B.A., M.A., Ph.D.; architecture and design editor, *The Dallas Morning News*. **[Architecture** Special Report: **Form Over Function: The Rise of Sculptural Architecture; Architecture]**

ELLIS, GAVIN, former Editor in Chief, *The New Zealand Herald & Weekend Herald*. **[New Zealand]**

ESTERHUYSEN, PIETER, B.A.; political analyst, Africa Institute of South Africa, Pretoria. **[Africa and African country articles]**

FARR, DAVID M. L., D.Phil., LL.D.; Professor Emeritus of History, Carleton University. **[Canada; Canada, Prime Minister of]**

FERRELL, KEITH, free-lance writer. **[Computer; Electronics]**

FISHER, ROBERT W., B.A., M.A.; free-lance writer. **[Bank; Labor and employment]**

FITZGERALD, MARK, B.A.; editor at large, *Editor & Publisher* magazine. **[Magazine; Newspaper]**

FRIEDMAN, EMILY, B.A.; health policy and ethics analyst. **[Health care issues]**

GADOMSKI, FRED, B.S., M.S.; Meteorologist, Pennsylvania State University. **[Global warming; Weather]**

GATTY, ROBERT C., free-lance writer, *Gatty Edits*. **[Food]**

GOLDBERG, BEVERLY, B.A.; Senior editor, American Library Association. **[Library]**

GOLDEN, JONATHAN J., B.A., M.J.Ed.; Chair, History Department at the Gann Academy, New Jewish High School of Greater Boston. **[Judaism]**

GOLDNER, NANCY, B.A.; free-lance dance critic. **[Dance]**

HARAKAS, STANLEY SAMUEL, B.A., B.Th., Th.D.; Archbishop Iakovos Professor (Emeritus) of Orthodox Theology, Holy Cross Greek Orthodox School of Theology. **[Eastern Orthodox Churches]**

HAVERSTOCK, NATHAN A., A.B.; affiliate scholar, Oberlin College. **[Latin America** Special Report: **Latin America Swings Left; Latin America and Latin American country articles]**

HENDERSON, HAROLD, B.A.; staff writer, *Chicago Reader*. **[Chicago]**

HOFFMAN, ANDREW J., B.S., M.S., Ph.D.; Holcim Professor of Enterprise, University of Michigan. **[Environmental pollution]**

JOHANSON, DONALD C., B.S., M.A., Ph.D.; Director and Professor, Institute of Human Origins, Arizona State University. **[Anthropology]**

JOHNSON, CHRISTINA S., B.A., M.S.; free-lance science writer. **[Global warming** Special Report: **The Great Meltdown; Ocean]**

JOHNSON, JULIET, A.B., M.A., Ph.D.; Associate Professor of Political Science, McGill University. **[Russia and other former Soviet republic articles]**

KATES, MICHAEL, B.S.J.; Associate sports editor, *Chicago Tribune*. **[Sports articles]**

KENNEDY, BRIAN, M.A.; free-lance writer. **[Australia; Australia, Prime Minister of; Australian rules football]**

KILGORE, MARGARET, B.A., M.B.A.; free-lance writer, Kilgore and Associates. **[Los Angeles]**

KING, MIKE, reporter, *The (Montreal) Gazette*. **[Montreal]**

KLINTBERG, PATRICIA PEAK, B.A.; Director of Constituent Affairs, Office of Communications, U.S. Department of Agriculture. **[Agriculture]**

KNIGHT, ROBERT, B.A., M.M.; free-lance writer. **[Gerald R. Ford; People in the news]**

4

KOPSTEIN, JEFFREY, B.A., M.A., Ph.D; Professor of Political Science and Director, Centre for European, Russian, and Eurasian Studies, University of Toronto. [Europe and Western European country articles]

KRONHOLZ, JUNE, B.S.J.; staff reporter, *The Wall Street Journal.* [Education]

LAWRENCE, ALBERT, B.A., M.A., M.Ed.; Executive Director, World Chess Hall of Fame. [Chess]

LEWIS, DAVID C., M.D.; Professor of Medicine and Community Health, Brown University. [Drug abuse]

MARCH, ROBERT H., A.B., M.S., Ph.D.; Professor Emeritus of Physics and Liberal Studies, University of Wisconsin at Madison. [Physics]

MARSCHALL, LAURENCE A., B.S., Ph.D.; W.K.T. Sahm Professor of Physics, Gettysburg College. [Astronomy]

MARTY, MARTIN E., Ph.D.; Fairfax M. Cone Distinguished Service Professor Emeritus, University of Chicago. [Protestantism]

MAY, SALLY-RUTH, B.A, M.A.; free-lance art writer. [Art]

McDONALD, ELAINE STUART, B.A.; free-lance public policy writer and editor. [State government]

McWILLIAM, ROHAN, B.A., M.A., D.Phil; Senior Lecturer in History, Anglia Polytechnic University, Cambridge, U.K. [Ireland; Northern Ireland; United Kingdom; United Kingdom, Prime Minister of]

MINER, TODD J., B.S., M.S.; Meteorologist, Pennsylvania State University. [Weather]

MORITZ, OWEN, B.A.; urban affairs editor, *New York Daily News.* [New York City]

MORRING, FRANK, Jr., B.A.; Senior Space Technology editor, *Aviation Week & Space Technology* magazine. [Space exploration]

MORRIS, BERNADINE, B.A., M.A.; free-lance fashion writer. [Fashion]

MOWATT, RAOUL, B.A.; free-lance writer. [Television]

MULLINS, HENRY T., B.S., M.S., Ph.D.; Professor of Geology, Syracuse University. [Geology]

NGUYEN, J. TUYET, M.A.; United Nations correspondent, Deutsche Presse-Agentur. [Population; United Nations]

OGAN, EUGENE, B.A., Ph.D.; Professor Emeritus of Anthropology, University of Minnesota. [Pacific Islands]

PAETH, GREGORY, B.A.; business writer, *The Cincinnati Post.* [Radio]

REINHART, A. KEVIN, B.A., M.A., Ph.D.; Associate Professor of Religious Studies, Dartmouth College. [Islam]

RICCIUTI, EDWARD, B.A.; free-lance writer. [Biology; Conservation; Zoos]

ROBERTS, THOMAS W., Editor, *The National Catholic Reporter.* [Roman Catholic Church]

ROSE, MARK J., B.A., M.A., Ph.D.; Executive editor, *Archaeology* magazine. [Archaeology]

RUBENSTEIN, RICHARD E., B.A., M.A., J.D.; Professor of Conflict Resolution and Public Affairs, George Mason University. [Terrorism]

RUBENSTONE, JEFFREY, B.A.; Editor, *Engineering News-Record* magazine. [Building and construction]

RUSSELL, MARY HARRIS, B.A., M.A, Ph.D.; Professor of English, Indiana University. [Literature for children]

SARNA, JONATHAN D., Ph.D.; Joseph H. & Belle R. Braun Professor of American Jewish History, Brandeis University. [Judaism]

SAVAGE, IAN, B.A., Ph.D.; Associate Professor of Economics and Transportation, Northwestern University. [Aviation; Transportation]

SHAPIRO, HOWARD, B.S.; staff writer and travel columnist, *The Philadelphia Inquirer.* [Philadelphia; Washington, D.C.]

SMUSKIEWICZ, ALFRED J., B.S., M.S.; free-lance writer. [AIDS; City; Crime; Energy supply Special Report: The Promise of Ethanol; Mental health; Nobel Prizes; Prison; Public health; Pulitzer Prizes; Safety]

STEIN, DAVID LEWIS, B.A., M.S.; former urban affairs columnist, *The Toronto Star.* [Toronto]

STOS, WILLIAM, B.A., M.A.; free-lance writer. [Canadian provinces; Canadian territories]

TANNER, JAMES C., B.J.; former news editor—energy, *The Wall Street Journal.* [Energy supply]

TATUM, HENRY K., B.A.; retired Associate editor, *The Dallas Morning News.* [Dallas]

VAN, JON, B.A., M.A.; technology writer, *Chicago Tribune.* [Telecommunications]

von RHEIN, JOHN, B.A.; classical music critic, *Chicago Tribune.* [Classical music]

WILLIAMS, BRIAN, B.A.; free-lance writer. [Cricket]

WILSON, DAVE, B.A.; Producer, Cable News Network. [Internet]

WOLCHIK, SHARON L., B.A., M.A., Ph.D.; Professor of Political Science and International Affairs, George Washington University. [Eastern European country articles]

WUNTCH, PHILIP, B.A.; former film critic, *The Dallas Morning News.* [Motion pictures]

YEZZI, DAVID, B.F.A., M.F.A.; Executive editor, *The New Criterion* magazine. [Poetry; Theater]

CONTENTS

FOCUS ON

PORTRAITS

417 **WORLD BOOK SUPPLEMENT**

Seven new or revised articles are reprinted from the 2007 edition of *The World Book Encyclopedia.*

481 **INDEX**

A 14-page cumulative index covers the contents of the 2005, 2006, and 2007 editions of *The Year Book.*

From the Republican Party's loss of control of the U.S. legislature to Pluto's loss of its status as a planet, 2006 was a year of extraordinary events. On these three pages are stories that the editors picked as some of the most important of the year, along with details on where to find more information about them in this volume.

The Editors

2006

LATIN AMERICA

Voters in several Latin American nations elected new leaders in 2006, continuing a continent-wide shift to the left. See **Bolivia**, page 100; **Brazil**, page 102; **Chile**, page 121; **Ecuador**, page 171; **Haiti**, page 219; **Latin America: A Special Report**, page 256; **Nicaragua**, page 299; **Venezuela**, page 409; **West Indies**, page 414.

MIDTERM ELECTIONS

The Democratic Party takes control of both the House of Representatives and the Senate in midterm elections in November, a triumph that political experts characterize as a display of the public's frustration over the war in Iraq and widespread corruption in the Republican-held Congress. See **Congress of the United States**, page 132; **Democratic Party**, page 160; **Elections**, page 173; **Republican Party**, page 338; **State government**, page 363; **United States, Government of the**, page 394; **United States, President of the**, page 408.

SITUATION IN IRAQ WORSENS

The Iraq Study Group issues a report in December in which it classifies the situation in Iraq as "grave and deteriorating." Just weeks before, Donald H. Rumsfeld resigns as secretary of the U.S. Department of Defense in the face of widespread disapproval of his tactics and policies in Iraq. President George W. Bush concedes in mid-December that the war was not progressing at the pace he had anticipated. See **Armed forces,** page 66; **Cabinet, U.S.,** page 105; **Iraq,** page 236; **United States, Government of the,** page 394.

PROSECUTION OF TERRORIST SUSPECTS

The United States Supreme Court rules in June that the military commissions that had been established by the administration of President George W. Bush in the aftermath of the attacks on the United Sates on Sept. 11, 2001, violated both U.S. and international law. In September, Congress passes legislation providing a legal framework for such commissions. President Bush reveals in September that the Central Intelligence Agency has held terrorism suspects at offshore, secret prisons, from which 14 suspects had been transferred to Guantánamo Bay, Cuba, for possible prosecution. See **Australia,** page 78; **Congress of the United States,** page 132; **Human rights,** page 225; **Supreme Court of the United States,** page 368; **United States, Government of the,** page 394; **United States, President of the,** page 408.

MIDDLE EAST

Members of the Lebanese militant group Hezbollah kidnap two Israeli soldiers, triggering Israeli retaliation that led to a month of deadly conflict. **Germany,** page 204; **Iran,** page 235; **Israel,** page 241; **Lebanon,** page 269; **Middle East,** page 280; **Syria,** page 371; **United Nations,** page 393.

SO LONG, PLUTO

Members of the International Astronomical Union, the scientific body responsible for naming celestial objects, redefine a "planet," eliminating Pluto. See **Astronomy,** page 76; **Astronomy Focus,** page 77.

continued

IMMIGRATION DEMONSTRATIONS

More than a million protesters demonstrated in March, April, and May throughout the United States against legislation passed by the House of Representatives in late 2005 that would have made felons of illegal immigrants. The Senate in 2006 passed a far less extreme immigration bill, which House conservatives refused to consider. See **Chicago,** page 120; **Congress of the United States,** page 132; **Immigration,** page 228; **United States, Government of the: A Special Report,** page 398.

NORTH KOREA

North Korea detonates a nuclear device in October, leading the United Nations and many governments to impose sanctions on the country. See **Asia,** page 72; **Congress of the United States,** page 132; **Korea, North,** page 247; **Korea, South,** page 249; **United Nations,** page 393.

MISSING LINK

Fossils from a 375-million-year-old aquatic animal that was evolving into a land animal, found in 2006, represent a key stage in the evolution of life on Earth. See **Paleontology,** page 316.

GLOBAL WARMING

Throughout the world, the ice cover is thinning, breaking up, and draining away, according to numerous studies published in 2006 that chart the continuing effects of global warming. See **Australia,** page 78; **Canadian territories,** page 116; **Environmental pollution,** page 188; **Global warming,** page 205; **Global warming: A Special Report,** page 206.

2006

YEAR IN BRIEF

A month-by-month listing of the most significant world events that occurred during 2006.

1 Russia shuts down a natural gas pipeline to Ukraine as negotiations over price unravel. International affairs experts note that in the face of Ukraine's pro-Western government, Russia is cutting off subsidies in the form of cheap energy.

2 President George W. Bush is not asking Congress for additional funds for Iraq reconstruction, confirm administration officials. Political experts suggest that the decision is a tacit admission of the failure of the rebuilding program in the face of the insurgency.

3 Jack Abramoff, a Washington, D.C., lobbyist, pleads guilty to defrauding several American Indian tribes of millions of dollars and conspiring to bribe public officials. Abramoff had close connections to a number of high-ranking members of Congress, including Representative Tom DeLay (R., Texas).

4 Only 1 of 13 miners trapped by an explosion in a coal mine in Sago, West Virginia, on January 2 is found to be alive. In 2005, federal inspectors fined International Coal Group some $24,000 for about 200 safety violations at the Sago mine.

4 Israeli Prime Minister Ariel Sharon suffers a stroke, which his physicians describe as "significant." The 77-year-old prime minister is unconscious and on a respirator in a Jerusalem hospital.

5 A wave of insurgent attacks across Iraq kill as many as 140 people, including 11 members of the U.S. armed forces.

7 Representative Tom DeLay (R., Texas) announces that he is relinquishing his post as majority leader of the House. DeLay temporarily gave up the position in September 2005 after he was indicted in Texas on two counts of money laundering. He resisted permanent forfeiture until it became clear that his ties to Jack Abramoff, a lobbyist who recently pleaded guilty on charges of fraud, had involved DeLay in a corruption scandal that political experts suggest would be far-reaching in its effects.

10 The Ukrainian parliament dismisses the government of Prime Minister Yuri Yekhanurov for agreeing to a deal with Russia that nearly doubles the price Ukrainians will pay for natural gas. The agreement was reached after Russia shut off the gas to much of Ukraine.

11 The U.S. Department of Defense will provide additional body armor to U.S. forces in Iraq, announces a department spokesperson. The report of a classified Defense Department investigation, leaked to the press this week, disclosed that extra side armor could have saved the lives of up to 80 percent of the U.S. Marines who died from torso wounds.

13 Severe storms and tornadoes sweep across Alabama and the Florida Panhandle, killing at least one person and damaging dozens of buildings.

15 Michelle Bachelet, with 53.5 percent of the vote, is elected Chile's first female president.

15 Representative Robert W. Ney (R., Ohio) announces that he will temporarily step down as chairman of the House Administration Committee, which oversees lobbying. Ney was implicated by former lobbyist Jack Abramoff, who after pleading guilty to various felony counts, informed the U.S. Department of Justice that he had provided Ney with campaign funds, gifts, and lavish trips in exchange for a number of political favors.

16 Representatives of China, France, Germany, Russia, the United Kingdom, and the United States meet in London to discuss Iran's resumption of a nuclear research program.

16 Members of Israel's new centrist Kadima political party choose Ehud Olmert, the acting Israeli prime minister, to lead the party into elections scheduled for March. Kadima was founded in late 2005 by Prime Minister Ariel Sharon, who suffered a debilitating stroke on January 4 and remains in critical condition.

Hamas supporters celebrate a January 25 election victory that gave the militant group control of the Palestinian parliament in Ram Allah. In response, Israel suspended paying taxes and customs duties totaling $55 million a month to the Palestinian Authority.

19 The National Aeronautics and Space Administration (NASA) launches the New Horizons probe to Pluto and its largest moon, Charon. The spacecraft is the fastest ever launched from Earth, reaching a velocity of approximately 36,250 miles (58,339 kilometers) per hour as it left Earth orbit. The 3-billion-mile (4.8-billion-kilometer) journey to Pluto will take 10 years.

21 More than 70 people in Moscow have died since January 17 from the severe cold gripping the city. Russia has cut natural gas exports as domestic consumption hits new highs. The cuts erode supplies in the Baltics, Belarus, Scandinavia, and Ukraine.

22 Evo Morales is sworn in as Bolivia's first indigenous president. Morales pledges to end "500 years" of injustice against Bolivia's native population and to "recover" Bolivia's considerable natural resources by renationalizing them.

24 Canadian voters end 12 years of Liberal rule, giving the Conservatives 36 percent of the vote and 124 seats in the House of Commons. Conservative leader Stephen Harper will become prime minister.

24 As much as $9 billion in cash earmarked for reconstruction in Iraq disappeared or simply cannot be accounted for, reports the Special Inspector General for Iraq Reconstruction.

25 The Islamic militant group Hamas claims victory in Palestinian parliamentary elections. International affairs experts note that with Hamas—which Israel considers a terrorist organization—leading the Palestinian government, there is little possibility for Israeli-Palestinian peace.

Iraqis inspect the ruin of the al-Åskari shrine in Samarra after a bomb destroyed its famous golden dome on February 22. Iraqi experts later pointed to the al-Åskari bombing as a tipping point in the escalation of violence between Sunni and Shi`ah Muslims in Iraq in 2006.

2 Republicans in the House of Representatives choose John Boehner of Ohio to replace Tom DeLay of Texas as House majority leader.

2 President George W. Bush asks the U.S. Congress for an additional $70 billion for military operations in Iraq and Afghanistan through September.

3 Areas of St. Petersburg, Florida, receive a record 12 to 15 inches (30 to 38 centimeters) of rain in three and one-half hours. The rain causes several roofs to collapse, including one at a Bed Bath & Beyond store, from which clerks, front windows, and merchandise are washed out through the storefront.

4 Demonstrators vent their anger over cartoons satirizing the Prophet Muhammad, published in a Danish newspaper in 2005, by setting fire to the Danish consulate in Lebanon and the Danish and Norwegian embassies in Syria. In one of the cartoons, the prophet is depicted wearing a turban shaped like a bomb.

5 The Pittsburgh Steelers defeat the Seattle Seahawks 21-10 in Detroit to win their fifth Super Bowl title.

6 President George W. Bush presents a 2007 budget to the U.S. Congress. The controversial $2.77-trillion budget boosts homeland security and military spending while cutting funding for education,

Medicare and Medicaid, and transportation. The proposed budget would make permanent tax cuts introduced in President Bush's first term.

6 U.S. Attorney General Alberto Gonzales, in testimony before the Senate Judiciary Committee, insists that President George W. Bush did not exceed his authority in ordering the National Security Agency to eavesdrop by phone on U.S. citizens without first obtaining a warrant. Gonzales asserts that the wiretaps were "only focused on international communications where one part of the communication is al-Qa'ida."

7 President George W. Bush; former presidents George H. W. Bush, Jimmy Carter, and Bill Clinton; a host of dignitaries; and more than 10,000 people gather in Lithonia, Georgia, for the funeral of Coretta Scott King, wife of slain civil rights leader Martin Luther King, Jr.

7 Scientists with a joint Australian-Indonesian-U.S. expedition report finding a "lost world" that may be the most pristine natural ecosystem in the Asia-Pacific region, in the Indonesian region of Papua on the island of New Guinea. The 1,200-square-mile (3,000-square-kilometer) mountaintop forest, which is uninhabited by people, contains dozens of previously unknown animal and plant species.

8 The discovery of the first intact ancient Egyptian tomb in the Valley of the Kings since the uncovering of the tomb of Tutankhamun in 1922 is announced in Egypt. The 3,000- to 3,500-year-old tomb, which contains seven wooden sarcophagi and about 20 alabaster jars, was discovered by archaeologists with the University of Memphis in Tennessee. One sarcophagus held a miniature pink-gold coffin. According to the archaeologists, the discovery of the tomb dispels the long-held belief that there is nothing left to be found in the Valley of the Kings.

10 The Winter Olympic Games open in Torino (Turin), Italy, with a spectacular ceremony featuring famed Italian tenor Luciano Pavarotti.

11 Vice President Dick Cheney accidentally shoots a hunting companion during a weekend quail-hunting outing on a ranch in Texas. Harry Whittington, a fund-raiser for the Bush-Cheney election campaigns, is sprayed with bird shot.

12 A massive snowstorm blankets the Northeastern United States, dropping a record 26.9 inches (68.3 centimeters) of snow in New York City's Central Park—the city's heaviest snowfall since record keeping began in 1869. A classic northeaster, the storm caused travel delays and power outages up the Eastern Seaboard from North Carolina to Maine.

13 The International Atomic Energy Agency, the Vienna-based United Nations nuclear watchdog organization, reports that Iran has begun uranium enrichment, a process that can produce either fuel for atomic reactors or a nuclear bomb.

15 U.S. military forces in Iraq uncover evidence of death squads functioning in the Iraqi Interior Ministry, announces Army Major General Joseph Peterson. More than 20 Interior Ministry policemen were arrested in late January at an Iraqi army checkpoint in Baghdad, as they were taking a Sunni man away to be executed. Hundreds of Sunni Iraqis have been found murdered execution style since the war was launched in 2003.

17 The amount of water Greenland's glaciers are dumping into the Atlantic Ocean has nearly doubled in the last five years, announce scientists with the Jet Propulsion Laboratory at the California Institute of Technology in Pasadena. As a result, sea levels are rising at a faster rate than predicted.

22 The al-Åskari shrine in Samarra, one of the holiest sites in Shi`ah Islam, is bombed, triggering massive protests across Iraq. Although no one is injured, the explosion severely damages the 1,000-year-old shrine, destroying its famous golden dome. Iraq's premier Shi`ah cleric, the Grand Ayatollah Ali al-Sistani, appeals for public calm. Political experts note that the attack was almost certainly designed to inflame tensions between Iraq's Shi`ah and Sunni groups.

23 Widespread sectarian violence continues unabated in Iraq in the wake of the bombing of the al-Åskari shrine in Samarra on February 22 with more than 100 people, including prominent Sunni clerics, killed in revenge attacks.

28 Five bomb blasts rock Baghdad one day after the lifting of a curfew to curb violence in response to the bombing of the al-Åskari shrine in Samarra. The explosions kill at least 75 people.

MARCH

2006

2 President George W. Bush, on a state visit to India, finalizes a nuclear agreement with Indian Prime Minister Manmohan Singh. The controversial pact would help energy-strapped India meet civilian energy needs, while allowing it to continue to develop its nuclear weapons program. If ratified by the U.S. Senate, the treaty guarantees that the United States will provide India with access to U.S. civil nuclear technology.

2 A rash of wildfires burn across some 8,000 acres (3,240 hectares) of grasslands in southern Oklahoma, destroying 40 houses.

5 AT&T Inc. of San Antonio announces plans to buy BellSouth Corporation of Atlanta, Georgia, for $67 billion in stock. If federal regulators approve the plan, the merger will reassemble much of the old AT&T telephone monopoly that the federal government broke up in 1984.

6 Governor Mike Rounds of South Dakota signs legislation that bans nearly all abortions with the exception of abortions to save a mother's life. According to legal experts, the new law was specifically designed to challenge *Roe v. Wade* before the Supreme Court.

7 The number of illegal immigrants in the United States may be nearly 12 million, accounting for 1 in every 20 workers, reports the Pew Hispanic Center. As many as 850,000 illegal immigrants have arrived in the United States annually since 2000.

8 A previously unknown crustacean has been discovered in the South Pacific, announces a U.S.-led team of scientists. The crustacean, which has been named *Kiwa hirsuta* and somewhat resembles a lobster covered in what appears to be silky fur, is so distinct that the scientists created a new taxonomic family for it, Kiwaida. The *Kiwa hirsuta*, which is blind, lives around hydrothermal vents at deep and dark levels of the ocean.

9 Sunni Arab leaders accuse Iraq's Shi`ah dominated government of operating anti-Sunni death squads from within the police force, which is under the control of the Interior Ministry. The accusation comes in the wake of the discovery of 26 bodies in different locations in Baghdad and the kidnapping of 50 employees of a Sunni-operated security company on March 8.

9 Dubayy Port (DP) World announces that it will "transfer fully to a U.S. entity" the Ports North American division of the P&O Navigation Company after it buys the British company. The announcement comes just days after the U.S. House Appropriations Committee voted 62 to 2 to block the acquisition, which would have placed various functions of six major U.S. ports under the control of a company owned by the government of the United Arab Emirates. The transaction, which proved extremely unpopular with the U.S. public, was backed by President George W. Bush, who threatened to veto any attempt by Congress to block it. Political experts describe DP World's pullout as an attempt to spare the president further humiliation in what had become a political debacle for his administration.

10 The Mars Reconnaissance Orbiter slips perfectly into orbit around the planet Mars, completing a 300-million-mile (483-million-kilometer) trip from Earth. NASA (the National Aeronautics and Space Administration) launched the orbiter on Aug. 12, 2005.

12 The militant Shi`ah cleric Moqtada al-Sadr appeals for calm among Iraq's Shi`ah majority after the nearly simultaneous explosion of six suicide car bombs leaves some 55 people dead and more than 300 others wounded in Sadr City, a largely Shi`ah Baghdad neighborhood. Declaring that Iraq was now in a state of civil war, al-Sadr asks his Mahdi militia not to respond to the violence. Other attacks in Baghdad kill 22 people.

13 President George W. Bush announces that control of most of Iraq will be turned over to newly trained Iraqi troops by the end of 2006.

An estimated 500,000 demonstrators march in downtown Los Angeles on March 25 to protest proposed federal legislation that would make felons of millions of illegal immigrants. Similar marches were staged in cities across the country.

12 A line of tornadoes cuts across Kansas, Missouri, Illinois, and Indiana, killing at least 10 people. Hail the size of baseballs is reported in Missouri, and the storms damage 60 percent of the buildings at the University of Kansas.

14 An oil pipeline has burst on Alaska's North Slope and has spread more than 267,000 gallons (1 million liters) of crude oil over more than 2 acres (0.8 hectares) that caribou herds regularly cross in their migrations, confirms British Petroleum (BP). Cleanup crews are working in subzero temperatures to vacuum up the thick mixture of snow and oil. A BP spokesperson notes that the break probably resulted from corrosion of the aging pipeline.

15 Firefighters continue to battle hundreds of wildfires in the Texas Panhandle and West Texas. The fires have blackened 840,000 acres (340,000 hectares) and left 11 people and some 10,000 horses and cattle dead since March 12.

19 Former Iraqi Prime Minister Ayad Allawi, in an interview in London, declares that Iraq is nearing a "point of no return." "We are losing each day, as an average, 50 to 60 people .... If this is not civil war, then God knows what civil war is."

21 President George W. Bush, speaking at a press conference, states that U.S. forces in Iraq are "making progress," but the U.S. involvement in Iraq is likely to last throughout his presidency.

25 At least 500,000 people march in downtown Los Angeles protesting possible changes in immigration laws that would make it a crime, rather than a civil offense, to be an illegal immigrant or to aid or hire an illegal immigrant.

In April, the price of a gallon of gas hits nearly $3.50 a gallon in San Francisco and averages $2.91 in the United States. By December 18, the average price of a gallon of gas nationwide had fallen to $2.32.

2 Eight Midwestern states—Arkansas, Kentucky, Illinois, Indiana, Iowa, Missouri, Ohio, and Tennessee—are battered by massive thunderstorms. Twenty-eight people are killed and hundreds of structures are destroyed by 86 tornadoes.

2 The University of Maryland women's basketball team wins the National College Athletic Association championship 81-70 over the University of North Carolina.

2 Nine U.S. service members die in Iraq's Anbar province—four in action and five in a truck accident—bringing to at least 13 the number of U.S. military personnel killed in Iraq since April 1.

3 The government of Venezuelan President Hugo Chávez seizes an oil field from the French oil company Total SA and terminates a contract with the Italian oil company Eni SpA after the companies refuse to turn over to Venezuela control of 32 oil fields.

3 The University of Florida beats the University of California at Los Angeles 73-57 in Indianapolis to win its first National College Athletic Association men's basketball championship.

3 Human bladders successfully grown in a laboratory from patients' own cells have been transplanted into those patients, announce scientists from Wake Forest University in North Carolina.

4 Representative Tom DeLay (R., Texas), the once-powerful majority leader of the U.S. House, announces his resignation from Congress in the face of a growing corruption scandal and a troubled reelection campaign.

4 Sectarian violence between Shi`ah and Sunni Muslims is markedly increasing the number of civilian deaths in Iraq, the Associated Press reveals. War-related violence killed at least 1,038 civilians in March, compared with 608 in January and 705 in February.

5 United States Customs and Border Protection officials take into custody 22 Chinese nationals leaving a cargo container at a Seattle, Washington, dock, after spending two weeks in a 40-foot- (12-meter-) long box to smuggle themselves into the United States from China.

6 The discovery of fossils of a fish that was evolving from an aquatic animal into a land animal is revealed by U.S. paleontologists. The 383-million-year-old fossils, from an animal named *Tiktaalik roseae*, represent a "missing link" from a key stage in the evolution of life on Earth.

6 Astrophysicists at the Massachusetts Institute of Technology (MIT) announce finding for the first time a swirling disk of debris from which planets likely arise. The debris disk probably was formed from metal-rich material that failed to escape a violent supernova explosion.

8 Some 110 people are killed when an overloaded boat capsizes in Lake Volta in Ghana, while residents from an island in the lake that had been designated as a nature reserve are being relocated to the mainland.

10 A French law designed to ease joblessness among the young but which triggered a month of massive nationwide protests will be struck from French law books, President Jacques Chirac announces. The law would have allowed businesses to dismiss new employees younger than 26 without cause during their first two years.

11 Iran has successfully enriched uranium, a major step in the development of its nuclear program, announces former Iranian President Hashemi Rafsanjani.

12 People seeking asylum in Australia who land illegally on the mainland face immediate deportation to offshore processing centers under tough new illegal-immigration laws, announces the government of Australian Prime Minister John Howard.

14 Two nearly simultaneous explosions injure at least nine people in the Jama Masjid (Grand Mosque) complex in Delhi, one of the largest and important Shi`ah mosques in India.

14 More than $1 billion of the $10 billion spent by the Federal Emergency Management Administration (FEMA) on relief for victims of Hurricane Katrina has been wasted, reports FEMA's inspector general.

15 Retired General Wesley Clark, who ran for the 2004 Democratic presidential nomination, joins six other retired U.S. generals in calling for the resignation of Secretary of Defense Donald Rumsfeld because of problems in Iraq.

16 The Danube River crests at its highest level since 1895 in Romania, where farmland and forests have been deliberately flooded to protect towns. Flooding is also widespread in Serbia and Bulgaria.

18 Chinese President Hu Jintao arrives in Seattle for a four-day visit to the United States and a meeting with President Bush.

22 The Shi`ah bloc in the Iraqi parliament, backed by Kurd and Sunni members, asks Shi`ah candidate Jawadal al-Maliki (originally Nouri Kamel al-Maliki) to form a Cabinet, breaking a four-month deadlock in the creation of a unity government.

24 King Gyanendra of Nepal reinstates the country's parliament, which he dissolved in 2002, in an attempt to end weeks of violent protests against his rule.

25 A suicide bomb attack on Sri Lanka's army headquarters in the capital by the rebel Liberation Tigers of Tamil Eelam—the biggest attack since the group agreed to a cease-fire in 2002—leaves at least nine people dead. The army launches air strikes against rebel positions.

25 The government of Panamanian President Martin Torrijos announces a $5.3-million plan to widen the Panama Canal to accommodate giant container ships.

27 Israel's Kadima Party, led by Prime Minister Ehud Olmert, allies with the Labor Party to form a coalition government, leaving Olmert six seats short of a majority in Israel's 120-seat parliament.

28 A severe funding shortfall forces the United Nations to cut by half the rations on which 3 million people in Sudan's Darfur region are depending.

29 Insurgent attacks in Iraq increased dramatically in 2005, the U.S. State Department's annual survey of global terrorism reveals, killing nearly 8,300 people and accounting for nearly one-third of all terrorist acts worldwide. About 100,000 Iraqi families have fled their residences to avoid sectarian violence, announces one of Iraq's newly elected vice presidents.

19

MAY

2006

1 President Evo Morales of Bolivia signs into law legislation that extends state control over all aspects of Bolivia's energy sector, fulfilling a 2005 campaign promise to end the foreign "looting" of Bolivia's natural resources.

1 A report by a United States watchdog agency auditing reconstruction spending in Iraq concludes that more than $265 million in U.S. taxpayer money invested in protecting and rebuilding Iraq's oil, gas and electric-power infrastructure has been wasted.

2 Silvio Berlusconi gives up contesting the results of recent parliamentary elections and resigns as prime minister of Italy, paving the way for Romano Prodi to form a center-left coalition government.

3 A suicide bomber blows himself up in a crowd of men waiting to join the police in the Iraqi city of Fallujah, killing 17 people and wounding another 20. In Baghdad, police discover the bodies of 37 Iraqis in 6 different locations, most of whom had been tortured and then murdered execution style.

3 A federal jury in Virginia votes to sentence Zacarias Moussaoui to life in prison, sparing him the death penalty. In 2005, Moussaoui pleaded guilty to conspiracy in the terrorist attacks on the United States on Sept. 11, 2001.

3 A portrait by Pablo Picasso entitled *Dora Maar With Cat* sells to an anonymous buyer for $95.2 million in New York City, the second-highest amount ever paid for a painting at auction.

4 The discovery of a royal burial site in the ruins of an ancient Maya city in the Guatemalan jungle is announced by archaeologists, who found jade jewelry, a jaguar pelt, and the remains of a king, who may have been the city's founder.

4 At least 300,000 U.S. children have been diagnosed with autism, announce government researchers who conducted the first comprehensive national survey of the developmental disorder.

5 British Prime Minister Tony Blair reshuffles his Cabinet after his Labour Party does poorly in local elections. The Cabinet has been plagued by scandals and by the unpopularity of the war in Iraq.

5 Porter Goss, the director of the Central Intelligence Agency, has resigned, announces President George W. Bush, whose failure to provide a reason prompts observers to suggest that Goss was dismissed.

6 The undefeated bay colt Barbaro pulls away from 19 challengers to win the Kentucky Derby by 6 ½ lengths, the fifth-best margin of victory in the race's 132-year history.

7 A U.S. soldier is killed near Tall Afar, northwest of Baghdad, bringing to 2,422 the number of U.S. military personnel who have died in Iraq since the war began in March 2003.

10 Whirlpool Corp. of Grand Rapids, Michigan, the largest U.S. appliance maker, announces plans to eliminate some 4,500 jobs by closing three manufacturing plants operated by the Maytag Corp., which it purchased in March.

11 At least 45 people are killed in a major sea battle between the Liberation Tigers of Tamil Eelam and Sri Lankan government forces in the Indian Ocean.

11 Seven U.S. soldiers are killed in Iraq—four by drowning when their tank rolls off a bridge and sinks in a canal and three by the detonation of roadside bombs.

12 At least 200 people die in a massive explosion at a gasoline pipeline near Lagos, Nigeria, that may have been caused by people drilling holes into the pipeline to steal gas.

14 More than 70 people, including 35 police officials, are killed in three days of gang violence in São Paulo, Brazil, and other towns in the state of São Paulo, after a series of coordinated attacks on patrolling police and on police stations ordered by imprisoned gang members.

Injured residents of Yogyakarta, Indonesia, receive medical treatment after a 6.5-magnitude earthquake on May 27. The earthquake on Java, Indonesia's main island, left more than 5,800 people dead, 30,000 injured, and an estimated 650,000 people homeless.

15 Four days of heavy rains across New England trigger the worst flooding since 1936. The rains submerge or damage more than 600 roads in New Hampshire.

20 Iraq's parliament approves a new unity government, which includes representatives of the country's three main groups, Shi`ah and Sunni Muslims and Kurds.

20 Bernardini wins the Preakness by 5 ¼ lengths after Kentucky Derby winner Barbaro suffers a broken leg.

21 The citizens of Montenegro vote to break away from Serbia and establish an independent country.

22 The U.S.-led coalition in Afghanistan carries out major air strikes on known Taliban strongholds in Kandahar province, in response to a major upsurge of Taliban attacks in southern Afghanistan.

25 Former top Enron executives Ken Lay and Jeffrey Skilling are found guilty of fraud and conspiracy for financial manipulations that caused the collapse of the Houston-based energy company in December 2001.

26 The U.S. Senate, in a 78-15 vote, confirms as head of the Central Intelligence Agency (CIA) General Michael Hayden, the first active or retired member of the U.S. military to lead the CIA in 25 years.

27 A 6.5-magnitude earthquake on Java, the main island of Indonesia, leaves more than 5,800 people dead, at least 30,000 others injured, and 650,000 homeless.

31 The U.S. Department of Homeland Security announces that the 2006 antiterrorism grants to U.S. cities total $711 million, with grants to New York City and Washington, D.C.—targets of the Sept. 11, 2001, terrorist attacks—substantially cut.

A spokesperson for the U.S. military announces the death of Abu Musab al-Zarqawi, leader of al-Qa`ida in Iraq, a major force in the Iraqi insurgency. Al-Zarqawi died on June 7 in a U.S. air strike on a house near the city of Baqubah. The air strike, which dropped two 500-pound (230-kilogram) bombs, also killed several of al-Zarqawi's associates.

1 The government of Iran announces its willingness to talk with the United States about its nuclear development program but refuses to stop enriching uranium first, a condition set by the administration of U.S. President George W. Bush before the start of any negotiations.

1 The U.S. Department of Defense offers condolences to relatives of 24 civilians killed in the Iraqi city of Hadithah on Nov. 19, 2005. The victims, who included elderly men, women, and children, were allegedly shot by Marines after a fellow Marine died in the explosion of a roadside bomb nearby.

1 Inflation in once-prosperous country of Zimbabwe reduces the value of the Zimbabwe dollar by half in just two weeks, forcing the government to issue a $100,000 bill that is worth approximately $1.50, the cost of a loaf of bread.

3 Police in Toronto arrest 17 men armed with guns and explosives suspected of planning terrorist attacks in Toronto and Ottawa, in what is believed to be Canada's largest counterterrorism operation.

3 President Evo Morales of Bolivia launches a land reform program that involves distributing more than 18,600 square miles (30,000 square kilometers) of land to indigenous communities, to restore land taken during the Spanish conquest in the 1500's and 1600's.

4 Former Peruvian President Alan García regains the presidency with 54.69 percent of the vote, compared with 45.3 percent for his populist rival Ollanta Humala.

5 Baghdad's main mortuary has received the bodies of 6,000 Iraqis who have died violently in 2006—the majority of whom are victims of sectarian killings—the Iraqi Ministry of Health announces.

6 Islamic militants who took control of Somalia's capital, Mogadishu, on June 5 announce their intention of establishing an Islamic nation ruled by Shari`ah, Islamic religious law, which triggers widespread rioting in the capital.

8 The U.S. Food and Drug Administration approves the first vaccine to protect against strains of the human papillomavirus (HPV) that cause most cases of cervical cancer, the most common sexually transmitted disease.

8 Representative Tom DeLay (R., Texas), under indictment for allegedly breaking state laws on political contributions and for money laundering, leaves the House, insisting on his innocence.

10 Three detainees at the U.S. government detention camp at Guantánamo Bay, Cuba, become the first prisoners there to commit suicide. Described as "committed jihadists," the men had never been charged with a specific crime.

11 Hamas militants in the Gaza Strip launch at least 60 rockets into Israel, seriously wounding one Israeli.

12 The Federal Bureau of Investigation announces that the violent crime rate in the United States rose significantly in 2005 for the first time in 13 years.

13 Ten people are killed in the Gaza Strip—including two children and three medical workers—in an Israeli air strike targeting a Palestinian leader who also is killed.

14 Some 40,000 Iraqi and U.S. troops patrol the streets of Baghdad as part of a crackdown on violence ordered by Iraqi Prime Minister Nouri Kamel al-Maliki, a day after U.S. President George W. Bush makes an unannounced visit there.

14 The Federal Emergency Management Administration gave out some $1.4 billion in aid to bogus victims of hurricanes Katrina and Rita, officials with the General Accountability Office report to Congress.

15 The U.S. Supreme Court rules 5-4 that evidence found by police who enter a residence with a search warrant but who do not follow the "knock and announce" rule may be presented at a trial, reinterpreting a rule long regarded as a basic protection against illegal entry by police.

15 The U.S. Department of Defense reports that 2,500 U.S. soldiers have died in Iraq since the war began in March 2003.

16 A man wearing shoes loaded with explosives blows himself up in a Shi`ah mosque in Bagdad, killing at least 11 people.

17 The painting *Adele Bloch-Bauer I*, a 1907 portrait by artist Gustav Klimpt that was looted by the Nazis during World War II (1939-1945), sells for $135 million, a record for a painting.

18 Katharine Jefferts Schori is elected presiding bishop of the Episcopal Church in the United States and the first woman leader of an Anglican Communion body.

19 The Carolina Hurricanes win the Stanley Cup, beating the Edmonton Oilers 3-1.

20 The bodies of two U.S. soldiers missing since June 16 are found near Baghdad, ending a search by 8,000 Iraqi and U.S. troops.

20 The Miami Heat win the National Basketball Association championship with a 95-92 victory over the Dallas Mavericks.

22 The Supreme Court votes 9-0 in favor of a female forklift operator punished after accusing her supervisor of sexual harassment, setting a broader standard favoring employees in retaliation claims.

26 Flooding caused by up to 12 inches (30.5 centimeters) of rain closes government buildings and engulfs rail and subway lines in Washington, D.C.

27 "Indisputable" evidence proves that secondhand smoke is responsible for tens of thousands of premature deaths each year among nonsmokers, U.S. Surgeon General Richard H. Carmona announces.

28 Nearly 200,000 people in Pennsylvania evacuate their homes as the Susquehanna River, fed by heavy rains, rises to 34.4 feet (10.5 meters) behind area levees.

29 The U.S. Supreme Court rules 5-3 that military tribunals created by the administration of President George W. Bush to try terror suspects violate both U.S. military law and the Geneva Conventions.

JULY

2006

1 More than 50 million people living in the United States must prove that they are citizens or lose their medical benefits or long-term care, according to a new Medicaid rule that goes into effect.

1 The explosion of a car bomb in a busy public market in Baghdad's Sadr City kills at least 62 people and leaves nearly 120 injured.

5 World leaders express deep concern after North Korea's military test-fires a series of missiles on July 4 and 5.

5 Israel destroys the Palestinian Interior Ministry in Gaza City, killing at least seven people, in a retaliatory missile strike made hours after the military wing of Hamas launches a rocket at the southern Israeli city of Ashkelon.

5 The price of oil on the New York City market climbs to a record $75 a barrel.

6 Felipe Calderón is declared the winner in Mexico's disputed July 2 presidential election, with 35.88 percent of the vote, compared with 35.31 percent for opponent Andrés Manuel López Obrador.

7 A plot to attack New York City's public transportation system has been disrupted, announces the Federal Bureau of Investigation.

9 An Iraqi mob, believed to be members of a Shi`ah militia, attacks a Sunni neighborhood in Baghdad, pulling some 40 people out of their houses and cars and shooting them in what is described as revenge for the bombing of a Shi`ah mosque the previous day.

9 Four U.S. soldiers in Iraq are charged with rape and murder and a fifth soldier is accused of "dereliction of duty" for failing to report crimes involving the deaths in March of a teen-age Iraqi girl and three members of her family.

11 The near-simultaneous explosions of eight bombs on the train network in Mumbai, India, during evening rush hour leave at least 200 people dead and some 700 others wounded.

11 The administration of U.S. President George W. Bush announces that guarantees of humane treatment specified by the Geneva Conventions are to be extended to detainees in the war on terror, a policy reversal triggered by a June ruling by the U.S. Supreme Court against the administration's detainee policy.

13 Israel blockades Lebanon by air and sea, a day after launching an air and ground assault into southern Lebanon in response to the capture of two Israeli soldiers by the militant group Hezbollah. Hezbollah responds with rocket attacks on Israeli border towns.

15 The United Nations Security Council votes unanimously to impose economic sanctions on North Korea in response to that country's recent testing of seven missiles, including a long-range missile that experts believe was designed to reach North America.

17 A 7.7-magnitude earthquake off the Indonesian island of Java triggers a tsunami that leaves more than 600 people dead and thousands of others homeless.

18 At least 14,000 Iraqi civilians have been killed in insurgent and sectarian violence in Iraq in the first half of 2006, reports the UN Assistance Mission for Iraq.

19 President George W. Bush vetoes legislation loosening restrictions on federal funding for stem-cell research, his first veto in five and one-half years in office.

21 The United States Department of Defense releases the names of 2,552 U.S. military personnel who have died since the start of the Iraq War in 2003.

24 The latest round of global free-trade talks sponsored by the World Trade Organization collapses over disagreements on cutting farm subsidies and lowering agricultural tariffs.

25 Four United Nations observers in southern Lebanon die when an Israeli bomb hits their bunker in Khiam.

Israeli soldiers lob shells into Lebanon near the beginning of Israel's 2006 conflict with Hezbollah. Israel launched the air and ground assault into southern Lebanon on July 12 after the militant group Hezbollah kidnapped two Israeli soldiers. The 34-day conflict ended in a stalemate.

25 Iraqi Prime Minister Nouri Kamel al-Maliki arrives in Washington, D.C., for the first visit to the United States by a democratically elected prime minister from Iraq since the fall of dictator Saddam Hussein in 2003.

27 Health department officials in France and Italy report that more than 80 people have died in Europe as the result of a heat wave that has engulfed the continent during the past two weeks.

27 Tour de France champion Floyd Landis fails an antidoping test for a segment of the race during which he moved from 11th to 3rd place in the overall standings, according to a statement from his team, Phonak—a charge Landis denies.

28 United States economic growth during the second quarter of 2006 not only drops sharply over first-quarter figures but also fails to reach economists' already-reduced forecast for the period.

28 The Israel Defense Force reports that total Israeli casualties during the conflict with Hezbollah include 33 soldiers killed and 110 soldiers wounded, with civilian casualties at 18 dead and 1,123 wounded. Lebanese security forces said the death toll in that country reached 398 with another 1,661 people wounded.

28 The suspected death toll in California from heat-related causes reaches 132, as temperatures remain above 100 °F (38 °C) for about two weeks.

30 At least 54 Lebanese civilians, including many children, are killed in Qana as their apartment building collapses after being bombed by Israeli warplanes.

31 The United Nations Security Council passes a resolution setting an August 31 deadline for Iran to suspend its uranium enrichment activities or face possible economic sanctions.

31 Cuban President Fidel Castro temporarily relinquishes power to his brother Raúl Castro, the commander of Cuba's military, after undergoing intestinal surgery.

AUGUST

2006

Members of the International Astronomical Union pass a resolution on August 24 that results in Pluto's reclassification as a dwarf planet.

1 President Mahmoud Ahmadinejad of Iran rejects a United Nations (UN) resolution demanding that Iran suspend its uranium enrichment program. In a television address, Ahmadinejad insists that Iran has every right to pursue a nuclear program, which he describes as "peaceful." International affairs experts have long noted that Iran, which has massive oil and natural gas reserves, has little need for nuclear fuel production technology, leading many world leaders to believe that Iran's program is aimed at the production of nuclear weapons.

1 At least 70 people are killed in Iraq in a series of bombings targeting soldiers and police. The U.S. military is moving approximately 3,700 soldiers into Baghdad from Mosul in an attempt to stem the violence.

4 Israeli air strikes in Lebanon sever the last major road connecting Lebanon with neighboring Syria in an effort to prevent Syria from providing support to the militant Islamic group Hezbollah battling Israel in southern Lebanon. The current wave of fighting began after Hezbollah fighters kidnapped two Israeli soldiers on July 12.

2 President George W. Bush signs the Central American Free Trade Agreement, a free-trade pact between the United States and six Latin American countries.

6 The oil company BP shuts down Alaska's Prudhoe Bay oil field after workers discover a severely corroded transit pipe. The field is one of the largest in the United States, producing 400,000 barrels of oil per day. Industry experts expect the shutdown to push up U.S. gasoline prices, which are already near record-high levels.

7 The price of crude oil spikes on markets worldwide. In New York City, light, sweet crude for September delivery climbs by $1.74 to $76.50 a barrel; in London, the price for Brent crude for September hits $77.39 a barrel.

11 Member nations of the United Nations (UN) Security Council vote unanimously to adopt a resolution designed to end four weeks of fighting in southern Lebanon between Israel and the Shi`ah militant organization Hezbollah. The agreement calls for UN peacekeeping forces to move into the area to enforce a cease-fire scheduled to go into effect on August 14.

12 Plans by the administration of President George W. Bush to cut federal Medicaid payments to hospitals and nursing homes meet growing opposition from state governors of both major political parties. The National Governors Association issues a statement that its members strongly oppose cuts that "would impose a huge financial burden on states." A group of 82 Republican members of the House of Representatives and a bi-partisan group of 50 U.S. senators also have called on the Bush administration to scrap the proposal. The new rules would both reduce federal funding and limit the ability of states to finance their share of Medicaid by taxing profits of health care providers, such as private hospitals and nursing homes. Medicaid provides health care to more than 50 million low-income people.

14 Israeli Prime Minister Ehud Olmert announces in the Knesset, the Israeli parliament, that the military will pursue Hezbollah leaders in Lebanon despite the UN-brokered cease-fire, which went into effect earlier that morning. According to Olmert, his government is doing its utmost to secure the release of two soldiers whose capture by Hezbollah sparked the four-week conflict.

17 The number of roadside bomb attacks on U.S. soldiers in Iraq was higher in July than in any previous month since the war began in March 2003, reveals *The New York Times* in an article based on a report by the Department of Defense. In July 2006, a total of 2,625 explosive devices either exploded or were dis-covered before detonating, compared

with 1,454 bombs in January 2006. According to the Defense Department analysis, 70 percent of the total was directed against the U.S. military. More civilians died violently in Iraq in July than in any previous month. The Iraqi Health Ministry announced on August 14 that an average of 110 civilians died daily in insurgent or sectarian violence in July. The count is a nearly 100-percent increase over the period from mid-February to mid-May.

18 Approximately 11 million illegal immi-grants are living in the United States, announces the Office of Immigration Statistics (OIS), a branch of the U.S. Department of Homeland Security. An estimated 6 million of the 11 million illegal immigrants are from Mexico. The OIS estimated that 8.5 million illegal immigrants lived in the country in January 2000.

20 Tiger Woods wins his second Professional Golfers' Association Championship, his 12th victory in a major, with a five-shot lead over Shaun Micheel at the Medinah Country Club in Medinah, Illinois.

24 The International Astronomical Union approves a definition for a "planet" and downgrades the status of Pluto to "dwarf planet" at its meeting in Prague, capital of the Czech Republic. Other dwarf planets include the asteroid Ceres and 2003 UB313, a spherical Kuiper belt object larger in diameter than Pluto.

25 European Union (EU) nations pledge to supply half of the 15,000 troops needed to enforce the United Nations-brokered cease-fire between Israeli forces and Hezbollah militants in southern Lebanon. The announcement comes in response to UN Secretary-General Kofi Annan's request for more troops at an emergency meeting of EU ministers. On August 24, French President Jacques Chirac pledged to increase the French contingent in Lebanon to 2,000 troops.

30 California legislators and Governor Arnold Schwarzenegger agree on a sweeping plan to cut carbon-dioxide (CO_2) emissions by 25 percent by 2020. The plan, which could result in controls on utilities and oil refineries, imposes the tightest restrictions on CO_2 emissions in the United States. The first major deadline calls for a reduction in emissions to 1990 levels by 2012.

1 Iraqi casualties increased by 51 percent from May 20 to Aug. 11, 2006, the U.S. Department of Defense reports in its quarterly assessment of conditions in Iraq. The authors of the assessment note that casualties among Iraqi military forces and civilians totaled almost 120 per day, a significant increase over the number during the period from mid-February to May 19. The average number of weekly attacks climbed to almost 800, about 50 percent higher than the number during the first reporting period. Although the overall number of attacks increased in all categories, the proportion of those attacks directed against civilians increased substantially.

3 American tennis star Andre Agassi plays the last match of his career at the U.S. Open in New York City. Plagued by a back injury, Agassi announced in June that he would retire after the tournament. "The scoreboard said I lost today," Agassi tells the crowd. "But what the scoreboard doesn't say is what it is I have found. Over the last 21 years, I have found loyalty. You have pulled for me on the court and also in life."

3 The SMART-1 spacecraft, the first European Space Agency probe to orbit the moon, successfully completes its mission by crashing into the lunar surface. Launched in September 2003, the probe followed a spiraling, 14-month-long route using a solar-electric engine for propulsion. In March 2005, SMART-1 began mapping the lunar surface and conducting a detailed survey of chemical elements.

5 Felipe Calderón is unanimously declared the winner of the July 2 presidential election by Mexico's Federal Electoral Judicial Tribunal. The special court certifies that Calderón won with a razor-thin margin of 233,831 votes out of a total of 41 million votes cast. However, political experts question whether the declaration will bring an end to an electoral crisis that began when the final tally had Calderón leading his opponent, Andrés Manuel López Obrador, by just one-half a percentage point.

López Obrador, a candidate for the leftist Democratic Revolutionary Party and a popular former mayor of the capital, Mexico City, continues to enjoy a strong following among Mexico's poorer classes. The closeness of the results brought claims of widespread election fraud, which in turn triggered a hard-fought legal battle and more than two months of massive public protests.

6 Seven junior aides resign from British Prime Minister Tony Blair's Labour government to protest his refusal to quit. Political experts speculate that the prime minister will be forced from office as more and more members of the party switch allegiance to Gordon Brown, Blair's heir apparent.

6 U.S. President George W. Bush acknowledges that the Central Intelligence Agency (CIA) operates a network of secret prisons around the world. Fourteen people suspected of terrorism are to be transferred from these installations to the U.S. military-operated prison at Guantánamo Bay, Cuba, to stand trial. The president proposes that Congress pass legislation authorizing the creation of military tribunals that would permit evidence to be withheld from a defendant if that evidence consisted of classified information. The president insists that the United States does not employ torture and that all of the suspects will be protected under the provisions of the Geneva Conventions.

7 Pakistan's President Pervez Musharraf denies that his government is assisting the international terrorist organization al-Qa`ida or the militant Islamic political group the Taliban along Pakistan's border with Afghanistan. Although Musharraf acknowledges that militants are crossing the border to launch attacks in Afghanistan, he insists that his government is working to halt such attacks. On September 5, Musharraf's representatives signed a peace agreement with pro-Taliban militants in Pakistan's north Warizistan region, which borders Afghanistan. Under the agreement, pro-Taliban forces

وعدنا الصادق
Our Truthful Pledge

Members of Hezbollah rally on September 23 in Beirut before a poster of their leader, Sayyed Hassan Nasrallah, in celebration of their "victory" over Israel. During the rally, Nasrallah declared that the Hezbollah militia emerged from the war stronger than ever and remained equipped with some 20,000 missiles. "Not a single army in the world will be able to dismantle our resistance," he noted.

will cease attacking Pakistani troops and stop crossing into Afghanistan to attack Afghan forces and troops from the North Atlantic Treaty Organization (NATO). In return, Pakistan will reduce the number of troops deployed to the region. International affairs experts suggest that the agreement provides Musharraf with an exit strategy from a campaign that is widely regarded as a failure. The experts note that hundreds of Pakistani troops have died in the region while local support for the Taliban continues to increase.

13 The amount of perennial Arctic sea ice, which stays frozen the year round, declined by 14 percent between 2004 and 2005, announce scientists at NASA's Goddard Space Flight Center. Researchers began monitoring the polar ice cap

in the 1970's, when perennial ice was fairly stable, with a decline of only 1.5 to 2 percent per decade. According to Goddard scientist Josefino Comiso, "the greenhouse phenomenon is actually becoming apparent in the Arctic." Because Arctic ice reflects sunlight, its decline increases the absorption of solar heat, accelerating global warming.

28 The Senate votes along party lines to pass a bill that allows the government to set up military commissions to try people accused of terrorism. The bill represents a compromise between President George W. Bush and powerful Republican senators who insisted that Bush's original plan violated international prohibitions on torturing prisoners.

A South Korean activist ignites a mock nuclear missile at a rally protesting North Korea's testing of a nuclear device on October 9. The test was condemned by South Korea, Japan, and the United States.

2 Dennis Hastert (R., Illinois), speaker of the U.S. House of Representatives, issues a statement denying that the Republican leadership in the House knew that Representative Mark Foley (R., Florida) had allegedly sent sexually explicit electronic messages to former House pages until the news broke on September 29. Foley resigned from the House soon after the media reported the story of his alleged e-mail and instant-message contacts with male pages. Before his resignation, Foley co-chaired the Congressional Missing and Exploited Children's Caucus and was a prominent advocate for legislation outlawing online sexual predators.

4 United States President George W. Bush signs into law legislation authorizing the construction of hundreds of miles of fencing along the border between the United States and Mexico to keep non-U.S. citizens from entering the United States illegally. The measure does not include funding for the fence, though a previous bill allotted about $1.2 million during fiscal year 2007 for fencing and other barriers.

9 The government of North Korea announces that it has successfully conducted a nuclear test. United States President George W. Bush describes the test as a "provocative act" and joins South Korea and Japan in condemning the move. China, North Korea's closest ally, expresses "resolute opposition" and describes the test as "brazen."

11 Sectarian violence continues to rage across Iraq. Police in Baghdad, the capital, report finding the bodies of 110 men who had been tortured before being murdered execution style. According to researchers at Johns Hopkins University in Baltimore, approximately 655,000 Iraqis have been killed since the war began in 2003. The estimate is based on a survey that compares prewar and postwar mortality rates from 47 randomly chosen areas. Critics, including U.S. President George W. Bush, dismiss the report as lacking credibility because the estimate is based on statistical prediction rather than actual body counts.

13 The foreign minister of South Korea, Ban Ki-moon, is elected secretary-general of the United Nations (UN). He will replace Kofi Annan, who will step down on December 31. Ban is described as "a consummate mediator and a world-class administrator." The first Asian to lead the UN in more than 30 years, Ban favors organizational reforms, noting that the UN must promise less and deliver more.

15 Eight American soldiers and Marines die in Iraq within 24 hours, announces the U.S. military in Baghdad, the capital. Their deaths bring to at least 58 the number of U.S. troops killed during the first half of October.

15 The Hawaiian Islands are hit by a 6.6-magnitude earthquake, which knocks out electric power in widespread areas and triggers a landslide onto a major highway on the Big Island of Hawaii. The epicenter is about 11 miles (18 kilometers) offshore from Kailua-Kona, a resort on Hawaii's Kona Coast. The United States Geological Survey reports at least 40 aftershocks.

17 U.S. President George W. Bush signs into law legislation that establishes military commissions to try terrorist suspects. The law authorizes the Central Intelligence Agency to continue operating a controversial and once-covert program of detaining and interrogating terrorist suspects in secret prisons outside the United States. The law gives the president the power to designate any non-U.S. citizen as an enemy combatant. In addition, statements obtained by "torture" are not admissible as evidence. However, statements extracted during "harsh interrogation" are allowed under certain conditions. The law bars the president from authorizing interrogation techniques specifically defined by the Geneva Conventions as war crimes. The president, however, is allowed to "interpret the meaning and application" of the Geneva Conventions.

19 The U.S.-led operation to suppress the insurrection and sectarian violence in Baghdad has not succeeded and a new approach is needed, announces Major General William B. Caldwell IV, the senior spokesman for the U.S. military in Iraq. According to the general, attacks in the Iraqi capital increased by 22 percent during the first three weeks of Ramadan compared with the three weeks before the Islamic holy season that began on September 23. At least 71 U.S. soldiers and hundreds of civilians have died in Iraq so far in October.

19 The St. Louis Cardinals beat the New York Mets 3-1 to win the National League Championship of Major League Baseball. The Cardinals will meet the Detroit Tigers in Detroit on October 20 in Game 1 of the World Series.

19 The Dow Jones Industrial Average closes above the 12,000 mark for the first time.

23 Ford Motor Company of Dearborn, Michigan, announces a third-quarter loss of $5.8 billion. Ford officials are attempting to stem the huge losses through restructuring and cost-cutting measures.

26 Exxon Mobil Corporation announces that its third-quarter profits are nearly $10.5 billion, the second largest quarterly profit ever recorded by a publicly traded corporation. The largest quarterly profit —$10.7 billion—was made by Exxon Mobil in the fourth quarter of 2005.

28 The St. Louis Cardinals win the World Series by beating the Detroit Tigers 4-2 in the fifth game of the best-of-seven championship series. The Cardinals took only 83 regular-season wins, the fewest of any World Series winner in history.

28 Hundreds of federal riot police and troops move into the besieged Mexican city of Oaxaca to end a protest that has essentially shut down the center of the resort city for five months.

31 Three U.S. soldiers are killed in Iraq, bringing to 105 the number of American military personnel killed in Iraq in October.

NOVEMBER 2006

1 A classified U.S. Department of Defense briefing, presented by the U.S. Central Command on October 18, describes conditions in Iraq as edging toward chaos. The report, leaked to *The New York Times*, says that "violence [is] at an all-time high, spreading geographically."

3 The International Monetary Fund (IMF) issues a report praising economic growth in Latin America. According to the 2006 IMF Regional Economic Outlook, average growth in the region in 2006 is expected to rise to 4.75 percent, mainly because of high oil prices and tighter inflation controls. The IMF reports that the incomes of the poorest half of the Latin American population is growing twice as fast as those of the top 10 percent.

3 Eleven U.S. soldiers and Marines are killed in Iraq over the last 24 hours, bringing to at least 2,829 the number of U.S. military personnel dying in Iraq since the war began in March 2003. In addition, at least 56 bodies are found in Baghdad, Iraq's capital, over the past 24 hours. All of the victims are men between ages 20 and 45 and show signs of having been tortured.

5 Former Iraqi dictator Saddam Hussein is sentenced to death by hanging for crimes against humanity. Hussein, a Sunni, was found guilty of ordering the killing of 148 people in the predominantly Shi`ah town of Dujail after a 1982 assassination attempt on his life.

7 A large voter turnout for the 2006 midterm elections gives Democrats control of the U.S. House of Representatives for the first time in 12 years. With the results of some races still uncertain, the Democrats appear to have gained at least 27 seats, 12 more than needed to take power. Democrats take five of six seats needed to control the Senate and are leading in Virginia. Political experts chalk up the Democratic victories to voter dissatisfaction with the war in Iraq and with Congressional corruption and scandal.

7 Daniel Ortega, Nicaragua's former Marxist guerrilla leader, regains power in a presidential election victory over Eduardo Montealegre, who was backed by the administration of U.S. President George W. Bush. Ortega takes 38 percent of the vote, compared with 29 percent for Montealegre.

8 Donald H. Rumsfeld resigns as secretary of the United States Department of Defense after serving in the position for nearly six years. President George W. Bush announces that he will nominate Robert Gates to replace Rumsfeld.

9 Senator George Allen (R., Virginia) concedes defeat to his Democratic challenger, Jim Webb, giving Democrats a 51-49 advantage in the U.S. Senate and control of Congress for the first time since 1994.

10 A huge hurricanelike storm with an eye surrounded by towering clouds is swirling over Saturn's South Pole, images from NASA's Cassini probe has revealed. The storm, the first of its kind seen on a planet other than Earth, measures 5,000 miles (8,000 kilometers) across, roughly two-thirds of Earth's diameter.

12 At least 159 Iraqis are killed in another surge of violence. A double suicide bomb attack on the police recruiting station in Baghdad leaves 33 young recruits dead. In addition, more than 75 bodies are found in Baghdad and Baqubah. The victims were murdered execution style.

13 President George W. Bush, meeting with the Iraq Study Group, a commission appointed by the U.S. Congress to study the war in Iraq, announces that conditions, not politics, will dictate troop levels. Press Secretary Tony Snow tells reporters that conditions in Iraq are "not getting better fast enough"

14 The Iraqi minister of higher education temporarily shuts down universities in Baghdad after some 80 gunmen abducted an estimated 100 to 150 men, primarily academics, from the Education Ministry. According to an eyewitness, the gunmen checked identity cards and released Sunnis. The head of the parliamentary education committee characterizes the mass kidnapping as a "national catastrophe."

President George W. Bush escorts outgoing Defense Secretary Donald H. Rumsfeld from the White House Oval Office after announcing Rumsfeld's resignation on November 8. Rumsfeld's abrupt departure came one day after Republicans lost control of both the House of Representatives and Senate in the 2006 midterm elections. Political experts attributed the losses in part to public dissatisfaction with the war in Iraq waged under Rumsfeld's leadership.

16 Democrats unanimously elect Nancy Pelosi (D., California) as speaker of the House of Representatives, the first woman to hold the position.

18 The Sudanese army and the Janjaweed militia launch new attacks on rebel groups in Darfur despite concluding a peace deal in May.

21 A leading anti-Syrian Lebanese minister, Pierre Gemayel, is murdered in Beirut, Lebanon's capital, the fifth prominent anti-Syrian politician killed since 2005.

23 The explosions of five closely timed car bombs in Baghdad's Sadr City leave more than 200 people dead and at least 250 others injured in the deadliest attack on Iraqi civilians since the U.S.-led invasion began in March 2003.

30 President George W. Bush praises Iraqi Prime Minister Nouri al-Maliki at a joint press conference in Amman, Jordan, and vows to strengthen the prime minister's authority over security forces in Iraq without announcing specific plans.

26 Israeli and Palestinian leaders agree to a cease-fire in the Gaza Strip, though rockets fired from Gaza continue to hit Israel.

26 Rafael Correa, a leftist economist who campaigned on a promise to cut Ecuador's dependence on international lenders, wins the Ecuadorean presidency.

27 Canada's Parliament passes a motion 266-16 to recognize the primarily French-speaking province of Quebec as a nation within a united Canada.

30 Heavy rain from Typhoon Durian triggers mudslides on the slopes of the Mayon Volcano in the Philippines, southwest of the capital of Manila, killing at least 1,000 people and leaving hundreds missing.

DECEMBER

2006

Members of the United States Senate and House of Representatives honor former U.S. President Gerald R. Ford, whose remains lie in state in the Capitol Rotunda on December 30.

1 The swearing-in ceremony of Mexico's conservative new president, Felipe Calderón, is marred by jeers and a fracas in Congress involving members of the left-wing Democratic Revolutionary Party, who claim that Calderón won the July election by fraud.

2 The explosions of two car bombs and three mortars in a market in a primarily Shi`ah neighborhood of Baghdad leave at least 50 people dead and more than 90 others wounded. Many of the victims were women shopping for food.

4 President Hugo Chávez of Venezuela is declared the winner of the December 3 presidential election with 61 percent of the vote.

5 Fiji's military ousts the prime minister, Laisenia Qarese, in the South Pacific island country's fourth coup in 20 years. The head of the army, Frank Bainimarama, appoints himself temporary president.

6 The Iraq Study Group, headed by former Secretary of State James Baker and former Representative Lee Hamilton, delivers its long-awaited report on the war in Iraq to President George W. Bush at the White House. The report calls the situation in Iraq "deteriorating" and "gravely dangerous" and reviews various new strategies to stanch the violence. The president says he will take their recommendations "very seriously" and act on them "in a timely fashion."

9 Some of the worst brush fires in nearly 70 years leave much of southeastern Australia swathed in thick smoke. Fires have burned at least 445,000 acres (180,000 hectares) in the state of Victoria.

11 Kofi Annan, in his farewell address as United Nations secretary-general, asks the government of the United States to respect human rights and not abandon its core principles in its "war on terror."

12 A suicide bomber drives an explosive-filled truck into a crowd of Iraqi Shi`ah laborers waiting in a Baghdad square to find day jobs, killing at least 57 people and injuring more than 220 others.

13 Saudi Arabia has informed the administration of President George W. Bush that if the United States pulls its military forces from Iraq, it may aid Iraq's Sunni minority, reveals *The New York Times*.

15 Florida Governor Jeb Bush suspends all executions there after a "botched job" carried out on December 13 and appoints a commission to study the humanity and constitutionality of lethal injections. A federal judge in California rules that lethal injections are cruel and unusual punishment and, thus, unconstitutional.

17 Zimbabwe's ruling Zanu-PF postpones the country's next presidential election from 2008 to 2010, giving President Robert Mugabe an additional two years in office.

18 Robert Gates is sworn in as secretary of the U.S. Department of Defense at a private ceremony at the White House. Gates replaces Donald Rumsfeld, who resigned on November 8 under increasingly heavy criticism for his Iraq War policies.

19 From mid-November 2005 to mid-November 2006, insurgent and sectarian militia attacks in Iraq jumped by 22 percent, to nearly 1,000 per week, the U.S. Defense Department reports.

20 U.S. President George W. Bush, speaking at his final news conference of 2006, calls for an increase in the overall size of the U.S. military without saying whether he plans to send more troops to Iraq. In an interview published on December 19 by *The Washington Post*, President Bush acknowledged for the first time that the United States is not winning the war.

21 The leader of the Union of Islamic Courts (UIC), an Islamist group that controls Som-alia's capital, Mogadishu, and much of southern Somalia, declares war on neighboring Ethiopia, which has some 8,000 troops in Somalia to prop up that country's official but powerless government.

21 Four U.S. Marines are charged with multiple counts of murder for allegedly killing 24 Iraqi civilians, including women, children, and elderly people, in the Iraqi town of Hadithah in 2005. Four U.S. Marine officers are charged with dereliction of duty for allegedly failing to investigate and report the incident.

23 The United Nations Security Council unanimously approves a resolution that imposes sanctions on Iran for its government's refusal to suspend its uranium enrichment program. The resolution calls on all countries to ban the sale of materials and technology that might contribute to Iran's nuclear program.

25 At least two tornadoes cut a swath from west to east across Florida, damaging hundreds of houses. The worst damage occurs around Daytona Beach.

26 A spokesperson for the U.S. military in Iraq announces the death of seven U.S. soldiers, pushing the December death toll of U.S. forces to 90 and the total number killed since the war began in 2003 to at least 2,978.

26 The explosion of an oil pipeline in Lagos, Nigeria, punctured by thieves kills more than 265 people, who are among at least 2,000 people to die in the past 10 years while stealing fuel from pipelines.

26 Iraq's Appeals Court rejects an appeal by Saddam Hussein's lawyers, upholding a death sentence imposed by an Iraqi court on November 5 for the killing of 148 Shi`ah Muslims in the town of Dujail.

26 Gerald R. Ford, the only person to serve as president and vice president of the United States without being elected to either office, dies at age 93.

28 Militias loyal to Somalia's transitional government, backed by Ethiopian forces, unexpectedly seize control of the capital, Mogadishu, from a disintegrating Islamist militia with alleged ties to the al-Qa`ida terrorist network.

30 Former Iraqi dictator Saddam Hussein is executed by Iraqi authorities.

2006 UPDATE

The major events of 2006 are summarized in more than 250 alphabetically arranged articles, from "Afghanistan" to "Zoos." Included are Special Reports that offer an in-depth look at subjects ranging from global warming to immigration. The Special Reports are found on the following pages.

SPECIAL REPORTS

FOCUS ON

PORTRAITS

Afghanistan in 2006 sank further into regional violence, political confusion, and increased production of narcotics—problems that cast doubts on the efforts of a 37-nation alliance to stabilize and rebuild Afghanistan. United States Marine General James Jones, the commander of the North Atlantic Treaty Organization (NATO) troops supporting the Afghan government, announced in September that NATO efforts to curb the country's booming drug trade are "losing ground."

Taliban resurgence. While warlords in northern Afghanistan continued fighting over territory and control of economic assets, the worst conflict was in the country's eastern and southern areas, which are dominated by Pashtuns, the largest of the nation's many ethnic groups. The Taliban, a fundamentalist Islamic element primarily composed of Pashtuns, was based in eastern and southern Afghanistan during its rule of the country from the mid-1990's until 2001. The Taliban had sheltered members of the international al-Qa`ida terrorist organization.

After the Sept. 11, 2001, terrorist attacks in the United States, U.S.-led forces combined with some Afghan elements to successfully drive the Taliban from power. They failed, however, in their second goal of capturing the al-Qa`ida leader, Osama bin Laden, and destroying his network. He remained at large in 2006. The Taliban slowly regrouped, and guerrilla attacks increased in 2006 against the government of President Hamid Karzai and its foreign supporters. In early 2006, Taliban forces began denying the government control of much of the southern part of the country.

Taliban militants also attacked such civilian targets as schools, medical stations, and road-building projects in an effort to drive out government influence. On August 4, officials from the United Nations (UN) Children's Fund cautioned that increased attacks on schools in southern Afghanistan left an estimated 100,000 children out of school. A senior female Afghan official was assassinated on September 25. Some experts suggested that Taliban militants might have assassinated her because they oppose women holding government positions.

Some 10,000 U.S. troops focused on trying to deny the insurgents access to Afghanistan from across its rugged border with Pakistan. Pakistan's president, General Pervez Musharraf, acknowledged in the Afghan capital, Kabul, on September 7 that Taliban insurgents and al-Qa`ida terrorists were "crossing from the Pakistani border and causing bomb blasts in Afghanistan." He denied that his government was "behind anything happening in Afghanistan."

NATO in 2006 commanded an International Security Assistance Force of some 31,000 troops. On July 31, responsibility for security in the south was transferred from U.S.-led coalition forces to some 8,000 NATO troops. The NATO force quickly ran into heavy fighting with Taliban militants. The NATO units, which were primarily British, Canadian, and Dutch, were supplemented by newly trained Afghan army soldiers. Coalition air power assisted the NATO force, but shortages of helicopters and transport aircraft proved problematic.

Intensified fighting in the south—the worst that NATO units had encountered since the alliance was formed in 1949—resulted in the deaths of dozens of NATO troops and hundreds of Afghans. Many were victims of suicide attacks and improvised explosive devices, which had been widely used in Iraq but had been absent from Afghanistan until late 2005. Military observers believed Taliban fighters were learning the techniques of Iraqi insurgents.

A suicide attack in the south on Aug. 3, 2006, killed 21 civilians shortly after 4 NATO soldiers had died in combat nearby. A suicide bomber rammed a U.S. military convoy in Kabul on September 8, killing 2 American soldiers and 14 civilians. Two days later, a suicide bomber killed a provincial governor who was a close friend of President Karzai. Another bombing at the governor's funeral killed five policemen and two children.

The worst violence in Kabul since the fall of the Taliban in 2001 occurred on May 29, 2006. The driver of a U.S. Army truck lost control during morning rush hour and crashed, killing 3 people. The incident touched off an anti-American riot in which 14 civilians died. According to Afghan police, U.S. troops in the runaway truck's convoy fired into the angry mob, killing 4 bystanders.

Opium. NATO's southern operational area was the center of Afghan cultivation of opium poppies used to make heroin. The UN Office on Drugs and Crime reported on September 2 that the poppy crop rose an estimated 59 percent in 2006, to produce a record 6,700 tons (6,100 metric tons), or 92 percent of the world supply. The Taliban encouraged poppy growth and funded much of their resurgence with drug money.

A $1-billion government and foreign effort to reduce poppy cultivation was "an absolute disaster," a Western narcotics official said. An estimated 35 percent of Afghanistan's economic output came from opium. One former Afghan minister noted that, "If you got rid of drugs overnight, the economy would collapse."

Christian trial. In March 2006, an Afghan man was put on trial after converting from Islam to Christianity. Muslim clerics called for his execution, but he was released in March and took asylum in Italy. Some members of parliament denounced the man's release from prison. They also blocked Karzai's efforts to name qualified jurists, rather than traditional Muslim clerics, to the supreme court.   ■ Henry S. Bradsher

See also **Armed forces; Drug abuse; Pakistan.**

AFRICA

Regional and international efforts to bring peace to a number of war-ravaged African countries continued in 2006. During the year, progress toward peace and stability was achieved in Angola, the Democratic Republic of the Congo (DRC)—also known as Congo (Kinshasa)—and Uganda. However, ongoing violence and instability in Chad, Côte d'Ivoire, and Somalia presented tough challenges to African and international leaders.

Global trade talks. The prospects for more peaceful conditions in Africa went hand in hand with economic revitalization, analysts noted. However, the suspension of trade talks under the auspices of the United Nations (UN) World Trade Organization (WTO)—the so-called "Doha Round"—was a major setback for the world's developing countries, including much of Africa. The negotiations, which took their name from a 2001 kickoff meeting in Doha, capital of Qatar, aimed at broadly reforming world trade. As the talks progressed, eliminating wealthy nations' agricultural subsidies to create a more level playing field for the trading of farm produce emerged as a major stumbling block. After an unproductive gathering of trade negotiators in July 2006 in Geneva, Switzerland, the WTO suspended the Doha Round.

Reducing agricultural subsidies as part of international trade reform was particularly important to agricultural regions of Africa. Unsubsidized farmers in those poorer countries could not hope to compete with heavily subsidized farmers in wealthy countries. According to agricultural experts, the prospects for many small farmers in Africa will not improve as long as world competition remained uneven.

Africa and Asia. Chinese involvement in Africa, already significant before 2006, increased during the year. As China's industrial sector expanded, Chinese industrialists looked increasingly toward resource-rich regions of the world. Africa, with its mineral and petroleum wealth, offered an attractive target for investment.

Both Chinese President Hu Jintao and Premier Wen Jiabao visited various African countries in 2006. In November, more than 40 African heads of state met in Beijing for a conference on Afro-Chinese relations. Chinese leaders used the opportunity to announce $3 billion in new loans to the continent and debt cancellation for a number of countries.

India, another rapidly industrializing Asian nation, pursued trade with and investment in a number of African countries in 2006. According to trade experts, India continued investing heavily in the South African economy during the year.

African Union. Human rights issues received much attention at the July summit of the African Union (AU) in Banjul, capital of the West African nation of Gambia. The AU is a political association of 53 African countries.

The AU delegates approved plans for a new judicial institution, the African Court on Human and Peoples' Rights, to be based in Arusha, Tanzania. A special panel, with full AU backing, ordered that former President Hissene Habre of Chad be tried in a Senegalese court on charges of mass murder and torture. Habre took power in Chad in a violent *coup* (overthrow) in 1982 and remained in power until 1990 when he was deposed. Habre had been prosecuted on human rights charges in a court in Senegal, but a judge later ruled that the court did not have jurisdiction over the former Chadian ruler. The 2006 AU decision was meant to remove this legal impediment so that the trial could go forward.

Women's roles. Across the sub-Saharan region of Africa, women played increasingly larger roles in politics, government, and business in the new millennium. The expanding political power of women was best symbolized in 2006 by the inauguration in January of Ellen Johnson-Sirleaf as president of Liberia. Africa's first elected female president explained her election as recognition by the people of Liberia that the men who had ruled the country before her had failed. She added that women leaders would be more likely to act as peacemakers in a region that desperately needed an end to endemic warfare.

Rwanda is one of Africa's most transformed societies in terms of women's roles. In that small central African nation, ethnic killings in 1994 had left 800,000 people dead, a high proportion of them men. One result of the genocide was that the country's surviving population was 70 percent female.

In the following years, Rwandan women assumed new roles in business and politics. By

Citizens of Congo (Kinshasa) wait to receive voter cards at an electoral commission office in July 2006. Holders of the cards were entitled to vote in the country's first multiparty presidential election in 41 years. Jean-Pierre Bemba and Joseph Kabila, the country's incumbent transitional president, emerged as the top votegetters in the poll. Kabila went on to defeat Bemba in an October 29 runoff election.

2006, women had achieved virtual parity with men in the legislature and courts. Women in government spearheaded reforms to remove anti-female discrimination, and women educators revitalized the school system. Sociologists noted that as Rwandan women acquired greater social and political power, the birth rate fell—from eight children per family in the 1980's to six per family in the mid-2000's. The decline proved to be a significant development in a poor and densely populated country.

Women took a greater share of political power in other African nations in 2006. In the parliaments of Burundi, Mozambique, and South Africa, the proportion of women legislators stood at 30 percent or greater in 2006. Mozambique had a female prime minister, South Africa and Zimbabwe had women vice presidents, and Tanzania had a female foreign minister.

Central Africa. Successful multiparty elections in Congo (Kinshasa) during the second half of 2006 signaled a new political beginning for a country that had last staged free elections in 1965 and had since endured decades of dictatorship and civil strife. The elections, which began in July 2006 and culminated in the October 29 election of Joseph Kabila as president (he had previously served as the interim president under a temporary government), gave the DRC a constitutional government with an elected parliament and executive.

In Chad, rebel forces—based in the eastern part of the country and allegedly supplied by neighboring Sudan—repeatedly challenged the administration of President Idriss Deby. Deby, Chad's leader since taking power in a 1990 military coup, won reelection to a third presidential term in February 2006. However, a boycott by opposition parties, angry over Deby's legal maneuvering to secure a constitutional amendment allowing him to run for reelection, marred the polling.

In the predawn hours of April 13, a column of rebels associated with the United Front for Change invaded the outskirts of Chad's capital,

FACTS IN BRIEF ON AFRICAN POLITICAL UNITS

Country	Population	Government	Monetary unit*	Foreign trade (million U.S.$)	
				Exports[†]	Imports[†]
Algeria	33,390,000	President Abdelaziz Bouteflika; Prime Minister Abdelaziz Belkhadem	dinar (71.35 = $1)	49,590	22,530
Angola	14,962,000	President José Eduardo dos Santos	kwanza (80.37 = $1)	26,800	8,165
Benin	7,284,000	President Thomas Yayi Boni	CFA franc (516.91 = $1)	827	1,043
Botswana	1,650,000	President Festus Mogae	pula (6.49 = $1)	3,680	3,370
Burkina Faso	14,209,000	President Blaise Compaore	CFA franc (516.91 = $1)	395	992
Burundi	7,561,000	President Pierre Nkurunziza	franc (1,058.51 = $1)	52	200
Cameroon	16,798,000	President Paul Biya	CFA franc (516.91 = $1)	3,236	2,514
Cape Verde	486,000	President Pedro Pires; Prime Minister José Maria Pereira Neves	escudo (86.68 = $1)	73	500
Central African Republic	4,021,000	President François Bozizé	CFA franc (516.91 = $1)	131	203
Chad	9,382,000	President Idriss Deby	CFA franc (516.91 = $1)	3,016	749
Comoros	666,000	President Ahmed Abdallah Mohamed Sambi	franc (387.73 = $1)	34	115
Congo (Brazzaville)	4,035,000	President Denis Sassou-Nguesso	CFA franc (516.91 = $1)	2,209	807
Congo (Kinshasa)	57,683,000	President Joseph Kabila	franc (540 = $1)	1,108	1,319
Côte d'Ivoire (Ivory Coast)	17,428,000	President Laurent Gbagbo	CFA franc (516.91 = $1)	6,490	4,759
Djibouti	731,000	President Ismail Omar Guelleh; Prime Minister Dileita Mohamed Dileita	franc (177.72 = $1)	250	987
Egypt	76,346,000	President Hosni Mubarak; Prime Minister Ahmed Nazif	pound (5.74 = $1)	14,330	24,100
Equatorial Guinea	534,000	President Teodoro Obiang Nguema Mbasogo; Prime Minister Ricardo Mangue Obama Nfubea	CFA franc (516.91 = $1)	6,727	1,864
Eritrea	4,603,000	President Issaias Afewerki	nafka (15.00 = $1)	34	677
Ethiopia	70,440,000	President Girma Woldegiorgis; Prime Minister Meles Zenawi	birr (8.75 = $1)	612	2,722
Gabon	1,400,000	President El Hadj Omar Bongo Ondimba; Prime Minister Jean Eyeghe Ndong	CFA franc (516.91 = $1)	5,813	1,533
Gambia	1,533,000	Head of State Yahya A. J. J. Jammeh	dalasi (27.95 = $1)	140	197
Ghana	21,210,000	President John Agyekum Kufuor	cedi (9,245.00 = $1)	3,010	3,699
Guinea	9,013,000	President Lansana Conté	franc (5,555.00 = $1)	612	680
Guinea-Bissau	1,629,000	President João Bernardo Vieira	CFA franc (516.91 = $1)	116	176
Kenya	33,260,000	President Mwai Kibaki	shilling (72.50 = $1)	3,173	5,126
Lesotho	1,868,000	King Letsie III; Prime Minister Pakalitha Mosisili	loti (7.80 = $1)	603	1,166

*Exchange rates as of Oct. 5, 2006.   [†]Latest available data.

Country	Population	Government	Monetary unit*	Foreign trade (million U.S.$)	
				Exports[†]	Imports[†]
Liberia	3,701,000	President Ellen Johnson-Sirleaf	dollar (59.50 = $1)	910	4,839
Libya	6,003,000	Leader Mu'ammar Muhammad al-Qadhafi; General People's Committee Secretary (Prime Minister) al-Baghdadi Ali al-Mahmudi	dinar (1.31 = $1)	30,790	10,820
Madagascar	18,910,000	President Marc Ravalomanana	ariary (2,165.00 = $1)	951	1,400
Malawi	12,806,000	President Bingu wa Mutharika	kwacha (138.13 = $1)	364	645
Mali	14,267,000	President Amadou Toumani Touré; Prime Minister Ousmane Issoufi Maïga	CFA franc (516.91 = $1)	323	1,858
Mauritania	3,153,000	Chairman, Military Council Ely Ould Mohamed Vall; Prime Minister Sidi Mohamed Ould Boubacar	ouguiya (271.30 = $1)	784	1,124
Mauritius	1,236,000	President Sir Anerood Jugnauth; Prime Minister Navinchandra Ramgoolam	rupee (32.40 = $1)	1,949	2,507
Morocco	29,631,000	King Mohamed VI Prime Minister Driss Jettou	dirham (8.72 = $1)	9,472	18,150
Mozambique	19,787,000	President Armando Guebuza	new metical (25.98 = $1)	1,690	2,041
Namibia	1,978,000	President Hifikepunye Pohamba	dollar (7.81 = $1)	2,040	2,350
Niger	13,333,000	President Mamadou Tandja	CFA franc (516.91 = $1)	222	588
Nigeria	133,205,000	President Olusegun Obasanjo	naira (128.00 = $1)	52,160	25,950
Rwanda	8,788,000	President Paul Kagame	franc (549.46 = $1)	98	243
São Tomé and Príncipe	177,000	President Fradique de Menezes	dobra (6,825.50 = $1)	8	38
Senegal	10,829,000	President Abdoulaye Wade; Prime Minister Macky Sall	CFA franc (516.91 = $1)	1,526	2,405
Seychelles	83,000	President James Michel	rupee (5.52 = $1)	312	460
Sierra Leone	5,439,000	President Ahmad Tejan Kabbah	leone (2,985.51 = $1)	185	531
Somalia	10,980,000	President Abdullahi Yusuf Ahmed	shilling (1,371.69 = $1)	241	576
South Africa	48,421,000	President Thabo Mvuyelwa Mbeki	rand (7.81 = $1)	50,910	52,970
Sudan	35,667,000	President Umar Hassan Ahmad al-Bashir	dinar (208.17 = $1)	6,989	5,028
Swaziland	977,000	King Mswati III; Prime Minister Absalom Themba Dlamini	lilangeni (7.81 = $1)	1,991	2,149
Tanzania	39,962,000	President Jakaya Kikwete	shilling (1,266.00 = $1)	1,581	2,391
Togo	5,243,000	President Faure Gnassingbé	CFA franc (516.91 = $1)	768	1,047
Tunisia	10,147,000	President Zine el-Abidine Ben Ali; Prime Minister Mohamed Ghannouchi	dinar (1.33 = $1)	10,300	12,860
Uganda	28,606,000	President Yoweri Kaguta Museveni	shilling (1,859.00 = $1)	768	1,608
Zambia	11,183,000	President Levy Mwanawasa	kwacha (3,750.00 = $1)	1,947	1,934
Zimbabwe	12,975,000	President Robert Gabriel Mugabe	dollar (250.00 = $1)	1,644	2,059

N'Djamena, and fought their way toward the city center. Forces loyal to the government, however, defeated and drove out the rebels, at a cost of several hundred dead. Observers alleged that French fighter planes had helped defeat the rebel forces. A small French military force was in Chad, at President Deby's invitation.

The rebel forces retreated to the eastern border areas, where they continued to raid settlements. In November, the Deby government declared a state of emergency in N'Djamena and in eastern Chadian towns as rebel forces again advanced westward. On November 25, rebels overran Abeche, the largest city in eastern Chad. The rebel forces quickly abandoned the city amid uncon-firmed rumors that they were advancing on N'Djamena.

In a November 30 visit to N'Djamena, French Prime Minister Dominique de Villepin pledged support to President Deby in the government's fight against the rebels. Villepin announced that France was expanding its military mission in Chad to 1,200 troops and would supply Deby's air force with additional airplanes.

Eastern Africa and the Horn. Events in Somalia in 2006 pushed the long-troubled country into civil war, which regional experts feared might engulf the Horn of Africa in a regional war. Government institutions had failed in Somalia in the early 1990's, when independent warlords toppled dictator Mohamed Siad Barre and took control of Mogadishu, the capital, and other areas of the country. In 2004, Somali leaders, under the auspices of international sponsors, had reconstituted a government-in-exile with a president and parliament based in Nairobi, Kenya. That government, recognized by most Western nations, relocated in 2005 to Baydhabo, Somalia, which is about 155 miles (250 kilometers) west of Mogadishu.

A group of Islamic leaders—the Union of Islamic Courts (UIC)—mobilized Islamic militias in 2006 to drive warlords out of Mogadishu, and in July the UIC militias took control of the capital. The clan-based religious courts in Somalia, which expounded fundamentalist Islamic values, had for years provided leadership and social cohesion in the fractured Somali society, recruiting their own militias and imposing Islamic law. By autumn 2006, the militias loyal to the UIC held most of southern and central Somalia.

As the UIC expanded its reach, neighboring Ethiopia sent a military force across the border into Somalia to bolster the Baydhabo-based transitional government. Ethiopia's leaders feared the influence on their own Muslim minority of a resurgent Islamic neighbor, analysts suggested. In response, UIC leaders based in Mogadishu declared *jihad* (holy war) on the Ethiopian troops. Terrorists allegedly linked to the UIC carried out suicide bombing attacks in Baydhabo in September and November.

Despite peace talks between representatives of the Baydhabo and UIC governments—which were sponsored by the AU in Khartoum, Sudan, and convened periodically between June and September—the situation in Somalia continued to deteriorate. In November, representatives of the United States presented a proposal to the UN Security Council for sending a peacekeeping force to Somalia to aid the transitional government at Baydhabo. In late November, Ethiopian Prime Minister Meles Zenawi declared that his country had completed its preparations for war and stood ready to fight the Mogadishu-based UIC.

On December 21, UIC leader Sheikh Hassan Dahir Aweys announced that Islamist militias were battling transitional government troops backed by Ethiopian forces outside Baydhabo. In what regional experts described as a "stunning reversal of fortunes," the UIC militias, the most powerful force in the country just weeks ago, disintegrated before the Ethiopian-led troops; and on December 28, Somalia's transitional government seized control of Mogadishu.

In February, Uganda held its first multiparty elections in 26 years. Ugandan voters reelected President Yoweri Museveni to a third term and gave Museveni's ruling National Resistance Movement a majority in Parliament. In late 2006, a truce and Sudan-based negotiations between the Ugandan government and the Lord's Resistance Army, a rebel group active in northern Uganda since the mid-1980's, raised new hopes for a lasting and comprehensive peace settlement.

Southern Africa. In July 2006 in Luanda, capital of Angola, representatives of the Angolan government and Cabinda-based rebels signed a peace agreement, ending a 30-year insurgency in the tiny, oil-rich province. Cabinda is a small enclave in the north, separated from the rest of Angola by a thin strip of land belonging to Congo (Kinshasa). The peace agreement authorized the establishment of a local government in Cabinda that would exercise considerable autonomy while remaining nominally under the authority of Angola's central government.

The Southern African Development Community held its annual summit in Maseru, capital of Lesotho, in August. The association of 14 southern African nations, strongly promoted by the government of South Africa, put forward an ambitious program of economic integration. Proposals included the establishment of a free trade zone by 2008, a *customs union* (a group of nations that abide by the same set of rules in international trade) by 2010, and a single-currency area by 2018. Observers reported, however, that the summit's accomplishments fell short of delegates' expectations and that the body had failed to meet any of its stated goals.

West Africa. Liberia's former president, Charles Taylor, was arrested and returned to Liberia from exile in Nigeria in March 2006. Taylor, charged with numerous war crimes, was expected to be tried at the UN Special Court in Freetown, Sierra Leone's capital. However, officials of the International War Crimes Tribunal in The Hague, Netherlands, moved Taylor's trial to that court for security reasons. Taylor's partisans were alleged to have committed numerous atrocities during Liberia's civil war. Taylor also stood accused of backing rebels in neighboring Sierra Leone, who were in turn accused of numerous atrocities and war crimes.

On August 14, 2006, Nigeria formally ceded the Bakassi Peninsula, a 400-square-mile (1,000-square-kilometer) patch of coastal swampland, to Cameroon. Possession of the oil-rich peninsula had been the subject of a 13-year dispute between the two countries.

In October 2002, the International Court of Justice in The Hague, Netherlands, had issued a ruling that awarded the peninsula to Cameroon, but the Nigerian government refused to accept the decision. The UN then intervened by setting up a joint commission to solve the dispute. In June 2006, presidents Olusegun Obasanjo of Nigeria and Paul Biya of Cameroon signed an agreement at the UN in New York City arranging for Nigeria's transfer of the territory to Cameroon. The agreement called for Nigeria to withdraw its troops and granted Nigerians residing on the peninsula a two-year grace period in which to choose whether to stay and become citizens of Cameroon or immigrate to Nigerian territory.

The UN Security Council in November approved a new peace plan for Côte d'Ivoire, a once-prosperous West African country that had been severely disrupted by fighting between rebel and government forces since 2002. The Security Council granted Prime Minister Charles Konan Banny expanded powers to restructure the armed forces, disarm militias, and stabilize the country ahead of elections to take place by October 2007. The council's plan curbed the powers of President Laurent Gbagbo, who according to international observers had failed to provide effective leadership and had tacitly encouraged the activities of progovernment militias.

Voters in the small West African nation of Benin elected Thomas Yayi Boni as president in March 2006. Political analysts regarded Boni, a former director of the West African Development Bank, as a political outsider not tainted by corruption scandals that had beset the administration of retiring President Mathieu Kerekou, who had ruled Benin for 30 years. ■ Pieter Esterhuysen

See also **AIDS; International trade; People in the news** (Ellen Johnson-Sirleaf); **United Nations;** and the various African country articles.

Agriculture. In 2006, drought reduced global supplies of wheat. Stocks of other feed grains, oilseeds, and cotton equaled or exceeded supplies in 2005. Globally, farmers increased plantings of genetically modified (GM) seed. Interest in replacing petroleum-based fuels with plant-based fuels soared.

World crop production. World wheat production totaled 589 million metric tons, down 5 percent from 2005, according to a report from the United States Department of Agriculture (USDA) released in November 2006. Extreme drought cut Australia's wheat crop by more than half to 10.5 million metric tons. Production also fell in the European Union (EU) by 8 percent, to 117 million metric tons. Russia, Kazakhstan, and Ukraine harvested 83 million metric tons of wheat, 10 percent below the 2005 crop. Drought also reduced U.S. wheat production in 2006 by 14 percent, to 49 million metric tons (1.8 billion bushels).

World production of coarse (or small) grains was projected at 965 million metric tons. (Coarse grains include corn, barley, sorghum, and oats, with corn making up two-thirds of this category.) Drought cut small grain production in Australia to 8 million metric tons, 43 percent below the 2005 harvest. China's corn crop rose in 2006 to 143 million metric tons. The United States harvested 273 million metric tons (10.7 billion bushels), the third largest total on record.

World oilseed production—soybeans, sunflower seeds, cottonseed, and rapeseed—was expected to total 396 million metric tons. In the United States, soybean production—the largest component of oilseeds—reached 97 million metric tons (3.2 billion bushels), a new record. Brazil and Argentina also increased crop totals in 2006, to 56 million and 41 million metric tons, respectively.

The global rice harvest totaled about 417 million metric tons. The U.S. crop, at 6 million metric tons (193 hundredweight), was 13 percent below the 2005 harvest. Expected harvests elsewhere included 128 million metric tons in China; 91 million metric tons in India; 18 million metric tons in Thailand; and 23 million metric tons in Vietnam.

World cotton production increased slightly to 115 million bales. (One bale is equivalent to 480 pounds (217 kilograms) of cotton.) China's 30-million-bale crop—expected to be 14.5 percent above 2005 levels—offset reductions in Australia, Greece, Pakistan, and Syria. Timely rains helped U.S. farmers produce 21 million bales in 2006, only 2 million bales fewer than a year earlier.

GM crops. The use of biotech crops—those genetically modified to resist herbicides or insects or both—continued to grow in 2006. The International Service for the Acquisition of Agri-Biotech Applications (ISAAA), an organization that promotes the use of biotechnology in developing countries, announced in 2005 that 90 percent of the 8.5 million farmers planting biotech crops were resource-poor farmers in developing countries. Argentina, Brazil, Canada, and the United States still had the most acres devoted to biotech soybeans, corn, cotton, and canola. However, 7.7 million poor subsistence farmers also benefited from biotech crops, according to the ISAAA. About 6.4 million of this number farmed in China, with India accounting for most of the rest.

Acreage planted with biotech crops in the United States increased in 2006 for the 10th year in a row. Biotech crops accounted for 61 percent of corn acreage, 89 percent of soybean acreage, and 83 percent of cotton acreage.

On August 18, Bayer CropScience in Monheim, Germany, announced that trace amounts of the protein Liberty Link 601, used to make plants resistant to herbicides, had been found in U.S. long grain rice. Although the U.S. Food and Drug Administration concluded that the rice posed no threat to people, it had not been approved for human consumption. As a result, U.S. long grain rice exports declined by 12 percent.

Organic food. Sales of organic food in the United States were expected to reach $16 billion in 2006, representing 2.5 percent of all retail food sales. According to a May survey by the Organic Trade Association, meat, condiments, and dairy products showed the largest sales increase among the food categories in 2005. Organic flowers, pet food, and fiber led purchases in the nonfood categories.

Higher gasoline prices and a backlash against foreign oil in 2006 increased interest in the development of home-grown, renewable fuels in the United States. In 2005, Brazil and the United States led the world in ethanol production, with more than 4 billion gallons each. In 2006, U.S. ethanol producers were expected to use about 20 percent of the domestic corn crop, or 2 billion bushels—up from 14 percent in 2005—to make about 5 billion gallons (19 billion liters) of ethanol.

The United States, Canada, and many EU countries also produced biodiesel using different *feedstocks* (primary materials). The United States uses soybeans, Canada uses canola, and the EU countries use oil from rapeseed and sunflower seeds. In 2005, the United States produced 75 million gallons (284 million liters) of biodiesel. About 13 percent of soybean oil went to biodiesel production.

The expected growth in ethanol production caused livestock producers and those involved in efforts to fight global hunger to question the wisdom of using food crops to make fuel. In November 2006, livestock producers and food companies paid an average of $3.00 per bushel for corn, 35 percent above the average harvest-time price of $1.95 per bushel.

Avian flu. A virulent form of *avian* (bird) influenza continued to spread among poultry and wild birds in Africa, Asia, and Europe in 2006. As of October, 57 countries had confirmed cases of the highly contagious H5N1 strain of the virus. From February through April, the number of countries reporting H5N1 cases in animals was more than twice the number reporting cases from 2003 through 2005. By late 2006, at least 220 million birds had died from the virus or had been killed in efforts to contain its spread.

In the United States, federal, state, and local governments established measures to prevent the importation of infected poultry and increased the testing of migratory birds and domestic poultry to detect any appearance of the virus. In 2006, the United States provided $392 million to help developing countries counter the virus by establishing prevention plans, building laboratories, and training scientists.

BSE. On January 20, Japan reimposed a ban on U.S. beef after finding veal with an attached vertebral column in a shipment. Vertebral column is considered a specified risk material associated with the transmission of bovine spongiform encephalopathy (BSE), a degenerative nervous system disease in cattle, also known as "mad cow disease." Japan had halted its beef trade with the United States in December 2003 after the discovery of a BSE-infected cow in Washington state. Japan had lifted the ban in December 2005.

Japan reopened its market to U.S. beef on July 27, 2006, but import levels were lackluster because of Japanese limitations on the age of cattle used for processing. Most countries accept beef and beef products from U.S. cattle that are up to 30 months old. Japan insists on products from cattle no older than 20 months. On November 13, Japan confirmed its 30th case of BSE. Since 2003, the United States has had two cases of BSE, one in a cow born in Canada.

Trade. On Aug. 1, 2006, U.S. officials ended a key component of the cotton subsidy program to comply with a 2004 World Trade Organization ruling. The same ruling suggested other potential problems with U.S. farm programs in which payments are tied to production.

The world trade talks—the so-called Doha Round—stalled in July 2006 over disagreements on agricultural issues. The United States wanted a substantial cut in the average global tariff of 62 percent to open markets to U.S. goods. The average U.S. tariff on imported agricultural products is 12 percent. The United States exported a record $68.7 billion in agricultural products in 2006.   ■ Patricia Peak Klintberg

See also **Africa; Energy supply: A Special Report; Food; International trade.**

AIDS. The year 2006 marked the 25th anniversary of the first-reported cases of AIDS. Since the first reports, HIV (the virus that causes AIDS) has led to the deaths of some 500,000 people in the United States and more than 22 million people worldwide.

Toronto AIDS conference. At the XVI International AIDS Conference, held in Toronto, Canada, in August 2006, attendees called for expanded access to both prevention and treatment. Some experts at the meeting noted that male circumcision could prevent many cases of AIDS in Africa, but religious and cultural barriers stood in the way. In December, researchers with the U.S. national Institutes of Health announced findings from two studies that circumcision reduces HIV infection rates by 50 percent among heterosexual men.

Three-in-one drugs. The first 3-in-1 antiretrovirus pill for use in U.S.-sponsored treatments of HIV/AIDS patients in poor nations was approved by the U.S. Food and Drug Administration in July. HIV is a type of retrovirus, a virus made of ribonucleic acid and containing an enzyme called reverse transcriptase. The approval was part of the President's Emergency Plan for AIDS Relief, a five-year, $15-billion program launched in 2003 to help treat HIV/AIDS patients in poor nations in Africa, Asia, and elsewhere.

The new pill combines three common drugs (Retrovir, Epivir, and Viramune), allowing patients to take one pill twice per day, rather than having to take multiple pills every day. Public health experts hoped the pill, manufactured by Aurobindo Pharma of India, would make it more likely that HIV/AIDS patients would take their proper doses of medication, thereby inhibiting the replication of HIV, slowing its spread, and reducing the risk of HIV becoming drug resistant.

Later in July, the FDA approved another 3-in-1 pill for HIV/AIDS patients in the United States. Named Atripia, the pill combined the existing medications of Viread, Emtriva, and Sustiva.

Malaria and AIDS. The spread of AIDS and malaria in Africa appear to be linked, according to a report issued in December by researchers at the Fred Hutchinson Cancer Research Center and the University of Washington, both in Seattle. The researchers found that the way the two diseases interact causes both to spread faster.

New testing guidelines. In September, the CDC released new guidelines on HIV testing. The guidelines recommended that doctors routinely screen all patients between ages 13 and 64 for HIV. The CDC explained that more widespread testing was needed to improve care for the estimated 250,000 Americans who do not know they are infected with HIV.   ■ Alfred J. Smuskiewicz

See also **Africa; Asia; Drugs; Public health.**

Albania. In 2006, Prime Minister Sali Berisha focused on improving Albania's position for admission to the European Union (EU) and North Atlantic Treaty Organization (NATO). In June, Albania signed a Stabilization and Association Agreement (SAA), which is regarded as a precursor to EU membership negotiations.

During 2006, Albania embraced reform initiatives tailored to meet EU requirements. The government aggressively prosecuted organized crime, and Parliament passed civil service reforms. In September, Prime Minister Berisha maneuvered EU-recommended election reforms through Parliament. In 2005, EU officials had postponed signing an SAA with Albania because of concerns about the conduct of elections.

At a September 2006 gathering of NATO-member defense officials in Tiranë, the capital, then-United States Secretary of Defense Donald Rumsfeld praised Albania for its participation in the U.S.-led war on terror. In 2006, Albania contributed about 200 troops to coalition forces in Iraq and Afghanistan.

Albania's economy grew by 5 percent in 2006. Analysts attributed some of the expansion to remittances sent back by as many as 1 million Albanians living abroad.   ■ Sharon L. Wolchik

See also **Europe.**

Alberta. See **Canadian provinces.**

Algeria. President Vladimir Putin of Russia visited Algeria in March 2006, the first such visit by a Russian leader since the 1991 fall of Communism in the Soviet Union. Putin's meeting reportedly led to an agreement to cancel Algeria's $4.7-billion debt to Russia in exchange for Algeria's purchase of an estimated $7.5 billion in Russian fighter planes and defense systems.

In 2006, Anadarko Petroleum Corporation of Houston, the largest United States firm in Algeria, more than doubled its 2005 investment there by earmarking $125 million for new and existing oil-development projects. In February 2006, the Anglo-Dutch company Royal Dutch Shell signed an agreement with Algeria's national energy company, Sonatrach, to cooperate on a number of energy-related projects.

The Peace and Reconciliation Charter, a six-month-long *amnesty* (pardon) for Islamic militants in Algeria, expired at the end of August. Only an estimated 250 to 300 militants laid down their arms and renounced violence under the terms of the charter. The government released more than 2,200 Islamic terrorists from prison as part of the amnesty.   ■ Mary-Jane Deeb

See also **Africa; Terrorism.**

Andorra. See **Europe.**

Angola. See **Africa.**

Animal. See **Biology; Conservation; Zoos.**

Anthropology. The 3.3-million-year-old fossils of a child found in Ethiopia represent the most complete skeleton of a juvenile early *hominid* (human ancestor) ever discovered. Zeresenay Alemseged, an Ethiopian scholar at the Max Planck Institute for Evolutionary Anthropology in Leipzig, Germany, and his co-workers announced the discovery in the Sept. 21, 2006, issue of *Nature.* The fossils were found from 2000 to 2003 in the remote Afar region at a site called Dikika .

The specimen's anatomy led the researchers to assign the fossil to the species *Australopithecus afarensis.* The most famous member of this species is the fossil nicknamed "Lucy," discovered in 1974 at Hadar, just north of Dikika.

The Dikika specimen is remarkably complete for such an ancient fossil. The specimen consists of a nearly complete skull; an attached lower jaw; several ribs; both collar bones and shoulder blades; many vertebrae; arm and hand bones; and portions of a lower limb.

The knee joint on the lower limb clearly shows that this individual walked upright. Surprisingly, the shoulder blades resemble those seen in gorillas and suggest that *A. afarensis* may have spent considerable time in trees, perhaps to find food or build sleeping nests at night. Curved finger bones, a feature of modern apes, also suggest these creatures led a more *arboreal* (tree-dwelling) lifestyle than later hominids.

Using computed tomography (CT) scanning, scientists were able to image internal structures of the skull. With African apes as a model for tooth development, they concluded that the child was about 3 years old when it died.

The "Dikika baby" fossils are providing invaluable insights into the growth and development of *A. afarensis.* Scientists calculated the fossil's cranial capacity, an indication of brain size, at 17 cubic inches (275 cubic centimeters). Cranial capacity would have expanded to roughly 24 cubic inches (400 cubic centimeters) had the child survived to adulthood. In contrast, modern adult human brains average about 73 cubic inches (1,200 cubic centimeters). Comparisons with human and ape brains suggest the child had a growth rate more similar to that of modern people than apes.

Neandertal DNA. New insights into Neandertals appeared in 2006, 150 years after the discovery of the first Neandertal skeleton in Germany's Neander Valley. A crucial issue surrounding the extinct Neandertals is whether they were a separate species from modern human beings or were simply a more primitive stage of *Homo sapiens.* Most anthropologists favor classifying Neandertals as a separate species, *Homo neanderthalensis.* This designation is based on differences in anatomy as well as genetic differences between modern people and Neandertals.

A paleontologist displays the 3.3- million-year-old fossil of a female child, perhaps 3 years of age, found at a site called Dikika in Ethiopia. The discovery was announced in 2006. Researchers describe the fossil as the most complete skeleton of a juvenile early hominid ever found.

Scientists extracted a form of DNA, called *mitochondrial DNA* (mtDNA), from several Neandertal fossils. DNA (deoxyribonucleic acid) is a chainlike molecule found in all living cells. MtDNA comes from mitochrondria, the power units of the cells, rather than the cell's nucleus. MtDNA extracted in 2006 from a fossil tooth of a Neandertal child, dating to about 100,000 years ago, supports the idea that Neandertals and modern human beings are different species. In addition, geneticist Svante Pääbo of the Max Planck Institute for Evolutionary Anthropology extracted nuclear DNA from a 45,000-year-old Neandertal fossil from Vindija, Croatia. He concluded that this DNA was very different from modern human DNA.

In 2006, anthropologist Clive Finlayson of the Gibraltar Museum and his colleagues excavated Neandertal artifacts from Gorhams's Cave on the Gibraltar peninsula. Radiocarbon dating suggested that these finds date from 24,000 to 28,000 years ago. Several nearby sites once occupied by *Homo sapiens* are about 32,000 years old. Therefore, it appears that both Neandertals and *H. sapiens* lived in the area for several thousand years. If the dates are correct, then the Gibraltar area may have been the last refuge for these intriguing human beings. ■ Donald C. Johanson

Antigua and Barbuda. See Latin America.

Archaeology. On March 5, 2006, archaeologists opened the first tomb discovered in Egypt's Valley of the Kings since that of Tutankhamun (who served as king from about 1332 B.C. until his death around 1322 B.C.), which was found in 1922. The tomb, dating to about 1300 B.C., held seven wooden coffins but no mummies. In the chamber, archaeologists also found jars filled with materials used in the mummification process, including *natron* (a natural salt) used to dry out bodies. A miniature pink-gold coffin found inside one coffin suggested that the tomb may have been intended for high-status members of society. Archaeologists think that the space was used to store materials leftover from other burials.

Cave burials. In September 2006, a Peruvian farmer led archaeologists to a burial cave used by the Chachapoyas, an Andean tribe conquered by the Inca in 1475. An exploration of the cave, which is 850 feet (250 meters) deep, revealed several mummies, some with their skin and hair preserved. Pottery, textiles, and wall paintings depicting faces and warrior figures were also found in the cave. The Chachapoyas were known as the "cloud people" by the Inca because their homeland lay in the cloud forests of what is now Peru's Amazon region. They ruled the area beginning about 800 and had a reputation as fierce warriors.

Earliest writing in the Americas. Inscriptions on a stone block found near Veracruz, Mexico, represent the oldest-known writing in the New World, a team of archaeologists from Mexico and the United States announced in September 2006. The stone, dated to between 800 and 900 B.C., is about 400 years older than any other example of writing found in the Americas. The stone, a slab of serpentine, has 62 signs inscribed in a number of horizontal rows. The inscriptions provide the first evidence that the Olmec, who developed what may have been the earliest civilization in the Americas—from about 1200 to about 400 B.C.—had a system of writing.

Foreign workers in ancient China. One of the workers who built the tomb of the first emperor of China apparently was not Chinese, according to genetic tests of the worker's skeletal remains reported in July. The skeletal remains were excavated from a pit near the tomb of Emperor Shi Huangdi, near Xi'an, China. Shi Huangdi, who died in 210 B.C., created the first united Chinese empire. His nearby tomb is famous for its army of life-sized *terra cotta* (baked clay) soldiers, found there in 1974.

The worker's *DNA* (deoxyribonucleic acid), the double-stranded chainlike molecule found in every living cell, more closely resembled that of the modern-day Parsi people of India and Pakistan than that of Chinese people. Several ancient Chinese texts contain references to foreigners. The discovery indicates that contacts between the Chinese and the peoples of central Asia occurred about 100 years earlier than previously supposed.

Scythian mummy. Archaeologists in July 2006 reported finding a 2,500-year-old mummy in an intact Scythian tomb in Mongolia's snowcapped Altai Mountains. The Scythians were warlike nomads who lived mainly north of the Black Sea in present-day Ukraine and southwestern Russia.

The international team of archaeologists said the frozen tomb contained the well-preserved body of a 30- to 40-year-old nobleman buried in a fur cloak. The preserved remains of two horses equipped with saddles, weapons, and metal vessels were also found in the tomb. The tomb is the first Scythian burial found on the Asian side of the Altai. Scythian tombs were previously known only from the Russian side of the mountain range.

Ancient surgery. In March, scientists announced that a 2,600-year-old skull of a woman from Abdera, an ancient Greek colony in Thrace on the northern coast of the Aegean Sea, bears signs of sophisticated and successful surgery. The woman had suffered a fractured skull in life. The fracture, which occurred in an area where two bones join at the back of the skull, was carefully scraped to smooth the injured area and

Archaeologists in 2006 discover the first intact tomb in Egypt's Valley of the Kings in 84 years.

Workers clear a shaft leading to the entrance of a 2,300-year-old tomb, the first to be found in the Valley of the Kings since British archaeologist Howard Carter discovered the tomb of Tutankhamun in 1922.

A view inside the tomb reveals painted wooden coffins. In all, seven coffins were discovered, but none contained a mummy. One held a miniature pink-gold coffin, indicating the tomb may have been intended for a high-status person. Jars inside the tomb held materials used in the mummification process. The tomb dates to approximately the same period as the reign of King Tutankhamun, about 2,300 years ago.

A close-up of one of the wooden coffins shows the painted face of a woman. Because the face bears a striking resemblance to Tutankhamun, Zahi Hawass, director of the Egyptian Supreme Council for Antiquities, suggested that the coffin may have been made for the king's mother.

remove bone fragments. This exact procedure was recommended 200 years later by the ancient Greek physician Hippocrates. The discovery suggests that Hippocrates, known as the father of medicine, wrote about long-established practices.

Ancient computer. An international team of scientists reported in November that a mysterious 2,100-year-old device recovered from a Roman-era shipwreck in 1900 is the world's oldest-known computer. Scientists have been trying for decades to understand how the device was made and what it was used for. The finding proves that ancient technology was much more complex than scientists had imagined.

Using computed tomography (CT) imaging, the scientists were able to make out faded inscriptions and reconstruct the device. The reconstruction showed that the device was a remarkably accurate mechanical astronomical computer that could predict the position of the sun and planets and even forecast lunar and solar eclipses.

Sponge divers found the ancient shipwreck near Antikythera, an island off the southern coast of Greece. Archaeologists investigating the wreck recovered many artifacts, including hand-cut bronze gears, dials, clocklike hands, and a wooden and bronze casing with ancient Greek writing.

■ Mark Rose

See also **Anthropology.**

Architecture.
In 2006, museums and performing arts centers once again topped the annual lists of notable buildings, continuing a trend that began with the turn of the new century. Such civic structures often serve as tools for revitalizing the slumbering economies of various American cities.

Denver Art Museum. The Frederic C. Hamilton Building, an addition to the Denver Art Museum designed by Daniel Libeskind, was the most anticipated building of 2006. The $90-million expansion, which opened in October, is a collage of gravity-defying cubes, squares, and triangles in which walls bow, ceilings tilt, and staircases spiral and swirl. From a distance, the building resembles a gigantic expressionist sculpture. Inside, it turns into a modernist maze with delightful surprises—but with so many twists and turns that some critics complained that it upstages the art it is supposed to serve.

Institute of Contemporary Art. Nearly as dramatic though not so aggressive as Libeskind's design is Boston's Institute of Contemporary Art, which opened in December. It was the first building in the United States created by the husband-and-wife team of Ricardo Scofidio and Elizabeth Diller, who are known for their bold, cutting-edge designs. The institute is a carved metal and glass cube in which the line between inside and

outside is intentionally blurred. It overlooks Boston's redeveloping waterfront with a monumental *cantilever* (projecting structure suspended at one end) that extends to the water's edge. The exhibition galleries are tall, airy spaces suitable for large contemporary works and multimedia performances, while the lobby and adjacent plaza are connected to the city's 40-mile (64-kilometer) harbor walk.

Morgan Library. Renzo Piano, a builder architect for whom materials and construction are more important than jaw-dropping forms, had half a dozen major projects completed or under development in the United States in 2006. He is at his best renovating and adding to existing buildings. Nowhere is that clearer than in his expansion of the Morgan Library & Museum, which opened in April on New York City's Madison Avenue.

Here, Piano slipped a pristine steel-and-glass cube between two historic masonry buildings—one of them designed by McKim, Mead, and White, one of the premier architectural firms in U.S. history. Piano thus set up a dialogue between old and new, past and present, continuity and change. He placed the bulk of the 75,000-square-foot (6,968-square-meter) addition belowground, thereby deferring to the street and the historic fabric instead of striving for a self-important architectural statement.

Carnival Center. Some 30 years after it was first proposed, the Carnival Center for the Performing Arts opened in Miami, Florida, in October. At a cost of more than $500 million, the center was the most expensive performing arts facility ever built. Designed by Pelli Clark Pelli Architects of New Haven, Connecticut, the Carnival Center features a 2,200-seat concert hall and a 2,400-seat opera house, plus a small black box theater. Early reports on the acoustics were enthusiastic, though reviews of the architecture were more mixed. Some reviewers praised the center for its transparency and openness to the city. Others described the mixture of public and performance spaces as bland and confusing.

Skyscraper stories. The major skyscraper story of 2006 involved Santiago Calatrava's spire-like condominium tower proposed for downtown Chicago. At 150 stories and 2,000 feet (610 meters) high, it would be the tallest building in the United States if built. The project's developer announced in November that the design team would include structural engineer Thornton Tomasetti, who helped shape the Petronas Towers in Malaysia. A redesign of the tower was unveiled in December.

Of the skyscrapers that opened in 2006, perhaps the most impressive was the Hearst Tower in Manhattan, designed by Foster and Partners

of the United Kingdom. Opening in October as the editorial offices of *Cosmopolitan, Esquire,* and other leading Hearst Corporation magazines, the 46-story skyscraper is New York City's first "green" building. It has a distinctive triangular framework, called a dia-grid, made of 90-percent recycled steel. The sky-scraper sits on a six-story masonry base that was constructed in 1928 for an art deco-style tower that was never built.

Awards. The 2006 American Institute of Architects' Gold Medal went to New Mexico architect Antoine Predock, whose bold sculptural work responds not only to the majestic landscape of the Ameri-can Southwest but also to that region's quirky sub-culture of truck stops, low-riders, and UFO's. Among Predock's best-known buildings are the Las Vegas (Nevada) Library and Discovery Museum; the American Heritage Center and Art Museum in Laramie, Wyoming; and the Nelson Fine Arts Center in Tempe, Arizona.

The 2006 Pritzker Prize, considered the "Nobel Prize" of architec-ture, was awarded to Paulo Mendes de Rocha. Widely considered to be Brazil's greatest modern designer, de Rocha is known for his innovative use of archi-tectural concrete in houses, churches, and major public buildings, including the Brazilian Museum of Sculpture in São Paolo. The Pritzker jury praised de Rocha not only for his technical mastery, but also for his skill at creat-ing lasting architecture with limited resources—a critical issue in such poor countries as Brazil. ■ David Dillon

The 46-story Hearst Tower, new headquar-ters of the media giant Hearst Corpora-tion, opened at Eighth Avenue and 57th Street in New York City in October. The gleaming glass and steel structure, which was designed by architect Lord Norman Foster, sits atop a 1920's-era, six-story masonry structure that was to provide the base for a tower that was never built.

By David Dillon

Architectural form no longer follows function—as American architect Louis Sullivan famously dictated that it should—it upstages function, even eclipsing it in some cases. Superstar architects are receiving commissions in virtually every major city to design signature buildings that will enhance that city's image and put it on the map architecturally. These buildings are not self-effacing background structures that blend into the urban landscape but bold, iconic sculptures that symbolize as graphically as possible the values and aspirations of institutions, cities, and entire regions—in the way the Eiffel Tower symbolizes Paris or the Empire State Building symbolizes New York City. In a world constantly scrambling for market share,

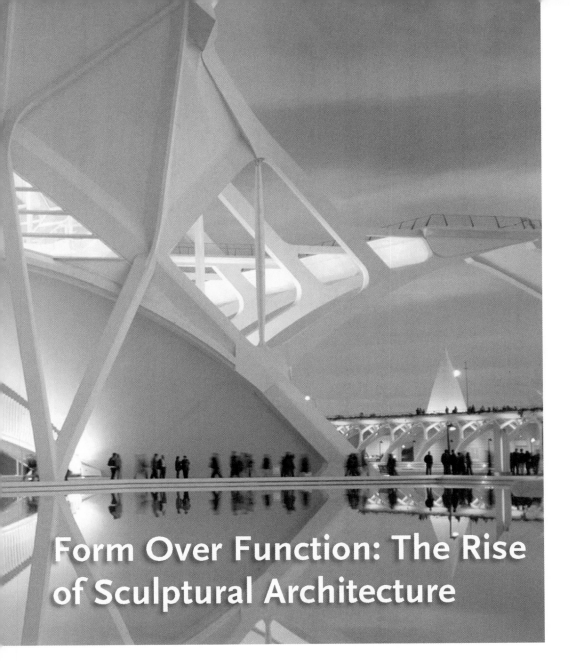

Form Over Function: The Rise of Sculptural Architecture

"starchitecture" has become a hot form of branding, a powerful phenomenon of the times.

"We want our buildings to be as diverse, forward thinking, and audacious as the community they are in," said former President Charles Vest of the Massachusetts Institute of Technology (MIT), whose Cambridge campus has become a laboratory of contemporary design. "They should stand as a metaphor for the ingenuity at work inside." In other words, iconic architecture should provide a visual "brand name" for a community's highly valued intellectual and cultural assets. Historically, the iconic buildings in a community were the cathedral, the city hall, and maybe the library, all expressing broadly shared beliefs

The eyelike entrance to Santiago Calatrava's City of Arts and Sciences in Valencia, Spain, is reflected in the community center's surrounding pool. Calatrava noted, "As the site is close to the sea, and Valencia is so dry, I [made] water a major element ... using it as a mirror for the architecture."

Curving titanium-clad shapes interconnect in Frank Gehry's Guggenheim Museum (1997) in Bilbao, Spain. The free-form structure inspired the current interest in sculptural architecture worldwide and transformed Bilbao into a major tourist destination.

The author:
David Dillon is the architecture and design editor of *The Dallas Morning News.*

and values. Today, a city's iconic buildings are just as likely to be office towers, museums, convention centers, and sports arenas.

Sculptural buildings are proliferating in cities across the globe. In London, the Tate Modern museum commissioned Swiss architects Jacques Herzog and Pierre de Meuron to design a $397-million addition, which will resemble a teetering stack of hatboxes. In the city of Santa Cruz de Tenerife in Spain's Canary Islands, Spanish architect Santiago Calatrava's Opera House (2003) has a roof shaped like a breaking wave. The competition to replace New York City's World Trade Center, destroyed in the terrorist attacks of Sept. 11, 2001, produced several sculptural designs. Polish-born architect Daniel Libeskind's winning entry included a tower that recalls the Statue of Liberty. The most popular design, British architect Sir Norman Foster's "Kissing Towers," featured a pair of intertwining skyscrapers reminiscent of the abstract sculptures of Romanian-born artist Constantin Brancusi.

The "Bilbao effect"

This explosion of sculptural architecture is called the "Bilbao effect," alluding to American architect Frank Gehry's twisting, billowing Guggenheim Museum (1997) in Bilbao, Spain. From its inception, the Bilbao Guggenheim was promoted as a unique structure that would "broadcast its presence and cast a wide sphere of influence." The

museum easily lived up to its publicity. Almost overnight, it transformed a gritty, industrial city into a cultural destination that annually
attracts hundreds of thousands of tourists who spend hundreds of
millions of dollars. The building has come to represent Bilbao in the
same way that Danish architect Jorn Utzon's exuberant Opera House
(1973) represents Sydney, Australia, or American architect Frank Lloyd
Wright's groundbreaking Johnson Wax Company administration
building (1939) distinguishes Racine, Wisconsin.

Naturally, public officials and civic leaders in other cities observed
this phenomenon and asked, "Why not us?" and the Bilbao effect
spread. The Milwaukee Art Museum commissioned a new wing from
Calatrava, who designed a free-standing structure, completed in 2003,
featuring a gigantic sunscreen that opens and closes like the wings of
bird or a butterfly—literally architecture as kinetic sculpture. Minneapolis's Guthrie Theater (2006), by French architect Jean Nouvel,
mimics the beefy round grain elevators located along the banks of the
adjacent Mississippi River. In Charlotte, North Carolina, the NASCAR
Hall of Fame, designed by the American firm Pei, Cobb, Freed, and
Partners, is to have an iconic racetrack shape, and a 50-story condominium tower in Mississauga, Canada, designed by MAD Studio, is
reminiscent of a gigantic Slinky toy.

"Some of my contemporaries believe that there are rules for architectural expression, and that they have to fit into certain channels,"

The Bilbao Guggenheim
was constructed on the
banks of the Nervión
River in the center of the
city. The building's
curving, billowing walls
allude to Bilbao's history
as a seaport.

says Frank Gehry, the most celebrated contemporary exponent of free-form architecture. However, for Gehry and some of his associates, such rules don't "mean anything." If a client wants a building that looks like a pickle, an ocean wave, or a pair of binoculars—and clients have asked for all three—then they should get it. The old rules—"form follows function" or the German-born architect Ludwig Mies van der Rohe's famous dictum that "less is more"—no longer apply.

The rise of contemporary sculptural architecture

Sculptural architecture is hardly new. Francesco Borromini, an Italian architect of the 1600's, built churches and palaces in Rome with daring curved forms. In the late 1800's and early 1900's, Spanish architect Antonio Gaudí designed undulating churches, houses, and apartment buildings in Barcelona that appear to have been poured rather than constructed. And Frank Lloyd Wright gave new three-dimensional life to the term "organic design" with his spiraling Guggenheim Museum (1959) on New York City's Fifth Avenue. Yet such buildings generally were considered *anomalies* (unusual departures) rather than parts of mainstream architectural practice.

Sculpture, of course, has long played an important role in the decoration of buildings. Until well into the 1900's, few architects would have designed a major building without incorporating the work of sculptors and stone carvers, painters, and other decorative artists to

Antonio Gaudí's Casa Mila (1910), a highly sculptural apartment building in Barcelona, Spain, appears to have been poured rather than built. While sculptural architecture has existed since ancient times, it was until recently the exception.

enrich their spaces. The Parthenon in Athens, Chartres Cathedral in France, and the United States Capitol in Washington, D.C., all represent the collaborative efforts of many artists. Architects and patrons alike believed that sculpture made architecture richer, more pleasurable, and more inspiring. However, sculpture and decoration were always subservient to the architecture, not its equal or master. Traditionally, buildings were not conceived of as works of sculpture in their own right.

Beginning in the early 1900's, architects of the International Modernism movement drove a wedge between architecture and the decorative arts. They rejected decorative buildings in favor of those with pure forms, clean lines, and machine-made industrial surfaces. Modernist Austrian architect Adolf Loos famously compared ornament with the tattoos on a criminal and proclaimed, "the evolution of culture requires the elimination of ornament from useful objects," especially in architecture. Decoration was considered a vestige of aristocratic privilege and *bourgeois* (European middle-class) decadence, to which modernism was supposedly the liberating alternative. This design philosophy held sway for decades. In the United States, architects of the International Modernism school, such as Philip Johnson, an avid art collector and patron, and Richard Meier, an accomplished painter and sculptor, allowed no decoration to distract from the purity of their designs.

By the 1970's and 1980's, however, a new architectural movement—Postmodernism—challenged this view. Architects such as Michael Graves and Robert A. M. Stern brought many traditional

The famed American architect Frank Lloyd Wright explored sculptural architecture throughout his long career. The central space of his Johnson Wax Building (1939, 1944) in Racine, Wisconsin, (upper left) has been likened to a pond with water lilies growing toward the light overhead. Wright compared his spiraling Guggenheim Museum (1959) in New York City to the coiled shell of a nautilus.

elements back into their buildings, including decorative sculpture and painting and a wider range of colors and patterns. Although their work looked nothing like Frank Gehry's, the Postmodernists paved the way for Gehry and others.

Gehry spent part of his early career as a sculptor who also designed studios for artist friends. As his architectural practice developed, he came to see his buildings as free-form alternatives to the hard-edged, straight-lined work of such designers as Mies van der Rohe. "I have never felt that what they [painters and sculptors] are doing is very different [from architecture]," noted Gehry in a statement that likely enrages architectural purists, but which Borromini and Michelangelo—who were painters and sculptors as well as architects—would certainly have understood.

At the same time, Gehry's architecture is very modern—that is, it is sleek and abstract. It is designed and built with sophisticated computer programs and clad in very modern, hard-edged materials—aluminum, stainless steel, and titanium. His gleaming Walt Disney Concert Hall (2003), a triumph of digital design, immediately became Los Angeles's new showpiece and helped spark the redevelopment of the city's downtown, which had been in decline for decades.

Sir Norman Foster's Swiss Re Tower (2003) in London has been dubbed the "gherkin" for its pickle-like shape. Nevertheless, critics have praised the office building's elegant sculptural form and reflective surface amid the City of London's predominantly gray-stone facades.

A marriage of art and marketing

The sculptural architecture movement is occurring in a media-saturated environment fixated on "signatures," "brands," and flashy ads. Inevitably, the buildings of this era are as much about marketing as about art.

The best of the new sculptural architecture affirms the power of buildings to entertain, instruct, and inspire: to change a city's image for tourists as well as for its citizens. The bold, graceful forms of the Bilbao Guggenheim or the Sydney Opera House have greatly enhanced the cultural images of these cities. When New York City began to recover from the 2001 terrorist attacks, it turned to architecture for hope and healing. The competition to replace the destroyed World Trade Center towers included several grandly sculptural skyscrapers that proclaimed that New York was still the business and cultural center of the world.

Although the starchitecture phenomenon can reflect lofty ideals, it also is very much about money, power, and prestige. The $400-million addition to London's Tate Modern museum has as much to do with economics as with exhibiting art. The addition will make the museum as big as the Louvre in Paris and the Museum of Modern Art in New York City. Supporters hope the addition will transform London into

With its spiraling observation decks, Sir Norman Foster's 1999 glass dome atop Germany's rebuilt Reichstag building in Berlin was designed to symbolize the transparency and openness of the country's post-World War II government.

The nautical shapes of Santiago Calatrava's City of Arts and Sciences, completed in stages from 1998 to 2002, are a reflection of its unusual site in Valencia, Spain, a dry riverbed near the Mediterranean Sea.

an international center of contemporary art, which it has never been. Moreover, politicians see the addition as a critical boost to the South Bank of the Thames, an area of the city in the midst of redevelopment. Commissioning internationally acclaimed architects Herzog and De Meuron as designers makes achieving both of these aims easier. Like most people, the donors who underwrite the costs of such structures are attracted to the power of stars and are, therefore, more likely to give money for projects designed by name architects than they are for designs by anonymous hometown architects, however talented they might be.

The leaders of corporations know the value of commissioning iconic structures by star designers. In London, Swiss Re, an insurance conglomerate, hired British architect Sir Norman Foster to design its new headquarters, which the locales refer to as the "gherkin" because of its pickle shape. Yet the building, completed in 2003, is more sophisticated than its nickname suggests. It curves and glitters and reflects, subtly swelling at the base and tapering at the top. In short, it has many of the qualities of good sculpture. In Chicago, Santiago Calatrava has proposed to redraw the city's skyline with a 124-story, 2000-foot- (610-meter-) high apartment tower, which has been variously compared with a corkscrew and a gigantic drill bit. The architect refers to the design as one of his "permeable sculptures."

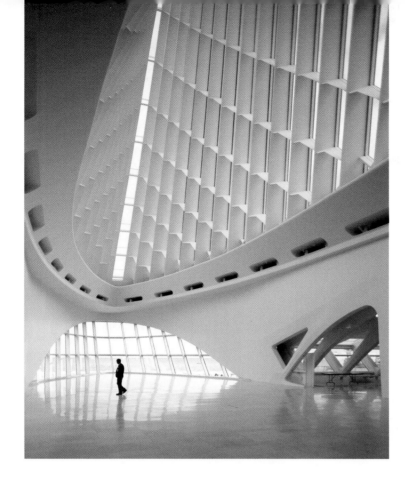

Santiago Calatrava's popular 2003 addition to the Milwaukee Art Museum (below), with its gigantic sunscreen that opens and closes like the wings of a bird, has been described as pure "kinetic sculpture." The interior (left), which consists almost entirely of a single grand space for public functions, also has been criticized for doing little to advance the museum's collections or curatorial reputation.

The Burj Al Arab, a billion-dollar hotel completed off the coast of Dubayy in 1999, is shaped like a billowing sail. Such fanciful, sculptural architecture has made the city of Dubayy a major tourist destination—the "Las Vegas of the Middle East." Critics worry that rising energy costs could make cooling such buildings too costly in the future.

The future of sculptural architecture

Will the proliferation of iconic architecture ultimately produce new and exciting cityscapes, or will it prove just another expensive fashion statement of no lasting significance? There is evidence for both outcomes.

The well-known definition of a celebrity as a person who is famous for being famous does not apply to Gehry, Nouvel, and the Dutch architect Rem Koolhaas. They are designers of real accomplishment who have broken new ground and raised the bar for others. Yet when they appear to have a monopoly on major important commissions, as they do today, a highly problematic star system develops.

The 20 or so winners of the Pritzker Prize—the architectural equivalent of a Nobel Prize—currently command a disproportionate share of major civic and institutional commissions, to the dismay of local architects who naturally feel frozen out. This situation is more of an issue in the United States than in Europe, where most major projects are awarded through competition, but the problem remains the same.

A vibrant architectural culture, like a vibrant local economy, cannot survive on imports alone. Sooner or later, it has to grow its own. Barcelona presents one of the best examples of a contemporary, home-grown architectural center. This city used the prestige and resources

gained from hosting the 1992 Olympics to inspire and support an entire generation of local architects. It imported the designs of a few international stars, but much of the best work has come from such local talent as Alfredo Arribas and the late Enric Miralles.

Cities must also ensure that their grandest new buildings do not compromise or overwhelm the activities that occur within those structures. Santiago Calatrava's addition to the Milwaukee Art Museum has turned out to be a mixed blessing. Although popular with the media, tourists, and many residents, the addition proved far more costly to build than initially expected. Cost overruns led to a lack of funds for other aspects of the museum, such as personnel salaries. Curators and other staff members lost their jobs in the process. Moreover, the museum's builders conceived of their new structure primarily as a social gathering place, featuring a grand entrance hall. Almost none of that addition was devoted to new gallery space, and the building has done little for the museum's collection or for its curatorial reputation.

Cities also must deal with the explosive growth that goes with high-profile architecture. Dubayy (also spelled Dubai), in the United Arab Emirates, may prove to be sculptural architecture's ultimate test. This instant city in the Persian Gulf, the "Las Vegas of the Middle East," has become a tourist destination not because of gambling, but on the strength of its fantastical architecture, which includes everything from a billion-dollar hotel shaped like a billowing sail to a blue-and-white,

Future Systems, architects of the metallic disk-clad Selfridges Department Store in Birmingham, England, deliberately set out to design a structure that would contrast sharply with its neighbors, including the famous Rotund Building and St. Martin's Church (far left). Critics question how such splashy structures affect the warp and weave of traditional city streets.

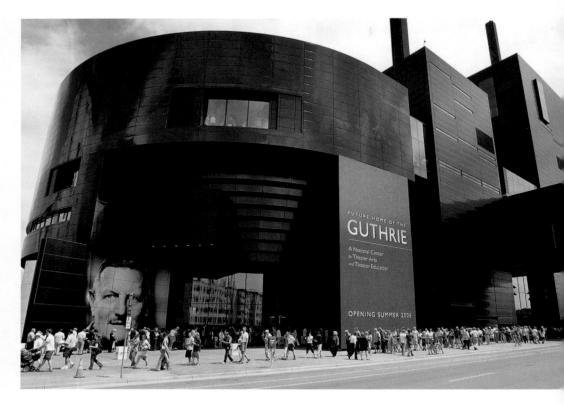

Minneapolis's new Guthrie Theater, completed in 2006, was designed by French architect Jean Nouvel to echo the stocky forms of 19th-century grain elevators lining the opposite bank of the Mississippi River.

high-rise minaret to what is be the world's tallest building. A sleepy port just a few years ago, Dubayy in 2006 had enough construction projects underway to occupy more than 15 percent of the world's large construction cranes. "Dubayy is an example of how to make something out of nothing," boasted an adviser to the ruling sheik.

Yet while runaway development has fueled an economic boom, it has also taken its toll on the environment and the quality of life. Tourists and residents alike complain that traffic is nightmarish and air quality is deteriorating. There are growing concerns, even in an oil-rich country, that a decade from now the cost of electric power will make all of these spectacular skyscrapers too expensive to cool.

Cities must also understand that signature buildings are one piece of a successful urban renovation plan. The Bilbao Guggenheim, for example, was accompanied by new bridges, a new subway system, and major improvements to the city's port and highways. Without these other infrastructure improvements, the museum's long-term success would have been dramatically diminished.

The case for more gradual urban development

Clearly, the current fascination with iconic architecture challenges traditional ideas about how cities should develop. There will always be boomtowns like Dubayy, but most great cities have grown slowly and organically. When spectacular architecture becomes a way to fix the

Iraqi-born British architect Zaha Hadid's Contemporary Art Center (2003) in Cincinnati, Ohio, evokes a sense of dynamic horizontal movement in a state of tension with the verticality of more traditional structures.

problems of ailing cities—or their major institutions and corporations—it can lead to the neglect of the small, everyday elements that make their communities livable and workable. American sociologist William H. Whyte referred to such elements—parks, trees, walkable streets, local shops—as "tremendous trifles." He pointed out that however trivial they might seem, and however little press they get, they can have a dramatic cumulative effect on the health of a city.

Paris, for example, has as many famous architectural monuments as any capital in the world. Yet it is also a city of cafes, gardens, and parks, with an inexhaustible supply of great walks. This interplay between big and little, grand and ordinary, makes the French metropolis such a memorable place. When people think of Florence, they may envision its cathedral, the Duomo, or the Uffizi Palace museum. Yet most of the city's buildings are anonymous background structures that frame streets and plazas without calling attention to themselves. The same can be said for London, New York, Boston, and Barcelona, where the connective tissue is as important as spectacular individual monuments.

Signature architecture alone, however dramatic, will not produce the kinds of transformations for which many cities are hoping. To create a truly distinctive urban environment, cities also need to provide decent, successful places in which people can live their ordinary lives. Such environments cannot develop overnight. One building, even a great building, is only a first step.

Argentina. Under President Nestor Kirchner, Argentina experienced its fourth consecutive year of economic expansion in 2006, with economists predicting that the Argentine economy would post an 8-percent rate of growth for the year. Economists also took note of collateral benefits of the economic boom—declining unemployment and a rising average standard of living. However, some among their ranks remained critical of policies they described as "unorthodox."

Price controls. The most controversial of Kirchner's economic policies was his campaign, beginning in late 2005, to curb inflationary pressures through mechanisms called "price agreements." Drawing on his high approval rating, Kirchner persuaded utility companies to accept a freeze on rate increases and businesses to comply with "temporary" price controls on more than 300 products commonly sold in supermarkets and stores. In late 2006, Kirchner requested an extension of these controls for another year.

Bolivian gas. President Kirchner in October announced a deal with Bolivia that would more than triple Argentina's imports of natural gas from that energy-exporting nation over a 20-year period. Responding to economists' warnings that power shortages could become a drag on Argentina's economic growth, the president characterized the deal as "a strategic step forward."

Memory Day. On March 24, Argentines observed a so-called "National Day of Memory for Truth and Justice" to commemorate the 30th anniversary of Argentina's 1976 military *coup* (government overthrow). To mark the occasion, which had been designated an official holiday by the Argentine Congress, Defense Minister Nilda Garre ordered all military archives of the so-called "Dirty War against Dissidents" to be opened to the public. The "Dirty War" was the period of brutal dictatorship that followed the coup and lasted from 1976 to 1983.

Public exposure of the archives facilitated trials of individuals accused of human rights violations allegedly committed during the Dirty War. In August 2006, Julio Simon, a federal police officer who had headed a detention center during that period, was sentenced to 25 years in prison on multiple criminal charges, including taking legal possession in 1978 of the 8-month-old daughter of a couple who disappeared under suspicious circumstances. Simon was the first official to be tried and convicted following nullification of amnesty laws by the Argentine Supreme Court in August 2005.

Restive armed forces. President Kirchner's advocacy of prosecutions against former military officers on human rights charges angered some members of the Argentine military. At an Army Day observance in May 2006, several officers interrupted a speech by the president while others turned their back on him. Kirchner responded to the affront by declaring, "I'm not afraid of you," and abruptly exiting.

Land reform. In February, Kirchner named Luis D'Elia head of a program to give land to millions of squatters. D'Elia, a media celebrity and former protest leader, identified 37.5 million acres (15.2 million hectares) for possible *expropriation* (taking land without due compensation), contending that the lands contained strategic resources or that the owners were infringing on the rights of *indigenous* (native) groups.

In August, D'Elia staged a media event when, with television cameras rolling, he cut through a fence and trespassed on land owned by Douglas Tompkins, an American millionaire businessman-turned-ecologist. Since 1990, Tompkins had bought up millions of acres in South America to create environmental parks, some of which he donated to governments for use as public parks.

"We don't want our natural resources in the hands of foreigners," declared Congresswoman Arceli Mendez, commenting on D'Elia's action. In late August 2006, she introduced a bill in the Argentine Congress to expropriate Tompkins's holdings. ■ Nathan A. Haverstock

See also **Latin America: A Special Report.**

Armed forces. The Iraq War, which entered a fourth year in March 2006, continued to dominate United States military affairs. The war also became a central issue in November's midterm elections. Public frustration with rising sectarian violence in Iraq helped the Democrats gain control of both houses of the U.S. Congress. In response to the Republicans' loss, Secretary of Defense Donald H. Rumsfeld, a major architect and supporter of President George W. Bush's war policy, resigned on November 8 after six years in office. To replace Rumsfeld, Bush appointed Robert Gates, who had served as head of the Central Intelligence Agency during the administration of President George H. W. Bush.

Reenergized by their election victory, Democrats strengthened their call for a phased withdrawal of U.S. forces from Iraq within six months. On November 15, however, General John P. Abizaid, commander of the U.S. Central Command with responsibility for the Middle East, warned against such a plan. At a Senate hearing, Abizaid insisted that cutting troop levels in Iraq so quickly would unleash greater sectarian violence and interfere with U.S. efforts to transfer greater responsibility for security to Iraqi forces.

Before and after the elections, Bush vowed that U.S. military forces would stay in Iraq until a democratic government could defend itself. He accused war critics of wanting to "cut and run" and insisted that any withdrawal would jeopardize the global war on terrorism.

Casualties in Iraq. In early 2006, three years after President Bush declared that major combat operations in Iraq had ended, 140,000 U.S. troops remained in Iraq. At year-end, that number had risen to 152,000. By December 31, 3,002 U.S. soldiers had died in Iraq. More than 21,000 had been wounded, most by roadside bombs known as improvised explosive devices that were detonated by insurgents.

The war exacted a heavy toll on the armed forces, particularly the Army and Marine Corps. Many units had tours of duty extended; some were ordered back to Iraq for second and third tours. Critics argued that the military was stretched so dangerously thin that it would have difficulty responding to other threats.

The Army raised its maximum enlistment age from 40 to 42 and hiked its promotion rate for junior officers as increasing numbers of younger officers left the service because of frequent combat deployments. The suicide rate for Army soldiers increased to the highest total since 1993.

Medal of Honor. On Nov. 10, 2006, President Bush announced that Marine Corporal Jason L. Dunham would become the second American to be awarded the Medal of Honor, the highest

U.S. military decoration, for service in Iraq. Dunham, who would be awarded the medal posthumously, died in April 2004, eight days after he threw himself on an exploding grenade to protect other members of his patrol.

Growing violence. Although some Iraqi provinces remained relatively peaceful throughout 2006, sectarian violence and insurgent attacks increased steadily. Upbeat appraisals of the war's progress by officials of the Bush administration increasingly gave way to more somber assessments. During the first half of 2006, officials at the U.S. Department of Defense (DOD) held out the possibility that the number of combat brigades in Iraq could be reduced by more than one-half by December 2007. The scenario envisioned two brigades (about 7,000 troops) leaving Iraq by the end of 2006. Military officials were forced to abandon any pullback plans, however, as the level of fighting, especially in and around Baghdad, the capital, escalated sharply. On July 25, after meeting with Iraqi Prime Minister Nouri al-Maliki at the White House, President Bush ordered 4,000 additional U.S. troops into the Baghdad area.

In August, General Abizaid said worsening violence made troop cuts unlikely until spring 2007 at the earliest. General Peter J. Schoomaker,

A United States soldier at a camp in eastern Afghanistan fires a mortar shell at Taliban fighters who launched a rocket attack on the outpost in late October. In 2006, Taliban forces regrouped in Afghanistan, especially in the south and east, and increased their attacks on U.S. and NATO forces as well as on civilian targets.

the Army chief of staff, disclosed in October 2006 that the Army was preparing contingency plans that envisioned maintaining about 140,000 U.S. troops in Iraq through 2010.

Rumsfeld under the gun. Dissatisfaction with Rumsfeld's performance by the U.S. military establishment escalated sharply in 2006. In April, several senior retired generals, including some who had commanded combat units in Iraq, publicly called for Rumsfeld's ouster. In November, a scathing editorial in the *Military Times* group of newspapers called on the president to fire Rumsfeld. Until the day after the November elections, however, President Bush offered strong public support for his secretary of defense.

Afghan War. Military operations in Afghanistan also deteriorated in 2006. Five years after a U.S.-led invasion toppled the Islamic fundamentalist Taliban government, 20,000 U.S. soldiers remained in Afghanistan. In May, heavily armed Taliban militants began flooding into southern Afghanistan as U.S. forces prepared to turn over security operations to peacekeepers from the North Atlantic Treaty Organization (NATO). Coalition forces were soon engaged in the fiercest fighting since the 2001 invasion. The fighting between NATO troops and the militants remained intense through the rest of the year.

In October 2006, about 12,000 U.S. troops were placed under the command of NATO, which took over counterinsurgency operations in the eastern part of the country. The remaining U.S. forces were engaged in counterterrorism, training, and reconstruction operations. By December, 346 U.S. soldiers had died and 1,000 had been wounded in the Afghan conflict.

The cost of the wars continued to rise in 2006. On September 29, Congress approved $70 billion in supplemental funding for military operations in Iraq and Afghanistan. Some of the money was earmarked for increased spending on body armor and recruiting incentives.

In 2006, DOD officials provided Congress with only average monthly costs of military spending for the two combat operations. In September, however, the Congressional Research Service (CRS) calculated that military operations in Iraq were costing $2 billion per week, a 20-percent increase over 2005. The CRS conducts nonpartisan research for Congress; CRS researchers reported that total war spending in Iraq would reach $379 billion by year-end. Since 2001, the U.S. government also had spent $97 billion in Afghanistan, according to the report.

Defense budget. On Feb. 6, 2006, the DOD submitted its budget for the 2007 fiscal year, which began on Oct. 1, 2006. The request totaled $439.3 billion, a 7-percent increase over appropriations for 2006. The budget included significant increases in spending for special operations and homeland security and a 13-percent spending increase for the Army. Heavy fighting in Iraq caused equipment costs to skyrocket. Military officials said the Army would need $17 billion beginning in 2007 to replace and repair tanks and other armored vehicles alone, double the budget for 2006.

Weapons. In 2006, the Defense Department continued to develop a variety of new weapons systems, including new armored fighting vehicles. The DOD's 2007 budget included $10.4 billion for the "Star Wars" strategic defense system; $3.1 billion for 12 C-17 airlift jets; and $2.8 billion for the F-22 Raptor jet fighter. Also in the budget was $3.7 billion for the Army's Future Combat System, which included unpiloted air and ground vehicles and battlefield command and communications systems.

Aircraft in development in 2006 included the Joint Strike Fighter F-35, named "Lightning II," scheduled for completion in 2013. At an estimated cost of $276 billion, the Strike Fighter program was expected to be the costliest weapons system in U.S. history. Three different versions of the aircraft were planned: a conventional version for the Air Force; a carrier version for the Navy; and a short take-off and landing model for the Marine Corps.

The DOD also asked Congress for $3.4 billion to help fund two DD(X) guided missile destroyers, a new generation of destroyers named for Admiral Elmo R. "Bud" Zumwalt, Jr., a former chief of naval operations. The destroyers were to serve as the centerpiece of a three-ship group that also included cruisers and Littoral Combat Ships (LCS), a new class of small, shallow-draft vessels capable of fighting at high speeds in coastal waters. The Navy christened the first LCS, the U.S.S. *Freedom*, on Sept. 23, 2006.

The DOD also requested $2.6 billion for another Virginia-class nuclear attack submarine, a vessel built with modules that can be replaced with more advanced components. The Navy commissioned the U.S.S. *Texas*, the second submarine in this class, on September 9.

National Guard. On May 15, President Bush announced that he was deploying members of the National Guard along the U.S. border with Mexico to help stem the flow of illegal immigrants into several southern states. The Guard troops would not have law-enforcement authority but would assist the U.S. Border Patrol. By July 31, at least 6,000 National Guard personnel were stationed along the border in four states.

The U.S. Air Force Memorial, the first memorial for the youngest U.S. military service, was dedicated on October 14 in ceremonies in Arlington, Virginia. The memorial's three soaring stainless steel spires overlook DOD headquarters and are adjacent to Arlington National Cemetery.

Command changes. Army General Bantz J. Craddock was appointed Supreme Allied Commander, EUROPE, in November. He replaced retiring General James Jones, the first Marine to hold the post. General Michael W. Hagee retired as commandant of the Marine Corps in November and was succeeded by General James T. Conway, a former commander in Iraq. In June, Major General Walter E. Gaskin, Sr., became the first African American commander of a Marine division. In March, then-Captain Nicole Malachowski became the first female member of the Thunderbirds, the Air Force's renowned precision flying squadron.

Christened, retired. The nuclear aircraft carrier *George H. W. Bush*, named for the naval aviator who became the 41st president of the United States, was christened on October 7 at Newport News, Virginia. The last of the giant Nimitz-class carriers, the *Bush* will join the fleet in 2008. The F-14 Tomcat jet fighter made its last flight for the Navy in September. The 1986 movie *Top Gun* made the carrier-based interceptor famous, but rising maintenance costs made it obsolete.

Death. Joe Rosenthal, a combat photographer who took one of the most famous photo images of World War II (1939-1945), died on Aug. 20, 2006. Rosenthal captured the moment when U.S. Marines and a Navy corpsman raised the flag on Mount Suribachi during the epic battle for the Pacific island of Iwo Jima in February 1945.

◼ Thomas M. DeFrank

See also **Afghanistan; Iraq; United States, Government of the; Washington, D.C.**

Art. Governments and museums in Europe and the United States continued in 2006 to resolve questions concerning art illegally moved from one country to another. Philippe de Montebello, director of the Metropolitan Museum of Art (Met) in New York City, reached an agreement in February with the Italian Culture Ministry to return 21 artifacts that Italy claimed were illegally excavated. In exchange, Italy agreed to lend the museum comparably prestigious objects on a long-term basis.

According to the agreement, the Metropolitan accepted no liability for acquiring objects deemed looted, claiming that it had acquired the 21 objects in good faith. The museum pledged to return four vessels to Italy. A vase from the 500's B.C., considered one of the world's finest vessels, will stay at the Met until 2008. The vase, which was once used to mix wine and water, is called the Euphronios krater after the celebrated Greek painter who decorated it. A set of 16 silver pieces from the 200's B.C. will remain at the Met until 2010.

The pact was the first of its kind between Italy and a foreign museum. It was hailed as a model for settling disputes with other museums that have antiquities with questionable *provenances* (histories of possession). In conjunction with the agreement, the Association of Art Museum Directors issued new ethical guidelines that defend a museum's right to exhibit antique artworks. However, the guidelines also urged museums to study ethical and legal issues when borrowing antiquities from a private collector.

Italian cultural officials in 2006 also examined works owned by Met trustee and benefactor Shelby White. With her late husband, financier and philanthropist Leon Levy, White acquired one of the finest private antiquities collections in the world. Pieces from their collection had been on view at the Met for several years.

Getty dispute. Italy and Greece pressed the J. Paul Getty Museum in Los Angeles for the return of dozens of ancient artifacts the countries claimed were illegally removed from their historical settings. Getty Director Michael Brand met with the Greek culture minister in May 2006, agreeing to recommend to the Getty's board of trustees that they return to Greece some of the museum's most prized antiquities.

In October, the Getty approved new acquisitions measures to screen out works that had not been properly documented going back to 1970. In December 2006, the Getty agreed to return to Greece an ancient gold funerary wreath and a marble statue from the 500's B.C.

The Getty had returned three disputed objects to Italy in November 2005, just before Marion True, the Getty's former antiquities curator, went on trial in Rome for conspiring to import illegally excavated ancient objects. American dealer Robert Hecht, who sold the Euphronios krater and the ancient silver to the Met, was indicted with True.

At the center of the debate was the Getty's acquisition in 1996 of the antiquities collection of Barbara Fleischman and her late husband, Lawrence. In 2006, many of these objects were on view at the Getty Villa, the $275-million, newly renovated home of the Getty's antiquities collection in Pacific Palisades, California, which reopened in January 2006 after nine years. On the eve of the reopening, Mrs. Fleischman resigned as a Getty trustee amid questions surrounding an undisclosed loan the Fleischmans had made to True to help finance True's vacation home in Greece. True received the loan just days after arranging the Getty antiquities acquisition. Accusations about this loan and related conflict-of-interest questions partially contributed to True's resignation in 2005.

Other antiquities investigations. In 2006, Italian officials also met with delegations from the Princeton University Art Museum in New Jersey and the Museum of Fine Arts in Boston to discuss

Worth, Texas, announced it would return a painting by British landscape master J. M. W. Turner to the heirs of John and Anna Jaffé of Nice, France. The 1841 painting, *Glaucus and Scylla*, along with other artworks, had been taken and sold at an auction of "Jewish property" in 1943 by France's Vichy government, which collaborated with the Nazis after France was occupied in 1942.

Record sales. During the spring 2006 auction season, a painting by the Spanish modern artist Pablo Picasso sold for $95.2 million at Sotheby's auction house in New York City. The 1941 portrait of Picasso's mistress, Dora Maar, was the second-highest price ever paid for a work of art at auction.

Records were also set for two Turner paintings. At Christie's auction house in New York City, an 1841 painting of the Venetian Giudecca Canal by Turner was sold for a record $35.8 million. And at Christie's in London, Turner's culminating watercolor, *The Blue Rigi: Lake of Lucerne, Sunrise* (1842), sold for nearly $11 million, breaking the world record for a British watercolor and for any British work on paper.

Sotheby's in New York City started its fall 2006 auction season with a sale of some $240 million worth of Impressionist and Modernist works in November—its best showing since 1990. Christie's in New York City broke a single-auction record with sales of $491 million the next day. Dominating the Christie's sale were four of the returned Klimt paintings, which fetched a total of $192 million. Klimt's 1912 portrait *Adele Bloch-Bauer II* was the auction's highest-selling work at $88 million.

The fifth returned Klimt painting, *Adele Bloch-Bauer I* (1907), was purchased for New York City's Neue Galerie in June 2006 by cosmetics magnate and gallery president Ronald S. Lauder for $135 million, the highest sum ever paid for a painting at the time.

In November, the Klimt painting's record sale was surpassed by the sale of a Jackson Pollock drip painting for $140 million. The 1948 work, titled *No.*

claims of illegally excavated art in both collections. In September, the Boston museum returned 13 Greek and Roman antiquities. The St. Louis Art Museum in Missouri declined to return a 3,200-year-old mummy mask unless Egypt could produce valid documentation that the mask was stolen.

Looted art returned. An Austrian arbitration panel unanimously decided in January that five paintings by Austrian Art Nouveau artist Gustav Klimt should be returned to the heirs of Austrian industrialist Ferdinand Bloch-Bauer, who fled Austria in 1938 as German troops seized the country. The five paintings, valued at some $300 million, had been seized by Germany's Nazi government during World War II (1939-1945) and had hung at the Belvedere Gallery in Vienna for more than 50 years. Bloch-Bauer's niece, Maria V. Altmann of California, began a lawsuit to recover the works in 1998. The case precipitated a landmark U.S. Supreme Court decision in June 2004 in which the court ruled that a foreign government could be sued in the United States over looted art. Binding arbitration ended further litigation.

In February 2006, the Dutch government announced one of the largest restitutions ever of art seized by the Nazis with the return of more than 200 Old Master paintings to the heir of Jacques Goudstikker. The wealthy Dutch Jewish art dealer and collector died while fleeing Amsterdam ahead of the advancing German troops in 1940. The restitution ended an eight-year campaign undertaken by the widow of Goudstikker's son, Marei von Saher of Greenwich, Connecticut.

In June 2006, the Kimbell Art Museum in Fort

5, 1948, was sold in a private sale by Los Angeles music and movie mogul David Geffen to international financier David Martinez. Later in November 2006, Geffen sold *Woman III* (1952-1953), a painting by Dutch-born Abstract Expressionist Willem de Kooning, to billionaire Steven Cohen for $137.5 million.

Major exhibitions. "Dada," the most comprehensive museum exhibition of Dada art ever mounted in the United States, premiered in February at the National Gallery of Art in Washington, D.C. The exhibition, which featured painting, sculpture, photography, film, collage, and ordinary objects treated as works of art, traveled to the Museum of Modern Art in New York City in June. In March, "Michelangelo Drawings: Closer to the Master" opened at the British Museum in London. The show presented 95 studies whose rarity was magnified by the knowledge that the great Renaissance artist destroyed many of his drawings. The works ranged from intimate early studies to the visionary "Crucifixion" scenes made just before his death. The exhibition drew such large crowds that the museum stayed open until midnight for the first time in its 247-year history.

Also opening in March was

"Andrew Wyeth: Memory and Magic" at the Philadelphia Museum of Art. The retrospective displayed more than 100 paintings, watercolors, and drawings by the popular American painter, some from the artist's personal collection that had never before been exhibited.

Another March exhibition, at the San Francisco Museum of Modern Art, was entitled "Beyond Real: Surrealistic Photography and Sculpture from Bay Area Collections." The exhibit showcased Surrealism's pinnacle in the 1920's and 1930's. Included were more than 200 photographs and sculptures that juxtaposed works by such Surrealist pioneers as German Hans Bellmer and American Man Ray with those of such contemporary artists as American Cindy Sherman and Japanese Hiroshi Sugimoto.

In November 2006, "Spanish Paintings From El Greco to Picasso: Time, Truth, and History," a blockbuster exhibition of some 135 paintings by Spanish masters, opened at the Solomon R. Guggenheim Museum in New York City.

■ Sally-Ruth May

See also **Architecture; Los Angeles.**

Ronald S. Lauder admires the 1907 painting *Adele Bloch-Bauer I* by Austrian artist Gustav Klimt at its opening at the Neue Galerie in New York City in June 2006. Lauder, the gallery's president and cofounder, purchased the work for $135 million. Seized by Nazis during World War II, the painting was returned to the heirs of the original owners in early 2006.

ASIA

Disease and natural disasters ravaged parts of Asia in 2006. In addition, North Korea's burgeoning weapons program caused tension worldwide, especially with its neighbors.

North Korea. Nations near North Korea expressed concern over its ballistic missiles test in July and detonation of a small nuclear device on October 9. North Korea's actions defied years of international efforts to keep it from developing nuclear weapons and warnings against provocative missile tests. On October 14, the United Nations (UN) imposed sanctions on North Korea, restricting sales of military equipment to, and allowing inspections of cargoes destined for, the Communist country. Japan imposed even tougher sanctions, but China and South Korea opposed severe economic penalties and failed to commit to how thoroughly they would check cargoes.

United States officials in 1994 had persuaded North Korea to agree to freeze its nuclear weapons development. In 2002, however, U.S. officials announced that the North had admitted that it had begun a secret program in violation of the agreement. China, Japan, Russia, South Korea, and the United States then began joint efforts to restrain the program and also limit development of missiles that might deliver nuclear weapons. The North broke off talks in 2005 after the United States imposed financial sanctions, partly because North Korea was counterfeiting U.S. money.

China, whose oil, food, and other support was vital to North Korea, announced on Oct. 31, 2006, that the North had agreed to resume talks. However, the North insisted that new talks be accompanied by discussions on lifting financial sanctions, which had hurt its already-crippled economy. The United States agreed to discuss these sanctions without making any promises.

Natural disasters struck hard in Asia in 2006. A typhoon in the Philippines in February caused a deforested mountainside to slide over a village on Leyte Island, killing more than 1,000 people. On May 27, an earthquake struck the Indonesian island of Java, killing more than 5,800 people. Floods caused by monsoon rains on Indonesia's Sulawesi Island in June killed more than 280 people. Another earthquake off Java's coast on July 17 caused a tsunami that killed more than 600 people. China was hit in August by its strongest typhoon in 50 years, which killed at least 436 people. Another typhoon struck the Philippines in November, causing mudslides that killed some 1,000 people.

Pollution became an ever-worsening problem in many parts of Asia during 2006. Since 2001, China, much of whose heat and electric energy production came from burning soft coal, had been listed by the World Bank, a UN affiliate, as having 16 of the world's 20 most polluted cities. Some Chinese cities made efforts to reduce pollution, and businesspeople in Hong Kong worried that increasing pollution there might reduce its attraction as a commercial center. India's capital, New Delhi, sought to reduce the smog from vehicle exhausts.

In Southeast Asia, a choking haze from vegetation burned by loggers and farmers from July to October was worse than at any time since 1998. Mostly originating in Indonesia, the smoke also affected Brunei, Malaysia, Singapore, and Thailand. The five countries' officials agreed on Nov. 2, 2006, on a series of joint measures to tackle the problem.

Economics. Trade and economic ministers from the 10-member Association of Southeast Asian Nations (ASEAN) agreed in August to hasten efforts to create a free trade market. They sought to attract more foreign investment and to stay competitive with growing economies in China and India. The Asian Development Bank, a UN affiliate, called on ASEAN to be more specific in listing steps being taken toward economic integration. On August 25, the United States signed a trade and investment pact with ASEAN.

On August 8, shipping insurers dropped a "war risk" designation for the Malacca Strait, which runs between Indonesia and Malaysia. The move cut insurance rates for ships using one of the world's busiest sea lanes, which had been plagued with piracy until the two bordering nations and Singapore began naval patrols in 2004 and aerial patrolling in 2005.

Brunei. Legal papers released in 2006 showed that the absolute ruler of Brunei, Sultan Haji Hassanal Bolkiah, had rewritten the constitution. A new passage declared that the sultan "can do no wrong in either his personal or any official capacity." The sultan's brother, Prince Jefri, was not so lucky. Bolkiah had fired Jefri in 2000 from the management of Brunei's oil and natural gas wealth after Jefri was responsible for the loss of billions of dollars. In 2006, the government made legal efforts in London and Brunei to recover some of the money Jefri had allegedly embezzled.

Laos. Lieutenant-General Choummaly Sayasone was named head of Laos's ruling Communist party on March 21, at the end of its party congress, which is held every five years. He succeeded 82-year-old Khamtai Siphandon, one of the last leaders of the Vietnamese-backed party that came to power in 1975. The party, the only one legal in Laos, won elections for a new

Archaeologists survey damage at the Prambanan Hindu temple complex at Yogyakarta caused by an earthquake on the Indonesian island of Java on May 27, 2006. The quake, one of several that had rocked the region in recent years, left more than 5,800 people dead and tens of thousands of others homeless.

100,000 people fled to refugee camps. As law and order broke down, Alkatiri was accused of arming hit squads to attack his political opponents.

Australian-led peacekeepers arrived in late May and restored order. After crisis talks among East Timor's divided leadership, the nominally nonpolitical president, Kay Rala Xanana Gusmão, claimed control of the remaining security forces on May 30. Alkatiri, who disputed Gusmão's authority, resigned on June 26.

National Assembly on April 30, 2006. On June 8, the party chose Choummaly to succeed Khamtai as the nation's president and named Bouasone Bouphavanh as prime minister.

East Timor, also known as Timor-Leste, suffered in 2006 through its worst violence since gaining independence from Indonesia in 2002. Trouble began in March 2006, after Prime Minister Mari Alkatiri discharged 600 of the 1,400 members of the country's army after a series of complaints over pay and promotions. Tensions also existed between corps members from different regions of the small nation. The ousted soldiers revolted and were brutally suppressed. The survivors then fled to the hills, calling for the authoritarian Alkatiri to resign.

The situation touched off clashes between soldiers and police as well as rioting by unemployed youths in the impoverished country. More than

Alkatiri was succeeded by Foreign Minister José Ramos-Horta. Ramos-Horta had been one of two recipients of the 1996 Nobel Peace Prize for his work against Indonesia's brutal occupation of his country. Taking office on July 10, 2006, he blamed "the inefficiency, the incompetence, the laziness" of the government and private business for the country's stunted development. He promised to change the way the country had been governed.

The UN Security Council voted on August 25 to establish a new UN peacekeeping command for East Timor to replace the Australian-led emergency force. The new force would maintain order during preparations for the first direct elections for parliament, scheduled for May 2007.

Maldives. Opposition activist Jennifer Latheef received a pardon from President

FACTS IN BRIEF ON ASIAN COUNTRIES

Country	Population	Government	Monetary unit*	Foreign trade (million U.S.$)	
				Exports[†]	Imports[†]
Afghanistan	26,929,000	President Hamid Karzai	afghani (49.58 = $1)	471	3,870
Armenia	3,400,000	President Robert Kocharian; Prime Minister Andranik Markaryan	dram (381.68 = $1)	800	1,500
Azerbaijan	8,616,000	President Ilham Aliyev; Prime Minister Artur Rasizade	manat (4,592.00 = $1)	6,117	4,656
Bangladesh	134,840,000	President Iajuddin Ahmed	taka (67.03 = $1)	9,372	12,970
Bhutan	814,000	King Jigme Khesar Namgyel Wangchuck; Prime Minister Lyonpo Khandu Wangchuk	ngultrum (45.58 = $1)	154	196
Brunei	382,000	Sultan and Prime Minister Haji Hassanal Bolkiah	dollar (1.59 = $1)	4,514	1,641
Cambodia (Kampuchea)	13,698,000	King Norodom Sihamoni; Prime Minister Hun Sen	riel (4,200.00 = $1)	2,663	3,538
China	1,338,331,000	President Hu Jintao; Premier Wen Jiabao	yuan (7.90 = $1)	752,200	631,800
East Timor	964,000	President Xanana Gusmão; Prime Minister José Ramos-Horta	dollar (1.00 = $1)	10	202
Georgia	4,244,000	President Mikhail Saakashvili; Prime Minister Zurab Nogaideli	lari (1.74 = $1)	1,400	2,500
India	1,103,121,000	President Abdul Kalam; Prime Minister Manmohan Singh	rupee (45.58 = $1)	76,230	113,100
Indonesia	226,875,000	President Susilo Bambang Yudhoyono	rupiah (9,207.50 = $1)	83,640	62,020
Iran	68,899,000	Supreme Leader Ayatollah Ali Khamenei; President Mahmoud Ahmadinejad	rial (9,159.00 = $1)	55,420	42,500
Japan	127,927,000	Emperor Akihito; Prime Minister Shinzo Abe	yen (118.98 = $1)	550,500	451,100
Kazakhstan	15,316,000	President Nursultan A. Nazarbayev; Prime Minister Daniyal Akhmetov	tenge (127.54 = $1)	30,090	17,510
Korea, North	22,954,000	Chairman of National Defense Commission Kim Jong-il	won (2.20 = $1)	1,275	2,819
Korea, South	48,360,000	President Roh Moo-hyun; Prime Minister Han Myung-sook	won (949.15 = $1)	288,200	256,000
Kyrgyzstan	5,345,000	President Kurmanbek Bakiev	som (39.21 = $1)	759	937
Laos	6,046,000	President Choummaly Sayasone; Prime Minister Bouasone Bouphavanh	kip (10,032.50 = $1)	379	541

*Exchange rates as of Oct. 6, 2006.   [†]Latest available data.

Maumoon Abdul Gayoom on Aug. 16, 2006, after 10 months of house arrest on charges of inciting a riot. The head of the opposition Maldivian Democratic Party, Mohamed Nasheed, was released from house arrest on September 21, but sedition charges against him were not withdrawn. Gayoom had been criticized by international human rights organizations for his authoritarian rule.

Mongolia. The Mongolian People's Revolutionary Party (MPRP), the former Communist party that had ruled Mongolia under Soviet influence for 70 years, withdrew in January from a deadlocked coalition government, accusing it of corruption and not doing enough to fight poverty. Parliament then elected Miyeegombo Enkhbold to replace Tsakhiagiyn Elbegdorj as prime minister on January 25. Enkhbold was the chairman of the MPRP and had served as the mayor of the capital, Ulaanbaatar.

Kyrgyzstan. Eight days of mass protests in Bishkek, the capital, in November led to a reduction in the powers wielded by President Kurmanbek Bakiev. Protesters accused Bakiev, who had won a landslide victory in 2005, of failing to introduce promised democratic reforms. On Nov. 9,

Country	Population	Government	Monetary unit*	Foreign trade (million U.S.$)	
				Exports[†]	Imports[†]
Malaysia	25,745,000	Paramount Ruler Mizan Zainal Abidin, the Sultan of Terengganu; Prime Minister Abdullah bin Ahmad Badawi	ringgit (3.69 = $1)	147,100	118,700
Maldives	321,000	President Maumoon Abdul Gayoom	rufiyaa (12.80 = $1)	123	567
Mongolia	2,580,000	President Nambaryn Enkhbayar; Prime Minister Miyeegombo Enkhbold	tugrik (1,168.00 = $1)	852	1,011
Myanmar (Burma)	51,223,000	Chairman of the State Peace and Development Council Than Shwe; Prime Minister Soe Win	kyat (6.42 = $1)	3,111	3,454
Nepal	25,636,000	King Gyanendra	rupee (72.93 = $1)	822	2,000
Pakistan	165,035,000	President Pervez Musharraf; Prime Minister Shaukat Aziz	rupee (60.55 = $1)	14,850	21,260
Philippines	84,093,000	President Gloria Macapagal-Arroyo	peso (50.00 = $1)	41,250	42,660
Russia	142,190,000	President Vladimir Putin; Prime Minister Mikhail Fradkov	ruble (26.90 = $1)	245,000	125,000
Singapore	4,240,000	President Sellapan Rama Nathan; Prime Minister Lee Hsien Loong	dollar (1.59 = $1)	204,800	188,300
Sri Lanka	19,500,000	President Mahinda Rajapakse	rupee (104.23 = $1)	6,442	8,370
Taiwan	22,781,000	President Chen Shui-bian; Premier (President of the Executive Yuan) Su Tseng-chang	dollar (33.09 = $1)	189,400	181,600
Tajikistan	6,574,000	President Emomali Rahmonov; Prime Minister Oqil Oqilov	somoni (3.38 = $1)	950	1,250
Thailand	64,645,000	King Bhumibol Adulyadej (Rama IX); Interim Prime Minister Surayud Chulanont	baht (37.55 = $1)	105,800	107,000
Turkmenistan	5,092,000	Deputy Prime Minister Gurbanguly Berdymukhamedov (acting)	manat (5,200.00 = $1)	4,700	4,175
Uzbekistan	27,250,000	President Islam A. Karimov; Prime Minister Shavkat Mirziyayev	som (1,229.21 = $1)	5,000	3,800
Vietnam	84,655,000	Communist Party Secretary-General Nong Duc Manh; President Nguyen Minh Triet; Prime Minister Nguyen Tan Dung	dong (16,054.00 = $1)	32,230	36,880

2006, Bakiev signed an amended Constitution that drastically cut his power. Under the new Constitution, the president no longer had the power to dissolve the country's Parliament, and the national security agency no longer reported to the president. In addition, in 2010, parliamentary membership was to increase from 75 to 90, and the majority party, rather than the president, was to choose the country's prime minister. In December, Bakiyev's Cabinet resigned in an attempt to speed the transition to a new government.

Abdication in Bhutan. Jigme Singye Wangchuck, king of Bhutan, announced his abdication on Dec. 14, 2006, more than a year earlier than was expected from the king's earlier statements. He did not announce when his son, Jigme Khesar Namgyel Wangchuck, will be crowned. King Jigme Singye Wangchuck had announced in December 2005 that he would step down in 2008, when the Himalayan nation will become a multiparty parliamentary democracy under a new constitution. ■ Henry S. Bradsher

See also **Disasters; Public health; Terrorism;** various Asian country articles.

Astronomy. Astronomers in 2006 found the first lakes outside Earth, approved an official definition of the word *planet*, discovered two new moons of Pluto, studied two remarkable planets orbiting stars other than the sun, and viewed planetary and satellite systems outside the solar system in the process of forming.

Pluto's "demotion." Members of the International Astronomical Union (IAU) meeting in August approved the first official definition of the word *planet*. The decision ejected Pluto, which was discovered in 1938, from the group comprising the solar system's true planets. Pluto is now categorized as a *dwarf planet* because there are several bodies similar in size in its neighborhood, a region in the distant reaches of the solar system known as the Kuiper belt.

Lakes of Titan. Astronomers announced in July the discovery of dozens of lakes near the north pole of Saturn's largest moon, Titan. Some of the lakes are nearly 20 miles (32 kilometers) wide. The longest covers about 60 miles (96 kilometers). Scientists identified the lakes on images taken by a radar system on-board the United States National Aeronautics and Space Adminis-

tration's (NASA) Cassini spacecraft. Radar can penetrate the dense clouds that surround Titan.

Titan's lakes are the only large bodies of liquid known on any object other than Earth, but they are highly unusual. Because Titan's surface is so cold—some –292 °F (–180 °C)—the lakes cannot contain liquid water, which would be frozen at such low temperatures. Instead, astronomers believe the lakes are filled with liquid methane or a mixture of liquid methane and ethane.

Data from the Huygens probe, a spacecraft that had parachuted from the Cassini spacecraft onto the surface of Titan in January 2005, confirmed the presence of liquid methane on Titan. Scientists at the NASA Ames Research Center in Moffett Field, California, announced in July 2006 that the clouds surrounding Titan contain liquid methane that continually drizzles onto Titan's surface.

Eris. In September 2006, the IAU gave the official name of Eris to 2003 UB_{313}, a Kuiper belt object discovered in 2005. Eris was the goddess of chaos and strife in ancient Greece.

More moons for Pluto. Astronomers in February 2006 confirmed the existence of two small moons that had first been spotted around Pluto in faint images taken by the Hubble Space Telescope in May 2005. Astronomers Hal Weaver of the Johns Hopkins University Applied Physics Laboratory in Laurel, Maryland, and Alan Stern of the Southwest Research Institute in Boulder, Colorado, used new Hubble images to identify the moons. Each of the new moons is about 10 times as small and 600 times as faint as Pluto's larger

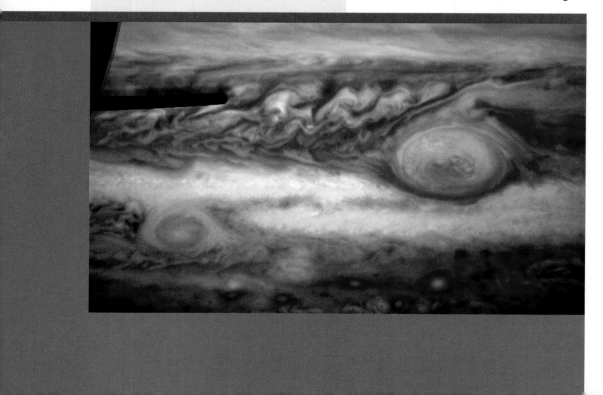

A new swirling storm (lower left), nicknamed "Red Spot, Jr.," rages near the famous Great Red Spot (right) in a photograph of Jupiter taken by the Hubble Space Telescope in April. The smaller spot gave astronomers an opportunity to observe how such storms develop.

Pluto, a ball of rock and ice in the outer reaches of the solar system (shown in an artist's illustration), lost its status as a planet in August 2006. Astronomers reclassified Pluto as a dwarf planet because it orbits the sun in a band of similar-sized objects known as the Kuiper belt.

Astronomers approved a formal definition of the term *planet* in 2006, reducing the solar system from nine to eight planets.

Astronomers in 2006 resolved a long-standing dispute about the definition of the term *planet* by removing Pluto from the list of planets in the solar system. At an August meeting of the General Assembly of the International Astronomical Union (IAU) in Prague, Czech Republic, astronomers voted to create an official definition. The IAU is the recognized authority in naming heavenly bodies.

According to the definition, a planet in our solar system is an object that meets all of the following three conditions: the body orbits the sun; it has enough *mass* (amount of matter) that its own gravitational pull squeezes it into a round shape; and its gravitational pull is strong enough to sweep the region of its orbit relatively free of other objects. The new definition means that the solar system has eight true planets: Mercury, Venus, Earth, Mars, Jupiter, Saturn, Uranus, and Neptune.

The astronomers also defined a *dwarf planet* as a body that orbits the sun, has enough mass to be round, but has not cleared its orbit of other objects. Some astronomers in 2006 disapproved of the definition and rejected its use.

Pluto became a dwarf planet under the definition because the neighborhood of its orbit contains several bodies of similar size. These bodies occupy the Kuiper belt, a swarm of icy objects at the edge of the solar system. Astronomers designated Eris, a Kuiper belt object that measures slightly larger than Pluto, as another dwarf planet. Ceres, the largest of the asteroids that orbit between Mars and Jupiter, also became a dwarf planet.

moon, Charon. In June 2006, the IAU approved the names Nix and Hydra for the two small bodies.

New Horizons. Pluto and its moons will be studied in greater detail by the New Horizons spacecraft, which was launched in January. It was scheduled to fly by Pluto in 2015.

Remarkable extrasolar planets. Two of several new planets discovered outside our solar system proved particularly interesting to astronomers in 2006. In September, astronomers using a network of robotic telescopes designed by astronomer Gaspar Bakos of the Harvard-Smithsonian Center for Astrophysics in Cambridge, Massachusetts, reported the discovery of a planet named HAT-P-1. The planet orbits very close to a star located about 450 light-years from the sun. (A light-year, the distance light travels in one year, equals 5.88 trillion miles [9.46 trillion kilometers]).

HAT-P-1 has a diameter about 1.4 times as great as Jupiter, but a *mass* (amount of matter) only half that of Jupiter. It is, thus, the lightest-known planetary body. Astronomers suspect its lightness may be related to the heat it receives from its host star, which would cause the object to expand like a hot-air balloon.

Another new extrasolar planet was described in January by an international team of astronomers. This planet, named OGLE-2005-BLG-390Lb, is the smallest, most Earthlike planet found outside the solar system. Orbiting a small star 25,000 light-years away, it is about 5 times as massive as Earth and circles its host star every 10 years. Astronomers believe it has a rocky surface mixed with frozen water.

Planemos. In June, astronomers led by Ray Jayawardhana of the University of Toronto in Canada announced the observations of small objects outside our solar system called *planetary mass objects*, or *planemos*. Planemos are similar to planets, with a mass several times that of Jupiter. Unlike planets, however, planemos seem to float through space rather than orbit a star.

The astronomers detected disks of dust and gas encircling the planemos. They concluded that these disks resemble the sun-circling disk of dust and gas from which the planets of our solar system formed.

The findings, noted astronomer Valentin D. Ivanov of the European Southern Observatory in Chile, "suggest similar infancies for our sun and for objects that are some hundred times less massive." For example, according to the astronomers, some of the moons of Jupiter and Saturn may have formed from disks of material that encircled these planets during their formation. Thus, the process of planet and moon formation from dusty disks around central objects appears to be widespread in the universe. ■ Laurence A. Marschall

See also **Space exploration.**

Australia continued to enjoy excellent economic conditions during 2006, as a boom in mining products offset the harmful effects of one of the longest droughts in living memory. During the course of the year, a wheat scandal reached the highest levels of government. In September, the nation mourned the death of Steve Irwin, the world-renowned "crocodile hunter" and naturalist, who was killed by a stingray. Sports fans will remember Nov. 7, 2006, as the day a Japanese jockey, Yasunari Iwata, riding Delta Blues, won the Melbourne Cup, the horse race that stops the nation each year. Iwata became the third foreign jockey to win the Cup.

Economy. The Australian Stock Exchange opened with several new records in January. In March, the Australian All Ordinaries Index, which represents Australia's leading 500 companies, passed the 5,000 mark for the first time. In August, the Australian-based international mining giant BHP-Billiton announced record profits.

Australia's booming economy in 2006 aroused fears that inflation, which was rising steadily toward 4 percent, might spiral out of control. To meet this threat, the Australian Reserve Bank, the nation's central bank, raised the rate at which banks lend to other banks three times during the year. In November, the prime interest rate reached

AUSTRALIA

6.25 percent, the highest level since 2000.

Other economic indicators were favorable in 2006. In April, Treasurer Peter Costello announced that Australia was free of all federal government debt. When he presented his 11th budget to Parliament on May 9, he was able to forecast a surplus for the ninth time in 10 years—this time, $10 billion. (All amounts in Australian dollars.) The budget included substantial cuts for most taxpayers. In June, Prime Minister John Howard announced that Australia's unemployment rate had fallen to a 30-year low of 4.9 percent.

Global warming became the subject of heated political debate in 2006. The conservative Liberal–National Coalition government, which had consistently refused to sign the Kyoto Protocol on greenhouse gas emissions, began serious discussions about ways to reduce the use of carbon fuels widely believed to be causing climate change. Australia has large reserves of coal and relies almost exclusively on coal to produce electric power. Australia is also one of the world's largest exporters of coal. In January, representatives from Australia, China, India, Japan, South Korea, and the United States met in Sydney, Australia's largest city, to discuss climate change and energy supplies. Clean coal technologies, industry-supported environment funds, and nuclear power were some of the issues discussed at the meeting. Later in the year, government officials announced plans to contribute $75 million toward building the world's largest solar power station, near Mildura in Victoria.

Energy. A report by the National Electricity Market issued in October confirmed fears that Australia was facing a future shortage of electric power and forecast that the demand for power in some states would outstrip supply as early as 2007. Prime Minister Howard, who had earlier in 2006 established a body to review the possibility of building the first nuclear plants in Australia, maintained that solar and wind power would remain peripheral, and that nuclear power could be competitive with coal in a few years. He argued that nuclear power could be the answer to both the demand for more electric power and the reduction of greenhouse gases. The proposal to build nuclear plants was opposed by conservationist groups and by many members of the Australian Labor Party.

Australian car owners, like those in the rest of the world, suffered from rising gasoline prices during 2006. In August, the federal government announced subsidies for private motorists to convert their automobiles from gasoline to liquefied petroleum gas. The government also offered

A wall of dust engulfs the town of Birdsville in southwestern Queensland in January 2006. The dust storm formed after years of lower-than-average rainfall. The extreme heat of Australia's summer caused evaporating raindrops to cool a column of air and send it plunging to the ground, where it raised the cloud of dust.

FACTS IN BRIEF ON AUSTRALIA

Population	20,324,000
Government	Governor General Michael Jeffrey; Prime Minister John Howard
Monetary unit*	dollar (1.34 = $1 U.S.)
Foreign trade (million U.S.$)	
Exports[†]	103,000
Imports[†]	119,600

*Exchange rate as of Oct. 5, 2006.
[†]Latest available data.

financial assistance to encourage retailers to sell gasoline blended with ethanol.

Climate. A heat wave struck Sydney on January 1, with the temperature soaring to a record 111.6 °F (44.2 °C). Fires raged in all of the country's southern states in January. Larry, the most powerful cyclone to hit Australia in several decades, struck Innisfail in Queensland in March. The cyclone caused millions of dollars in damage and destroyed much of the nation's banana crop.

Despite some rain early in the year, drought continued to grip much of southeastern Australia for the fifth year in succession, making it the longest period of sustained low rainfall in the area since the 1930's. Economists estimated that the 2006 wheat crop would be down by about two-thirds, and livestock production would also suffer greatly. By October, farmers in more than half of Australia's agricultural areas were being subsidized by the federal government through special-assistance drought payments.

The centerpiece of the federal budget in May was a grant of $500 million to improve water management in the Murray-Darling Basin, where *salinity* (saltiness) is a major problem. In October, an audit of water supplies by the National Water Commission criticized the performance of state and territory authorities in planning for future water needs. Flows into the Murray-Darling Basin in 2006 were the lowest on record, and, in November, the federal government called a meeting of state leaders in Canberra, the capital, to address the crisis.

Australian cities also suffered from a shortage of water. In April, the main dammed reservoir supplying the city of Goulburn in New South Wales was officially declared dry. Restrictions on the use of water for gardens in Sydney continued as levels behind the Warragamba Dam, the city's main source of water, remained at about 40 percent of capacity. In October, local councils in Gosford and Wyong, north of Sydney, began looking for sites to build temporary desalination units.

Politics. In June, the federal government overturned laws passed by the government of the Australian Capital Territory permitting same-sex marriages. Voters in Tasmania and South Australia went to the polls in March and returned the two Labor premiers, Paul Lennon and Mike Rann, respectively, to office. In Queensland, the government of Labor Premier Peter Beattie was reelected on September 9. Victoria's Labor Premier Steve Bracks was also reelected to another term at state elections held in November. On December 4, the Australian Labor Party voted to replace Kim Beazley, its leader in the federal parliament, with Kevin Rudd, the party's spokesperson on foreign affairs.

In July, legislation came into effect that put all new workers on a 90-day probation period during which they were not allowed to file complaints against their employers. Hundreds of workers throughout Australia protested the legislation, which critics argued would encourage exploitation. Later in July, the government unveiled plans for sweeping changes to the laws governing Australian media outlets. The new proposals involved lifting restrictions that had prevented foreign ownership and kept corporations from owning both newspapers and television stations in the same markets. As soon as the changes had passed the Senate in October, Australia's richest media owner, James Packer, announced a $5.5-billion sale of half of his interest in the Channel Nine television network and Australian Consolidated Press magazines to a European private equity group to increase his investments in casinos. Rupert Murdoch, whose New York City-based News Corporation in 2006 owned a large proportion of Australia's newspapers and had shares in a cable television company, bought a 7-percent stake in Fairfax, the public company that owned *The Sydney Morning Herald* and *The Age* in Melbourne.

Security. In March, Joseph Thomas, a convert to Islam known in the Australian media as "Jihad Jack," became the first Australian to be sentenced to prison under new antiterrorism laws. He was found guilty of receiving money from the al-Qa'ida terrorist network. Thomas walked free in August after an appeals court quashed his conviction, ruling that some evidence used against him was inadmissible. He was then placed under a control order that restricted his movements.

Also in August, Faheem Khalid Lodhi, a Pakistani-born architect working in Sydney, was sentenced to 20 years in prison for planning a terrorist attack on Australian soil. Evidence showed that he intended to attack Australia's electric power grid. Meanwhile, David Hicks spent his fifth year imprisoned at Guantánamo Bay, Cuba, despite the U.S. Supreme Court's June ruling that the military commissions set up to try detainees at the prison camp in Cuba were illegal. Hicks is an

Australian convert to Islam who was arrested in Afghanistan in 2001 on suspicion of being an enemy combatant. In August 2006, Attorney General Philip Ruddock announced that he would press the U.S. authorities to return Hicks to Australia if they did not bring charges quickly.

Middle East. In June, the government announced that the approximately 450 Australian troops in Iraq were to be moved to Talil Air Base southeast of Baghdad. In August, the government sent an additional 240 troops to Afghanistan to help with reconstruction. Later in August, the government outlined plans to recruit more soldiers.

AWB scandal. In January, the Australian government established a commission under former Judge Terence Cole to investigate the conduct of AWB, a private company that was formerly the government-owned Australian Wheat Board. AWB executives had allegedly breached the rules of the 1996 United Nations oil-for-food program by paying kickbacks to Iraqi dictator Saddam Hussein to ensure sales of Australian wheat. Senior AWB executives admitted in 2006 that they had paid millions of dollars to a Jordanian trucking firm that they knew was partly owned by the Iraqi government. Evidence showed that the departments of Foreign Affairs and Trade had received a series of cables from 1998 to 2004 raising allegations

about the AWB. In April 2006, Minister of Foreign Affairs Alexander Downer testified that he could not remember the specifics. Deputy Prime Minister and Trade Minister Mark Vaile and Prime Minister Howard testified that they had no knowledge of the cables. In November, the commission cleared the government of involvement in the scandal.

International relations. Australian officials pledged $3 million in aid after a 6.5-magnitude earthquake struck the Indonesian island of Java in May. Earlier in the year, Australia's delicate relationship with Indonesia was strained after refu-

Bindi Irwin reads a tribute to her father, internationally known conservationist and self-styled "crocodile hunter" Steve Irwin, at a memorial service for him on Sept. 20, 2006. Irwin was killed by a stingray while filming a nature documentary at the Great Barrier Reef.

THE CABINET OF AUSTRALIA*

John Howard—prime minister
Warren Truss—minister for transport and regional services
Peter Costello—treasurer
Mark Vaile—minister for trade; deputy prime minister
Brendan Nelson—minister for defence
Helen Coonan—minister for communications, information technology, and the arts
Alexander Downer—minister for foreign affairs
Kevin Andrews—minister for employment and workplace relations
Amanda Vanstone—minister for immigration and multicultural affairs
Ian Campbell—minister for the environment and heritage
Philip Ruddock—attorney general
Nick Minchin—minister for finance and administration; leader of the government in the Senate
Peter McGauran—minister for agriculture, fisheries, and forestry
Mal Brough—minister for families, community services, and indigenous affairs
Julie Bishop—minister for education, science, and training
Tony Abbott—minister for health and ageing
Ian Macfarlane—minister for industry, tourism, and resources

*As of December 7, 2006.

PREMIERS OF AUSTRALIAN STATES

State	Premier
New South Wales	Morris Iemma
Queensland	Peter Beattie
South Australia	Mike Rann
Tasmania	Paul Lennon
Victoria	Steve Bracks
Western Australia	Alan Carpenter

CHIEF MINISTERS OF AUSTRALIAN MAINLAND TERRITORIES

Australian Capital Territory	Jon Stanhope
Northern Territory	Clare Martin

government's displeasure at the release of Abu Bakar Bashir, a Muslim cleric jailed for his role in the 2002 resort bombings on the Indonesian island of Bali, in which 88 Australians were among the people killed. Many Australians saw Bashir's release in strong contrast to the treatment of four Australians given lengthy prison sentences in Indonesia for smuggling heroin through Bali in 2005. After the four appealed their sentences, the Indonesian government sentenced them to death. Later in 2006, the two countries made arrangements to swap prisoners in the future. This would mean that many Australians convicted of smuggling drugs into Indonesia could be allowed to serve their sentences in Australian jails.

When Prime Minister Howard visited Indonesian President Yudhoyono in the Indonesian capital of Jakarta in June, the two leaders agreed to negotiate a new security agreement. The agreement, which was signed in November, included plans to cooperate on border patrols and to help Indonesia develop nuclear power and suppress Papuan independence movements in Indonesia.

In May, Australia sent troops to help quell violence that broke out in Dili, the capital of East Timor. Australia also sent police to help restore order following riots in the Solomon Islands. Relations with its Pacific Island neighbors came under stress in October after both Papua New Guinea and the Solomon Islands refused to return Julian Moti, an Australian lawyer and the attorney general of the Solomon Islands, to Australia to face child-sex charges.

Arts. In April, Geraldine Brooks became the first Australian to win a Pulitzer Prize. Her award-winning novel, *March,* was inspired by American writer Louisa M. Alcott's classic *Little Women* (1868). In June, Roger McDonald won the Miles Franklin Literary Award, Australia's leading literary prize, for *The Ballad of Desmond Kale,* a novel set in the early days of the wool industry.

In March, Melbourne-based painter Marcus Wills won the Archibald Prize, Australia's most prestigious award for painting. His surreal, Medieval-styled work, *The Paul Juraszek monolith (after Marcus Gheeraerts),* contained more than 200 individual figures, 29 of which were portraits of Melbourne-based sculptor Juraszek.

Steve Irwin. On September 4, conservationist, television personality, and self-styled "crocodile hunter" Steve Irwin was killed by a stingray while filming a documentary at the Great Barrier Reef in Queensland. A family memorial service was shown on television in Australia, the United States, and many other countries, and included tributes by Prime Minister Howard, celebrities, and Irwin's daughter, Bindi.   ■ Brian Kennedy

gees from Indonesia's Papua province landed in Australian territory in an outrigger canoe and sought asylum. Indonesia protested by withdrawing its ambassador from Australia. Australia's government introduced legislation that would have allowed future refugees arriving by boat to have their cases processed on the island of Nauru, but it was withdrawn in August, when it became obvious that the bill would not pass the Senate.

Prime Minister Howard wrote to Indonesian President Susilo Bambang Yudhoyono to voice his

See also **Australia, Prime Minister of; Indonesia; Literature; Pacific Islands; Pulitzer Prizes.**

MEMBERS OF THE AUSTRALIAN HOUSE OF REPRESENTATIVES

The House of Representatives of the 41st Parliament first met Nov. 16, 2004. As of Dec. 7, 2006, the House of Representatives consisted of the following members: 74 Liberal Party of Australia, 60 Australian Labor Party, 12 National Party of Australia, 3 independents, and 1 Northern Territory Country Liberal Party. This table shows each legislator and party affiliation. An asterisk (*) denotes those who served in the 40th Parliament.

Australian Capital Territory
Annette Ellis, A.L.P.*
Bob McMullan, A.L.P.*

New South Wales
Tony Abbott, L.P.*
Anthony Albanese, A.L.P.*
John Anderson, N.P.*
Peter Andren, Ind.*
Bruce Baird, L.P.*
Bob Baldwin, L.P.*
Kerry Bartlett, L.P.*
Sharon Bird, A.L.P.*
Bronwyn Bishop, L.P.*
Chris Bowen, A.L.P.*
Tony Burke, A.L.P.*
Alan Cadman, L.P.*
Ian Causley, N.P.*
John Cobb, N.P.*
Justine Elliot, A.L.P.*
Pat Farmer, L.P.*
Laurie Ferguson, A.L.P.*
Joel Fitzgibbon, A.L.P.*
Peter Garrett, A.L.P.*
Joanna Gash, L.P.*
Jennie George, A.L.P.*
Sharon Grierson, A.L.P.*
Jill Hall, A.L.P.*
Luke Hartsuyker, N.P.*
Michael Hatton, A.L.P.*
Chris Hayes, A.L.P.
Kelly Hoare, A.L.P.*
Joe Hockey, L.P.*
John Howard, L.P.*
Kay Hull, N.P.*
Julia Irwin, A.L.P.*
Jackie Kelly, L.P.*
Sussan Ley, L.P.*
Jim Lloyd, L.P.*
Louise Markus, L.P.*
Robert McClelland, A.L.P.*
Daryl Melham, A.L.P.*
John Murphy, A.L.P.*
Gary Nairn, L.P.*
Brendan Nelson, L.P.*
Julie Owens, A.L.P.
Tanya Plibersek, A.L.P.*
Roger Price, A.L.P.*
Philip Ruddock, L.P.*
Alby Schultz, L.P.*
Ken Ticehurst, L.P.*
Malcolm Turnbull, L.P.*
Mark Vaile, N.P.*
Danna Vale, L.P.*
Tony Windsor, Ind.*

Northern Territory
Warren Snowdon, A.L.P.*
David Tollner, C.L.P.*

Queensland
Arch Bevis, A.L.P.*
Mal Brough, L.P.*
Steven Ciobo, L.P.*
Peter Dutton, L.P.*
Kay Elson, L.P.*
Craig Emerson, A.L.P.*
Warren Entsch, L.P.*
Teresa Gambaro, L.P.*
Gary Hardgrave, L.P.*
Michael Johnson, L.P.*
David Jull, L.P.*
Robert Katter, Ind.*
De-Anne Kelly, N.P.*
Andrew Laming, L.P.*
Peter Lindsay, L.P.*
Kirsten Livermore, A.L.P.*
Ian Macfarlane, L.P.*
Margaret May, L.P.*
Paul Neville, N.P.*
Bernie Ripoll, A.L.P.*
Kevin Rudd, A.L.P.*
Bruce Scott, N.P.*
Peter Slipper, L.P.*
Alexander Somlyay, L.P.*
Wayne Swan, A.L.P.*
Cameron Thompson, L.P.*
Warren Truss, N.P.*
Ross Vasta, L.P.*

South Australia
Alexander Downer, L.P.*
Trish Draper, L.P.*
Kate Ellis, A.L.P.*
David Fawcett, L.P.*
Steve Georganas, A.L.P.*
Christopher Pyne, L.P.*
Kym Richardson, L.P.*
Rodney Sawford, A.L.P.*
Patrick Secker, L.P.*
Andrew Southcott, L.P.*
Barry Wakelin, L.P.*

Tasmania
Dick Adams, A.L.P.*
Mark Baker, L.P.*
Michael Ferguson, L.P.*
Duncan Kerr, A.L.P.*
Harry Quick, A.L.P.*

Victoria
Kevin Andrews, L.P.*
Fran Bailey, L.P.*
Phillip Barresi, L.P.*
Bruce Billson, L.P.*
Russell Broadbent, L.P.*
Anna Burke, A.L.P.*
Anthony Byrne, A.L.P.*
Ann Corcoran, A.L.P.*
Peter Costello, L.P.*
Simon Crean, A.L.P.*
Michael Danby, A.L.P.*
Martin Ferguson, A.L.P.*
John Forrest, N.P.*
Petro Georgiou, L.P.*
Steve Gibbons, A.L.P.*
Julia Gillard, A.L.P.*
Alan Griffin, A.L.P.*
David Hawker, L.P.*
Greg Hunt, L.P.*
Harry Jenkins, A.L.P.*
Catherine King, A.L.P.*
Jenny Macklin, A.L.P.*
Stewart McArthur, L.P.*
Peter McGauran, N.P.*
Sophie Mirabella, L.P.
Brendan O'Connor, A.L.P.*
Gavan O'Connor, A.L.P.*
Chris Pearce, L.P.*
Andrew Robb, L.P.*
Nicola Roxon, A.L.P.*
Bob Sercombe, A.L.P.*
Tony Smith, L.P.*
Sharman Stone, L.P.*
Lindsay Tanner, A.L.P.*
Kelvin Thomson, A.L.P.*
Maria Vamvakinou, A.L.P.*
Jason Wood, L.P.*

Western Australia
Kim Beazley, A.L.P.*
Julie Bishop, L.P.*
Graham Edwards, A.L.P.*
Barry Haase, L.P.*
Stuart Henry, L.P.*
Dennis Jensen, L.P.*
Michael Keenan, L.P.*
Carmen Lawrence, A.L.P.*
Judi Moylan, L.P.*
Geoffrey Prosser, L.P.*
Don Randall, L.P.*
Stephen Smith, A.L.P.*
Wilson Tuckey, L.P.*
Mal Washer, L.P.*
Kim Wilkie, A.L.P.*

Australia, Prime Minister of.

On March 2, 2006, John Howard celebrated 10 years in office, making him the second-longest-serving prime minister in Australia's history. Howard made it clear that he had no intention of stepping down in the immediate future and would lead his party to the next general election, due in 2007.

During 2006, Howard received several important visitors, including Queen Elizabeth II and Prime Minister Tony Blair of the United Kingdom; Secretary of State Condoleezza Rice of the United States; and Premier Wen Jiabao of China. In May, Howard met with U.S. President George W. Bush in Washington, D.C., before making official visits to Canada and Ireland. In June, Howard visited China, where he signed a deal to supply that country with liquid natural gas worth $25 billion (Australian). In October, Howard flew to Fiji to attend a meeting with leaders of Pacific Island nations.

During 2006, Howard appeared to change his attitude toward global warming and began discussing ways in which Australia could reduce greenhouse gas emissions. In June, he announced the launch of a study to determine if Australia should develop nuclear power.

■ Brian Kennedy

See also **Australia.**

Australian rules football.

The West Coast Eagles defeated the Sydney Swans 12 goals 13 behinds (85 points) to 12 goals 12 behinds (84 points) to win the Australian Football League (AFL) premiership in Melbourne on Sept. 30, 2006. The Swans started badly, but managed to cut the margin to 5 points just 12 seconds into the last quarter. However, West Coast held on to the lead to win by 1 point. For West Coast, it was a sweet revenge for their 2005 loss to Sydney in the grand final. The Eagles' Andrew Embley won the 2006 Norm Smith medal for the best player on the ground in the grand final. The Swans' Adam Goodes won his second Brownlow Medal for the best and fairest player during the season.

Three regional finals were held on September 24. Subiaco won the West Australian Football League premiership, beating South Fremantle 24.9 (153) to 10.10 (70). Sandringham beat Geelong 13.13 (91) to 11.7 (73) to win their third consecutive Victorian Football League premiership. In the AFL Queensland grand final, the Southport Sharks defeated the Zillmere Eagles 17.14 (116) to 16.8 (104). The Woodville West Torrens Eagles won the 2006 South Australian National Football League premiership over the Central District Bulldogs by 17.19 (121) to 7.3 (45) on October 8.   ■ Brian Kennedy

Austria.

The governing center-right coalition led by Chancellor Wolfgang Schussel's Austrian People's Party lost in national elections in October 2006. The winning Social Democratic Party took 36 percent of the vote under the leadership of Alfred Gusenbauer. The Social Democrats profited especially from the splintering of the far right into two parties, the Alliance for Austria's Future and the Freedom Party, which took 4 percent and 11 percent of the total vote, respectively. Both parties ran on platforms that were anti-immigrant and *xenophobic* (based on fear or hatred of foreigners and strangers). Together, they took enough votes from the conservative Austrian People's Party to hand the election to the Social Democrats.

The Social Democrats found it difficult to form a majority government, however. They refused to include the far right in the government. In addition, a coalition between the Social Democrats and the Greens fell short of a majority. The only possibility for a stable majority was to adopt a "grand coalition" between the Social Democrats and the Austrian People's Party. The two parties negotiated throughout the fall in an attempt to form a Cabinet. However, disagreements over whether to push on with an unpopular contract to buy Eurofighter military aircraft and over the level of social and educational spending divided the two parties.

Economy. The Austrian economy performed better than expected in 2006. European Union economists projected that the country's *gross domestic product* (GDP, the total value of all goods and services produced in a country in a given year) would increase by 3.1 percent in 2006, up from 2 percent in 2005. A stronger-than-expected labor market and demand for Austria's exports helped nudge unemployment down from 5.2 percent in 2005 to 5.1 percent in 2006.

The past on trial. An Austrian court sentenced British historian David Irving to three years in prison in February for denying, during a speech in Austria in 1989, the fact of the Holocaust. The Holocaust was the systematic killing of Jews and other people by Germany's Nazi government during World War II (1939-1945). In Austria, as well as in at least nine other European countries and in Israel, it is a crime to deny the Holocaust or to diminish its reality.

Some critics viewed the sentence as overly harsh, because Irving pleaded guilty and acknowledged that he had been wrong about certain aspects of the Holocaust. Others considered the trial to be a suppression of the right of free speech. In late December 2006, an Austrian appeals court released Irving from jail and converted the remainder of his sentence to probation.   ■ Jeffrey Kopstein

See also **Europe.**

Automobile and light truck sales in the United States dipped in 2006 as higher gasoline prices and higher interest rates kept customers away from dealers' showrooms. Sales through September hit 12.7 million units, 3.7 percent below 2005's figures. Analysts anticipated that year-end sales would total about 16.5 million, 3 percent below 2005's total.

There were definite winners and losers in 2006. On the losing end were the traditional Big Three—General Motors (GM) Corporation of Detroit; Ford Motor Company of Dearborn, Michigan; and the U.S. division of DaimlerChrysler AG of Germany. The Big Three's market share dropped to 55.3 percent through September, compared with 59.1 percent for the same period in 2005. The big winner for 2006 was Toyota, which took a 15.2-percent market share, surpassing Chrysler and becoming the third-largest seller in the United States. The Japanese company led the surge of Asian automakers, which captured 39.4 percent of the U.S. market for the first nine months, compared with 36.1 percent for the same period in 2005. European automakers took 5.4 percent of the U.S. market for the first nine months of 2006, compared with 4.8 percent for the same period in 2005.

The Big Three lost domestic market share in 2006 despite offering higher incentives than their Asian competitors. Average GM incentives totaled $3,093 through September; Ford's were $3,396 and Chrysler's, $3,684. In October, incentives offered by Big Three manufacturers averaged $3,129 per vehicle, compared with $1,074 for Japanese automakers, $1,715 for Korean companies, and $2,419 for European automakers.

High gasoline prices and environmental concerns boosted the popularity of gas-electric hybrid models in 2006. Hybrid sales for the first nine months climbed to 192,170 units, for an increase of nearly 25 percent over the same period a year earlier. The most popular models for the year were the same as in 2005. Through September 2006, the Ford F-series pickup sold 579,294 units to lead other light trucks, and the Toyota Camry was the number-one automobile with combined sales of its standard and hybrid models reaching 340,905 units.

Big Three. Ford's sales fell 9 percent to 2.2 million units through September, and its market share declined from 18.6 percent in 2005 to 17.7 percent during the same period in 2006. Ford was hurt by declining sport utility sales. For example, sales for Ford Explorers dropped 27 percent to 143,270 units. Declining sales numbers were reflected in Ford's financial statements. The company lost nearly $7 billion through the first nine months of 2006, compared with a net income of $1.5 billion a year earlier. In January 2006, Ford announced a program of plant closings, white-collar job cuts, and other measures to improve the company's finances. As

problems worsened, the nation's number-two automaker put its Aston Martin sports car unit up for sale in August. Ford intensified its turnaround and in September brought in Alan Mulally as president and chief executive officer. Mulally had previously served as executive vice president of the Chicago-based Boeing Company, an aerospace equipment manufacturer. William Ford remained the company's executive chairman.

In September, Ford executives announced the company was reducing costs in North America by further cutting its salaried workforce, offering buyouts to factory workers, and closing 16 North American plants. In all, the moves may cut more than 40,000 of Ford's 110,000 North American employees. To improve the company's fortunes in 2007, Ford executives announced in November 2006 a plan to pledge corporate assets as collateral for $18 billion in loans.

GM's sales for the first nine months fell 11 percent to 3.1 million units, and its market share declined to 24.8 percent, compared with 26.9 percent a year earlier. The company reported a net loss of $3 billion through September 2006, compared with a $3.9-billion loss for the same period a year earlier. Analysts said the declining losses showed the restructuring program that GM implemented in 2005 was beginning to pay off. As part of that program, about 34,400 hourly workers accepted buyouts. In February 2006, GM cut its dividend in half to save $500 million a year. To raise cash, GM agreed in April to sell its 51-percent interest in its finance company, General Motors Acceptance Corp. Also in April, GM sold its 7.9-percent interest in Isuzu Motors of Japan for $300 million. During 2006, GM opened negotiations with Renault of France and Nissan of Japan about a possible business alliance but eventually broke off talks. For 2007, GM hoped for better sales from its new Chevrolet Silverado and GMC Sierra pickup trucks and from the Saturn Aura.

Sales by DaimlerChrysler's U.S. division dropped 11 percent in the first nine months of 2006 to 1.6 million units, and its market share declined to 12.9 percent from 13.1 percent for the same period in 2005. Through September 2006, Chrysler's operating loss totaled $1.3 billion, compared with a 2005 operating profit of $1.4 billion. The company attributed the loss in part to lower sales for its sport utility vehicles, such as the Dodge Durango. Durango sales fell about 40 percent to 53,417 units. The company hoped to appeal to buyers interested in more fuel-efficient vehicles with its Chrysler Sebring, a midsize car.

Asian manufacturers. Toyota's sales jumped 12 percent to 1.9 million units through the first nine months of 2006, and its market share rose to 15.2 percent, compared with 13 percent in 2005. The company benefited in 2006 from sales of its

GM retired the Hummer H1 in 2006. The enormous sport utility vehicle, which had been a status symbol, fell out of favor when gas climbed above $3 per gallon.

Mitsubishi officials experimented in 2006 with the possibility of introducing to the United States their "i" car, which is popular in Japan. According to industry experts, the car's 3-cylinder engine would get an upgrade if sold in the United States.

High gas prices in 2006 inspired automakers to retire some gas-guzzlers and bring back the subcompact.

Dieter Zetsche, chairman of German-American automaker DaimlerChrysler (below right), introduces Roger Penske, chairman of U.S. car dealer United Auto Group, to the Smart car in Detroit in June. Popular in such congested European cities as Paris and Rome, the car, which is less than 10 feet (3 meters) long, was scheduled to enter the U.S. market in 2008.

small vehicles. Nine-month sales of Toyota's RAV-4 sport utility more than doubled to 115,684 units, and the subcompact Yaris posted sales of 51,748. In October, Toyota's Georgetown, Kentucky, plant began producing the Camry hybrid, which uses gas and electric power. The company intended to grow sales even more in 2007 with its new Tundra full-size pickup, which will be produced at a recently opened San Antonio plant.

Japan-based Honda also had a good year in 2006. Honda's sales rose 4 percent to 1.2 million units through the first nine months, in part because of better sales of the new Civic. Honda's U.S. market share grew to 9.2 percent through the first nine months, compared with 8.5 percent a year earlier. In June 2006, the automaker announced it would build a $550-million assembly plant near Greensburg, Indiana, to produce 4-cylinder vehicles beginning in 2008. The plant, Honda's sixth in North America, was expected to employ about 2,000 workers. Kia, a South Korean company, announced in March 2006 that it would build its first U.S. assembly plant in West Point, Georgia. The $1.2-billion facility will create about 2,500 jobs and was expected to start production in 2009. Through the first nine months of 2006, Kia sold 221,997 vehicles in the United States—1.8 percent of the market. ■ Mike Casey

See also **Transportation.**

Automobile racing.
Jimmie Johnson captured his first NASCAR Nextel Cup championship, but once again in 2006, many racing fans were more focused on 24-year-old Indy Racing League (IRL) driver Danica Patrick's quest to become the first woman to win a race on a major circuit. Fans also speculated on whether she would leave open-car racing for the glamour and high profile of NASCAR, but she opted to stay with the IRL.

The IRL and the Champ Car World Series, which split in 1996, appeared to move closer to reuniting in 2006. Tony George, founder and president of the IRL, announced in June that the two racing bodies had "agreed conceptually" to merge but needed to work out specific details.

Indianapolis 500. Sam Hornish, Jr., captured the Indy 500 on May 28, after slipping past 19-year-old rookie Marco Andretti on the final straightaway. The race, decided by .0635 second, was the second-closest Indy 500 in history. (The closest was the 1992 race, settled by .043 second.) Andretti's father, Michael, who had come out of retirement to race with his son, finished in third place, 1.0087 seconds behind Hornish.

Formula One. Defending champion Fernando Alonso defeated seven-time champion Michael Schumacher to win the Formula One Championship in Brazil on Oct. 22, 2006. Alfonso established an early points lead with 6 wins in the first 9 races

of the 18-race series. Schumacher captured 3 straight races but lost to Alonso in the final race. On September 10, Schumacher announced that he would retire at the end of the season. He finished his career with a record 90 Grand Prix victories.

NASCAR. Johnson captured the Nextel Cup championship on November 19 in Homestead, Florida, with a ninth-place finish, 51 points ahead of Matt Kenseth. In the first 20 races, Johnson notched 16 top-10 finishes, including 3 wins and 7 top-5 finishes, to surge to a sizable lead in the point standings. Struggles in the middle of the season left defending points winner Tony Stewart and Dale Earnhardt, Jr., in jeopardy of not making the final 10-race "Chase for the Championship."

Champ Car. France's Sebastien Bourdais won the season's first four races, then added three more victories to win his third straight Champ Car World Series title on November 12. He finished with 387 points, 89 ahead of Justin Wilson.

In July, Champ Car announced a new chassis for its 2007 cars. The chassis—developed by Georgia-based Panoz Auto Development Company—is lighter than the previously used Lola chassis and allows for closer racing.

IRL. With just three races to go, Hornish was locked in a tight points battle with Helio Castroneves and Dan Wheldon. Hornish captured the championship on Sept. 10, 2006, with a third-place finish at the Peak Antifreeze Indy 300 in Joliet, Illinois. Wheldon finished second in the points standings, and Castroneves, third.

Patrick failed to capture any IRL races in her second season on the circuit, finishing ninth in the point standings. She announced plans in July to switch from the Rahal Letterman Racing team to the powerful Andretti Green Racing team.

Endurance. On June 18, Audi became the first team to win the Le Mans (France) 24 Hour endurance race with a diesel-powered car, its sixth title overall. The car was driven by Frank Biela, Marco Werner, and Emanuele Pirro.

Scott Dixon and Dan Wheldon of the IRL teamed with Casey Mears to take the Rolex 24 at Daytona Beach, Florida, on January 29. The winners averaged 108.826 miles (175.138 kilometers) per hour.

Dragsters. Tony Schumacher won the 2006 National Hot Rod Association (NHRA) top fuel division championship, John Force won the funny car division, and Greg Anderson won the pro stock division.

Paul Dana, a former motor-sports reporter and IRL rookie, died on March 26 during a warm-up lap in the season-opening race in Homestead, Florida. Dana's car, traveling nearly 200 miles (325 kilometers) per hour, slammed into a car that had crashed and spun to a stop moments earlier.

■ Michael Kates

Aviation. The discovery of a suspected terrorist plot shook the aviation industry in 2006, causing widespread travel delays and new airport security measures.

On August 10, British police arrested 24 people who were allegedly involved in a plot to blow up a number of airplanes traveling from the United Kingdom to the United States. Seventeen people were eventually charged. The British government claimed that the suspects planned to construct bombs from liquid explosives disguised as common beverages, toiletries, and other liquids. The bombs would then be detonated using electronic devices.

For the next five days, passengers were not allowed to bring carry-on baggage aboard flights departing from the United Kingdom. Passengers were allowed to pass through security checkpoints only with the barest essentials, such as a wallet and required medications, contained in a transparent plastic bag. There were extensive delays and flight cancellations because of the lines at security checkpoints and the need for passengers to check all their baggage.

In the United States, the Transportation Security Administration (TSA), an agency of the Department of Homeland Security, immediately banned passengers from taking most types of liquids and gels onto aircraft. In late September, the TSA relaxed the ban and allowed passengers to transport small amounts of certain liquids and gels.

It was widely reported that the alleged plotters—most of whom were British-born citizens of Pakistani descent or converts to Islam—had links to the Islamist terrorist organization al-Qaʿida. Qaʿida operatives were reportedly behind a foiled 1995 plot to destroy aircraft using liquid explosives.

Improving profitability. Prior to the midsummer terrorist threat and security alert, the financial fortunes of the airline industry had been improving in 2006. Despite high oil prices, airlines were operating flights at close to capacity and were even able to moderately increase fares. Air travel remained relatively high even after the security alert, though many airlines had to offer discounts.

United Airlines—a division of UAL Corporation of Elk Grove Village, Illinois—emerged from bankruptcy protection in February 2006. The company announced in July that it had a profitable second quarter for the first time since 2000. Nevertheless, United's profits still lagged behind those of its closest competitor, American Airlines. American—a subsidiary of AMR Corporation, based in Fort Worth, Texas—avoided seeking bankruptcy protection.

United's other main rivals—Delta Air Lines Inc., based in Atlanta, Georgia, and Northwest Airlines, based in Eagan, Minnesota—remained in bankruptcy protection throughout 2006. Both airlines struggled to persuade their employees to accept wage and benefit concessions to reduce costs. In addition, Delta discontinued its Song brand in May. Delta started Song to provide a low-fare competitor to the New York City-based JetBlue Airways in leisure markets along the Atlantic seaboard. Song's aircraft and routes reverted to the standard Delta brand.

Troubles at Airbus. European aircraft manufacturer Airbus faced major problems in 2006. Deliveries of its new large passenger aircraft, the Airbus A380, were significantly delayed. The first commercial flights were rescheduled for 2008, and aircraft were to be delivered at a slower rate than was originally planned.

Airbus found little interest among airlines for its proposed new midsize jet, called the Airbus A350. The aircraft was designed to compete with the Chicago-based Boeing Company's 787 Dreamliner, which was expected to make its debut in 2008. In contrast to the Airbus model, the Boeing 787 Dreamliner had attracted considerable attention from airlines looking to add a fuel-efficient jet to serve smaller international markets. Airbus announced in July 2006 that it was redesigning the A350—now designated the A350XWB (extra wide body)—to make the jet more attractive to purchasers. The aircraft was reconfigured to compete with both the Boeing 787 and the larger Boeing 777.

At the start of 2006, Airbus was co-owned by the European Aeronautic Defence and Space Company (EADS) and BAE Systems of the United Kingdom. In April, however, BAE Systems announced that it would try to sell its 20-percent share of Airbus to EADS. The transaction was made in October.

The troubles at Airbus led to the ouster in July of Gustav Humbert, the Airbus chief executive, and Noël Forgeard, the co-chief executive of EADS. The new Airbus chief executive, Christian Streiff, lasted only three months before resigning in October. He was replaced by Louis Gallois.

Distance record. On February 11, United States adventurer Steve Fossett set the world record for the longest nonstop flight. His 25,766-mile (41,467-kilometer) trip took him from the Kennedy Space Center in Florida eastbound around the world, back over Florida, and then across the Atlantic Ocean for a second time, before landing in Bournemouth, England. The flight, in a single-engine jet aircraft, took 76 hours 43 minutes. The flight bested the nonstop jet aircraft record, set in 1986, and the balloon record, set in 1999. ■ Ian Savage

See also **Energy supply.**

Azerbaijan. The governing Yeni Azerbaijan Party (YAP) of President Ilham Aliyev won 5 of the 10 parliamentary seats contested in a by-election held on May 13, 2006. Independents took 3 seats and opposition parties took 2. Voting irregularities in the Nov. 6, 2005, parliamentary elections led to the annulment of the original results. After the 2006 by-election, the YAP held 61 of the 125 parliamentary seats. Although the by-election was boycotted by most opposition parties, the Council of Europe's election monitors deemed the election a "step forward" in comparison with the flawed November elections.

The government took legal action against several independent journalists in 2006. Most notably, Sakit Mirza Zahidov, a writer for the opposition daily *Azadliq,* was arrested for heroin possession on June 23. On October 4, he was found guilty and sentenced to three years in prison. Zahidov accused the police of planting the heroin on him. Opposition journalists called the arrest and trial politically motivated. Because of increased threats against the editors, two leading independent newspapers ceased publication on October 3.

■ Juliet Johnson

See also **Asia.**

Bahamas. See **Latin America; West Indies.**

Bahrain. See **Middle East.**

Ballet. See **Dancing.**

Baltic states. Estonia, Latvia, and Lithuania were all forced to postpone their anticipated adoption of the euro currency from 2007 to at least 2009 after experiencing higher-than-expected inflation in 2006. The European Union holds strict economic criteria for new euro-zone entrants.

Estonia's parliament failed to elect a new president after three rounds of voting in August 2006. No candidate reached the required majority of 68 votes in the 101-seat parliament. The failures sent the decision to a 345-member electoral college, which on September 23 chose Toomas Hendrik Ilves over incumbent Arnold Ruutel. Ilves received 174 votes to Ruutel's 162. Ilves had previously served as foreign minister and had held a seat in the European Parliament since 2004.

Latvia's ruling conservative People's Party triumphed in October 7 parliamentary elections. Incumbent Prime Minister Aigars Kalvitis formed a coalition from his People's Party (which won 19.5 percent of the vote), the Union of Greens and Farmers (16.7 percent), the First Party of Latvia and Latvia's Way (8.6 percent), and For Fatherland and Freedom (7 percent). The new government held 59 seats in the 100-seat Saeima at the end of 2006. The leading opposition party, the center-right New Era, received 16.4 percent of the vote.

■ Juliet Johnson

See also **Europe.**

Bangladesh. Some 31 Muslim extremists were sentenced to death in Bangladesh in 2006 for their roles in a wave of bombings the previous year. The bombings of courts, police stations, and other government buildings occurred between August and December 2005 and killed at least 30 people, including two judges. The bombings were carried out by two banned Islamic groups that demanded that Bangladesh, a predominantly Muslim nation with secular laws, be ruled by Islamic law, Shari`ah. Leaders of the two groups, along with some 800 militants, entered police custody in March 2006.

Since the 1990's, control of Bangladesh has switched back and forth between Khaleda Zia, who served as prime minister from 2001 to October 2006, and former Prime Minister Sheikh Hasina Hajed. In October 2006, Zia was required by Bangladeshi law to hand over control to a neutral caretaker government that would conduct the January 2007 parliamentary elections. Hajed's Awami League staged angry demonstrations and boycotted the September 2006 session of Parliament to protest election preparations. After at least 20 people died in clashes over who would lead the caretaker government, President Iajuddin Ahmed named himself to the post and was sworn in on October 29, angering Hajed. ■ Henry S. Bradsher

See also **Asia; Disasters; Nobel prizes.**

Bank. In June 2006, the Federal Reserve (the Fed), the central bank of the United States, raised its key short-term interest rate from 5 to 5.25 percent, the 17th consecutive boost since June 2004, and the last increase in 2006. The rate, known as the federal funds rate, is the interest charge for interbank borrowing and for the most creditworthy borrowers. In July, the Fed expressed continuing concern about inflationary pressures in the rapidly expanding 2006 economy but declined to increase the rate again. By the late fall, the Fed's forbearance was rewarded when gasoline and some energy prices tumbled precipitously. However, some experts expressed concern that the "core" rate of inflation (price change minus changes in energy and food prices) was, at nearly 3 percent, too high.

Bank profits. Banks and savings institutions continued to rack up record quarterly profits in 2006, according to data published by the Federal Deposit Insurance Corporation (FDIC), the federal agency that insures individual bank deposits up to $100,000 against loss. In recent years, bank profits have been on a winning streak in net profits. In the third quarter of each year beginning in 2002, banking institutions posted profits of $27.3 billion (2002), $30.4 billion (2003), $32.5 billion (2004), $34.7 billion (2005), and $37.6 billion in 2006. The 2006 third-quarter profits were the second highest in history, surpassed only by the $38 billion posted in the second quarter of 2006. The FDIC attributed the higher net income to strong growth in loans, which produced higher interest income, and lower expenses resulting from lower losses on loans.

Bank assets. In a Sept. 30, 2006, report, the FDIC outlined key statistics on 8,743 commercial banks and savings institutions. Together, the institutions held a total of $11.8 trillion in assets. Of these assets, $7.2 trillion were loans and nearly $2 trillion were securities. Bank and savings institutions' liabilities totaled $10.5 trillion, of which $7.6 trillion was deposits and $1.3 trillion was borrowed funds. Of the total assets, commercial banks alone held $9.8 trillion, with the balance held by savings institutions. Commercial banks' liabilities totaled $8.8 trillion, of which $6.4 trillion was customers' deposits. The biggest banks (those with assets of $1 billion or more) held about 88 percent of all bank and savings institutions' assets, liabilities, and capital, yet they represented only six percent of the total number of these institutions.

According to economists, the FDIC report documented the increasing size and importance of financial institutions in general and commercial banks in particular in both the U.S. and global economies. The four largest banks in the third quarter of 2006, according to the report, were the Bank of America of Charlotte, North Carolina ($1.19 trillion in domestic and foreign assets); JPMorgan Chase & Company of Columbus, Ohio ($1.17 trillion in assets); Citibank, Inc. of New York City ($816 billion); and Wachovia Bank, also of Charlotte ($517 billion).

Bank loans. In 2006, banking institutions loaned more to commercial customers than to individuals, continuing a trend that began in 2005. In the third quarter, banks loaned $1.1 trillion to commercial borrowers and $847 billion to individuals. Of those loans, 30 percent went for residential mortgages, 17 percent were commercial and industrial loans,12 percent were for commercial real estate, and 5 percent were on credit cards, with the balance scattered among other consumer loans (8 percent), construction loans (8 percent), and other types of loans (about 20 percent).

Charge-offs. The proportions of commercial and consumer debt that banks write off as uncollectible ("charge-offs") are a clue to the health of the banking industry and the economy. According to Fed data (seasonally adjusted at annual rates), the charge-off rate on loans and leases deemed uncollectible in the third quarter of 2006 was less than half a percent of that quarter's holdings. Charge-off rates ranged from less than a tenth of a percent on commercial and residential real estate loans to almost 4 percent on credit card loans.

Mergers and consolidations. After the passage of key banking laws in 1994 and 1999, the regulations that had allowed the banking industry to be involved in only certain activities since the Glass-Steagall Act of 1933 were largely removed. Since the passage of these laws, banks have been freer to merge and consolidate, to operate across state and international boundaries, to underwrite municipal bonds, and to be affiliated with firms that sell insurance. Several mergers took place in 2006, including the $25-billion acquisition of the Golden West Financial Corporation of Oakland, California, by the Wachovia Corporation.

Bank notes. In November, an investment consortium won a bid to pay $3.1 billion for a more-than 85-percent stake in China's Guangdong Development Bank. The consortium includes Citigroup, Inc., which will have a 20-percent share; International Business Machines Corp., which will have about 5 percent; and four Chinese companies, which will have the remaining approximately 60 percent. The yearlong negotiations for the sale were aided by China's obligations under its entry into the World Trade Organization in 2001 and by support from the U.S. government.

Exotic mortgages. Economists warned in 2006 against the growing practice of lenders granting mortgages that require low initial payments that may escalate sharply depending on economic conditions. Economists worry that such debt instruments as the interest-only and "pick your monthly payment" starter mortgages could cause massive foreclosures in the future if required payments increase dramatically. The warnings did not appear to have the desired effect, as preliminary data suggest that more such "nontraditional" mortgages were issued in the first six months of 2006 than in the same period in 2005.

New FDIC premiums. In November, the FDIC issued final regulations to implement the Federal Deposit Insurance Corporation Reform Act of 2005. The U.S. Congress had passed the act to strengthen the federal deposit insurance fund. The new regulations would vary the premiums paid into the fund by banks and other financial institutions that receive insured deposits. The new rates would be based on how each bank compares with (1) ratings for all insured institutions, (2) financial ratios for most institutions, and (3) ratings by long-term debt issuers. The new premiums would follow a point system based on the institution's risk rating. In the 2005 law, Congress provided that banks that had paid higher premiums in the past into the deposit insurance fund would receive credit against the newly required premiums that kick in on Jan. 1, 2007.

■ Robert W. Fisher

See also **Economics; Stocks and bonds.**

Barbados. See **Latin America; West Indies.**

Baseball. The St. Louis Cardinals in 2006 captured their 10th World Series championship, stunning the heavily favored Detroit Tigers four games to one. The Cardinals won just 83 regular-season games, the lowest full-season total of any series winner in history. St. Louis shortstop David Eckstein was named Most Valuable Player, finishing the series with eight hits in his final three games.

The loss ended a Cinderella season for the Tigers. After 12 straight losing seasons, Detroit surged through a phenomenal first half of the 2006 season. The team then blew its American League (AL) Central lead in the season's last few weeks, entering the play-offs as a wild-card team. Detroit became the overwhelming favorite to win the series when it rolled through the first two play-off rounds, earning nearly a week off before the opening game.

World Series. The series began in Detroit on October 21, with the Cardinals winning 7-2. The Tigers took Game 2 by a score of 3-1 behind left-hander Kenny Rogers. Rogers, who turned 42 in November, pitched eight shutout innings, becoming the oldest starter to earn a World Series win. Controversy arose over a brown smudge seen on his hand during the first inning. Some observers suspected it was a sticky substance called pine tar used to improve the grip on a baseball. The umpires made Rogers wash off the smudge, but St. Louis did not request further investigation.

The Cardinals rebounded as the series moved to St. Louis, winning 5-0 in Game 3 on October 24. Two days later, in Game 4, they fell behind 3-0

before rallying to a 5-4 victory, with Eckstein racking up four hits. On October 27, the Cardinals finished at home, coming from behind to win 4-2. Throughout the series, St. Louis took advantage of Detroit's mistakes. The Tigers committed eight errors in five games—a record five by pitchers.

Play-offs. The Tigers made it to the series by sweeping the Oakland Athletics four games to none in the American League Championship Series (ALCS). Detroit had advanced to the ALCS by toppling the overwhelmingly favored New York Yankees three games to one in the American League Division Series (ALDS). Oakland had swept the Minnesota Twins three games to none in the ALDS.

The Cardinals reached the World Series by besting the New York Mets four games to three in the National League Championship Series. St. Louis had beaten the San Diego Padres three games to one in the National League Division Series (NLDS), while the Mets had swept the Los Angeles Dodgers.

Regular season. The Mets easily topped the National League (NL) East, posting a league-leading 97-65 record and ending the 11-year reign of the Atlanta Braves. St. Louis won the NL Central at 83-78, edging out the Houston Astros, who won 10 of their last 12 games. In the NL West, the Padres and

The St. Louis Cardinals play their first night game at the new Busch Stadium on April 12, 2006. The stadium, which partially covers the site of the previous Busch Stadium, features an open design that embraces views of such downtown landmarks as the Gateway Arch.

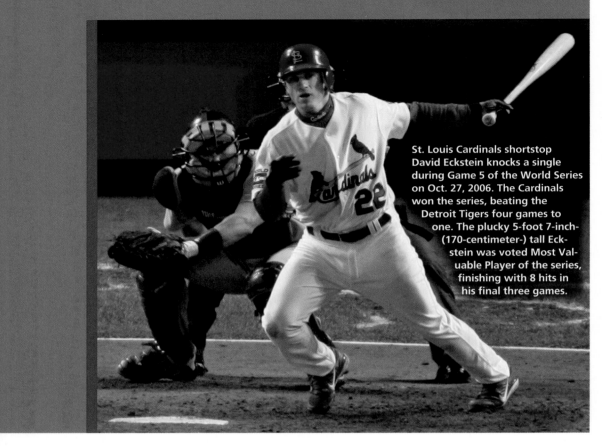

St. Louis Cardinals shortstop David Eckstein knocks a single during Game 5 of the World Series on Oct. 27, 2006. The Cardinals won the series, beating the Detroit Tigers four games to one. The plucky 5-foot 7-inch- (170-centimeter-) tall Eckstein was voted Most Valuable Player of the series, finishing with 8 hits in his final three games.

the Dodgers tied at 88-74, but San Diego got the title, having won the season series.

Minnesota, also a surprise contender, started the season 25-33 and trailed Detroit by 10 ½ games on August 8. But when the Tigers lost their last five games, the Twins snatched the AL Central, finishing 96-66. The Yankees won their ninth straight AL East title despite trailing the Boston Red Sox by three games at the All-Star break. New York eventually blew past Boston to a 97-65 mark. Oakland won the AL West with a 93-69 record.

Embattled Bonds. San Francisco Giants slugger Barry Bonds suffered another troubled season. Two books published in the spring detailed allegations that Bonds had used performance-enhancing drugs—*Love Me, Hate Me: Barry Bonds and the Making of an Antihero* by Jeff Pearlman and *Game of Shadows* by Mark Fainaru-Wada and Lance Williams. Both works addressed Bonds's ties to the Bay Area Laboratory Co-Operative (BALCO), whose founder had pleaded guilty in 2005 to distributing steroids. In 2006, grand juries investigated whether Bonds had committed perjury during a government investigation into BALCO and had evaded taxes by not reporting income from the sale of memorabilia.

On the field, Bonds hit 26 home runs in 2006, bringing his career total to 734, just 21 short of

Hank Aaron's all-time mark. Bonds became a free agent at the end of the season but in December signed to play for the Giants in 2007.

Drug scandals. Following the publication of *Game of Shadows*, Major League Baseball officials appointed former U.S. Senate Majority Leader George Mitchell to investigate past steroid use by players. However, many critics doubted that the investigation would be effective because Mitchell lacked the authority to subpoena players and coaches—that is, to legally compel them to testify.

On June 6, 2006, federal agents raided the home of Arizona Diamondbacks pitcher Jason Grimsley for evidence that he had distributed a performance-enhancing drug called *human growth hormone* (HGH). Grimsley admitted to using HGH, steroids, and amphetamines and named other players who had allegedly done the same. The Diamondbacks released Grimsley on June 7.

Milestones. Florida Marlins rookie Anibal Sanchez pitched a no-hit game against Arizona on September 6, ending the longest no-hitter drought in major-league history at 6,364 games. On September 22, Alfonso Soriano of the Washington Nationals became the first major-league player to hit 40 home runs and 40 doubles and to steal 40 bases in a single season.

FINAL STANDINGS IN MAJOR LEAGUE BASEBALL

AMERICAN LEAGUE

American League champions—
Detroit Tigers
(defeated Oakland Athletics, 4 games to 0)

Eastern Division	W.	L.	Pct.	G.B.
New York Yankees	97	65	.599	—
Toronto Blue Jays	87	75	.537	10
Boston Red Sox	86	76	.531	11
Baltimore Orioles	70	92	.432	27
Tampa Bay Devil Rays	61	101	.377	36

Central Division	W.	L.	Pct.	G.B.
Minnesota Twins	96	66	.596	—
Detroit Tigers*	95	67	.586	1
Chicago White Sox	90	72	.566	6
Cleveland Indians	78	84	.481	18
Kansas City Royals	62	100	.383	34

Western Division	W.	L.	Pct.	G.B.
Oakland Athletics	93	69	.574	—
Los Angeles Angels	89	73	.549	4
Texas Rangers	80	82	.494	13
Seattle Mariners	78	84	.481	15

Offensive leaders

Batting average	Joe Mauer, Minnesota	.347
Runs scored	Grady Sizemore, Cleveland	134
Home runs	David Ortiz, Boston	54
Runs batted in	David Ortiz, Boston	137
Hits	Ichiro Suzuki, Seattle	224
Stolen bases	Carl Crawford, Tampa Bay	58
Slugging percentage	Travis Hafner, Cleveland	.659

Leading pitchers

Games won	Johan Santana, Minnesota	19
Earned run average (162 or more innings)—	Johan Santana, Minnesota	2.77
Strikeouts	Johan Santana, Minnesota	245
Saves	Francisco Rodriguez, L.A.	47
Shut-outs	John Lackey, Los Angeles	2
	C. C. Sabathia, Cleveland	2
	Jeremy Sowers, Cleveland	2
	Jake Westbrook, Cleveland	2
Complete games	C. C. Sabathia, Cleveland	6

Awards†

Most Valuable Player....................Justin Morneau, Minnesota
Cy Young ....Johan Santana, Minnesota
Rookie of the Year...............................Justin Verlander, Detroit
Manager of the Year ....Jim Leyland, Detroit

NATIONAL LEAGUE

National League champions—
St. Louis Cardinals
(defeated New York Mets, 4 games to 3)

World Series champions—
St. Louis Cardinals (defeated Detroit Tigers, 4 games to 1)

Eastern Division	W.	L.	Pct.	G.B.
New York Mets	97	65	.599	—
Philadelphia Phillies	85	77	.525	12
Atlanta Braves	79	83	.488	18
Florida Marlins	78	84	.481	19
Washington Nationals	71	91	.438	26

Central Division	W.	L.	Pct.	G.B.
St. Louis Cardinals	83	78	.516	—
Houston Astros	82	80	.506	1.5
Cincinnati Reds	80	82	.494	3.5
Milwaukee Brewers	75	87	.463	8.5
Pittsburgh Pirates	67	95	.414	16.5
Chicago Cubs	66	96	.407	17.5

Western Division	W.	L.	Pct.	G.B.
San Diego Padres	88	74	.543	—
Los Angeles Dodgers*	88	74	.543	—
San Francisco Giants	76	85	.472	11.5
Arizona Diamondbacks	76	86	.469	12
Colorado Rockies	76	86	.469	12

Offensive leaders

Batting average	Freddy Sanchez, Pittsburgh	.344
Runs scored	Chase Utley, Philadelphia	131
Home runs	Ryan Howard, Philadelphia	58
Runs batted in	Ryan Howard, Philadelphia	149
Hits	Juan Pierre, Chicago	204
Stolen bases	Jose Reyes, New York	64
Slugging percentage	Albert Pujols, St. Louis	.671

Leading pitchers

Games won	Aaron Harang, Cincinnati	16
Earned run average (162 or more innings)—	Roy Oswalt, Houston	2.98
Strikeouts	Aaron Harang, Cincinnati	216
Saves	Trevor Hoffman, San Diego	46
Shut-outs	Chris Carpenter, St. Louis	3
	Brandon Webb, Arizona	3
Complete games	Aaron Harang, Cincinnati	6

Awards†

Most Valuable Player ....Ryan Howard, Philadelphia
Cy Young..Brandon Webb, Arizona
Rookie of the Year ....Hanley Ramirez, Florida
Manager of the Year....................................Joe Girardi, Florida

*Qualified for wild-card play-off spot.
†Selected by the Baseball Writers Association of America.

World Baseball Classic. Japan defeated Cuba 10-6 on March 20 in San Diego to win the first World Baseball Classic (WBC). The international tournament drew more fans than expected.

Daisuke Matsuzaka, the star pitcher of Japan's WBC team, in October announced his intention to enter the U.S. major leagues. Matsuzaka later signed with the Red Sox, who had bid $51 million just for the opportunity to negotiate with him.

Deaths. Yankees pitcher Cory Lidle, 34, died on October 11 when his small plane crashed into a New York City high-rise. Former Twin Kirby Puckett, 45, died on March 6 after suffering a massive stroke. Negro League standout John "Buck" O'Neil, 94, who fell just one vote short of winning entry to the Hall of Fame, died on October 6. Knuckleball pitcher Joe Niekro, 61, the Houston Astros' all-time wins leader with 144, died on October 27.

College. Oregon State University won its first National Collegiate Athletic Association World Series in 2006 with a 3-2 victory over the University of North Carolina on June 26 in Omaha, Nebraska.

Youth. On August 28 in Williamsport, Pennsylvania, a team from Columbus, Georgia, beat a team from Kawaguchi City, Japan, 2-1 to win the Little League World Series. ■ Michael Kates

Basketball. The Miami Heat, riding the spectacular play of guard Dwyane Wade, clinched the franchise's first National Basketball Association (NBA) title in its 18-season existence with a 95-92 victory over the Dallas Mavericks on June 20, 2006, in Dallas. Each team had reached the NBA finals for the first time.

In the National Collegiate Athletic Association (NCAA), two schools claimed their first national championships. The University of Florida men denied the University of California at Los Angeles (UCLA) a record 12th title, and the University of Maryland women edged Duke University.

George Mason University captured the imagination of college basketball fans with a dramatic run as an 11th seed to the Final Four. The unheralded Patriots knocked off both North Carolina and the University of Connecticut (UConn)—the last two national champions—en route to the Final Four. George Mason matched the 1986 Louisiana State University team as the lowest seed to make it to the Final Four and became the first team not from a major conference to get there since the University of Pennsylvania and Indiana State in 1979.

Professional men. Miami captured the NBA title 4 games to 2 over Dallas in one of the most dramatic turnarounds in NBA Finals history. After losing the first two games in Dallas—by double-digit margins—Miami trailed the Mavericks by 13 points in the fourth quarter in Game 3 on June 13, 2006, in Miami. Wade led a remarkable comeback to seize that game, and the Heat evened the series by routing the Mavericks in Game 4 on June 15. Wade scored 43 points in Game 5 on June 18 as the Heat won 101-100. With its victory in Game 6, Miami joined Boston (1969) and Portland (1977) as the only teams to rally from 0-2 to win a title.

The Mavericks earned a Finals berth by eliminating the Phoenix Suns 4 games to 2. The Mavericks had beaten the defending champion San Antonio Spurs 4 games to 3. The Suns, by topping the Los Angeles Clippers, became just the eighth team in NBA history to rally from a 3-games-to-1 deficit to win a series in its conference semifinal against the Los Angeles Clippers. The Suns had also rallied from 3 games to 1 in the first round against the Los Angeles Lakers, dealing coach Phil Jackson his first opening-round play-off loss in 15 tries. The Mavericks beat the Vancouver Grizzlies 4 games to none in the opening round.

The Heat earned its spot by eliminating Detroit 4 games to 2 in the conference finals. Miami eliminated the Chicago Bulls 4 games to 2 in the first round and the New Jersey Nets, 4 games to 1 in the conference semifinals.

In the regular season, Detroit easily won the Central Division with the best record in the NBA: 64 wins and 18 losses. Miami won the Southeast Division with a 52-30 mark; New Jersey won the Atlantic Division with a 49-33 record.

San Antonio captured the Southwest Division with a 63-19 record. Phoenix, behind guard Steve Nash—who captured his second straight regular-season Most Valuable Player (MVP) award—won the Pacific Division with a 54-28 record. Denver won the Northwest Division with a mark of 44-38.

Milestones. On January 22, Kobe Bryant of the Los Angeles Lakers scored 81 points (55 in the second half), the second-highest single-game total in the history of the NBA. Wilt Chamberlain continued to hold the record, with 100 points on March 2, 1962.

Professional women. The Detroit Shock won the WNBA championship, defeating the Sacramento Monarchs 3 games to 2. The Shock rallied to win the final two games to take the title. Deanna Nolan of Detroit was named the MVP of the Finals. Leslie Leslie of the Los Angeles Sparks was named the MVP for the regular season. Leslie also won the honor in 2001 and 2004. Diana Taurasi of the Phoenix Mercury set a single-season WNBA scoring record, averaging 25.3 points per game.

FIBA (International Basketball Federation) **World Championship.** The United States men's national team suffered disappointment in seeking the gold medal. The U.S. team lost to Greece 101-95 in the semifinals and then defeated Argentina 96-81 to win the bronze medal. Spain defeated Greece 70-47 to win the championship.

The U.S. women's team also met with disappointment. American squads had won 26 consecutive games dating back to 1994 before losing in the semifinals to Russia. The U.S. team defeated Brazil 99-59 to win the bronze medal. Australia defeated Russia 91-74 to win the title.

College men. Led by Joakim Noah, the son of French tennis great Yannick Noah, Florida used a punishing defense to overwhelm UCLA 73-57 on April 3 in Indianapolis. Noah, named the Final Four's MVP, set a championship game record for blocked shots with six.

Florida reached the title game on April 1 by ending George Mason's run 73-58. The Gators hit 12 three-pointers—the second-highest total in an NCAA national semifinal. George Mason had beaten UConn, the top seed in the Washington, D.C., regional, to make the Final Four. Florida, a third seed, blasted the Minneapolis (Minnesota) regional top seed Villanova to get to the Finals at Indianapolis. UCLA, the second seed in the Oakland regional, beat Louisiana State, the fourth seed out of the Atlanta regional, 59-45, to advance to the title game.

College women. Maryland rallied from 13 points down on April 4 in Boston to topple

THE 2005-2006 COLLEGE BASKETBALL SEASON

COLLEGE TOURNAMENT CHAMPIONS

NCAA (Men)	Division I:	Florida
	Division II:	Winona State
	Division III:	Virginia Wesleyan
(Women)	Division I:	Maryland
	Division II:	Grand Valley State
	Division III:	Hope College

NAIA (Men)	Division I:	Texas Wesleyan
	Division II:	College of the Ozarks
(Women)	Division I:	Union
	Division II:	Hastings College

NIT (Men)	South Carolina

Joakim Noah of the University of Florida Gators dunks the ball in the Finals of the NCAA tournament in Indianapolis on April 3, 2006. Florida defeated UCLA 73-57. The victory gave Florida its first men's NCAA basketball championship.

MEN'S COLLEGE CHAMPIONS

CONFERENCE	SCHOOL
America East	Albany*
Atlantic 10	George Washington
	Xavier (tournament)
Atlantic Coast	Duke*
Atlantic Sun	Belmont–Lipscomb* (tie)
Big 12	Kansas*–Texas (tie)
Big East	Connecticut–Villanova (tie)
	Syracuse (tournament)
Big Sky	Northern Arizona
	Montana (tournament)
Big South	Winthrop*
Big Ten	Ohio State
	Iowa (tournament)
Big West	Pacific*
Colonial	George Mason–
	North Carolina (Wilmington)* (tie)
Conference USA	Memphis*
Horizon League	Wisconsin (Milwaukee)*
Ivy League	Pennsylvania†
Metro Atlantic	Manhattan
	Iona College (tournament)
Mid-American	
East Division	Kent State*
West Division	Northern Illinois
Mid-Continent	IUPUI–Oral Roberts* (tie)
Mid-Eastern	Delaware State
	Hampton (tournament)
Missouri Valley	Wichita State
	Southern Illinois (tournament)
Mountain West	San Diego State*
Northeast	Farleigh Dickinson
	Monmouth (tournament)
Ohio Valley	Murray State*
Pacific 10	UCLA*
Patriot League	Bucknell*
Southeastern	Florida (tournament)
East Division	Tennessee
West Division	Louisiana State
Southern	Davidson (tournament)
North Division	Elon
South Division	Georgia Southern
Southland	Northwestern State
	Texas (Arlington) (tournament)
Southwestern	Southern*
Sun Belt	
East Division	Western Kentucky
West Division	South Alabama*
West Coast	Gonzaga*
Western Athletic	Nevada*

*Regular season and conference tournament champion.
†No tournament played.
Sources: National Collegiate Athletic Association (NCAA); National Association of Intercollegiate Athletics (NAIA); National Invitation Tournament (NIT); Conference Web sites.

Shaquille O'Neal (left) and Dwyane Wade of the Miami Heat wait for the ball to drop during the sixth game of the NBA finals on June 20, 2006. The Heat beat the Dallas Mavericks, 4 games to 2.

NATIONAL BASKETBALL ASSOCIATION STANDINGS

EASTERN CONFERENCE

Atlantic Division

	W.	L.	Pct.	G.B.
New Jersey Nets*	49	33	.598	—
Philadelphia 76ers	38	44	.463	11
Boston Celtics	33	49	.402	16
Toronto Raptors	27	55	.329	22
New York Knicks	23	59	.280	26

Central Division

	W.	L.	Pct.	G.B.
Detroit Pistons*	64	18	.780	—
Cleveland Cavaliers*	50	32	.610	14
Chicago Bulls*	41	41	.500	23
Indiana Pacers*	41	41	.500	23
Milwaukee Bucks*	40	42	.488	24

Southeast Division

	W.	L.	Pct.	G.B.
Miami Heat*	52	30	.634	—
Washington Wizards*	42	40	.512	10
Orlando Magic	36	46	.439	16
Atlanta Hawks	26	56	.317	26
Charlotte Bobcats	26	56	.317	26

WESTERN CONFERENCE

Northwest Division

	W.	L.	Pct.	G.B.
Denver Nuggets*	44	38	.537	—
Utah Jazz	41	41	.500	3
Seattle SuperSonics	35	47	.427	9
Minnesota T'wolves	33	49	.402	11
Portland Trail Blazers	21	61	.256	23

Pacific Division

	W.	L.	Pct.	G.B.
Phoenix Suns*	54	28	.659	—
Los Angeles Clippers*	47	35	.573	7
Los Angeles Lakers*	45	37	.549	9
Sacramento Kings*	44	38	.537	10
Golden State Warriors	34	48	.415	20

Southwest Division

	W.	L.	Pct.	G.B.
San Antonio Spurs*	63	19	.768	—
Dallas Mavericks*	60	22	.732	3
Memphis Grizzlies*	49	33	.598	14
New Orleans Hornets	38	44	.463	25
Houston Rockets	34	48	.415	29

INDIVIDUAL LEADERS

Scoring

	G.	F.G.	F.T.M.	Pts.	Avg.
Kobe Bryant, Los Angeles L	80	978	696	2,832	35.4
Allen Iverson, Philadelphia	72	815	675	2,377	33.0
LeBron James, Cleveland	79	875	601	2,478	31.4
Gilbert Arenas, Washington	80	746	655	2,346	29.3
Dwyane Wade, Miami	75	699	629	2,040	27.2
Paul Pierce, Boston	79	689	627	2,116	26.8
Dirk Nowitzki, Dallas	81	751	539	2,151	26.6
Carmelo Anthony, Denver	80	756	573	2,122	26.5
Michael Redd, Milwaukee	80	678	491	2,017	25.2
Ray Allen, Seattle	78	681	324	1,955	25.1
Elton Brand, Los Angeles C	79	756	440	1,953	24.7

Rebounding

	G.	Off.	Def.	Tot.	Avg.
Kevin Garnett, Minnesota	76	214	752	966	12.7
Dwight Howard, Orlando	82	288	734	1,022	12.5
Marcus Camby, Denver	56	132	536	668	11.9
Shawn Marion, Phoenix	81	249	710	959	11.8
Ben Wallace, Detroit	82	301	622	923	11.3
Tim Duncan, San Antonio	80	231	650	881	11.0
Yao Ming, Houston	57	148	433	581	10.2
Troy Murphy, Golden State	74	195	548	743	10.0
Emeka Okafor, Charlotte	26	94	167	261	10.0
Elton Brand, Los Angeles C	79	236	554	790	10.0
Chris Webber, Philadelphia	75	184	557	741	9.9

NBA champions—Miami Heat
(defeated Dallas Mavericks, 4 games to 2)

*Made play-offs.

Atlantic Coast Conference (ACC) rival Duke 78-75 in overtime. Freshman Kristi Toliver's three-pointer at the end of regulation play forced the extra session, and her two free throws with 34 seconds left in overtime capped the second-largest comeback in a title game.

Maryland, the second seed in the Albuquerque (New Mexico) regional, reached the title game with an 81-70 victory over the ACC's North Carolina, the top seed in the Cleveland (Ohio) regional. Duke, the top seed in the Bridgeport (Connecticut) regional, throttled Louisiana State, the top seed in the San Antonio regional 64-45 to advance to the title game.

Deaths. Arnold "Red" Auerbach, 89, who coached the NBA's Boston Celtics to nine titles—including an unprecedented eight in a row—died on Oct. 28, 2006. An NBA trailblazer, Auerbach was the first to pick an African American player in the draft, the first to start five black players in one lineup, and the first to hire a black coach.

Ray Meyer, who coached DePaul University basketball for 42 years and reached the Final Four twice, died on March 17 at age 92. Army women's coach Maggie Dixon, 28, died suddenly on April 6. One month before her death, Dixon had led the U.S. Military Academy to its first berth in the women's NCAA tournament. ■ Michael Kates
See also **Sports**.

Belarus. President Aleksandr Lukashenko claimed a third term in office after elections held on March 19, 2006. Lukashenko took 83 percent of the vote; his closest rival, Aleksandr Milinkevich, took only 6 percent. Russian observers judged the elections fair, but observers from the Organization for Security and Co-operation in Europe condemned the elections as "severely flawed." Prior to the election, government agents had arrested, detained, and harassed opposition politicians and their supporters. Thousands of people protested the election results in October Square in Minsk, the capital, for several days, until police dispersed the demonstrators, arresting hundreds of others.

Four opposition leaders, including Milinkevich, were convicted of attending an unsanctioned rally on April 26, the 20th anniversary of the Chernobyl nuclear disaster. In April, the European Union (EU) agreed to refuse Lukashenko and 30 other government officials entry into EU nations. In June, United States officials froze Lukashenko's U.S.-held assets and banned U.S. organizations from doing business with him. Unfazed by international criticism, the Belarusian government in July sentenced former presidential candidate Aleksandr Kazulin to 5 ½ years in prison for organizing protests after the disputed presidential vote. ■ Juliet Johnson
See also **Europe**.

Demonstrators in Minsk, Belarus, on March 23, 2006, protest elections that gave Aleksandr Lukashenko a third term in office. Observers from the Organization for Security and Co-operation in Europe called the elections, in which Lukashenko took 83 percent of the vote, "severely flawed."

Belgium. Local elections held throughout Belgium in October 2006 weakened the power of the Flemish Liberal Party of Prime Minister Guy Verhofstadt, who became prime minister in 1999. The result strengthened the possibility that Yves Leterme, leader of the opposition Christian Democratic Party, would become the new prime minister after parliamentary elections scheduled for mid-2007.

After the 2003 parliamentary elections, Verhofstadt formed a coalition made up of four parties: his own Flemish Liberal Party, based in the economically dominant, Dutch-speaking northern region of Belgium; the sister Francophone Liberal Party in Wallonia, the French-speaking southern region of the country; the Flemish Socialist/Spirit Alliance; and the Francophone Socialist Party. Political observers had predicted that one of Europe's most successful far-right parties, *Vlaams Belang* (Flemish Interest), would perform well enough in the 2006 elections for municipal councils to gain representation in a large number of local governments. However, the group managed to win only 20 percent of the regional vote in Flanders in 2006, a 4-percent decline compared with the vote in 2004. Verhofstadt's Liberals won 19 percent of the vote in Flanders, and Leterme's Christian Democrats took 32 percent.

Vlaams Belang campaigned on a platform of independence for Flanders and a crackdown on crime. It also called for a reversal of the 1974 recognition of Islam as an official religion. In 2006, the government created new state-funded institutions for training Muslim *imams* (clerics), in the hope of better integrating the large Muslim immigrant population. Vlaams Belang advocated a hard-line anti-immigrant, assimilationist policy. Political observers attributed the continued strength of the far-right party—and the decline in support for the Flemish Liberals—to a dissatisfaction among voters with the government and the mainstream party alternatives.

Belgium's economy grew by only 2.7 percent in 2006, according to estimates by European Union economists. The growth rate was an improvement, however, over the 1.1-percent rate of 2005 and reflected an increase in household disposable income and domestic spending on goods and services. Unemployment remained high at 8.6 percent, a slight increase from 8.4 percent in 2005.

Foreign relations. In October 2006, the United Nations General Assembly elected Belgium to the decision-making Security Council for a period of two years. Belgium's term was to begin in January 2007.   ■ Jeffrey Kopstein

See also **Europe.**

Belize. See Latin America.

Benin. See Africa.

Bhutan. See Asia.

Biology. A tiny fish made news in 2006 in contrast to 2005, when a 9-foot (3.7-meter) Mekong catfish captured in Thailand was recognized as the largest recorded freshwater fish. In January 2006, scientists—including biologists at the Raffles Museum of Biodiversity in Singapore and the Max Planck Institute in Germany—reported finding a mosquito-sized relative of carp on the Indonesian islands of Sumatra and Borneo. *Paedocypris progenetica* is 0.31 inch (7.9 millimeters) long, making it both the smallest-known fish and the smallest-known vertebrate.

Crustacean curiosities. Scientists reported several discoveries about animals in 2006. In March, biologists at the Monterey Bay Aquarium Research Institute in California described a "furry lobster" found near hydrothermal vents on the floor of the Pacific Ocean. Hydrothermal vents are volcanic cracks that spew hot water and minerals from beneath the seafloor. The animal is not a true lobster but a relative constituting a new family of crustaceans.

The 5.9-inch (15-centimeter) *Kiwa hirsuta* has a thick coating of hairlike filaments covering its pincers. Investigators proposed that bacteria living in the filaments may serve as food for the crustacean, or they may break down poisonous chemical compounds flowing from the hot vents.

Caribbean spiny lobsters, which are true lobsters, can sense when other members of their species are infected with a deadly virus—even before the animals show signs of disease. Scientists at Old Dominion University in Norfolk, Virginia, and the Virginia Institute of Marine Sciences in Gloucester reported in May that these lobsters shunned any individuals infected with the PaV1 virus. The isolation of the infected lobsters was very noticeable, because Caribbean spiny lobsters are normally social. The researchers believed the behavior was an adaptation that helps prevent the spread of disease.

Venomous fish. There are more *venomous* (poison producing) fish than venomous snakes, according to a study published in August by biologists at the American Museum of Natural History in New York City. The scientists examined more than 100 species of fish for body structures that might contain venom. Based on these examinations, the investigators estimated that at least 1,200 species of fish secrete venom from glands and carry it in their spines.

Scientists previously thought that only a few hundred fish were venomous. The venom in most fish species is not life-threatening to people, but some species—the stonefish of the Indo-Pacific region, for example—produce strong toxins that can kill people.

Biologists believe that approximately 400 species of snakes produce venom. The exact number is uncertain, however, because some snakes may have venom glands but not an effective means of delivering poison when biting.

Ape revelations. The reason that mountain gorillas chew rotting wood is no longer a puzzle. In April, scientists at Cornell University in Ithaca, New York, reported that gorillas in Uganda obtain most of their sodium requirements from rotting wood, which constitutes 4 percent of their diet. Observations indicated that the gorillas select the saltiest wood in the forest to eat.

In May, researchers at the Max Planck Institute for Evolutionary Anthropology in Germany reported that some apes have the ability to plan —at least in laboratory tests. Researchers positioned grapes in a container so that only certain tools could be used to extract them. They then showed bonobos (pygmy chimpanzees) and orangutans tools that would work to extract the grapes and tools that would not work. The test animals selected the correct tools to obtain the grapes. When the apes were moved to another room, they took the correct tools with them— presumably thinking that they might need them in the future. When allowed to return to the room with the grapes, they brought the proper tools along again—14 hours after the initial test.

Animals and plants signal warming? Unusual behavior in animals and excessive growth in plants may be linked to global warming, a gradual increase in temperatures that most climate scientists believe is being caused by the build-up of carbon dioxide gas in the atmosphere. The carbon dioxide is produced mainly by the burning of fossil fuels.

In May, officials with the Canadian Wildlife Service announced that a bear shot in Canada's Northwest Territories in April was a hybrid of a polar bear and a grizzly bear. The conclusion was based on an analysis of the animal's DNA (deoxyribonucleic acid). The hybrid was the first known offspring of a polar and grizzly bear in the wild—though members of the two species have mated and produced fertile offspring in zoos.

Wildlife officials said the cross probably occurred because of the movement of grizzly bears into northern lands that had previously been the exclusive province of polar bears. They added that an increase in Arctic temperatures could have prompted the grizzlies to move north.

In mid-2006, a number of people reported seeing grizzlies around Barrow, Alaska, which is north of the grizzlies' normal range. Some of the grizzlies were even seen to venture onto the sea ice. The mix of grizzly and polar bears raised the possibility that a new kind of bear might eventually evolve in the Far North.

Poison ivy is growing larger and faster as the burning of fossil fuels increases the concentration of carbon dioxide in the atmosphere, scientists at Duke University in Durham, North Carolina, and Harvard University in Cambridge, Massachusetts, reported in May. The plants absorb carbon dioxide from the atmosphere to carry out photosynthesis, in which they produce carbohydrates for their food and growth.

The scientists, who studied poison ivy in a forest at Duke University, found that increased concentrations of carbon dioxide seem to enhance poison ivy's production of urushiol. Urushiol is the oily fluid that triggers the familiar itch when people touch the plant's leaves.

Roots of homosexuality? Research published in June added to evidence that homosexuality may stem from physical causes rather than social interaction or learned behavior. The findings, by psychologist Anthony Bogaert of Brock University in Ontario, Canada, indicate that a boy's chances of being gay increase according to the number of brothers born before him.

Bogaert analyzed 902 male subjects and their brothers. He found that family interactions did not influence the sexual preferences of his subjects. He also determined that the chances of a boy being homosexual increased by 33 percent for each brother born before him. According to some estimates, the rate of homosexuality among men is 2 percent, so Bogaert's finding indicates that it would take 11 older brothers to make the odds of being gay 50–50.

Bogaert's conclusion was consistent with the idea that homosexuality may be caused by elevated concentrations of *antibodies* (proteins that destroy harmful substances) in the womb. Some researchers believe that a male fetus increases antibody production in the mother. If so, each male fetus would make the mother's immune response stronger. This high antibody concentration may somehow affect the development of male fetuses. Psychologists said this study may explain not only why some boys are homosexuals, but also why boys are more likely than girls to be autistic, dyslexic, and hyperactive.

Other new insights into homosexuality were reported in May by physician Ivanka Savik of the Karolinska Institute in Stockholm, Sweden. Savik's group discovered that both homosexual men and heterosexual women were attracted by body odors containing the pheromones of men. Pheromones are chemical substances produced by one animal that affect another animal's behavior by causing certain chemical reactions. The investigators also reported that homosexual women and heterosexual men were both attracted by body odors containing pheromones produced by women.

■ Edward Ricciuti

See also **Global warming; Ocean; Zoos.**

Boating. Tragedy, an open-sea rescue, and major changes for the future marked the 2005-2006 running of the Volvo Ocean Race. The daunting 36,000-mile (58,000-kilometer) journey for carbon fiber yachts began on Nov. 12, 2005, in Vigo, Spain, and concluded on June 17, 2006, in Göteborg, Sweden.

The Dutch yacht *ABN Amro One,* skippered by Mike Sanderson, won six of the race's nine legs and finished in first place with a total of 96 points. The United States yacht *Pirates of the Caribbean* won the race's ninth and final leg and finished second overall, with 73 points.

On May 18, tragedy struck the race's other Dutch entry, *ABN Amro Two,* as crewman Hans Horrevoets, 32, was swept overboard about 1,300 miles (2,100 kilometers) off Land's End, England. His fellow crew members lowered the boat's sails and pulled Horrevoets from the ocean, but he later died. Three days later, *ABN Amro Two* successfully rescued the 10-man crew from the Spanish boat *movistar,* which was abandoned southwest of Cornwall, England, because of a severe leak in its keel box.

During June, organizers introduced a number of changes to the event. They announced that the four-year cycle of the race would be changed to a three-year cycle, with the next event beginning in late 2008. They also announced plans to alter the route to include ports in Asia, the Middle East, and the West Coast of the United States.

America's Cup. During the final warm-ups for the 2007 America's Cup, Team New Zealand dethroned champion Alinghi of Switzerland on July 2, 2006, off the coast of Valencia, Spain. San Francisco's BMW Oracle Racing finished the season ranked second among the challengers.

World championships. Chris Draper and Simon Hiscocks of England won the 49er Gold Fleet title off Aix-les-Bains, France, in June. Spain's Monica and Sandra Azon and Graciela Pisonero won the Yngling women's title, and John Ingalls, James Randall, and Mikael Komar of the United States won the Yngling open title in La Rochelle, France, in July. Singapore's Colin Cheng and Victoria Chan won the men's and women's Laser 4.7 World Championships on Lake de Hourtin, France, in July. Hamish Pepper and Carl Williams won New Zealand's first Star World Championship, off San Francisco in October. Kowk Fai Cheng of Hong Kong took the men's title in the Mistral World Championship, held in China in October. China's Shuijia Wang won the women's title.

Powerboats. Jean Theoret of Canada drove the *U-37 Miss Beacon Plumbing* to victory in the 102nd running of the Gold Cup race for Unlimited hydroplanes in Detroit on July 16. Theoret became the first non-U.S. citizen since 1938 to win the event. ■ Michael Kates

Bolivia. Juan Evo Morales Ayma of the leftist Movement Toward Socialism was sworn in as president of Bolivia on Jan. 22, 2006, after winning a December 2005 presidential election. Morales, an Aymara Indian, became Bolivia's first *indigenous* (native) president. Previously, he had led Bolivia's coca growers' federation. Coca is the source of cocaine, an illegal drug. However, use of coca leaves for chewing or for brewing tea is legal in Bolivia. Morales's involvement with the coca growers' federation and his opposition to the United States-led war on drugs put him at odds with the administration of U.S. President George W. Bush, U.S. analysts observed.

Constitutional crisis. Within Bolivia, substantial opposition to Morales's leftist political agenda surfaced during a referendum in July 2006 to elect a national assembly charged with constitutional reform. Supporters of Morales won the largest share of seats in the assembly but did not have the two-thirds majority required to carry important motions. However, on September 29, the assembly declared by majority vote that it held the power to rewrite the nation's Constitution without reference to the Bolivian Congress or the country's courts. Critics described the move as a Morales "power grab," and some opposition parties withdrew from the assembly.

Another source of constitutional strain was the vote by four eastern lowland *departments* (administrative regions) in a separate July ballot issue to seek greater autonomy from the central government. The four departments hold most of Bolivia's natural gas reserves. Their support for autonomy, analysts said, could impede President Morales's efforts to increase governmental representation of long-neglected Indian populations in Bolivia's western highlands. Predominantly European-descended or mixed-race populations have traditionally dominated the government.

Nationalization. On May 1, President Morales dispatched troops to occupy foreign-owned natural gas fields in Bolivia as the first dramatic step in his program to nationalize all energy production in the country. Ownership of gas and oil fields was transferred to the Bolivian state energy company YPFB, which then granted leases to foreign energy companies operating in Bolivia. As a result of this arrangement, foreign energy companies that had owned Bolivia's largest gas fields began paying $32 million per month to YPFB. The state company's annual revenues soared to $240 million in 2006, compared with $10 million in 2005. ■ Nathan A. Haverstock

See also **Latin America; Latin America: A Special Report; People in the news** (Evo Morales).
Books. See **Literature; Literature for Children; Poetry.**

Bosnia-Herzegovina. An election campaign culminating in polling on Oct. 1, 2006, opened wide political rifts in Bosnia-Herzegovina (generally called Bosnia). The country is an ethnic patchwork of Bosnian Muslims, called *Bosniaks;* Bosnian Serbs; and Croats. Bosnia consists of two ministates: the Serb enclave, called Republika Srpska (RS); and the Muslim-Croat Federation (MCF), populated mainly by Bosniaks and Croats. These ministates are loosely linked under a national government, headed by a tripartite presidency of one Croat, one Bosniak, and one Bosnian Serb representative.

Voters elected the three members of the national presidency and members of parliament. Constitutional issues dominated the campaign, due to a proposed timetable to end international oversight of Bosnian political institutions in 2007. By that time, Bosnia was expected to have created a new constitutional government to replace the 1995 Dayton Accords, the peace pact that ended the Bosnian war (1992–1995).

During the campaign, Haris Silajdzic, Bosniak candidate for the presidency (later elected), recommended unifying the two ministates, which would abolish the RS. Prime Minister Milorad Dodik of the RS then called for an independence referendum in the Serb enclave, which analysts suggested would likely endorse independence and prompt ethnic partition of Bosnia. Christian Schwarz-Schilling, United Nations High Representative for Bosnia, responded by threatening to remove Dodik from his post. Under the Dayton Accords, the High Representative was empowered to enforce provisions of that agreement.

The October 2006 election results also caused potential political instability in the MCF. Voters elected Zeljko Komsic as the Croat member of Bosnia's tripartite presidency. Croat nationalists, however, claimed that Komsic, the head of a multiethnic political party, owed his election to Bosniak votes and did not truly represent Croats.

European Union (EU) officials expressed disappointment at the failure of Bosnia's national parliament in April to approve governmental reforms designed to strengthen central institutions. Constitutional experts regarded the proposed reforms as a first step toward drawing up a new constitution. During 2006, EU and Bosnian leaders failed to finalize a preliminary agreement for starting EU membership negotiations.

Army reform. In July, Bosnian leaders announced that the separate Bosniak, Croat, and Serb armies in Bosnia would be unified by the end of 2007. Analysts viewed army unification as a prerequisite to Bosnia's eventual admission to NATO.   ■ Sharon L. Wolchik

See also **Europe.**

Botswana. See Africa.

Bowling. Tommy Jones, in just his fifth season on the Professional Bowlers Association (PBA) tour, captured Player of the Year honors in 2006 for his performance during the 2005-2006 season.

The 2005-2006 season. Jones, of Simpsonville, South Carolina, led all bowlers in titles—four—and earnings—$301,700. He was second in points and fifth in average at 221.68. He tied for tops on the tour with 19 match-play appearances.

Jones won the season's second major on February 19 in North Brunswick, New Jersey, by capturing the U.S. Open 237-223, beating top-seeded Ryan Shafer. Mike Scroggins had won the first major, defeating Norm Duke 245-238 on Nov. 20, 2005, in Milwaukee.

In 2006, Walter Ray Williams surpassed the late Earl Anthony as the PBA's all-time number-one bowler by capturing his 41st tournament in March and 42nd in September. Williams took the third major of the season—the Denny's World Championship—on March 26. He defeated Pete Weber 236-213 in the final in Indianapolis.

Chris Barnes gained his second career major title by defeating Steve Jaros 234-227 at the Dexter Tournament of Champions on April 9 in Windsor Locks, Connecticut, the final major of the season.

The 2006-2007 season. In the first major of the new season, Doug Kent of Newark, New York, captured the Masters on Oct. 29, 2006, in West Allis, Wisconsin. Kent rolled nine straight strikes to oust top seed Jack Jurek 277-230 in the title match. Kent became the first non-top-two seed in history to win the event since 1980.

Breakthrough. Kelly Kulick, 29, of Union, New Jersey, became the first woman to earn a full-time tour exemption by finishing sixth in the PBA Tour Trials, which ended on June 4, 2006, in Hammond, Indiana. She had been the 2001 Rookie of the Year in the Professional Women's Bowling Association, which folded in the fall of 2003.

Seniors. Tom Baker, 51, of Buffalo, New York, dominated the nine-tournament circuit to win Player of the Year honors in 2006 for a second straight year. Baker won four titles—including three in a row and both majors—and led the tour in points, earnings, and average—finishing with a 226.32 average, less than a pin off the record he set in 2005. Baker captured the Senior U.S. Open on June 23, 2006, in Las Vegas, defeating Dick Baker 215-176 in the final match. Tom Baker became the first bowler to win back-to-back Senior U.S. Opens. The only senior bowler with an exemption for the PBA tour, Tom Baker captured the Senior Masters in Dayton, Ohio, on July 14, winning nine straight matches after slipping to the losers bracket. He defeated Bob Kelly in back-to-back two-game total pinfall matches.   ■ Michael Kates

Boxing. With a last-minute flurry, Oleg Maskaev defeated World Boxing Council (WBC) heavyweight champion Hasim Rahman on Aug. 12, 2006, in Las Vegas, Nevada. Maskaev, a former Russian Army officer, battered Rahman in the 12th round until the referee stopped the fight. His victory gave boxers from the former Soviet Union possession of all four heavyweight title belts for the first time in history. Maskaev, a naturalized U.S. citizen, joined champions Wladimir Klitschko of Ukraine (International Boxing Federation [IBF]), Russia's Nikolay Valuev (World Boxing Association), and Sergei Lyakhovich of Belarus (World Boxing Organization).

In-ring melee. An IBF welterweight title fight between Floyd Mayweather, Jr., and Zab Judah turned into a brawl after Judah punched Mayweather in the groin and the back of the head in the 10th round of their April 8 fight in Las Vegas. Both corners jumped into the ring and exchanged punches. After police and security guards restored order, Mayweather won a unanimous 12-round decision to stay unbeaten at 36-0.

The Nevada Athletic Commission levied huge punishments for the brawl. On April 13, Roger Mayweather, the uncle and trainer for Floyd Mayweather and first corner person into the ring, was fined $200,000 and had his license revoked in Nevada for one year. In early May, the commission revoked Judah's license for a year and fined him $250,000. Under federal law, Judah was banned from fighting anywhere in the United States until April 8, 2007. Yoel Judah, his son's trainer, also had his license revoked in Nevada for one year and was fined $100,000.

Holyfield's comeback. Former heavyweight champion Evander Holyfield returned to the ring in 2006 after a nearly two-year hiatus. He began his quest to become the first man to win the title five times, with victories over two lesser-known opponents—Jeremy Bates and Fres Oquendo.

Notable deaths. Floyd Patterson, 71, who in 1956 became the youngest heavyweight champion in history, died on May 11, 2006, in New Paltz, New York, after battling Alzheimer's disease and prostate cancer. Patterson posted a record of 55-8-1 with 40 knockouts in his 20-year professional career, first winning the title at age 21. That mark was broken by Mike Tyson, who won the heavyweight title in 1986 at age 20. Patterson lost his title to Ingemar Johansson in 1959 but won it back in 1960 to become the first man to recapture a heavyweight title.

Willie Pep (born Gugliermo Papaleo), considered by many the greatest featherweight of all time, died on Nov. 23, 2006, at age 84. Pep won 230 fights and lost only 11 bouts. ■ Michael Kates

See also **Deaths; Sports.**

WORLD CHAMPION BOXERS

WORLD BOXING ASSOCIATION

Division	Champion	Country	Date won
Heavyweight	Nikolay Valuev	Russia	12/05
Light heavyweight	Silvio Branco	Italy	10/06
Middleweight	Jermain Taylor	United States	7/05
Welterweight	(Vacant)		
Lightweight	Juan Diaz	United States	7/04
Featherweight	Chris John	Indonesia	9/03
Bantamweight	Wladimir Sidorenko	Ukraine	2/05
Flyweight	Lorenzo Parra	Venezuela	12/03

WORLD BOXING COUNCIL

Division	Champion	Country	Date won
Heavyweight	Oleg Maskaev	Kazakhstan	8/06
Light heavyweight	Tomasz Adamek	Poland	5/05
Middleweight	Jermain Taylor	United States	7/05
Welterweight	Floyd Mayweather	United States	11/06
Lightweight	Joel Casamayor	Cuba	10/06
Featherweight	Rodolfo Lopez	Mexico	7/06
Bantamweight	Hozumi Hasegawa	Japan	4/05
Flyweight	Pongsaklek Wonjongkam	Thailand	3/01

Brazil. President Luiz Inácio Lula da Silva turned back a strong challenge from Geraldo Alckmin of the Brazilian Social Democratic Party to win reelection to the presidency in a runoff election on Oct. 29, 2006. Da Silva, representing the Workers Party, had first been elected president in 2002. Alckmin, a former governor of São Paulo state, touted his managerial skills in having turned a deficit into a surplus in Brazil's largest state government. He attacked the da Silva administration for a series of scandals involving some of the president's close aides and the Workers Party. Political analysts suggested that Brazil's surging economy helped turn the tide for da Silva, who after failing to draw 50 percent of votes in the first polling on Oct. 1, 2006, garnered 61 percent in the runoff election.

Economists forecast that Brazil's economy, stimulated by demand in Asia for the country's raw materials and agricultural products, would expand by 3.5 percent in 2006. The Brazilian government was able to pay off its debts to the International Monetary Fund, a United Nations–affiliated financing body, in early 2006 by drawing upon the nearly $60 billion in foreign reserves that the Central Bank of Brazil had amassed by late 2005.

Two giant government-owned companies contributed to Brazil's large trade surplus in

2006. The Companhia Vale do Rio Doce (CVRD), headquartered in Rio de Janeiro, earned record profits from sales to China and India, both rapidly industrializing countries. CVRD ranked as the world's largest producer of iron ore in 2006. In September, the company announced a joint venture with two Chinese steel companies to operate a steel plant at Zhuhai in China's southern Guangdong Province. Other acquisitions in 2006 positioned CVRD to dominate the world nickel market, economists noted.

Another huge Brazilian multinational, the state energy company Petróleo Brasileiro (Petrobras), anticipated record sales and earnings in 2006, after having doubled its production of oil in less than a decade through investments in 18 countries on three continents. Drawing on its leadership in deep-water drilling technology, Petrobras, whose proven oil reserves increased by nearly 50 percent between 2000 and 2005, announced plans to invest $2 billion to develop oil fields in the Gulf of Mexico.

Within Brazil, Petrobras continued to work closely with farmers to increase consumption of sugar-cane-based ethanol as an automotive fuel. By 2006, ethanol, which is cleaner-burning than gasoline, accounted for 40 percent of all fuel used in automobiles in Brazil.

New fuel. Hailing the arrival of "the age of agro-energy," Brazil's agriculture minister unveiled a new renewable source of energy called "H-Bio" in June. The H-Bio formula, though as yet undisclosed, involved mixing vegetable oil extracted from oil-rich crops such as soybeans or sunflowers with ordinary mineral diesel oil. Petrobras announced plans to produce H-Bio at three Brazilian refineries in 2007.

First astronaut. On March 29, 2006, Colonel Marcos C. Pontes of the Brazilian Air Force became his country's first astronaut, blasting into space from the Russian launch site in Kazakhstan in the company of a Russian cosmonaut and a United States astronaut. Pontes returned safely to Earth in early April after having spent eight days aboard the International Space Station. The cost of the mission to the Brazilian government was $10.5 million.

Crash. On September 29, the collision of two airplanes at 37,000 feet (11,278 meters), above a remote area of Mato Grosso in Brazil's interior, resulted in the crash of a Brazilian jet airliner, killing all 155 people aboard. The crash was the worst in Brazil's aviation history. The other plane involved in the collision, a small business jet, landed safely.   ■ Nathan A. Haverstock
See also **Latin America: A Special Report.**

British Columbia. See **Canadian provinces.**

Brunei. See **Asia.**

Building and construction. Structural work was completed in May 2006 on the main wall of the Three Gorges Dam, located near the town of Sandouping on the Yangtze River in China. The Three Gorges Dam, which workers began to construct in 1994, was in 2006 the largest dam and hydroelectric facility in the world. The dam is 7,575 feet (2,309 meters) long and 607 feet (185 meters) high. The hydroelectric facility was designed to supply power to areas that had long relied on coal-fired power plants.

Although the dam itself was completed in 2006, much work remained, including the construction of a ship elevator alongside the dam's navigational locks and the installation of several of the project's 26 massive turbines. The dam was expected to become fully operational in 2009. Project managers in China estimated the final cost of the structure at $22 billion, though Western observers estimated that the actual cost would be much greater.

The reservoir behind the dam was flooded in 2003, inundating approximately 150,000 acres (60,700 hectares) of land and displacing more than 1 million residents of Hubei and Chongqing provinces. Critics of the dam—both inside and outside of China—condemned the forced relocation of people who lived in the flooded area. Environmentalists worried about pollution caused by garbage and untreated industrial waste submerged by the water behind the dam. Brushing off these concerns, Chinese officials emphasized that the Three Gorges Dam would generate much-needed electric power for China's growing economy.

"Roof of the world." The Qinghai-Tibet Railway, the highest railway in the world, opened in Qinghai Province, China, in July 2006—one year ahead of schedule. The railway, which is more than 13,100 feet (4,000 meters) above sea level and 1,216 miles (1,956 kilometers) long, connects Lhasa, the capital of Tibet, to Xining, capital of Qinghai Province.

Workers laid 506 miles (814 kilometers) of the track, from Xining to Golmud, in 1984. Construction of the remaining 710 miles (1,142 kilometers) of track began in 2001. The highest point of the new track is 16,640 feet (5,072 meters) above sea level. Project managers estimated the total cost of the railway would be $3.2 billion.

The Qinghai-Tibet Railway was the first railway ever built in Tibet, where rugged, mountainous geography presents many engineering challenges. Approximately 340 miles (550 kilometers) of the track were laid over *permafrost* (permanently frozen soil), which is difficult to build on. Furthermore, workers performed much of the construction in subzero temperatures and in the thin air of the Himalayas.

Emergency workers (below) inspect the scene where part of a tunnel roof collapsed in Boston's "Big Dig" project along Interstate 90 on July 10. A 10-ton (9-metric ton) chunk of concrete crushed a car, killing a motorist, when anchor bolts (left) holding concrete slabs to the roof of the tunnel failed. After the tunnel was closed, inspectors discovered more than 240 loose anchor bolts.

In addition to being the world's highest railway, the Qinghai-Tibet Railway also features the world's highest rail tunnel. The Fenghuoshan Tunnel is 16,092 feet (4,905 meters) above sea level.

Olympic footbridge fixed. The unofficial symbol of the 2006 Winter Olympic Games, which were held in February in Turin, Italy, was a distinctive red arch that anchored a footbridge linking the Olympic Village to the Lingotto commercial center. The arch and bridge, unveiled in January, made up one of the major projects designed for the games. The arch, which is 226 feet (69 meters) tall and 180 feet (55 meters) wide, forms a type of curve called a parabola. The 1,207-foot (368-meter) bridge is supported by eight pairs of cable stays.

In the months leading up to the Olympic Games, engineers had to solve the problem of excess swaying of the footbridge when it carried heavy foot traffic. This was the same embarrassing problem that forced the closing of the Millennium Bridge in London three days after it opened in June 2000. Engineers stopped the swaying of the bridge in Turin by using a method similar to that used to fix the Millennium Bridge. They added a series of *dampers* (massive weights) designed to counteract the force of large crowds crossing the bridge.

Tunnel collapse in Boston. On July 10, 2006, part of a tunnel roof collapsed in a section of the Central Artery/Tunnel (CA/T) Project in Boston, Massachusetts. The collapse killed one motorist. This was the first death directly related to the CA/T Project, also known as the "Big Dig." The project, which had undergone multiple delays and setbacks since construction began in 1991, was in its final stages in 2006.

The main purpose of the CA/T Project was to reroute Interstate 93 (the Central Artery) through the heart of Boston using a system of tunnels. The tunnel ceiling that fell was part of the portal that links Interstate 90 to the Ted Williams Tunnel and Logan Airport. According to investigators, the collapse occurred when numerous epoxy-coated anchor bolts failed, allowing a 10-ton (9-metric-ton) section of precast concrete panels to fall onto the traffic below. Such bolts are often used to bear heavy loads. Further investigation revealed at least 240 loose epoxy-coated bolts in the closed tunnel, with an additional 40 loose bolts found in the westbound connector tunnel from I-90 to I-93. This tunnel was also subsequently closed.

The failure of the bolts led to much public discussion and criticism of the CA/T Project, which was estimated to have cost in excess of $14.5 billion. The tunnel collapse also sparked several official investigations into the project.

■ Jeffrey Rubenstone

See also **Architecture; China.**

Bulgaria. European Union (EU) officials announced in September 2006 that Bulgaria would be admitted to the EU in January 2007. Previously, EU officials had criticized Bulgarian leaders for insufficient progress in curbing organized crime and accomplishing judicial reform. In response, Bulgarian lawmakers in March 2006 approved constitutional amendments to reform the judicial system and in June adopted measures to inhibit money laundering. Along with Romania, which was scheduled to join the EU at the same time, Bulgaria was to be subjected to continued monitoring by EU officials in the areas of combating crime and corruption, food safety, proper use of EU funds, and aviation safety.

Bulgaria's economy grew by 6.6 percent in the first half of 2006. In the same period, inflation declined from 7.9 percent to 6.8 percent. Unemployment dropped to the lowest level in 15 years, registering slightly less than 9 percent in August.

◼ Sharon L. Wolchik

See also **Europe**.

Burkina Faso. See **Africa**.

Burma. See **Myanmar**.

Burundi. See **Africa**.

Bush, George W. See **United States, President of the**.

Business. See **Bank; Economics, U.S.; Economics, world; International trade**.

Cabinet, U.S. Four Cabinet officials left President George W. Bush's administration in 2006.

Defense. On November 8—one day after Bush's Republican Party lost control of both houses of Congress—the president announced the resignation of Donald Rumsfeld, secretary of the Department of Defense, and the nomination of Robert Gates to replace Rumsfeld. President Bush, who had strongly defended Rumsfeld on many occasions, said the time was right for a fresh perspective. Rumsfeld had faced harsh criticism over his role in the U.S.-led war in Iraq. In early 2006, at least eight retired Army and Marine generals had called for his resignation.

The Senate confirmed Gates on December 6, and he was sworn in on December 18. Gates spent much of his career with the Central Intelligence Agency, serving as its director from 1991 to 1993. In 2002, he became the president of Texas A&M University, located in College Station.

Treasury. On May 30, 2006, Bush announced John W. Snow's resignation as secretary of the U.S. Department of the Treasury and the nomination of Henry M. Paulson, Jr., to replace Snow. The Senate confirmed Paulson on June 28, and he was sworn in on July 10. Snow had been treasury secretary since 2003. Paulson had been employed by the New York City-based investment firm Goldman Sachs Group, Inc., for which he served

United States Defense Secretary Donald Rumsfeld faced harsh criticism over the U.S.-led war in Iraq through much of 2006, during which at least eight retired Army and Marine generals called for his resignation. He resigned on November 8, one day after the midterm elections switched control of Congress from the Republicans to the Democrats.

as chairman and chief executive officer from 1999 to 2006.

Interior. On March 16, President Bush nominated Dirk Kempthorne as secretary of the U.S. Department of the Interior. The Senate confirmed him on May 26. He replaced Gale A. Norton, who had resigned in March. She had served since 2001 and was the first woman to hold the post. Many environmental groups had criticized her, in part because of her support for oil and gas development in Alaska's Arctic National Wildlife Refuge. Kempthorne had served as U.S. senator (R., Idaho) from 1993 to 1999 and as governor of Idaho from 1999 to 2006.

Transportation. Bush nominated Mary E. Peters as secretary of the U.S. Department of Transportation on Sept. 5, 2006. The Senate confirmed her on September 30, and she took office on October 17. Peters replaced Norman Y. Mineta, who ended his term as transportation secretary in July. Mineta, the only Democrat in Bush's Cabinet, had served since 2001. Peters had held the position of national director for transportation policy and consulting for HDR, Inc., an engineering firm based in Omaha, Nebraska. She also headed the Federal Highway Administration from 2001 to 2005.   ■ Geoffrey A. Campbell

See also **Armed forces; People in the news** (Henry Paulson).

Cambodia. Legal proceedings began in July 2006 against surviving leaders of the Khmer Rouge (KR), the Communist regime that was responsible for the deaths of more than 1.5 million Cambodians during its rule of the nation from 1975 to 1979. Cambodia's prime minister, Hun Sen, a former KR officer installed in power by a 1979 Vietnamese invasion, had stalled for years on allowing trials, finally relenting under pressure from the United Nations (UN). The proceedings, under guidance from the UN, were expected to lead to trials by 2008.

Only Kaing Khek Iev, the commandant of a torture and death house in the capital, Phnom Penh, was in custody as legal work began. The top KR leader, Pol Pot, died of natural causes in 1998, and the KR military commander, Ta Mok, died on July 21, 2006. Several other KR leaders remained free.

A UN human rights envoy, Kenyan lawyer Yash Ghai, completed a fact-finding tour of Cambodia in March. Upon his return, Ghai reported that Hun Sen was centralizing power in himself and concluded that the Cambodian government was "not very committed to human rights." Hun Sen, who in 2006 began threatening his critics with imprisonment for defamation, dismissed Ghai's claims as "deranged."   ■ Henry S. Bradsher

See also **Asia.**

Cameroon. See Africa.

The Conservative Party, led by Stephen Harper, succeeded the waning Liberal administration of Paul Martin after a national election on Jan. 23, 2006. The Conservatives also increased their representation in the House of Commons, building on gains from the June 2004 election. However, Canada remained in political uncertainty, as the governing Conservatives—like the Liberals before them—held a minority of seats in the Commons.

The Liberal Party fell from power because of political misconduct that occurred in Quebec in the 1990's. The government had allocated funds for an advertising campaign to undermine the separatist cause in the province and promote the image of a united Canada. Some Liberal officials used some of the funds for the party's own election campaigns.

In 2005, a judicial commission investigated the proceedings and issued a report charging some Liberal Party members with illegal financial practices. The report seriously damaged the standing of the Liberal Party in Quebec and across the country. The Liberals clung to office through 2005, surviving votes of confidence brought by the opposition parties. Finally, in a vote on Nov. 28, 2005, the government was defeated in the Commons. Paul Martin announced a national election for January 2006.

The Liberal Party fumbled its election campaign, opening the door to a rejuvenated Conservative Party. Stephen Harper ran a campaign on traditional conservative principles, stressing sound financial management, a balanced budget with tax reductions, and a limited social program. Harper claimed that the Liberal government represented a "culture of entitlement" and vowed that his party would bring a "culture of accountability." The Conservatives convinced Canadians that the Liberals, who had ruled for 13 years, had been in power too long.

The January election altered Canada's balance of political power. Before the election, the Liberals held 135 seats in a 308-seat House of Commons. Their standing fell to 103 seats. The Conservatives, with 99 seats before the election, emerged with 124 seats. They expanded their traditional support base in western Canada by gaining 40

CANADA

seats in vote-rich Ontario. In addition, to the surprise of political commentators, the Conservatives won 10 seats from the Liberals in Quebec, a province in which they had no representation before the election. The loss dealt a severe blow to the Liberals. Over the years, Quebec had provided the party with solid support among both French- and English-speaking residents.

The two smaller opposition parties also felt the shift in power. The separatist Bloc Québécois (BQ) lost 3 seats, although it still won 51 of the 75 seats in Quebec. The party's total vote count in the province fell slightly. The socialist New Democratic Party (NDP) gained 10 seats, for a total of 29 seats in the new Parliament, benefiting from voter disenchantment with the Liberals.

New Cabinet. The Conservative Party took office on February 6. Harper formed a new Cabinet of 26 members, with 10 members from the four Western provinces, 9 from Ontario, and 5 from Quebec. Six women held posts in the new government. Harper chose Peter MacKay from Nova Scotia, a man whom he had previously replaced as party leader, as foreign minister. James Flaherty of Ontario, a 10-year member of the provincial government, assumed the role of finance minister.

Harper made two controversial Cabinet choices. With no Conservative elected from Montreal, Harper chose Michael Fortier, a Quebec member of the Senate—to which representatives are appointed, not elected—to be minister of public works.

Harper appointed David Emerson from Vancouver as minister of international trade. A former Liberal Cabinet minister, Emerton changed parties immediately after he won reelection. He argued that he had been responsible for the early negotiations on the softwood lumber agreement with the United States and that he wanted to continue his work under the new government.

Accountability Act. The Conservative Party's top priority was to pass an Accountability Act to prevent the kind of improper financial practices that had damaged the Liberal Party in the Quebec scandal. The act encouraged "fairness, openness

A large area of British Columbia's Great Bear Rainforest became off-limits to loggers in a deal reached in February 2006. The deal, between provincial officials, Native Canadian nations, logging companies, and environmental protection groups, guards 4.4 million acres (1.8 million hectares) that contain the world's largest remaining temperate coastal rain forest.

and transparency" in government. The act set out 250 pages of new procedures for government operations and created a range of new public officers to ensure ethical behavior among ministers, political aides, and public servants. It also regulated lobbyists. The act lowered legal contributions to political parties and banned donations from corporations and labor unions. The Commons passed the act on June 21. In November, the Senate sent an amended bill back to the Commons. It was formally approved on December 12, after the amendments were accepted by the Commons.

Quebec. On November 27, Parliament voted to recognize the province of Quebec as "a nation within a united Canada." Harper had brought the motion to preempt a BQ motion to declare Quebec an independent nation. Quebecers have twice voted against independence, most recently in 1995, but separatist debate continued in the province. Some political experts noted that the motion would not grant the BQ more power on a national level.

Budget. The Conservatives presented their budget on May 2, 2006, fulfilling two of their election promises. A national child-care program that provided parents with $100 a month for each child under 6 years of age was launched in July (all amounts in Canadian dollars). The measure replaced a child-care program, started by the Liberals, that was based on grants to the provinces. The budget also reduced the federal government's goods-and-services tax from 7 to 6 percent. The act, which also took effect in July, brought some financial relief to all Canadians.

The budget ended the tight control on expenditures that had marked the previous Liberal administration of Jean Chrétien and the first year of Paul Martin's government. It contained 28 tax reductions and concessions, representing tax cuts of $26 billion to be introduced over the next three years. The budget exempted postgraduate scholarships from the federal income tax and gave tax credits to users of public transport. In spite of the

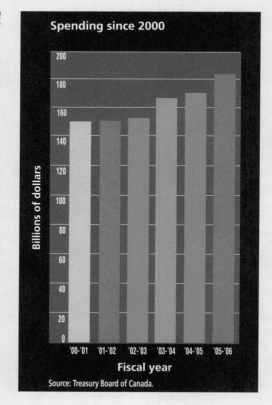

FEDERAL SPENDING IN CANADA
Estimated budget for fiscal 2006-2007*

Department or agency	Millions of dollars†
Agriculture and agri-food	2,802
Atlantic Canada opportunities agency	382
Canada revenue agency	3,228
Canadian heritage	3,548
Citizenship and immigration	1,344
Economic development agency of Canada for the regions of Quebec	382
Environment	1,454
Finance	73,755
Fisheries and oceans	1,513
Foreign affairs and international trade	5,238
Governor general	19
Health	4,334
Human resources and skills development	36,662
Indian affairs and northern development	6,196
Industry	4,420
Justice	2,356
National defence	14,799
Natural resources	1,714
Parliament	525
Privy Council	292
Public safety and emergency preparedness	6,022
Public works and government services	2,573
Transport	3,529
Treasury board	2,816
Veterans affairs	3,203
Western economic diversification	316
Total	**182,493**

*April 1, 2006, to March 31, 2007.
†Rounded in Canadian dollars; $1 = U.S. $0.89 as of Oct. 5, 2006.

Spending since 2000

Billions of dollars

Fiscal year

'00-'01   '01-'02   '02-'03   '03-'04   '04-'05   '05-'06

Source: Treasury Board of Canada.

budget's massive expenditures, the government reported a surplus of $12 billion for fiscal year 2005 (April 1-March 31, 2006). The credit marked Canada's ninth consecutive surplus.

A robust economy fueled Canada's expenditures in 2006. Energy reserves—in oil, gas, uranium, and water—proved the key to Canada's success and its bright economic future. For example, the tar sands of northern Alberta contained oil reserves second only to those of Saudi Arabia. High energy prices throughout 2005 led to a record surplus of $30.2 billion in Canada's trade and investment figures. As a result, in May 2006, the value of the Canadian dollar increased to 91.4 U.S. cents, its highest level since the 1970's.

Under these conditions, Canada enjoyed strong employment growth. In May 2006, the rate of unemployment dipped to 6.1 percent, the lowest figure since the 1970's. Inflation held steady between 2 and 3 percent in 2006. The reduction in the goods-and-services tax slightly moderated the gains from rising energy costs.

Financial transfers. Provincial and federal territorial leaders held their annual summit in St. John's, Newfoundland, on July 27 and 28. At the meeting, they attempted to draw up a common proposal on financial transfers to present to the federal government. Harper had promised during the election campaign to resolve a long-standing imbalance between federal revenues and the financial needs of the provinces. As of 2006, the federal government has unlimited taxing power, but the provincial governments must provide basic social services to Canada's citizens. This imbalance has plagued Canada for most of its history.

The federal government transfers funds to the provinces through two sets of policies: direct transfers and equalization grants. Direct transfers involve distributing federal revenues and income tax points based on the population of each province. Such transfers finance health, education, and social services. Equalization grants are designed to provide comparable services across Canada. Under this plan, the wealthier provinces assist the poorer provinces to provide a reasonable level of services.

The premiers failed to achieve a consensus at the summit. A dispute between Ontario and Quebec blocked the agreement. Ontario, the largest and richest province, claimed that it had been deprived of about $86 per person each year in direct transfers from the federal government. As a result, it demanded an increase in the funding by direct transfers to all provinces. However, the poorer provinces, led by Quebec, opposed increasing this fund out of concern that it would reduce the amount available for equalization grants.

The lack of consensus meant that the federal government would define new terms for the transfers. Such terms would probably be decided on an

individual basis with each province. Prime Minister Harper had previously stated that he planned to review Quebec's demands for additional revenues. Some observers noted that such action could improve the Conservative Party's electoral position in Quebec. The Conservatives needed more seats from that province to win a majority in Parliament.

Environment. The Conservatives, some of whom have strong ties with energy-rich Alberta,

2006 CANADIAN POPULATION ESTIMATES

PROVINCE AND TERRITORY POPULATIONS

Alberta	3,308,900
British Columbia	4,309,800
Manitoba	1,184,700
New Brunswick	752,000
Newfoundland and Labrador	514,500
Northwest Territories	43,100
Nova Scotia	937,900
Nunavut	30,300
Ontario	12,679,400
Prince Edward Island	138,400
Quebec	7,651,300
Saskatchewan	994,100
Yukon Territory	31,100
Canada	32,575,500

CITY AND METROPOLITAN AREA POPULATIONS

	Metropolitan area	City
Toronto, Ont.	5,394,300	2,583,100
Montreal, Que.	3,661,100	1,854,800
Vancouver, B.C.	2,243,600	580,100
Ottawa-Hull	1,155,700	
Ottawa, Ont.		832,600
Hull, Que.		*
Calgary, Alta.	1,082,600	1,013,200
Edmonton, Alta.	1,029,200	721,700
Quebec, Que.	724,100	516,200
Hamilton, Ont.	719,200	514,300
Winnipeg, Man.	711,100	620,600
London, Ont.	467,600	347,900
Kitchener, Ont.	465,500	203,500
St. Catharines-Niagara Falls	398,100	
St. Catharines, Ont.		127,400
Niagara Falls, Ont.		80,800
Halifax, N.S.	382,300	376,500
Oshawa, Ont.	348,500	144,000
Victoria, B.C.	339,700	74,800
Windsor, Ont.	334,000	220,000
Saskatoon, Sask.	237,500	200,000
Regina, Sask.	199,800	176,100
St. John's, Nfld. Lab.	184,300	96,500
Abbotsford, B.C.	166,900	126,900
Sherbrooke, Que.	165,300	75,100
Greater Sudbury, Ont.	161,100	146,000
Kingston, Ont.	156,400	116,400
Saguenay	152,200	
Chicoutimi, Que.		57,200
Jonquiere, Que.		53,200
Trois-Rivieres, Que.	143,300	44,200
Saint John, N.B.	126,800	67,000
Thunder Bay, Ont.	126,400	104,600

*Hull became part of the city of Gatineau in 2002. Gatineau's projected 2006 population was 241,800.

Source: World Book estimates based on data from Statistics Canada.

MEMBERS OF THE CANADIAN HOUSE OF COMMONS

The House of Commons of the first session of the 39th Parliament convened on April 3, 2006. As of Nov. 30, 2006, the House of Commons consisted of the following members: 102 Liberal Party, 51 Bloc Québécois, 124 Conservative Party of Canada, 29 New Democratic Party, and 2 Independent. This table shows each legislator and party affiliation. An asterisk (*) denotes those who served in the 38th Parliament.

Alberta
Diane Ablonczy, C.P.C.*
Rona Ambrose, C.P.C.*
Rob Anders, C.P.C.*
Leon E. Benoit, C.P.C.*
Blaine Calkins, C.P.C.
Rick Casson, C.P.C.*
Ken Epp, C.P.C.*
Peter Goldring, C.P.C.*
Art Hanger, C.P.C.*
Stephen Harper, C.P.C.*
Lurie Hawn, C.P.C.
Rahim Jaffer, C.P.C.*
Brian Jean, C.P.C.*
Jason Kenney, C.P.C.*
Mike Lake, C.P.C.
Ted Menzies, C.P.C.*
Rob Merrifield, C.P.C.*
Bob Mills, C.P.C.*
Deepak Obhrai, C.P.C.*
Jim Prentice, C.P.C.*
James Rajotte, C.P.C.*
Lee Richardson, C.P.C.*
Monte Solberg, C.P.C.*
Kevin Sorenson, C.P.C.*
Brian Storseth, C.P.C.
Myron Thompson, C.P.C.*
Chris Warkentin, C.P.C.
John Williams, C.P.C.*

British Columbia
Jim Abbott, C.P.C.*
Alex Atamanenko, N.D.P.
Catherine Bell, N.D.P.
Don H. Bell, Lib.*
Dawn Black, N.D.P.
Ron Cannan, C.P.C.
Raymond Chan, Lib.*
Jean Crowder, N.D.P.*
Nathan Cullen, N.D.P.*
John Cummins, C.P.C.*
Libby Davies, N.D.P.*
Stockwell Day, C.P.C.*
Sukh Dhaliwal, Lib.*
Ujjal Dosanjh, Lib.*
David Emerson, C.P.C.*
Ed Fast, C.P.C.
Hedy Fry, Lib.*
Nina Grewal, C.P.C.*
Richard Harris, C.P.C.*
Russ Hiebert, C.P.C.*
Jay Hill, C.P.C.*
Betty Hinton, C.P.C.*
Peter Julian, N.D.P.*
Randy Kamp, C.P.C.*
Gary Lunn, C.P.C.*
James Lunney, C.P.C.*
Keith Martin, Lib.*
Colin Mayes, C.P.C.
James Moore, C.P.C.*
Stephen Owen, Lib.*
Penny Priddy, N.D.P.
Denise Savoie, N.D.P.
Bill Siksay, N.D.P.*
Chuck Strahl, C.P.C.*

Mark Warawa, C.P.C.*
Blair Wilson, Lib.

Manitoba
James Bezan, C.P.C.*
Bill Blaikie, N.D.P.*
Rod Bruinooge, C.P.C.
Steven Fletcher, C.P.C.*
Tina Keeper, Lib.
Inky Mark, C.P.C.*
Pat Martin, N.D.P.*
Anita Neville, Lib.*
Brian Pallister, C.P.C.*
Raymond Simard, Lib.*
Joy Smith, C.P.C.*
Vic Toews, C.P.C.*
Merv Tweed, C.P.C.*
Judy Wasylycia-Leis, N.D.P.*

New Brunswick
Mike Allen, C.P.C.
Jean-Claude D'Amours, Lib.*
Yvon Godin, N.D.P.*
Charles Hubbard, Lib.*
Dominic LeBlanc, Lib.*
Rob Moore, C.P.C.*
Brian Murphy, Lib.
Andy Scott, Lib.*
Greg Thompson, C.P.C.*
Paul Zed, Lib.*

Newfoundland and Labrador
Gerry Byrne, Lib.*
Norman Doyle, C.P.C.*
Loyola Hearn, C.P.C.*
Fabian Manning, C.P.C.
Bill Matthews, Lib.*
Todd Russell, Lib.*
Scott Simms, Lib.*

Northwest Territories
Dennis Bevington, N.D.P.

Nova Scotia
Scott Brison, Lib.*
Bill Casey, C.P.C.*
Rodger Cuzner, Lib.*
Mark Eyking, Lib.*
Gerald Keddy, C.P.C.*
Peter MacKay, C.P.C.*
Alexa McDonough, N.D.P.*
Geoff Regan, Lib.*
Michael Savage, Lib.*
Peter Stoffer, N.D.P.*
Robert Thibault, Lib.*

Nunavut
Nancy Karetak-Lindell, Lib.*

Ontario
Harold Albrecht, C.P.C.
Omar Alghabra, Lib.
Dean Allison, C.P.C.*
Charlie Angus, N.D.P.*
Navdeep Bains, Lib.*

John Baird, C.P.C.
Sue Barnes, Lib.*
Colleen Beaumier, Lib.*
Mauril Bélanger, Lib.*
Carolyn Bennett, Lib.*
Maurizio Bevilacqua, Lib.*
Raymond Bonin, Lib.*
Ken Boshcoff, Lib.*
Bonnie Brown, Lib.*
Gord Brown, C.P.C.*
Patrick Brown, C.P.C.
John Cannis, Lib.*
Colin Carrie, C.P.C.*
Brenda Chamberlain, Lib.*
Chris Charlton, N.D.P.
Michael Chong, C.P.C.*
Olivia Chow, N.D.P.
David Christopherson, N.D.P.*
Tony Clement, C.P.C.
Joe Comartin, N.D.P.*
Joe Comuzzi, Lib.*
Roy Cullen, Lib.*
Patricia Davidson, C.P.C.
Del Mastro, C.P.C.
Barry Devolin, C.P.C.*
Paul Dewar, N.D.P.
Ruby Dhalla, Lib.*
Ken Dryden, Lib.*
Rick Dykstra, C.P.C.
Diane Finley, C.P.C.*
Jim Flaherty, C.P.C.
Royal Galipeau, C.P.C.
Cheryl Gallant, C.P.C.*
John Godfrey, Lib.*
Gary Goodyear, C.P.C.*
Bill Graham, Lib.*
Albina Guarnieri, Lib.*
Helena Guergis, C.P.C.*
Mark Holland, Lib.*
Michael Ignatieff, Lib.
Susan Kadis, Lib.*
Jim Karygiannis, Lib.*
Wajid Khan, Lib.*
Daryl Kramp, C.P.C.*
Guy Lauzon, C.P.C.*
Jack Layton, N.D.P.*
Derek Lee, Lib.*
Pierre Lemieux, C.P.C.
Dave Mackenzie, C.P.C.*
Gurbax Malhi, Lib.*
John Maloney, Lib.*
Diane Marleau, Lib.*
Wayne Marston, N.D.P.
Tony Martin, N.D.P.*
Brian Masse, N.D.P.
Irene Matthyssen, N.D.P.
John McCallum, Lib.*
David McGuinty, Lib.*
John McKay, Lib.*
Dan McTeague, Lib.*
Larry Miller, C.P.C.
Peter Milliken, Lib.*
Maria Minna, Lib.*
Peggy Nash, N.D.P.
Rob Nicholson, C.P.C.

Rick Norlock, C.P.C.
Gordon O'Connor, C.P.C.*
Bev Oda, C.P.C.*
Glen Pearson, Lib.
Jim Peterson, Lib.*
Pierre Poilievre, C.P.C.*
Joe Preston, C.P.C.*
Yasmin Ratansi, Lib.*
Karen Redman, Lib.*
Scott Reid, C.P.C.*
Anthony Rota, Lib.*
Gary Schellenberger, C.P.C.*
Judy Sgro, Lib.*
Bev Shipley, C.P.C.
Mario Silva, Lib.*
Lloyd St. Amand, Lib.*
Brent St. Denis, Lib.*
Bruce Stanton, C.P.C.
Paul Steckle, Lib.*
Belinda Stronach, Lib.*
David Sweet, C.P.C.
Paul Szabo, Lib.*
Andrew Telegdi, Lib.*
Lui Temelkovski, Lib.*
David Tilson, C.P.C.*
Alan Tonks, Lib.*
Garth Turner, Ind.
Roger Valley, Lib.*
Dave Van Kesteren, C.P.C.
Peter Van Loan, C.P.C.*
Joseph Volpe, Lib.*
Mike Wallace, C.P.C.
Tom Wappel, Lib.*
Jeff Watson, C.P.C.*
Bryon Wilfert, Lib.*
Borys Wrzesnewskyj, Lib.*

Prince Edward Island
Wayne Easter, Lib.*
Lawrence MacAulay, Lib.*
Joe McGuire, Lib.*
Shawn Murphy, Lib.*

Quebec
Guy André, B.Q.*
Arthur André, Ind.
Gérard Asselin, B.Q.*
Claude Bachand, B.Q.*
Vivian Barbot, B.Q.
André Bellavance, B.Q.*
Maxime Bernier, C.P.C.
Bernard Bigras, B.Q.*
Jean-Pierre Blackburn, C.P.C.
Raynald Blais, B.Q.*
Steven Blaney, C.P.C.
France Bonsant, B.Q.*
Robert Bouchard, B.Q.*
Sylvie Boucher, C.P.C.
Diane Bourgeois, B.Q.*
Paule Brunelle, B.Q.*
Lawrence Cannon, C.P.C.
Serge Cardin, B.Q.*
Robert Carrier, B.Q.*
Denis Coderre, Lib.*
Irwin Cotler, Lib.*
Paul Crête, B.Q.*

THE MINISTRY OF CANADA*

Claude DeBellefeuille, B.Q.
Nicole Demers, B.Q.*
Johanne Deschamps, B.Q.*
Stéphane Dion, Lib.*
Gilles Duceppe, B.Q.*
Meili Faille, B.Q.*
Raymonde Folco, Lib.*
Carole Freeman, B.Q.
Christiane Gagnon, B.Q.*
Roger Gaudet, B.Q.*
Michel Gauthier, B.Q.*
Jacques Gourde, C.P.C.
Raymond Gravel, B.Q.
Monique Guay, B.Q.*
Michel Guimond, B.Q.*
Luc Harvey, C.P.C.
Marlene Jennings, Lib.*
Maka Kotto, B.Q.*
Jean-Yves Laforest, B.Q.
Mario Laframboise, B.Q.*
Francine Lalonde, B.Q.*
Jean Lapierre, Lib.*
Carole Lavallée, B.Q.*
Marc Lemay, B.Q.*
Yves Lessard, B.Q.*
Yvon Lévesque, B.Q.*
Yvan Loubier, B.Q.*
Marcel Lussier, B.Q.
Luc Malo, B.Q.
Paul Martin, Lib.*
Réal Ménard, B.Q.*
Serge Ménard, B.Q.*
Maria Mourani, B.Q.
Richard Nadeau, B.Q.
Christian Ouellet, B.Q.
Massimo Pacetti, Lib.*
Pierre Paquette, B.Q.*
Christian Paradis, C.P.C.*
Bernard Patry, Lib.*
Gilles-A. Perron, B.Q.*
Daniel Petit, C.P.C.
Pauline Picard, B.Q.*
Louis Plamondon, B.Q.*
Marcel Proulx, Lib.*
Lucienne Robillard, Lib.*
Pablo Rodriguez, Lib.*
Jean-Yves Roy, B.Q.*
Francis Scarpaleggia, Lib.*
Thierry St.-Cyr, B.Q.
Caroline St.-Hilaire, B.Q.*
Louise Thibault, B.Q.*
Josée Verner, C.P.C.
Robert Vincent, B.Q.*

Saskatchewan
David Anderson, C.P.C.*
Dave Batters, C.P.C.*
Garry Breitkreuz, C.P.C.*
Brian Fitzpatrick, C.P.C.*
Ralph E. Goodale, Lib.*
Ed Komarnicki, C.P.C.*
Tom Lukiwski, C.P.C.*
Gary Mersaty, Lib.
Gerry Ritz, C.P.C.*
Andrew Scheer, C.P.C.*
Carol Skelton, C.P.C.*
Bradley Trost, C.P.C.*
Maurice Vellacott, C.P.C.*
Lynne Yelich, C.P.C.*

Yukon Territory
Larry Bagnell, Lib.*

Stephen Harper—prime minister
Marjory LeBreton—leader of the government in the Senate
Robert Nicholson—leader of the government in the House of Commons and minister for democratic reform
Jason Kenney—parliamentary secretary
James Flaherty—minister of finance
Peter Van Loan—president of the Queen's Privy Council for Canada, minister of intergovernmental affairs, and minister for sport
Peter MacKay—minister of foreign affairs and minister of the Atlantic Canada Opportunities Agency
David Emerson—minister of international trade
Jim Prentice—minister of Indian affairs and Northern development and federal interlocutor for Métis and nonstatus Indians
Chuck Strahl—minister of agriculture and agri-food and minister for the Canadian Wheat Board
Gregory Thompson—minister of veterans affairs
Michael Fortier—minister of public works and government services
Gordon O'Connor—minister of national defence
Monte Solberg—minister of citizenship and immigration
Diane Finley—minister of human resources and social development
Jean-Pierre Blackburn—minister of labour and minister of the Economic Development Agency of Canada for the Regions of Quebec
Carol Skelton—minister of national revenue and minister of Western economic diversification
Tony Clement—minister of health and minister for the Federal Economic Development Initiative for Northern Ontario
John Baird—president of the Treasury Board
Loyola Hearn—minister of fisheries and oceans
Lawrence Cannon—minister of transport, infrastructure, and communities
Vic Toews—minister of justice and attorney general of Canada
Beverley Oda—minister of Canadian heritage and status of women
Gary Lunn—minister of natural resources
Rona Ambrose—minister of the environment
Maxime Bernier—minister of industry
Stockwell Day—minister of public safety
Josée Verner—minister of international cooperation and minister for La Francophonie and official languages

*As of Dec. 15, 2006

PREMIERS OF CANADIAN PROVINCES

Alberta ....Ed Stelmach
British Columbia ....Gordon Campbell
Manitoba ....Gary Doer
New Brunswick.........................Shawn Graham
Newfoundland and Labrador ....Danny Williams
Nova Scotia ....Rodney MacDonald
Ontario ....Dalton McGuinty
Prince Edward Island................Patrick George Binns
Quebec ....Jean Charest
Saskatchewan..........................Lorne Albert Calvert

GOVERNMENT LEADERS OF TERRITORIES

Northwest Territories ....Joe Handley
Nunavut...................................Paul Okalik
Yukon Territory........................Dennis Fentie

moved cautiously on environmental legislation in 2006. They claimed that the 1997 Kyoto Protocol targets for reducing greenhouse gas emissions, which had been set by the former Liberal government, were unattainable.

On Oct. 19, 2006, the government announced a Clean Air Act that promised to cut greenhouse gas emissions in half by 2050. The act called for new auto emissions standards, comparable to those of the United States, by late 2007. The three opposition parties claimed that the act was ineffective and vowed to vote against the bill.

Apologies. The government apologized in 2006 for Canada's role in two episodes. In June, Harper expressed regret for an injustice dealt to about 81,000 Chinese immigrants brought to Canada to build a transcontinental railway in the 1880's. The Chinese laborers, who were not allowed to bring their wives and children, were forced to pay a "head tax" for each family member to enter Canada. By the early 1900's, the tax amounted to the equivalent of two years' wages. Harper's apology was accompanied by "symbolic" payments of $20,000 to about 20 surviving head-tax payers and around 200 surviving spouses.

The House of Commons apologized in September 2006 to Maher Arar, a Canadian citizen who was wrongly arrested and was then tortured by foreign agents shortly after the terrorist attacks on the United States on Sept. 11, 2001. Agents of the United States, operating under faulty Royal Canadian Mounted Police (RCMP) reports that Arar had links to al-Qa`ida, arrested him at John F. Kennedy International Airport in New York City in 2002. He was held for nearly one year in Syria and freed in October 2003.

Justice Dennis O'Connor issued a report in September 2006 that exonerated Arar. It stated that the RCMP had supplied U.S. officials with bad intelligence and provided the Canadian government with inaccurate information about its actions. Prime Minister Harper planned to compensate Arar once negotiations had been completed.

Military. In June, Harper announced the largest military spending plan in Canadian history. The plan called for $15 billion in defense spending over the next several years. The money would be used to buy heavy-lift aircraft and helicopters, supply ships, and a variety of tanks and other armored vehicles. The government sought to enhance the military's ability to fight in foreign conflicts.

Foreign affairs. Canada remained engaged in the Middle East during 2006. Canadian soldiers fought in Afghanistan, in company with U.S. and British forces, in an effort to restore stability to the country. Canadians had served in Afghanistan since 2002, when they were stationed at the capital, Kabul, to help stabilize and rebuild the city.

In 2005 and early 2006, Canada substantially increased its presence and transferred its forces to Kandahar, a center of resistance by forces loyal to the former Taliban government. By February, Canada had 2,300 troops stationed in Afghanistan.

Parliament held two debates in 2006 about the purposes of the intervention. On April 10, most members of the Commons expressed support for the mission. However, NDP leader Jack Layton called for a vote on Canada's continued presence. Harper rejected the motion.

On May 15, the government scheduled a second debate for May 17 that would be followed by a vote. Harper asked the Commons to extend the mission to February 2009. At the debate, members of the opposition parties expressed concerns about the long-term prospects for the mission's success. Their misgivings may also have arisen from the combat death on the same day of Captain Nichola Goddard, the first woman to be killed on the front lines in Canadian history. The government won the vote to extend the mission by a small margin.

Canadian forces engaged the Taliban opposition in hard fighting in the Kandahar area in mid-2006. From 2002 to early November 2006, Canadian troops suffered 42 casualties. In addition, a Canadian diplomat serving with the mission was killed by enemy forces.

In 2006, Canada moved away from its traditional balanced attitude toward the Arab-Israeli struggle. On March 30, the Harper government suspended official aid to Hamas, a major Palestinian radical Islamist organization and the governing party of the Palestinian Authority. Canada claimed that Hamas was a terrorist organization. It cut funds to Hamas out of concern that money might be diverted from civil tasks to the armed struggle with Israel. Canada was the second country, after Israel, to take this step.

The Harper government also sided with Israel during its summer fighting with Hezbollah, a radical Islamist group in Lebanon. In July, Hezbollah captured two Israeli soldiers near the border of Lebanon and Israel. The resulting conflict caused the deaths of over 1,000 people, most of them Lebanese, before ending in August. In July, Harper said he believed that Israel had a right to defend itself and called its response "measured." Many Canadians criticized Harper's comments, calling for the government to adopt a more neutral stance and to work toward a cease-fire agreement.

U.S. relations. Harper's policies indicated that he planned to work more closely with the administration of U.S. President George W. Bush than did his predecessor, Paul Martin. Harper met with President Bush a number of times during 2006.

In March, the two leaders met at a conference of North American countries held in Mexico. They announced that they had instructed their staffs to settle the dispute over Canadian exports of softwood lumber to the United States. In 2002, the United States imposed a duty on lumber imports, imperiling trade worth $10 billion annually to Canadian provinces. The United States had charged that Canada had provided unfair assistance to its lumber producers. In August 2005, a North American Free Trade Agreement (NAFTA) panel called for an end to the U.S. duty, but the United States refused to abide by the ruling.

Negotiators worked steadily during spring 2006 to resolve the dispute. They reached a preliminary agreement on April 26. However, the deal did not please some Canadian lumber interests, particularly in British Columbia and Ontario. On July 1, trade officials from Canada and the United States agreed on the final text. The deal allowed Canada full access on lumber exports to the United States for seven years. However, if the cost of Canadian lumber fell below a settled price, it would be subject to either a Canadian export tax or to a mutually acceptable quota system. The deal also required the United States to return $4.4 billion of the $5.3 billion it had collected to the Canadian companies that had paid the duties. Some critics noted that the deal could collapse before the end of the seven-year term.

The Harper government worked with U.S. officials to revise the agreement and signed it in September. The deal came into force on October 12. However, a depressed lumber market led Canada to impose a tax on its exports. ■ David M. L. Farr

See also **Afghanistan; Canada, Prime Minister of; Canadian provinces; Canadian territories; Montreal; People in the news** (Stephen Joseph Harper); **Toronto; United States, Government of the.**

Canada, Prime Minister of.

Stephen Harper became Canada's 22nd prime minister when he took office on Feb. 6, 2006. Harper's Conservative Party toppled Paul Martin's administration in a January national election, ending 13 years of Liberal Party rule.

Harper, a 47-year-old economist, was from the Western province of Alberta. He served in the House of Commons from 1993 to 1997 and from 2002 to 2006. Harper chaired the National Citizens' Coalition, a conservative advocacy group, in the late 1990's and the early 2000's. In 2003, Harper cofounded a new Conservative Party by combining Canada's two former conservative parties.

The new prime minister was an economic conservative, interpreting Canada's federal constitution to give more power to the provinces, arguing

Stephen Harper and his family celebrate Harper's Conservative Party's victory of the Liberal Party government on January 23. Harper subsequently succeeded Paul Martin as prime minister.

that they best represent their people's interests.

Harper sought in 2006 to establish closer relations with the administration of United States President George W. Bush. In March, he worked with Bush to settle the softwood lumber dispute that had strained bilateral relations since 2002.

Harper's main goal in 2006 was to win a parliamentary majority. He focused on building Conservative Party support in Quebec, whose votes were essential to reaching that goal. ■ David M. L. Farr

See also **Afghanistan; Canada; Canadian provinces; Canadian territories; People in the news** (Stephen Joseph Harper).

Canadian provinces. Finance ministers in 8 out of 10 Canadian provinces reported balanced budgets or surpluses in 2006, marking an end to a long period in the 1990's and parts of the early 2000's of deficit financing by many provincial governments. With most of their books in order, the provinces attempted to attract businesses by cutting personal and corporate taxes and reinvesting in social programs and crumbling infrastructure.

Alberta. Record-high oil prices in 2006 fueled Alberta's continuing economic boom and increased interest in exploration and development of the province's tar sands, which can be processed to produce crude oil. In addition, royalties from existing operations swelled Alberta's coffers.

On March 22, Finance Minister Shirley McLellan presented the province's 13th consecutive balanced budget and forecast a $4.1-billion surplus for fiscal year 2006 (April 1-March 30, 2007). Predicted spending topped $28 billion (all amounts in Canadian dollars). The budget included a plan to invest in health care, infrastructure, education, and the environment. The province also cut its corporate tax rate from 11.5 percent to 10 percent, effective April 1, 2006, in a bid to boost Alberta's appeal to large corporations.

The government shared its wealth in January by issuing rebate checks to nearly every Albertan. With the exception of prisoners, every man, woman, and child in the province received a $400 dividend from the 2005 surplus. The government mailed about 2.3 million checks over the course of 2006. Albertans dubbed the money "Ralphbucks" in honor of Premier Ralph Klein.

Klein faced a disappointing exit from Albertan politics after being endorsed by only 55.4 percent of delegates at the Progressive Conservative Party convention in March. Many party loyalists were displeased by his delayed retirement plans. Klein took the vote as a sign to step down. On August 31, he left the provincial legislature after more than 14 years as premier. Klein formally announced his resignation on September 20.

On December 3, Ed Stelmach won a Progressive Conservative Party vote to become the 13th premier of Alberta. Stelmach, a farmer and the first Alberta premier of Ukrainian descent, defeated frontrunner and former Finance Minister Jim Dinning and Ted Morton, a social conservative and former political science professor.

British Columbia. The province's Liberal government released a budget on February 21 that focused on spending initiatives for children's services. Finance Minister Carole Taylor restored funding to the Ministry of Children and Family Development that had been cut in the early 2000's. The budget provided $421 million over four years for child care, including funds to reduce waiting lists for children with special needs and their families. A September 2006 update forecast a $1.2-billion surplus—double the February forecast—due to rising employment, greater retail sales, and a strong housing market.

In January, British Columbia hog farmer Robert Pickton, 56, entered innocent pleas on 27 counts of first-degree murder in the British Columbia Supreme Court in New Westminster. Pickton chose a trial by jury in the largest suspected serial-killing case in Canadian history. He was arrested in 2002 as part of a police investigation into the disappearance of as many as 60 women from Vancouver from 1995 through 2001. Authorities found many human remains on Pickton's farm in Port Coquitlam, a Vancouver suburb. In August 2006, Justice James Williams ruled that Pickton would initially face trial on only six counts so as not to risk a mistrial or confuse and discourage jurors.

Manitoba. Finance Minister Greg Selinger presented a budget in March that included modest tax relief for families and businesses and an average spending increase of 6.8 percent across all government departments. The budget projected a $148-million surplus on an $8.6-billion budget for fiscal year 2006. The province increased its net debt by the same amount as the surplus to finance such long-term infrastructure projects as the expansion of the Red River Floodway, a channel used to divert water around Winnipeg.

The province's growing online pharmacy industry, which provides inexpensive prescription medication to many customers in the United States, faced criticism from the U.S. government in August. The U.S. Food and Drug Administration (FDA), an agency that seeks to protect the public by ensuring the safety of food, drugs, and other biological products, accused Minnedosa-based Mediplan Global Health of shipping counterfeit products. The FDA claimed that some intercepted drugs ordered from the Canadian online pharmacy were not shipped from Canada, but the FDA could not verify their origin. Canadian industry consultants accused the FDA of trying to scare away customers in an attempt to discourage pharmaceutical trade across the border.

The Nisichawayasihk Cree Nation in Nelson House signed an agreement in June with Winnipeg-based Manitoba Hydro, the province's primary energy utility, to construct the Wuskwatim hydroelectric dam project. The First Nation's representatives said the deal would allow residents to train for and obtain jobs at the dam. The First Nation was also eligible for construction contracts that could result in $100 million in revenues over the six years it will take to complete the dam.

New Brunswick. Progressive Conservative Premier Bernard Lord lost a provincial election on September 18. Lord, who became New Brunswick's youngest premier at age 33 in 1999, faced a challenging term in 2006 as his small majority in the provincial legislature teetered on the verge of collapse. After a close campaign, the Liberal Party won a small three-seat majority. The Progressive Conservatives won a slightly larger share of the popular vote, but a seat redistribution conducted in early 2006 favored some urban areas that tended to support the Liberals.

On October 3, Liberal leader Shawn Graham was sworn in as premier. At age 38, he became one of the older incoming premiers in New Brunswick's modern history. Graham promised to restore the province's pride by making it less dependent on federal equalization payments. He also vowed to work to develop job opportunities to keep New Brunswick's young people from migrating to wealthier areas.

Finance Minister Jeannot Volpe announced a balanced budget on March 28 that featured a surplus of $22.2 million for fiscal year 2006 and record spending of $6.2 billion. The budget included a corporate tax rate cut from 13 to 12 percent; a $100-million energy consumer relief program to fight rising home heating costs; and new education and health care spending.

Newfoundland and Labrador announced plans in March to hold the third-largest offshore drilling rights auction in its history. The surging price of oil and gas in the early 2000's prompted development of many underwater oil fields in Newfoundland and Labrador. Such resources enabled the province to recover from economic troubles that began in the early 1990's when its lucrative fish stocks collapsed and the government imposed a moratorium on certain types of large commercial fishing.

The province called for bids by November 2006 to the rights to more than 4.2 million acres (1.7 million hectares) of exploration properties. According to the National Energy Board, Canada's federal energy-regulation agency, Newfoundland and Labrador produced about 12 percent of the country's oil output in 2005. The province was second only to Alberta in overall production.

In February 2006, the Conference Board of Canada, a research organization based in Ottawa, the capital, projected that Newfoundland and Labrador would lead all the provinces in economic growth in 2006—after a poor year in 2005—with an expected increase of 6.4 percent in real gross domestic product (GDP). (GDP is the total value of goods and services produced within a region in a year.) The board cited a full production year at the Voisey Bay nickel mine and the White Rose offshore oil project as key factors in the increase.

Finance Minister Loyola Sullivan canceled his warning of a nearly $500-million deficit in 2005 when he presented a balanced budget on March 30, 2006. Sullivan noted that the 2005 results

yielded a surplus of about $76.5 million. The budget marked the first time that Newfoundland and Labrador had projected a fully consolidated surplus—$6.2 million. The surplus resulted from high oil revenues and money from the Atlantic Accord, an agreement signed by the federal government in February 2005 that allowed the province to keep more of its oil and gas royalties.

Nova Scotia. Rodney MacDonald won the leadership of the province's Progressive Conservative minority government in February 2006. At age 34, he became Canada's youngest serving premier. The former tourism and immigration minister replaced outgoing Premier John Hamm.

MacDonald called a general election for June 13 in hopes of turning his minority in the provincial legislature into a majority. However, his party lost 2 seats for a total of 23 and returned to office with reduced control. The opposition New Democratic Party won 5 additional seats for a total of 20. The third-place Liberals lost 1 seat for a total of 9. Only 61 percent of voters turned out for the election, a record low for Nova Scotia.

In May, the province announced its fifth consecutive balanced budget—one filled with tax cuts and spending increases. The budget included an 8-percent rebate on soaring home heating bills that effectively removed the provincial sales tax; an increase to the personal tax exemption; a $1,000 income tax credit for new post-secondary graduates; and a plan to reduce the capital tax for large corporations to zero by 2012.

In September 2006, Mayann E. Francis, a descendant of black loyalists to the British monarchy who left the United States after the Revolutionary War in America (1775-1783), was appointed lieutenant governor of the province. Elizabeth II, queen of Canada and the United Kingdom, was in 2006 represented in Canada by two black women—Francis and Governor General Michaëlle Jean, a Haitian immigrant who served as the queen's national representative.

Ontario. A land claims dispute over the building of a subdivision in southern Ontario raged between Native Canadians and other local residents in early 2006. On February 28, a small group of protesters from the Six Nations of the Grand River Territory moved onto the construction site near Caledonia—about 50 miles (80 kilometers) southwest of Toronto. The group erected a protest camp and defied court orders to leave.

In early 2006, members of the First Nation and nonindigenous residents had violent clashes. On April 20, the Ontario Provincial Police raided the area and arrested several protesters. On June 22, provincial officials announced that the province had purchased the disputed land for about $12.3 million and would hold it until the developers and the First Nation resolved the claim.

In March, about 9,100 college faculty members, represented by the Ontario Public Services Employees Union, held a strike against 24 Ontario colleges. The strike ended on March 24 after Premier Dalton McGuinty called for teachers to return to their classrooms. The two sides agreed to binding arbitration. Approximately 150,000 college students missed three weeks of classes.

Ontario's deficit of $1.4 billion made it one of only two provinces to present an unbalanced budget in 2006. Finance Minister Dwight Duncan's March 23 budget invested $1.2 billion in crumbling infrastructure and heavily burdened public transit systems. The plan included funds for roads and bridges, a Toronto subway extension, and bus transit initiatives in Brampton and Mississauga. The budget also created a $2.1-billion skills-training and employment-services strategy program.

Prince Edward Island (P.E.I.) Treasurer Mitch Murphy's March 30 budget estimated a $12.5-million deficit for fiscal year 2006 and a balanced budget for 2007. The budget featured a $45-million increase in expenditures. About 40 percent of the province's budget, or $459 million, came from the federal government in 2006.

Canada's smallest and least-populated province faced international attention in March 2006 as former Beatle Paul McCartney and his wife, Heather, visited the island to conduct media interviews as they protested Canada's seal hunt. The McCartneys, who toured ice floes in the Gulf of St. Lawrence to view newborn seal pups, lent their celebrity to a campaign by animal rights activists to end the annual hunt. Federal Fisheries Minister Loyola Hearn stated that Canada would not end the regulated hunt, citing abundant seal populations. Many P.E.I. residents regard the hunt as a tradition and an important supplement to their winter livelihood as well as a method to protect vulnerable fish stocks from a predator.

Quebec. The provincial government in June imposed a pay settlement on about 8,000 Quebec medical specialists. The specialists, who earned about $233,000 annually, sought a salary closer to the national average of $343,000. In August, the Montreal-based Quebec Medical Association published a poll that revealed that almost 25 percent of physicians were considering setting up a practice outside of Quebec within five years.

Justice Nicole Benard of Quebec Superior Court ruled in August that the province had misinterpreted its Medicare law with respect to abortions and ordered the government to reimburse 45,000 women with more than $13 million. Some women seeking the procedure had been charged from $200 to $300 at certain health centers and private clinics from 1999 through 2005. The justice ruled that a patient cannot be charged a supplemental fee.

Finance Minister Michel Audet's March 23, 2006, budget outlined plans to fund the province's new debt-reduction plan through royalties on commercial water users. A large portion of the royalties were to be collected from Hydro-Québec, the provincial electric utility that operated a network of hydroelectric dams. Some observers noted that the plan echoed Alberta's successful program of using oil and gas royalties to eliminate its debt. Quebec's budget also heralded $1.5 billion in new spending for environmentally friendly modes of transportation, $925 million in tax credits and loans to aid the forestry sector, and personal income tax cuts of $362 million.

Saskatchewan. In January, 72 workers became trapped within a mine near Esterhazy, about 130 miles (210 kilometers) northeast of Regina, after a fire broke out in plastic piping. The miners waited in sealed-off safe rooms as smoke filled the tunnels. Everyone was rescued.

Finance Minister Andrew Thomson presented a balanced budget on April 6 that promised a $95-million corporate tax cut that would grow to $240 million after three years. The 2006-2007 budget also increased health care spending, welfare rates, and funding for education. The government forecast a $27-million surplus.   ■ William Stos

See also **Canada; Canadian territories; Montreal; Toronto.**

Canadian territories.
Industry boomed in Canada's Far North in 2006 as the three territories expanded development of their natural resources. However, they continued to face the challenges wrought by the higher temperatures resulting from global warming.

The three territorial premiers sought changes to federal funding formulas that would allow them to keep more of their resource revenues and borrow more money for capital expenditures. They also lobbied the federal government for more provincelike powers and responsibilities.

Northwest Territories. The Northwest Territories' diamond mining industry continued to expand in 2006. A report released in June by Statistics Canada revealed that the value of diamonds exported from the territory surged to $1.7 billion in 2005, almost triple the value from 1999—the industry's first year of production. (All amounts are in Canadian dollars.) The agency reported that, by 2004, Canada had become the world's third largest diamond producer in terms of value and its sixth largest producer by volume.

The industry's growth slowed in January 2006, when unseasonably warm weather led mining companies to delay opening an ice road that runs over frozen lakes to the territory's two diamond mines. The companies use the roads to truck fuel and supplies to the mines during the winter months. In

February, Premier Joe Handley proposed building all-weather roads and bridges.

The first hybrid grizzly-polar bear in the wild was discovered in 2006 in the Northwest Territories. In April, an American big-game hunter shot the animal on Banks Island. The bear had the white fur of a polar bear and the claws and humped back of a grizzly. Differences in mating seasons make hybrid offspring rare, but some grizzlies have been observed moving into polar bear territory in search of food. Canadian wildlife officials considered naming the hybrid bear a "pizzly," "grolar bear," or "nanulak"—a combination of the Inuit words *nanuk,* polar bear, and *aklak,* grizzly bear.

Northwest Territories Finance Minister Floyd Roland presented a balanced budget on February 2 that forecast a $31-million surplus for fiscal year 2006 (April 1-March 31, 2007). Spending increased by 7 percent, and the territory cut its corporate tax rate from 14 to 11.5 percent to stay competitive with its southern neighbor, Alberta.

Nunavut. Prime Minister Stephen Harper visited the three territories in August. In Nunavut, he reiterated the federal government's desire to enforce Canadian sovereignty in the Far North. Some scientists contend that rising temperatures could melt enough ice to open the storied Northwest Passage to shipping. Local leaders expressed concern that other countries could begin shipping in waters that Canada claims as its own. Melting ice could also promote exploration for such underwater resources as oil and gas. Harper vowed to continue to lobby the international community to sign a treaty that recognizes a country's right to a 230-mile (370-kilometer) economic zone off its coasts.

During his visit, Harper officially opened the Jericho diamond mine owned by Toronto-based Tahera Diamond Corporation. In 2006, the mine, Nunavut's first, yielded about 2,000 carats of diamonds every day and employed about 180 people in Canada's least-populated territory. The mine has an expected life span of about eight years.

Territorial Finance Minister David Simailak presented a budget on February 22 that forecast a small deficit of $7.6 million on about $1 billion in revenues for fiscal year 2006. The budget included fuel tax rebates for Nunavut's hunting, fishing, mining, and tourism industries. Simailak noted that the territory's growing population faced serious housing shortages that could be addressed by a new funding agreement with the federal government. About 82 percent of the territory's revenues in 2006 came from the federal government.

Yukon. Premier Dennis Fentie and his conservative Yukon Party won reelection in a territorial vote on October 10. The party took a total of 10 of the province's 18 seats. Fentie had governed since 2002.

Scientists off the coast of Yukon in the Beaufort Sea reported in June 2006 that they had found evidence of cannibalism in polar bears. Researchers had previously observed the behavior in grizzlies and black bears, but never before in polar bears. The scientists cited climate change as the most likely culprit. Successive years of warmer weather has reduced the amount of sea ice and, as a result, the mating and birthing grounds of ring seals, the bears' main source of food.

Climate change also had an acute impact on Yukon's Dawson City. The community of 1,500, which lies about 60 miles (100 kilometers) east of the Alaskan border, is built on a slowly melting layer of frozen water and *permafrost* (ground that remains frozen for two or more years). The town's dirt roads, water pipes, and buried sewer system could be among the first casualties of the melting. In February, a thaw shifted the ground and tore open a large section of a waterline. The town increased its public works budget for 2006 by about 50 percent to combat the problems.

On March 30, Fentie, also the territory's finance minister, unveiled Yukon's largest budget ever. The balanced budget featured $191.7 million in capital spending projects. About 71 percent of Yukon's revenues came from federal transfers.

■ William Stos

See also **Biology; Canada; Canada, Prime Minister of; Global warming: A Special Report.**

Cape Verde. See Africa.

Census. The population of the United States reached 300 million on Oct. 17, 2006, according to U.S. Census Bureau estimates. At that time, the bureau projected a net gain of 1 person every 11 seconds—that is, 1 birth every 7 seconds, 1 death every 13 seconds, and a net gain of 1 immigrant every 31 seconds. The bureau also projected that the population would reach 400 million in 2043. It hit 200 million in 1967 and 100 million in 1915.

Diversity on the rise. On May 10, 2006, the bureau reported that the country was continuing to diversify, with minority groups making up about one-third of all residents in 2005. The minority population—that is, people other than non-Hispanic, single-race whites—was 98 million, or 33 percent of the total of 296.4 million.

The country's 42.7 million Hispanics made up the largest minority group. They were also the fastest-growing group, with a 3.3-percent rise in population from July 1, 2004, to July 1, 2005. Hispanics may be of any race. African Americans were the second-largest minority group and the largest racial minority group. The 2005 black population, including Hispanics and non-Hispanics, was 39.7 million. In the bureau's three other racial minority categories—Asians, American Indians and Alaska natives, and native Hawaiians and other Pacific Islanders—the 2005 populations were 14.4 million, 4.5 million, and 990,000, respectively. All these racial groups had grown since 2004, with Asians posting the largest increase (3 percent). The white population, including Hispanics and non-Hispanics, stood at 241.8 million in 2005. The numbers for all five racial groups included both single-race and mixed-race people, which means mixed-race people were counted in two or more groups.

Delaying marriage, living alone. On May 25, 2006, the bureau reported that the median age of first marriage in 2005 was 27.1 years for men and 25.8 years for women. In 1970, it was 23.2 and 20.8 years, respectively. The proportion of U.S. households consisting of one person living alone rose from 17 percent in 1970 to 26 percent in 2005. Average household size fell from 3.14 to 2.57 people during that period.

An aging United States. A December 2005 census report projected rapid growth in the country's elderly population. By 2030, one-fifth of U.S. residents—about 72 million—were expected to be 65 or older. People 85 and older were the fastest-growing age group. The report revealed that the percentage of people 65 and older with disabilities fell from 26.2 percent in 1982 to 19.7 percent in 1999. Most disabilities reported in Census 2000 were linked to such chronic ailments as arthritis and heart disease. The rate of older people living in poverty fell from 35 percent in 1959 to 10 percent in 2003. The report attributed the drop to Social Security benefits, which by the 1950's were being paid to nearly all retirees.

Disabilities. In 2002, 51.2 million people—about 18 percent of the population—reported having a disability, and 32.5 million people (12 percent) had severe disabilities, according to bureau findings released on May 12, 2006. In the 21-to-64 age group, about 56 percent of people with disabilities had a job. The employment rate for people without disabilities was 88 percent.

Income and poverty. A census report released on Aug. 29, 2006, revealed that the country's real median household income grew by 1.1 percent from 2004 to 2005, reaching $46,326. In the same period, the proportion of Americans in poverty (12.6 percent, or 37 million people) showed no statistical change. The number of people without health insurance coverage rose to 46.6 million (15.9 percent).

Speedy growth. In late 2005 and in 2006, the bureau announced which U.S. areas had the fastest population growth rates from July 1, 2004, to July 1, 2005. Nevada was the fastest-growing state, with a rate of 3.5 percent. Arizona was a close second. Flagler County, Florida, was the fastest-growing large county (10.7 percent). Elk Grove, California, was the fastest-growing large city (12 percent).   ■ Geoffrey A. Campbell

See also **City; Population; State government.**

Chemistry. An important step toward making artificial bones and new metal-ceramic *composites* (solid substances made of at least two different ingredients) was reported in January 2006 by materials scientist Sylvain Deville and colleagues at the Lawrence Berkeley National Laboratory in California. By taking advantage of the crystal formation that occurs as salt water freezes, the scientists made artificial mother of pearl, or nacre, that was the closest yet to the natural substance.

The secret to nature's ability to make materials that are both strong and flexible lies in the architecture of the materials. Both nacre and bones consist of alternating, ultrathin layers of minerals and proteins. Either substance alone is fragile, but together, they carry great strength.

Previous attempts to imitate this natural architecture had limited success, because the alternating layers were too thick. The key to the new process was freezing. The scientists took advantage of the way water can freeze in the presence of salts. Ice forms as sheets of *hexagons* (figures with six sides), which can trap material in-between. Deville's team used the sheets as scaffolding for thin layers of ground ceramic and *polymer* (long-chain) molecules. They then freeze-dried this assembly and sintered, or baked, it in an oven.

To make the bonelike material, the scientists placed *epoxy* (a chainlike compound containing oxygen) between layers of hypoxyapatite, which forms the mineral part of bone. In addition, to make an example of an advanced, nonbiological ceramic, the scientists filled *alumina* (the mineral used in making aluminum) plates with titanium and other metals.

The new technique held promise for making materials that are strong enough to replace artificial joints, which tend to cause inflammation and sometimes need later adjustments. For nonjoint bones, the voids between mineral crystals might be filled with materials that can be absorbed by the body, along with other substances that encourage bone growth.

Planet-friendly plastics. Each year, North Americans use 5 million tons (4.5 million metric tons) of polystyrene, a type of plastic used in everything from hamburger clamshells (disposable food containers) to toys to packing peanuts. Most polystyrene is made from petroleum, a nonrenewable resource. In July, a team led by James A. Dumesic, a chemical engineer at the University of Wisconsin in Madison, described a practical technique for using a renewable resource in the manufacture of polystyrene.

The researchers synthesized hydroxymethylfurfural (HMF)—a key building block for polystyrene and other plastics—with a chemical process involving the simple sugar fructose. Fructose is the sugar found in fruits, corn, syrup, and honey. Scientists had previously made HMF from fructose, but those experiments were plagued by low yields and by difficulties separating the HMF from other compounds.

In the new method, fructose was mixed in water with an organic solvent—methylisobutylketone—and an acid *catalyst* (a substance that causes a chemical reaction without being changed in the reaction). Stirring the mixture caused the molecules to polymerize, or bind together in chains. The larger HMF molecules floated to the surface, where they could evaporate as a pure compound. The scientists reported that this process had an overall yield of 80 percent.

Tiny colors. The first carbon-based quantum dots were reported in a June article by chemist Ya-Ping Sun of Clemson University in South Carolina. The tiny *semiconductors* (materials that conduct electric current better than insulators but not as well as conductors) had the potential of providing a nontoxic approach to quickly identifying biological and environmental threats, including poisons and germs used in warfare or terrorism.

Quantum dots are *nanostructures* (atom-sized structures) that can be used to hold and confine the movement of electrons, negatively charged particles. The electrons in quantum dots can *fluoresce*—that is, they can emit light of different colors when they absorb electromagnetic energy. These small but highly stable structures can be joined to *antigens* (foreign substances such as bacteria) and other biological substances, making them useful as tagging agents for medical and environmental tests. Tagging agents help scientists observe and keep track of substances in the body and in the environment. For example, the quantum dot tags could attach themselves to bacteria and be made to glow under colored light. Because the color given off by the dots depends on their size, a rainbow of tagging agents—each associated with a different biological chemical—could be available in one test solution. The colors would provide physicians with information about the nature of illnesses.

The scientists created the quantum dots from a small disk of carbon atoms. Using a laser, they broke off tiny dots (each about 25 atoms in diameter), which they then chemically activated with nitric acid. The dots were turned into tagging agents by "bathing" them with the long-chain molecule polyethylene glycol.

Previous uses of this type of quantum dot technology were based on toxic materials, such as cadmium selenide and lead sulfide. Although safety testing on the carbon-based dots was not completed in 2006, the researchers believed that the new dots could lead to tagging agents and medical imaging applications with less risks than applications of current dots. ■ Peter Andrews

Chess. Vladimir Kramnik of Russia in 2006 became the first undisputed world champion of chess in 13 years, after defeating Veselin Topalov of Bulgaria in the World Chess Championship. The championship match—held in Elista, in the Russian republic of Kalmykia—marked the reunification of the two main championship crowns that had been recognized in the chess world. The game had been split into rival groups since 1993, after then-champion Garry Kasparov of Russia broke away from the Fédération Internationale des Échecs (FIDE), the international governing body of chess.

Heading into the 2006 championship match, Topalov, nicknamed the "Bulgarian Chainsaw," held the FIDE championship, while Kramnik, who defeated Kasparov in 2000, was considered the "classical" champion. The match, scheduled for 12 games, became controversial after the fourth game, when Topalov and his manager accused Kramnik of taking too many bathroom breaks. They lodged a formal protest, suggesting that Kramnik may have received outside help while within his private lavatory. Following the complaint, the private lavatories were locked, and the players had to use a shared bathroom.

Kramnik refused to play the fifth game, and Topalov was declared the winner of the game by forfeit. Kramnik threatened to withdraw from the match, but he resumed play. By the end of the 12 games, the match was tied. On October 14, 2006, Kramnik won the championship by defeating Topalov in a rapid-play overtime series.

Chess Olympiad. During late May and early June, 148 national teams from around the world competed at the 37th Chess Olympiad in Turin, Italy. The Armenian team won the gold medal in the men's tournament. China finished second, and the United States, third. In the women's tournament, the Ukrainian team won gold, followed by Russia and then China.

U.S. events. Alexander Onischuk of Baltimore won the 2006 U.S. Chess Championship in San Diego in March. Anna Zatonskih of Holtsville, New York, captured the women's championship at the same event. In August, Yury Shulman of Barrington, Illinois, won the U.S. Open Chess Championship in Oak Brook, Illinois.

Young champions. Robert Hess of New York City won the U.S. Junior Invitational Chess Championship in Dallas in July. In April and May, schools battled for championships in three U.S. locations. In Milwaukee, Edward R. Murrow High School of New York City won the National High School Championship. The Hunter College Campus Schools of New York City won the National Junior High Championship in Louisville, Kentucky, and the National Elementary School Championship in Denver. ■ Al Lawrence

Chicago. July 2006 was a difficult month for Chicago Mayor Richard M. Daley. On July 6, a federal jury convicted his patronage chief, Robert Sorich, on two counts of mail fraud for arranging city jobs for the mayor's political supporters.

In a report released on July 19, special prosecutors concluded that Chicago police under former Commander Jon Burge frequently used torture to obtain confessions from crime suspects during the 1970's and 1980's. The report accused top officials, including Daley (who was then Cook County state's attorney) of failing to notice or stop the abuse.

On July 26, 2006, the City Council—in an unprecedented gesture of mayoral defiance—voted 35-14 to require such "big box" stores as Wal-Mart and Target to pay employees at least $9.25 per hour and $1.50 in fringe benefits beginning in July 2007. Big box stores are those that cover at least 90,000 square feet (8,400 square meters). Labor and liberal political groups hailed the ordinance, but the mayor opposed it, claiming that it would drive the stores (and their sales tax revenues) out of the city to the suburbs. The mayor vetoed the ordinance in September 2006.

Reelection drive. Despite his reduced clout, Mayor Daley made plans to run for a sixth term in the February 2007 city election. Chicago Housing Authority director Terry Peterson resigned in August 2006 to manage the campaign.

Landmark changes. A number of developments affected Chicago's commercial landmarks in 2006. The storied Berghoff restaurant in the Loop closed its doors in February after 107 years in business. In September, the nameplate of New York City-based Macy's went up on the former Marshall Field's stores, which had long been a Chicago shopping institution.

Bon-Ton Stores, Inc., of York, Pennsylvania, announced in August that the State Street store of Carson Pirie Scott & Co. would close by March 2007. The building, an architectural landmark created by renowned architect Louis H. Sullivan, was to be turned to other uses.

Sullivan losses. Fire claimed three of Sullivan's Chicago buildings in 2006. The Pilgrim Baptist Church on the South Side, considered the birthplace of gospel music and a landmark in the African American community, was gutted by a fire on January 5. Two less distinguished Sullivan-designed structures—the commercial Wirt Dexter Building in the Loop and a private residence—burned in October and November, respectively.

Transportation. Chicago's O'Hare International Airport regained its status as the nation's busiest airport—in terms of number of flights—during the first half of 2006, according to the Federal Aviation Administration. In 2005, O'Hare had fallen behind Hartsfield-Jackson Atlanta International Airport, which continued to lead the nation in number of passengers.

Loyal customers of Chicago's Marshall Field's State Street department store protest its conversion into a Macy's in September. Federated Department Stores of Cincinnati, Ohio, changed the names of more than 400 stores across the United States to Macy's in 2006.

Construction in 2006 snarled traffic on Chicago's South Side Dan Ryan Expressway and on the Chicago Transit Authority's Northwest Side Brown Line. The city's Bike 2015 plan, unveiled in midyear, called for the development of a 500-mile (800-kilometer) network of bicycle paths to encourage bicycling to work and shopping.

Historic *el* car. In January 2006, Chicago's first *el* (elevated railroad) car was installed in the renovated Chicago History Museum in the Lincoln Park neighborhood. The el car went into operation in 1893 to carry visitors to the World's Columbian Exposition. It served Loop riders until 1930.

Grass-roots activism returned to Chicago on March 10 and May 1, 2006, when hundreds of thousands of people gathered in the Loop to show their support for legalizing the status of *undocumented* (illegal) immigrants. The rallies were part of a national effort to oppose legislation proposed in Congress that would create stricter rules for undocumented immigrants.

Deaths. Legendary former DePaul University basketball coach Ray Meyer died on March 17. North Side politician George Dunne, who served as Cook County board chairman for 21 years, died on May 28.   ■ Harold Henderson

See also **Baseball.**

Children's books. See Literature for children.

Chile. On March 11, 2006, Verónica Michelle Bachelet Jeria, leader of the incumbent *Concertación* (Convergence) coalition of left-of-center parties, became Chile's first female president after having won a runoff election in January. The new president divided her Cabinet appointments equally between men and women, honoring a campaign pledge to expand opportunities for women. Bachelet also spearheaded legislation providing free child care to enable impoverished single mothers to enter the work force.

Contraception controversy. In September, Bachelet's minister of health ordered public clinics to begin distributing free "morning-after" birth control pills to girls as young as 14 years old. Conservative politicians and leading *lay* (nonclergy) Roman Catholics had sued in court to stop the policy's implementation, but a Chilean court ruled against them. The pill contains a hormone that can stop an egg from implanting in a woman's womb. To be effective, it must be taken within 72 hours of intercourse. Bachelet's administration defended the use of the contraceptive to curb a high incidence of teen-age pregnancy, but conservatives and religious groups vowed to continue their opposition. Chile's population is predominantly Catholic and has traditionally been socially conservative.

Mine workers strike. In 2006, record-high copper prices buoyed the economy of Chile, the world's largest copper exporter. Chile's Escondida Mine, the world's largest copper mine, reported $2.9 billion in profits for the first half of 2006— triple the figure for the same period in 2005.

In August 2006, union workers at Escondida went on strike for better pay and benefits. Union and company representatives reached an agreement on a new contract in early September, after mining operations had been idle for 25 days at a cost to the mining company of nearly $17 million per day. Under the settlement, miners were to receive an 8-percent salary increase, a bonus, interest-free loans, and education funding.

Human rights. In March, 13 retired Chilean army officers were indicted on homicide charges stemming from the aftermath of a 1973 *coup* (government overthrow) led by General Augusto Pinochet Ugarte. The men were accused of complicity in the so-called "Caravan of Death," in which troops were ferried about the country by helicopters to kill 75 prominent dissidents.

Pinochet, military dictator of Chile from 1973 to 1990, died on Dec. 10, 2006. At his death, Pinochet was under investigation for his role in various human rights violations associated with his 1973 military coup and subsequent dictatorship.   ■ Nathan Haverstock

See also **Latin America: A Special Report** and **People in the news** (Bachelet, Michelle).

China. The Chinese Communist Party (CCP) tried in 2006 to combat threats to its ruling power arising from extensive corruption, a widening gap between rich and poor, and publicity for its failures. Party efforts also served to tighten control by CCP General Secretary and President Hu Jintao.

On June 30, during celebrations marking the 85th anniversary of the party's founding, Hu reiterated earlier warnings that corruption threatened to undermine its rule. "There are continued cases of leading officials abusing power for private gain, engaging in graft, and bending the law and falling into corruption and dissolution," he declared.

After middle-level officials in several cities were removed on corruption charges, Hu carried out the highest-level purge since 1995. Chen Liangyu, the CCP's top official in Shanghai, was put under house arrest on Sept. 24, 2006. Chen was accused of corruption in the handling of Shanghai's public welfare funds and of illegally helping relatives. Chen had been a close colleague of Jiang Zemin, Hu's predecessor as China's top leader. Some Chinese saw the purge of Chen as part of Hu's continuing process of installing his own supporters in key CCP jobs. By late October, more than 50 others had also been arrested for roles in the scandal.

The Beijing-Lhasa Express crosses a bridge outside the Tibetan capital of Lhasa on July 1, 2006, on its maiden voyage. The new railway—the highest in the world—connects China with the remote Tibet Autonomous Region, which came under Chinese control in 1951.

"Social harmony." The CCP's 350-member Central Committee met in the capital, Beijing, from October 8 to October 11. It adopted Hu's proposal to "build a harmonious socialist society." A quarter-century of emphasizing economic growth had caused China's overall wealth to soar but had produced "many conflicts and problems affecting social harmony," according to an official committee statement. These conflicts included a widening income gap, worsening pollution, and declines in educational and medical systems.

At its annual session in March 2006, the National People's Congress (NPC), a parliament that, in general, automatically approves policies set by the party's Politburo, voted a 15-percent increase in money for agricultural development and services to rural areas. Prime Minister Wen Jiabao noted that bringing rapid and significant change to rural areas was "a major historic task."

Under Wen's influence, the NPC promised increased benefits for rural people. They included ending agricultural taxes; extending experimental health care insurance to 40 percent of counties; and eliminating, by the end of 2007, tuition and other fees for rural students receiving compulsory education. However, the increased spending amounted to only $7 a year per rural person.

Complaints of corruption and abuse of power by local officials had led in recent years to increasing public unrest. During 2006, fewer riots and demonstrations were reported in the tightly controlled media, though it was not clear whether the actual number of incidents had declined. Chinese academics in universities and think tanks became increasingly critical of party policies.

Economy. Since the 1980's, China's economy as a whole had grown about 9 percent a year. In 2006, it grew at a rate of more than 10 percent, creating dangers of inflation. Despite problems looming ahead, China's trade surplus—the excess value of what it sold abroad compared with what it bought—continued to grow, setting a record of $18.8 billion in August.

China's foreign exchange reserves hit $1 trillion in early November. The imbalance increased foreign pressure, particularly from the United States, for China to raise the value of its currency, the yuan. A higher value compared with other countries' currencies would make Chinese exports more expensive and imports cheaper. However, officials allowed only a small value increase.

In 2006, rising pay scales and higher energy costs combined to raise prices of Chinese goods in the world market, and competitiveness with such neighbors as Vietnam and India declined. A shortage of trained workers, despite the massive reservoir of rural people needing jobs, led to higher pay. In July, the booming industrial zone adjacent to Hong Kong raised the mandatory minimum wage by 17 percent to $101 a month. Nonetheless, the region lost workers to higher-paying industrial areas farther north on China's coast. In recent years, more than 100 million Chinese have migrated from farmlands to fill new urban jobs. However, 200 million or more remained underemployed among the approximately 800 million rural people in China's population of 1.3 billion.

Mao. In 2006, increasing criticism of party policies led to renewed questioning of the role of Mao Zedong, who led the CCP to power in 1949 before subjecting China to decades of turmoil marked by famine and internal conflict. The year 2006 marked the 40th anniversary of the start of Mao's Cultural Revolution, which ended with his death in 1976. Scholars estimated that well over 1 million people were killed or driven to suicide by political struggles during the Cultural Revolution. Hundreds of millions of others had their lives shattered, a generation of Chinese missed out on education, and the economy was greatly damaged.

As part of the CCP's attempt to dissociate itself with the negative impact of the Cultural Revolution, the anniversary passed without official notice. Mao's image remained prominent throughout the nation as a unifying symbol, but schoolchildren were no longer saturated with praise of him. In 2006, some new textbooks scarcely mentioned him or the collectivist policies that he imposed on a nation with a long tradition of small farms.

Although Communist ideology seemed to be fading away, the CCP continued to argue that one-party rule was best for China.

Censorship. Authorities in 2006 also intensified efforts to bury current conditions that they thought might show CCP rule in a bad light. Many publications that exposed corruption and other sensitive subjects were forced to close, and authorities dismissed editors and jailed reporters. The party's propaganda department had always issued instructions on what could and could not be published, but rules were tightened in 2006. In addition to banning news of corruption and abuses of power, the rules dictated keeping information on industrial accidents, many social issues, and natural disasters from the public.

In February, some former senior CCP officials complained publicly after the forced closure of a prominent newspaper. The officials criticized the act, claiming that it violated China's constitutional guarantee of free speech. However, rules were tightened on the media and on access to the Internet to prevent the spread of what officials called "harmful information." Officials increased the monitoring of computer Web discussions, search engines, and instant messages to block politically sensitive subjects. Officials imposed stricter limits on the distribution of news by foreign agencies and sources of economic data.

Visitors watch the demolition of a temporary cofferdam at China's Three Gorges Dam, the largest construction project in the world, on the Yangtze River on June 6, 2006. The main wall of the dam was completed in May.

Authorities also cracked down on Chinese lawyers and civic activists who tried to assist people claim constitutional rights, correct social problems, and resist abuses of power. Chen Guangcheng, a blind peasant who advocated peasants' rights, was sentenced to more than four years in prison in August. State-run media were banned from reporting on his trial. On October 31, however, a court threw out Chen's verdict, claiming he had not received a fair trial, and he was granted a retrial.

Independent churches that operated without official authorization had grown rapidly in recent years. In 2006, the government moved forcefully to repress this challenge to state-appointed religious leaders. A Christian advocacy group based in the United States estimated in 2006 that the Chinese government had arrested some 1,958 pastors between mid-2005 and mid-2006. Muslims and Tibetan Buddhists also came under pressure from government officials.

On August 25, Roman Catholic Bishop An Shuxin was released after more than 10 years in prison. However, a Catholic organization announced that dozens of other bishops and priests remained in jail. The Vatican estimated that underground congregations in China had 10 million members, and the state organization had only 4 million. In China, underground Roman Catholic churches stood in opposition to the state-sanctioned Catholic church, which does not recognize the authority of the pope.

Railroads. Minister for Railways Liu Zhijun announced in March plans to build more than 3,300 miles (5,400 kilometers) of high-speed rail lines by the year 2010. One line would link two main cities: China's capital, Beijing, and its economic center, Shanghai. Other plans called for building and refurbishing railroads to ease bottlenecks in the transportation system.

The first railroad into Tibet opened on July 1, 2006. The 710-mile (1,140-kilometer) line from Qinghai province to Lhasa, Tibet's capital, crossed mountain passes more than 16,000 feet (5,000 meters) high, making it the world's highest railroad.

Surveillance. After a lengthy debate, Hong Kong's Legislative Assembly passed legislation on August 6 authorizing police to conduct covert surveillance for the sake of public security. Pro-democracy legislators walked out of the Assembly during the debate, after pro-Beijing legislators blocked a provision to ban political surveillance.

Typhoons. Saomai, the strongest typhoon to hit China in 50 years, struck the southeast coast on August 10 with winds as high as 135 miles (216 kilometers) per hour. The typhoon killed at least 435 people and forced more than 1.5 million others to relocate. Two typhoons in July killed more than 600 others. ■ Henry S. Bradsher

See also **Asia; Disasters.**

City. More than 200 United States mayors gathered in Las Vegas, Nevada, from June 2 to June 6, 2006, for the 74th annual meeting of the United States Conference of Mayors (USCM). The Washington, D.C.-based USCM is a *nonpartisan* (politically unaffiliated) organization made up of mayors of cities with populations of at least 30,000. Among the topics addressed by the municipal leaders were immigration reform, homelessness, homeland security, and the use of *fossil fuels* (oil, natural gas, and coal).

Immigration reform. One resolution passed at the USCM meeting urged U.S. President George W. Bush and the U.S. Congress to pass comprehensive reforms of immigration policies, including instituting a "guest worker" program. Such a program would encourage illegal immigrants to legally register for temporary work. President Bush repeatedly called on Congress to pass such a program in 2006, but no such plan was approved.

Border security was a major issue in many Southwestern States in 2006. In May, President Bush announced plans to deploy 6,000 National Guard troops to assist the U.S. Border Patrol in securing the border. The government also made funds available for improved fencing and other security enhancements along the border.

In a related issue at the USCM meeting, Sam Lagrone, the mayor of Roswell, New Mexico, called for more action by the Border Patrol to stop the flow of such illegal drugs as *methamphetamine* across the border. Methamphetamine is an addictive stimulant that can lead to depression, anxiety, and cardiovascular problems.

Homelessness. Philip Mangano, executive director of the U.S. Interagency Council on Homelessness, told mayors at the USCM meeting that U.S. cities had "turned the corner" on poverty. He noted decreases in the number of chronically homeless people in many cities, including New York City and San Francisco. The Interagency Council on Homelessness, consisting of several federal agencies, is charged with providing leadership to assist homeless people.

Several mayors expressed frustration with federal policies on homelessness. Mayor Mark Begich of Anchorage, Alaska, asked Mangano to urge the U.S. Department of Housing and Urban Development (HUD) to broaden the definition of "chronically homeless" so that federal funds designated for such people could help more families.

Homeland security. Many mayors at the USCM meeting expressed concerns about cuts in federal homeland security grants to certain cities. Mayor Gavin Newsom of San Francisco—which had $5 million in federal money cut from its homeland security funding—noted that the cuts could lead to job losses in the affected cities and could force cities to find alternative sources of funding.

50 LARGEST CITIES IN THE UNITED STATES

Rank	City	Population*
1.	New York, NY	8,121,745
2.	Los Angeles, CA	3,852,273
3.	Chicago, IL	2,824,119
4.	Houston, TX	2,022,060
5.	Phoenix, AZ	1,507,426
6.	Philadelphia, PA	1,455,350
7.	San Antonio, TX	1,278,300
8.	San Diego, CA	1,247,318
9.	Dallas, TX	1,218,842
10.	San Jose, CA	922,005
11.	Detroit, MI	874,392
12.	Jacksonville, FL	789,197
13.	Indianapolis, IN	785,583
14.	San Francisco, CA	735,678
15.	Columbus, OH	732,411
16.	Austin, TX	699,889
17.	Memphis, TN	671,035
18.	Fort Worth, TX	645,798
19.	Baltimore, MD	629,745
20.	Charlotte, NC	623,963
21.	El Paso, TX	605,511
22.	Seattle, WA	576,473
23.	Milwaukee, WI	574,661
24.	Denver, CO	559,850
25.	Louisville, KY	557,494
26.	Las Vegas, NV	556,000
27.	Nashville, TN	552,016
28.	Boston, MA	550,539
29.	Washington, DC	546,828
30.	Oklahoma City, OK	535,989
31.	Portland, OR	533,967
32.	Tucson, AZ	519,333
33.	Albuquerque, NM	504,851
34.	Atlanta, GA	475,810
35.	Long Beach, CA	472,281
36.	Fresno, CA	465,106
37.	Sacramento, CA	458,892
38.	New Orleans, LA	448,696
39.	Mesa, AZ	448,491
40.	Cleveland, OH	446,411
41.	Kansas City, MO	445,732
42.	Virginia Beach, VA	437,607
43.	Omaha, NE	420,097
44.	Miami, FL	394,339
45.	Oakland, CA	393,441
46.	Tulsa, OK	381,536
47.	Honolulu, HI	378,051
48.	Minneapolis, MN	371,916
49.	Colorado Springs, CO	370,317
50.	Arlington, TX	366,447

*2006 World Book estimates based on data from the U.S. Census Bureau.

50 LARGEST METROPOLITAN AREAS IN THE UNITED STATES

Rank	Metropolitan area*	Population†
1.	New York–Northern New Jersey–Long Island, NY-NJ	18,826,595
2.	Los Angeles–Long Beach–Santa Ana, CA	13,032,018
3.	Chicago–Naperville–Joliet, IL-IN-WI	9,510,380
4.	Dallas–Fort Worth–Arlington, TX	5,959,033
5.	Philadelphia–Camden–Wilmington, PA-NJ-DE-MD	5,849,749
6.	Miami–Fort Lauderdale–Miami Beach, FL	5,507,045
7.	Houston–Sugar Land–Baytown, TX	5,400,047
8.	Washington–Arlington–Alexandria, DC-VA-MD-WV	5,299,745
9.	Atlanta–Sandy Springs–Marietta, GA	5,063,838
10.	Detroit–Warren–Livonia, MI	4,494,367
11.	Boston–Cambridge–Quincy, MA-NH	4,413,902
12.	San Francisco–Oakland–Fremont, CA	4,155,864
13.	Riverside–San Bernardino–Ontario, CA	4,060,412
14.	Phoenix–Mesa–Scottsdale, AZ	4,003,528
15.	Seattle–Tacoma–Bellevue, WA	3,235,058
16.	Minneapolis–St. Paul–Bloomington, MN-WI	3,176,862
17.	San Diego–Carlsbad–San Marcos, CA	2,956,076
18.	St. Louis, MO–IL	2,794,290
19.	Tampa–St. Petersburg–Clearwater, FL	2,701,261
20.	Baltimore–Towson, MD	2,676,086
21.	Denver–Aurora, CO	2,395,842
22.	Pittsburgh, PA	2,377,590
23.	Portland–Vancouver–Beaverton, OR-WA	2,130,467
24.	Cleveland–Elyria–Mentor, OH	2,121,994
25.	Sacramento–Arden-Arcade–Roseville, CA	2,095,078
26.	Cincinnati–Middletown, OH-KY-IN	2,081,943
27.	Orlando–Kissimmee, FL	1,997,884
28.	Kansas City, MO-KS	1,969,858
29.	San Antonio, TX	1,927,250
30.	Las Vegas–Paradise, NV	1,788,481
31.	San Jose–Sunnyvale–Santa Clara, CA	1,757,989
32.	Columbus, OH	1,727,563
33.	Indianapolis–Carmel, IN	1,664,089
34.	Virginia Beach–Norfolk–Newport News, VA-NC	1,661,356
35.	Providence–New Bedford–Fall River, RI-MA	1,629,811
36.	Charlotte–Gastonia–Concord, NC–SC	1,562,464
37.	Milwaukee–Waukesha–West Allis, WI	1,514,980
38.	Austin–Round Rock, TX	1,495,725
39.	Nashville–Davidson–Murfreesboro, TN	1,445,285
40.	New Orleans–Metairie–Kenner, LA	1,320,095
41.	Jacksonville, FL	1,275,457
42.	Memphis, TN-MS-AR	1,271,877
43.	Louisville–Jefferson County, KY–IN	1,217,437
44.	Hartford–West Hartford–East Hartford, CT	1,195,916
45.	Richmond, VA	1,191,805
46.	Oklahoma City, OK	1,169,256
47.	Buffalo–Niagara Falls, NY	1,143,545
48.	Birmingham–Hoover, AL	1,097,729
49.	Salt Lake City, UT	1,047,717
50.	Rochester, NY	1,039,141

*The U.S. Census Bureau defines a metropolitan area as a large population nucleus with adjacent communities having a high degree of economic and social integration.

†2006 World Book estimates based on data from the U.S. Census Bureau.

50 LARGEST URBAN CENTERS IN THE WORLD

Rank	Urban center*	Population
1.	Tokyo, Japan	35,250,000
2.	Mexico City, Mexico	19,658,000
3.	New York City, U.S.	18,849,000
4.	São Paulo, Brazil	18,575,000
5.	Mumbai, India	18,547,000
6.	Delhi, India	15,412,000
7.	Shanghai, China	14,750,000
8.	Kolkata, India	14,521,000
9.	Jakarta, Indonesia	13,586,000
10.	Dhaka, Bangladesh	12,834,000
11.	Buenos Aires, Argentina	12,652,000
12.	Los Angeles, U.S.	12,384,000
13.	Karachi, Pakistan	11,916,000
14.	Rio de Janeiro, Brazil	11,605,000
15.	Lagos, Nigeria	11,389,000
16.	Cairo, Egypt	11,304,000
17.	Osaka, Japan	11,276,000
18.	Beijing, China	10,913,000
19.	Manila, Philippines	10,898,000
20.	Moscow, Russia	10,716,000
21.	Istanbul, Turkey	9,872,000
22.	Paris, France	9,827,000
23.	Seoul, South Korea	9,627,000
24.	Chicago, U.S.	8,887,000
25.	Guangzhou, China	8,618,000
26.	London, U.K.	8,525,000
27.	Bogotá, Colombia	7,876,000
28.	Tehran, Iran	7,409,000
29.	Shenzhen, China	7,399,000
30.	Lima, Peru	7,265,000
31.	Wuhan, China	7,180,000
32.	Tianjin, China	7,123,000
33.	Hong Kong, China	7,114,000
34.	Chennai, India	7,036,000
35.	Taipei, Taiwan	6,774,000
36.	Bangkok, Thailand	6,665,000
37.	Bangalore, India	6,605,000
38.	Lahore, Pakistan	6,459,000
39.	Chongqing, China	6,427,000
40.	Kinshasa, Congo	6,313,000
41.	Hyderabad, India	6,235,000
42.	Baghdad, Iraq	6,034,000
43.	Santiago, Chile	5,741,000
44.	Madrid, Spain	5,680,000
45.	Miami, U.S.	5,493,000
46.	Philadelphia, U.S.	5,436,000
47.	Belo Horizonte, Brazil	5,424,000
48.	Toronto, Canada	5,394,000
49.	St. Petersburg, Russia	5,323,000
50.	Ahmadabad, India	5,233,000

Source: 2006 estimates based on data from the United Nations and other official government sources.

*The United Nations defines an urban center as a city surrounded by a continuous built-up area having a high population density.

Green buildings. At its Las Vegas meeting, the USCM endorsed a call by the American Institute of Architects (AIA) to reduce the amount of fossil fuels used to operate city buildings. Many scientists have blamed the burning of fossil fuels for a build-up of atmospheric carbon dioxide and other *greenhouse gases* (gases that trap heat near Earth's surface, contributing to global warming).

A resolution passed by the USCM set a goal of zero use of fossil fuels by new buildings by 2030. This goal could be achieved, according to the resolution's supporters, by new building designs that incorporate elements of natural heating, cooling, and ventilation, as well as by using more energy-efficient building materials.

Mayors honored. The USCM honored two mayors at its meeting with awards for helping make their cities more "livable." Chicago Mayor Richard M. Daley was acknowledged for the Chicago Bicycle Program, which established 100 miles (160 kilometers) of bike lanes on streets and 50 miles (80 kilometers) of off-street bike trails throughout the city. Mary Lib Saleh, mayor of Euless, Texas, was recognized for the creation of a *garbage-composting* program, which used a state grant to give away compost bins, thermometers, and worms to city residents. In composting, microbes, worms, and other organisms *decompose* (break down) wastes into substances that can be used to fertilize soil.

Disaster preparedness. In July 2006, the USCM reported the results of a survey of municipal leaders from 183 cities regarding preparedness for terrorist attacks and natural disasters. The results were announced as the United States approached the fifth anniversary of the terrorist attacks of Sept. 11, 2001, and the first anniversary of the devastation caused by Hurricane Katrina along the Gulf Coast in August 2005.

According to the survey, 80 percent of municipal leaders said their cities had not received sufficient federal resources to upgrade the communications capabilities that would be needed in the event of a disaster. When asked how much each city's level of disaster preparedness had improved since the terrorist attacks of 2001, the average response—with 1 being the lowest and 10 being the highest—was 6.3. When asked about the level of confidence that the Federal Emergency Management Agency would respond quickly to a major disaster, the average response was 5.2.

Fifty-six percent of the respondents said their cities had recently created or updated evacuation plans. However, 72 percent said their city had no plans in place to use personnel or equipment from nearby military bases to help stabilize the city during emergencies.

The USCM noted that the survey results indicated that much more needed to be done at every

A mountain of debris remains at a New Orleans, Louisiana, waste collection point in August 2006, a full year after Hurricane Katrina devastated the city. Experts believed that more needed to be done at all levels of government to better prepare cities for natural disasters and to speed their recovery in the wake of such catastrophes.

level of government to ensure that cities could meet the challenges of homeland security and emergency response.

The State of America's Cities, an annual survey of U.S. municipal officials, was released in March 2006 by the National League of Cities, a Washington, D.C.-based organization representing cities throughout the country. According to the survey, which included responses from 511 officials, 43 percent of the municipal leaders believed that the fiscal conditions of their cities had improved during the past year—an increase from 32 percent who expressed a similar opinion in the 2005 survey.

Respondents expressed concerns in several areas, including health care costs, traffic congestion, and affordable housing. More than half the respondents said that the cost and availability of health services had worsened over the past year. Nearly three-quarters of the officials reported that health care was a major or moderate problem. Officials identified traffic congestion as the problem that had deteriorated the most in their communities during the past five years. Thirty-five percent of the surveyed officials reported that the availability of affordable housing had worsened during the past year.

Population trends. In April 2006, Peter Linneman and Albert Saiz—real estate professors at the Wharton School of the University of Pennsylvania in Philadelphia—presented an analysis of population statistics. Titled *Forecasting 2020 U.S. County and MSA* (metropolitan statistical area) *Populations,* the paper predicted a number of future population trends in the United States.

The authors of the study stated that major population growth is likely to take place in the West, the Sunbelt (the southern rim of the United States, from Virginia to southern California), and along the Interstate 85 corridor between Raleigh, North Carolina, and Atlanta,

Georgia. The report highlighted Clark County, Nevada—which includes Las Vegas—as the region that will experience the greatest population growth in the nation.

The analysis predicted that the largest population drops, or slowdowns in growth, are likely to occur in the Northeast, the Mid-Atlantic, and the Midwest. The report noted that the hardest-hit area will be the city and county of Baltimore, which could lose 100,000 residents—15 percent of its 2000 population—by 2020.

■ Alfred J. Smuskiewicz

See also **Chicago; Disasters; Global warming; Los Angeles; New York City; Terrorism; United States, Government of the: A Special Report.**

Classical music. In October 2006, the Carnival Center for the Performing Arts opened in Miami, Florida. The music complex, which cost $446 million to construct, includes the 2,200-seat John S. and James L. Knight Concert Hall and the 2,400-seat Sanford and Dolores Ziff Ballet Opera House. The Carnival Center was built to host the Concert Association of Florida, the Florida Grand Opera, the Miami City Ballet, and pop, jazz, and world music events. Argentine-born American architect Cesar Pelli designed the complex, and acoustician Russell Johnson of Artec Consultants, Inc. of New York City crafted the hall's acoustics.

Pelli and Johnson also designed the Renee and Henry Segerstrom Concert Hall, which opened in Costa Mesa, California, in September. The building, which cost $200 million, includes two auditoriums: the 2,000-seat Segerstrom venue (home of the Pacific Symphony and Pacific Chorale) and the 500-seat Samueli Theater. The Philharmonic Society of Orange County planned to use both facilities. The concert hall's inaugural concert featured tenor Placido Domingo in the premiere of *Canciones de Lorca,* a song cycle by William Bolcom.

The $120-million Schermerhorn Symphony Center opened in September as the new cultural hub of Nashville, Tennessee. The facility houses the 1,870-seat Laura Turner Concert Hall, home of the Nashville Symphony. Architect David M. Schwarz of Washington, D.C., and acoustical experts at Akustics, Inc., of Norwalk, Connecticut, designed the center. Leonard Slatkin conducted the inaugural program, which included the premiere of *Triple Concerto for Banjo, Double Bass and Tabla,* composed and performed by soloists Bela Fleck, Edgar Meyer, and Zakir Hussain.

All hail Mozart and Shostakovich. The classical music world celebrated birthday anniversaries of two major composers in 2006—the 250th anniversary of the birth of Austrian composer Wolfgang Amadeus Mozart (1756-1791) and the 100th anniversary of the birth of Russian composer Dmitri Shostakovich (1906-1975). Mozart's birth was marked by a host of performances, publications, recordings, and broadcasts. After two centuries, Mozart's rich body of masterpieces remains the lifeblood of the classical repertory. Shostakovich was also honored with many performances and other commemorations. Shostakovich's creative output represents a musical diary of his difficult life as a Soviet citizen during a turbulent period in Russian history.

Music lessons make better brains. Young children who take music lessons show more advanced brain development, more memory capacity, and greater attention skills than those who do not, according to a Canadian study reported in September 2006. Researchers at McMaster University's Institute for Music and the Mind in Hamilton, Ontario, and the Rotman Research Institute of the University of Toronto compared the brain functions of two groups of children aged 4 to 6 years. The six children in one group took music lessons for one year, while the six children in the other group did not. The researchers measured the electrical activity of the children's brains and gave the children memory tests associated with intelligence skills.

The researchers concluded that studying and playing music improve children's brain function. They recommended that music education be part of the preschool and primary school curriculum.

Oldest Bach manuscripts. An August report described the discovery of the oldest known manuscripts by German composer Johann Sebastian Bach (1685-1750) at the Duchess Anna Amalia Library in Weimar, Germany. The two manuscripts are copies in Bach's hand of chorale fantasias by two other composers—Dietrich Buxtehude and Johann Adam Reinken. The 15-year-old Bach made the copies around 1700.

New operas. *Grendel* had its premiere by the Los Angeles Opera in June 2006. The opera is based on John Gardner's 1971 novel that retells the ancient Anglo-Saxon saga *Beowulf* from the viewpoint of the monster, Grendel. It was the first opera by film composer Elliot Goldenthal. The opera was directed by Julie Taymor, who also cowrote the libretto with poet J. D. McClatchy.

In February 2006, the Indiana University Opera Theater in Bloomington presented the premiere of Ned Rorem's *Our Town,* with a libretto by J. D. McClatchy. The opera is based on the classic play of the same name by Thornton Wilder.

The Glimmerglass Opera in Cooperstown, New York, gave the premiere of Stephen Hartke's *The Greater Good, or The Passion of Boule de Suif,* in July. The libretto, by Philip Littell, is based on a short story by French author Guy de Maupassant about middle-class French citizens during the Franco-Prussian War (1870-1871).

Miss Lonelyhearts, with music by Lowell Liebermann and text by J. D. McClatchy, had its premiere performance in April 2006 by the Juilliard Opera Center in New York City. The opera's plot, based on Nathanael West's 1933 novella, illustrates how the tragedies of people who write to a newspaper advice columnist affect the columnist's life.

New orchestra works. In February 2006, pianist Peter Serkin performed in the premiere of Charles Wuorinen's *Flying to Kahani,* a concert piece for piano and orchestra in New York City. Roberto Abbado conducted the Orchestra of St. Luke's in the work. Pop music icon Billy Joel's piano concerto, *Symphonic Fantasies for Piano and Orchestra,* premiered in June at the Eastern Music Festival in Greensboro, North Carolina. Jeffrey Biegel was the piano soloist.

Two hundred and fifty years after his birth, Wolfgang Amadeus Mozart remains one of the most revered and beloved figures in classical music.

The 250th anniversary of the birth of Austrian composer Wolfgang Amadeus Mozart (left) was commemorated by an entire year of special performances, publications, recordings, and broadcasts of his operas, including *The Marriage of Figaro, Don Giovanni, and The Magic Flute.* On Mozart's birthday, January 27, a visitor lays flowers on the grave of the great composer in Vienna, Austria (below).

In March, the Metropolitan Opera of New York City staged Tchaikovsky's rarely performed *Mazeppa*, an opera based on a poem by Alexander Pushkin. Baritone Nikolai Putilin portrayed the title character, an 18th-century Ukrainian separatist. George Tsypin designed the sets, and Tatiana Noginova created the costumes.

In July, composer John Musto was the soloist in the premiere of his *Piano Concerto* at the Caramoor International Music Festival in Katonah, New York. Michael Barrett conducted the Orchestra of St. Luke's. *Concierto para Mendez* by composer Lee Holdridge and librettist Richard Sparks had its first performance in October by soloists and the Los Angeles Opera Orchestra under Richard Kaufman. The multimedia piece celebrates the life of Hollywood trumpeter, composer, and teacher Rafael Mendez.

Deaths. György Ligeti, a Hungarian composer whose music was among the most innovative of the second half of the 20th century, died in June at age 83. German soprano Dame Elisabeth Schwarzkopf—one of the most beloved singers of opera and German lieder—died in August at age 90. Astrid Varnay, an American soprano who was one of the leading Wagnerian singers of the 1950's, died in September at age 88.

Other notable deaths in 2006 included American mezzo-soprano Lorraine Hunt Lieberson, American soprano Anna Moffo, and Canadian lyric tenor Leopold Simoneau. ■ John von Rhein

See also **Deaths; Popular music.**

Clothing. See Fashion.

Coal. See Energy supply.

GRAMMY AWARD WINNERS IN 2006

Classical Album, *Bolcom: Songs of Innocence and of Experience;* University of Michigan School of Music Symphony Orchestra; Leonard Slatkin, conductor; Jerry Blackstone, William Hammer, Jason Harris, Christopher Kiver, Carole Ott, Mary Alice Stollak, choir directors; Tim Handley, producer.

Orchestral Performance, *Shostakovich: Symphony No. 13;* Symphonieorchester und Chor des Bayerischen Rundfunks; Mariss Jansons, conductor.

Opera Recording, *Verdi: Falstaff;* London Symphony Chorus and Orchestra; Sir Colin Davis, conductor; Carlos Alvarez, Bülent Bezdüz, Marina Domashenko, Jane Henschel, Ana Ibarra, Maria José Moreno, Michele Pertusi, soloists; James Mallison, producer.

Choral Performance, *Bolcom: Songs of Innocence and of Experience;* University of Michigan School of Music Symphony Orchestra; Leonard Slatkin, conductor; Jerry Blackstone, William Hammer, Jason Harris, Christopher Kiver, Carole Ott, Mary Alice Stollak, choir directors.

Instrumental Soloist with Orchestra, *Beethoven: Piano Concertos Nos. 2 & 3;* Mahler Chamber Orchestra; Claudio Abbado, conductor; Martha Argerich, piano.

Instrumental Soloist without Orchestra, *Scriabin, Medtner, Stravinsky;* Evgeny Kissin, piano.

Chamber Music Performance, *Mendelssohn: The Complete String Quartets;* Emerson String Quartet.

Small Ensemble Performance, *Boulez: Le Marteau Sans Maître, Dérive 1 & 2;* Ensemble Intercontemporain; Pierre Boulez, conductor.

Classical Vocal Performance, *Bach: Cantatas;* Thomas Quasthoff, bass-baritone.

Classical Contemporary Composition, *Bolcom: Songs of Innocence and of Experience;* William Bolcom, composer.

Classical Crossover Album, *4 + Four;* Turtle Island String Quartet and Ying Quartet.

Colombia. President Alvaro Uribe Vélez took the presidential oath of office for a second four-year term on Aug. 7, 2006. Uribe won reelection in a landslide victory on May 28. In March, political allies of the popular president won substantial majorities in congressional elections.

Under Uribe's leadership, the Colombian government continued to prosecute a decades-long civil war against guerrilla fighters belonging to the Revolutionary Armed Forces of Colombia (FARC). The leftist group controlled large parts of rural Colombia and funded their operations through drug trafficking. Colombia is the world's largest producer of coca, the plant from which the illegal drug cocaine is derived.

Embarking upon his second term, President Uribe pledged to continue the hard-line policies that observers credited with having restored law and order to Colombia's cities. Uribe also promised to continue demobilizing right-wing paramilitary forces that had long engaged in independent warfare against FARC. However, the president suffered a political setback in November, when four of his allies in Congress were arrested on charges of having conspired with right-wing paramilitary groups to assassinate dissidents and rig polling in some election districts of northern Colombia.

Stagnant war on drugs. According to figures released by the United States State Department in August 2006, Colombia was making little or no progress in eradicating the illicit production of coca. The Colombian and U.S. governments had in 2000 jointly launched a $4.7-billion initiative called "Plan Colombia," funded largely by the United States, to attack drug trafficking at its source: cultivation of the coca plant. Despite a massive program of aerial spraying to destroy coca crops, Colombia produced as much coca in 2006 as it had in 2000. According to observers familiar with FARC-controlled areas, the coca growers were adapting to eradication tactics by practicing more intensive cultivation on small fields in remote, forested locales.

Dangers to trade unionists. A report released on June 15, 2006, by the Solidarity Center of the American Federation of Labor-Congress of Industrial Organizations (AFL-CIO) claimed that as many as 4,000 labor union leaders and activists had been murdered since the mid-1980's in Colombia. The report also stated that Colombian authorities had investigated fewer than 400 of the homicides and secured only five convictions of the perpetrators.   ■ Nathan A. Haverstock

See also **Latin America**.

Commonwealth of Independent States. See Asia; Azerbaijan; Belarus; Georgia; Kazakhstan; Russia; Ukraine.

Comoros. See Africa.

Computer. In 2006, Apple Computer, Inc., of Cupertino, California, began putting microprocessors made by Intel Corporation of Santa Clara, California, in all new Macintosh computers. This key change in the "brains" of the Mac had startled many in the industry when Apple announced the move in 2005. Previous Mac models contained PowerPC microprocessors, originally developed in the early 1990's to challenge the dominance of Intel computer chips. The PowerPC chip was a joint creation of Apple; International Business Machines Corporation (IBM) of Armonk, New York; and Motorola, Inc., of Schaumburg, Illinois.

Apple executives said they made the switch in part to help Apple gain ground in personal computer sales, because Intel-based Macs could run a wider range of software—including the popular Windows operating system made by Microsoft Corporation of Redmond, Washington.

Burning batteries. In 2006, computer and electronics companies recalled nearly 10 million lithium-ion batteries used in portable computers after reports of overheating, fires, and explosions. The batteries had been made by Sony Corporation of Tokyo. In June, images of burning computers began appearing on the Internet. In August, Dell Inc. of Round Rock, Texas, recalled 4.1 million Sony batteries used with Dell notebook computers. Days later, Apple recalled 1.8 million batteries. Other firms soon followed suit. The recalls cost Sony about $250 million.

Stolen computers. Concerns about identity theft remained high in 2006, partly because of a rash of high-profile thefts of government and corporate computers containing sensitive data. Identity theft involves using another individual's personal information—such as a Social Security number or credit card number—to commit fraud.

The most notable data breach occurred in May, when a United States Department of Veterans Affairs (VA) laptop computer and external hard drive were stolen from a VA employee's residence. The equipment contained the personal records of over 28 million military veterans and active-duty personnel. The VA recovered the equipment in June, and police said there was no indication that the data had been used to create false identities.

Computing with light. Advances were made in 2006 in the field of *silicon photonics,* which seeks to integrate laser light technology into silicon computer chips. Researchers at Intel and the University of California, Santa Barbara, developed a hybrid chip that used indium phosphide to emit light and silicon to contain and route it. Light signals can transmit data much faster than the electrical signals in electronic chips.   ■ Keith Ferrell

See also **Electronics; Internet**.

Congo (Brazzaville). See Africa.

Congo (Kinshasa). In 2006, a series of democratic elections in the Democratic Republic of the Congo (DRC) signaled a new political beginning for Africa's fourth largest country and its 60 million people. Not since 1965 had Congo (Kinshasa) held free, multiparty elections. In the interim, the country had been ravaged by dictatorship and a brutal civil war (1998–2002). These events had wrecked the country's infrastructure and left social turmoil and widespread poverty in their wake.

On Oct. 29, 2006, Joseph Kabila won election as president of the DRC in a runoff, besting rival Jean-Pierre Bemba. Kabila was serving as president of the country's power-sharing interim government, and Bemba was serving as one of the four interim vice presidents. These arrangements had been prescribed by a 2003 peace accord negotiated under the auspices of South Africa President Thabo Mbeki to end the civil war.

The first round of the 2006 presidential voting took place in July. At that time, Congolese voters also elected a new parliament, resulting in a majority of legislators backing Kabila.

Referring to the October 29 polling, the United Nations Security Council in November praised the Congolese people for conducting a generally orderly election under the rule of law. In the October round of voting, 70 percent of eligible voters cast their ballots under the watchful eyes of more than 2,000 election monitors sponsored by the European Union (EU), observers from the Atlanta, Georgia-based Carter Center, and thousands of Congolese pollwatchers.

Ominous violence. On August 20, open warfare broke out in Kinshasa, the capital, between an armed militia loyal to Vice President Bemba and forces loyal to President Kabila. The fighting took place near television stations supporting Bemba's candidacy for the presidency and outside Bemba's residences and office in the city. Intensive diplomatic efforts by South African President Mbeki and other regional leaders brought an end to the fighting on August 22, but only after 23 people had been killed and 43 others wounded.

Analysts said that tensions over the results of the first presidential round of voting on July 30 had led to the violence. Kabila had expected to win that poll outright but fell short of the 50-percent threshold of votes necessary for victory.

In September, President Kabila and Vice President Bemba signed an agreement to demilitarize the capital. International observers continued to warn of the corrosive effect of armed militias on democratic development, noting that a number of such militias remained active in Congo (Kinshasa) in late 2006. ■ Pieter Esterhuysen

See also **Africa; Conservation; South Africa.**

Congress of the United States. Republican lawmakers endured a number of setbacks in 2006 that contributed to a stunning Democratic take-over of both houses of Congress in the November elections. Political scandals dogged a number of Republican legislators during the year, and the low approval ratings of Republican U.S. President George W. Bush contributed to the party's woes. One key bill that Congress passed in 2006 set guidelines for the trial and treatment of terrorism suspects.

Elections. On November 7, voters switched both the House of Representatives and the Senate from Republican to Democratic control. In the 435-member House, Democrats won 233 seats compared with the Republicans' 202. In the 100-member Senate, Democrats and Republicans emerged with 49 seats apiece. Two independents won seats and planned to caucus with the Democrats. (Two years earlier, Republicans had won a 232-202-1 advantage in the House and a 55-44-1 advantage in the Senate.)

According to many political analysts, the election results were an expression of voter dissatisfaction with the war in Iraq—which the Bush administration had begun in 2003 and which became increasingly violent in 2006—and with congressional corruption scandals. Democrats retained all seats they already held and picked up 6 Senate and 31 House seats. The third-ranking Senate Republican, Rick Santorum of Pennsylvania, lost his seat, as did Republican senators from Missouri, Montana, Ohio, Rhode Island, and Virginia. In the House, 22 Republican incumbents lost.

After the elections, Democrats chose Nancy Pelosi (D., California) to become the speaker of the House at the start of the 110th Congress in January 2007. She is the first woman speaker in U.S. history. Democrats chose Steny Hoyer (D., Maryland) to be the House majority leader. Republicans chose John Boehner (R., Ohio) to become minority leader after outgoing House Speaker Dennis Hastert (R., Illinois) opted not to run for the job. Senate Democrats selected Harry Reid (D., Nevada) as majority leader, and Senate Republicans picked Mitch McConnell (R., Kentucky) as minority leader.

On Dec. 13, 2006, Senator Tim Johnson (D., South Dakota) had emergency surgery after suffering a brain hemorrhage. He remained hospitalized at year's end. His condition threatened to swing the Senate back to Republican control. If he died or was forced to resign, South Dakota's Republican governor, Mike Rounds, was likely to appoint a Republican to finish the term, creating a 50-50 split in which Republican Vice President Dick Cheney would cast tie-breaking votes.

Detainees. In September, Congress passed the Military Commissions Act of 2006, which

House approved the bill 250-170 the next day, and President Bush signed the bill on October 17.

The act required a military commission to consist of at least five active-duty military officers. A suspect on trial by a military commission was to be presumed innocent, with guilt needing to be established beyond a reasonable doubt. The suspect was to be provided with defense counsel and could not be forced to testify against himself. He could present evidence and witnesses in his defense and cross-examine witnesses against him. The act provided a route of appeal in civilian courts for either a conviction or an acquittal. However, a commission could convict a defendant with only a two-thirds vote, as opposed to the unanimity required in civilian trials. The defendant was to be banned from seeing any evidence containing classified information. Also, certain kinds of evidence normally prohibited in civilian trials was to be allowed—including hearsay evidence and evidence obtained by coercion before Dec. 30, 2005. (On that date, the Detainee Treatment Act, outlawing "cruel, inhuman, or degrading treatment," went into force.)

The act did not prohibit the president from holding many detainees indefinitely without charge. In 2006, hundreds of foreign detainees designated as "unlawful enemy combatants" were being held at a military prison camp at Guantánamo Bay, Cuba, and most of them were neither scheduled for release nor expected to be charged and tried. Under the act, a detainee could get a court review of his "unlawful enemy combatant" status. However, a detainee could not submit a petition of *habeas corpus* in federal court. Such a petition would allow a detainee to have a court decide whether he was being wrongfully detained or mistreated. (A Senate amendment to strike the habeas corpus ban from the bill was narrowly defeated.)

The act also addressed the treatment of detainees during interrogations. It classified a number of specific interrogation methods as war

established interrogation guidelines and trial procedures for people detained in the U.S. "war on terror." The act legalized special military commissions for trying foreign terrorism suspects designated by the United States as "unlawful enemy combatants" and accused of war crimes. The commissions were designed to provide some but not all of the legal rights that would normally be provided in a regular civilian or military court.

President Bush had authorized special tribunals for terrorism suspects shortly after the Sept. 11, 2001, terrorist attacks against the United States. However, on June 29, 2006, the U.S. Supreme Court ruled in *Hamdan v. Rumsfeld* that the tribunals were unauthorized by U.S. law and violated the international treaties known as the Geneva Conventions, which govern the treatment of wartime prisoners. In response to the ruling, Bush asked Congress to pass legislation authorizing special tribunals. The Senate approved a compromise bill by a 65-34 vote on September 28. The

MEMBERS OF THE UNITED STATES HOUSE OF REPRESENTATIVES

The House of Representatives of the first session of the 110th Congress consisted of 233 Democrats and 202 Republicans (not including representatives from American Samoa, the District of Columbia, Guam, Puerto Rico, and the Virgin Islands) when it convened on Jan. 4, 2007. This table shows congressional district, legislator, and party affiliation. Asterisk (*) denotes those who served in the 109th Congress; dagger (†) denotes "at large."

Alabama
1. Jo Bonner, R.*
2. Terry Everett, R.*
3. Mike Rogers, R.*
4. Robert Aderholt, R.*
5. Bud Cramer, D.*
6. Spencer Bachus, R.*
7. Artur Davis, D.*

Alaska
†Donald E. Young, R.*

Arizona
1. Rick Renzi, R.*
2. Trent Franks, R.*
3. John Shadegg, R.*
4. Ed Pastor, D.*
5. Harry E. Mitchell, D.
6. Jeff Flake, R.*
7. Raul Grijalva, D.*
8. Gabrielle Giffords, D.

Arkansas
1. Marion Berry, D.*
2. Vic Snyder, D.*
3. John Boozman, R.*
4. Mike Ross, D.*

California
1. Mike Thompson, D.*
2. Wally Herger, R.*
3. Dan Lungren, R.*
4. John Doolittle, R.*
5. Doris O. Matsui, D.*
6. Lynn Woolsey, D.*
7. George E. Miller, D.*
8. Nancy Pelosi, D.*
9. Barbara Lee, D.*
10. Ellen Tauscher, D.*
11. Jerry McNerney, D.
12. Tom Lantos, D.*
13. Pete Stark, D.*
14. Anna Eshoo, D.*
15. Mike Honda, D.*
16. Zoe Lofgren, D.*
17. Sam Farr, D.*
18. Dennis Cardoza, D.*
19. George Radanovich, R.*
20. Jim Costa, D.*
21. Devin Nunes, R.*
22. Kevin McCarthy, R.
23. Lois Capps, D.*
24. Elton Gallegly, R.*
25. Howard McKeon, R.*
26. David Dreier, R.*
27. Brad Sherman, D.*
28. Howard Berman, D.*
29. Adam Schiff, D.*
30. Henry Waxman, D.*
31. Xavier Becerra, D.*
32. Hilda Solis, D.*
33. Diane Watson, D.*
34. Lucille Roybal-Allard, D.*
35. Maxine Waters, D.*

36. Jane Harman, D.*
37. Juanita Millender-McDonald, D.*
38. Grace Napolitano, D.*
39. Linda Sanchez, D.*
40. Ed Royce, R.*
41. Jerry Lewis, R.*
42. Gary Miller, R.*
43. Joe Baca, D.*
44. Ken Calvert, R.*
45. Mary Bono, R.*
46. Dana Rohrabacher, R.*
47. Loretta Sanchez, D.*
48. John Campbell, R.*
49. Darrell Issa, R.*
50. Brian Bilbray, R.*
51. Bob Filner, D.*
52. Duncan Hunter, R.*
53. Susan Davis, D.*

Colorado
1. Diana DeGette, D.*
2. Mark Udall, D.*
3. John Salazar, D.*
4. Marilyn Musgrave, R.*
5. Doug Lamborn, R.
6. Tom Tancredo, R.*
7. Ed Perlmutter, D.

Connecticut
1. John Larson, D.*
2. Joe Courtney, D.
3. Rosa DeLauro, D.*
4. Christopher Shays, R.*
5. Christopher S. Murphy, D.

Delaware
†Michael Castle, R.*

Florida
1. Jeff Miller, R.*
2. Allen Boyd, D.*
3. Corrine Brown, D.*
4. Ander Crenshaw, R.*
5. Virginia Brown-Waite, R.*
6. Clifford B. Stearns, R.*
7. John Mica, R.*
8. Ric Keller, R.*
9. Gus Bilirakis, R.
10. C. W. Bill Young, R.*
11. Kathy Castor, D.
12. Adam Putnam, R.*
13. Vern Buchanan, R.
14. Connie Mack, R.*
15. Dave Weldon, R.*
16. Tim Mahoney, D.
17. Kendrick Meek, D.*
18. Ileana Ros-Lehtinen, R.*
19. Robert Wexler, D.*
20. Debbie Wasserman Schultz, D.*
21. Lincoln Diaz-Balart, R.*
22. Ron Klein, D.
23. Alcee Hastings, D.*
24. Tom Feeney, R.*
25. Mario Diaz-Balart, R.*

Georgia
1. Jack Kingston, R.*
2. Sanford Bishop, Jr., D.*
3. Jim Marshall, D.*
4. Hank Johnson, D.
5. John Lewis, D.*
6. Tom Price, R.*
7. John Linder, R.*
8. Lynn Westmoreland, R.*
9. Charles Norwood, R.*
10. Nathan Deal, R.*
11. Phil Gingrey, R.*
12. John Barrow, D.*
13. David Scott, D.*

Hawaii
1. Neil Abercrombie, D.*
2. Mazie K. Hirono, D.

Idaho
1. Bill Sali, R.
2. Mike Simpson, R.*

Illinois
1. Bobby Rush, D.*
2. Jesse L. Jackson, Jr., D.*
3. Daniel Lipinski, D.*
4. Luis Gutierrez, D.*
5. Rahm Emanuel, D.*
6. Peter J. Roskam, R.
7. Danny Davis, D.*
8. Melissa Bean, D.*
9. Janice Schakowsky, D.*
10. Mark Kirk, R.*
11. Gerald Weller, R.*
12. Jerry F. Costello, D.*
13. Judy Biggert, R.*
14. J. Dennis Hastert, R.*
15. Timothy Johnson, R.*
16. Donald Manzullo, R.*
17. Phil Hare, D.
18. Ray LaHood, R.*
19. John Shimkus, R.*

Indiana
1. Peter J. Visclosky, D.*
2. Joe Donnelly, D.
3. Mark Souder, R.*
4. Steve Buyer, R.*
5. Dan Burton, R.*
6. Mike Pence, R.*
7. Julia Carson, D.*
8. Brad Ellsworth, D.
9. Baron P. Hill, D.

Iowa
1. Bruce Braley, D.
2. David Loebsack, D.
3. Leonard Boswell, D.*
4. Thomas Latham, R.*
5. Steve King, R.*

Kansas
1. Jerry Moran, R.*
2. Nancy E. Boyda, D.

3. Dennis Moore, D.*
4. Todd Tiahrt, R.*

Kentucky
1. Edward Whitfield, R.*
2. Ron Lewis, R.*
3. John A. Yarmuth, D.
4. Geoff Davis, R.*
5. Harold (Hal) Rogers, R.*
6. Ben Chandler, D.*

Louisiana
1. Bobby Jindal, R.*
2. William J. Jefferson, D.*
3. Charles Melancon, D.*
4. Jim McCrery, D.*
5. Rodney Alexander, R.*
6. Richard Hugh Baker, R.*
7. Charles Boustany, Jr., R.*

Maine
1. Thomas Allen, D.*
2. Michael Michaud, D.*

Maryland
1. Wayne T. Gilchrest, R.*
2. C. A. Ruppersberger, D.*
3. John P. Sarbanes, D.
4. Albert Wynn, D.*
5. Steny H. Hoyer, D.*
6. Roscoe Bartlett, R.*
7. Elijah Cummings, D.*
8. Chris Van Hollen, D.*

Massachusetts
1. John W. Olver, D.*
2. Richard E. Neal, D.*
3. James McGovern, D.*
4. Barney Frank, D.*
5. Martin Meehan, D.*
6. John Tierney, D.*
7. Edward J. Markey, D.*
8. Michael Capuano, D.*
9. Stephen F. Lynch, D.*
10. William Delahunt, D.*

Michigan
1. Bart Stupak, D.*
2. Peter Hoekstra, R.*
3. Vernon Ehlers, R.*
4. Dave Camp, R.*
5. Dale Kildee, D.*
6. Frederick S. Upton, R.*
7. Timothy Walberg, R.
8. Mike Rogers, R.*
9. Joseph Knollenberg, R.*
10. Candice Miller, R.*
11. Thaddeus McCotter, R.*
12. Sander M. Levin, D.*
13. Carolyn Kilpatrick, D.*
14. John Conyers, Jr., D.*
15. John Dingell, D.*

Minnesota
1. Timothy J. Walz, D.
2. John Kline, R.*

3. Jim Ramstad, R.*
4. Betty McCollum, D.*
5. Keith Ellison, D.
6. Michele Bachmann, R.
7. Collin C. Peterson, D.*
8. James L. Oberstar, D.*

Mississippi
1. Roger Wicker, R.*
2. Bennie Thompson, D.*
3. Charles Pickering, R.*
4. Gene Taylor, D.*

Missouri
1. William Clay, D.*
2. Todd Akin, R.*
3. Russ Carnahan, D.*
4. Ike Skelton, D.*
5. Emanuel Cleaver II, D.*
6. Samuel Graves, R.*
7. Roy Blunt, R.*
8. Jo Ann Emerson, R.*
9. Kenny Hulshof, R.*

Montana
†Dennis Rehberg, R.*

Nebraska
1. Jeff Fortenberry, R.*
2. Lee Terry, R.*
3. Adrian Smith, R.

Nevada
1. Shelley Berkley, D.*
2. Dean Heller, R.
3. Jon Porter, Sr., R.*

New Hampshire
1. Carol Shea-Porter, D.
2. Paul W. Hodes, D.

New Jersey
1. Robert E. Andrews, D.*
2. Frank LoBiondo, R.*
3. H. James Saxton, R.*
4. Christopher H. Smith, R.*
5. Scott Garrett, R.*
6. Frank Pallone, Jr., D.*
7. Mike Ferguson, R.*
8. William Pascrell, Jr., D.*
9. Steven Rothman, D.*
10. Donald M. Payne, D.*
11. Rodney Frelinghuysen, R.*
12. Rush Holt, D.*
13. Albio Sires, D.*

New Mexico
1. Heather Wilson, R.*
2. Steve Pearce, R.*
3. Thomas Udall, D.*

New York
1. Tim Bishop, D.*
2. Steve Israel, D.*
3. Peter King, R.*
4. Carolyn McCarthy, D.*
5. Gary L. Ackerman, D.*
6. Gregory Meeks, D.*
7. Joseph Crowley, D.*
8. Jerrold Nadler, D.*
9. Anthony Weiner, D.*
10. Edolphus Towns, D.*
11. Yvette D. Clarke, D.

12. Nydia Velazquez, D.*
13. Vito J. Fossella, R.*
14. Carolyn Maloney, D.*
15. Charles B. Rangel, D.*
16. Jose E. Serrano, D.*
17. Eliot L. Engel, D.*
18. Nita M. Lowey, D.*
19. John J. Hall, D.
20. Kirsten E. Gillibrand, D.
21. Michael R. McNulty, D.*
22. Maurice Hinchey, D.*
23. John McHugh, R.*
24. Michael Arcuri, D.
25. James Walsh, R.*
26. Thomas Reynolds, R.*
27. Brian Higgins, D.*
28. Louise M. Slaughter, D.*
29. Randy Kuhl, R.*

North Carolina
1. G. K. Butterfield, D.*
2. Bob Etheridge, D.*
3. Walter Jones, Jr., R.*
4. David Price, D.*
5. Virginia Foxx, R.*
6. Howard Coble, R.*
7. Mike McIntyre, D.*
8. Robin Hayes, R.*
9. Sue Myrick, R.*
10. Patrick McHenry, R.*
11. Heath Shuler, D.
12. Melvin Watt, D.*
13. Brad Miller, D.*

North Dakota
†Earl Pomeroy, D.*

Ohio
1. Steve Chabot, R.*
2. Jean Schmidt, R.*
3. Michael Turner, R.*
4. Jim Jordan, R.
5. Paul E. Gillmor, R.*
6. Charles A. Wilson, D.
7. David L. Hobson, R.*
8. John A. Boehner, R.*
9. Marcy Kaptur, D.*
10. Dennis Kucinich, D.*
11. Stephanie Tubbs Jones, D.*
12. Pat Tiberi, R.*
13. Betty Sutton, D.
14. Steven LaTourette, R.*
15. Deborah Pryce, R.*
16. Ralph Regula, R.*
17. Timothy Ryan, D.*
18. Zachary T. Space, D.

Oklahoma
1. John Sullivan, R.*
2. Dan Boren, D.*
3. Frank Lucas, R.*
4. Tom Cole, R.*
5. Mary Fallin, R.

Oregon
1. David Wu, D.*
2. Greg Walden, R.*
3. Earl Blumenauer, D.*
4. Peter A. DeFazio, D.*
5. Darlene Hooley, D.*

Pennsylvania
1. Robert Brady, D.*
2. Chaka Fattah, D.*
3. Philip English, R.*
4. Jason Altmire, D.
5. John Peterson, R.*
6. Jim Gerlach, R.*
7. Joe Sestak, D.
8. Patrick J. Murphy, D.
9. Bill Shuster, R.*
10. Christopher P. Carney, D.
11. Paul E. Kanjorski, D.*
12. John P. Murtha, D.*
13. Allyson Schwartz, D.*
14. Michael Doyle, D.*
15. Charles Dent, R.*
16. Joseph Pitts, R.*
17. Tim Holden, D.*
18. Tim Murphy, R.*
19. Todd Platts, R.*

Rhode Island
1. Patrick Kennedy, D.*
2. James Langevin, D.*

South Carolina
1. Henry Brown, Jr., R.*
2. Joe Wilson, R.*
3. J. Gresham Barrett, R.*
4. Bob Inglis, R.*
5. John M. Spratt, Jr., D.*
6. James Clyburn, D.*

South Dakota
†Stephanie Herseth, D.*

Tennessee
1. David Davis, R.
2. John J. Duncan, Jr., R.*
3. Zach Wamp, R.*
4. Lincoln Davis, D.*
5. Jim Cooper, D.*
6. Bart Gordon, D.*
7. Marsha Blackburn, R.*
8. John S. Tanner, D.*
9. Steve Cohen, D.

Texas
1. Louis Gohmert, R.*
2. Ted Poe, R.*
3. Sam Johnson, R.*
4. Ralph M. Hall, R.*
5. Jeb Hensarling, R.*
6. Joe Barton, R.*
7. John Culberson, R.*
8. Kevin Brady, R.*
9. Al Green, D.*
10. Michael McCaul, R.*
11. Mike Conaway, R.*
12. Kay Granger, R.*
13. Mac Thornberry, R.*
14. Ron Paul, R.*
15. Ruben Hinojosa, D.*
16. Silvestre Reyes, D.*
17. Chet Edwards, D.*
18. Sheila Jackson Lee, D.*
19. Randy Neugebauer, R.*
20. Charlie Gonzalez, D.*
21. Lamar S. Smith, R.*
22. Nick Lampson, D.
23. Ciro Rodriguez, D.

24. Kenny Marchant, R.*
25. Lloyd Doggett, D.*
26. Michael Burgess, R.*
27. Solomon P. Ortiz, D.*
28. Henry Cuellar, D.*
29. Gene Green, D.*
30. Eddie Bernice Johnson, D.*
31. John Carter, R.*
32. Pete Sessions, R.*

Utah
1. Rob Bishop, R.*
2. Jim Matheson, D.*
3. Christopher Cannon, R.*

Vermont
†Peter Welch, D.

Virginia
1. Jo Ann Davis, R.*
2. Thelma Drake, R.*
3. Robert Scott, D.*
4. J. Randy Forbes, R.*
5. Virgil Goode, Jr., R.*
6. Robert Goodlatte, R.*
7. Eric Cantor, R.*
8. James P. Moran, Jr., D.*
9. Rick C. Boucher, D.*
10. Frank R. Wolf, R.*
11. Tom Davis, R.*

Washington
1. Jay Inslee, D.*
2. Rick Larsen, D.*
3. Brian Baird, D.*
4. Doc Hastings, R.*
5. Cathy McMorris, R.*
6. Norman D. Dicks, D.*
7. Jim McDermott, D.*
8. Dave Reichert, R.*
9. Adam Smith, D.*

West Virginia
1. Alan B. Mollohan, D.*
2. Shelley Moore Capito, R.*
3. Nick J. Rahall II, D.*

Wisconsin
1. Paul Ryan, R.*
2. Tammy Baldwin, D.*
3. Ron Kind, D.*
4. Gwen Moore, D.*
5. James Sensenbrenner, Jr., R.*
6. Thomas E. Petri, R.*
7. David R. Obey, D.*
8. Steve Kagen, D.

Wyoming
†Barbara Cubin, R.*

Nonvoting representatives
American Samoa
Eni F. H. Faleomavaega, D.*

District of Columbia
Eleanor Holmes Norton, D.*

Guam
Madeleine Bordallo, D.*

Puerto Rico
Luis Fortuño, R.*

Virgin Islands
Donna Christian-Christensen, D.*

MEMBERS OF THE UNITED STATES SENATE

The Senate of the first session of the 110th Congress consisted of 49 Democrats, 49 Republicans, and 2 Independents when it convened on Jan. 4, 2007. The first date in each listing shows when the senator's term began. The second date in each listing shows when the senator's term expires.

STATE	TERM
Alabama	
Richard C. Shelby, R.	1987-2011
Jeff Sessions, R.	1997-2009
Alaska	
Theodore F. Stevens, R.	1968-2009
Lisa Murkowski, R.	2003-2011
Arizona	
John McCain III, R.	1987-2011
Jon Kyl, R.	1995-2013
Arkansas	
Blanche Lambert Lincoln, D.	1999-2011
Mark Pryor, D.	2003-2009
California	
Dianne Feinstein, D.	1992-2013
Barbara Boxer, D.	1993-2011
Colorado	
Wayne Allard, R.	1997-2009
Ken Salazar, D.	2005-2011
Connecticut	
Christopher J. Dodd, D.	1981-2011
Joseph I. Lieberman, I.	1989-2013
Delaware	
Joseph R. Biden, Jr., D.	1973-2009
Thomas Carper, D.	2001-2013
Florida	
Bill Nelson, D.	2001-2013
Mel Martinez, R.	2005-2011
Georgia	
Saxby Chambliss, R.	2003-2009
Johnny Isakson, R.	2005-2011
Hawaii	
Daniel K. Inouye, D.	1963-2011
Daniel K. Akaka, D.	1990-2013
Idaho	
Larry E. Craig, R.	1991-2009
Mike Crapo, R.	1999-2011
Illinois	
Richard J. Durbin, D.	1997-2009
Barack Obama, D.	2005-2011
Indiana	
Richard G. Lugar, R.	1977-2013
Evan Bayh, D.	1999-2011
Iowa	
Charles E. Grassley, R.	1981-2011
Tom Harkin, D.	1985-2009
Kansas	
Sam Brownback, R.	1996-2011
Pat Roberts, R.	1997-2009
Kentucky	
Mitch McConnell, R.	1985-2009
Jim Bunning, R.	1999-2011

STATE	TERM
Louisiana	
Mary L. Landrieu, D.	1997-2009
David Vitter, R.	2005-2011
Maine	
Olympia Snowe, R.	1995-2013
Susan M. Collins, R.	1997-2009
Maryland	
Benjamin L. Cardin, D.	2007-2013
Barbara A. Mikulski, D.	1987-2011
Massachusetts	
Edward M. Kennedy, D.	1962-2013
John F. Kerry, D.	1985-2009
Michigan	
Carl Levin, D.	1979-2009
Debbie Stabenow, D.	2001-2013
Minnesota	
Amy Klobuchar, D.	2007-2013
Norm Coleman, R.	2003-2009
Mississippi	
Thad Cochran, R.	1978-2009
Trent Lott, R.	1989-2013
Missouri	
Christopher S. (Kit) Bond, R.	1987-2011
Claire C. McCaskill, D.	2007-2013
Montana	
Max Baucus, D.	1978-2009
Jon Tester, D.	2007-2013
Nebraska	
Chuck Hagel, R.	1997-2009
Ben Nelson, D.	2001-2013
Nevada	
Harry M. Reid, D.	1987-2011
John Ensign, R.	2001-2013
New Hampshire	
Judd Gregg, R.	1993-2011
John E. Sununu, R.	2003-2009
New Jersey	
Robert Menendez, D.	2006-2013
Frank R. Lautenberg, D.	2003-2009
New Mexico	
Pete V. Domenici, R.	1973-2009
Jeff Bingaman, D.	1983-2013
New York	
Charles E. Schumer, D.	1999-2011
Hillary Rodham Clinton, D.	2001-2013
North Carolina	
Elizabeth Dole, R.	2003-2009
Richard Burr, R.	2005-2011
North Dakota	
Kent Conrad, D.	1987-2013
Byron L. Dorgan, D.	1992-2011

STATE	TERM
Ohio	
Sherrod Brown, D.	2007-2013
George V. Voinovich, R.	1999-2011
Oklahoma	
James M. Inhofe, R.	1994-2009
Tom Coburn, R.	2005-2011
Oregon	
Ron Wyden, D.	1996-2011
Gordon Smith, R.	1997-2009
Pennsylvania	
Arlen Specter, R.	1981-2011
Bob Casey, D.	2007-2013
Rhode Island	
Jack Reed, D.	1997-2009
Sheldon Whitehouse, D.	2007-2013
South Carolina	
Lindsey Graham, R.	2003-2009
Jim DeMint, R.	2005-2011
South Dakota	
Tim Johnson, D.	1997-2009
John Thune, R.	2005-2011
Tennessee	
Bob Corker, R.	2007-2013
Lamar Alexander, R.	2003-2009
Texas	
Kay Bailey Hutchison, R.	1993-2013
John Cornyn, R.	2003-2009
Utah	
Orrin G. Hatch, R.	1977-2013
Robert F. Bennett, R.	1993-2011
Vermont	
Patrick J. Leahy, D.	1975-2011
Bernie Sanders, I.	2007-2013
Virginia	
John W. Warner, R.	1979-2009
Jim Webb, D.	2007-2013
Washington	
Patty Murray, D.	1993-2011
Maria Cantwell, D.	2001-2013
West Virginia	
Robert C. Byrd, D.	1959-2013
John D. Rockefeller IV, D.	1985-2009
Wisconsin	
Herbert Kohl, D.	1989-2013
Russell D. Feingold, D.	1993-2011
Wyoming	
Craig Thomas, R.	1995-2013
Mike Enzi, R.	1997-2009

crimes—including torture, maiming, intentional infliction of serious bodily harm, and rape. Other coercive methods, such as sleep deprivation, were not outlawed. The act gave the president broad authority to decide which methods were appropriate. The act also gave retroactive legal protection to military and intelligence personnel who had participated in harsh interrogations.

In Congress, the legislation encountered resistance not only from Democrats concerned about possible civil liberties violations but also from three key Republicans on the Senate Armed Services Committee: John Warner (R., Virginia), John McCain (R., Arizona), and Lindsay Graham (R., South Carolina). The three Republicans opposed President Bush's proposal to reinterpret U.S. obligations under the Geneva Conventions. They feared that if other countries also decided to reinterpret their Geneva obligations, U.S. prisoners of war would be at risk for torture or other abuse. The differences between these senators and the Bush administration provided considerable drama, as the Bush administration conducted intensive lobbying to win Senate support, and the maverick senators held their ground. Eventually, the differences were resolved when the president agreed to drop his demand for power to reinterpret the Geneva Conventions and also assented to a more expansive list of war crimes.

Other antiterror measures. In March, Congress permanently extended several expiring provisions of the USA PATRIOT Act, a broad law passed in 2001 that granted U.S. law enforcement agencies sweeping powers to combat terrorism. Since its original passage, critics had contended that it eroded civil liberties while yielding dubious benefits in protecting the country. The act strengthened the government's power to seize certain records and conduct surveillance, and it also revised various immigration, banking, and money laundering statutes. President Bush signed the PATRIOT Act extension bill on March 9, 2006.

In December, Congress reauthorized a program for coordinating research and vaccine development to prepare the United States to respond to a bioterrorism attack. President Bush signed the reauthorization bill on December 22.

Congress considered legislation in 2006 that would have established oversight for a National Security Agency (NSA) wiretapping program for monitoring possible terrorism activity. News reports had revealed in 2005 that President Bush had secretly authorized the NSA to intercept calls and e-mails between people in the United States and overseas without a court warrant. In September 2006, the House passed a bill to allow such warrantless surveillance on a restricted basis. However, the Senate took no floor action on the issue.

Immigration. Lawmakers in September approved a bill to erect 700 miles (1,100 kilometers) of fencing along portions of the U.S. border with Mexico. The action was part of a national debate about illegal immigration. President Bush signed the bill on October 26. By the end of the year, however, it was unclear whether the fencing would ever be constructed.

Budget. Congress in June approved $94.5 billion in emergency appropriations for the U.S. military efforts in Iraq and Afghanistan, related diplomatic and foreign aid efforts, aid for Gulf Coast states pummeled by hurricanes in 2005, and preparations for a possible avian flu pandemic. In September 2006, Congress approved fiscal year 2007 (Oct. 1, 2006-Sept. 30, 2007) appropriations for defense and homeland security programs. The $447.6 billion defense bill included $70 billion in emergency funds, almost all for the Iraq and Afghanistan wars. The $34.8 billion homeland security bill included $1.8 billion in emergency funds for border security. Congress failed to finish work on nine other appropriations bills for fiscal year 2007. Lawmakers had to pass three continuing resolutions in late 2006 to fund programs covered by the unfinished appropriations bills.

Scandals. Former House Majority Leader Tom DeLay (R., Texas) resigned his seat in Congress on June 9, 2006. DeLay was forced to step down as House majority leader after he was charged in September 2005 with campaign finance violations in Texas. Representative Roy Blunt (R., Missouri) became interim majority leader. In January 2006, DeLay announced that he would not try to reclaim the majority leader job. House Republicans on February 2 selected Representative Boehner as DeLay's replacement in a contest pitting Boehner against Blunt.

In addition to the campaign finance charges, DeLay also had been tainted by his association with Washington, D.C., lobbyist Jack Abramoff, who pleaded guilty in 2006 to a variety of political corruption charges. DeLay had received trips, gifts, and political contributions from Abramoff, but by late 2006, law enforcement officials had not linked the gifts to DeLay's public acts, and no Abramoff-related charges had been filed against DeLay. However, two former DeLay aides who went to work for Abramoff, Michael Scanlon and Tony Rudy, pleaded guilty to corruption charges in November 2005 and March 2006, respectively.

Representative Bob Ney (R., Ohio) resigned from Congress on Nov. 3, 2006, after pleading guilty in October to charges of conspiracy and making false statements in connection with the Abramoff scandal. Ney's troubles had begun early in the year after his name surfaced in guilty pleas entered by Abramoff and the House Ethics Committee announced an investigation of Ney.

On September 29, Representative Mark Foley

(R., Florida) resigned from Congress after it was revealed that he had sent sexually explicit e-mails and instant messages to teen-age boys who had served as congressional pages. The messages spanned a 10-year period from 1995 to 2005. Foley had been chairman of the House Caucus on Missing and Exploited Children. The House Ethics Committee investigated the response of House leaders to warnings about Foley's conduct. Some observers suspected that House leaders had known about Foley's conduct and tried to cover it up. However, on December 8, the committee reported that, though House leaders were negligent in not shielding teen-agers from inappropriate advances by Foley, the leaders had broken no House ethics rules.

Republicans were not the only ones to be dogged by congressional scandals in 2006. On May 20, Federal Bureau of Investigation agents raided the congressional office of Representative William Jefferson (D., Louisiana) as part of a corruption probe against him. Jefferson had been accused of taking bribes. FBI agents had found thousands of dollars in a raid on his home in August 2005.   ■ Geoffrey A. Campbell

See also **Democratic Party; Elections; Human rights; Immigration; Republican Party; Taxation; United States, Government of the; United States, Government of the: A Special Report; Welfare.**

Conservation.

Many conservationists compare the battle to preserve the natural world to fighting fires. A May 2006 report by the World Conservation Union (IUCN) revealed that conservationists have plenty of fires to put out. According to the 2006 Red List compiled by the IUCN, an international organization based in Gland, Switzerland, more than 16,000 species of animals and plants were threatened with global extinction. The endangered list included one out of three amphibian species, one in eight bird species, and a quarter of Earth's mammal species.

Tigers and lions. By most estimates, fewer than 8,000 wild tigers remained in Asia in 2006, hemmed into only 7 percent of their original range. In October, the WWF (formerly known as the World Wildlife Fund), a conservation organization based in Geneva, Switzerland, blasted an international meeting of 30 nations for not acting to solve the tiger crisis.

The meeting of the Standing Committee of the Convention on International Trade in Endangered Species (CITES) featured a report describing how tiger conservation efforts have failed. CITES is an international treaty to control trade in wildlife and wildlife products. Despite the report, the CITES committee put off any action until the next full meeting of the approximately 160 CITES nations, scheduled for June 2007.

Habitat loss and *poaching* (illegal killing) of tigers for skins were the main reasons for the tiger's troubles. The WWF urged immediate action to save the large cats.

About 40,000 lions lived in Africa in 2006, but conservationists worried that these felines might eventually follow the tiger to the brink of extinction. Conservationists and representatives from African governments met in Johannesburg, South Africa, in January, to find ways of preventing the threat to lions from growing worse.

Lion habitat was shrinking in 2006 as exploding human populations in Africa cultivated more land for farming. Lions in small, isolated populations engage in inbreeding, which can lead to genetic problems. They also often prey on livestock and people.

One controversial proposal discussed at the January meeting advocated trophy hunting of lions in those areas where their populations thrive. Advocates said this action would eliminate problem cats and provide income for local people. Animal rights advocates, however, opposed the proposal.

Habitat protection in the United States. Two new wildlife sanctuaries in the United States came under federal protection in 2006—one on land and the other in the sea. In January, U.S. Secretary of Agriculture Mike Johanns dedicated the El Toro Wilderness Area, which had been created by President George W. Bush the previous month. The protected area comprises 10,000 acres (4,000 hectares) of Puerto Rico's Caribbean National Forest, the only tropical rain forest in the U.S. Forest Service system. The forest has 240 species of native trees, the most of any national forest.

In June, President Bush created the world's largest marine sanctuary, in the northwest Hawaiian Islands. He invoked the little-used National Antiquities Act to establish a California-sized *archipelago* (broad expanse of water containing islands) as a national monument. It was the second time President Bush had used the 100-year-old act, which allows the president to establish national monuments of special significance. All fishing was to be phased out in the sanctuary.

International habitat protection. In September, Congo (Brazzaville) granted protected status to 3,800 square miles (9,800 square kilometers) of remote forests, swamps, sand dunes, and savannahs. This area is inhabited by chimpanzees, elephants, gorillas, hippopotamuses, and leopards—among many other animals.

Canada contributed to wilderness conservation in February by creating a 4.4-million acre (1.8-million hectare) park on the Pacific coast of

British Columbia. The region teems with large mammals, including cougars, grizzly bears, moose, mountain goats, and wolves.

Also in February, Brazil designated a protected area of almost 25,000 square miles (64,700 square kilometers) in the Amazon Basin, where the world's richest rain forests are threatened by logging and agriculture. The area protected not only wildlife but also *indigenous* (native) people whom land developers were expelling from their homes.

Animal recoveries. China pursued plans in 2006 to preserve the giant panda by breeding the species in captivity so that the animals could be released into the wild as their numbers built up. In April, biologists for the first time released a

captive-bred panda in a protected area. The animal was a 4-year-old male that had been trained to survive on its own. There were only 1,600 wild pandas in 2006, all of them in China.

In September, wildlife officials in Colorado searched an area in the San Isabel Mountains by helicopter after hunters reported seeing three grizzly bears. The last-known grizzly in Colorado was trapped and killed in 1952, but there had been periodic, unconfirmed grizzly sightings since then. Although the officials did not find the reported bears, the descriptions of the animals by the experienced hunters suggested that the animals were indeed grizzlies.

Evidence increased in 2006 that jaguars were returning to the southwestern United States,

A bluefin trevally fish swims over a coral reef in the Northwestern Hawaiian Islands Marine National Monument, which was created by President George W. Bush in June. The sanctuary is home to more than 7,000 species, a quarter of them found nowhere else on Earth.

from which they had vanished in the mid-1900's. In February 2006, a jaguar that was being tracked with dogs was photographed in the Animas Mountains of New Mexico. Scientists believed that the cats were straying north from Mexico, and that they were not a resident group.

Last-ditch effort. In May, the government of India banned the use of the anti-inflammatory drug diclofenac by farmers and veterinarians. The drug, which had long been used to treat cattle, was linked to fatal liver damage in three species of vultures that feed on dead cattle. Wildlife biologists described in 2004 how diclofenac caused populations of white-backed, long-billed, and slender-billed vultures to decline from perhaps 40 million to a few thousand birds in about 15 years. Another drug, meloxicam, was a potential replacement for diclofenac.

Doomsday vault. In June 2006, engineers in Norway began digging a "doomsday vault" into a mountain on the Arctic island of Svalbard. The vault was designed to hold as many as 3 million seeds, from all known varieties of the world's crops. These seeds might be needed in the future to reestablish crops destroyed by major disasters.
■ Edward R. Ricciuti

See also **Biology; Ocean; Zoos.**

Costa Rica. See Latin America.
Côte d'Ivoire. See Africa.

Courts in the United States ruled in 2006 on several cases involving high-ranking corporate and government officials. Many state courts also ruled on same-sex marriage cases.

Enron. A jury on May 25 convicted two top executives of Houston-based Enron Corporation of fraud and conspiracy in connection with their management of the company. The jury found Kenneth L. Lay, Enron's former chairman, guilty on six counts of fraud and conspiracy and four counts of bank fraud. Jeffrey K. Skilling, Enron's former chief executive, was convicted of 18 counts of fraud and conspiracy and 1 count of insider trading.

Enron, once a leading energy company, filed for bankruptcy in 2001 in one of the largest corporate bankruptcy claims in U.S. history. Investigators charged that the company had used dishonest accounting practices to hide its financial problems from investors. Many Enron employees and other investors lost large amounts of money as a result of the company's collapse.

Lay died on July 5, 2006, before he could be sentenced, and on October 17, Federal District Judge Simeon T. Lake III erased Lay's convictions. The judge based his decision on a legal principle under which convictions of defendants who die before they can appeal are voided.

On October 23, Lake sentenced Skilling to 24 years and 4 months in federal prison. "His crimes have imposed on hundreds if not thousands of people a life sentence of poverty," Lake said. Skilling insisted he was innocent and vowed to appeal the conviction. He started serving his sentence on December 12 at a prison in Minnesota.

Plamegate. Valerie Plame Wilson, a former Central Intelligence Agency (CIA) officer, and Joseph C. Wilson IV, her husband, filed a federal lawsuit on July 13 against several members of the administration of President George W. Bush. In a case often referred to as "Plamegate," the Wilsons charged that Vice President Dick Cheney, former Cheney aide I. Lewis (Scooter) Libby, Jr., and presidential adviser Karl Rove conspired to violate their constitutional rights. The suit claimed that the three men tried to destroy Valerie Wilson's career by leaking to the press that she was an undercover employee of the CIA. The Wilsons charged that the men leaked her identity to retaliate against a 2003 newspaper article by Joseph Wilson questioning the Bush administration's use of what was later found to be faulty intelligence as justification for launching the Iraq War. A spokesman for Rove called the charges "utterly without merit." The trial was set to begin in January 2007.

Former White House aide sentenced. Claude A. Allen, a former domestic policy adviser to President Bush, pleaded guilty on Aug. 4, 2006, to shoplifting from a Maryland Target store. Security cameras at the store filmed Allen charging items to his credit card and taking the items to his car. He then returned to the store, picked up identical items, and sought refunds for them. Under the plea agreement, Allen must serve two years of supervised probation and perform 40 hours of community service. He also must pay a $500 fine and pay $850 to Target Corp.

Congressman pleads guilty. Representative Patrick J. Kennedy (D., Rhode Island) pleaded guilty on June 13 to driving under the influence of prescription drugs. Kennedy, a son of Senator Edward M. Kennedy (D., Massachusetts), had crashed his car into a security barrier near the Capitol in the early morning hours of May 4. The District of Columbia Superior Court sentenced him to undergo drug treatment, pay a $350 fine, and spend a year on probation.

Same-sex marriage was the subject of a number of 2006 court rulings. On July 6, the New York Court of Appeals, the state's highest court, ruled that a state law defining marriage as a union between a man and woman does not violate New York's Constitution. On the same day, the Georgia Supreme Court upheld a Georgia constitutional amendment that barred homosexual couples from marrying or claiming benefits under civil unions.

On July 14, the Eighth U.S. Circuit Court of

Appeals reimposed a ban on same-sex marriage approved by Nebraska voters in 2000. A federal district judge had overturned the ban in 2005 on the grounds that it discriminated against gays and lesbians. Also on July 14, 2006, the Tennessee Supreme Court ruled that a proposed constitutional amendment banning same-sex marriage could stay on the ballot. Tennessee voters approved it by a wide margin on November 7. The Washington Supreme Court on July 26 upheld a state law prohibiting same-sex marriages.

Despite the rulings banning same-sex marriage, the Vermont Supreme Court on August 4 ruled that estranged homosexual couples may retain parental rights. The New Jersey Supreme Court held on October 25 that the state Constitution gives same-sex couples all the rights that heterosexual couples have. The court left it up to the state Legislature to carry out its decision.

Moussaoui sentenced. Zacarias Moussaoui, called the "20th hijacker," was sentenced to life in prison for his role in the Sept. 11, 2001, terrorist attacks. He had pleaded guilty to conspiracy charges in 2005. On May 3, 2006, a federal jury rejected the death penalty for him. Moussaoui shouted, "America, you lost!" He was sent to a prison in Colorado.   ■ Geoffrey A. Campbell

See also **Crime; Supreme Court of the United States.**

Cricket. In 2006, cricket fans prepared for a renewed battle between England and Australia amid a hectic international schedule that included a unique confrontation between a test match umpire and an international team; the International Cricket Council (ICC) Champions Trophy one-day tournament in India; and the build-up to the 2007 World Cup, to be staged in the West Indies.

Test matches. Following their Ashes victory over the Australians in 2005, England lost key players to injury, notably captain Michael Vaughan. All-rounder Andrew Flintoff led England in Pakistan, where they lost 2-0 but squared the series against India 1-1, with one match drawn (March-April 2006). Back home, England shared the series with Sri Lanka (each side winning one game, with one draw) but beat Pakistan 3-0, with one match drawn. Promising newcomers spin bowler Monty Panesar and batsman Alastair Cook were named in the squad, captained by Flintoff, to contest the 2006-2007 Ashes series in Australia.

Australia bounced back in 2006, to dispel any suggestions that aging stars Shane Warne and Glenn McGrath were past their best. Emerging talents such as Shane Watson, Shaun Tait, Michael Hussey, and Mitchell Johnson augured well for the team's future. Under the captaincy of Ricky Ponting, Australia topped the world test rankings,

comfortably beating South Africa 3-0 (February-March) and Bangladesh 2-0 in April. England was ranked second, followed by Pakistan and India.

In other test series, New Zealand defeated the unpredictable West Indies 2-0 but lost 0-2 to South Africa, which in turn went down 2-0 to Sri Lanka. In the first match of this series (Colombo, July), Sri Lankan batsmen Mahela Jayawardene (374) and Kuma Sangakkara (287) set a world record partnership of 624 runs. Jayawardene's score was the fourth-best in test cricket history.

India lost a tense series to Pakistan (1-0) but won on tour in the West Indies (1-0), helped by star batting from Rahul Dravid. Bottom-ranked Bangladesh recorded a rare 2-0 win over Sri Lanka, for whom Muttiah Muralitharan remained, with Australia's Warne, the most inventively successful wicket-taker in test cricket.

World Cup. The West Indies looked for a revival, ahead of the World Cup in the Caribbean in 2007. For this tournament, the 11 major cricket nations would be joined by Bermuda, Canada, Ireland, the Netherlands, and Scotland.

One-Day Internationals (ODI's). One-day cricket continued to be a money-spinner. India had a successful year, beating Pakistan 4-1 and England 5-1. England drew at home with Pakistan, but crashed to Sri Lanka 5-0. In the last match, Sri Lankan veteran Sanath Jayasuriya scored 152 runs during a record opening partnership of 286 with Upul Thuranga. It was Jayasuriya's 362nd one-day appearance. Critics blamed England's failings (only seven wins in 24 ODI's in the year) on relative inexperience in this form of international cricket.

Australia lost a thrilling series 3-2 to South Africa, which scored a world record ODI total of 438 for 9 wickets to win the fifth match. The Australians remained formidable, however, crushing Bangladesh 3-0, and winning a triangular series against India and West Indies. New Zealand outplayed the West Indies 4-1 and beat Sri Lanka 3-1. Pakistan beat Sri Lanka 2-0, while Bangladesh defeated Kenya 4-0. Strife-torn Zimbabwe managed a 2-2 result against Kenya.

The International Cricket Council Champions Trophy was played in India (October-November), and non-Asian teams dominated. Australia, New Zealand, South Africa, and West Indies reached the semifinals, Australia beating West Indies by eight wickets.

Twenty20. All-action Twenty20 (only 20 'overs,' or 120 balls, bowled in each innings) drew enthusiastic crowds. The World Cricket Classic in April matched eight teams, with South Africa beating Bermuda in the final. Sri Lanka beat England in June, and Pakistan did likewise in their first-ever Twenty20 international. An inaugural Twenty20 world championship was scheduled for 2007.

Women's cricket. In the first Asia Cup final, India beat Sri Lanka with the help of a century from captain Mithali Raj. Visiting England, India lost the one-day series 4-0. Claire Taylor of England scored 156 runs at Lord's, making hers the first woman's name on its honors board. India gained revenge by winning the test series.

Other competitions. Pakistan won the Under-19 World Cup in February 2006. The Intercontinental Cup, designed to give second-ranking cricket nations experience, switched in 2006 from a regional to a global format, with eight teams playing four-day matches to replicate test cricket.

Personalities. In 2006, cricket lost two stars of yesteryear. Fans mourned the deaths of West Indian batsman Sir Clyde Walcott and England fast bowler Fred Trueman—the first player to take 300 test wickets.

The 2006 England-Pakistan series was marred by a dispute during the fourth test; Australian umpire Darrell Hair claimed the ball had been altered to aid the bowler, and the incensed Pakistani team refused to restart play. After they finally returned to the field, the umpires awarded the match to England by forfeit, a first in the 129-year history of test cricket. Pakistan was later cleared of "ball-tampering," but captain Inzamam ul-Haq was censured for his team's action. The ICC subsequently barred Hair from umpiring international matches.   ■ Brian Williams

Crime. The rate of violent crime in the United States increased by 1.3 percent in 2005, while the rate of property crime decreased by 2.4 percent, compared with 2004 levels, reported the Federal Bureau of Investigation (FBI) in 2006. The FBI's annual "Crime in the United States" report includes data from more than 17,000 U.S. law enforcement agencies on the violent crimes of murder, nonnegligent manslaughter, forcible rape, robbery, and aggravated assault, as well as the property crimes of burglary, larceny-theft, motor vehicle theft, and arson. Data on arrests are also included in the FBI report.

According to the report, there were almost 1.4 million violent crimes in the United States in 2005. The majority of these crimes involved aggravated assault (62.1 percent of the total) and robbery (30.0 percent). Forcible rape was the only violent crime to decrease, by 1.2 percent, in 2005.

The report stated that there were more than 10 million property crimes in 2005. Two-thirds of these crimes were larceny-thefts. Burglary was the only property crime to increase, by 0.5 percent.

The FBI estimated that authorities made 14.1 million arrests across the United States in 2005. This number represented an increase of 0.2 percent over 2004—though arrests for murder rose 7.3 percent. There were more arrests for drug

abuse violations than for any other offense—1.8 million (13.1 percent of the total).

Enron convictions. In May 2006, a jury in federal court in Houston convicted Kenneth Lay and Jeffrey Skilling on charges of accounting fraud and corruption that led to the financial collapse in 2001 of Enron Corp. The convictions of Lay, the founder and former chairman of Enron, and Skilling, the company's former chief executive officer, came after four months of testimony, some of it from former Enron chief financial officer Andrew Fastow. Fastow already had pleaded guilty to fraud charges.

Enron, based in Houston, was the world's largest energy trading firm before its bankruptcy filing in December 2001 destroyed thousands of jobs and wiped out at least $1 billion in employee retirement funds. The scandal led to a government crackdown on other corporate crime.

Skilling, who was also convicted of using insider information to sell his shares of Enron stock soon before the company's collapse, was sentenced to 24 years and 4 months in prison in October 2006. Lay died of a heart attack in July.

Former Governor Ryan convicted. Former Illinois Governor George Ryan, a longtime Republican dealmaker in the state, was convicted on 18 counts of federal corruption charges in April. The counts included steering state business to friends and political allies for bribes, misusing state resources for political gain, and blocking efforts at fighting corruption. Lawrence Warner, Ryan's friend and lobbyist, was found guilty on 12 counts.

Ryan served as governor from 1999 to 2003. Before that, he was Illinois secretary of state. A key part of his trial focused on allegations that Ryan blocked investigations into the sale of truck drivers' licenses for bribes while he was secretary of state. This scandal was symbolized by a highway accident that killed six children in 1994. A truck driver, with a record of driving under the influence and who had obtained his license by bribing a state official, caused the accident.

Ryan, who was the third former governor of Illinois to be convicted of crimes, was sentenced to 6 ½ years in prison in September 2006.

School shootings. United States President George W. Bush arranged a national conference of law enforcement and education experts in early October to discuss a recent rash of school shootings. Many of the experts called for stricter security measures at schools to help prevent violence.

On September 27, a man held six teen-age girls hostage and sexually molested them at a high school in Bailey, Colorado. After police stormed the classroom, the man, Duane Morrison, fatally shot 16-year-old student Emily Keyes before shooting and killing himself.

On September 29, Eric Hainstock, a 15-year-old

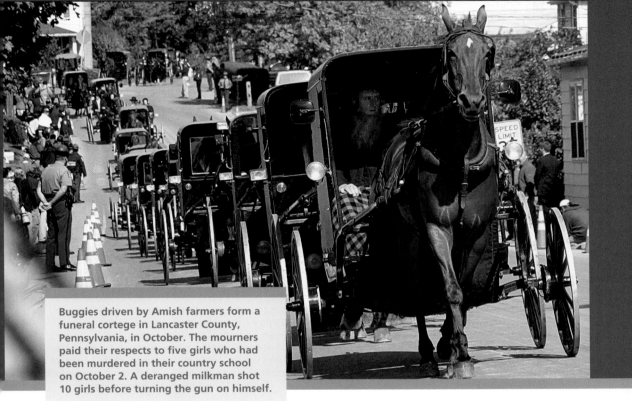

Buggies driven by Amish farmers form a funeral cortege in Lancaster County, Pennsylvania, in October. The mourners paid their respects to five girls who had been murdered in their country school on October 2. A deranged milkman shot 10 girls before turning the gun on himself.

student at a high school in Cazenovia, Wisconsin, shot and killed school principal John Klang. Hainstock was reportedly angry at being disciplined for bringing tobacco to school.

On October 2, milk deliveryman Charles Carl Roberts bound and shot 10 girls at an Amish school in Lancaster County, Pennsylvania, before committing suicide. Five of the girls, aged 7 through 13, died from their wounds.

JonBenet Ramsey case. The latest bizarre twist of events concerning the Christmastime 1996 murder of 6-year-old beauty pageant queen Jon-Benet Ramsey came to an end in August 2006, after the case against John Mark Karr collapsed. Earlier in the month, the 41-year-old schoolteacher had held a press conference in Thailand to confess to the long-unsolved crime. Prosecutors in Boulder, Colorado, then arranged for his deportation to the United States.

After comparing a sample of Karr's *DNA* (deoxyribonucleic acid, the molecule that makes up genes) with a male's DNA found on the beaten and strangled body of JonBenet, the prosecutors announced that the two samples did not match. They concluded that Karr could not have been the murderer. ■ Alfred J. Smuskiewicz

See also **Courts; Prison; Terrorism; United States, Government of the: A Special Report.**

Croatia. In September 2006, a new dispute erupted between Croatian Prime Minister Ivo Sanader and Carla Del Ponte, chief prosecutor for the International War Crimes Tribunal in The Hague, Netherlands, over the prosecution of Ante Gotovina. The Croatian general, whose years-long evasion of capture had strained relations between Croatia and the European Union (EU), was apprehended in the Canary Islands in December 2005 and turned over to the Tribunal. Gotovina was alleged to have committed war crimes including ethnic cleansing and genocide in the 1995 war between Croatia and Serbia during the breakup of Yugoslavia.

Prime Minister Sanader requested that the Croatian government be granted the status of *amicus curiae* (friend of the court) in proceedings against Gotovina and two other Croatian generals at the Tribunal. *Amicus curiae* gives parties not involved in a court case the right to file legal briefs with the court about issues touching on the case. Sanader had made the request as part of a protest against charges in the generals' indictments that their actions had been part of a "joint criminal enterprise" involving the Croatian government. On Sept. 30, 2006, prosecutor del Ponte rejected Sanader's request, asserting that "judicial processes should be left beyond the reach of politics and the interference of governments."

EU candidacy. The Tribunal controversy played out in a larger context of the desire of Croatia's leaders, including Prime Minister Sanader and President Stipe Mesic, to obtain the country's *accession* (admission) to the EU as early as 2009. Formal accession talks between EU officials and representatives of the Croatian government officially began in February 2006.

Economy. Croatia continued to experience economic expansion throughout 2006. The *gross domestic product* (the value of all goods and services produced in a country in a given year) increased at an annual rate of 6 percent in the first quarter of 2006. The rate of inflation remained relatively low in 2006, hovering around 3.5 percent. Unemployment declined to 16 percent in August, the lowest level Croatia had experienced in 10 years.

In an annual report released in September 2006, the World Bank (a United Nations-affiliated agency that loans money to countries for development) ranked Croatia seventh among the world's nations in enacting economic and business reforms. The report credited electronic land registers and a single registration point for new companies with streamlining the business environment in Croatia since the publication of the 2005 report, in which Croatia had ranked 118th.   ■ Sharon L. Wolchik

See also **Europe.**

Cuba. President Fidel Castro appointed his brother, Raul Castro, provisional president and head of the Communist Party on July 31, 2006, as Fidel prepared to undergo intestinal surgery for an unspecified ailment. As the year progressed, speculation about Fidel Castro's true condition abounded, and many analysts wondered if the transfer of power would prove to be permanent. In early December, Castro failed to appear at a celebration marking both his 80th birthday and the start of the revolution in Cuba in 1956, sparking a flurry of speculation by the international news media about the seriousness of his illness.

Upon taking the reins of power at the end of July 2006, Raul Castro, who had served for decades as Cuba's military commander, announced that he had mobilized the nation's armed forces to fend off a possible invasion. "We could not rule out the risk of somebody going crazy within the U.S. government," he said.

Although officials of the administration of President George W. Bush of the United States denied any intention of intervening in Cuban affairs, the U.S. State Department announced an $80-million initiative in July to influence Cuba's transition to democracy. Cuban authorities responded with threats to crack down on illegal satellite television dishes to prevent Cubans from receiving "destabilizing" U.S. broadcasts.

Economy. In the 2005–2006 fiscal year, the government of Venezuelan President Hugo Chávez provided Cuba with economic assistance worth $2.1 billion, including development funds and heavily subsidized supplies of oil. During 2006, Cuba entered into lease agreements with international companies for oil and gas drilling in Cuban waters of the Florida Straits. Experts estimated that those fields contained 4.6 billion barrels of oil and 9.8 trillion cubic feet (277.5 million cubic meters) of natural gas.

Analysts noted that the strengthened Cuban economy, boosted by Venezuelan aid and the drilling leases, would possibly ease the transition of leadership in government. They speculated, however, that Cuba's highly nationalized economy would face major challenges in transforming into a more market-oriented model, if the country's leaders chose to embrace significant economic reforms in 2007 and afterward.

Revival of the sugar industry. In September 2006, Cuba's agriculture minister announced that sugar production on the island would increase by 25 percent during the current year, following years of decline. The increased production was aimed at exploiting global demand for the crop, from which such "environment-friendly" fuels as ethanol can be distilled.   ■ Nathan A. Haverstock

See also **Latin America: A Special Report.**

Czech Republic. The Czech government spent most of the final six months of 2006 in political stalemate, the result of June elections that gave parties of the left and right approximately equal strength in Parliament. The center-right Civic Democratic Party (CDP) narrowly outpolled the left-of-center ruling Social Democratic Party (SDP) of Prime Minister Jiri Paroubek, giving the CDP the opportunity to try to form a government. After negotiations, Mirek Topolanek, leader of the CDP, forged a governing coalition and was sworn in as prime minister on September 4. However, Topolanek's government fell on a no-confidence vote in Parliament in early October, a mere 38 days after its inception.

On November 8, Czech President Vaclav Klaus again asked Topolanek to try to form a ruling coalition. Political analysts speculated that Klaus refrained from tapping Paroubek of the SDP for fear that the SDP might be forced to bring the Communist Party into coalition to achieve a majority. Legislators continued negotiating into December to forge some kind of workable parliamentary majority.

As a result of the political stalemate, legislation to enact a number of reforms keyed to European Union (EU) standards stalled. Such measures included pension reform, various proposals to reform the tax code, and revision of the criminal code. Further privatization of state-owned companies was also delayed.

Economic trends. Despite the Czech Republic's political impasse, its economy continued to boom. The country's gross domestic product (GDP)—the measure of all goods and services produced in a country in a given year—expanded by 7.4 percent in the first quarter of 2006 and by 6.1 percent in the second quarter. According to a survey published in June 2006, the Czech Republic was the seventh most attractive country in the world for investors. Foreign investment was boosting employment in the Czech Republic, economists noted. In 2006, the country's unemployment rate hovered well below 8 percent, a four-year low.

Foreign policy. In 2006, Czech forces continued to participate in North Atlantic Treaty Orgnization coalition peacekeeping activities in Afghanistan and Kosovo, in United States-led coalition peacekeeping activities in Iraq, and in European Union-led peacekeeping activities in Bosnia-Herzegovina. In late 2006, the Czech caretaker government gave authorization to increase the 120 troops in Afghanistan to 225 and the 500 troops in Kosovo to 660. Troop levels in Iraq (100) and Bosnia (70) were to remain stable.

■ Sharon Wolchik

See also **Europe.**

Dallas.
Voters went to the polls on Nov. 7, 2006, and approved a record $1.3-billion city bond issue. The proposal was more than double the city's last bond issue of 2003. Included in the package were funds to build a downtown performance hall and a 5.2-acre (2.1-hectare) park over portions of the Woodall Rodgers Freeway downtown and to renovate the Cotton Bowl and the Farmers Market. Dallas officials considered the bond issue critical to the city's continuing economic rebound.

Dallas Mayor Laura Miller announced on July 6, that she would not seek reelection in 2007. Miller, a former investigative reporter for an alternative newspaper, had frequently clashed with her City Council colleagues during her four years as mayor. In 2005, she pushed unsuccessfully for a ballot proposition that would have greatly increased the governing powers of the mayor.

Police chief cracks down. Dallas Police Chief David Kunkle fired at least 12 police officers during 2006 for offenses ranging from harassment of citizens to stealing supplies from stations. The crackdown by Kunkle was aimed at rebuilding the Dallas Police Department's image, which was tarnished by a scandal in 2001 in which dozens of immigrants were wrongly arrested after police informants planted fake drugs on them. In 2006, Dallas had the highest crime rate per capita among all major cities in the United States, though the statistics had improved by year's-end.

School credit card scandal. In July, the Dallas Independent School District (DISD) launched an investigation into employee misuse of school credit cards that could involve millions of dollars in unauthorized expenditures. DISD Superintendent Michael Hinojosa ordered more than 1,200 school credit cards to be canceled after *The Dallas Morning News* reported school workers were using the cards to purchase everything from iPods to motorized scooters. Former U.S. Attorney Paul Coggins was appointed to lead the probe.

Housing bargains. A national survey in June concluded that Dallas had the most undervalued housing of any major city in the country. The median home price in Dallas was almost 19 percent below market value in 2006, according to financial analysts Global Insight, based in Waltham, Massachusetts, and National City Corp. of Cleveland, Ohio. In contrast, the survey found that 71 metro areas were "extremely overvalued." The findings provided encouraging news that Dallas would suffer less than other cities from the decline in residential property sales during 2006.

Calatrava bridge. Bids submitted in June for a suspension bridge over the Trinity River designed by renowned Spanish architect Santiago Calatrava were twice the budgeted amount. However, a second round of bids in September lowered the price from $113 million to $69 million. City officials questioned how costs to build the bridge could be reduced by 40 percent but approved the bid. The bridge is one of three designed by Calatrava as part of the city's plans to turn the riverway into Dallas's version of Central Park with pathways, lakes, athletic fields, and an equestrian center.

The Wright Amendment, which limited commercial airline flights into and out of Dallas Love Field to Texas and eight adjoining states, was repealed by the U.S. Congress on Sept. 29, 2006. Named for former Speaker of the House Jim Wright, the amendment was designed to move most major airline traffic to Dallas/Fort Worth International Airport, which opened five years before the bill was passed in 1979. The legislation will phase out the Wright Amendment over eight years. However, it will permit air carriers to immediately fly anywhere in the United States from Love Field, providing the airlines stop first in one of the surrounding states.

Mavericks in NBA finals. For the first time in the franchise's 26-year history, the Dallas Mavericks made it to the National Basketball Association finals. The Mavericks defeated the Phoenix Suns in June to win the Western Conference but lost to the Miami Heat in the championship series.

■ Henry Tatum

See also **Basketball.**

Dance. There was much to celebrate in the world of dance in 2006. The Mark Morris Dance Group, the Royal Ballet, and the Joffrey Ballet celebrated anniversaries, and a new group was formed by ballet legend Mikhail Baryshnikov to train the next generation of dancers.

Anniversary. Celebrating its 25th anniversary in 2006, the Mark Morris Dance Group embarked on a tour of more than 20 cities in the United States and a 10-city tour of the United Kingdom. While in London, Morris premiered *King Arthur,* a new work with the English National Opera, staged to a semi-opera by Henry Purcell. The piece was given its U.S. premiere in September in Berkeley, California. Although *King Arthur* was not Morris's

first operatic undertaking, it was his first staging of a full-length work with an episodic storyline.

Joining the worldwide celebration in 2006 that marked the 250th anniversary of Wolfgang Amadeus Mozart's birth, Morris choreographed three dances set to music by the composer. The *Mozart Dances,* performed in August at the Mostly Mozart Festival at New York City's Lincoln Center for the Performing Arts, was set to Piano Sonata No. 11, the Sonata in D Major for Two Pianos, and Piano Sonata No. 27.

Works premiered. The star roster of the American Ballet Theatre (ABT) continued to attract large audiences in 2006, though the company's artistic productivity lagged. The ABT presented only one

A version of *Swan Lake,* performed in 2006 in China by the Guangdong Military Acrobatic Troupe, fuses classical ballet with traditional Chinese acrobatics. The troupe planned to take its wildly popular *Swan Lake* on a 2007 world tour that included Germany, Japan, Russia, and the United States.

world premiere, by the Finnish-born choreographer Jorma Elo on October 19 at the New York City Center. Called *Glow-Stop*, it was set to Mozart's Symphony No. 28 and Philip Glass's *Tirol Concerto for Piano and Orchestra*. Elo, whose style was marked by intricate partnering and off-balance movement, was highly sought as a choreographer in 2006.

In contrast, new works were heavily featured in the New York City Ballet's 2006 season. City Ballet's sixth Diamond Project festival consisted of seven new ballets sprinkled through the company's two-month season at the Lincoln Center. The Diamond Project was founded by philanthropist Irene Diamond in 1992 to commission new works by well-known choreographers. Mauro Bigonzetti, Jean-Pierre Bonnefoux, Jorma Elo, Eliot Feld, Peter Martins, Alexei Ratmansky, and Christopher Wheeldon were the choreographers for the 2006 festival.

Russian dance and the West. Ratmansky's *The Russian Seasons* was the work that stirred most interest at the City Ballet's Diamond Project festival. Ratmansky was born and trained in the Soviet Union in a Russian-style of ballet, but his experience in dance has been very international. Ratmansky became artistic director of Moscow's Bolshoi Ballet in 2004, but he had previously danced in the West with the Royal Danish Ballet and the Royal Winnipeg Ballet and had choreographed for such troupes as the San Francisco Ballet. *The Russian Seasons* reflected Ratmansky's varied background and his unique dance vocabulary. Critics noted an unusual mixture of lyricism and startling blunt movement. The American premiere of his *Middle Duet* by the City Ballet in November 2006 was also well received.

In another sign that the traditional barriers and differences between Russian and Western ballet were softening, St. Petersburg's Kirov Ballet presented a full evening of works by choreographer William Forsythe in June at the Kennedy Center for the Performing Arts in Washington, D.C. For some in the audience, it was a shock to see the usually tutu-clad ballerinas of the Kirov gyrate in leotards to avant-garde choreography. Some wished the Kirov had chosen a more varied repertory to showcase its new-found internationalism, but both fans and detractors agreed that the dancers looked amazingly comfortable in a foreign style of ballet.

A shuffled score. Merce Cunningham, a founder of American avant-garde dance, continued to explore new ways of presenting movement in 2006. In October, at the Joyce Theater in New York City, the Merce Cunningham Dance Company premiered *eyeSpace*. Members of the audience were loaned iPods to download a score by Mikel Rouse. With the iPods set on shuffle, audience members were likely to be listening to different scores to accompany the dance. Cunningham had been experimenting with chance and randomness in dance for decades.

Hell's Kitchen Dance. In his 50's, Mikhail Baryshnikov has found new avenues for artistic expression. In 2005, he created the Baryshnikov Arts Center as a laboratory for artists in different disciplines. Baryshnikov's latest project was created with of a group of resident choreographers and dancers from the center and was called Hell's Kitchen Dance. The name is derived from the New York City neighborhood where the center is located. Baryshnikov included himself as one of the dancers, and in June 2006 the ensemble debuted at the University of Buffalo in New York. The performance featured three new pieces— Aszure Barton's *Over/Come* and *Come In,* and Benjamin Millepied's *Years Later.* The latter featured Baryshnikov dancing live along with video of himself, sometimes shown dancing at earlier periods in his career.

New homes. New York's Alvin Ailey American Dance Theater, which moved into a spacious new home at the Joan Weill Center for Dance in 2005, thrived in 2006 with an opening that left critics enthusiastic. The Joffrey, which celebrated its 50th anniversary in 2006, purchased new accommodations in Chicago's downtown theater district. The company will occupy two floors of a hig-hrise named Joffrey Tower when construction is completed in 2008.

Ashton's legacy. Two stars from the Joffrey Ballet in the 1970's, Gary Chryst and Christian Holder, returned to the troupe in October 2006. They danced the roles of the stepsisters in Frederick Ashton's *Cinderella*. Ashton choreographed the piece for the United Kingdom's Royal Ballet, and the stepsisters were intended to be danced by men in the style of English pantomime. Ashton danced the part of a stepsister at the ballet's opening in 1948.

The Royal Ballet observed its 75th anniversary in 2006 in part by looking back to its glory days. It reproduced the 1946 version of *The Sleeping Beauty* that wowed American audiences on the troupe's first U.S. tour in 1949.

Deaths. Katherine Dunham died in May 2006. In the 1930's, Dunham introduced black dance from the West Indies to the American public with her glamorous revues. In the 1940's and 1950's, her Dunham School of Dance and Theater in New York was a training ground for actors and dancers. An anthropologist as well as a dancer, she was active in civil rights and in her later years conducted inner-city cultural programs in East St. Louis, Illinois.   ■ Nancy Goldner

See also **Classical music; Deaths.**

DEATHS

in 2006 included those listed below, who were Americans unless otherwise indicated.

Aarons, George Allen "Slim" (1916–May 30), photographer whose images of film stars, royalty, and socialites enlivened the pages of *Holiday*, *Life*, and *Town & Country* in the 1950's and 1960's.

Allen, Jay Presson (1922–May 1), writer who crafted the highly successful stage and screen adaptations of Muriel Spark's novel *The Prime of Miss Jean Brodie* and the equally successful screen adaptation of *Cabaret*.

Robert Altman, film director

Allyson, June (Ella Geisman) (1917–July 8), film actress who most famously played steadfast wives opposite James Stewart in *The Stratton Story* (1949), *The Glenn Miller Story* (1953), and *Strategic Air Command* (1955).

Altman, Robert (1925–November 20), maverick director who received an honorary Academy Award in 2006 for "repeatedly reinvent[ing] the art form" in such landmark films as *M*A*S*H* (1970), *McCabe and Mrs. Miller* (1971), *Nashville* (1975), and *The Player* (1992).

Anderson, Lew (1922–May 14), musician and bandleader who was best known as Clarabell the Clown, Howdy Doody's sidekick on the children's television program that ran from 1947 to 1960.

Arizin, Paul (1928–December 12), Hall of Fame forward who led the Philadelphia Warriors to the 1956 NBA championship, pioneered the jump-shot, and was chosen as one of the 50 greatest NBA players.

Arnold, Sir Malcolm (1921–September 23), popular British composer who completed 9 symphonies and scored 132 films, including *The Bridge on the River Kwai* (1957), for which he won an Academy Award.

Asplund, Lillian Gertrud (1906–May 6), woman who was the last American survivor of the 1912 sinking of the *Titanic*.

Auerbach, Arnold "Red" (1917–October 28), basketball coach, manager, and club executive who led the Boston Celtics to 16 NBA championships while building one of most successful franchises in sports.

Barbera, Joseph (1911–December 18), partner in the Hanna-Barbera film production team, which created such beloved cartoon characters as Tom and Jerry, the Flintstones, Jetsons, and Yogi Bear.

Barnett, Isabel Bigley (1926–September 30), musical comedy star who portrayed Laurey in the first London production of *Oklahoma*, won a Tony for her performance as Sarah Brown in *Guys and Dolls*, and starred in *Juliet and Me,* in a part crafted for her by Rodgers and Hammerstein.

Barrett, Syd (Roger Keith Barrett) (1946–July 7), guitarist and influential songwriter who was one of the founding members of Pink Floyd and who composed many of the rock group's early hits.

Benchley, Peter (1940–February 12), writer who promoted oceanic conservation after his novel *Jaws* became a 1974 best seller.

Bennett, Louise (1919–July 26), Jamaican poet and who became the island's cultural ambassador.

Bentsen, Lloyd (1921–May 23), former senator who as the 1988 Democratic candidate for vice president famously told Dan Quayle, who had compared himself to a late president, "Senator, you're no Jack Kennedy."

Berg, Patty (1918–September 10), Ladies Professional Golf Association founder who won a record 15 major championships.

Botha, P. W. (1916–October 31), South African politician who served as president (1978-1989) during the height of the anti-apartheid struggle.

Boyle, Peter (1935–December 12), character actor who initially made a name for himself as a hate-filled factory worker in *Joe* (1970) and as the bumbling monster in *Young Frankenstein* (1974) and who capped his career as the father on the hit TV sitcom "Everybody Loves Raymond."

June Allyson, actress

Peter Boyle, actor

Ed Bradley, journalist

Carrol, Lou (1923– April 3), gentleman who sent Tricia and Julie Nixon a puppy that lent its name—Checkers—to a 1952 speech in which Richard Nixon defended himself against charges of fiscal impropriety.

Carter, Janette (1923–January 22), singer of Appalachian folk music who was the last surviving child of the Carter family of country music fame.

Cassini, Oleg (1913–March 17), French-born couturier who was the first designer to exploit licensing agreements and who designed clothes for film stars, including his wife, Gene Tierney, and for Jacqueline Kennedy when she was first lady.

Chamberlain, Owen (1920–February 28), physicist who shared the 1959 Nobel Prize in physics for the discovery of the antiproton, one of two main components of the atomic nucleus.

Chandler, Otis (1927–February 27), scion of a powerful California family who transformed the family-owned *Los Angeles Times* into one of most respected and widely read U.S. newspapers.

Coffin, Reverend William Sloane (1924–April 12), former Yale University chaplain who became a leading figure in the civil rights and anti-Vietnam War movements of the 1960's and 1970's.

Colzano, Anselmo (1918–March 19), Italian baritone who performed with the Metropolitan Opera for 18 consecutive seasons in the 1960's and 1970's.

Bradley, Ed (1941–November 9), journalist whose career spanned both the Vietnam and Iraq wars and who appeared for more than 25 years on the CBS Sunday night fixture "60 Minutes."

Brown, James (1933-December 25), "Godfather of Soul" whose energetic performances of such hits as "Papa's Got A Brand New Bag" and "I Got You (I Feel Good)" earned him the reputation as "the hardest working man in show business." A black activist, Brown's "Say It Loud—I'm Black and I'm Proud" was a civil rights anthem in the 1960's.

Brown, Ruth (1928–November 17), rhythm-and-blues singer who won a Tony for *Black and Blue* and a Grammy for "Blues on Broadway."

Butcher, Susan (1954–August 5), musher who won the Iditarod dog sled race four times.

Butler, Octavia (1947–February 24), science-fiction writer who explored alienation and survival in hostile worlds in such novels as *Kendrid* (1979), *Dawn* (1987), *Adulthood Rites* (1988), and *Imago* (1989).

Buttons, Red (Aaron Chwatt) (1919–July 13), burlesque comedian who became a star of Broadway and early television, then revived a declining career in such films as *Sayonara* (1957), *They Shoot Horses, Don't They?* (1969), and *The Poseidon Adventure* (1972).

Caldwell, Sarah (1924–March 23), opera director and conductor who founded the Opera Company of Boston and was the first woman to conduct at the Metropolitan Opera House in New York City.

Calvello, Ann (1929–March 14), roller derby star whose eccentric personal style, "bad-girl" image, and longevity in the sport—more than 50 years—made her a roller derby legend.

Campbell, Bebe Moore (1950–November 27), novelist (*Your Blues Ain't Like Mine*), essayist, and commentator who explored race and class in the United States, particularly the world of upwardly mobile African Americans.

James Brown, entertainer

Comden, Betty (Elizabeth Cohen) (1917– November 23), lyricist who with Adolph Green wrote lyrics and librettos for the musicals *On the Town* (1944), *Wonderful Town* (1953), and *Bells Are Ringing* (1956) and for the film musicals *Singin' in the Rain* (1952) and *The Band Wagon* (1953).

Connally, Nellie (1919–September 1), former Texas first lady who was riding in President John F. Kennedy's limousine when he was assassinated in Dallas on Nov. 23, 1963.

Coombs, Doug (1957–April 3), revered extreme skier who slipped over a cliff in France while attempting to aid a fellow skier who had gone over the same precipice.

Cowsill, Barry (1954–August? 2005, reported January 2006) and **William** (1948–February 17), members of the Cowsills, the family band of the 1960's on which "The Partridge Family" TV series was based. Barry Cowsill disappeared in New Orleans during the Hurricane Katrina disaster.

Crossfield, A. Scott (1921–April 19), pilot who in 1953 became the first man to fly twice the speed of sound.

D'Aquino, Iva Toguri (1916–September 26), Japanese American who in 1949 was convicted of treason as the World War II propagandist "Tokyo Rose." Doubts about her actual guilt prompted President Gerald Ford to pardon her in 1977.

Davis, Raymond, Jr., (1937– May 31), chemist and physicist who was awarded the 2002 Nobel Prize in physics for the detection of cosmic neutrinos.

Vernon Ingram, biologist

Dekker, Desmond, (Desmond Dacres) (1941–May 25), Jamaican singer who helped popularize reggae music.

Douglas, Mike (1925–August 11), affable talk-show host whose "Mike Douglas Show" ruled afternoon television from 1961 to 1982.

Drabowsky, Moe (1935–June 10), Polish-born baseball player who pitched for eight major league teams from 1956 to 1972 and who set a World Series record for a relief pitcher by striking out 11 batters in Game 1 of the 1966 series.

Dunham, Katherine (1909–May 21), dancer, choreographer, and anthropologist who introduced into serious dance the heritage of African and African-colonial culture as well as important physical innovations.

Ecevit, Bülent (1925–November 5), former prime minister of Turkey who reoriented his country away from the Middle East toward the West.

Epstein, Barbara (1928–June 16), editor and cofounder of *The New York Review of Books*. Epstein championed the publication of Anne Frank's *Diary of a Young Girl* and guided the works of such authors as Joyce Carol Oates and Gore Vidal.

Ertegün, Ahmet (1923–December 14), Turkish-born music executive who founded Atlantic Records and shaped the careers of Ray Charles, John Coltrane, Aretha Franklin, and the Rolling Stones.

Fallaci, Oriana (1929–September 15), provocative Italian journalist who in interviews was renowned for challenging the authority of powerful world leaders.

Faludy, György (1910–September 1), Hungarian poet and novelist and a leading figure in the Hungarian resistance against Nazism and Communism. Faludy won international fame for his interpretation of Francois Villon ballads and his 1962 autobiographical novel *My Happy Days in Hell*.

Farrell, Henry (Charles Henry Myers) (1920–March 29), writer whose novel *Whatever Happened to Baby Jane?* (1960) and short story "Hush, Hush Sweet Charlotte" launched a new genre, the psychological horror film.

Fender, Freddy (Baldemar Huerta) (1937–October

Katherine Dunham, dancer and anthropologist

Glenn Ford, actor, with Rita Hayworth

Betty Friedan, feminist writer

14), singer who had hit records in Spanish and English, including "Before the Next Teardrop Falls," "Wasted Days and Wasted Nights," and "You'll Lose a Good Thing."

Ferguson, Maynard (1928–August 23), Canadian-born jazz trumpeter who was known for his soaring, shrieking high notes and for the "Rocky" movies theme, "Gonna Fly Now."

Feuer, Cy (1911–May 17), producer who with partner Ernest Martin brought a string of hit musicals to Broadway—*Guys and Dolls* (1950), *Can-Can* (1953), *How to Succeed in Business Without Really Trying* (1961)—and produced the film *Cabaret* (1971).

Flaherty, Paul A. (1964–March 16), computer engineer who conceived the idea of indexing the World Wide Web, which resulted in AltaVista, the first Internet search engine to become popular with the public.

Fleischer, Richard (1916–March 25), film director whose works included the noir classic *The Narrow Margin* (1952), *20,000 Leagues Under the Sea* (1954), *Fantastic Voyage* (1966), and *The Boston Strangler* (1968).

Ford, Gerald (1913–December 26), the 38th president of the United States. See Special Report at Deaths.

Ford, Glenn (Gwyllyn Samuel Newton Ford) (1916–August 30), Canadian-born veteran film actor who starred in *The Big Heat* (1953) and *The Blackboard Jungle* (1955) and opposite Rita Hayworth in *Gilda* (1947).

Franciosa, Anthony (Anthony Papaleo) (1928–January 19), "method" actor whose realistic portrayals of troubled characters in such films as *A Hatful of Rain* (1957) and *The Long, Hot Summer* (1958) made him a star in the 1950's.

Friedan, Betty (1921–February 4), visionary feminist whose 1963 bestseller *The Feminine Mystique* reawakened the American feminist movement and helped launch a profound social revolution.

Friedman, Milton (1912–November 16), Nobel laureate economist who championed free market economics and led the post-World War II challenge of Keynesian economic theory. See Portrait at Economy, U.S.

Galbraith, John Kenneth (1908–April 29), Canadian-born economist, author, teacher, and diplomat who served as an adviser to presidents John F. Kennedy and Lyndon Johnson. See Portrait at Economy, U.S.

Gardiner, John Reynolds (1946–March 4), author of the children's books *Top Secret* (1985), *General Butterfingers* (1986), and *Stone Fox* (1980), which sold more than 3 million copies.

Geoffrion, Bernie "Boom Boom" (1931– March 11), Canadian hockey player who popularized the slap shot and starred in six Stanley Cup championship teams in his 14 seasons (1951-1964) with the Montreal Canadiens.

Gilbert, Michael (1912–February 8), British author of dozens of meticulously plotted detective, crime, and espionage stories and novels and stage, radio, and television plays.

Gowdy, Curt (1919–February 20), television sportscaster who called hundreds of sporting events, including seven Olympics and eight Super Bowls.

Green, Gerald (1922–August 29), author of nearly 20 novels, including the 1956 best-seller *The Last Angry Man*, and TV producer who was a creator of the "Today" show, first broadcast in 1952.

Hargitay, Mickey (1926–September 14), Hungarian-born bodybuilder—Mr. America and Mr. Universe in 1955—who married Jayne Mansfield and fathered actress Mariska Hargitay.

Haughey, Charles (1925–June 13), Irish politician who served as prime minister three times between 1979 and 1992 and was credited with laying the foundation for Ireland's economic boom of the 1990's.

Hayden, Melissa (Mildred Herman) (1923–August 9), Canadian-born ballerina who was one of the first international stars of George Balanchine's New York City Ballet.

Jane Jacobs, urban philosopher

Don Knotts, comic actor

Hill, Arthur (1922–October 22), Canadian-born actor who originated the role of George in the Broadway production of *Who's Afraid of Virginia Woolf?*.

Hunt, Lamar (1932–December 13), longtime owner of the Kansas City Chiefs who helped name the Super Bowl.

Hussein, Saddam (1937–December 30), former president of Iraq who was executed by Iraqi authorities for the murder of 148 Shi`ahs in Dujail.

Hyde, Philip J. (1921–March 30), the Sierra Club's primary photographer, whose images of Western landscapes were potent weapons in the organization's battle for conserving the environment.

Imamura, Shohei (1926–May 30) Japanese film director who twice won the Palme d'Or at the Cannes Film Festival—in 1983 for *The Ballad of Narayama* and in 1997 for *The Eel.*

Ingram, Vernon (1924–August 17), German-born biologist who discovered the cause of sickle cell anemia and who was known as the "father of molecular medicine."

Irwin, Steve (1962–September 4), Australian conservationist who became internationally known as the "Crocodile Hunter" and who died after being pierced in the heart by a stingray. See Australia.

Jacobs, Jane (1916–April 25), writer and intellectual whose *The Death and Life of Great American Cities* (1961), which advocated urban complexity, diversity, and density, changed the direction of urban planning.

Jessie, Ron (1948–January 13), Pro Bowl wide receiver who played 11 seasons in the National Football League with the Los Angeles Rams, Detroit Lions, and Buffalo Bills.

Kaduri, Yitzha (1899?–January 28), Israeli rabbi who was the leader of the Kabala school of Jewish mystical thought and was one of the most politically influential holy men in Israel.

Kimball, Narvin (1909–March 17), Dixieland jazz banjoist whose career began on Mississippi riverboats and who was the last surviving founder of New Orleans' Preservation Hall Jazz Band.

King, Coretta Scott (1927–January 30), widow of the Reverend Martin Luther King, Jr., and "first lady of the civil rights movement." See Portrait at Human rights.

Kirby, Bruno (Bruno Giovanni Quidaciolu) (1949–August 14), character actor who most famously played Billy Crystal's best friend in *When Harry Met Sally* (1989) and *City Slickers* (1991).

Kirkpatrick, Jeane (1926–December 7), former U.S. ambassador to the United Nations who served as an international affairs adviser to President Ronald Reagan.

Knotts, Don (1924–February 24), actor whose high-strung, bumbling comic persona achieved television immortality as Deputy Barney Fife on "The Andy Griffith Show."

Kunitz, Stanley (1905–May 24), poet who won a Pulitzer Prize in 1959 for his collection *Selected Poems 1928-1958* and was appointed poet laureate of the United States in 2000.

Laker, Sir Freddie (1922–February 10), British businessman who in 1977 changed the face of commercial aviation by challenging industry giants with the launch of low-cost transatlantic flights on the "Skytrain."

Lawford, Patricia (1924–September 17), sister of President John F. Kennedy. Lawford founded the National Committee for the Literary Arts.

Lem, Stanislaw (March 27–1921), Polish master of science fiction whose many works, including *Solaris* (1961) and *His Master's Voice* (1968), contemplate humanity's place in and inability to comprehend the universe.

Lewis, Al (Albert Meister) (1923–February 3), political candidate, radio host, and actor who played Leo in the TV series "Car 54, Where Are You?" and Grandpa on "The Munsters."

Lieberson, Lorraine Hunt (1954–July 3), mezzo-soprano who was described as the greatest artist in contemporary opera. Lieberson specialized in singing the work of husband Peter Lieberson.

Ligeti, György Sandor (1923–June 12), Romanian-born composer whose highly innovative and often eerie and fantastic music gained an international audience after Stanley Kubrick blended various Ligeti works into the "moon music" in *2001: A Space Odyssey* (1968).

Mahfouz, Naguib (1911–August 30), Egyptian philosopher, man of letters, and novelist who in 1988 became the first Arab writer to be awarded the Nobel Prize in literature.

al-Maktoum, Sheik Maktoum bin Rashid (1949?– January 4), emir of Dubayy, prime minister of the United Arab Emirates, and founder of the Dubai Cup, the world's richest horse race.

Mathias, Bob (1930–September 2), athlete who won the gold medal in the Olympic decathlon in 1948 and 1952 and who served four terms in Congress as a Republican from California.

McFerrin, Robert (1921–November 24), baritone who was the first African American to sing with the Metropolitan Opera Company.

McGavin, Darren (1922–February 25), actor who most famously played Mike Hammer in the 1950's TV series of the same name, Carl Kolchak in the cult series "The Night Stalker," and the gruff dad in the 1983 holiday classic "A Christmas Story."

McLean, Jackie (1931–March 31), jazz saxophonist, composer, and educator who worked with Miles Davis, Art Blakey, and Charles Mingus before developing his own highly distinctive style.

Merrifield, Robert Bruce (1921–May 14), biochemist who won the 1984 Nobel Prize in chemistry for producing chains of polypeptides.

Meyer, Ray (1913–March 17), Hall of Fame college basketball coach who won 724 games and made 21 postseason appearances over 42 seasons with DePaul University.

Bob Mathias, athlete

Miller, G. William (1925–March 17), investment banker who served as secretary of the U.S. Department of the Treasury in the Jimmy Carter administration and chairman of the Federal Reserve Board (1978-1979).

Milosevic, Slobodan (1941-March 11), Serbian leader who in the 1990's presided over the disintegration of Yugoslavia in a series of wars so brutal that he came to be called the "butcher of the Balkans."

Moffo, Anna (1932–March 9), soprano whose hugely successful career in the 1950's and 1960's was cut short with the premature decline of her voice.

Money, John (1921–July 7), New Zealand-born psychologist who pioneered research into sexual ambiguity and who coined the phrase "gender identity."

Mosteller, Frederick (1916–July 23), Harvard statistics department founder who applied statistical data to a range of diverse fields, from public health and politics to sports.

Murray, Jan (Murray Janofsky) (1916–July 2), "Borscht Belt" stand-up comic who hosted a number of popular game shows in the early days of television.

Nelson, Byron (1912–September 26), renowned golfer who in 1945 won a record 11 consecutive professional tournaments.

Newman, Arnold (1918–June 6), photographer whose celebrated images of such people as Igor Stravinsky and Pablo Picasso popularized a style of photography that became known as environmental portraiture.

Nicholas, Fayard (1914–January 24), legendary tap dancer and the elder half of the Nicholas Brothers, whom dancer Mikhail Baryshnikov one described as "the most amazing dancers I have ever seen in my life—ever."

Nilsson, Birgit (Märta Birgit Svensson) (1918– Dec. 25, 2005; reported January 2006), Swedish soprano whose stupendous voice and rich interpretations of the roles of Wagner's Isolde,

Birgit Nilsson, soprano

Ann Richards, politician

Buck Owens, singer

Hollywood's Nudie's Rodeo Tailors, which provided actors and country music and rock 'n'roll singers—including Roy Rogers, Hank Williams, Sr., and Elvis—with the wildly embroidered, rhinestone-studded "Nudie Suit."

O'Day, Anita (Anita Belle Colton) (1919– November 23), big-band singer who transformed herself into one of the great song stylists and jazz singers of the post-World War II era.

O'Neil, Buck (John Gordon O'Neil, Jr.) (1911–October 6), star first baseman of the Negro Leagues, the Leagues' last surviving veteran, and Major League Baseball's first African American coach.

Brünnhilde, and Sieglinde; Strauss's Salome and Elektra; and Puccini's Turandot—made her one of opera's legendary performers.

Niyazov, Saparmurad (1940-December 21), president for life and prime minister of Turkmenistan who had ruled since the nation gained independence in 1992 after serving as the president of the Turkmen Soviet Socialist Republic.

Nudie, Bobbie (Helen Kruger Cohn) (1913–April 7), costumer who with husband Nudie Cohn ran

Owens, Buck (1929–March 25), singer and "Hee Haw" TV show cohost whose more than 20 number-one hits—including "Act Naturally" (1963), "I've Got a Tiger by the Tail" (1964), and "Waitin' in Your Welfare Line" (1966)—influenced the sound of country music.

Paik, Nam June (1932–January 29), Korean-born avant-garde artist and composer who is credited with inventing video art.

Palance, Jack (Vladimir Palahniuk) (1918?– November 10), actor who specialized in menacing characters but won an Academy Award for a selfparodying performance in *City Slickers* (1991).

Parks, Gordon (1912– March 7), chronicler of the African American experience as a photographer and photojournalist; magazine editor; poet; and novelist—*The Learning Tree* (1963); film director—*The Learning Tree* (1969) and *Shaft* (1971); and composer—"Martin" (1989).

Patterson, Floyd (1935–May 11), heavyweight boxer, admired as "a gentlemen of the ring," who took the championship title in 1956 from Archie Moore, lost it to Ingemar Johansson in 1959, and regained it in 1960.

Petrone, Rocco (1926–August 24), NASA engineer who directed the countdown for launching the first mission to land astronauts on the moon and headed the Apollo space program.

Pickett, Wilson (1941–January 20), early soul music star whose 1960's classics include "In the Midnight Hour" and "Mustang Sally."

Pinochet, Augusto (1915–December 10), Chilean general who was accused of being responsible for the deaths of 3,000 people during his 17-year regime as dictator.

Gordon Parks, photographer, editor, writer, film director, and composer

Pitney, Gene (1941–April 5), songwriter ("Hello Mary Lou," "He's a Rebel") and singer who became a teen-age idol with "Town Without Pity" and "Only Love Can Break a Heart."

Platner, Warren (1919–April 17) architect whose 1960's furniture line for Knoll, with bases fashioned from nickel-plated steel rods in sheaflike patterns, became icons of Modernist design.

Pointer, June (1954–April 11), the youngest of the Pointer Sisters, the singing group that became known in the 1970's and 1980's for "I'm So Excited," "Fire," and "Slow Hand."

Profumo, John (1915–March 9), British politician who was the center of the "Profumo affair," a 1963 sex and espionage scandal that forced him to resign as secretary of state for war and eventually brought down Prime Minister Harold Macmillan's government.

Puckett, Kirby (1960–March 6), Hall of Fame Minnesota Twins outfielder who played in 10 consecutive All-Star Games and led the Twins to two World Series championships (1987 and 1991).

Puskás, Ferenc (1927–November 17), Hungarian athlete who was considered one of the all-time great soccer players.

Rawls, Lou (1933–January 6), singer whose suave baritone and distinctive blend of gospel and jazz sold more than 40 million records, including the hit single "You'll Never Find Another Love Like Mine" (1976).

Redman, Dewey (1931–September 2), tenor saxophonist and bandleader who was at the cutting edge of jazz through a career that spanned nearly half a century.

Reeve, Dana (1961–March 6), singer and actress who after her husband's paralysis in 1995 devoted herself to fund-raising for medical research and championing stem-cell research.

Richards, Ann (1933–September 13), charismatic former governor of Texas and high-profile Democrat who famously described former President George H. W. Bush as having been "born with a silver foot in his mouth."

Floyd Patterson, boxer

Lou Rawls, singer

Rosenthal, A. M. (1922–May 10), Canadian-born journalist who began his career with *The New York Times* in 1943 as a stringer and rose to become the executive editor who led the *Times* through the challenges of the Vietnam War, the publication of the Pentagon Papers, and Watergate scandal.

Rosenthal, Joe (1911–August 20), Pulitzer Prize-winning photographer whose World War II photograph of Marines raising the U.S. flag on Iwo Jima became one of the iconic images of the 20th century.

Rukeyser, Louis (1933–May 2), author and host of "Wall Street Week," the public television program on which he delivered, with some wit, common-sense commentary on the marketplace.

al-Sabah, Sheik Jabir al-Ahmad (1926– January 15), emir of Kuwait whose control of its vast oil revenues made him among the world's richest and most influential figures.

Schembechler, Glenn E. "Bo" (1929–November 17), legendary University of Michigan football coach and athletic director who won or shared 13 Big Ten Conference championships during his coaching career.

Schwartz, Melvin (1932–August 28), physicist who shared the 1988 Nobel Prize in physics with Leon M. Lederman and Jack Steinberger for their development of the neutrino beam and the discovery of the muon-neutrino.

William Styron, novelist

Elisabeth Schwarzkopf, soprano

Schwarzkopf, Elisabeth (1915–August 3), German soprano whose beauty, refined voice, and musical intelligence shone in her three signature roles: Donna Elvira in *Don Giovanni*, the countess in *The Marriage of Figaro*, and above all, the Marschallin in Richard Straus's *Der Rosenkavalier*.

Scott, Robert Lee, Jr., (1908–February 27), celebrated World War II fighter pilot who wrote the best-selling *God Is My Co-Pilot*, a memoir of his wartime missions in Burma (now Myanmar) and India and with the Flying Tigers in China.

Shearer, Moira (Moira Shearer King) (1926–January 31), Scottish ballerina whose luminous performance as the doomed heroine in the film *The Red Shoes* (1948) somewhat overshadowed her career with Sadler's Wells Ballet and the subsequent Royal Ballet.

Sherman, Vincent (1906–June 18), one of the last of the studio-era Hollywood directors. While at Warner Brothers, Sherman directed Humphrey Bogart, Joan Crawford, Bette Davis, Errol Flynn, and Ronald Reagan.

Shugart, Alan (1930–December 12), engineer who helped develop the first disk drive, profoundly changing the computer industry.

Shumway, Norman (1923–February 10), surgeon who in 1968 performed the first successful heart transplant in the United States.

Skinner, Todd (1958–October 23), internationally renowned mountain climber who championed "free climbing" methods and who fell to his death from Leaning Tower in Yosemite Park.

Smith, Claydes Charles (1948–June 20), cofounder of Kool & the Gang, a funk-pop band whose 1970's and 1980's hits included "Jungle Boogie," "Joanna," and "Celebration."

Smith, Louise (1916–April 15), NASCAR driver who was the first woman inducted into the International Motorsports Hall of Fame.

Spark, Muriel (1918–April 13), Scottish writer whose more than 20 macabre, humorous novels include *The Prime of Miss Jean Brodie* (1961).

Spelling, Aaron (1923–June 23), prolific producer of such critically scorned but hugely popular television series as "Charlie's Angels," "Fantasy Island," "Love Boat," "Dynasty," and "Beverly Hills, 90210."

Spillane, Mickey (Frank Morrison Spillance) (1918–July 17), pulp-fiction novelist whose most famous hero, Mike Hammer, inspired numerous films and at least two television series.

Stanton, Frank (1908–December 25), television executive who was president of the CBS network for 26 years and who helped build it into what was referred to in the 1950's and 1960's as the "Tiffany Network."

Stapleton, Maureen (1925–March 13), actress who created the heroines of two Tennessee Williams plays—*The Rose Tattoo* (1951) and *Orpheus Descending* (1957)—and won an Academy Award for Best Supporting Actress for her portrayal of anarchist Emma Goldman in *Reds* (1981).

Stroessner, General Alfredo (1912–August 16), Paraguayan dictator who ruled from 1954 until 1989 when he was ousted by a military coup.

Styron, William (1925–November 1), Pulitzer Prize-winning novelist whose principal works—*Lie*

Down in Darkness (1951), *The Confessions of Nat Turner* (1967), and *Sophie's Choice* (1979)—explore the effects of corruption, evil, and redemption on the individual and society, particularly in the author's native South.

Te Atairangikaahu, Dame Te Arikinui (1933–August 15), queen of New Zealand's indigenous Maori population. She was the longest serving head of the Kingitanga movement.

Thomson, Kenneth (1923–June 12), Canadian billionaire and art collector who transformed his family's newspaper business into a highly successful provider of electronic data and specialized information to students and professionals.

Taufa'ahau Tupou IV, King of Tonga (1918–September 10), sovereign who ruled his South Pacific islands nation for more than 40 years.

Van Allen, James A. (1914–August 9), physicist who in 1958 discovered the Van Allen belts, two zones of electrically charged particles that surround Earth.

Varnay, Astrid (1918–September 4), Swedish-born soprano whose first appearance in a leading role—as a last-minute replacement as Sieglinde in Wagner's *Die Walkure* at the Metropolitan Opera in 1941—provided one of the most sensational debuts in opera history.

Wagner, Phyllis Cerf (Helen Brown Nichols) (1916–November 24), widow of publisher Bennett Cerf and former New York City Mayor Robert F. Wagner. She appeared in films, collaborated with Theodor Seuss Geisel (Dr. Seuss) on learning-to-read books, wrote columns, and hob-nobbed with the most famous people of her day while raising millions for New York City parks.

Walker, Cindy (1918–March 23), highly prolific country-western composer who wrote "Dream Baby" for Roy Orbison; "In the Misty Moonlight," sung by Dean Martin; and "You Don't Know Me," recorded by Jerry Vale, Ray Charles, and Elvis Presley.

Warden, Jack (Jack Warden Lebzelter) (1920–July 19), Emmy award-winning character actor who appeared on Broadway, in more than 10 television series, and in nearly 100 films.

Wasserstein, Wendy (1950–January 30), Pulitzer Prize and Tony Award-winning playwright whose studies of the struggles and triumphs

James Van Allen, physicist

confronted by liberated intelligent women include *Uncommon Women and Others* (1977), *The Heidi Chronicles* (1988), and *The Sisters Rosensweig* (1993).

Weaver, Dennis (1924–February 24), actor who achieved television fame playing Chester on "Gun-smoke" and the title character in "McCloud."

Weinberger, Caspar W. (1917–March 28), public servant who held Cabinet posts under presidents Richard M. Nixon, Gerald Ford, and Ronald Reagan.

Williamson, Jack (1908–November 10), science-fiction genre pioneer who wrote more than 50 novels, including *The Legion of Time* (1938), *Darker than You Think* (1948), and *The Humanoids* (1949).

Winters, Shelley (Shirley Schrift) (1920–January 14), stage, film, and television actress who graduated from playing "sexpots" to character roles to campy mothers, picking up along the way, two Academy Awards—for *The Diary of Anne Frank* (1959) and *A Patch of Blue* (1965).

Woods, Earl (1932–May 3), the man who taught his son, Tiger Woods, to play golf and mentored the golf champion's career.

Wyatt, Jane (1910–October 20), actress who most famously played Sonya in Frank Capra's *Lost Horizon* (1937) and Margaret Anderson on the television series "Father Knows Best."

Shelley Winters, actress

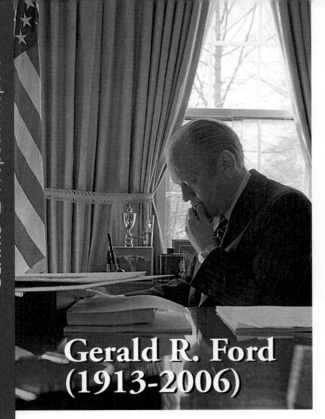

Gerald R. Ford
(1913-2006)

By Robert N. Knight

Former United States President Gerald R. Ford died on Dec. 26, 2006, at the age of 93. Ford, who came to the presidency upon the resignation of President Richard M. Nixon on Aug. 9, 1974, was unique in U.S. history for having served as president and vice president without being elected to either of those offices. Ford became vice president on Dec. 6, 1973, under the terms of the Twenty-Fifth Amendment to the Constitution, replacing Spiro T. Agnew, who had resigned as vice president the previous October. Ford was the longest-living former president in U.S. history, surpassing by one month the record set by Ronald Reagan, who died at age 93 in 2004.

Ford became president at one of the most troubled times in U.S. history, during a political scandal involving the cover-up of the June 1972 Watergate break-in, a burglary of Democratic Party headquarters in Washington, D.C., committed by operatives allied with Nixon subordinates. Faced with the almost certain threat of impeachment for his role in the cover-up, President Nixon resigned.

Ford's calming presence and his reputation for decency helped restore respect for the presidency at this crucial moment of history. Many tributes issued following the announcement of Ford's death in December 2006 cited Ford's healing effect on a wounded nation as his greatest presidential achievement. President George W. Bush observed that "for a nation that needed healing and for an office that needed a calm and steady hand, Gerald Ford came along when we needed him most."

Midwestern roots

Gerald Ford was born Leslie Lynch King, Jr., on July 14, 1913, in Omaha, Nebraska. Ford's mother, Dorothy, later divorced Ford's father and moved to Grand Rapids, Michigan. There she married Gerald R. Ford (Sr.). Dorothy's three-year-old son then acquired a stepfather and a new name, Gerald R. Ford—or "Jerry."

Jerry excelled at sports and scouting, attaining the rank of Eagle Scout, the highest rank in Boy Scouting. In 1931, he entered the University of Michigan at Ann Arbor, where he performed well academically and was a star player on the football team. After graduating in 1935, he accepted a job as an assistant coach at Yale University in New Haven, Connecticut. In 1938, Ford entered Yale Law School. He received his law degree there in 1941.

Ford the politician

Like millions of other young men of his generation, Gerald Ford served in the armed forces during World War II (1939-1945). He joined the U.S. Navy in 1942, returning to Grand Rapids to practice law after his

The author:
Robert N. Knight is a free-lance writer.

discharge in 1946. Soon he was being urged by local leaders to run for Congress. In 1948, he won election as a Republican to the U.S. House of Representatives from the Michigan district containing Grand Rapids. Ford won 13 successive elections to that seat. Meanwhile, Ford met and married Betty Bloomer, a fashion coordinator and dancer. During Ford's presidency, Betty Ford became one of the most popular first ladies in U.S. history.

President Ford

During his long career in Congress, Ford gained respect for his ability to work in a *bipartisan* (two-party) manner for common goals and became the Republican minority leader in the House. After Republican Vice President Spiro T. Agnew was forced to resign in October 1973 while under criminal investigation for bribery, Congressional leaders persuaded President Nixon to nominate Ford as Agnew's replacement. Ford's tenure in the vice presidency was brief, however. Less than one year later, in August 1974, he became president upon Nixon's resignation.

Initially, President Ford enjoyed broad popular support. On Sept. 8, 1974, however, he created a political firestorm when he issued a blanket pardon to former President Nixon. With the advantage of hindsight, most historians now judge Ford's pardon an act of statesmanship, intended to spare the American people the corrosive political drama of a Nixon trial. However, the pardon seriously eroded public support for Ford and may have led to his defeat for reelection in a close contest with Democratic candidate Jimmy Carter in 1976. Eight days after pardoning Nixon, President Ford offered amnesty to draft dodgers and deserters of the Vietnam War period (1957-1973).

Ford's presidency (1974-1977) was occasionally contentious. With Democrats in control of both houses of Congress, he found little support for his proposals. He also delivered 66 vetoes, mostly for bills that he feared would increase inflation, which he considered "public enemy Number 1." His administration also faced congressional opposition to resupplying South Vietnamese forces as they came under increasing military pressure from North Vietnam following the 1973 peace accord that ended the U.S. role in the Vietnam War. Nevertheless, Ford achieved a lasting legacy in foreign policy by signing the Helsinki Accords in 1975, a set of international agreements that set standards for basic human rights.

A nation's respect

In death, Ford was accorded full ceremonial honors. During the final days of 2006, Ford lay in state in the rotunda of the U.S. Capitol. President George W. Bush declared Tuesday, Jan. 2, 2007—the date of Ford's funeral at the National Cathedral in Washington, D.C.— a national day of mourning. Ford was buried on January 3 at the Gerald R. Ford Presidential Library and Museum in Grand Rapids.

President Gerald R. Ford and First Lady Betty Ford (left) escort former President Richard M. Nixon and wife Pat (right) from the White House to a waiting jet on Aug. 9, 1974, following Nixon's resignation from the presidency.

Democratic Party. Democrats celebrated a major victory in the midterm elections on Nov. 7, 2006, in which voters demonstrated widespread dissatisfaction with the Republican Party and its role in conducting the war in Iraq. Control of both the United States House of Representatives and U.S. Senate passed from Republican to Democratic hands, paving the way for Democratic Representative Nancy Pelosi of California to become the first woman speaker of the House. Alluding to scandals that brought down a number of Republicans during during 2006, Pelosi promised that Democrats would "lead the most ethical Congress in history."

Democratic National Committee Chairman Howard Dean said the results represented a rejection of Republican rule. Dean said Americans had voted for "hope and opportunity" and an end to "the politics of fear and smear."

Illinois Representative Rahm Emanuel, chairman of the Democratic Congressional Campaign Committee, had recruited candidates who would appeal to moderate voters. He said the election showed that "vital center politics beat polarization politics."

Aggressive agenda. Following the election, Pelosi outlined an ambitious agenda for the House. She said that within the first 100 hours of the 110th Congress, Democrats would raise the minimum wage, cut interest rates on student loans, reduce subsidies to oil companies, boost stem cell research, and strengthen homeland security. Although many Democratic initiatives put the party in direct opposition to the policies of President George W. Bush, Pelosi promised that Democrats would reach out to the administration and attempt to find *bipartisan* (two-party) solutions to national problems. She also ruled out any attempt by Democrats to initiate impeachment proceedings against President Bush.

House of Representatives. Democrats picked up 31 seats in the House, including 1 seat that had been held by a Democratic-leaning independent. They retained all their seats from the previous Congress and ousted 22 Republican incumbents. Democrats fared well even against moderate candidates, reflecting the depth of voters' disappointment with the Republican Party.

Senate races. Control of the Senate swung to the Democrats following two races that remained in doubt well after the polls had closed. In Virginia, Democrat James H. Webb, Jr., defeated incumbent Republican Senator George F. Allen. Webb, a former Republican who had served as Navy secretary under President Ronald Reagan, was aided in his bid when Allen used an ethnic slur in describing a man at an Allen rally. Democrats also won a close race in Montana, where Jon Tester beat three-term Senator Conrad R. Burns, who had been tainted by a scandal involving lobbyist Jack Abramoff.

Democrats also defeated several other incumbents. Pennsylvania Treasurer Robert P. Casey, Jr., defeated Senator Richard J. Santorum, and Demo-

Democratic U.S. Senate candidate Jim Webb celebrates in Vienna, Virginia, on the night of Nov. 7, 2006, despite the election being too close to call. Incumbent Senator George Allen did not concede until November 9. Webb's victory secured Democratic control of the Senate.

crat Sherrod Brown of Ohio pushed out incumbent Republican Senator Michael DeWine. Missouri State Auditor Claire McCaskill beat incumbent Republican Senator James M. Talent, and Rhode Island Democrat Sheldon Whitehouse defeated incumbent Senator Lincoln D. Chafee, a moderate Republican who had often voted with Democrats.

Party holds vulnerable seats. Incumbent Democratic Senator Robert Menendez of New Jersey, who faced widespread allegations of corruption, fended off a challenge from Republican Tom Kean, Jr., the son of a popular former governor. In Maryland, Representative Benjamin L. Cardin beat Republican Lieutenant Governor Michael Steele, keeping the Senate seat in Democratic hands. In Minnesota's Senate race, Amy Klobuchar beat Republican Representative Mark Kennedy, preserving the seat for Democrats.

Independent victories. Connecticut voters reelected incumbent Senator Joseph I. Lieberman. Lieberman had lost in the Democratic primary but decided to run as an independent. Lieberman, who had supported the Iraq War, defeated Democrat Ned Lamont, who ran an antiwar campaign. In Vermont, voters elected independent Representative Bernard Sanders to the Senate. Both Lieberman and Sanders will organize with Senate Democrats, giving the party a 51-49 majority.

Governors' races. Democratic gubernatorial candidates also fared well on Election Day, giving Democrats a majority of the nation's governorships. Prior to the election, Democrats held 22 governorships, compared with the Republicans holding 28. The elections reversed the ratio.

In New York, State Attorney General Eliot Spitzer handily beat Republican John Faso. Democrats also won in Maryland, where Baltimore Mayor Martin O'Malley beat incumbent Republican Governor Robert L. Ehrlich, Jr.

Presidential race. In late 2006, outgoing Iowa Governor Tom Vilsack, U.S. Representative Dennis Kucinich (D., Ohio), and former U.S. Senator John Edwards (D., North Carolina) officially declared their intention to seek the Democratic presidential nomination in 2008.

Fund-raising. The Democratic National Committee, Democratic Senatorial Campaign Committee, and the Democratic Congressional Campaign Committee raised a total of $332.7 million through mid-October 2006, according to the Federal Election Commission. The Republican National Committee, Republican Senatorial Committee, and the National Republican Congressional Committee raised a total of $435.4 million over the same period.   ■ Geoffrey A. Campbell

See also **Cabinet, U.S.; Congress of the United States; Elections; Republican Party; State government; United States, Government of the; United States, President of the.**

Denmark. Prime Minister Anders Fogh Rasmussen continued in 2006 to preside over a center-right coalition government consisting of the Liberal Party and the Conservative People's Party. The coalition, which ruled as a minority government, remained in power by cooperating with the populist, anti-immigrant Danish People's Party (DPP). The government passed budgets through parliament by making occasional concessions on immigration issues. In addition, though tens of thousands of Danes protested in September and October against proposed reductions in spending for such social services as child care and care for the elderly, the government used budget surpluses to expand spending in other areas. Such flexibility, along with simmering anti-immigrant sentiment among some segments of the population, allowed for a stable working collaboration between the government and the DPP.

Cartoon controversy. A controversy set off in September 2005 by the publication of 12 cartoons of the Muslim Prophet Muhammad in the Danish newspaper *Jyllands-Posten* spilled over into 2006. The incident led to Denmark's most significant foreign policy crisis since World War II (1939-1945).

The controversy began when a Danish *imam* (Islamic religious leader), Abu Laban, toured the Middle East with copies of the offensive cartoons. According to international affairs experts, he hoped to generate outrage among Muslims. The drawings included a cartoon of Muhammad wearing a bomb-shaped turban. In January and February 2006, Danish embassies and missions in several Muslim countries were vandalized, and several Muslim governments enacted embargoes on Danish imports. At least 15 people were killed during the protests.

Prime Minister Rasmussen called for respect for all religions. However, he also defended the right of the newspaper to publish the cartoons on the grounds of freedom of speech and independence of the press. According to experts, radical Muslims in Europe and elsewhere used the incident in an attempt to increase their influence. In mid-February, the European Union's (EU) foreign policy chief, Javier Solana, embarked on a tour of Muslim countries to assure their leaders of the EU's respect for Islam. Eventually, amid calls for calm by moderate Muslims in Denmark and the United Kingdom, the protests subsided.

Denmark's economy grew by an encouraging 3 percent in 2006, according to estimates by EU economists. The country's unemployment rate fell from 4.8 percent in 2005 to 3.8 percent in 2006. The resulting drop in social spending yielded a significant budget surplus.   ■ Jeffrey Kopstein

See also **Europe.**

Dinosaur. See Paleontology.

Disability. The United Nations (UN) General Assembly on Dec. 13, 2006, unanimously adopted an agreement called the Convention on the Rights of Persons with Disabilities. The agreement, reached after five years of negotiations, would require countries to guarantee people with disabilities such rights as equality; independent living; accessibility; health; education; employment; and participation in political and cultural life, recreation, leisure, and sport. To enter into force, the convention required ratification by 20 UN member countries.

In 2006, only 45 countries had legislation that guaranteed people with disabilities such rights. According to advocates, about 650 million people—or 10 percent of the world's population—had disabilities in 2006. Some 90 percent of children with disabilities in less developed nations were not able to attend school. In some countries, 80 percent of people with disabilities were unemployed.

New voting law assures privacy. The Help America Vote Act (HAVA), which went into effect in 2006, assured for the first time that people with a wide range of disabilities could cast their ballot in private. Previously, voters with disabilities were often accompanied into voting booths by election judges from both parties and could be overheard indicating their choices to poll workers.

The HAVA was passed in 2002, in response to problems with punch-card voting machines that had contributed to contested results in the 2000 presidential election. The law provided $3.9 billion in federal funds to states to update their voting machines, improve voter education, and train poll workers. Included in the law were regulations that called for making polling places—including entrances and voting areas—accessible to people with disabilities; assuring that people with disabilities could vote privately and independently; and training election workers on ways to inform people with disabilities of the new procedures.

Each polling place was required to have at least one voting machine that could accommodate a variety of different kinds of disabilities, including visual impairments, hearing impairments, mobility impairments, and emotional and intellectual impairments. By late October 2006, 34 states had purchased new machines that allow voters with visual impairments to hear their choices through headphones or to enlarge the type on a touch screen. Voters with mobility impairments can inhale or puff into an air tube to indicate their choice. After voting is completed, the machines allow voters to double-check their choices and make changes.

■ Kristina Vaicikonis

Disasters. The deadliest disaster of 2006 was an earthquake that struck Indonesia on May 27, killing more than 5,800 people. Disasters that resulted in 25 or more deaths include the following:

Aircraft crashes

January 20—Hungary. Forty-two Slovakian troops are killed when their An-24 military aircraft crashes in northern Hungary. The troops, part of a NATO-led peacekeeping force, were en route from Pristina in Kosovo to Kosice in Slovakia.

July 9—Russia. At least 124 people are killed when a Russian S7 airline jet bursts into flames after landing on a runway in Irkutsk in southern Siberia. The plane was en route from Moscow carrying 201 passengers and crew members.

August 22—Ukraine. A Russian TU-154 aircraft traveling from the Black Sea resort town of Anapa to St. Petersburg crashes in eastern Ukraine about 30 miles (45 kilometers) north of Donetsk. All 170 people aboard are killed.

August 27—United States. A Comair commuter jet crashes shortly after take-off from the Lexington, Kentucky, airport, killing all 47 passengers and 2 of 3 crew members. According to aviation officials, the jet, bound for Atlanta, Georgia, took off from a runway too short for its size.

September 1—Iran. A Russian-built TU-154 jet skids off a runway and bursts into flames as it attempts to land in Masshad in northeastern Iran. Eighty of 147 people aboard are killed. The plane was traveling from the southern port city of Bandar Abbas.

September 29—Brazil. A Brazilian Gol airline Boeing 737 traveling from Manaus to Brasilia, the capital, collides in midair with an executive jet and crashes in the Amazon jungle, killing all 155 passengers and crew members aboard the Gol flight. The smaller jet lands safely.

October 29—Nigeria. A Nigerian ADC airliner crashes immediately after take-off from Abuja, the capital, killing 96 of the 100 passengers and 5 crew members aboard. The pilot had ignored traffic controllers' advice to wait out a storm.

Earthquakes

March 31—Iran. At least 66 people are killed and more than 900 others are injured when earthquakes measuring 4.7 to 6.0 in magnitude strike western Iran. The quakes occurred about 210 miles (338 kilometers) southwest of Tehran, the capital.

May 27—Indonesia. A 6.5-magnitude earthquake on Java leaves more than 5,800 people dead and more than 30,000 injured. The district of Bantul is hardest hit.

July 17—Indonesia. A 7.7-magnitude earthquake off the island of Java triggers a tsunami that leaves more than 600 people dead. Much of the damage is in the resort town of Pangandaran.

Explosions and fires

February 24—Bangladesh. A fire in a textile mill in the southeastern port of Chittagong leaves at least 50 people—primarily women—dead and more than 100 others injured. According to rescuers, the fire spread quickly through yarn piled on the floors of the four-story mill.

April 10—India. A fire engulfs three huge tents at a consumer electronics fair in the northern city of Meerut, killing at least 42 people.

May 12—Nigeria. As many as 200 people are killed when a pipeline from which gas is seeping bursts into flames. Villagers from Ilado, near Lagos, the main city, were collecting the fuel.

Mine disasters

February 19—Mexico. Sixty-five miners are killed when an explosion causes a tunnel to collapse at a coal mine in San Juan de las Sabinas, about 80 miles (130 kilometers) southwest of Eagle Pass, Texas.

September 6—India. At least 50 miners are killed when methane and carbon-dioxide gas explode in a state-owned coal mine near Dhanbad in the eastern state of Jharkhand.

September 20—Kazakhstan. Forty-one miners are killed when methane gas explodes in a coal mine in Shakhtinsk in northern Kazakhstan.

Shipwrecks

February 3—Egypt. An Egyptian ferry carrying 1,310 passengers and 96 crew members from the Saudi Arabian port of Duba to Bur Safajah on Egypt's east coast sinks in the Red Sea. Only 401 people survive.

March 23—Cameroon. At least 123 people drown when their boat capsizes in the Gulf of Guinea off the coast of Cameroon. According to the 27 survivors, the ship was en route from the port of Oron in Nigeria to Gabon's Port Gentil when it was engulfed by waves during a storm.

March 30—Bahrain. A boat carrying some 140 employees involved in the construction of the Bahrain World Trade Center towers capsizes in the Persian Gulf during a dinner cruise. At least 58 people are killed.

April 6—Djibouti. A ferry carrying more than 250 pilgrims to a religious festival in the port city of Tadjoura capsizes in the Gulf of Aden near Djibouti, the capital. At least 69 people drown.

April 8—Ghana. About 110 people are killed when an overloaded boat capsizes in Lake Volta. Forty others are rescued. The passengers were being relocated to the mainland from an island that had been designated as a nature reserve.

April 17—Indonesia. A ferry swamped by heavy waves sinks in the Java Sea, about 1,180 miles (1,900 kilometers) east of Jakarta, the capital. The Indonesian Navy rescues 19 of the approximately 100 passengers. About 40 people drowned in the area in March during a similar ferry accident.

Storms and floods

January 4—Indonesia. Heavy rain triggers a landslide that buries 75 people in Cijeruk (also called Sijeruk) in central Java, about 215 miles (350 kilometers) east of the capital, Jakarta. Flooding and landslides caused by tropical downpours killed at least 79 people in East Java on January 2.

February 17—Philippines. More than 1,000 people are killed when a mudslide buries the village of Guinsaugon on Leyte Island, about 420 miles (670 kilometers) southeast of Manila.

April 2—United States. Twenty-eight people are killed when more than 60 tornadoes strike the Midwest during massive thunderstorms. One tornado kills 24 people in an area between Newbern and Bradford in Tennessee.

June 3—Vietnam. Government officials call off the search for sailors killed when Typhoon Chanchu sank a fleet of boats in the South China Sea in mid-May. The bodies of about 20 people were recovered, and more than 220 others were missing and presumed dead.

June 25—Indonesia. Government officials report that more than 280 people are dead and dozens more are missing after a 48-hour torrential rain triggered flash floods and landslides on June 20 in the eastern province of Sulawesi.

July 10—North Korea. Typhoon Ewiniar brings catastrophic rains and landslides to North Korea. According to a pro-North Korean newspaper published in Japan, at least 549 people die and 295 others are missing. A South Korean relief agency estimates that nearly 55,000 people are dead or missing.

July 14—China. At least 612 people are killed as Typhoon Bilis drenches southern China with more than 24 inches (60 centimeters) of rain. Hardest hit is the province of Hunan.

August 8—India and Pakistan. Authorities in India report that at least 150 people were killed during the past week as rains triggered flooding in the states of Gujarat, Maharashtra, and Andhra Pradesh. More than 140 people in northwest Pakistan also die in the floods.

August 10—China. At least 435 people are killed and 1.5 million others are evacuated as Typhoon Saomai—the strongest typhoon to hit China in 50 years—strikes the eastern province of Zhejiang. The typhoon packs winds as high as 135 miles (216 kilometers) per hour.

August 13—Ethiopia. At least 125 people are killed in flash floods when heavy rains cause the Omo River in southern Ethiopia to overflow its banks. One week earlier, more than 250 people were killed when the Dechatu River flooded the city of Dire Dawa in eastern Ethiopia.

October 4—Philippines and Vietnam. Government officials report that the death toll from Typhoon Xangsane, which struck the Philippines on September 28 and Vietnam on September 30, has reached 250 people.

November 30—Philippines and Vietnam. An estimated 1,000 people are killed across the central and northern Philippines when heavy rain from Typhoon Durian triggers mudslides on the Mayon Volcano in southern Luzon. At least 50 people are killed in Vietnam when Durian strikes the country's southern coast on December 4.

Train wrecks

January 23—Montenegro. At least 45 people are killed and nearly 200 others are injured as a passenger train derails and plunges into a ravine near the capital, Podgorica. Many of the passengers are children returning to the coastal city of Bar from a skiing trip in northern Montenegro.

July 3—Spain. A subway train traveling at twice its normal speed derails in the coastal city of Valencia. Forty-one people are killed and an additional 47 people are injured.

August 21—Egypt. A passenger train pulling into a station in Qalyoub, north of Cairo, the capital, plows into a second train, killing 58 people. More than 140 others are injured.

Other disasters

January 12—Saudi Arabia. At least 345 people are killed and nearly 300 others are injured outside of Mecca in a stampede during the stoning of the devil, a ritual that takes place during the hajj, an annual Muslim pilgrimage. One week earlier, at least 76 pilgrims were killed when the hotel in which they were staying collapsed.

January 24—Central and Eastern Europe. Russian officials report that more than 50 people have died as weeklong Arctic temperatures settled in across the nation. In Moscow, the capital, temperatures fell to -24 °F (-31 °C) on January 19, the lowest temperature for that date since 1927. In Poland, at least 60 people die from the cold. In Romania, temperatures plunged to -29 °F (-34 °C) on January 23, and a cold snap that continued for three weeks caused the deaths of 82 people.

January 28—Poland. The roof of a trade hall collapses in the southern city of Katowice, killing at least 67 people and injuring about 150 others. Government authorities report that heavy snow may have contributed to the collapse.

February 4—Philippines. Seventy-four people are killed outside a stadium in Manila when a crowd that had gathered to watch a television game show stampedes at an entry gate.

February 13—Ukraine. Health ministry officials report that 844 people have died of exposure across Ukraine during a month-long cold snap.

February 23—Russia. The roof of a Moscow market collapses, killing at least 66 people. Authorities believe that snow build-up on the building's concave roof may have caused the collapse.

April 17—Mexico. Fifty-eight people are killed when a bus traveling from Guadalajara to Veracruz plunges more than 650 feet (200 meters) into a ravine. The bus was transporting a religious group home from an Easter week festival.

April 28—Angola. Officials from the international group Doctors Without Borders report that more than 900 people have died over the past 10 weeks from cholera.

August 1—United States. A heat wave that began on July 16 in California causes the deaths of at least 164 people throughout the state, according to public health authorities. Temperatures remained in the triple digits for almost two weeks.

August 3—France. Health department officials in France report that 112 people have died from a heat wave that engulfed Europe in July.

September 12—Yemen. Fifty-one people are killed and more than 200 others are injured during a stampede in a stadium in Ibb, south of Sanaa, the capital. The victims—most of whom were schoolchildren and teen-agers—were attending a campaign rally for Yemeni President Ali Abdullah Saleh.   ■ Kristina Vaicikonis

See also **Asia; Indonesia; Weather.**

Drug abuse. An estimated 126 million Americans were current (within the past month) drinkers of alcoholic beverages, 71.5 million were current smokers, and 19.7 million were current users of illegal drugs in 2005, according to the National Survey on Drug Use and Health (NSDUH) released in September 2006. The NSDUH is an annual survey by the United States Substance Abuse and Mental Health Services Administration.

Alcohol. The 2005 NSDUH revealed that an estimated 126 million Americans age 12 or older—about 51.8 percent of all Americans in this segment of the population—were current drinkers. Almost 23 percent of Americans identified themselves as having participated in *binge drinking* (five or more drinks on the same occasion on at least one day) in the past month. The rate of binge drinking for youth ages 18 to 25 was 41.9 percent.

Tobacco. According to the NSDUH, 71.5 million Americans age 12 or older—or 29.4 percent of this population—were current users of tobacco products in 2005. In addition, the survey found that current cigarette smoking by youth ages 12 to 17 decreased from 11.9 percent in 2004 to 10.8 percent in 2005.

The 2005 Monitoring the Future Survey, an annual survey conducted by researchers at the University of Michigan in Ann Arbor, found that 50 percent of Americans in 2005 had tried smoking cigarettes by the 12th grade. Twenty-three percent of current 12th-graders were cigarette smokers in 2005.

Illegal drugs. Marijuana was the illegal drug most commonly used by youth in the United States in 2005. The NSDUH found that 9.9 percent of people ages 12 to 17 currently used illicit drugs, and 74.2 percent of those individuals also used marijuana. Among adults ages 18 to 25, 16.6 percent used marijuana in 2005.

Between 2001 and 2005, the use of ecstasy (MDMA), a mild hallucinogen, decreased among 8th-, 10th-, and 12th-graders by more than 50 percent, according to the Monitoring the Future Survey. The Monitoring the Future Survey found that cocaine use, which had decreased steadily among youth since 2000, appeared to be leveling off in 2005. Approximately 2.3 percent of 12th-graders used cocaine in the past month in 2005.

Methamphetamine. The 2005 NSDUH found that 10.4 million Americans—approximately 4.3 percent of the population—reported methamphetamine use during their lifetime. Methamphetamines are a class of addictive stimulants that have powerful effects on the central nervous system. According to the Monitoring the Future Survey, 2.5 percent of 12th-graders had used methamphetamines.   ■ David C. Lewis

See also **Drugs.**

Drugs. On Aug. 24, 2006, the United States Food and Drug Administration (FDA) approved over-the-counter (OTC) sales of the emergency contraceptive Plan B for women age 18 and older. Plan B, often called the "morning-after pill," usually prevents pregnancy if taken within 72 hours of unprotected sexual intercourse. The drug, made by Barr Pharmaceuticals, Inc., of Woodcliff Lake, New Jersey, had been available by prescription since 1999. Backers of Plan B applauded the FDA decision but criticized the age restriction, saying the prescription requirement should also be eliminated for girls younger than 18. Many social conservatives denounced the FDA decision, arguing that it would encourage promiscuity. Some conservatives also compared Plan B to abortion because of the drug's possible ability to stop a fertilized egg from lodging in the uterus.

Barr had applied for OTC status for Plan B in 2003, but the FDA initially rejected the application in 2004, even though the agency's scientific advisers had recommended approval. At the time, FDA officials said their rejection was based on a lack of safety data about Plan B's use by younger teens. However, backers of Plan B said the rejection was driven more by politics than by science.

Potential Tylenol risk. Extra Strength Tylenol, at its highest recommended dose, may increase the risk of liver damage, according to a

A U.S. Army humvee passes an opium poppy field in southern Afghanistan in April. While the U.S. military in 2006 trained Afghan forces to destroy the country's enormous opium crop, Afghanistan continued to supply much of the morphine and heroin sold in Europe and the United States.

clinical study published in July 2006 by a research team led by physician Paul Watkins of the University of North Carolina at Chapel Hill. Doctors had previously known that overdoses of Tylenol could harm the liver, but this was the first study to identify a possible risk in adults taking the nonprescription pain reliever as directed. McNeil Consumer & Specialty Pharmaceuticals of Fort Washington, Pennsylvania, produces Tylenol. In the United States, Tylenol is the leading brand of the pain-relieving and fever-reducing drug acetaminophen.

Watkins's team studied 145 people over 14 days. Some took Tylenol, at the maximum recommended dose of 4 grams a day; some took an acetaminophen-opiate combination; and some took a *placebo* (inactive substance). The researchers measured the subjects' levels of aminotransferase—an enzyme that, when found at elevated levels, can indicate possible liver damage. About 39 percent of the nonplacebo subjects had aminotransferase of more than three times the normal amount.

Help for smokers. On May 11, the FDA approved Chantix as a potential aid in reducing some smokers' cravings and withdrawal symptoms when they try to quit. Chantix, made by Pfizer Inc. of New York City, is a brand name for the drug varenicline. It is designed to partly mimic the effects of nicotine, the addiction-causing substance in tobacco. Nicotine stimulates receptor cells in the brain that produce dopamine, a chemical that causes a sensation of pleasure. Chantix also stimulates dopamine production, but not as much as nicotine. In addition, if a person smokes while taking Chantix, the medication has the potential to diminish the pleasure sensation associated with nicotine. A number of clinical studies released in 2006 indicated that varenicline helped more study participants quit smoking than other cessation treatments. Nevertheless, a majority of the varenicline users in the studies failed to quit.

Cancer vaccine for girls. On June 8, the FDA approved Gardasil, a vaccine that protects against the four strains of human papillomavirus (HPV) that cause most cases of cervical cancer and genital warts. Worldwide, cervical cancer is the second most common cancer in women. The FDA approved Gardasil for females age 9 to 26 years.

Gardasil, manufactured by Merck & Co., Inc., of Whitehouse Station, New Jersey, became the first FDA-approved HPV vaccine. A London-based firm, GlaxoSmithKline PLC, was expected to seek approval in 2007 for a second HPV vaccine. In the early 2000's, HPV was the most common sexually transmitted disease in the United States, affecting millions of women and men. Because Gardasil is effective only prior to HPV infection, experts recommend giving the vaccine to girls at an early age, before they begin having sex. By 2006, there was not yet an approved HPV vaccine for males.

On June 29, the U.S. Advisory Committee on Immunization Practices recommended that all 11- and 12-year-old girls receive an HPV vaccine. The panel is part of the U.S. Centers for Disease Control and Prevention. Federal officials were expected to accept the panel's recommendation and add the HPV vaccine to the federal list of immunizations recommended for children.

Inhaled insulin. On January 27, the FDA approved a Pfizer product called Exubera, a powder form of insulin that is inhaled rather than injected into the body. It was the first new insulin treatment for diabetes since insulin was discovered in 1921. Insulin is a hormone that regulates the body's use of sugars. Diabetes results when the body cannot produce or use enough insulin. Before inhaled insulin was developed, the only way for people with diabetes to put insulin into their systems was through frequent, painful needle injections. Clinical trials of Exubera indicated that it was safe and effective in the short term. However, many experts remained concerned about the possible long-term effects of Exubera on the lungs. The FDA recommended that smokers and people with asthma, bronchitis, or emphysema avoid Exubera. ■ Alfred J. Smuskiewicz

See also **AIDS; Health care issues; Medicine; Mental health.**

East Timor. See Asia.

Eastern Orthodox Churches.
Ecumenical Patriarch Bartholomew, the leader of Orthodox Christians, visited St. Nicholas Cathedral in Tarpon Springs, Florida, in January 2006. He presided over the 100th anniversary of the parish's Epiphany festival, celebrating the baptism of Jesus. In September, after Pope Benedict XVI made comments that offended many Muslims, Bartholomew called for "sincere dialogue based on tolerance." The patriarch asked people of all faiths to "avoid situations which can offend each other's beliefs."

Russia. The government of Vladimir Putin tightened its relationship with the Russian Orthodox Church in 2006. On Russian Airborne Forces Day in August, troops marched in a religious procession with church priests. In September, some public schools introduced a course on Orthodox Christian culture, sparking debate. In the same month, Putin attended the consecration of a cathedral in Kaliningrad in western Russia.

Church leaders restored unity to the Russian Orthodox Church in 2006. The Patriarchate of Moscow and the breakaway Russian Orthodox Church Outside Russia reached an agreement in September that helped heal a division caused by the Communist October Revolution of 1917.

Jerusalem. In December 2006, Attalla Hanna, a Palestinian priest, was ordained Theodosios, Archbishop of Sabastia. He joined the ethnic

Greek bishops of the Patriarchate as the first Palestinian bishop since the early 1980's.

Tensions between the Patriarch Theophilos III and his deposed predecessor, Irineos I, continued in 2006. During a February holiday celebration, the church held two processions—one by followers of Theophilos and the other by Irineos's supporters.

United States. The Standing Conference of the Canonical Orthodox Bishops in the Americas (SCOBA) met in Chicago in October for its third national meeting to promote unity among the Orthodox Churches. SCOBA asked the churches to "bear public witness on matters of spiritual and moral concern" in the nation and called for a "Commission on Canonical and Pastoral Issues."

The Orthodox Church in America, a branch of the Russian Orthodox Church, was shaken in February by charges of financial corruption. The scandal, involving top church officials, centered on large sums misused in the 1990's. In September 2006, the church borrowed $1.7 million to cover the missing funds and the costs of an investigation.

A New York appeals court in June dismissed a lawsuit against the Greek Orthodox Archdiocese of America challenging its 2003 Charter. Plaintiffs from Orthodox Christian Laity, a lay advocacy group based in West Palm Beach, Florida, sought a return to the 1977 Charter.   ■ Stanley S. Harakas

See also **Islam; Roman Catholic Church.**

Economics, United States. The economy of the United States began 2006 on a solid footing and weathered a growth-sapping surge in fuel costs in the first eight months of the year. Fuel prices were moderating by September, but by then, housing values had plunged, and consumers had slowed their spending. In 2006, the Federal Reserve System, the nation's central bank, halted its two-year program of raising interest rates designed to curb inflationary pressures, and some analysts wondered whether the economy was merely experiencing a temporary slow spell or might weaken further in 2007.

The housing bubble. News from several sources in the second half of 2006 suggested that a housing "bubble" (overly high prices) might be about to burst. According to the National Association of Realtors, sales of new houses in October slid into the greatest monthly decline since 1970. A survey of home builders published by the National Association of Home Builders in August 2006 revealed the lowest level of confidence in 15 years. Sales of existing houses—a much larger market—sustained a 10-percent decline in October, also the sharpest drop since 1970.

The overheated housing market had long underpinned vigorous growth in the U.S. economy, analysts pointed out. Moreover, many home-buyers had obtained adjustable-rate or

SELECTED KEY U.S. ECONOMIC INDICATORS

Gross domestic product
Billions of dollars

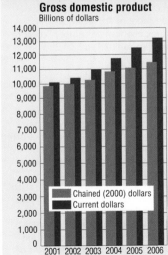

Chained (2000) dollars
Current dollars

2001 2002 2003 2004 2005 2006

Unemployment rate
Percent of labor force

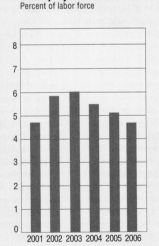

2001 2002 2003 2004 2005 2006

Consumer Price Index
Percent change from previous year

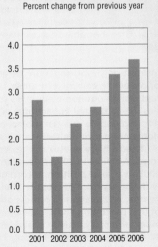

2001 2002 2003 2004 2005 2006

Sources: U.S. Department of Commerce and U.S. Department of Labor, except 2006 figures, which are estimates from The Conference Board.

The gross domestic product (GDP) measures the value in current prices of all goods and services produced within a country in a year. Many economists believe the GDP is an accurate measure of the nation's total economic performance. Chained dollars show the amount adjusted for inflation. The unemployment rate is the percentage of the total labor force that is unemployed and actively seeking work. The Consumer Price Index measures inflation by showing the change in prices of selected goods and services consumed by urban families and individuals.

John Kenneth Galbraith on the left

John Kenneth Galbraith, the Canadian-born economist whose persuasive, skillfully written books influenced political leaders and excited the public, died on April 29, 2006. During a long career as an author, teacher, and public servant, Galbraith never abandoned his belief in the need for a strong governmental role in economic affairs to balance the inequities of the free enterprise system.

Born in 1908 in Ontario, Galbraith intended to follow his politically active father into farming. However, the economic aspects of farming—seen against the backdrop of the farming crisis of the Great Depression—attracted his attention. He completed his education with a Ph.D. in agricultural economics in 1934 from the University of California, Berkeley, becoming a U.S. citizen in 1937.

In 1949, Galbraith joined the economics department at Harvard University, a post he held until his retirement in 1975. Also in the 1940's, Galbraith launched his career as an influential advisor to U.S. presidents, including Franklin D. Roosevelt, John F. Kennedy, and Lyndon Johnson. From 1961 to 1963, he served as ambassador to India. He also played a major role in developing Johnson's Great Society, a liberal program designed to help the poor and improve general economic security.

Galbraith wrote nearly 50 books. His most famous was the best-selling *The Affluent Society* (1958). In it, he contended that the greatest threat to economic and political stability was the widening gap between the rich and the poor. To establish a "good society," he argued for increased spending on society's "public goods"—that is, education, highways, and parks—to be funded by consumption taxes on consumer goods. More conservative free market economists strongly criticized Galbraith's belief in government spending and economic regulation. They also challenged his examination of economics within a social and cultural context, seeing mathematical models as a more accurate and realistic foundation for economic theory.

In 2000, U.S. President Bill Clinton awarded Galbraith the Medal of Freedom. At the awards ceremony, Galbraith was praised for making "complex economic theories...comprehensible to a wide audience" and for "resolutely promot[ing] social justice."

interest-only mortgages on the assumption that prices would continue to surge, and many others had cashed out home equity to fund other activities. The potential impact of a collapse of the housing bubble was the subject of much discussion among economists in late 2006.

The factory sector of the economy performed tepidly in 2006. The sector had ended 2005 in a good position, according to analysts with the Institute for Supply Management (ISM), a Tempe, Arizona-based professional organization of U.S. purchasing managers. The ISM monthly index of factory activity peaked at 59.2 in October 2005, dipped to 54.8 in January 2006, but rebounded to 56.7 in February. However, the index sagged as 2006 wore on, sinking to 49.5 in November, which indicated contraction in the sector. (An index value of 50 is the dividing line between growth and contraction.)

One obvious contributor to the factory sector's

stagnation, economists noted, was the steady rise in fuel costs through the first half and into the third quarter of the year. Fuel price inflation worked its way through the economy in many directions, but analysts noted that manufacturing, which requires considerable amounts of energy and uses such energy products as petroleum as raw materials, was hit especially hard.

Automakers. The outlook for the U.S. auto industry, a major source of manufacturing jobs, darkened in 2006 as Ford Motor Company of Dearborn, Michigan, and General Motors (GM) Corporation of Detroit both announced plans for plant closings and job cuts. Product lines of these former powerhouses of U.S. manufacturing continued to lose market share in 2006, reflected in multibillion-dollar losses per each quarter by GM, Ford, and the other member of the U.S. "Big Three," the U.S. division of DaimlerChrysler AG of Germany.

and on the right, Milton Friedman

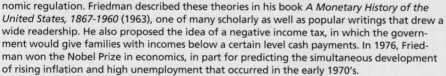

Milton Friedman, a Nobel Prize-winning economist who championed the power of the free enterprise system to create prosperity and support individual freedom, died on Nov. 16, 2006. Friedman argued against government intervention in the economy, claiming that the forces of a free market would efficiently solve most economic problems. He also insisted that political freedom was impossible without economic freedom. Although Friedman's conservative theories aroused heated debate, they made him one of the most influential economists of the 20th century.

For most of his career, Friedman, who was born in 1912, was associated with the University of Chicago, where he earned his master's degree in 1933 and to which he returned as a faculty member in 1946. There, Friedman established himself as the leader of what became known as the Chicago School of economics. He and like-minded economists argued that governments could keep prices stable and promote growth by increasing the supply of money in circulation at a constant rate. They also argued that this should be the chief—if not the only—form of government economic regulation. Friedman described these theories in his book *A Monetary History of the United States, 1867-1960* (1963), one of many scholarly as well as popular writings that drew a wide readership. He also proposed the idea of a negative income tax, in which the government would give families with incomes below a certain level cash payments. In 1976, Friedman won the Nobel Prize in economics, in part for predicting the simultaneous development of rising inflation and high unemployment that occurred in the early 1970's.

Friedman's theories found their strongest support during the 1980's among such conservatives as U.S. President Ronald Reagan and Prime Minister Margaret Thatcher of the United Kingdom. Officials in Chile and other countries and at international lending institutions were also influenced by his theories. In the mid-1980's, however, monetarism began to lose its credibility after the U.S. economy failed to respond to monetarist policies as predicted. Despite these problems, Friedman never abandoned his belief that an unrestrained economy is essential for individual success and political liberty. "The free market," he wrote, "is the only mechanism that has ever been discovered for achieving participatory democracy."

According to analysts, U.S. automakers had stayed too long with product lines of big, gas-hungry vehicles without investing resources in the development of energy-thrifty hybrid-fuel models. The latter became hot sellers for foreign car makers in 2006, as U.S. pump prices soared.

On November 13, the heads of Chrysler, Ford, and GM were invited to the White House for an auto industry summit with President George W. Bush. Although the three executives underscored that they were not asking for a federal bailout, they did ask for federally sponsored reforms of the U.S. health care and pension systems. According to a report jointly issued by Chrysler, Ford, and GM, the U.S. Big Three spent $12.2 billion in 2005 on employee health care costs, compared with $1.6 billion spent by their top foreign competitors.

The services sector, which constitutes a larger part of the U.S. economy than manufacturing, presented a mixed picture in 2006. The ISM's nonmanufacturing index tracked the progress of the group of businesses that cater to consumers' service needs from a high in late 2005 through a trough in mid-2006 and to an apparent recovery in October. Specific months' readings included 59.2 in October 2005; 56.8 in January 2006; 52.9 in September; and 57.1 in October. As with the factory sector index, a value of 50 serves as the division between expansion and contraction.

The nation's largest service industry, passenger airlines, began 2006 with many top carriers in bankruptcy, operating under court protection from creditors while they reorganized. However, United Airlines of Elk Grove Village, Illinois, emerged from bankruptcy in February, and as the year went on, Atlanta-based Delta AirLines and Eagan, Minnesota-based Northwest Airlines—both still under bankruptcy protection—won battles with unions to slash labor costs and benefits. Airlines overall appeared to have turned a corner by the end of 2006 in fighting cost pressures. Costs had built up gradually over many years and had become critical for many airlines in the wake of the economically destabilizing September 2001 terrorist attacks on the United States. In 2006, many jetliners were flying with their seats filled, but rising fuel prices substantially increased the airlines' operating costs and cut into profits.

Consumers. Average incomes grew modestly, but layoffs or pay cuts swept some industries, and consumers felt the impact of gasoline prices, which peaked in mid-2006 at around $3 a gallon for regular. Pump prices siphoned off disposable income, leading analysts to blame fuel prices for dampening sales of the nation's largest retailer, Wal-Mart of Bentonville, Arkansas. According to figures released by the company, sales in the third quarter of 2006 rose by a lackluster 1.5 percent, and monthly sales actually declined marginally in November. Economists had long warned that households were relying too much on home equity loans to cover normal expenses as well as special costs. As housing prices declined steadily in 2006, consumers lost that source of ready cash, further crimping spending.

The Conference Board, a New York City-based research group that measures consumer attitudes monthly, reported its index starting the year at 107, rising to 110 in the spring, and then dipping to 100.2 in August. However, fuel prices finally began to decline in August, helping lift the gauge to 105.9 in September.

The Fed stops pushing. To curb inflationary pressures, the Federal Reserve (the Fed) had raised short-term interest rates 17 consecutive times in quarter-point increments since June 2004. The policy began under Fed Chairman Alan Greenspan, who retired in early 2006, and continued under his successor, Ben Bernanke. However, the Fed's governing board declined to post another raise at its August meeting, leaving the rate unchanged at 5.25 percent. The decision helped spur a previously lackluster stock market, pushing the Dow Jones Industrial Average above 12,000 in mid-October for the first time in history.

The U.S. gross domestic product (GDP), the total value of all goods and services produced in a country in a year, reflected the generally perceived economic slowdown in mid- to late 2006. The nation's GDP grew at a robust 5.6-percent annual pace in the first quarter of 2006, comparing favorably with the 3.2-percent GDP growth reported for calendar year 2005. However, growth slowed to 2.6 percent in the second quarter—with fuel prices then at record highs—and sagged to 2.2 percent in the third quarter.   ■ John D. Boyd

See also **Automobile; Economics, world; Energy supply; People in the news** (Ben Bernanke); **Transportation.**

Economics, world. Global commerce proved resilient in 2006, absorbing record-high oil prices in the first half of the year and a slow-down in the key United States economy in the second half. According to economists' forecasts, global economic growth for 2006 was expected to match or exceed that of 2005. The worldwide expansion broadened during the year partly because key European economies began to rally and Japan continued a recovery from the *deflationary* era (period of falling prices) that had plagued that country since the mid-1990's.

China, the world's most populous nation, was again an important engine of international economic growth. Its economy continued to surge at a 10-percent annual rate of growth in 2006, and China once again was a major source of world trade expansion in 2006.

Resilient global economy. In September, the International Monetary Fund (IMF)—a United Nations-affiliated agency that provides short-term credit to member nations—revised its estimate of global economic growth upward, forecasting 5.1-percent growth for 2006. That figure compared favorably with the 4.9-percent rate of global economic growth that occurred in 2005.

One wild card for future growth, economists noted, was the performance of the massive U.S. economy, the world's largest. The U.S. economy started out strong in 2006, posting a vigorous 5.6-percent rate of growth in the first quarter. However, the expansion cooled progressively during the year, with government economists reporting a lackluster 2.2-percent rate of growth in the third quarter.

Typically, a slowdown like the one in mid-2006 in the United States with its huge consumer market—which pulls in far more goods from other countries than it sells abroad—would be a cause for concern about economic performance in other regions of the world. However, it appeared to economists by late 2006 that strong consumer demand in other key world economies could take up the slack—barring an unexpectedly sharp drop in U.S. demand.

The world's major central banks—government bodies that control their nations' money supply—reacted to a variety of pressures through 2006. Strong economic growth and rising prices of key *commodities* (raw materials) early in the year kept central bankers pushing up interest rates in an attempt to rein in inflation. As consumer markets slowed in the United States, however, that nation's central bank, the Federal Reserve (the Fed), found it necessary to change course. Although the Fed raised U.S. interest rates through June—continuing a policy of previous years—its governing board declined to raise rates further when it met in August.

However, the European Central Bank (ECB) continued pushing rates upward in the Eurozone, the group of 12 European Union (EU) member nations using the euro as their common currency. The Bank of England, the central bank for the United Kingdom, also continued its policy of raising interest rates. In July, the Bank of Japan raised interest rates a quarter-point for the first time in six years. The action signaled a recovery of confidence in the Japanese economy, which had been stagnant for many years.

Regional trends. Forecasts by IMF economists in September indicated that European economies were gaining momentum in 2006. The IMF forecast a 2.4-percent growth rate for the Eurozone in 2006. That figure compared favorably with the region's lackluster performance in 2005, when economic growth was 1.3 percent. Germany, the Eurozone's largest single economy, was poised to post 2-percent growth in 2006, according to the IMF, after stalling at 0.9 percent in 2005. France's 2.4-percent estimated growth in 2006 doubled that of 2005, and Italy's predicted 1.5-percent growth represented an upsurge for an economy that was essentially flat in 2005. In Europe outside of the Eurozone, the important economy of the United Kingdom was forecast to expand by 2.7 percent in 2006, up from 1.9 percent in 2005.

Latin America's largest economies, Mexico and Brazil, both improved in 2006, compared with 2005. The IMF forecast a 4-percent rate of growth for Mexico and 3.5 percent for Brazil. Resource-rich Brazil sent record exports abroad, notably to supply the rapidly industrializing nations of China and India, analysts noted.

In Asia, China's 10-percent forecast rate of growth for 2006 and India's 8.3 percent were both down slightly from 2005, but nonetheless, these two countries' economies remained the fastest-growing among nations with major populations. Growth in both economies continued to be fueled by exports as well as robust domestic demand for goods and services. Economists forecast that Russia's resource-rich economy would match or surpass its 2005 performance, posting a growth rate of at least 6.5 percent.

Economists noted that economic activity was severely interrupted in regions afflicted with internal strife or warfare. Such areas included Afghanistan, Congo (Kinshasa), Iraq, Israel, Lebanon, and the territories administered by the Palestinian Authority, and Sudan in Africa. Excluding these troubled areas, many parts of the Middle East and Africa experienced broad economic growth in 2006.

Troubled industries. In the United States, the "Big Three" automakers—Ford Motor Company of Dearborn, Michigan; General Motors

(GM) Corporation of Detroit; and the U.S. division of DaimlerChrysler AG of Germany—all lost money in 2006 and underwent retrenchment that included plant closings and layoffs, even as global rivals such as Japan's Toyota Motor Corporation posted record profits. Analysts noted that the Big Three cutbacks were sending ripples through the U.S. economy, affecting industries ranging from parts suppliers to trucking firms.

Airbus, one of Europe's biggest manufacturers, recorded huge losses in 2006 as a result of delays in promised deliveries of the company's "super-jumbo" A380 passenger jet. Airbus representatives said that production problems had unexpectedly slowed down the completion and testing of the airplanes. In November, the FedEx Corporation of Memphis, Tennessee—the world's largest cargo airline—canceled its order for 10 Airbus A380's, announcing that it would buy Boeing 777 freighters instead. A few weeks later, officials of Korean Air of South Korea announced that they had placed a $5.5-billion order with the Chicago-based Boeing Company. News that Airbus was losing highly competitive bids to Boeing depressed the European aviation giant's stock values further. ■ John D. Boyd

See also **Automobile; Aviation; Bank; Economics, United States; Energy supply; International trade; Latin America: A Special Report.**

Ecuador. In a Nov. 26, 2006, presidential runoff, voters elected Rafael Correa as president of Ecuador. Correa, a leftist politician with close ties to Venezuela's President Hugo Chávez, decisively defeated opponent Alvaro Noboa, a pro-market conservative and billionaire banana planter. Correa pledged to seek membership for Ecuador, South America's second largest oil producer, in the Organization of the Petroleum Exporting Countries (OPEC). He also vowed to revoke a lease agreement with the United States for use of an air base on the Ecuadorean coast.

In May, Ecuadorean officials revoked a contract with Occidental Petroleum Company of Los Angeles to operate oil fields in Ecuador. The action followed unsuccessful efforts to resolve a legal dispute with the U.S. company—Ecuador's biggest foreign investor—and protests by Ecuadoreans against foreign energy companies.

In March, thousands of Ecuadoreans blocked roads leading into Quito, the capital, to protest free trade talks between Ecuadorean and U.S. representatives in Washington, D.C. Protest leaders claimed that the proposed free trade pact would flood Ecuador with cheap agricultural imports from the United States. The government of President Alfredo Palacio deployed troops to clear the roads. ■ Nathan A. Haverstock

See also **Latin America: A Special Report.**

Education. The United States Department of Education estimated that a record 55.5 million students enrolled in the nation's prekindergarten, elementary, and high schools in fall 2006. Much of the growth was attributed to a high rate of immigration and to high birth rates among Hispanic immigrants.

The Pew Hispanic Center, a nonpartisan group that studies the U.S. Latino population, said Hispanic enrollment increased by 1.3 million students from 2000 to 2005 and accounted for 19 percent of the student population. White enrollment fell by 1.8 million in five years and accounted for 57 percent of all public school students, down from 78 percent in 1972. Black enrollment dropped by 75,000 in five years and accounted for 16 percent of all students, about the same as in 1972.

About 6.5 million students were enrolled in private schools in 2006—about 12 percent of all students, a percentage only slightly higher than that in 1996. The share of private school students enrolled in parish-run Roman Catholic schools fell from 55 percent in the 1989-1990 school year to 46 percent in 2003-2004 (the latest year for which figures are available). At the same time, the share of students in conservative Christian schools increased to 15 percent from 11 percent of all private school enrollment.

The Education Department reported that 1.1 million students were home-schooled in 2003 (latest figure available). Twenty-nine percent of those students were studying at a high school level.

College enrollment reached a record 17.6 million students in 2006 as children born in the late 1980's to the youngest baby boomers reached college age. About 40 percent of students attended college part-time, and 75 percent attended public colleges and universities. Women accounted for 58 percent of college students and earned 58 percent of all bachelor's degrees, 61 percent of master's degrees, and 48 percent of doctorates.

Single-sex education. New rules announced by the Education Department allowed public schools, as of November 24, to offer single-sex classes if "substantially equal" coed classes are available as well and if attendance in the single-sex classes is voluntary. Districts may also offer single-sex schools if a "substantially equal" coed school is available to students of the opposite gender. Although single-sex private schools have long been permitted, public school districts could offer a same-sex school for one gender only if one was available for the other gender as well.

Education spending. The Education Department estimated that states would spend an average of $9,562 on each of their elementary and secondary students in the 2006-2007 academic year. In the 2003-2004 school year (latest figures available), New Jersey's spending was the highest,

at $13,338 per student, while Utah's $4,991 per-pupil spending was the lowest. Estimates indicated that states would spend an average of $24,821 for each public four-year college or university student and $10,674 per student at each two-year college.

College costs. The College Board released its survey of college costs in October 2006. According to the report, tuition and fees at public four-year colleges rose 6.3 percent in 2006, to an average of $5,836. With the addition of room and board, the total annual cost at a four-year public college averaged $12,796. Tuition and fees at private four-year colleges averaged $22,218, with total costs reaching $30,367, an increase of 5.9 percent. Two-year community college tuition and fees rose only 4.1 percent, to $2,272. The government's Commission on the Future of Higher Education warned that rising costs will keep 2 million students from attending college from 2000 to 2010.

Dropout rates. According to the Education Department, nearly 3.2 million students graduated from high school in 2006. An average 75 percent of students graduated with a diploma four years after they entered high school (based on 2003-2004 school year figures, the latest available). A study released in 2006 by the Bill & Melinda Gates Foundation, however, reported that only 22 percent of Detroit students graduated on time and that 13 other urban school districts had on-time graduation rates lower than 50 percent.

A study by the National Center for Public Policy and Higher Education in San Jose, a *nonpartisan* (not politically affiliated) think tank, raised similar concerns about college completion rates. The group reported that 35 percent of Americans ages 18 to 24 attend college but only 17 percent of those who enroll complete their degrees. Fifteen other industrialized nations, led by Japan, have higher completion rates.

Early admission. In September, Harvard University in Cambridge, Massachusetts, announced that it will drop its early-admission process beginning with students applying in 2007 for the 2008-2009 school year. Under Harvard's program, called *early action,* students who applied in the fall were notified by December 15 whether they had been admitted to the school. (Other institutions follow a process called *early decision,* under which students learn of acceptance in late fall and then are honor-bound to enroll at the school.) Some universities admit as much as half of their freshman class through early admission programs, cutting recruiting costs. But critics say the process favors students who do not need to compare financial aid offers from other colleges. Several other prominent universities quickly followed Harvard's lead.

Test scores. According to ACT Inc., the average composite score on its ACT college-admissions test was 21.1 out of a possible 36 points in 2006, up from 20.9 a year earlier—the biggest increase in 20 years. On its new writing test, students averaged 7.7 points on a scale of 2 to 12. The company noted that the results indicated that only 42 percent of test takers are ready for college-level math and only 27 percent are prepared for college-level biology.

The College Board reported that scores fell on its SAT admissions test in 2006. The company attributed the drop to a declining number of students who take the test more than once. Students who take the test a second time typically show a 30-point score increase, officials said, but the longer, costlier version of the redesigned test seems to be discouraging repeat test taking. The average math score was 518 out of a possible 800 points, down two points from the year earlier. The average score on the critical-reading test was 503, a five-point drop. The average score on the new SAT writing test was 502 points.

Earlier in 2006, the College Board was forced to rescore nearly 6,000 SAT tests administered in October 2005 because the tests were incorrectly scored. In most cases, the corrected scores were within 100 points of a student's original score. Nevertheless, the problem created anxiety for students and colleges alike, as it came to light just as the admissions process was ending at most schools. ■ June Kronholz

Egypt. The Egyptian government continued in 2006 to suppress any secular opposition to the administration of President Hosni Mubarak. The leader of the political party al-Ghad (Tomorrow), Ayman Nour, who ran against Mubarak in the presidential elections of 2005, remained in prison in 2006, serving a five-year term. A court rejected Nour's appeal on May 18. According to political experts, the charges against Nour are politically motivated—essentially punishment for daring to run against Mubarak—and the court's rejection of his appeal suggests that Mubarak is able to manipulate the judiciary for political ends. By contrast, the government continued in 2006 to prop up the Islamic opposition (Muslim Brotherhood), and allowed it to increase its representation in parliament from 17 seats to 88. Analysts noted that Egyptian authorities use the Muslim Brotherhood as a "bogeyman" to scare the West, particularly the United States.

Attacks on Coptic Christians. Knife-wielding Muslim fundamentalists attacked Coptic Christians in three churches in Alexandria on April 14. (Copts are the native Christians of Egypt.) One worshiper was killed and at least 15 others were wounded. The official government explanation that a single deranged individual carried out the attacks in three churches at different locations in a span of one hour was derided by Coptic Church leaders. Hundreds of Copts subsequently staged a demonstration in Alexandria, demanding that the government stop persecuting them. The approximately 10 million Copts living in Egypt complain that Egyptian authorities treat them as second-class citizens.

Dahab attacks. Terrorists detonated three coordinated bombings on April 24 at Dahab, a Red Sea resort frequented by both Egyptians and foreign tourists. At least 30 people were killed in the attacks, and more than 115 others were wounded. The attacks coincided with an Egyptian holiday celebrating the Israeli withdrawal from the Sinai Peninsula in 1982. Terrorism experts noted that all evidence suggests that the operation was executed by al-Tawhid wal-Jihad, a local Islamic fundamentalist organization with links to Osama bin Laden's al-Qa`ida terrorist network.

Death. The Egyptian novelist Naguib Mahfouz died on Aug. 30, 2006, at the age of 94. He had been awarded the Nobel Prize in literature in 1988. In 1994, he was stabbed by a Muslim fundamentalist who objected to *Children of Gebelawi*, Mahfouz's allegorical novel on religion. A product of Egypt's liberal era, which lasted from 1919 until 1952, Mahfouz never wavered in his support for secularism and liberal democracy.

■ Marius Deeb

See also Deaths; Middle East; Terrorism.

Elections for federal, state, and local offices were held across the United States on Nov. 7, 2006. For the first time since 1994, the Democratic Party won control of both houses of Congress and a majority of state governorships. Political experts suggested that the results showed voters' dissatisfaction with the Republican Party, which had endured a number of high-profile scandals in 2005 and 2006 and had championed an increasingly unpopular U.S.-led war in Iraq.

Senate races. The Democratic take-over of the Senate—considered a long shot before the elections—was confirmed on November 9 when two Republicans conceded races that had been too close to call on election night. The two senators, Conrad R. Burns of Montana and George F. Allen of Virginia, joined four other ousted Republican incumbents—James M. Talent of Missouri, Michael DeWine of Ohio, Richard J. Santorum of Pennsylvania, and Lincoln D. Chafee of Rhode Island. The Democrats' gain of these 6 seats raised their total to 49. Two independents who won their Senate elections announced they would caucus with the Democrats, creating a 51-seat majority over the Republicans' 49.

In Virginia, Democrat James Webb—a former Republican who was secretary of the Navy under President Ronald Reagan—squeaked past Allen by about 9,300 votes out of over 2.3 million cast.

Allen's campaign had been damaged in August when he used a derogatory ethnic slur to describe a Webb campaign worker of Indian descent. In Montana, Democrat Jon Tester, the state Senate president, defeated Burns by about 3,500 votes out of over 400,000 cast. Burns's campaign had been hurt because of his links to Jack Abramoff, a Washington, D.C., lobbyist who in 2006 pleaded guilty to a variety of political corruption charges. From 2001 to 2004, Burns had received campaign contributions from Abramoff and his associates.

In Pennsylvania, Santorum—the third-ranking Republican U.S. senator—lost to State Treasurer Bob Casey, Jr. In Missouri, Talent lost to State Auditor Claire McCaskill in a close race. In Ohio, DeWine fell to U.S. Representative Sherrod Brown, and in Rhode Island, Chafee lost to Sheldon Whitehouse, a former state attorney general.

Democrats' hopes of filling the seat of retiring U.S. Senator Bill Frist (R., Tennessee) were dashed when Republican Bob Corker, a former Chattanooga mayor, edged past Democratic U.S. Representative Harold Ford, Jr. However, Democrats kept seats that had been vulnerable to Republican take-over. Senator Bob Menendez (D., New Jersey), dogged by allegations of ties to corrupt state officials and contractors, survived a challenge from Republican Tom Kean, Jr., son of a former governor. In Maryland, Democratic U.S. Representative Benjamin L. Cardin defeated Republican Lieutenant Governor Michael Steele to replace departing Democratic U.S. Senator Paul Sarbanes. In Minnesota, Democrat Amy Klobuchar, the Hennepin County attorney, beat Republican U.S. Representative Mark Kennedy to replace retiring U.S. Senator Mark Dayton (D.).

In an unusual contest in Connecticut, U.S. Senator Joe Lieberman was reelected as an independent after having lost the August Democratic primary to Ned Lamont, a businessman. Lamont's stance against the war in Iraq had propelled his primary victory, but Lieberman, who had supported the war, won the general election with support from many Republicans and moderates.

U.S. House races. Democrats defended all their seats in the U.S. House of Representatives and picked up 31 more—including 1 seat that had been held by a Democratic-leaning independent—to finish with a 233-202 majority over Republicans. The list of defeated Republicans included such House veterans as Nancy Johnson of Connecticut; E. Clay Shaw, Jr., of Florida; and Jim Leach of Iowa.

A big factor in many House races was the involvement of several Republican House members in scandals. Democrat Zack Space won the election to succeed Bob Ney (R., Ohio), who had resigned after pleading guilty in October to corruption in connection with the Abramoff scandal. Democrat Tim Mahoney won the seat vacated by Mark Foley

(R., Florida), who had resigned in September after it was revealed that he had sent sexually explicit electronic messages to male teen-age congressional pages. Don Sherwood (R., Pennsylvania) lost his reelection bid amid publicity about an extramarital affair. Curt Weldon (R., Pennsylvania) lost his race after coming under federal investigation for corruption. John Sweeney (R., New York) was dogged by a police report alleging that he had physically abused his wife. Republicans even lost the Texas seat that had been held by the once-powerful House Majority Leader Tom DeLay. A Texas grand jury indicted DeLay in 2005 on charges of violating state campaign finance laws, and he resigned his House seat in June 2006 amid the scandal.

Gubernatorial races. The governorships of six states—Arkansas, Colorado, Maryland, Massachusetts, New York, and Ohio—switched from Republican to Democratic hands in the 2006 elections, leaving the country with 28 Democratic and 22 Republican state governors. In a tight race in Maryland, voters rejected the incumbent, Republican Governor Bob Ehrlich, Jr., in favor of his Democratic challenger, Baltimore Mayor Martin O'Malley. In the other five states, Democrats won open races for seats vacated by Republicans.

Massachusetts voters chose Democrat Deval Patrick, a businessman, over Republican Lieutenant Governor Kerry Healey. Patrick became the second African American to be elected as a state governor in U.S. history. The first was L. Douglas Wilder, Virginia's governor from 1990 to 1994. In Ohio, Democratic U.S. Representative Ted Strickland defeated Republican J. Kenneth Blackwell, the Ohio secretary of state. In New York, Democrat Eliot Spitzer, the state attorney general, beat Republican John Faso, a former minority leader in the state House of Representatives. In Arkansas, Democrat Mike Beebe, the state attorney general, beat Republican Asa Hutchinson, a former high-level official in the U.S. Department of Homeland Security. In Colorado, Denver District Attorney Bill Ritter, a Democrat, beat Republican U.S. Representative Bob Beauprez.

Democrats also kept all governor's offices they already controlled. In Iowa, the seat of departing Governor Tom Vilsack (D.) was captured by Iowa's Democratic secretary of state, Chet Culver. Incumbent Democratic governors who won reelection were Janet Napolitano, Arizona; Rod Blagojevich, Illinois; Kathleen Sebelius, Kansas; John Baldacci, Maine; Jennifer Granholm, Michigan; John Lynch, New Hampshire; Bill Richardson, New Mexico; Brad Henry, Oklahoma; Ted Kulongoski, Oregon; Ed Rendell, Pennsylvania; Phil Bredesen, Tennessee; Jim Doyle, Wisconsin; and Dave Freudenthal, Wyoming.

Alaskans made history when they elected Republican Sarah Palin as their first female governor. She beat Democrat Tony Knowles, a former governor. Palin had already ousted the incumbent, Frank

Democratic congressional leaders—(from left) Representative Rahm Emanuel of Illinois, Representative Nancy Pelosi of California, Senator Harry Reid of Nevada, and Senator Chuck Schumer of New York—celebrate their party's success in the Nov. 7, 2006, midterm elections, which gave the Democrats control of both houses of Congress.

Murkowski, in the August Republican primary. In Florida, Idaho, and Nevada, Republicans were elected to open seats vacated by Republican governors. These winning Republicans, respectively, were Florida Attorney General Charlie Crist, Idaho U.S. Representative C. L. "Butch" Otter, and Nevada U.S. Representative Jim Gibbons. Meanwhile, incumbent Republican governors who retained their offices were Bob Riley, Alabama; Arnold Schwarzenegger, California; M. Jodi Rell, Connecticut; Sonny Perdue, Georgia; Linda Lingle, Hawaii; Tim Pawlenty, Minnesota; Dave Heineman, Nebraska; Donald Carcieri, Rhode Island; Mark Sanford, South Carolina; Mike Rounds, South Dakota; Rick Perry, Texas; and Jim Douglas, Vermont.

Ballot initiatives. South Dakota voters resoundingly repealed a measure, approved by state lawmakers, that would have outlawed almost all abortions, even in cases of incest and rape. The law had been aimed to spark court proceedings that would cause the U.S. Supreme Court to revisit its 1973 *Roe v. Wade* ruling in favor of abortion rights. Meanwhile, voters in California and Oregon rejected proposals that would have required parental notification before abortions could be performed on minors.

In Colorado, Idaho, South Carolina, South Dakota, Tennessee, Virginia, and Wisconsin, voters approved state constitutional amendments to ban gay marriage. Similar constitutional prohibitions had already been approved by voters in 20 states. Arizona, however, became the first state in which voters rejected a proposed gay marriage ban. In Colorado, the anti-gay-marriage campaign had prompted a former male prostitute to accuse a key leader of the campaign—Ted Haggard, president of the National Association of Evangelicals (NAE)—of having had a three-year sexual relationship with him. Haggard initially denied the accusation, but he later resigned as NAE president and said he was guilty of what he called "sexual immorality."

In Missouri, voters amended the state constitution to legalize embryonic stem cell research. Michigan voters approved a measure to end affirmative action in public college admissions and government hiring. Voters in six states approved minimum wage increases. In Arizona, Nevada, and Ohio, voters enacted strict smoking bans in public places. Marijuana legalization proposals lost in Colorado, Nevada, and South Dakota. Measures to cap state spending were rejected in Maine, Nebraska, and Oregon. ■ Geoffrey A. Campbell

See also **Congress of the United States; Democratic Party; Disability; Republican Party; State government; United States, Government of the; United States, Government of the: A Special Report; United States, President of the.**

Electronics. Two new optical disc formats, both capable of storing high-definition movies, reached consumer markets in 2006. The HD DVD (High-Definition DVD or High-Density DVD) and the Blu-ray Disc both resemble a standard DVD but hold more digital data and support higher-quality video and audio. The blue lasers used on HD DVD and Blu-ray can write and read more data than standard DVD lasers. As a result, they can include more sophisticated "extras" on movie and television-show discs and larger animated worlds on video-game discs. Players for both new formats typically can also play standard DVD's and CD's.

Neither HD DVD nor Blu-ray established clear market dominance in 2006, because of the high price of the players ($500 and up), the fact that many people did not yet own high-definition TV sets, and the limited movie selection. By the end of 2006, from 100 to 150 movies were available in each format in the United States. Several film studios released titles in both formats, but other studios opted to release titles in only one format.

Among high-tech firms, the main producers and supporters of HD DVD technology included Toshiba Corporation of Tokyo; NEC Corporation of Tokyo; Microsoft Corporation of Redmond, Washington; and Intel Corporation of Santa Clara, California. The key manufacturers promoting Blu-ray technology included Sony Corporation of Tokyo; Samsung Corporation of Songnam, South Korea; Apple Computer, Inc., of Cupertino, California; and Dell Inc. of Round Rock, Texas.

New video-game consoles. Competition in the video-game market heated up in 2006 with the introduction of new game consoles from Sony and from Nintendo Co., Ltd., of Kyoto, Japan. Sony's PlayStation 3 and Nintendo's Wii (pronounced *wee*) both went on sale in North America in November 2006. The PlayStation 3 cost $500 to $600, while Wii sold for $250. Their main competitor, Microsoft's Xbox 360, had debuted in November 2005 with a price tag of $300 to $400.

PlayStation 3 featured advanced Blu-ray technology, which provided massive storage space, high-definition graphics, and the ability to play movies and other media on Blu-ray Discs, DVD's, or CD's. Wii featured a position-sensing controller, which allowed for more physical motion than a normal controller. For example, in a tennis video game, players could swing the controller with the same arm motion used to swing a tennis racket.

Zune takes aim at iPod. In November 2006, Microsoft released its Zune digital media player. The Zune was intended to compete with Apple Computer's market-leading iPod player. The Zune had 30 gigabytes of storage and could hold up to 7,500 songs, 25,000 pictures, or 100 hours of video. It cost $250, the same as a 30-gigabyte iPod. Unlike an iPod, a Zune could send songs

and photos—but not video—wirelessly to other Zunes. Microsoft also launched the online Zune Marketplace, the counterpart to Apple's iTunes Store. Zune users could download songs from the Zune Marketplace for a per-song fee or a $15-per-month subscription. Also, just as songs downloaded from iTunes could not be played on non-iPod players, songs from the Zune Marketplace could not be played on non-Zune players.

Tech industry. Worldwide, the information and communications technology (ICT) industry was expected to grow by 6 percent in 2006, according to a 2006 report from the Organisation for Economic Co-operation and Development, a Paris-based association of 30 developed countries. The report indicated that ICT growth was likely to continue, especially in Internet-related investments, servers using the Linux operating system, digital storage, personal digital assistants, and new portable consumer products. The report also detailed the rise of ICT production in emerging economies, especially that of China. In 2004, China overtook the United States as the world's leading exporter of computer, electronic, and telecommunications goods.   ■ Keith Ferrell

See also **Computer; Telecommunications.**

Employment. See Economics, U.S.; Labor and employment.

Endangered species. See Conservation.

El Salvador. Responding to mounting criticism of his administration's failure to curb violent crime, President Elias Antonio Saca in August 2006 unveiled his third major security plan in three years. The new plan's objectives were to apprehend more high-profile criminals, strengthen police and judicial investigations, and restructure the country's police force.

Previous security plans, implemented in 2003 and 2004, had failed to reduce the rate of violent crime in El Salvador. During the first five months of 2006, the number of murders in the country climbed to 1,873, a 7.5-percent rise over the comparable period in 2005. According to law enforcement officials, many of the killings were the result of gang warfare to control lucrative drug trafficking operations. In a poll published in September 2006, 68 percent of respondents judged that President Saca was failing to deal effectively with violent crime.

Two police officers were killed in San Salvador, the capital, in July when a student demonstration to protest increased bus fares and utility rates turned violent. Salvadoran authorities blamed the violence on radicals of the Farabundo Marti National Liberation Front, a former guerrilla group that in 1992 became a political party.

■ Nathan A. Haverstock

See also **Latin America.**

Energy supply. In 2006, for the second straight year, energy prices surged to record levels on fears of possible fuel shortages. After midyear, however, prices fell as worries over supply disruptions began to ease. A relatively calm hurricane season in the Gulf of Mexico that produced no major storms was a major contributor to the increase in supplies of petroleum and natural gas. In 2005, Hurricanes Katrina and Rita had severely interrupted the production of oil and gas in the region.

Oil and gasoline prices. After approaching $80 a barrel in the summer of 2006, crude oil prices fell to $50 to $70 a barrel—still high by historical standards. The lower crude oil prices were reflected in cheaper per-gallon costs of such fuels as gasoline and heating oil in late 2006. (A barrel contains 42 gallons [159 liters].)

The average price of regular-grade gasoline in the United States peaked at a record $3 a gallon at the pump in July. By September, retail prices of motor fuel in the United States averaged $2.59 a gallon, according to the Energy Information Agency (EIA), a government agency in Washington, D.C. Later months brought even lower prices.

Natural gas prices fell in 2006 after surging to as much as $11 per 1,000 cubic feet (28.3 cubic meters) at the wellhead in late 2005. By mid-2006, the average wellhead price of natural gas had fallen below $6 per 1,000 cubic feet. In November, the EIA projected that spot prices of natural gas would average $7.06 per 1,000 cubic feet in 2006 and increase to an average of $7.79 per 1,000 cubic feet in 2007.

Electric power costs. The cost of electric power continued to increase in 2006 as demand outpaced generating capacity. The average residential price of electric power in the United States, according to government statistics, was 9.6 cents per kilowatt hour in January 2006, 1 cent higher than a year earlier. By July, the price had climbed to 11 cents per kilowatt hour.

World events. Risks of disruptions in the availability of energy, especially oil and natural gas, continued throughout 2006. Contributing to the energy supply worries were the ongoing war in Iraq, the debate over Iran's ambitions regarding nuclear power, and other political tensions in the Middle East, which is home to many of the world's most abundant oil fields.

Under fire for soaring energy prices, U.S. oil executives blamed high petroleum costs on rising world demand. Some also pointed to energy constraints in the Organization of the Petroleum Exporting Countries (OPEC), an association of 11 oil-exporting nations that are located mostly in the Middle East. OPEC accounted for nearly 40 percent of the world's total petroleum supply. The ministers of OPEC, however, claimed they were doing all they could to keep petroleum prices stable.

OPEC's spare capacity was at historically low levels at the beginning of 2006, and most of the OPEC nations pumped at nearly maximum capacity for much of the year. In late 2006, however, OPEC ministers announced that they would cut output because of a weakness in oil markets. "With some reduction in OPEC oil production, the price of WTI (West Texas Intermediate) crude oil is projected to rise over the next several months," the EIA reported in November. The EIA projected that the price of WTI, which is the U.S. benchmark crude, would average approximately $66 a barrel in 2006 and $65 a barrel in 2007.

United States petroleum demand. The United States remained the world's largest oil user in 2006, consuming nearly 20.7 million barrels of petroleum a day, according to the EIA. Although this amount was down slightly from the 20.8 million barrels a day consumed in 2005, it still accounted for nearly one-fourth of the world's petroleum demand. The EIA estimated that total U.S. demand for petroleum would average 21 million barrels a day in 2007.

Demand for gasoline in the United States hit 9.25 million barrels a day in 2006, up slightly from 9.16 million barrels a day in 2005, the EIA estimated. The EIA forecast that motor fuel use would rise to an average 9.36 million barrels a day in 2007.

World petroleum demand. Thriving economies around the globe and rising oil demands by such rapidly developing countries as China and India combined to push up world petroleum demand in 2006. In China, the feverish growth in energy consumption slowed in 2006, but the trend in that nation's demand for energy remained upward.

Oil consumption worldwide increased in 2006 by nearly 1 million barrels a day, reaching a record annual rate of 84.5 million barrels a day, according to a November report by the International Energy Agency (IEA), an energy policy organization based in Paris. IEA officials estimated that worldwide petroleum consumption would average nearly 86 million barrels a day in 2007. In a midyear report, however, the IEA noted that there was little doubt that high prices were tempering global demand for petroleum, and the organization forecast that increases in demand would trail the growth in global supply capacity through 2010.   ■ James Tanner

See also **China; Economics, U.S.; Economics, world; Energy supply: A Special Report; India; International trade; Iran; Iraq; Latin America; Middle East.**

The Promise of ETHANOL

In 2006, ethanol seemed to be moving into the fast lane as an automotive fuel. However, there were still roadblocks ahead.

By Alfred J. Smuskiewicz

Ethanol has been pumped as the automotive fuel of the future for at least 100 years. Its advocates have ranged from American automobile pioneer Henry Ford in the early 1900's to Brazil's military dictators in the 1970's to United States President George W. Bush in 2006. In the United States, conservationists, farmers, business executives, and government officials have promoted plant-derived ethanol as a home-grown vehicle fuel that would lower both U.S. dependence on foreign oil—especially from the troubled Middle East—and emissions of heat-trapping greenhouse gases. In mid-2006, ethanol was being blended into only about 3 percent of the country's transportation fuel. However, ethanol seemed to be nudging its way into the fast lane of the transportation highway thanks to a combination of factors, including a spike in prices for both crude oil and gasoline and federal legislation mandating increased use of this alternative fuel.

In 2006, the United States produced about 4.5 billion gallons (17 billion liters) of ethanol used for fuel, slightly more than second-ranked Brazil. Ethanol plants under construction in the United States promised another 2 billion gallons (7.6 billion liters) per year. Ethanol's success was hardly assured, however. Technical and commercial problems as well as environmental and political issues were putting up formidable roadblocks.

The basics of ethanol

Ethanol, also known as *ethyl alcohol* and *grain alcohol,* is a colorless, flammable liquid usually produced from plant material. Throughout the late 1900's and early 2000's, nearly all the ethanol fuel produced in the United States came from corn. Other countries were producing ethanol fuel primarily from sugar cane, sugar beets, wheat, or some other *feedstock* (primary material). People have actually been making ethanol for thousands of years—it is the intoxicating ingredient in alcoholic beverages. Over the centuries, ethanol has become a common component in many other products, including perfumes, paints, lacquers, antibacterial medical products, and even explosives.

Automobile pioneer Henry Ford designed his Model T (above) to run on ethanol, gasoline, or a combination of the two. In 2006, about 700 of the 170,000 gas stations in the United States sold E85, a blend of 85 percent ethanol and 15 percent gasoline.

Ethanol's rocky history

Ethanol was the fuel of choice for Henry Ford and some other automobile pioneers. In fact, Ford's first vehicle, built in 1896, ran on pure ethanol. Ford noted, "There is enough alcohol in one year's yield of an acre of potatoes to drive the machinery necessary to cultivate the fields for a hundred years." Ford was referring to the fact that green plants make their own food through *photosynthesis,* in which light energy from the sun is used to chemically combine water and carbon dioxide to create high-energy carbohydrates. This energy can be recovered in certain ways, such as through burning the plant material or by chemically converting the energy into a usable form. Ford planned to use ethanol as the primary fuel for his highly successful Model T as well. However, commercially, ethanol was no match for petroleum-derived gasoline. The discovery of new oil fields around the world, particularly in the Middle East, and a more efficient process for producing gasoline from petroleum helped make gasoline abundant and relatively cheap.

Although Ford's Model T could run on ethanol, gasoline, or a combination of the two, ethanol was sidelined as an additive, used to boost gasoline's *octane number* (a number indicating how evenly a motor fuel burns in an engine). In the 1930's, fuel blends called *gasohol,* which were from 6 to 12 percent ethanol, could be found at more than 2,000 gas stations in the Midwest. By the 1940's, however, ethanol had largely disappeared from the transportation fuel landscape.

The oil crisis of 1973 renewed U.S. interest in ethanol and other alternative fuels. Gas prices skyrocketed after Arab oil producers stopped shipping petroleum to the United States in retaliation for U.S. support of Israel in the 1973 Arab-Israeli Yom Kippur War. In

The author:
Alfred J. Smuskiewicz is a free-lance writer specializing in science and medicine.

response, the U.S. Congress began offering tax breaks and other incentives to boost commercial ethanol production. By 1979, a number of oil companies were marketing a form of gasohol called *E10*, which consisted of 10 percent ethanol and 90 percent gasoline. In the mid-1990's, oil companies introduced *E85* (85 percent ethanol, 15 percent gasoline). Both ethanol blends were most commonly sold in the Midwest, though by the early 2000's, they were spreading to other parts of the country.

Ethanol got another boost in 1999 when states began prohibiting the use of methyl tertiary butyl ether (MTBE), which was then the most commonly used octane-boosting fuel additive. MTBE, which is made from petroleum and natural gas, had been embraced as a way to reduce vehicle emissions of carbon dioxide, a major greenhouse gas. However, scientific studies linked MTBE to the pollution of ground water and, possibly, to cancer in human beings. By mid-2006, 26 states had banned MTBE. The bans left ethanol and an ethanol-based compound called ethyl tertiary butyl ether as the only safe, clean, cost-effective gas additives in the United States.

How ethanol fuel is produced

Corn-derived ethanol fuel is made in a multistep process that closely resembles the process used to make alcoholic beverages. In the early 2000's, most ethanol in the United States was being made using the *dry milling* process. Free-swinging metal hammers connected to a spinning rotor inside a drum grind corn kernels into a fine powder, called *meal*. (In a variation of this first step, called *wet milling*, the corn is soaked in water and sulfur dioxide to facilitate the separation of the grain into its component parts.)

Next, the meal is mixed with water and *enzymes* (molecules that speed up chemical reactions) and heated. During this liquefaction stage, the meal turns into a mash. An enzyme is added to the cooled mash to convert the liquefied cornstarch into a simple sugar called glucose. Yeast is then added to the mash to *ferment* (break down) the glucose, which produces a mixture containing a weak solution of ethanol and carbon dioxide. (The carbon dioxide is often used to carbonate soft drinks.)

The fermented mash is pumped through vertical cylinders, where the alcohol is separated from nonfermentable solids and water. (Nonfermentable solids can be used as a high-protein livestock feed.)

This distillation process—which requires energy, typically from the burning of natural gas or coal—leaves a solution that is 96 percent alcohol. Any remaining water is then removed using a molecular sieve so that only pure ethanol is left. In the final step, called *denaturing*, a small amount of a toxic substance or a substance with an unpleasant taste or odor is added to the ethanol to make it unfit for human consumption. The ethanol is then ready to use as fuel.

Ethanol can also be produced with sugar—a feedstock used with great success in Brazil. Although sugar beets and sugar cane are grown in the United States, corn has historically been a more economical crop to grow and harvest.

Corn (right) is the source of nearly all ethanol made in the United States. Corn is also used in Australia, Canada, China, and Europe. Switchgrass (above), a common, fast-growing, deep-rooted prairie grass, was being closely studied in the early 2000's for its ethanol-producing potential.

Many experts in 2006 believed that the best feedstock for ethanol was not corn, sugar cane, or sugar beets but *cellulosic biomass*—that is, plant material that has a carbohydrate called *cellulose* in its cell walls. Examples of cellulosic biomass include trees, corn stalks, prairie grass, spoiled grain, straw, wood chips, forestry residues, sawdust, and waste paper. The optimism about cellulosic biomass was based on the material's widespread availability, as well as producers' ability to make ethanol from all parts of the plants.

Switchgrass, a common, fast-growing, deep-rooted prairie grass, became a major focus of cellulosic biomass research in the early 2000's. Switchgrass is a *perennial* (plant that lives for more than two growing seasons). Researchers were also examining trees for their ethanol-producing potential—especially such fast-growing varieties as black locusts and hybrid poplars that can be harvested after only a few years.

The U.S. ethanol industry

As of mid-2006, U.S. companies were operating more than 100 ethanol production plants in about 20 states, with another 30 plants under construction. Most ethanol plants were in the Midwest, home of such giant agribusinesses as Archer Daniels Midland (ADM) of Decatur, Illinois. ADM was the country's largest ethanol maker in 2006, accounting for about one-fourth of the national output. The top ethanol-producing states were Illinois, Iowa, Minnesota, and Nebraska.

Advantages of ethanol as fuel

Unlike petroleum, ethanol is considered a *renewable* source of energy— that is, energy that is replaced by natural processes faster than it is

Sugar cane (right) is the crop from which Brazil produces nearly all of its ethanol. Australia, India, and Thailand also use sugar cane. Wheat (below) is used to produce ethanol in Australia, Canada, China, South Africa, and a number of European countries.

Total World Ethanol Production 2005 (billions of gallons)*

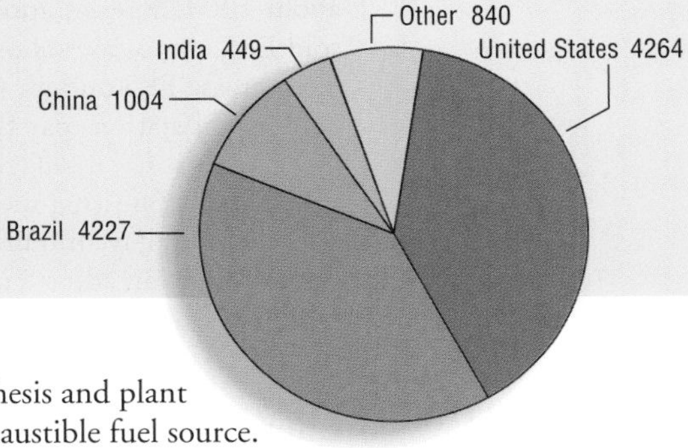

India 449
China 1004
Brazil 4227
Other 840
United States 4264

*Fuel, industrial uses, alcoholic beverages.

consumed. The natural processes of photosynthesis and plant reproduction make ethanol an essentially inexhaustible fuel source.

Ethanol fuel also burns cleaner than petroleum-derived gasoline—that is, it gives off lower amounts of smog-causing hydrocarbons and nitrogen oxides. In addition, when burned, ethanol returns to the atmosphere only as much carbon dioxide as its feedstock removed through photosynthesis. In other words, burning ethanol causes no net increase in atmospheric carbon dioxide. The burning of petroleum, on the other hand, has contributed to a gradual build-up in atmospheric carbon dioxide, widely linked to global warming.

Ethanol fuel production and use, advocates claimed, would also offer economic benefits. In addition to reducing dependence on foreign oil, these benefits would include an increase in corn prices for farmers and economic growth and job creation in rural areas, where most ethanol production facilities were located.

Challenges to ethanol use

Ethanol fuel faced some major challenges in production, transportation, distribution, and use. In 2006, ethanol production consumed about 14 percent of the U.S. corn crop—a figure that was expected to grow to more than 20 percent in 2007. One economic forecaster quoted in *The New York Times* predicted a "food fight" between producers of livestock and ethanol over corn—a struggle that could result in higher food prices for consumers or general inflation. Some environmentalists worried that an ethanol boom would encourage farmers to plant corn on land that the government was paying them to leave idle for conservation purposes. In addition, the production of ethanol requires large amounts of water, diminishing water supplies available for residential, agricultural, or industrial uses. Cultivating the large amounts of corn and other crops needed for ethanol production would also increase the use of chemical fertilizers and herbicides, which contribute to increased water and air pollution.

Transporting ethanol fuel through long pipelines—as gasoline normally is—presented its own difficulty. Unlike gasoline, ethanol picks up and incorporates the water and impurities commonly found in fuel pipelines. To avoid this contamination problem, ethanol suppliers usually transport the fuel by trucks, trains, and barges, an option that is more expensive.

In 2006, consumers wishing to buy E85 had few outlets—only about 700 U.S. gas stations, the majority of them in the Midwest, sold E85, out of a total of about 170,000 gas stations nationwide. To increase E85 outlets, California and some other states were helping gas stations pay the costs of installing ethanol pumps. Vehicle makers, most notably General Motors Corporation of Detroit, were substantially boosting their production of *flexible fuel vehicles* (FFV's). Such vehicles have modified engines with fuel supply and injection systems that can adjust automatically to using gasoline, ethanol, or a mixture of the two. A gasoline-powered vehicle can be converted to run on E85, but it is a complex, costly procedure.

Energy efficiency

One of the most contentious issues surrounding ethanol involved *fuel efficiency*—that is, the amount of energy per gallon released by burning. Ethanol provides less mileage per gallon than unleaded gasoline does, meaning that drivers need to fill their tanks more frequently. In addition, some energy experts questioned whether government incentives to automakers to encourage FFV production might be lowering fuel efficiency instead of raising it. Since the 1970's, automakers have had to meet minimum federal standards for fuel efficiency. In 1988, Congress passed legislation giving automakers credits toward meeting the standards if they manufactured FFV's, under the assumption that these vehicles would promote the use of ethanol-based fuel in place of gasoline. Most FFV's rolling out of auto plants, however, fed the American desire for large vehicles and had relatively poor fuel efficiency. In addition, because of E85's relative unavailability in most of the country, lower energy content per gallon, and higher cost in many areas, many people were simply filling up their FFV's with gasoline.

Energy experts also debated whether ethanol production—particularly the process of distillation—consumed more energy than the ethanol could deliver. Studies of ethanol efficiency produced contradictory results. For example, scientists at Cornell University in Ithaca, New York, and the University of California at Berkeley reported in 2005 that ethanol production is inefficient. They calculated that ethanol production from corn requires 29 percent more energy than the fuel produces. Scientists at Argonne National

U.S. Fuel Ethanol Production (billions of gallons)

In the United States, fuel ethanol production increased from next to nothing in the late 1970's to nearly 4 billion gallons (15 billion liters) in 2005. The country produced about 4.5 billion gallons (17 billion liters) of ethanol fuel in 2006, mostly at facilities in the Midwest.

Source: U.S. Energy Information Administration; Renewable Fuels Association

Laboratory in Illinois, however, reached the opposite conclusion. According to their study, also done in 2005, making ethanol takes less energy than the fuel generates, thanks to technological advances made since the 1980's. The Argonne researchers found that, on average, the production of 1 million British thermal units (BTU's) of ethanol requires only 0.74 million BTU's of energy.

Will ethanol reduce America's oil addiction?

In the early 2000's, the U.S. government renewed efforts to promote ethanol fuel as an alternative to petroleum. The Energy Policy Act of 2005, for example, called for an increase in U.S. production of gasoline additives from renewable biological sources. The act set a production target of 7.5 billion gallons (28 billion liters) per year by 2012. Most energy experts expected ethanol to fill the bulk of this requirement.

In his 2006 State of the Union address, President Bush called for U.S.-made biofuels and other fuel alternatives to replace more than 75 percent of U.S. oil imports from the Middle East by 2025. According to energy industry experts, achieving such a goal would require the domestic production of more than 50 billion gallons (189 billion liters) per year of corn-derived ethanol. Many experts said that despite corn's status as the country's most abundant and heavily subsidized crop, such an ambitious goal was unrealistic. John Ashworth, an alternative fuel expert at the U.S. Department of Energy's National Renewable Energy Laboratory, noted in 2006 that U.S. farmers produced only enough corn to fulfill about 10 percent of U.S. vehicle fuel needs.

An ethanol boom could greatly benefit regions of the Midwest economically depressed by the shuttering of manufacturing plants. Ethanol production facilities have provided new jobs and boosted local economies.

Other experts, however, believed that Bush's goal could be achieved through advances in science and technology. For example, genetic research could lead to higher corn yields. New manufacturing techniques could result in the development of cheaper and more efficient methods for making ethanol from cellulosic biomass. Some experts predicted that cellulosic biomass might have the potential to yield as much as 100 billion gallons (378 billion liters) of ethanol every year.

By 2006, the U.S. government had invested millions of dollars into the commercialization of cellulosic biomass, with the goal of producing at least 250 million gallons (946 million liters) of ethanol from this material by 2013. Federal grant programs and loan guarantees were in place to encourage the production of ethanol from cellulosic biomass. However, according to a July 2006 report from the United States Department of Agriculture, the process of breaking down the starch in cellulosic biomass and fermenting the resulting sugars still made ethanol production more expensive than the production process used to make corn-based ethanol or gasoline. The successful commercialization of cellulosic biomass was, therefore, probably several years away in 2006.

Lessons from Brazil

Many energy experts, environmentalists, and leaders in the U.S. automobile industry looked to Brazil as a model of how ethanol might be successfully integrated into a country's economy. By 2006, most new automobiles manufactured in Brazil were FFV's, widely available there since 2002. In addition, drivers could buy E85 at virtually every Brazilian gas station. Moreover, Brazil had gained independence from

foreign oil. These achievements were partly the result of a commitment
Brazil's government made in the 1970's to use ethanol derived from
sugar cane as the country's primary vehicle fuel. The government,
which was then a military regime, set up a distribution system that
made ethanol fuel available throughout the country. Strong domestic
oil production also played a role in eliminating the Brazilian demand
for foreign oil.

According to experts, however, Brazil had fewer obstacles to overcome than those facing the United States in its quest for energy
independence. Even in its pre-ethanol era, Brazil consumed far less
gasoline than the United States does. In addition, Brazil's military
government had the power to establish mandates for the sale of
ethanol blends and regulate the retail prices of the fuels as well as
intervene directly in agricultural production, politically challenging
tasks for the U.S. government. Moreover, sugar cane is a more energy-
rich feedstock than corn, and Brazil has plenty of arable land on which
to grow sugar cane for both ethanol and food. As a result, Brazil has
been able to convert sugar cane into ethanol more easily and less
expensively than the United States has been able to convert corn into
ethanol. In 2006, ethanol made up more than 40 percent of Brazil's
vehicle fuel consumption.

Most energy supply experts in 2006 agreed that, for the foreseeable
future, ethanol was likely to be only a small part of the U.S. transportation fuel picture. Still, ethanol's use as a fuel seemed likely to grow.
Many Americans hoped ethanol might provide at least a partial
cushion in the event of a new energy crisis, spurred by some unforeseen
event in the conflict-ridden world of the early 2000's.

Environmental pollution. The government of California took two dramatic steps in 2006 that went further than the actions of any other state to combat global warming. Global warming is a gradual increase in Earth's average temperature that many scientists believe is being caused by emissions of carbon dioxide and other greenhouse gases. Such gases trap heat in the atmosphere. In 2006, California was the second-largest emitter of greenhouse gases in the United States (behind Texas) and produced 2.5 percent of the world's total emissions of these gases.

In September, California Governor Arnold Schwarzenegger signed the Global Warming Solutions Act of 2006. The act required power plants, oil refineries, cement plants, and other industrial polluters in the state to reduce their emissions of greenhouse gases by 25 percent by 2020.

Also in September 2006, California Attorney General Bill Lockyer filed suit in the U.S. District Court of Northern California against the world's six largest automobile manufacturers (Chrysler, Ford, General Motors, Honda, Nissan, and Toyota). The suit alleged that these companies created a "public nuisance" that has cost the state millions of dollars. The suit also argued that because vehicle emissions have contributed to global warming, the carmakers should be held responsible for the past and future costs of fighting this problem.

Climate change and disease. A surface-temperature increase of 0.09 °F (0.05 °C) between 1950 and 2002 is a likely cause of an increase in malaria-carrying mosquitoes in the East African Highlands, according to an April 2006 report by scientists with the National Center for Ecological Analysis and Synthesis in Santa Barbara, California. The report linked rising levels of a greenhouse gas to the rising incidence of malaria that has been observed since the 1970's in Africa.

This study supported findings that were reported in November 2005 by scientists at the World Health Organization (a United Nations agency) and the University of Wisconsin at Madison. Those findings showed that malaria and many other diseases are likely to increase in some of the world's poorest countries as a result of climate change.

Climate change and crops. Researchers at the University of Illinois at Urbana-Champaign reported in June 2006 that food crops produced dramatically smaller yields when grown in the higher atmospheric concentrations of carbon dioxide and ozone that are projected for 2050. Ozone is a form of oxygen that, in the lower atmosphere, forms part of smog. The scientists found the reduced productivity in maize (corn), rice, sorghum, soybeans, and wheat—contradicting previous studies that had found increased carbon dioxide levels to be beneficial for plant growth.

The Illinois researchers warned that without changes in food production strategies, global food supplies may decline during the next 50 to 60 years.

Slow ozone layer recovery. The protective ozone layer above Antarctica will take about 20 years longer to fully recover than previously estimated, according to a June 2006 report by researchers at the National Aeronautics and Space Administration, the National Oceanic and Atmospheric Administration, and the National Center for Atmospheric Research. The high-altitude ozone layer blocks harmful ultraviolet rays from the sun. Every spring, an "ozone hole" develops in this layer as a result of temperature-related chemical reactions involving compounds called chlorofluorocarbons (CFC's). CFC's were widely used in many products until they were banned by most countries in the 1990's.

Although CFC's are banned, they remain in the atmosphere, where they attack the ozone layer. Previous studies had found that these compounds will diminish over time, with the ozone hole filling in by 2050. The new study examined the problem using a more advanced *computer model* (simulation) in which the latest measurements of CFC levels were plugged in. Future projections of these levels led the scientists to conclude that the ozone hole will not be filled in until 2068.

Mail delivery gets greener. The United States Postal Service (USPS) put its first hybrid mail delivery van into test service in May 2006 in the Boston, Massachusetts, area. The vehicle was a converted mail van that was altered to use a combination of gasoline and electric power for propulsion. Hybrid vehicles emit fewer air pollutants than vehicles that run only on gasoline. The USPS planned to monitor the environmental and economic performance of the hybrid before putting more such vehicles into production.

The hybrid van was the latest addition to the postal service's fleet of 30,000 alternative fuel vehicles. Other vehicles in this fleet use compressed natural gas, propane, ethanol, or biodiesel as alternatives to gasoline.

Pesticides in U.S. streams. A March report by the U.S. Geological Survey (USGS) concluded that most streams in the United States carry traces of pesticides. The USGS scientists tested water samples from 51 large streams and *aquifers* (ground water supplies) throughout the United States. The researchers found one or more pesticide chemicals in all the surface water and in 33 percent of the ground water, as well as in 96 percent of the fish tested from the streams.

More than 80 percent of sampled urban streams and more than 50 percent of agricultural streams contained pesticides at concentrations that pose a hazard to aquatic life and to animals that eat aquatic life. However, the pesticides were seldom at concentrations high enough to harm people. Fewer than 10 percent of the streams and less than 1 percent of the ground-water supplies had pesticide concentrations above U.S. drinking water standards.

Largest marine reserve. In June, U.S. President George W. Bush created the world's largest marine reserve when he designated a chain of small Hawaiian islands and surrounding waters and coral reefs as a national monument. The chain stretches for more than 1,200 miles (1,900 kilometers), and the entire protected area covers 140,000 square miles (362,600 square kilometers)—nearly the size of California.

The Northwestern Hawaiian Islands Marine National Monument is made up of a variety of reefs, *atolls* (circular formations of coral), *seamounts* (volcanoes on the sea floor), and *shoals* (shallow parts of the sea). It includes habitat that is home to more than 7,000 species, including Hawaiian monk seals, breeding seabirds, and endangered green sea turtles.

The designation of the area as a national monument resulted in strict new conservation rules. These rules included a phase-out of all commercial and recreational fishing by 2011 and bans on the removal of corals and the mining of minerals and petroleum.

Species extinction update. According to a May 2006 report by the World Conservation Union (IUCN), 16,199 species of plants and animals are threatened with extinction. The 2006 Red List by the IUCN, an international conservation organization based in Gland, Switzerland, includes one-third of the world's amphibian species, one-fourth of all species of mammals and *coniferous* (cone-bearing) trees, and one-eighth of bird species. Habitat destruction is the main reason behind the population declines of most species. Well-known species on the 2006 Red List included hippopotamuses, desert gazelles, ocean sharks, and stingrays.

The IUCN blamed climate change for the decline of polar bears, which are highly adapted for life in the Arctic environment. Polar bears depend on Arctic ice floes as platforms for hunting seals. As the Arctic warms, some scientists project that summer sea ice will decrease by 50 percent by 2040. As ice floes become rarer, polar bear numbers might decrease by more than 30 percent over this time.   ■ Andrew Hoffman

See also **Conservation; Global warming: A Special Report; Ocean.**

Equatorial Guinea. See **Africa.**

Eritrea. See **Africa.**

Estonia. See **Baltic states; Europe.**

Ethiopia. See **Africa.**

Workers clean up an oil spill at a field operated by BP Exploration (Alaska) Inc., at Prudhoe Bay, Alaska, in August. The oil company began a phased shutdown of the field following the spill, which was caused by severely corroded pipes. The shutdown was expected to result in a reduction of about 400,000 barrels per day in Alaska's North Slope oil production.

EUROPE

The European Union (EU), Europe's main political and economic bloc, continued to operate without a constitution in 2006. Voters in France and the Netherlands rejected the constitutional treaty in 2005, effectively postponing indefinitely the adoption of such a document. (The treaty must be ratified by all EU members to go into effect.)

Although a deadline of October 2006 had originally been established for the ratification of the constitution, after its rejection by French and Dutch voters, the EU member nations agreed to postpone the treaty ratification deadline to allow for a "period of reflection." Throughout 2006, Austria, which held the rotating EU presidency from January to June, and Finland, which held the presidency from July to December, continued to conduct the work of the bloc but did not actively pursue passage of the treaty. Chancellor Angela Merkel of Germany, the country that was to assume the presidency in January 2007, promised to set a timetable for ratification of the constitution and called for the treaty to be in place before elections to the European Parliament, scheduled for 2009.

Despite the failure to agree on a constitution, the nations of Europe continued in 2006 to discuss the need for EU institutional reform. According to EU rules, a unanimous vote is required to pass EU legislation on many issues. Such a requirement was not an insurmountable difficulty in 1958, when the organization began as a trading bloc of six members. In 2007, however, the addition of Bulgaria and Romania was to bring the number of EU members to 27, making the decision process much more difficult. In August 2006, French Interior Minister Nicolas Sarkozy, a contender for the presidency of France in 2007, suggested changing the rule of unanimity.

In addition, members expressed concerns about the number of highly paid administrative positions at EU headquarters in Brussels. EU treaties require that each member nation appoint a commissioner to hold an administrative post. Critics argued that it would be difficult to find meaningful posts for 27 administrators. The rejected constitution addressed the problem by reducing the number of commissioners to two-thirds of the number of member nations, beginning in 2014.

The EU did make progress in 2006 on the issue of passport-free border crossing. Most older EU member countries—with the exception of Ireland and the United Kingdom (U.K.)—had by 2006 signed the Schengen Treaty, which allows citizens of acceding countries to travel freely between cooperating countries. With the exception of Cyprus, the newest members of the EU, which had joined the bloc in 2004, were eager to participate in the no-border zone. At a meeting in Brussels on Dec. 5, 2006, EU interior ministers announced that the passport-free zone would be extended to the new members in 2008. EU members were to formally approve the decision in 2007, after verifying that the requesting nations had met specified security requirements and that the border control database, called the Schengen Information System, was secure.

Economy. Economic growth increased modestly in the EU in 2006; EU economists projected that the *gross domestic product* (GDP—the value of all goods and services produced in a year) would increase by an average 2.6 percent for the 12 countries using the euro and 2.8 percent for the 25 EU member nations as a whole. GDP had increased by an average 1.4 percent in the euro area and 1.7 percent in the EU as a whole in 2005. The improvement in GDP came in part from the rapidly growing new member states. Economic growth in Estonia and Latvia in 2006, for example, was estimated at 10.9 percent and 11 percent, respectively.

In May 2006, the EU ratified a new and larger budget for the period from 2007 to 2013. The budget agreement, which involved intense negotiations between the member nations, was finalized only after France received guarantees that its agricultural subsidies would continue and Germany agreed to fund a portion of the aid for the poorer member countries of Eastern Europe. The countries of the EU agreed to reevaluate the budget in 2009. For 2007, the greatest share of spending continued to be earmarked for agricultural subsidies and for transfer payments from wealthier regions to poorer ones.

Enlargement. In September 2006, the European Commission (the executive arm of the EU) officially invited Bulgaria and Romania to join the bloc in January 2007. Nevertheless, significant concerns remained over whether either country had fulfilled all membership requirements, especially in the areas of judicial reform, corruption, and food safety. The EU called for additional reforms and outlined sanctions to be imposed if the conditions were not met. The sanctions included reductions in transfer payments to Bulgaria and Romania in the case of corruption; the right not to recognize judicial decisions if judicial

In March, Paris police wear riot gear to face off hundreds of thousands of demonstrators angry over a new labor law. The law, later rescinded, allowed employers to fire workers under age 26 without stating a reason during their first two years on the job. The law was designed to encourage greater employment of young people.

reform was suspended; and the possible ban of pork and pork products if an animal disease called swine fever has not been eradicated.

Because the incomes of Bulgarians and Romanians in 2006 remained about one-third of the EU average, current member nations also imposed restrictions (of varying numbers of years) on the right of Bulgarian and Romanian workers to move to other areas of the EU. Countries such as the U.K. feared a mass immigration of workers from Bulgaria and Romania in light of the fact that, after 10 new countries were admitted to the EU in 2004, more than 500,000 Eastern European workers immigrated to the U.K.

Turkey. The issue of Turkey joining the EU remained controversial in 2006, despite official negotiations between Turkey and the EU that began in October 2005. These negotiations hit a number of roadblocks throughout 2006. One issue involved Turkey's refusal to allow Greek Cypriot ships the right to dock in Turkish ports and Greek Cypriot aircraft the right to land in its airports. Turkish leaders argued that the continued isolation of Turkish Northern Cyprus needed to be resolved first. The Greek-controlled government of Cyprus maintained that because Cyprus is an EU member nation, Turkey must first recognize its Greek government

FACTS IN BRIEF ON EUROPEAN COUNTRIES

Country	Population	Government	Monetary unit*	Foreign trade (million U.S.$) Exports†	Imports†
Albania	3,243,000	President Alfred Moisiu; Prime Minister Sali Berisha	lek (97.75 = $1)	650	2,473
Andorra	77,000	Co-sovereigns bishop of Urgel, Spain, and the president of France; Head of Government Albert Pintat Santolària	euro (0.79 = $1)	145	1,077
Austria	8,143,000	President Heinz Fischer; Chancellor Alfred Gusenbauer	euro (0.79 = $1)	122,500	118,800
Belarus	9,769,000	President Aleksandr Lukashenko; Prime Minister Sergei Sidorsky	ruble (2,141.95 = $1)	16,140	16,940
Belgium	10,372,000	King Albert II; Prime Minister Guy Verhofstadt	euro (0.79 = $1)	269,600	264,500
Bosnia-Herzegovina	4,221,000	Chairman of the presidency Haris Silajdzic	marka (1.55 = $1)	2,700	6,800
Bulgaria	7,702,000	President Georgi Parvanov; Prime Minister Sergei Stanishev	lev (1.55 = $1)	11,670	15,900
Croatia	4,380,000	President Stjepan Mesic; Prime Minister Ivo Sanader	kuna (5.87 = $1)	10,300	18,930
Czech Republic	10,236,000	President Václav Klaus; Prime Minister Mirek Topolanek	koruna (22.41 = $1)	78,370	76,590
Denmark	5,408,000	Queen Margrethe II; Prime Minister Anders Fogh Rasmussen	krone (5.91 = $1)	84,950	74,690
Estonia	1,283,000	President Toomas Hendrik Ilves; Prime Minister Andrus Ansip	kroon (12.42 = $1)	7,439	9,189
Finland	5,231,000	President Tarja Halonen; Prime Minister Matti Taneli Vanhanen	euro (0.79 = $1)	67,880	56,450
France	60,093,000	President Jacques Chirac; Prime Minister Dominique de Villepin	euro (0.79 = $1)	443,400	473,300
Germany	82,636,000	President Horst Koehler; Chancellor Angela Merkel	euro (0.79= $1)	1,016,000	801,000
Greece	10,981,000	President Carolos Papoulias; Prime Minister Costas Caramanlis	euro (0.79 = $1)	18,540	48,200
Hungary	9,956,000	President Laszlo Solyom; Prime Minister Ferenc Gyurcsany	forint (215.77 = $1)	61,750	64,830
Iceland	296,000	President Olafur Ragnar Grimsson; Prime Minister Geir H. Harde	krona (68.43 = $1)	3,215	4,582
Ireland	4,076,000	President Mary McAleese; Prime Minister Bertie Ahern	euro (0.79 = $1)	102,000	65,470
Italy	58,029,000	President Giorgio Napolitano; Prime Minister Romano Prodi	euro (0.79 = $1)	371,900	369,200 (includes San Marino)
Latvia	2,244,000	President Vaira Vike-Freiberga; Prime Minister Aigars Kalvitis	lat (0.55 = $1)	5,749	8,559
Liechtenstein	34,000	Prince Hans-Adam II; Prime Minister Otmar Hasler	Swiss franc (1.26 = $1)	2,470	917

*Exchange rates as of Oct. 6, 2006.   †Latest available data.   **Montenegro separated from Serbia on June 15, 2006.

as the sole legitimate government of Cyprus. (Cyprus has been divided since 1974 into the Republic of Cyprus and the Turkish Republic of Northern Cyprus. The Republic of Cyprus is controlled by Cypriots of Greek origin. That government is recognized by all countries except Turkey. The Turkish Republic of Northern Cyprus is controlled by Cypriots of Turkish origin. Their government is recognized by Turkey alone.)

In October 2006, the EU presidency under the leadership of Finnish Prime Minister Matti Vanhanen set a Dec. 6, 2006, deadline for Turkey to open Turkish ports and airports to Cypriot vessels. By mid-December, the issue remained unresolved, and European Union foreign ministers agreed to partially freeze membership negotiations with Turkey.

Other issues revolved around Turkey's poor record on protecting freedom of speech, espe-

Country	Population	Government	Monetary unit*	Foreign trade (million U.S.$)	
				Exports[†]	Imports[†]
Lithuania	3,391,000	President Valdas Adamkus; Prime Minister Gediminas Kirkilas	litas (2.74 = $1)	10,950	13,330
Luxembourg	467,000	Grand Duke Henri; Prime Minister Jean-Claude Juncker	euro (0.79 = $1)	13,390	18,740
Macedonia	2,085,000	President Branko Crvenkovski; Prime Minister Nikola Gruevski	denar (48.11 = $1)	2,047	3,196
Malta	398,000	President Edward Fenech Adami; Prime Minister Lawrence Gonzi	lira (0.34 = $1)	2,744	3,859
Moldova	3,598,000	President Vladimir Voronin; Prime Minister Vasile Tarlev	leu (13.25 = $1)	1,040	2,230
Monaco	34,000	Prince Albert II; Minister of State Jean-Paul Proust	euro (0.79 = $1)	no statistics available	
Montenegro	650,000	President Filip Vujanovic; Prime Minister Zeljko Sturanovic	euro (0.79 = $1)	no statistics available**	
Netherlands	16,357,000	Queen Beatrix; Prime Minister Jan Peter Balkenende	euro (0.79 = $1)	365,100	326,600
Norway	4,586,000	King Harald V; Prime Minister Jens Stoltenberg	krone (6.70 = $1)	111,200	58,120
Poland	38,485,000	President Lech Kaczynski; Prime Minister Jaroslaw Kaczynski	zloty (3.11 = $1)	92,720	95,670
Portugal	10,777,000	President Aníbal Cavaco Silva; Prime Minister José Sócrates	euro (0.79 = $1)	38,800	60,350
Romania	21,422,000	President Traian Basescu; Prime Minister Calin Popescu-Tariceanu	new leu (2.79 = $1)	27,720	38,150
Russia	142,190,000	President Vladimir Putin; Prime Minister Mikhail Fradkov	ruble (26.89 = $1)	245,000	125,000
San Marino	30,000	2 captains-regent appointed by Grand Council every 6 months	euro (0.79 = $1)	371,900	369,200 (includes Italy)
Serbia	9,860,000	President Boris Tadic	euro (0.79 = $1) dinar (64.30 = $1)	no statistics available**	
Slovakia	5,415,000	President Ivan Gasparovic; Prime Minister Robert Fico	koruna (29.46 = $1)	32,390	34,480
Slovenia	1,975,000	President Janez Drnovsek; Prime Minister Janez Jansa	tolar (190.20 = $1)	18,530	19,620
Spain	41,205,000	King Juan Carlos I; Prime Minister José Luis Rodríguez Zapatero	euro (0.79 = $1)	194,300	271,800
Sweden	9,003,000	King Carl XVI Gustaf; Prime Minister Fredrik Reinfeldt	krona (7.37= $1)	126,600	104,400
Switzerland	7,298,000	President Micheline Calmy-Rey	franc (1.26 = $1)	148,600	135,000
Turkey	74,204,000	President Ahmet Necdet Sezer; Prime Minister Recep Tayyip Erdogan	new lira (1.49 = $1)	72,490	101,200
Ukraine	46,691,000	President Viktor Yushchenko; Prime Minister Viktor Yanukovych	hryvnia (5.03 = $1)	38,220	37,180
United Kingdom	60,715,000	Queen Elizabeth II; Prime Minister Tony Blair	pound (0.53 = $1)	372,700	483,700

cially Turkey's official unwillingness to acknowledge that the massacre of Armenians in Turkey from 1915 to 1918 constituted *genocide* (the systematic extermination of a cultural or racial group). In October 2006, the lower house of France's parliament approved a controversial bill imposing fines and prison time on anyone who denied that there had been an Armenian genocide. Turkey claimed that Armenians abroad and Europeans who opposed Turkey's EU member-

ship were using the issue to prevent Turkey's accession. By late 2006, the French bill had not become law.

Foreign policy. The determination of EU foreign policy continued to be a cumbersome process in 2006, in part because of the unanimity requirement. The requirement allows a veto by any member nation to prevent the adoption of a foreign policy issue.

Critics of EU foreign affairs argued that the

EU lacks clear lines of authority in formulating and implementing policy. This reflects not only the member nation veto power but also the fact that the EU has neither a foreign minister nor a diplomatic corps that reports to the same authority. (EU High Representative for Common Foreign and Security Policy Javier Solana reports to the Council of the EU; the diplomatic corps reports to the European Commission.) The constitution would have resolved the issue by creating a post of foreign minister who would hold a seat as a commissioner.

In addition, critics maintained, the capacity of the EU to deploy military force to hot spots around the world remained underdeveloped. Plans for the creation of an EU rapid-reaction force of 60,000 troops remained in the planning stages in 2006.

Russian energy. During 2006, EU leaders were particularly eager to renew their Partnership and Cooperation Agreement with Russia. The 1997 agreement, which addresses European access to Russian oil and natural gas supplies, was set to expire at the end of 2007. About one-fourth of the EU's gas and oil comes from Russia, making it the EU's largest energy supplier. The leaders of many EU nations were concerned that the Russian government could one day use these resources in political disputes, a tactic Russia has employed in the past with its non-EU neighbors. In January 2006, Russia cut off gas supplies to Ukraine for three days in a dispute over pricing. The move triggered energy shortages in other European countries, because the same gas lines that supply Ukraine carry gas to Europe. Renewing the agreement would have allayed some of the concerns.

The Russian government, for its part, maintained that its own energy companies should not only be suppliers of oil and gas to Europe but should also have the right to purchase refining and distribution capacity within the EU. European governments, however, have resisted large-scale Russian investments. By late November, hopes for renegotiating the agreement were dim. Poland announced that it would veto any such agreement as long as Russia persisted in banning meat and plant imports from Poland. (Russia imposed the ban in November 2005, ostensibly because of safety concerns.) Despite considerable pressure from the EU presidency, the Polish government's stance continued to block the start of the treaty talks.

Relations with Iran. In 2006, the EU spearheaded negotiations with Iran in an attempt to use diplomacy to persuade Iran to freeze its nuclear enrichment program, a first step toward developing nuclear weapons. Under the leadership of France, Germany, and the U.K., Javier Solana regularly consulted with Iranian, European, and American officials. No progress was made toward ending the crisis. By December, the United Nations (UN) Security Council was debating the imposition of sanctions on Iran.

Middle East. As part of a UN-brokered deal to end hostilities between Israel and the militant Islamist group Hezbollah that broke out in southern Lebanon in July, the EU offered peacekeeping troops. Together with UN Secretary General Kofi Annan, European foreign ministers agreed that a European contribution to the peacekeeping force was essential. The French government initially agreed to send up to 2,000 troops. Facing a skeptical French public with memories of other French peacekeeping missions in the region having gone bad, the government reduced this number to 200. After being criticized for not backing an agreement it helped design, France increased this number again to 2,000. Italy agreed to contribute as many as 3,000 troops, a move that the Israelis welcomed because they considered the Italians more impartial than the French in the Arab-Israeli conflict.   ■ Jeffrey Kopstein

See also **Disasters** and various European country articles.

European Union. See Europe.
Explosion. See Disasters.
Farm and farming. See Agriculture.

Fashion. A bottle of water in one hand, a cell phone in the other, and books, papers, and an iPod tucked into a backpack, wearing jeans with a thin sweater or T-shirt—this was the basic look for both male and female high-school and college students for 2006. They might add a coat when the weather was really cold, but a hoodie sweatshirt was a more likely substitute. Similar outfits were worn by younger office workers. Formal dress during the day was certainly not the thing in 2006. Even the middle-aged wore more casual clothing. Only weddings and proms were seen as worthy occasions for really dressing up.

Style. Fashion companies featuring name designers insisted that their luxury business was gaining, but this was not apparent among mainstream customers. Nevertheless, consumers were interested in fashion. The cable-television show "Project Runway," hosted by model Heidi Klum, drew high ratings, providing evidence of the public's interest in clothing design. Further, consumers certainly liked to look at extravagant fashion photographs in magazines. When it came to putting down their credit cards, however, buyers focused on such accessories as watches and handbags or, more likely still, such electronics as computer notebooks.

Certain well-known designers, including Karl Lagerfeld and Marc Jacobs, continued to thrive.

In Paris, Nicolas Ghuesquière was applauded for his renewal of the fashion house Balenciaga. Christian Lacroix staged his own revival. Lacroix broke away from fashion conglomerate LVMH Moët Hennessey-Louis Vuitton to once again design under his own name in 2006. He had made a big impact on fashion in 1987 with his first couture collection, where he introduced his widely copied pouf dress, a dress with a short skirt fitted at the waist that then swelled out in a bubble shape. Although there was nothing as groundbreaking in his 2006 collection, it was still generally commended.

Other acclaimed designers were less able to turn the favor of critics into financial success. A case in point was Olivier Theyskens, the Council of Fashion Designers of America's international designer in 2006. His beautiful gowns were worn by Hollywood stars and featured in fashion magazines, but the fashion branch of the Paris house he designed for, Rochas, closed in summer 2006. Theyskens was hired subsequently as creative director at Nina Ricci, but the closing at Rochas was seen as more evidence of the difficulties in designing in the current climate. The financial backers of fashion houses saw haute couture as a business, desiring clothing that sold well above clothing as art.

Trends in 2006 included some return in women's clothing to styles of the 1970's and 1980's. Shoes with wedge heels were popular. Shoes and boots with high platforms were seen in the fall. Leggings worn under long, tunic-style tops and knee-length cardigan sweater-coats also seemed to recall earlier decades.

After several seasons of jeans with a bootcut leg or flared leg, the skinny jean became hip. This straight-leg jean was cut narrow at the ankle, sometimes with a circumference of 10 inches (25 centimeters). Pants in unusual lengths were also popular in the fall. Some women's suits in formal fabrics showed knee-length shorts instead of skirts. Gaucho-styled pants were also popular. Plaid was featured in unusual ways on diverse items from evening gowns to boots.

In menswear, designer Hedi Slimane won approval for his collection at Dior. Slimane's designs for men featured a very narrow silhou-

Models parade down a spiral stair, presenting the spring-summer collection by Karl Lagerfeld for Chanel. The show was held in Paris at the Grand Palais exhibition hall.

ette, which began to appear in less exaggerated forms in men's ready-to-wear.

Fashion-conscious men were willing to follow a trend shown by a number of designers, including Ralph Lauren, of mixing formal and informal clothing elements—for example, pin-striped trousers worn with a sweater, white shirt, bow tie, and a leather bomber jacket. For many men, however, substituting a French-blue shirt for a white shirt was as far as they were willing to venture in business attire. ■ Bernadine Morris

Finland. In February 2006, voters reelected Tarja Halonen, who became Finland's first woman president in 2000, to another six-year term. Halonen, who was backed by the Social Democratic Party, won a runoff election against Sauli Niinistö, a former finance minister and the candidate of the opposition Conservative Party. Prime Minister Matti Vanhanen of the governing Center Party, who also ran in the election, came in third.

The three-party coalition government led by Vanhanen—consisting of the Center Party, the Social Democratic Party, and the Swedish People's Party—remained stable in 2006. National elections were scheduled for March 2007.

European Union presidency. In July 2006, Finland assumed the rotating presidency of the European Union (EU) for a period of six months. During that time, the EU addressed the issue of Turkey's accession to the bloc. Turkey had begun membership talks with the EU in October 2005. However, continued concerns by many EU members over Turkey's record on human rights and freedom of speech and the Turkish government's refusal to recognize the legitimacy of the Greek Cypriot government on the island of Cyprus raised doubts over whether the membership bid would succeed. In December 2006, EU foreign ministers agreed to partially freeze membership negotiations with Turkey until the issue with Cyprus was resolved.

The Finnish EU president also attempted to reach an agreement with Russia regarding oil and gas imports. Many EU countries depend heavily on Russia for their energy supplies but fear that Russian investment in European refining and delivery capacity could undermine their national security. By December, the issue remained unresolved.

Economy. Finland's economy grew rapidly in 2006, continuing to outperform all other nations using the euro. EU economists projected that the country's *gross domestic product* (GDP—the value of all goods and services produced in a country in a year) would grow by 4.9 percent in 2006. Finland's sizable budget surplus—at 2.9 percent of GDP, the largest among the euro-zone countries—allowed for tax cuts that were planned to continue in 2007. Although unemployment remained high in 2006 at 7.7 percent—down from 8.4 percent in 2005—Finland remained one of the most competitive economies in the world. The country's top producer, cell phone manufacturer Nokia Corporation, continued to thrive despite intense competition from other consumer electronic giants.

Music scene. Finnish rock band Lordi won the 2006 Eurovision song contest held in May in Athens, Greece. Lordi's winning entry, "Hard Rock Hallelujah," represented a radical departure from the pop fare of previous Eurovision entries.

◼ Jeffrey Kopstein

See also **Europe.**

Food. Concern about the prevalence of obesity in the United States grew in 2006. The Federal Trade Commission (FTC) and the Department of Health and Human Services (HHS) released a report on May 2 recommending that the food industry take steps to curtail childhood obesity. Among their recommendations, the agencies urged food companies to make products lower in calories and more nutritious, while still being appealing to children and convenient to prepare and eat. The FTC and HHS also urged companies to develop packaging with smaller portions to help consumers control calories, to revise marketing practices for foods aimed at children, and to improve nutritional education efforts.

On May 3, the nation's top three soft drink companies announced that they would start removing sweetened drinks from school cafeterias and vending machines in the fall of 2006. The voluntary agreement was negotiated with the companies by the Alliance for a Healthier Generation, led by former U.S. President Bill Clinton together with the Dallas-based American Heart Association (AHA). On October 6, a similar agreement involving snack foods was reached between the alliance and five major manufacturers of snack foods sold in school vending machines, stores, and cafeterias.

Allergens and trans fats. The Food Allergen Labeling and Consumer Protection Act took effect on Jan. 1, 2006. The act requires that food product labels state—in plain language—the presence of ingredients that contain such major food allergens as eggs, shellfish, peanuts, wheat, or soy.

Federal law also required food manufacturers, effective January 1, to report the amount of trans fat a product contains on the Nutrition Facts and some Supplement Facts panels of food labels. Trans fat forms when hydrogen is added to vegetable oil, a process used to increase the shelf life and flavor stability of some foods. Trans fats are believed to contribute to high levels of cholesterol in the blood. According to the AHA, no more than 1 percent of calories should come from trans fats. In December, New York City became the first U.S. city to ban the use of trans fats in restaurants. The ban was to be phased in by July 2008.

Organic foods. Buoyed by increased interest in healthy eating among many consumers, organic food sales continued to increase as mainstream supermarket companies—including Wal-Mart Stores Inc. of Bentonville, Arkansas, the nation's largest food retailer—increased their offerings of organic products. According to the 2006 Manufacturer Survey of the Organic Trade Association, organic food sales in 2005 reached $13.8 billion, or 2.5 percent of total U.S. food sales, an increase of 16.2 percent over 2004.

Food safety. In late September 2006, the Food and Drug Administration (FDA) recalled

A student purchases a snack from a vending machine stocked with junk food in a high school cafeteria. In October, the Alliance for a Healthier Generation, a group concerned about the rise in child obesity, reached an agreement with five major food manufacturers to keep junk foods out of schools.

California-grown fresh spinach that was tainted with a particularly lethal strain of the microbe *Escherichia coli,* O157:H7. As of October 6, 199 cases of illness—including three deaths—caused by the infection had been reported to the U.S. Centers for Disease Control and Prevention (CDC) in Atlanta, Georgia. The outbreak affected 26 states. On September 29, the FDA said all spinach implicated in the case had been traced to Natural Selection Foods, LLC, of San Juan Bautista, California. Food safety officials later found the same deadly bacteria in cattle manure in pastures located near the spinach-growing fields. On October 8, the Nunes Company Inc. of Salinas, California, voluntarily recalled bags of green-leaf lettuce from seven Western states because of possible *E. coli* contamination in water that had been used to irrigate the lettuce. However, multiple samples of the lettuce tested negative for O157:H7.

In late November and early December, the CDC confirmed that 71 people who had eaten at fast-food restaurants in five Northeastern states had also been sickened by *E. coli* bacteria. Researchers reported that shredded lettuce was the most likely source of contamination.

In December, the FDA tentatively concluded that milk and meat from some *cloned* animals is safe to eat. Cloning is the process of making a genetic duplicate.   ■ Robert C. Gatty

Football. The University of Florida derailed the chances of Ohio State for a perfect season and a national championship with a stunning 41-14 victory in the Bowl Championship Series (BCS) title game on Jan. 8, 2007, in Glendale, Arizona. The Florida Gators (13-1) won their second national title since 1996, defeating the previously unbeaten Buckeyes (12-1), the number-one team in the United States from the preseason on.

The selection of Florida to play in the title game was somewhat controversial because the Gators leapfrogged over the University of Michigan in the final BCS poll after winning the Southeastern Conference title game on Dec. 2, 2006. The Michigan Wolverines had lost only one game during the season—to Ohio State by three points. Many observers still considered Michigan the second-best team in the land, until they were defeated by the University of Southern California (USC) in the Rose Bowl on Jan. 1, 2007.

In the National Football League (NFL), the Pittsburgh Steelers won their first Super Bowl in 26 years, toppling the Seattle Seahawks 21-10 on Feb. 5, 2006, in Detroit. The victory tied Pittsburgh with the Dallas Cowboys and San Francisco 49ers as the only teams with five Super Bowl titles.

In the 2006-2007 NFL season, the Indianapolis Colts became the first team in league history to start back-to-back seasons 9-0. But their attempt to join the 1973 Miami Dolphins (17-0) as the only unbeaten team in history was derailed by the surging Dallas Cowboys on Nov. 19, 2006. The New Orleans Saints, returning to the city ravaged by Hurricane Katrina in 2005, surprised football fans by entering the final weeks of the season as one of the top teams in the league. The Saints won the NFC South division after finishing last in the division in 2005.

Running back LaDainian Tomlinson of the San Diego Chargers scored 100 touchdowns in fewer games than any other NFL player, posting 102 touchdowns through 89 games. He scored 31 touchdowns during the season, breaking the record of 28 set in the 2005-2006 season by running back Shaun Alexander of the Seattle Seahawks. Tomlinson was the NFL's leading rusher and also named the Most Valuable Player for the 2006 season.

The Chicago Bears' Devin Hester set an NFL record for kick returns for a touchdown with two returns on December 11 in a 42-27 win over the St. Louis Rams. Hester finished the season with six return touchdowns.

College. On Jan. 8, 2007, Florida upset top-ranked Ohio State 41-14 in the BCS title game to win their second national championship. Florida quarterback Chris Leak was named the game's Most Valuable Player. Florida outgained Ohio State with 370 yards of total offense to 82.

In other major bowl games, undefeated Boise State upset Oklahoma 43-42 in the Fiesta Bowl; Louisville defeated Wake Forest 24-13 in the Orange Bowl; USC defeated Michigan 32-18 in the Rose Bowl; and Louisiana State defeated Notre Dame 41-14 in the Sugar Bowl.

Trouble at Miami. A tumultuous season for the University of Miami ended in the MPC Computers Bowl, but not before head coach Larry Coker was fired after six seasons, a 59-15 record, and a national championship. Coker was dismissed on November 24, a day after his team upset number-18 Boston College to finish the regular season 6-6. On October 14, Miami was also involved in a sideline-clearing brawl with Florida International. Thirteen Miami players and 18 Florida International players were suspended. Tragedy also struck the Miami team when senior defensive lineman Bryan Pata was shot and killed on November 7.

Big East rising. Through seven games, the Big East Conference had three unbeaten teams—West Virginia, Louisville, and, the biggest surprise, Rutgers. When number-five Louisville toppled number-three West Virginia on November 2, the Cardinals moved to 8-0 for the first time since 1926 and had a chance to play for the national title. That chance fizzled the following week—on Nov. 9, 2006,— when Rutgers moved to 9-0 with a stunning come-from-behind win over Louisville.

Heisman Trophy. Ohio State quarterback Troy Smith decisively won the Heisman Trophy as the top U.S. college player on December 9 in New York City. Smith received 801 first-place votes and 2,540 points, well ahead of Arkansas running back Darren McFadden, who had 45 first-place votes and 878 points. Notre Dame quarterback Brady Quinn finished third with 13 first-place votes and 782 points.

NFL. On Feb. 5, 2006, Pittsburgh defeated Seattle in the Seahawks' first Super Bowl appearance, despite being outgained in yardage, losing the time-of-possession battle, and having more turnovers. The Steelers' Willie Parker set a Super Bowl record with a 75-yard touchdown run early in the third quarter.

Ben Roethlisberger, the youngest quarterback to win a Super Bowl, rushed for a touchdown but completed just 9 of 21 passes for 123 yards with two interceptions. His wide receiver, Hines Ward, was named Most Valuable Player for his five catches for 123 yards and one touchdown.

THE 2006 COLLEGE FOOTBALL

NATIONAL CHAMPIONS

NCAA Div. I-A	Florida	41	Ohio State	14
NCAA Div. I-AA	Appalachian State	28	Massachusetts	17
NCAA Div. II	Grand Valley State	17	N.W. Missouri State	14
NCAA Div. III	Mount Union	35	Wisc.-Whitewater	16
NAIA	Sioux Falls (S.D.)	23	St. Francis (Ind.)	19

BOWL CHAMPIONSHIP SERIES GAMES

BOWL	RESULT			
Rose	Southern California	32	Michigan	18
Orange	Louisville	24	Wake Forest	13
Fiesta	Boise State	43	Oklahoma	42
Sugar	Louisiana State	41	Notre Dame	14

OTHER BOWL GAMES

BOWL	RESULT			
Alamo	Texas	26	Iowa	24
Capital One	Wisconsin	17	Arkansas	14
Car Care	Boston College	25	Navy	24
Champs Sports	Maryland	24	Purdue	7
Chick-fil-A	Georgia	31	Virginia Tech	24
Cotton	Auburn	17	Nebraska	14
Armed Forces	Utah	25	Tulsa	13
Emerald	Florida State	44	UCLA	27
GMAC	So. Mississippi	28	Ohio	7
Gator	West Virginia	38	Georgia Tech	35
Hawaii	Hawaii	41	Arizona State	24
Holiday	California	45	Texas A&M	10
Independence	Oklahoma State	34	Alabama	31
Insight	Texas Tech	44	Minnesota	41
Las Vegas	BYU	38	Oregon	8
Liberty	South Carolina	44	Houston	36
MPC Computers	Miami	21	Nevada	20
Motor City	Central Michigan	31	Middle Tennessee	14
Music City	Kentucky	28	Clemson	20
New Orleans	Troy	41	Rice	17
Outback	Penn State	20	Tennessee	10
Poinsettia	TCU	37	Northern Illinois	7
Sun	Oregon State	39	Missouri	38
Texas	Rutgers	37	Kansas State	10

The offseason wasn't as kind to Roethlisberger, who was involved in a motorcycle accident on June 23. While the injuries were serious—and he wasn't wearing a helmet—he missed only the 2006-2007 season opener—because of an emergency appendectomy. He later suffered a concussion during the season, and the Steelers missed the play-offs.

2006 play-offs. In the American Football Conference (AFC) wild-card play-offs, the New England Patriots ripped the Jacksonville Jaguars 28-3 on Jan. 7, 2006, in Foxborough, Massachusetts, while the Steelers defeated the Cincinnati Bengals 31-17 on January 8. The Denver Broncos handed New England quarterback Tom Brady his first loss in 11 play-off games the following weekend in Denver, forcing five turnovers in a 27-13 victory. The Steelers built a 21-3 lead on the top-seeded Colts and then held on 21-18 as Indianapolis missed a last-second field goal. The Steelers continued their unlikely run as the sixth (and last) seed in the AFC playoffs, earning a trip to the Super Bowl

SEASON

CONFERENCE CHAMPIONS

NCAA DIVISION I-A

CONFERENCE	SCHOOL
Atlantic Coast	Wake Forest
Big 12	Oklahoma
Big East	Louisville
Big Ten	Ohio State
Conference USA	Houston
Mid-American	Central Michigan
Mountain West	Brigham Young
Pacific 10	Southern California
Southeastern	Florida
Sun Belt	Troy
Western Athletic	Boise State

NCAA DIVISION I-AA

CONFERENCE	SCHOOL
Atlantic 10	Massachusetts
Big Sky	Montana
Big South	Coastal Carolina
Gateway	Youngstown State
Great West	North Dakota State
Ivy League	Princeton
Metro Atlantic	Duquesne
Mid-Eastern	Hampton
Northeast	Monmouth
Ohio Valley	Eastern Illinois
Patriot	Lafayette—Lehigh (tie)
Pioneer	San Diego
Southern	Appalachian State
Southland	McNeese State
Southwestern	Alabama A&M

ALL-AMERICAN TEAM, DIVISION I-A

(as chosen by the Associated Press)

OFFENSE
Quarterback—Troy Smith, Ohio State
Running backs—Darren McFadden, Arkansas; Steve Slaton, West Virginia
Wide receivers—Dwayne Jarrett, USC; Calvin Johnson, Georgia Tech
Tight end—Matt Spaeth, Minnesota
Center—Dan Mozes, West Virginia
Other linemen—Josh Beekman, Boston College; Justin Blalock, Texas; Jake Long, Michigan; Joe Thomas, Wisconsin
Place-kicker—Justin Medlock, UCLA
All-purpose player—DeSean Jackson, California

DEFENSE
Linemen—Gaines Adams, Clemson; Glenn Dorsey, LSU; Quinn Pitcock, Ohio State; LaMarr Woodley, Michigan
Linebackers—James Laurinaitis, Ohio State; Paul Posluszny, Penn State; Patrick Willis, Mississippi
Backs—Leon Hall, Michigan; Daymeion Hughes, Callifornia; LeRon Landry, LSU; Reggie Nelson, Florida
Punter—Daniel Sepulveda, Baylor

PLAYER AWARDS
Heisman Trophy (best player)—Troy Smith, Ohio State
Bednarik Trophy (best defensive player)—Paul Posluszny, Penn State

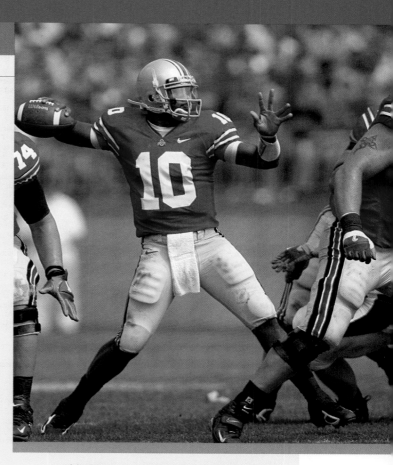

Ohio State quarterback Troy Smith, winner of the 2006 Heisman Trophy, throws a pass against the University of Cincinnati in a September match that Ohio won 37-7. Behind their star quarterback, the Buckeyes (12-0) rolled through the college football season as the country's number-one ranked team, until they were defeated by Florida 41-14 in the BCS title game.

on January 22 in Denver with a 34-17 win. The Steelers joined the 1985 Patriots as the only teams to win three road games to make the Super Bowl.

The Washington Redskins beat the Tampa Bay Buccaneers 17-10 In the National Football Conference (NFC) wild-card play-offs on Jan. 7, 2006, in Tampa. Washington gained only 120 yards of offense in the game, the lowest ever by a winning NFL play-off team. The Carolina Panthers shut out the host New York Giants 23-0 on January 8, the first road postseason shut-out in the NFL in 25 years. A week later, top-seeded Seattle topped Washington 20-10, and Carolina beat the Bears in Chicago 29-21. Seattle trampled Carolina 34-14 on January 22 in the NFC title game.

2006 NATIONAL FOOTBALL LEAGUE FINAL STANDINGS

AMERICAN CONFERENCE

North Division	W.	L.	T.	Pct.
Baltimore Ravens*	13	3	0	.813
Cincinnati Bengals	8	8	0	.500
Pittsburgh Steelers	8	8	0	.500
Cleveland Browns	4	12	0	.250

East Division	W.	L.	T.	Pct.
New England Patriots*	12	4	0	.750
N.Y. Jets*	10	6	0	.625
Buffalo Bills	7	9	0	.438
Miami Dolphins	6	10	0	.375

South Division	W.	L.	T.	Pct.
Indianapolis Colts*	12	4	0	.750
Tennessee Titans	8	8	0	.500
Jacksonville Jaguars	8	8	0	.500
Houston Texans	6	10	0	.375

West Division	W.	L.	T.	Pct.
San Diego Chargers*	14	2	0	.875
Kansas City Chiefs*	9	7	0	.563
Denver Broncos	9	7	0	.563
Oakland Raiders	2	14	0	.125

*Made play-offs

NATIONAL CONFERENCE

North Division	W.	L.	T.	Pct.
Chicago Bears*	13	3	0	.813
Green Bay Packers	8	8	0	.500
Minnesota Vikings	6	10	0	.375
Detroit Lions	3	13	0	.188

East Division	W.	L.	T.	Pct.
Philadelphia Eagles*	10	6	0	.625
Dallas Cowboys*	9	7	0	.563
New York Giants*	8	8	0	.500
Washington Redskins	5	11	0	.313

South Division	W.	L.	T.	Pct.
New Orleans Saints*	10	6	0	.625
Carolina Panthers	8	8	0	.500
Atlanta Falcons	7	9	0	.438
Tampa Bay Buccaneers	4	12	0	.250

West Division	W.	L.	T.	Pct.
Seattle Seahawks*	9	7	0	.563
St. Louis Rams	8	8	0	.500
San Francisco 49ers	7	9	0	.438
Arizona Cardinals	5	11	0	.313

*Made play-offs

TEAM STATISTICS

Leading offenses	Plays	Yards per game
Indianapolis	1,011	379.4
San Diego	1,016	365.0
Pittsburgh	1,041	357.8
Cincinnati	994	341.4
Jacksonville	989	338.9

Leading defenses	Avg. points against	Yards per game
Baltimore	12.6	264.1
Jacksonville	17.1	283.6
Oakland	20.8	284.8
Miami	17.7	289.1
New England	14.8	294.4

TEAM STATISTICS

Leading offenses	Plays	Yards per game
New Orleans	1,075	391.5
Philadelphia	988	381.4
Dallas	1,015	360.8
St. Louis	1,065	360.4
Green Bay	1,085	341.1

Leading defenses	Avg. points against	Yards per game
Chicago	15.9	294.1
Carolina	19.1	296.1
Minnesota	20.4	300.2
New Orleans	20.1	307.3
Green Bay	22.9	320.9

INDIVIDUAL STATISTICS

Leading scorers, touchdowns	TD's	Rush	Rec.	Ret.
LaDainian Tomlinson, San Diego	31	28	3	0
Larry Johnson, Kansas City	19	17	2	0
Maurice Jones-Drew, Jacksonville	16	13	2	1
Willie Parker, Pittsburgh	16	13	3	0

Leading kickers	PAT made/att.	FG made/att.	Longest FG	Pts.
Nate Kaeding, San Diego	58/58	26/29	54	136
Matt Stover, Baltimore	37/37	28/30	52	121
Josh Scobee, Jacksonville	41/41	26/32	48	119
Jason Elam, Denver	34/34	27/29	51	115

Leading quarterbacks	Att.	Comp.	Yds.	TD's	Ints.
Peyton Manning, Indianapolis	557	362	4,397	31	9
Carson Palmer, Cincinnati	520	324	4,035	28	13
Tom Brady, New England	516	319	3,529	24	12
Ben Roethlisberger, Pittsburgh	469	280	3,513	18	23
Philip Rivers, San Diego	460	284	3,388	22	9

Leading receivers	Passes caught	Rec. yards	Avg. gain	TD's
Chad Johnson, Cincinnati	87	1,369	15.7	7
Marvin Harrison, Indianapolis	95	1,366	14.4	12
Reggie Wayne, Indianapolis	86	1,310	15.2	9
Lee Evans, Buffalo	82	1,292	15.8	8

Leading rushers	Rushes	Yards	Avg.	TD's
LaDainian Tomlinson, San Diego	348	1,815	5.2	28
Larry Johnson, Kansas City	416	1,789	4.3	17
Willie Parker, Pittsburgh	337	1,494	4.4	13
Rudi Johnson, Cincinnati	341	1,309	3.8	12

Leading punters	Punts	Yards	Avg.	Longest
Shane Lechler, Oakland	77	3,660	47.5	67
Kyle Larson, Cincinnati	77	3,428	44.5	67
Hunter Smith, Indianapolis	47	2,085	44.4	61
Dustin Colquitt	71	3,145	44.3	72

INDIVIDUAL STATISTICS

Leading scorers, touchdowns	TD's	Rush	Rec.	Ret.
Marion Barber, Dallas	16	14	2	0
Steven Jackson, St. Louis	16	13	3	0
Terrell Owens, Dallas	13	0	0	0
Brian Westbrook, Philadelphia	11	7	4	0

Leading kickers	PAT made/att.	FG made/att.	Longest FG	Pts.
Robbie Gould, Chicago	47/47	32/36	49	143
Jeff Wilkins, St. Louis	35/35	32/37	53	131
Jason Hanson, Detroit	30/30	29/33	53	117
Joe Nedney, San Francisco	29/29	29/35	51	116

Leading quarterbacks	Att.	Comp.	Yds.	TD's	Ints.
Drew Brees, New Orleans	554	356	4,418	26	11
Marc Bulger, St. Louis	588	370	4,301	24	8
Jon Kitna, Detroit	596	372	4,208	21	22
Brett Favre, Green Bay	613	343	3,885	18	18
Eli Manning, New York	522	301	3,244	24	18

Leading receivers	Passes caught	Rec. yards	Avg. gain	TD's
Roy Williams, Detroit	82	1,310	16.0	7
Donald Driver, Green Bay	92	1,295	14.1	8
Anquan Boldin, Arizona	83	1,203	14.5	4
Torry Holt, St. Louis	93	1,188	12.8	10

Leading rushers	Rushes	Yards	Avg.	TD's
Frank Gore, San Francisco	312	1,695	5.4	8
Tiki Barber, New York	327	1,662	5.1	5
Steven Jackson, St. Louis	346	1,528	4.4	13
Brian Westbrook, Philadelphia	240	1,217	5.1	7

Leading punters	Punts	Yards	Avg.	Longest
Mat McBriar, Dallas	56	2,697	48.2	75
Jason Baker, Carolina	98	4,483	45.7	70
Ryan Plackemeir, Seattle	84	3,778	45.0	72
Nick Harris, Detroit	66	2,967	45.0	67

Notable deaths. Northwestern University football coach Randy Walker, considered one of the brightest young coaching minds in college football, died on June 29 from an apparent heart attack. Walker, 52, had guided the Wildcats, once perennial losers, to three bowls since 2000—winning a share of the Big Ten title in 2000. His 37-46 record since joining the school in 1999 made him the second most successful coach in Northwestern's history.

Legendary former University of Michigan coach Bo Schembechler, 77, died on Nov. 17, 2006, from a heart condition after collapsing on the day before the "Game of the Year" between number-one Ohio State and number-two Michigan. Schembechler, who won 13 Big Ten titles in 21 seasons at the school, was honored before the game, which Ohio State won 42-39.

Wellington Mara, 87, a long-time New York Giants owner who helped build the NFL, died on October 25. Wellington and his father, Timothy J. Mara, were the first father-son inductees to the Pro Football Hall of Fame. Under Wellington's direction, the Giants won six NFL championships.

Canadian Football League. The British Columbia Lions won their fifth Grey Cup—and first since 2000—with a 25-14 victory over the Montreal Alouettes on Nov. 19, 2006, in Winnipeg, Manitoba. ■ Michael Kates

France. In his 11th year in office, President Jacques Chirac in 2006 fended off challenges not only from his potential successors but also from street protesters who resisted economic reforms. After the government backed down under pressure from striking students and unionists in April, Prime Minister Dominique de Villepin saw his popularity wane, and experts noted that he appeared to be out of the 2007 presidential running.

In 2006, political experts predicted that Chirac would not seek reelection and that the front-runner for the election would be Nicolas Sarkozy, the leader of Chirac's Union for a Popular Movement. Sarkozy advocated economic reforms that reminded many French citizens of United States policies. Sarkozy's populist approach and public education reinforced his U.S.-style image. On the center-left, Ségolène Royal defeated two rivals to become the Socialist Party's candidate for president, as well as the first woman from a major party to contest a French presidential election. Like Sarkozy, Royal presented herself as an outsider to the French establishment. Another force within French politics in 2006 was the leader of the far-right National Front, Jean-Marie Le Pen. In 2002, Le Pen finished second in the first round of voting, which propelled him to a runoff against President Chirac in which Le Pen received nearly 17 percent of the total vote. All three potential successors

based their campaigns on the distrust of government that had become widespread in France after more than a decade of Chirac's rule.

Labor reforms and street protests. In March and April 2006, more than a million students, trade unionists, and sympathizers protested throughout France against legislation intended to reduce unemployment among youth, which at the time was more than 20 percent. Universities remained closed for more than a month, and the protests affected rail travel. The legislation, called the "First Employment Contract," was introduced by Prime Minister de Villepin by government decree without consultation with France's powerful trade unions and without parliamentary debate. It permitted French firms to dismiss first-time employees under 26 years old within two years of being hired without going through cumbersome administrative procedures. The legislation was intended to stimulate job creation by increasing employers' flexibility with the labor force.

Student groups and labor unions maintained the law was unfair because it created, in effect, two classes of workers, one protected by the law and one not. The protesters also argued that the law represented a scheme to "Americanize" the French economy and reduce the broad range of welfare benefits and social protections that French citizens currently enjoy. The Socialist Party challenged the law at the Constitutional Court, the highest in France, but the court refused to declare it unconstitutional. Having remained silent for weeks and letting his prime minister take the brunt of criticism, President Chirac finally stepped in at the beginning of April and capitulated to the students' demands to cancel the legislation.

Reform failure. For the remainder of 2006, French commentators focused on the long string of governmental failures over the past two decades in reforming the economy. They cited instances in which the government backed down on legislation after being confronted with street protests. Books and documentaries on the decline of France appeared on the bookshelves and on television. President Chirac failed to keep 1995 campaign promises to reduce taxes and the share of governmental ownership of the economy. Attempts to increase the working hours of France's workers—at 35 hours per week French workers spend less time at work than the workers in any other industrialized country—also proved elusive. In the face of the government's inability to reform the economy, Chirac's popularity plummeted in 2006. An October poll saw his approval rating at 24 percent, making him the least popular French president in decades.

New legislation and directives. In October, the lower house of the French parliament voted in support of a bill to make it a criminal offense to deny that Turkey in 1915 committed genocide against the Armenian people. A precedent existed for such a law—in France and other European nations, it is illegal to deny the Nazi Holocaust against Europe's Jews during World War II (1939-1945). Even so, foreign affairs experts considered the bill a bad idea, aimed more at discrediting Turkey in its bid for admission to the European Union than at protecting the memory of an event important to France's Armenian population. Experts noted that the bill stood little chance of becoming law, but Turkish officials threatened France with economic sanctions.

In November, the French government banned smoking in most public places beginning on Feb. 1, 2007. Exempt from the ban until 2008 were bars, cafes, casinos, discothèques, and hotels.

Economy. France's overall unemployment rate remained high in 2006, hovering just above 9 percent. Despite concerns over long-term economic decline, economic growth improved in 2006, reaching 2.2 percent, up from 1.2 percent in 2005.

■ Jeffrey Kopstein

See also **Europe; Middle East.**

Gabon. See Africa.
Gambia. See Africa.
Gas and gasoline. See Energy supply.
Genetic engineering. See Biology; Medicine.

Geology. A magnitude-6.3 earthquake shook the floor of the Indian Ocean about 10 miles (16 kilometers) southeast of Yogyakarta, Java, in Indonesia, on May 27, 2006. The quake occurred along the boundary of the colliding Eurasian and Indo-Australian tectonic plates at a depth of approximately 6.2 miles (10 kilometers). These plates are among the approximately 30 rigid pieces of rock that make up Earth's outer shell.

The displacement of the sea floor caused by the earthquake unleashed a *tsunami* (series of powerful ocean waves) in the Yogyakarta region. As the waves crashed onto shore, they killed more than 5,800 people and displaced more than 650,000 others.

On July 17, a magnitude-7.7 earthquake struck the bottom of the Indian Ocean 220 miles (354 kilometers) south of Jakarta, the capital of Indonesia. The tsunami resulting from this tremor swamped local villages and resorts along the southwest coast of Java, killing at least 600 people, displacing more than 54,000 others, and destroying hundreds of buildings. Despite the devastating tsunami of December 2004 that killed more than 200,000 people along coastal areas of the Indian Ocean, a planned tsunami warning system had not been completed in 2006.

Hawaiian earthquake. On October 15, the most powerful earthquake to strike Hawaii since 1983 cut electric power to much of the state for several hours. The magnitude-6.7 quake, which occurred about 18 miles (29 kilometers) below the west coast of the Big Island, was followed by more than 50 aftershocks. No deaths and only minor injuries were reported.

Monitoring a volcano. Augustine Volcano in southern Alaska ended 20 years of dormancy with 13 eruptions over a 20-day period in January 2006. Geophysicist John A. Power and colleagues with the United States Geological Survey (USGS) described in September how careful monitoring of this volcano allowed scientists to study the geological changes that led to the eruptions.

Geologists have long been concerned about Augustine Volcano because ash injected into the atmosphere by its eruptions can pose a health hazard to people for hundreds of miles downwind. Eruptions of Augustine can also affect commercial aviation and generate tsunamis.

Seismometers (instruments to measure earthquake intensity) were installed on Augustine as early as 1970. In 1986, instruments to measure changes in the elevations of the land were installed on the volcano and upgraded in 2004. Scientists also installed Web cameras—to display real-time images of the volcano on the Internet—and ash-collection devices. Scientists also employed overflights to measure gas emissions and make visual observations.

Scientists at the USGS's Alaska Volcano Observatory documented eight months of earthquakes, land deformation, and gas and steam emissions preceding the January 2006 eruptions. A steady increase in minor earthquakes was followed by a strong earthquake swarm that led to the first eruption and ash plumes, which rose more than 14 miles (22 kilometers) into the atmosphere. Over the next few days, a series of powerful eruptions destroyed many of the instruments deployed on the volcano. In February, the volcano began to deflate because of the loss of *magma* (partially melted rock that erupts as lava) below the surface. Reduced volcanic activity continued until late March.

The USGS scientists noted that extensive monitoring of hazardous volcanoes around the world—similar to the monitoring of Augustine—could serve as the basis for early warning systems.

Collapsing ice shelves. The breakup of the ice shelves on the Antarctic Peninsula because of increasing temperatures was described in August by glacial geologist Dominic A. Hodgson of the British Antarctic Survey and colleagues. The scientists said the breakup served as a warning of the dangerous effects of global warming, an increase in Earth's surface temperatures that many scientists believe is being caused primarily by the burning of such fossil fuels as coal, oil, and natural gas.

The scientists reported that the average annual temperature on the Antarctic Peninsula is increasing at a rate of 6.1 °F (3.4 °C) per century—a rate that is approximately five times the global average increase. In response, many of the region's *ice shelves* (ice that sticks out from land into the sea) have collapsed. The researchers estimated that 22,400 square miles (58,000 square kilometers) of ice has broken off the Antarctic Peninsula and drifted into the sea over the past 20 years.

Geological evidence in ocean sediment suggests that the peninsula's ice shelves collapsed naturally during previous warm intervals over the past 11,500 years, according to Hodgson's team. However, measurements made with radar by Earth-orbiting satellites indicate that the present collapse is more dramatic than those previous disintegrations. The measurements show that as much as 10 feet (3 meters) of ice is being lost from the base of some ice shelves every year.

The scientists concluded that Antarctica's ice shelves are breaking up and melting from a combination of warming atmospheric temperatures and warming ocean waters. Large-scale melting of Antarctica's land-based ice could cause a rise in sea level that could lead to severe flooding in many coastal areas. ■ Henry T. Mullins

See also **Disasters; Global warming: A Special Report; Indonesia.**

Georgia. Relations between the governments of Georgia and Russia reached a new low in 2006, as Georgian President Mikheil Saakashvili increased his efforts to restore control over the breakaway regions of Abkhazia and South Ossetia. Tensions grew in July when Georgia's military took control of the Kodori Gorge on the Abkhaz-Georgian border. The tensions escalated further after the Georgian government on September 27 detained four Russian military officers for spying.

Although the Georgian government released the officers to the Organization for Security and Co-operation in Europe on October 2, the Russian government responded on October 3 by severing all transportation, trade, and postal links with Georgia. Russian authorities then raided the offices of Georgian-owned businesses in Moscow and deported hundreds of Georgian citizens from Russia.

In retaliation, the Georgian government in November announced that it would suspend World Trade Organization (WTO) talks with Russia, leaving Georgia and Moldova as the only two WTO members standing in the way of Russia's entry bid. In a move promising to further exacerbate tensions, 99 percent of South Ossetian voters approved on November 12 a referendum advocating independence . ■ Juliet Johnson

See also **Asia; Moldova; Russia.**

Lava flows down the side of Mount Merapi in Yogyakarta, Indonesia, on May 10. The eruption of Merapi came just days before a magnitude-6.3 earthquake on May 27 shook the bottom of the Indian Ocean southeast of Yogyakarta. That quake generated a *tsunami* (series of large ocean waves) that killed more than 5,800 people.

Germany. The "grand coalition" government of Angela Merkel, Germany's first woman chancellor, remained in power in 2006. The coalition was formed after Merkel's center-right Christian Democratic Union (CDU)—with its sister party, the Christian Social Union of the state of Bavaria only—won a narrow victory over the center-left Social Democratic Party (SPD) in September 2005.

Merkel's government began 2006 with several successful reforms, including redesigning the federal system to reduce the power of state premiers to block legislation, raising the pension age from 65 to 67, and reducing subsidies to poorer areas of the country. However, the coalition ran into difficulties tackling other issues. Merkel proposed reforming Germany's health care system—among the most expensive in the world—by introducing more competition, increasing insurance premiums, and creating a central health fund. However, the reform was watered down by her SPD coalition partners and the powerful CDU state premiers. In addition, neither party was able to find an alternative source of revenue to finance a much-needed corporate tax cut. The government also squabbled over such wage reforms as the introduction of a minimum wage to help Germany's large numbers of workers in low-paying jobs.

Because of the deadlocks, both parties fared poorly in state elections, especially in the former Communist East, where unemployment remained high. In addition, in an effort to decrease Germany's large budget deficit, the government announced plans to raise the *value-added tax* (a tax on consumer goods) by 3 percentage points to 19 percent on Jan. 1, 2007—the largest increase since World War II (1939-1945). By October 2006, public opinion polls showed that support for the CDU and SPD had fallen to 33 percent and 36 percent, respectively, the lowest levels since German reunification in 1990.

Foreign relations. Merkel visited the United States in January 2006 to improve relations between the two countries. Relations had deteriorated during the administration of Merkel's predecessor, Gerhard Schröder, who opposed the U.S.-led war in Iraq. Merkel largely succeeded in reestablishing a balance in German foreign policy between the United States and Europe.

In 2006, the German parliament debated the role of the nation's troops abroad. Because of the country's Nazi past, many German politicians hesitated to deploy soldiers in situations where they might have to use force. Under pressure from its democratic allies, however, Germany contributed about 8,000 soldiers to a number of United Nations, North Atlantic Treaty Organization, and European Union (EU) missions, including efforts in Afghanistan, Bosnia, Congo (Kinshasa), Georgia, the Horn of Africa, Kosovo, and Sudan. In Septem-

ber, the German Cabinet committed an additional 2,400 naval and air troops to patrol the coast of Lebanon as part of the cease-fire that ended the Hezbollah-Israeli conflict. The government resisted any deployment of ground troops, fearing the possibility of a military clash with Israel in light of Germany's continued sensitivity about the *Holocaust* (the systematic murder of Jews and others by Germany's Nazi government during World War II).

In Afghanistan during 2006, the German government rejected a combat role for its troops. Germany's participation was confined mostly to assisting in the reconstruction of civilian institutions, providing security for development aid workers, and helping train Afghan police officers in the less violent northern part of the country.

In fall 2006, Germany began preparations for assuming the rotating presidency of the EU for a six-month period starting in January 2007. Germany announced plans to revive the Constitutional Treaty, rejected by France and the Netherlands in 2005. Most EU members agreed that some sort of institutional reform within the EU was necessary to streamline decision-making procedures and permit the expansion to new members after Bulgaria and Romania joined in 2007. Germany was also to assume the presidency of the G8 (a group of wealthier industrialized nations) in 2007.

Günter Grass affair. Nobel Prize-winning author Günter Grass's memoir, *Peeling the Onion,* raised a storm of controversy after it was published in 2006. After many years of urging Germans to come to terms with their Nazi past, Grass revealed that, contrary to his previous assertions that he served merely as an assistant in an anti-aircraft battery during World War II, he had, in fact, had been drafted into a tank division in the Waffen-SS in the last few months of the war. Grass had previously admitted his attraction to Nazism as a 17-year-old youth but had never revealed his membership in the elite Nazi military unit. Critics in Germany and abroad accused him of hypocrisy for his long silence on such an important matter.

Economy. Germany's budget deficit in 2006—2.3 percent—fell below the EU-mandated level of 3 percent of *gross domestic product* (GDP—the total value of goods and services produced in a country in a year) for the first time since 2002. Following positive growth trends throughout the EU, Germany's economy grew in 2006 by 2.4 percent. Unemployment, though high at 8.9 percent, declined for the third straight year.

World Cup. In June and July, Germany hosted the World Cup soccer tournament. Thirty-two teams competed for the championship. Italy defeated France in the final match to take the cup.

■ Jeffrey Kopstein

See also **Europe; Soccer: A Special Report.**

Ghana. See Africa.

Global warming. January 2006 began with a rare—for winter—tropical storm roaming the unusually warm waters of the Atlantic Ocean. Tropical Storm Zeta was the record-setting 27th storm of the Atlantic hurricane season, which had begun in June 2005.

The first month of 2006 was also the warmest January in the United States since record keeping began in 1895. Furthermore, the United States in 2006 had its second warmest summer since 1934.

The period from May through September 2006 was the warmest in central England since records were first kept there in the 1600's. During June and July 2006, sea ice in the Arctic shrank to its lowest values on record for those months.

Temperature trends reevaluated. In June, the National Research Council, a private research organization that advises the U.S. government, issued a report reevaluating a 2,000-year reconstruction of global surface temperatures that had been published in the 1990's by climatologist Michael Mann and colleagues. Mann's reconstruction was based on *proxy data*—that is, data from such sources as tree rings, ocean and lake sediments, ice cores, cave deposits, and historic drawings of glaciers. Scientists rely on proxy data to reconstruct long-term surface temperatures, because geographically widespread records of temperatures measured with instruments date back to only the mid-1800's.

Mann's reconstruction showed an unprecedented rapid rise in temperature since about 1970. His reconstruction also showed temperatures in the late 1990's reaching their highest values of the last 2,000 years.

The council concluded with high confidence that the proxy data demonstrates that the last few decades of the 1900's—averaged around the globe—have been warmer than any period since 1600. However, the report noted that much less confidence can be placed in temperature data before 1600.

Shrinking polar ice. Scientists from the National Snow and Ice Data Center at the University of Colorado in Boulder reported in October 2006 that the extent of sea ice in the Arctic reached its annual minimum in September at 2.2 million square miles (5.7 million square kilometers). This measurement was the second lowest value since records began in the 1970's. Only in 2005, when the minimum was 2.0 million square miles (5.2 million square kilometers), was there less Arctic sea ice. The researchers suggested that unusually cold weather in August probably prevented a new record from being established.

Polar sea ice is an important indicator of climate change, because it is sensitive to initial warming trends. As sea ice, which reflects much sunlight, melts, more of the darker ocean water is exposed. This darker surface absorbs more of the sun's heat energy, which further increases air temperatures near the water, ocean temperatures themselves, and the melting of sea ice.

Unexpected ocean cooling. Researchers at the National Oceanic and Atmospheric Administration's Pacific Marine Environmental Laboratory in Seattle reported in September 2006 that the average temperature of the top layer of Earth's oceans dropped slightly from 2003 to 2005. According to the scientists, the heat content of the upper 2,500 feet (750 meters) of ocean water decreased by 0.055 °F (0.031 °C)—an amount that was equal to approximately 20 percent of the total heat gained by the world's oceans between 1955 and 2003.

The researchers noted that ocean water was still warmer in 2005 than it had been in the 1980's, but they had no explanation for the observed cooling, which was not predicted by any climate model. Because the ocean is a vast storehouse of energy that helps to drive the world's climate system, temperature changes in the ocean are a key to understanding long-term climate change.

The role of the sun. A study published in March 2006 by scientists at Duke University in Durham, North Carolina, concluded that changes in the amount of energy from the sun can account for as much as 50 percent of the observed global temperature increase between 1900 and 2000 and as much as 35 percent of the warming between 1980 and 2000. The scientists noted that these results suggested that human-induced warming may have played a progressively greater role during the 1900's.

In October 2006, researchers at the Center for Sun-Climate Research in Denmark provided experimental evidence demonstrating how *cosmic rays,* high-speed atomic particles streaming from distant exploding stars, can affect the formation of clouds in Earth's atmosphere. Their experiment, which involved cosmic radiation passing through a chamber filled with atmospheric gases, showed that cosmic rays can promote chemical processes in the atmosphere that form *condensation nuclei.* Condensation nuclei are microscopic particles that aid the development of cloud droplets.

The Danish researchers explained that the strength of the sun's magnetic field, which helps shield Earth from cosmic rays, doubled during the 1900's. This fact led the researchers to propose that reduced cosmic radiation resulting from the stronger magnetic field would lead to less cloud formation—and subsequent higher global temperatures.   ■ Fred Gadomski

See also **Disasters; Environmental pollution; Global warming: A Special Report; Weather.**

THE GREAT

By Christina Johnson

MELTDOWN

Scientists warn that global warming is leading to the rapid and potentially catastrophic disappearance of ice sheets and glaciers worldwide.

The hard, cold fact about Earth's ice is that it is melting. In the Arctic, in the Antarctic, and on even the highest mountains, the ice cover is thinning, breaking up, and draining away. Ice in the Arctic Ocean is retreating so quickly that by 2100 the ocean could be ice free in summer, opening the year-round seaway from the North Atlantic to the North Pacific oceans sought by early explorers to North America. From 1996 to 2006, the amount of Greenland's ice sliding into the North Atlantic each year jumped by about 250 percent, an amount equal to the volume of water in Lake Erie. The collapse of Antarctica's Larsen B ice shelf in 2002 dumped enough ice into the sea to give every person on Earth 1,800 bags of ice weighing 22 pounds (10 kilograms) each.

Most scientists agree that Earth's ice cover is eroding because of global warming—the increase of from 0.7 to 1.4 °F (0.4 to 0.8 °C) in the planet's average surface temperature since the late 1800's. In fact, Earth is warmer now than at any time in the past 11,500 years, the National Academy of Sciences reported in September 2006. While cycles of cooling and warming as well as other natural processes affect Earth's climate, a widespread scientific consensus points to human activities, particularly emissions of heat-trapping greenhouse gases, as the main driving force behind the current warm-up. The most significant of these gases is carbon dioxide, produced by the burning of coal, gasoline, and wood.

Although the meltdown has—so far—hit hardest in the Arctic, its effects have been global and diverse. In 2005, the chairperson of the 150,000-member Inuit Circumpolar Conference said that the thinning and loss of Arctic *sea ice* (frozen seawater) was threatening the traditional lifestyles of *indigenous* (native) peoples. Also in 2005, scientists reported the first evidence that polar bears, which use sea ice as a platform for hunting seals, are drowning because of the growing distance between ice floes. Scientists also have linked a decline in sea ice to a 70-percent drop in the number of Adélie penguins living on one part of the Antarctic Peninsula. In the central Asian countries of Nepal and Bhutan, an

Ice sheets and glaciers cover about 10 percent of Earth's land surface. *Sea ice* (frozen seawater) covers about 15 percent of the world's oceans during parts of the year.

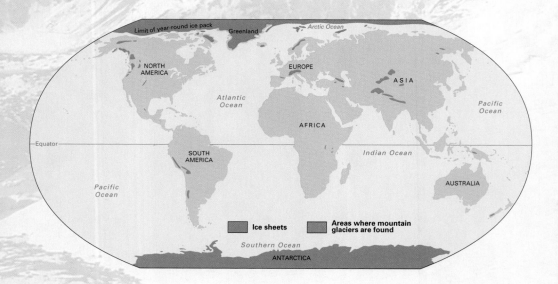

Ice sheets

Areas where mountain glaciers are found

international survey found at least 44 mountain lakes filling so rapidly with meltwater from Himalayan glaciers that they could burst their banks within five years, causing potentially catastrophic floods in the populated valleys below.

Earth is unlikely to become ice free for at least a few centuries, even at current rates of warming. Nevertheless, the melting is seriously affecting human and animal populations as well as the environment. Numerous studies have predicted even more disturbing consequences for human health and safety as well as for ecosystems in the near future.

Ice in the Arctic

The Arctic, which is often described as the barometer of global environmental health, is experiencing dramatic changes in both its seasonal and *perennial* (year-round) ice packs. Seasonal ice, which grows and melts throughout the year, has been declining since at least 1978, the time when scientists began using satellites to monitor the ice. Historically, by March, all of the Arctic Ocean except for an area along the coasts of Norway and western Russia is locked in ice. By mid-September, only about 30 percent of the ice remains.

The amount of perennial ice surviving the summer melting season dropped by about 6.5 percent per decade from 1979 to 2001. After 2001, the retreat began to seem more like a rout. Between 2004 and 2005, perennial ice shrank by 14 percent to a record low of 2.05 million square miles (5.32 million square kilometers), according to a September 2006 report by scientists from NASA's Jet Propulsion Laboratory in Pasadena, California. The shrinkage represented an area equal to the size of Texas.

Just as disturbing, a 2006 study found that the amount of the Arctic Ocean covered by seasonal ice in March had dropped to its lowest average

A house in Shishmaref, an island village in Alaska, has tumbled onto the beach after rising surface temperatures caused its permafrost foundation to thaw and crumble. Retreating sea ice also has left the shoreline of the village, a Inuit winter home for 4,000 years, dangerously vulnerable to erosion.

The author:
Christina Johnson is a free-lance science writer.

since 1978. The so-called winter ice maximum shrank by a record 6 percent—equivalent to an area roughly the size of New Mexico—from 2005 levels, the previous record. Moreover, in 2006 the winter ice shrank more than twice as fast as it did in the 1980's and 1990's.

The Arctic is experiencing "some of the most rapid and severe climate change on earth," according to the 2004 Arctic Climate Impact Assessment (ACIA). The ACIA emerged from a four-year study by hundreds of scientists working under a mandate from the United States and seven other Arctic nations, six organizations representing indigenous Arctic people, and 18 national academies of science. Signs of climate change documented by ACIA scientists included rising temperatures, shrinking and thinning sea ice, melting glaciers, and rising sea levels.

Melting's ripple effect

For indigenous people, mushy ice and unexpectedly early thaws have made hunting on what used to be well-known ice highways more difficult and dangerous. Some hunters, for example, have been forced to travel farther to find seals, walruses, and other Arctic prey. In addition, accidents on the ice are reportedly increasing, resulting in injuries and death, loss of valuable equipment, and expensive rescues, according to the National Snow and Ice Data Center (NSIDC) in Boulder, Colorado. The melting of the highways is also limiting the time available to truckers trying to deliver heating oil, gasoline, and other supplies to Far North communities. "The land is becoming a stranger to the Inuit," one Inuit official said in an interview.

Deteriorating sea ice is also threatening numerous animal species that depend on the ice for their survival. Seals give birth, raise their pups, and rest on the ice. In February 2006, Canadian scientists reported that about 1,500 grey seal pups were swept out to sea in a storm and drowned because a scarcity of sea ice forced females to give birth on the vulnerable beaches of a small island.

The increasingly earlier break-up of sea ice in the spring is likely the cause of a startling drop in the average weight of polar bears in western Hudson Bay. The bears feed almost exclusively in winter, when they hunt seals from the ice. Between 1980 and 2004, the average weight of adult female polar bears in that area fell from 650 to 507 pounds (295 to 230 kilograms). Because the female's ability to reproduce and care for cubs depends on her fat stores, a shortened hunting season may be contributing to an observed decline in birth and survival rates.

The dwindling of the ice has set off a scramble by the United States, Canada, Denmark, and other countries with borders in the Arctic to establish territorial claims in the Far North. Opening the Arctic, in addition to increasing ship traffic, would allow the development of what is reportedly about 25 percent of the world's remaining oil and gas reserves. Such development could further disrupt these troubled ecosystems.

Global changes

The effects of climate change in the Arctic may extend far beyond the frozen north. Although the Arctic Ocean is the smallest of the world's oceans, it plays a crucial role in regulating global climate. For example,

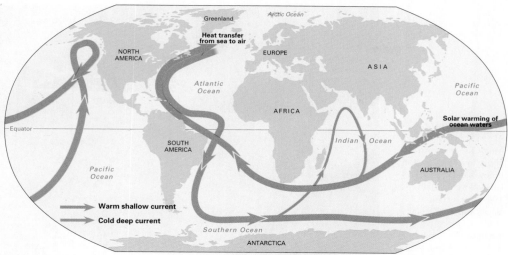

Source: US Global Change Research Program.

the Arctic acts like a giant mirror, reflecting back into space up to 90 percent of incoming sunlight and, in the process, helping to cool the planet. By contrast, the open ocean reflects only about 6 percent of the sunlight reaching it. In addition, thin ice, such as seasonal ice, reflects less solar energy than perennial ice. Using measurements made by U.S. submarines, scientists have found that, from the 1960's to the mid-1990's, the average thickness of Arctic ice in deep-water areas of the ocean dropped by about 40 percent, from 10 to 6 feet (3.1 to 1.8 meters). As the Arctic's ice cover disappears, more of the sun's heat is absorbed. The result is a "feedback loop" of rising temperatures that promote melting, which increases energy absorption and further raises temperatures.

Another possible consequence of Arctic melting involves the worldwide ocean current known as the thermohaline circulation (THC). Often described as a conveyor belt, the THC helps move solar energy from the tropics to polar regions and is partially responsible for the moderate winter temperatures in northwestern Europe, including the United Kingdom.

The THC exists because of regional differences in the density of seawater caused by temperature and *salinity* (saltiness). As seawater freezes, its salt separates from the growing ice crystals, creating *briny* (highly salty) pockets within the ice. Over time, the brine drips through the ice into the ocean, forming unusually dense layers of water. Briny water formed in the Arctic and other northern seas travels southward to the North Atlantic, where it joins and helps cool warm, salty water carried northward by the Gulf Stream. Several million cubic kilometers of the cold, briny water, which is denser than warm water, sinks toward the ocean bottom and begins moving south. After a 1,000-year journey through the South Atlantic, Indian, Pacific, and Southern (Antarctic) oceans, the water returns to the North Atlantic, where another circuit begins.

Many scientists have warned that rising surface temperatures and a loss of sea ice in the Arctic could disrupt the THC, causing dramatic

A worldwide ocean current that helps move solar energy from the tropics to polar regions could be slowed or shut down by melting Arctic ice. The current helps warm the Northern Hemisphere—particularly northwestern Europe—and cool the Southern Hemisphere.

The eastern arm of Alaska's once-massive Muir Glacier (shown above in a 1941 photo) is now a deep glacial lake (above right). In 1941, this section of the glacier was 3,000 feet (1,000 meters) thick and 1.8 miles (3 kilometers) wide. Since 1899, Muir Glacier has retreated 28 miles (45 kilometers) from the sea, with 12 miles (20 kilometers) of that amount occurring from 1941 to 2004.

changes in the global climate. For example, some computer models predict that if the THC were to slow or shut down, the Northern Hemisphere could become significantly cooler, while the Southern Hemisphere could become warmer. Fresh water flooding into the North Atlantic from melting glaciers in the Arctic and Greenland also could stall the THC by lowering the salinity of the water and forming a "cap" over the ocean.

The rising threat of higher sea levels

Perhaps the most discussed impact of a global ice meltdown is rising sea levels. The ACIA predicted that global sea levels could rise from 4 inches to 3 feet (10 to 90 centimeters) by 2100, with even faster increases as the century progresses. Currently, about half of the world's population lives within 125 miles (200 kilometers) of a coast, with many people residing much closer. A 1.5-foot (0.5-meter) increase in sea levels could cause shorelines in relatively flat areas to move inland by about 150 feet (50 meters). Higher sea levels would pollute underground freshwater aquifers and require the massive reengineering and reconstruction of coastal roads, power plants, and other basic infrastructure. Wetlands, marshes, and estuaries would be submerged, disrupting animal life on land and in the sea. Rising water would also result in major shifts in plant habitats, likely causing some species to become extinct.

In fact, sea levels have risen by about 4 to 9 inches (10 to 25 centimeters) since the early 1900's, according to the United Nations Environmental Programme (UNEP). Surprisingly, melting Arctic sea ice accounts for almost none of that total because the ice floats and, thus, occupies nearly the same volume as its meltwater would. About half of

As Muir Glacier has retreated, the stony hillsides of the valley have been transformed by thickly growing trees and shrubs.

the increase has resulted from *thermal expansion* (the expansion and rise of the ocean caused directly by higher temperatures), UNEP scientists concluded. Meltwater from the world's two main *ice sheets* in Greenland and Antarctica and, to a much lesser degree, from glaciers outside polar regions accounts for the other half. (An ice sheet is a dome-shaped glacier covering an area greater than 19,300 square miles [50,000 square kilometers]).

Greenland's ice sheet, which covers the island's central plateau, ranks second only to Antarctica's ice sheets in volume. Two miles (3 kilometers) thick in places, it holds about 9 percent of the world's glacial ice and 10 percent of its fresh water, enough water to maintain the Mississippi River for at least 4,700 years, according to the U.S. Geological Survey. Surrounding the ice sheet are coastal mountains with glaciers that flow down the valleys to the sea. If Greenland's ice sheet were to melt completely, scientists have calculated, world oceans would rise by 20 feet (66 meters).

Vanishing glaciers

Glaciers outside Earth's polar regions are retreating because of both modern global warming and natural causes, particularly a gradual warm-up in Earth's temperature that followed a mini-ice age ending in the mid-1800's. A 2003 report by the conservation group WWF noted, "Since the early 1960's, mountain glaciers worldwide have experienced an estimated net loss of 960 cubic miles (4,000 cubic kilometers) of water—more than the annual discharge of the Orinoco, Congo, Yangtze, and Mississippi rivers combined; this loss was more than twice as fast in the 1990's than during the previous decades."

The retreat of the Gangotri Glacier in the Himalaya (inset), shown in a composite of satellite images, has accelerated since 1971. The Gangotri helps supply the Ganges River, on which millions of people depend for farming (above), drinking water, and electric power.

In Alaska, glaciers are thinning by an average of 6 feet (1.8 meters) a year, twice the rate in the mid-1990's. From 1850 to 2006, Glacier National Park lost 123 of its 150 glaciers. If current warming trends continue, all the park's glaciers—11,000-year-old remnants of the last Ice Age—will disappear sometime before 2050, according to the U.S. National Park Service.

Glaciers in Asia's Himalaya-Hindu Kush region are retreating at the rate of about 30 to 50 feet (10 to 15 meters) annually, according to the WWF. Glaciers in the European Alps have lost from 10 to 20 percent of their volume since 1980, a number projected to rise to 80 percent by 2100. Because of the loss of the ice—and the reduction of the glaciers' weight on Earth's crust—Alpine peaks are rising. Mount Blanc in Switzerland, for example, is being lifted by about one-third inch (0.9 millimeter) per year.

Glaciers in equatorial regions are also draining away. In the Andes, glaciers are retreating at a rate exceeding anything seen in 5,000 years, according to a study released in June 2006. The Qori Kalis Glacier in

the Peruvian Andes was retreating about 30 times faster in 2001 than it was in 1978. The Upsala Glacier in Argentina, the largest glacier in South America, is shrinking by 46 feet (14 meters) per year. Under current conditions, scientists predict, the Chacaltaya Glacier in Bolivia will disappear by about 2015. Once famous for the world's highest ski slope, Chacaltaya has lost 98 percent of its volume, most of it in the 1990's.

In Africa, about 80 percent of the ice on Mount Kilimanjaro, the continent's highest mountain, has disappeared since the early 1900's. Ice on Mount Kenya has shrunk by 40 percent since 1963. Glaciers in the mist-shrouded Ruwenzori Mountains of East Africa, known since ancient times as the Mountains of the Moon, have almost vanished.

The disappearance of Earth's glaciers has been described as a "time bomb." Tourists who visit the glaciers each year provide revenues crucial to the economies of numerous countries, especially in the developing world. Meltwater from glaciers powers hydroelectric dams. Peru, for example, depends on hydropower, mainly from glacial runoff, for a significant amount of its electric energy. Glacial meltwater also supports mining activities and is often essential for farming.

Most important, one-sixth of the world's population relies on glaciers and snow packs for its water supply. Glaciers in the Himalaya-Hindu Kush region, for example, help supply seven of Asia's most important rivers, including the Ganges, Yangtze, and Yellow. Municipal water systems in La Paz and El Alto, two of Bolivia's largest cities, depend on the Chacaltaya Glacier for their water. Glacier-fed rivers worldwide are also a crucial source of water for birds and other animals as well as for river and lake ecosystems. Computer models indicate that many of these rivers could all but disappear up during the dry season.

Ice in the Antarctic

If all the glaciers outside Greenland melted, sea levels would rise only slightly. The melting of Antarctica's two enormous ice sheets would be another story. Antarctica is Earth's largest storehouse of ice, holding about 90 percent of all the planet's ice and 70 percent of its fresh water. Most of this ice lies in two massive ice sheets that can be as thick as 11,500 feet (3,500 meters). If both ice sheets melted, Earth's oceans would rise nearly 230 feet (70 meters).

Several important studies published in 2006 demonstrated that Antarctica is losing ice faster than it can be replaced by the continent's sparse snowfall. One study, by German and U.S. scientists analyzing gravity variations, showed that Antarctica's ice sheets decreased by 36 cubic miles (152 cubic kilometers) annually from 2002 to 2005. Most of that amount—equal to the total amount of water used in the United States for three months—came from West Antarctica, much of which lies below sea level. Air temperatures there have risen faster than any other place on Earth since the mid-1900's.

The second study was the first comprehensive survey of glaciers on the Antarctic Peninsula, a mountainous finger of West Antarctica. Since 1940, British and U.S. scientists found, 87 percent of the glaciers have retreated, by an average of 165 feet (50 meters) every year for the last five years. This retreat is faster than in earlier years.

The 2002 collapse of the northern section of the massive Larsen B ice shelf on the eastern side of the peninsula provided dramatic evidence of the changes occurring in the Antarctic. Over a 35-day period, 1,250 square miles (3,250 square kilometers) of the shelf shattered and separated from the continent, the largest single retreat of an ice shelf on the peninsula since the mid-1970's. At that time of its collapse, Larsen B, which was once 720 feet (220 meters) thick, had already lost 60 percent of its volume. In 2006, British and Belgian scientists determined that climate warming linked to human activity strengthened the westerly winds that blow across the northern part of the peninsula, allowing them to rise over mountains that normally block their flow.

Like melting sea ice, melting ice shelves have little effect on sea level. However, the ice shelves act as brakes on the ice flowing off the

A polar bear sloshes through melting ice on Hudson Bay, near Churchill, Canada, in winter 2006. Scientists report that the disappearance of sea ice, which the bears use as hunting platforms, has contributed to a 22-percent drop in bear populations in the bay since 1987.

continent in glaciers. In fact, the four glaciers that had fed the northern section of Larsen B flowed up to eight times faster after the collapse. By contrast, the speed of nearby glaciers flowing toward the surviving section of the shelf remained unchanged. Moreover, the four glaciers that had been feeding Larsen B thinned by as much as 124 feet (38 meters) within six months.

Melting sea ice, aggravated by warming temperatures in the Southern Ocean, is affecting Antarctica's wildlife, particularly migratory birds. A 2006 study by French researchers found that nine species of sea birds that summer in Antarctica were migrating to the region an average of nine days later in 2004 than they were in the early 1950's. According to the scientists, one reason for the delay was a dramatic decline in populations of krill, tiny shrimplike animals that feed on algae that grow on the underside of the ice. A 2004 study by French researchers found that the number of krill, which form the base of the Antarctic food chain, had plunged by 80 percent since the 1970's. Shorter breeding seasons and less food threaten the birds' ability to reproduce.

Scientists know enough about the extent and effects of global warming to warn that actions should be taken to stabilize or reduce carbon-dioxide emissions. For this reason, the political and regulatory decisions made by governments and the choices made by individuals will continue to have a major influence on the future of climate change and Earth's icescape. In his 2006 book, *An Inconvenient Truth*, environmentalist and former U.S. Vice President Al Gore notes, "Our new technologies, combined with our numbers, have made us, collectively, a force of nature. And those with the most technology have the greatest moral obligation to use it wisely."

A scientist examines one of the plant species colonizing a warmer Antarctica. The plant population at this research station rose from zero in 1995 to 234 cushion plants—normally found on the tundra— and 5,129 grass plants in 2004.

Golf. Tiger Woods overcame the death of his father and a nine-week break in 2006 to capture his 11th and 12th career major Professional Golfers' Association of America (PGA) championships, winning both the British Open and PGA Championship. Woods also became the youngest player to win 50 PGA events by capturing the Buick Open on August 6 in Grand Blanc, Michigan, at age 30. Jack Nicklaus won his 50th event when he was 33.

Corey Pavin established a new low score for nine holes with a 26 on July 27 in Milwaukee at the U.S. Bank Championship. Pavin birdied eight of the first nine holes. The previous best was 27 by Robert Gamez in 2004.

Swedish-born golfer Annika Sorenstam captured her 10th major title on the Ladies Professional Golf Association (LPGA) tour in 2006. Three other women also claimed major titles.

PGA. Phil Mickelson captured his second Masters title in three years on April 9, 2006, in Augusta, Georgia. He finished at 7-under par for the tournament after a 3-under par 69 on the final day. At the U.S. Open in Mamaroneek, New York, in June, Mickelson's poor performance on the final hole wrecked his chance to win his third straight major. He needed a par but double-bogeyed. The collapse let Geoff Ogilvy of Australia capture his first major with a 5-over par 285, the first time a

U.S. Open winner finished over par since 1978.

Woods took an extended break from the tour after the final round of the Masters to spend time with his ailing father, Earl, who died on May 3, 2006, from cancer. Woods returned for the U.S. Open but failed to make the cut at a major for the first time in his 10 years as a pro.

In July, Woods returned to form, becoming the first player to win consecutive British Open titles since Tom Watson in 1982 and 1983. Woods shot a 5-under 67 in Hoylake, United Kingdom, to finish at 18-under and defeat Chris DiMarco by two shots. At the final major, Woods captured the PGA Championship on Aug. 20, 2006, in Medinah, Illinois. He rolled behind a hot putter to an 18-under 270, good for a five-stroke victory over Shaun Micheel.

LPGA. Karrie Webb of Australia captured her seventh career major, winning the Kraft Nabisco Championship in Rancho Mirage, California, on April 2. Webb finished the final round with a 7-under 65. Her 9-under put her in a play-off with Loren Ochoa of Mexico, who shot a tournament-record 62 earlier in the event. Webb birdied the first play-off hole for victory.

Se Ri Pak of South Korea topped Webb on the first play-off hole of the LPGA Championship in Havre de Grace, Maryland, on June 11, shooting a 7-under for the tournament. The victory was the seventh for South Korean women in the tour's first 14 events.

Sorenstam captured an 18-hole play-off with Pat Hurst by four strokes on July 3 in Newport, Rhode Island, to win the U.S. Women's Open. They tied at even par. Sherri Steinhauer won her third Women's British Open with a 7-under, capturing the title in Royal Lytham and St. Annes, United Kingdom, on August 6.

Senior PGA Tour. Jay Haas captured his first major championship, topping Brad Bryant on the third play-off hole of the Senior PGA Championship on May 28 in

Tiger Woods walks off the 18th green in tears with his caddy, Steve Williams, in July 2006 after winning his third British Open Championship. The title was his first major since the death in May of his father, Earl Woods, who strongly influenced Tiger's golfing career.

Edmond, Oklahoma. Haas shot a 3-under 68 on the final day to finish at 5-under. Bobby Wadkins fired a 4-under 68 on July 16 to capture the Senior Players Championship in Dearborn, Michigan. Wadkins rallied from a four-stroke deficit to finish at 14-under and win his first major by a single shot.

Allen Doyle claimed his second straight U.S. Senior Open on July 9 in Hutchinson, Kansas. Loren Roberts captured the Senior British Open on the first play-off hole on July 30 in Turnberry, Scotland. Australia's Eduardo Romero won the final major, The Tradition, on August 27 in Aloha, Oregon, sinking a birdie putt on the first play-off hole to beat Lonnie Nielsen. The pair had tied at 13-under.

The Ryder Cup. The European team routed the United States team 18 ½ to 9 ½ to win its third straight Ryder Cup competition. The victory was the Europeans' 8th in the last 11 Ryder tournaments.

◼ Michael Kates

Great Britain. See **United Kingdom.**

Greece. The center-right New Democracy (ND) government, under the leadership of Costas Caramanlis, remained stable in 2006. Countrywide local elections bolstered support for the ND party, which the prime minister hailed as support for continuing the party's reform program. According to most public opinion surveys, through the end of 2006, Caramanlis remained far ahead of his potential challenger, the leader of the Panhellenic Socialist Movement (PASOK), George Papandreou.

Budget. Greece remained on track in 2006 to keep its budget deficit under 3 percent of *gross domestic product* (GDP), which it is obliged to do as one of the countries using the euro as a currency. (GDP is the value of all goods and services produced in a country in a year.) Since 2004, the European Union (EU) statistical agency, Eurostat, has carefully audited Greece's budget. Earlier, Eurostat had objected to Athens' bookkeeping methods and suggested that its budget deficits were actually higher than those officially reported.

Student protests. In June 2006, students in Athens staged a violent protest against government plans to privatize the country's higher education system. Most of Greece's political elite have degrees from foreign universities, and the country's wealthier residents tend to send their children abroad for higher education. The education reform plan called for allowing the creation of nonprofit private universities in Greece that would charge tuition and would attract donations from the business community. Although the government did not back down from its reform plans, implementing them would require a constitutional change that could take several years to bring about.

Foreign policy. In 2006, Greek diplomats attempted to mediate the conflict between Cyprus and Turkey. As part of Turkey's negotiations to enter the EU, the nation must recognize the Greek Cypriot government as the sole legitimate representative of the island and allow Greek Cypriot ships and aircraft to use Turkey's ports and airstrips. Turkey refused, insisting that EU nations lift the general embargo on goods and services from Turkish Northern Cyprus. Turkish officials also proposed a plan for overcoming the divide in the island that had been in place since the Turkish invasion of 1974. The Greek Cypriot government threatened to derail Turkey's accession to the EU over the dispute.

Economy. EU economists estimated that Greece's economy grew by 3.8 percent in 2006. In addition, the country's unemployment rate fell to 9.3 percent from 9.8 percent in 2005.

◼ Jeffrey Kopstein

See also **Europe; Turkey.**

Grenada. See **Latin America.**

Guatemala. In September 2006, Guatemalan soldiers and police stormed the Pavon prison near Guatemala City, the capital, leaving seven soldiers dead. Following decades of neglect, prisoners had assumed control of the overcrowded facility, which housed twice as many inmates as it was designed to hold, and made it the headquarters of a lucrative drug-trafficking operation.

In a July massacre on a farm in central Guatemala, five people were killed by guns or machetes. The violence resulted from a clash between landless peasants attempting to settle on the privately owned farmland. Tens of thousands of subsistence farmers, similarly displaced during Guatemala's decades-long civil war, had occupied idle farmland following the end of the fighting in 1996. A policy of evicting the squatters, begun in 2004 by President Óscar Berger, heightened tensions in rural Guatemala, observers reported.

On Oct. 30, 2006, Mexico's government approved the extradition to Guatemala of former Guatemalan President Alfonso Portillo Cabrera. Portillo was to stand trial on charges of having stolen $4 million from Guatemala's defense budget from 2000 to 2003. ◼ Nathan A. Haverstock

See also **Latin America.**

Guinea. See **Africa.**

Guinea-Bissau. See **Africa.**

Guyana. See **Latin America.**

Haiti. René Préval was sworn in as president of Haiti on May 14, 2006, after having been declared the winner of a controversial presidential election in February. He had previously served as Haiti's president from 1996 through 2001.

In June 2006, 14 member nations of the Caribbean Community reinstated Haiti as a member of

Voters mass in front of a polling station in Haiti in February 2006 to cast ballots in the country's presidential election. United Nations-sponsored police maintained order during the polling, which resulted in the election of René Préval.

their regional association. Haiti's membership had been suspended following the rebellion that led to the United States-endorsed ouster of President Jean-Bertrand Aristide in 2004 and his replacement by a transitional president backed by a United Nations (UN) peacekeeping force.

In July 2006, President Préval released Yvon Neptune, prime minister during the Aristide administration, from prison. Neptune had been imprisoned in 2004 and held without trial on unsubstantiated charges of human rights abuses. UN officials hailed the release as a first step toward judicial reform.

In September, the UN peacekeeping mission in Haiti redeployed many of its 8,000 troops from stabilized rural areas to gang-controlled slums of Port-au-Prince. The UN mission also launched an incentive program, offering money, food, and job training to gang members who agreed to turn in their arms.   ■ Nathan A. Haverstock

See also **Latin America: A Special Report.**

Harness racing. See **Horse racing.**

Health care issues. Medicare, the United States government program that pays many health care costs for seniors and some disabled Americans, launched its initiative for coverage of prescription drugs on Jan. 1, 2006. Medicare Part D, as the plan was named, allows beneficiaries to purchase private insurance that will partially pay the cost of prescription medications for those patients who are not in hospitals or nursing homes.

Implementation of the program did not go smoothly. Hundreds of plans were available, and many beneficiaries were confused by the variety. Participants reported that information about prices and about which drugs were covered was difficult to find. Critics also challenged the accuracy of various plans' advertising. At the end of 2006, 22.5 million people had enrolled in the program.

After winning control of Congress in the 2006 midterm elections, Democratic leaders announced plans to pass legislation that would make changes to Medicare Part D. One of the more significant changes would require the Medicare program to negotiate with pharmaceutical companies for lower prices.

State and local insurance initiatives. In August 2006, the U.S. Census Bureau announced that 46.6 million Americans lacked health insurance, the highest figure on record. The legislatures of several U.S. states, including Tennessee and Vermont, passed laws in 2006 that attempted to broaden access to health insurance. Massachusetts implemented a plan that required all legal residents to acquire coverage by July 2007. The plan called for the state to partially subsidize the cost for families with annual household incomes of less than $60,000.

The Maryland legislature approved a law requiring large employers to devote a certain percentage of profits to health insurance for employees. Governor Robert Ehrlich vetoed the measure, but the legislature overrode his veto. In July 2006, a federal judge overturned the law. A bill passed by the California legislature creating a state-run universal insurance program was vetoed by Governor Arnold Schwarzenegger. The city of San Francisco also attempted to establish a universal coverage program. A restaurant association responded by suing the city, claiming that the program violated federal law.

Stem-cell research. On July 19, U.S. President George W. Bush exercised his first presidential veto by rejecting a bill passed by Congress that would have expanded federal funding for stem cell research. Stem cells are largely derived from embryos created through artificial fertility enhancement.

Birth control debate. On August 24, the Food and Drug Administration (FDA), a part of the U.S. Department of Health and Human Services, approved nonprescription sales of the drug Plan B, the so-called "morning-after pill" that usually prevents pregnancy if taken within 72 hours after a woman has sex. Plan B contains progestin, a synthetic hormone that can inhibit or delay ovulation, inhibit the transport of the egg or sperm, or prevent implantation of a fertilized egg. Under FDA directives, Plan B could be sold only to women age 18 or older. Many religious and antiabortion groups condemned the decision to make the pill available over the counter.

Gulf Coast woes. Health care services in New Orleans, Louisiana, and the rest of the Gulf Coast battered by hurricanes Katrina and Rita in 2005 struggled in 2006. Some hospitals remained closed, notably Charity Hospital, the largest health care facility in New Orleans and the city's only public health care institution. The city had no plans to reopen the hospital, which will likely be razed.

Leadership changes. Surgeon General of the United States Richard Carmona resigned in August. Rear Admiral Kenneth P. Moritsugu was named acting surgeon general. Mark McClellan, administrator of the Centers for Medicare and Medicaid Services, resigned on September 5 and was replaced by Deputy Administrator Leslie Norwalk. ■ Emily Friedman

See also **Drugs; Medicine; Public health.**

Hockey. In the National Hockey League (NHL), the Carolina Hurricanes beat the Edmonton Oilers in 2006 to capture their first Stanley Cup. The Hurricanes clinched the title with a 3-1 victory in Raleigh, North Carolina, beating Edmonton 4 games to 3. Hurricanes netminder Cam Ward became only the third rookie goaltender to lead his team to a title in the last 35 years, joining the Montreal Canadiens' Ken Dryden in 1971 and Patrick Roy in 1986. Ward was the fourth rookie to be named the play-offs' Most Valuable Player (MVP).

Play-offs. In the 2006 Western Conference finals, the Oilers advanced to their first Stanley Cup finals since 1990 with a 4-games-to-1 triumph over the Anaheim Ducks. In the 2006 Eastern Conference, Carolina defeated the Buffalo Sabres 4 games to 3 in the finals.

In Game 1 of the finals, Edmonton's stellar goalie, Dwayne Roloson, suffered a season-ending knee injury with about six minutes left on the clock, as Carolina rallied from a 3-0 deficit to win 5-4. The Oilers trailed the series 3 games to 1 but rallied to force a decisive seventh game.

Regular season. In the Western Conference, the Detroit Red Wings posted the best record in the NHL with 58 wins and 124 points to win the Central Division. Dallas won the Pacific Division with 53 wins and 112 points, while Calgary took the Northwest Division with 46 wins and 103 points. In the Eastern Conference, Ottawa captured the Northeast Division with 52 wins and 113 points. Carolina led the Southeast Division with 52 wins and 112 points. New Jersey took 46 wins and 101 points to win the Atlantic Division.

NHL awards. Joe Thornton of the San Jose Sharks won the Hart Memorial Trophy as the league's MVP. Thornton also won the

A pharmacist explains the intricacies of the Medicare Part D prescription drug benefit program to a possible beneficiary after the launch of the program in January 2006. Despite a rocky start, 22.5 million seniors had enrolled in the program by the year's end.

NATIONAL HOCKEY LEAGUE STANDINGS

WESTERN CONFERENCE

Central Division	W.	L.	OTW.†	OTL.††	Pts.
Detroit Red Wings*	58	16	7	8	124
Nashville Predators*	49	25	9	8	106
Columbus Blue Jackets	35	30	14	9	95
Chicago Blackhawks	26	43	9	13	65
St. Louis Blues	21	46	7	15	57
Northwest Division					
Calgary Flames*	46	25	4	11	103
Colorado Avalanche*	43	30	6	9	95
Edmonton Oilers*	41	28	13	13	95
Vancouver Canucks	42	32	8	8	92
Minnesota Wild	38	36	6	8	84
Pacific Division					
Dallas Stars*	53	23	15	6	112
San Jose Sharks*	44	27	10	11	99
Anaheim Ducks*	43	27	6	12	98
Los Angeles Kings	42	35	10	5	89
Phoenix Coyotes	38	39	10	5	81

EASTERN CONFERENCE

Northeast Division	W.	L.	OTW.	OTL.	Pts.
Ottawa Senators*	52	21	4	9	113
Buffalo Sabres*	52	24	11	6	110
Montreal Canadiens*	42	31	9	9	93
Toronto Maple Leafs	41	33	10	8	90
Boston Bruins	29	37	6	16	74
Atlantic Division					
New Jersey Devils*	46	27	13	9	101
Philadelphia Flyers*	45	26	11	11	101
New York Rangers*	44	26	11	12	100
New York Islanders	36	40	12	6	78
Pittsburgh Penguins	22	46	5	14	58
Southeast Division					
Carolina Hurricanes*	52	22	12	8	112
Tampa Bay Lightning*	43	33	12	6	92
Atlanta Thrashers	41	33	10	8	90
Florida Panthers	37	34	12	11	85
Washington Capitals	29	41	9	12	70

*Made play-offs   †Overtime wins   ††Overtime losses

STANLEY CUP CHAMPIONS—Carolina Hurricanes
(defeated Edmonton Oilers, 4 games to 3)

LEADING SCORERS	Games	Goals	Assists	Pts.
Joe Thornton, San Jose	81	29	96	125
Jaromir Jagr, New York R	82	54	69	123
Alexander Ovechkin, Wash.	81	52	54	106
Dany Heatley, Ottawa	82	50	53	103
Daniel Alfredsson, Ottawa	77	43	60	103

LEADING GOALIES (26 or more games)	Games	Goals against	Avg.
Miikka Kiprusoff, Calgary	74	151	2.07
Dominik Hasek, Ottawa	43	90	2.09
Manny Legace, Detroit	51	106	2.19
Cristobal Huet, Montreal	36	77	2.20
Henrik Lundqvist, New York R	53	116	2.24

AWARDS

Adams Award (coach of the year)—Lindy Ruff, Buffalo

Calder Trophy (best rookie)—Alexander Ovechkin, Washington

Clancy Trophy (leadership)—Olaf Kolzig, Washington

Hart Trophy (most valuable player)—Joe Thornton, San Jose

Jennings Trophy (team[s] with fewest goals against)—Miikka Kiprusoff, Calgary

Lady Byng Trophy (sportsmanship)—Pavel Datsyuk, Detroit

Masterton Trophy (perseverance, dedication to hockey)—Teemu Selanne, Anaheim

Norris Trophy (best defenseman)—Nicklas Lidstrom, New Jersey

Pearson Award (best player as voted by NHL players)—Jaromir Jagr, New York R

Ross Trophy (leading scorer)—Joe Thornton, San Jose

Selke Trophy (best defensive forward)—Rod Brind'Amour, Carolina

Smythe Trophy (most valuable player in Stanley Cup)—Cam Ward, Carolina

Vezina Trophy (best goalkeeper)—Miikka Kiprusoff, Calgary

Carolina Hurricanes goalie Cam Ward stops a shot from Radek Dvorak of the Edmonton Oilers in the sixth game of the NHL Stanley Cup finals. Carolina defeated the Oilers 4 games to 3. Ward was named the series' Most Valuable Player.

Art Ross Trophy as the league's leading scorer. Miikka Kiprusoff of the Calgary Flames won the Vezina Trophy as the league's leading goalkeeper. Nicklas Lidstrom of the Detroit Red Wings won the James Norris Trophy as the league's leading defenseman.

World championships. In 2006, Sweden became the first hockey team to capture an Olympic gold medal and a world title in the same year. Sweden defeated Finland 3-2 in the Olympic championship in Turin, Italy. Sweden then beat the defending champion, the Czech Republic, 4-0 on May 21 in Riga, Latvia, for the world title.

Colleges. The University of Wisconsin-Madison swept both the men's and women's 2006 National Collegiate Athletic Association championships. The men's team edged Boston College 2-1 for its sixth title. The women's team took its first championship with a 3-0 shutout of the University of Minnesota.   ■ Michael Kates

Honduras. See Latin America.

Horse racing. Barbaro's decisive victory in the 2006 Kentucky Derby raised hopes that the Thoroughbred would become the first Triple Crown winner since Affirmed in 1978. Just a few hundred yards into the May running of the 2006 Preakness Stakes in Baltimore, however, Barbaro suffered potentially life-threatening fractures above and below his right rear ankle. His jockey, Edgar Prado, pulled the horse to a stop and jumped off. Barbaro came through emergency surgery well and, despite one setback due to a dangerous inflammation, appeared to be on the road to recovery by the end of 2006.

Three-year-olds. At the Derby, held on May 6 in Louisville, Barbaro crushed 19 rivals to win by 6 ½ lengths, the largest margin in that race in 60 years. The Derby title was Barbaro's sixth straight win.

In the Preakness Stakes, a record crowd watched Bernardini beat Sweetnorthernsaint after Barbaro pulled up. Two weeks later, on June 10 in Elmont, New York, Jazil took the Belmont Stakes, the final leg of the Triple Crown, surging from the back to beat Bluegrass Cat by 1 ¼ lengths. Neither Barbaro nor Bernardini raced, the third time in 36 years that the Belmont failed to draw the winners of the Kentucky Derby and the Preakness Stakes.

New record. On December 1, Canadian-born Russell Baze set a record for career victories by a jockey. Baze broke the record of 9,530 wins set by Panamanian-born jockey Lafitt Pincay, Jr., in 1999.

International. Electrocutionist captured the $6-million Dubai World Cup, on March 25, 2006, in the United Arab Emirates (UAE), storming past Brass Hat to win the world's richest race by 1 ¼ lengths. On the same day, Discreet Cat won the $2-million UAE Derby by 6 lengths.

In European racing, Sir Percy took the Epsom Derby on June 3, winning by less than a head in a four-way photo finish. Rail Link won the Prix de l'Arc de Triomphe on October 1.

Dylan Thomas, with jockey Kieren Fallon aboard, captured the Irish Derby on July 2. On July 7, Fallon was barred from riding in the United Kingdom pending a criminal trial on race-fixing charges. Fallon, one of 11 charged on July 3, was accused of defrauding customers on an

MAJOR HORSE RACES OF 2006

THOROUGHBRED RACING

Race	Winner	Value to Winner
Belmont Stakes	Jazil	$600,000
Blue Grass Stakes	Sinister Minister	$450,000
Breeders' Cup Classic	Invasor	$2,700,000
Breeders' Cup Distaff	Round Pond	$1,220,400
Breeders' Cup Filly & Mare Turf	Ouija Board	$1,188,000
Breeders' Cup Juvenile	Street Sense	$1,080,000
Breeders' Cup Juvenile Fillies	Dreaming of Anna	$1,080,000
Breeders' Cup Mile	Miesque's Approval	$1,171,800
Breeders' Cup Sprint	Thor's Echo	$1,150,200
Breeders' Cup Turf	Red Rocks	$1,620,000
Canadian International Stakes	Collier Hill	$1,067,627
Epsom Derby (United Kingdom)	Sir Percy	£740,695
Dubai World Cup (United Arab Emirates)	Electrocutionist	$3,600,000
Haskell Invitational Stakes	Bluegrass Cat	$600,000
Hollywood Gold Cup Stakes	Lava Man	$450,000
Irish Derby (Ireland)	Dylan Thomas	780,000 euros
Jockey Club Gold Cup	Bernardini	$450,000
Kentucky Derby	Barbaro	$1,453,200
Kentucky Oaks	Lemons Forever	$400,000
King George VI and Queen Elizabeth Diamond Stakes (United Kingdom)	Hurricane Run	£425,850
Lane's End Stakes	With a City	$300,000
Oaklawn Handicap	Buzzards Bay	$300,000
Pacific Classic Stakes	Lava Man	$600,000
Preakness Stakes	Bernardini	$650,000
Prix de l'Arc de Triomphe (France)	Rail Link	1,143,000 euros
Santa Anita Derby	Brother Derek	$450,000
Santa Anita Handicap	Lava Man	$600,000
Stephen Foster Handicap	Seek Gold	$502,647
Travers Stakes	Bernardini	$600,000
Woodbine Mile (Canada)	Becrux	$600,000

HARNESS RACING

Race	Winner	Value to Winner
Cane Pace	Total Truth	$150,000
Hambletonian	Glidemaster	$750,000
Kentucky Futurity	Glidemaster	$256,425
Little Brown Jug	Mr. Feelgood	$270,500
Meadowlands Pace	Artistic Fella	$500,000
Messenger Stakes	Palone Ranger	$546,830
Woodrow Wilson	Fox Valley Barzgar	$205,000
Yonkers Trot	Glidemaster	$728,930

Jockey Edgar Prado and a handler struggle with Barbaro after the Kentucky Derby winner broke bones in his right hind leg during the Preakness Stakes on May 20. After major surgery—unusual in such cases—and lengthy care, Barbaro appeared to be recovering by the year's end.

online betting exchange. In November, he was banned from French racing after testing positive for a prohibited substance.

Harness. Glidemaster won the trotting triple crown on November 25 by clinching the Yonkers Trot. He captured the Hambletonian on August 5 and the Kentucky Futurity on October 7. In the pacing triple crown, Total Truth captured the Cane Pace on September 4; Mr. Feelgood won the Little Brown Jug on September 21; and Palone Ranger won the Messenger Stakes on November 25.

■ Michael Kates

Hospital. See Health care issues.
Housing. See Building and construction.

Houston. The aftermath of Hurricane Katrina remained a serious issue for Houston in 2006, as tensions escalated between former residents of New Orleans, Louisiana, and native Houstonians. After the hurricane swamped New Orleans in August 2005, hundreds of thousands of evacuees streamed into Texas. Many stayed into 2006 because federal funds allowed them to live rent-free in Houston-area apartments.

The Houston Police Department blamed the evacuees—who were largely poor and African American—for an increase in violent crime. Houston's homicide rate rose 25 percent in 2006, reaching its highest point in more than a decade. Due to concerns about violent crime, many Houston residents became less welcoming toward the evacuees. On August 30, more than 1,700 residents crowded a Houston church to urge Mayor Bill White to send the evacuees back to New Orleans. White told the crowd that he expected the evacuees to become productive, working members of the community, and that lawbreakers would be arrested.

The controversy over the evacuees prompted Richard "Kinky" Friedman, an independent candidate for Texas governor, to single out evacuees as "the thugs and the crackheads" responsible

for the crime surge. The comments drew widespread criticism, and Friedman did not win the election. Nevertheless, Friedman's sentiments were shared by others. Defenders of the evacuees claimed that many Houstonians blamed all of the city's problems on the newcomers.

By the end of 2006, many evacuees had left Houston. According to the Texas Education Agency, an organization of the state government, some Houston-area school districts had their evacuee enrollment plunge by 40 to 50 percent during the course of the year.

Enron rulings. Nearly five years after the collapse of Enron Corp.—the energy trading corporation that was once Houston's largest company—former employees gained a measure of closure with the convictions of top executives. In May 2006, Kenneth Lay, Enron's founder, and Jeffrey Skilling, the former chief executive, were found guilty of fraud and conspiracy. Weeks later, in July, Lay died of heart disease. In October, Skilling received a prison sentence of more than 24 years.

Enron's stockholders in 2006 continued to seek repayment for money lost in the company's collapse. By November, they had recovered more than $7 billion through settlements with Enron's former accountants, lawyers, and lenders.

No smoking. Houston in October joined a growing number of United States cities by banning smoking in most workplaces, including bars. Sparked by workplace safety concerns, Houston's

City Council approved the measure by a 13-2 vote. The ban—which provides exceptions for cigar shops and certain other businesses—was scheduled to go into effect in September 2007.

Immigration policy. As federal lawmakers struggled over immigration reform in 2006, the Houston Police Department toughened its own policy on October 1. The move came less than two weeks after Rodney Johnson, a Houston police officer, was fatally shot in the line of duty. An illegal immigrant who had previously been deported was charged in the shooting.

The police department's new policy called for police to work more closely with federal agencies in reporting illegal immigrants suspected of crimes. The policy called for officers to ask all arrested suspects about their citizenship status and to run criminal background checks on those who could not provide identification. Police were instructed to hold suspects for immigration authorities if background checks showed that the suspects had violated orders to leave the United States. Prior to the new policy, critics had called Houston a "sanctuary city" for illegal immigrants, because they believed the city's police took a hands-off approach to immigration enforcement.
■ Eric Berger

See also **City; Courts; Immigration; United States, Government of the: A Special Report.**

Human rights.
The United States and other countries continued to be accused of human rights violations in 2006 during their campaigns against terrorism. International human rights groups, such as London-based Amnesty International, New York City-based Human Rights Watch, and United Nations (UN) human rights bodies, issued reports and statements criticizing the U.S. government and the government of the United Kingdom for their policies on captured terrorism suspects. The groups claimed that thousands of suspects were being detained worldwide—some at known facilities, others at secret sites—without having been charged with crimes or provided with judicial due process. The groups also claimed that suspects were being transferred illegally across borders and that torture and other abusive tactics were being used during interrogations.

A U.S. military prison camp for terrorism suspects at Guantánamo Bay, Cuba, continued to be a lightning rod for criticism. As of late 2006, the camp held about 430 detainees, most of whom were not expected to face trial or be designated for release. President George W. Bush of the United States had classified the detainees as "unlawful enemy combatants" and declared that they did not qualify for the wartime prisoner rights set forth in the international treaties known as the Geneva Conventions. Throughout 2006, many individuals and groups,

including the UN Committee against Torture, alleged abusive treatment of Guantánamo detainees and called for the camp to be closed.

On June 10, three Guantánamo detainees committed suicide by hanging themselves with makeshift nooses. Camp officials, citing several prior incidents of harassment and violence by prisoners against guards, suggested that the three detainees may have been motivated more by martyrdom or hatred than by desperation. Human rights advocates questioned this explanation and called for an independent probe.

Hamdan ruling. The U.S. Supreme Court on June 29 rejected the military commissions that Bush had established in 2001 to try foreign terrorism suspects, including suspected members of al-Qa`ida. The court, ruling in *Hamdan v. Rumsfeld,* stated that the commissions violated the Geneva Conventions and were unauthorized by U.S. law. The case involved Salim Ahmed Hamdan, a Guantánamo detainee alleged to have been an aide to al-Qa`ida leader Osama bin Laden. Hamdan faced trial before a military commission. This commission would have offered fewer legal protections than a regular U.S. civilian or military court. Legal experts said the Hamdan ruling challenged Bush's claims of expansive executive power to fight terrorism and gave detainees at least some protection under international law. The ruling required the Bush administration either to operate the commissions according to established law or to seek congressional approval to operate them differently. In July 2006, the Bush administration announced that it would apply Geneva protections to all terrorism suspects in U.S. custody.

Secret prisons. On September 6, President Bush publicly acknowledged for the first time that the U.S. Central Intelligence Agency (CIA) had been holding terrorism suspects in secret prisons outside the country. He said the CIA program had used "an alternative set of procedures" to interrogate suspects, but he said he could not reveal what those procedures were. He claimed that the program had gleaned information that had helped thwart a number of terrorist plots. Human rights groups suspected that the secret prisons were meant to hide illegal treatment and possible torture of detainees, but Bush said no torture had taken place. Bush also called on Congress to authorize new military commissions for detainees.

Military Commissions Act. In September, Congress passed the Military Commissions Act of 2006, and Bush signed it on October 17. The act set forth the rules for trying foreign terrorism suspects in special military commissions and also enacted guidelines for detainee interrogations. Under these guidelines, coercive interrogation tactics were allowed, but torture, rape, and cruel or inhuman treatment were prohibited. Human

Coretta Scott King
Building the Beloved Community

Coretta Scott King, widow of civil rights activist and Nobel Peace Prize winner Martin Luther King, Jr.— and an international activist in her own right—died on Jan. 30, 2006. As a newlywed and young mother in the 1950's and 1960's, King put aside her considerable musical talent and her interest in such causes as world peace and disarmament to devote herself to her family and to support the work of her husband. After the assassination of Martin Luther King, Jr., on April 4, 1968, she became a prominent activist in the movement to which her husband had devoted his life and the caretaker of his legacy.

Coretta Scott was born on April 27, 1927, in the small country crossroads of Heiberger, near Marion, Alabama. Her parents, Obadiah and Bernice (McMurry) Scott, owned and worked a small farm, and Coretta, as well as her sister and brother, often helped in the fields. The farm was successful enough that all three children were able to attend college.

Coretta attended Antioch College in Yellow Springs, Ohio. She earned a Bachelor of Arts degree in music and education in 1951 and was awarded a scholarship to study voice at the New England Conservatory of Music in Boston, Massachusetts. While at the conservatory, a mutual friend introduced her to Martin Luther King, Jr., who was a doctoral student at Boston University's School of Theology at the time. King's father, who was also a minister, presided over the couple's wedding on June 18, 1953.

In September 1954, King accepted the position of pastor of the Dexter Avenue Baptist Church, and the young couple moved to Montgomery, Alabama. Barely a year later—and two weeks after the birth of the Kings' first child—Rosa Parks refused to give up her seat on a bus to a white man, and King was chosen to lead the massive, citywide boycott that paralyzed the Montgomery bus system for more than a year. Mrs. King accompanied her husband to the marches, rallies, and protest meetings that drew the world's attention to the reality of racial segregation in the United States.

As three more children were born to the couple, Mrs. King participated in the civil rights movement by assuming administrative chores, filling in as a speaker when her husband was unavailable, and raising funds for the Southern Christian Leadership Conference (SCLC, of which King was the first president) by organizing and singing at events called "freedom concerts." In 1957, she accompanied her husband to Ghana to celebrate that country's independence from the United Kingdom. In 1959, they traveled to India to study the nonviolent principles of Mohandas Gandhi. Mrs. King was a delegate for the Women's Strike for Peace to the 17-nation Disarmament Conference in Geneva, Switzerland, in 1962. In 1965, she spoke at an anti-Vietnam War rally in Madison Square Garden in New York City, and in 1967, she appeared in Chicago in support of "Operation Breadbasket," an SCLC program to improve the economic conditions of black communities.

Four days after Martin Luther King, Jr., was shot and killed in Memphis, Mrs. King led a march in the city—attended by an estimated 50,000 people—to call for peace. In 1968, she established the Martin Luther King, Jr., Center for Nonviolent Social Change in Atlanta and served as the center's president, chairwoman, and chief executive officer until 1995. The King Center, which includes Martin Luther King, Jr.'s, tomb, amassed one of the largest archives of civil rights movement documents in the United States. One of Mrs. King's greatest endeavors was to have her husband's birthday declared a national holiday in the United States. President Ronald Reagan signed the bill establishing the holiday in 1983, and Martin Luther King, Jr., Day was first celebrated in January 1986.

Coretta Scott King died in Rosarito Beach, Mexico, at the age of 78. She spent her life, in her own words, in pursuit of "a free and true and peaceful society," a vision to which her husband referred as "the beloved community."

■ Kristina Vaicikonis

rights advocates criticized a number of provisions in the new law. They especially objected to the provision barring detainees from obtaining a *writ of habeas corpus.* A writ of habeas corpus would allow detainees to have a court decide whether their detention was justified.

The United Nations. In March, the UN General Assembly voted to eliminate its 53-country Commission on Human Rights. Many critics believed that the commission had become ineffective and lacked credibility after countries with poor human rights records—such as Sudan and Zimbabwe—had held appointments. The General Assembly replaced the commission with a new 47-country Human Rights Council, charged with promoting and protecting human rights. However, when elections for the council were held in May, some countries considered to be rights violators won council seats. These countries included China, Cuba, Pakistan, Russia, and Saudi Arabia. The United States did not seek a seat on the council. U.S. officials said that further reforms would be necessary before the council could be effective, but they also said that the United States would support the council's goals.

■ Geoffrey A. Campbell

See also **Congress of the United States; Courts; Disability; Sudan; Supreme Court of the United States; United States, Government of the.**

Hungary. A political firestorm threatened to bring down the government of Prime Minister Ferenc Gyurcsány in late 2006. The trouble stemmed from the disclosure of a speech that Gyurcsány made to a closed meeting of members of his governing Socialist Party in May. He stated that he and other party leaders lied to the public, falsely promising cuts in taxes and increases in social services in order to win parliamentary elections in April. (In those elections, the Socialists outpolled the main opposition party and retained their parliamentary majority.) The release of a tape recording of the speech to the media in mid-September incited massive protest demonstrations and rioting in Budapest, the capital.

As the protests continued, Gyurcsány won a vote of confidence in parliament on October 6. However, ceremonies marking the 50th anniversary of the 1956 Hungarian uprising against the Soviet Union provided opportunities for further antigovernment protests. On Oct. 23, 2006, the anniversary of the start of the 1956 uprising, riots in the streets of Budapest resulted in more than 150 injuries and at least 100 arrests. Prominent among the rioters, noted reporters, were right-wing extremists sporting Nazi symbols and flags.

On Nov. 4, 2006, an estimated 50,000 people participated in a candlelight march in Budapest to observe the 50th anniversary of the crackdown by Soviet forces on Hungary that ended the 1956 rebellion. Participants were peaceful, but many carried signs demanding Gyurcsány's resignation.

Budget deficit. Analysts speculated that public anger over austerity measures passed by the Socialist-led government to reduce Hungary's large budget deficit aggravated anti-Gyurcsány opinion. These included tax hikes, increases in energy costs, the introduction of tuition payments for formerly free higher education, and increases in costs for health care services.

Economists projected that in 2006 Hungary's deficit would grow to more than 10 percent of the country's *gross domestic product* (the value of all goods and services produced in a year). The deficit threatened Hungary's target date for adopting the euro, the common currency of 12 of the 25 members of the European Union (EU). Hungarian leaders had committed to euro adoption by 2010, but an EU member nation must meet various economic requirements to qualify.

The Hungarian economy grew steadily at around 4 percent in 2006, comparable with the pace of growth in 2005. In mid-2006, unemployment stood at around 7 percent and the annual rate of inflation at about 3.5 percent. Both of these indexes were relatively unchanged from 2005. ■ Sharon L. Wolchik

See also **Europe.**

Ice skating. Teen-ager Kimmie Meissner of the United States shocked the skating world in 2006 with a dynamic performance that made her a world champion. In 2006, Stéphane Lambiel retained his title, one year after becoming the first Swiss man in 58 years to win gold at the world skating championships.

Michelle Kwan, a five-time world champion, struggled with injuries in 2006. She could not compete in the U.S. championships, but a panel of judges let her join the U.S. Olympic team. She then withdrew from the team when a groin pull kept her from skating at a peak level.

U.S. Championships. In January 2006, Sasha Cohen won the women's title in St. Louis, Missouri, after two straight second-place finishes. Meissner took the silver, and Emily Hughes earned the bronze. Johnny Weir captured his third straight men's title, with newcomer Matt Savoie taking the silver and Evan Lysacek claiming the bronze. Garrett Lucash and Katie Orscher garnered their second pairs title. The bigger story, though, was the silver medal won by Aaron Parchem and Marcy Hinzmann, which earned them a place with the U.S. Olympic skating team. Parchem was the first African American male skater—and only the second African American skater, after Debi Thomas—to represent the United States at the Olympics. Ice dancers Tanith

Kimmie Meissner of the United States performs her short program at the 2006 World Figure Skating Championships in Calgary, Canada, on March 24. Meissner won the women's world championship title on March 25.

Belbin and Ben Agosto took their third straight gold medal at the U.S. championships.

World championships. Meissner won the women's world championship title on March 25 in Calgary, Canada. She executed seven triple jumps to post a personal best of 129.70 points in the free skate. Sasha Cohen led the field after the short program and was considered an overwhelming favorite to win her first world title. However, she struggled in her free skate with a fall and missed jumps and finished third. Japan's Fumie Suguri took the silver.

Lambiel claimed his second straight world title on March 23, edging French skater Brian Joubert by 3.39 points. Joubert led after the short program and was dazzling in the free skate but could not hold off an even better Lambiel. Lysacek took the bronze, his first world medal.

European championships. At Lyon, France, in late January, the Russians won all four disciplines for the second straight year and for the third time in four years. Evgeni Plushenko won his second straight and fifth overall European men's title, with Lambiel finishing second and Joubert third. Irina Slutskaya won a record-breaking seventh women's title. Fellow Russian Elena Sokolova took the silver, and Italy's Carolina Kostner won the bronze. ■ Michael Kates

See also **Olympics: A Special Report.**
Iceland. See Europe.

Immigration took center stage in 2006 as a volatile political issue in the United States. President George W. Bush and Congress grappled with finding a way to combat illegal immigration—particularly from Mexico—while also acknowledging that millions of illegal immigrants had already integrated into the U.S. economy.

Mass rallies. In March, April, and May, millions of immigrants—both illegal and legal—and their supporters participated in demonstrations throughout the United States. The main days of protest were April 10, when rallies were held in more than 100 cities, and May 1, when hundreds of thousands of immigrants boycotted work and school and avoided spending money to show their worth to the economy. The protesters, most of whom were Hispanic, favored lenient immigration laws and opposed a bill passed by the U.S. House of Representatives in December 2005. The bill would have established tough criminal penalties for undocumented immigration and for assisting in such immigration and would have required fencing along parts of the 1,952-mile (3,141-kilometer) U.S.-Mexican border.

Congress. On May 25, 2006, the U.S. Senate passed a competing immigration bill. It would have toughened border security and called for a border fence, but it also would have established a guest-worker program and a path for citizenship for many of the estimated 12 million illegal immigrants already in the United States. Unlike the House bill, which focused mainly on law enforcement, the Senate bill embodied a moderate and more comprehensive approach that had been endorsed by President Bush. However, differences between the two bills were not reconciled in 2006.

In September, the two houses passed legislation authorizing fencing along 700 miles (1,100 kilometers) of the U.S.-Mexican border. President Bush signed the measure on October 17. However, it was unclear whether funds would ever be appropriated to build the fence.

National Guard. More than 6,000 National Guard members were sent to the U.S.-Mexican border region in 2006 to aid U.S. Customs and Border Protection (CBP) agents with surveillance and construction. The support mission, dubbed Operation Jump Start, was intended to allow CBP agents to focus more on their primary patrol duties.

Border deaths. The number of people who died crossing illegally into the United States from Mexico more than doubled from 1995 to 2005, the U.S. Government Accountability Office reported in August 2006. In 2005, there were more than 470 such deaths, many attributed to heat exposure in the Arizona desert.   ■ Geoffrey A. Campbell

See also **United States, Government of the: A Special Report.**

India suffered from terrorism and insurgency in 2006. Nevertheless, its economy improved and steps were made toward banning child labor. In addition, a nuclear agreement between India and the United States was solidified.

Terrorism. On July 11, bombs exploded almost simultaneously on seven commuter trains in Mumbai (formerly Bombay), the nation's financial capital and largest city, during the evening rush hour. The explosions killed more than 200 people and wounded some 700 others.

Mumbai's police commissioner announced on September 30 that the attack had been planned by Pakistan's Directorate for Inter-Services Intelligence and carried out by Lashkar-e-Taiba, a militant Islamist group based in Pakistan. The commissioner based his information on the confessions of 15 people arrested after the attack, 11 of whom were Pakistani. Pakistan's Foreign Office denounced the accusation as irresponsible and baseless. It came amid continuing hostility between India and Pakistan over Jammu and Kashmir, a Himalayan state over which the two nations have fought since 1947.

Some Indian commentators suggested, however, that the Mumbai bombings may have been in retaliation for the murder of Indian Muslims, crimes that were seldom punished by officials from India's Hindu majority. A 1993 bombing in Mumbai that killed 257 people was officially listed as retaliation for Hindu fanatics having destroyed a Muslim mosque built in the 1500's.

Explosions on March 7, 2006, in Varanasi, a Hindu holy city formerly known as Benares, left 15 people dead at a railway station and at a temple where Hindus were gathered for prayers. At least four people were killed by a grenade in a Hindu temple in Manipur state on August 16. On September 8, explosions at a mosque at Malegaon, 160 miles (250 kilometers) northeast of Mumbai, killed 31 people.

Rebels. In a speech on August 15, Prime Minister Manmohan Singh declared that the two largest threats to India's internal security were terrorists and rebels. In 2006, members of a Maoist rebel group calling themselves Naxalites were active in rural and forested areas in at least 160 of India's 604 administrative districts, mostly in the southeast of the country. The Naxalites claimed to fight oppression by corrupt officials and brutal landlords in some of the poorest and least accessible parts of India.

Clashes between Naxalites and law enforcement in 2005 and 2006 left an estimated 1,000 people dead. A Naxalite land mine killed 12 police officers in June. On July 17, rebels attacked a police station and refugee camp, killing some 50 people, apparently in retaliation for government-backed counterinsurgency efforts.

Politics. Four states elected new governments in April and May 2006. Communist parties retained control of West Bengal and won power in Kerala. The India National Congress Party and its allies took control of the state governments in Assam and in Tamil Nadu. Congress also won in the union territory of Pondicherry.

The Congress leader, Sonia Gandhi, was reelected to Parliament in May. She had resigned from Parliament in March after controversy over her simultaneously holding a paid job as chairperson of the National Advisory Council, which advises the prime minister. She resigned from this post as well. Her return to Parliament in May was widely viewed as a personal triumph.

The Bharatiya Janata Party (BJP), dedicated to increasing Hindu influences in India, had governed India until the 2004 elections. In January 2006, former Prime Minister Atal Bihari Vajpayee and BJP President Lal Krishna Advani both gave up leadership roles in the party. The party then selected a low-profile politician, Rajnath Singh, as its president, and the BJP continued to drift without a clear sense of how to appeal to voters.

Economy. During Independence Day celebrations on August 15, Prime Minister Singh claimed, "The going has never been as good for India in the past as it is now." He applauded the nation's three successive years of 8-percent annual economic growth. Observers credited the growth to economic reforms begun by Singh a decade earlier when he was finance minister.

However, economic growth was uneven. An official with the World Bank, a United Nations affiliate, announced in March that half of all India's children suffered from malnutrition. In addition, conditions of extreme poverty and debt that caused 100,000 farmers to kill themselves from 1993 to 2003 remained severe. Another 1,000 debt-ridden farmers committed suicide in 2006.

In October, a new law came into effect that banned the employment of children under 14 years old as domestic servants or hotel and restaurant workers. Laws banning child labor in hazardous industries have been widely ignored, however, and many observers were skeptical that the new ban would have much effect.

Nuclear agreement. On a visit to India on March 2, U.S. President George W. Bush and Prime Minister Singh announced an agreement for U.S. help in India's development of civilian nuclear energy. President Bush said that cooperation on peaceful nuclear energy would boost America's "strategic relationship" with India. The U.S. Senate overwhelmingly approved the agreement on November 16.

■ Henry S. Bradsher

See also **Asia; Disasters; Pakistan.**

Indian, American. A decade-long lawsuit against the United States government on behalf of nearly 500,000 Indians continued in 2006. The suit, brought by Elouise Cobell, a member of the Montana Blackfeet tribe, charged that the Department of the Interior had mishandled more than $100 billion in trust funds that the department has administered for the Indians since 1887. The accounts contain royalties from mining, oil and gas extraction, timber, and grazing on lands that the department manages for individual Indians and tribes.

Since the lawsuit began in 1996, the plaintiffs had won several victories in the U.S. District Court for the District of Columbia. However, in July 2006, a federal appeals panel voted to remove the presiding judge, Royce C. Lamberth, from the case. According to the panel, Lamberth had lost his objectivity. The judge had held two secretaries of the interior in contempt of court for failing to provide an accounting of the funds and had accused the department of racism.

Also in July, U.S. Senate Indian Affairs Committee Chairman John McCain (R., Arizona) and Vice Chairman Byron Dorgan (D., North Dakota) presented an offer to settle the lawsuit for $8 billion. In 2005, the Indians had proposed a settlement of $27.5 billion. The government maintained that account losses totaled less than $500 million. By the end of 2006, no settlement had been reached.

Indian fire officers inspect a train coach that was destroyed by a bomb on July 11, 2006, in Mumbai, India's largest city and financial capital. Seven near-simultaneous explosions killed more than 200 people and wounded some 700 others.

Lawsuit over casino closing. The Alabama-Coushatta tribe of Livingston, Texas, filed a lawsuit in July against former Washington, D.C., lobbyist Jack Abramoff and his associates. The suit alleged that the defendants had defrauded the tribe of millions in revenue by mounting a campaign—ostensibly based on moral grounds—to close the tribe's nine-month-old casino in 2002. Because of the closure, many tribe members lost their jobs, and the tribe was unable to make planned improvements to housing, roads, and education on its reservation. Abramoff pleaded guilty in January 2006 to other charges of fraud, tax evasion, and conspiracy to bribe public officials. Abramoff's associates included Ralph Reed, a former Christian Coalition of America leader who lost a primary election for lieutenant governor of Georgia in 2006; Michael Scanlon, an aide to former U.S. Representative Tom DeLay (R., Texas); Jon Van Horne, a former Abramoff partner; and Neil Volz, a former aide to U.S. Representative Bob Ney (R., Ohio).

According to the suit, Abramoff and his associates campaigned to defeat a bill that would have legalized Indian casinos in Texas on the grounds that gambling was immoral. In truth, the group had been paid by a tribe in neighboring Louisiana to protect its own competing casino.

Canadian compensation for school abuse. In May 2006, the federal Cabinet of Canada agreed to pay $2 billion (Canadian) to about 80,000 Native Canadians who had been forced to attend government-financed residential schools in which they were physically and sexually abused. The 130 boarding schools, which operated from the 1800's to the 1980's, were run primarily by various Christian churches and were part of an effort to assimilate Inuit, Cree, and other native children into Canadian culture. The children were punished for speaking their own language or practicing their religion, experiences that sociologists say may have led to the high rates of alcoholism, domestic violence, unemployment, and poverty in many Native Canadian communities.

Each eligible former student was to receive $10,000, plus an additional $3,000 for each year of school beyond the first year attended. The Cabinet also agreed to provide $120 million to establish a foundation to promote native healing therapies and a "truth and justice commission." The settlement, one of the largest ever awarded in Canada, required approval by courts in nine jurisdictions.

Seminoles rock. The Seminole tribe of Florida announced in December that it had purchased Hard Rock International, a chain of restaurants, hotels, and casinos, for $965 million. The deal, which was to be completed in March 2007, was one of the largest purchases ever made by an American Indian tribe.   ■ Kristina Vaicikonis

See also **Congress of the United States.**

Indonesia was plagued in 2006 with earthquakes, volcanic activity, floods, and disease.

On May 27, an earthquake with a magnitude of 6.3 caused a *tsunami* (series of powerful ocean waves) that devastated the south-central coastal area of Java, Indonesia's most populous island. The Social Affairs Ministry subsequently announced that more than 5,800 people had been killed and more than 30,000 others injured. In addition, nearly 650,000 people were left homeless. The quake occurred near Mount Merapi, one of Indonesia's most active volcanoes. It began belching lava in early 2006, causing fears of a major eruption over densely populated farmland. On July 17, a 7.7-magnitude earthquake off Java's south coast triggered a tsunami that, according to Indonesian officials, killed about 600 people and left more than 74,000 others homeless.

Bird flu. The number of Indonesian deaths from avian influenza (also known as bird flu), a disease usually associated with farmers' poultry, reached 57 by December 2006, the highest total in any country. Although the number of avian flu cases declined in some Southeast Asian countries as officials vaccinated flocks and destroyed sick birds, cases continued to be reported from remote areas of Indonesia. International health officials said the country's lack of strong and efficient centralized health controls hindered efforts to restrict the illness in backyard birds and to treat people who became infected.

Terrorism that had repeatedly afflicted Indonesia in recent years raised legal issues in 2006. On June 14, police freed Abu Bakar Bashir after 26 months in prison. Bashir was the spiritual head of an Islamic organization, Jemaah Islamiyah, that was affiliated with the terrorist group al-Qa`ida. United States and Australian officials accused Bashir of a key role in the 2002 bombings on the island of Bali that killed 202 people, including 88 Australians. In December 2006, Indonesia's Supreme Court cleared Bashir of involvement in the bombings.

In 2003, three Indonesians who had confessed to roles in the Bali bombings were sentenced to death. In July 2006 their execution date was set, but on August 21, the day before their scheduled executions, the three men filed legal appeals, further delaying their executions.

Economy. Indonesia's government announced in September plans to allocate more money to a program intended to create 15 million jobs within three years. Of these, 12.5 million new jobs were to empower residents of small villages. Others were to be generated by the government-sponsored biofuel industry. Officials estimated that in 2006, 39 million people, out of a population of 220 million, lived below the poverty line, which was set at just $16.80 a month.

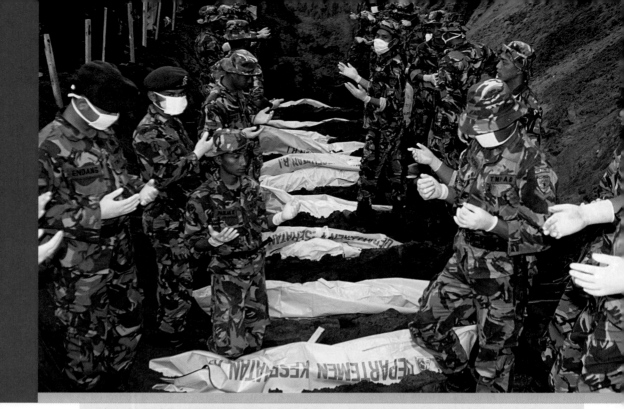

Indonesian soldiers pray over the bodies of tsunami victims in July 2006. The tsunami, triggered by a 7.7-magnitude earthquake, killed about 600 people and left more than 74,000 others homeless.

Some academic observers contended that the number of poor Indonesians was as high as 80 million people. They added that the 2006 economic growth rate of approximately 5 percent was too low to reduce unemployment or generate a sufficient number of new jobs to employ people entering the work force. They also noted that poverty was increasing because import controls kept the price of rice, a basic staple, too high.

Aceh. On July 11, the Indonesian parliament passed a law that gave greater autonomy to Aceh province on the island of Sumatra. A peace agreement signed on Aug. 15, 2005, had ended three decades of secessionist struggle that cost some 15,000 lives. Preliminary results from gubernatorial elections held on Dec. 11, 2006, suggested that former separatist leader Irwandi Yusuf would be the first directly elected representative of Aceh.

Separatist trouble continued at the other end of Indonesia, in the Papua region on the island of New Guinea. On January 18, 43 people from Papua landed by boat in northeastern Australia. The Papuan separatists claimed to be fleeing *genocide* (extermination of a cultural or racial group) by Indonesian forces. On March 23, Australia granted 42 of them temporary political asylum despite Indonesia's call for their return.

■ Henry S. Bradsher

See also **Asia; Australia; Disasters.**

International trade. The flow of goods and services between nations grew solidly during 2006, even as the system of global trading rules suffered major policy setbacks that were expected to affect future terms of trade. World leaders in international trade, such as the United States and China, instead pursued bilateral accords—individual deals with other countries or regional trading blocs—on such trade issues as tariffs and market access to achieve their commercial goals without waiting for worldwide consensus.

Doha talks collapse. In July, trade representatives meeting in Geneva, Switzerland, failed in a last-ditch effort to get the struggling "Doha Round" of world trade negotiations back on track. The Doha negotiations were named for the capital of Qatar, where talks had begun in 2001 to achieve comprehensive reform of world trade. As the negotiations proceeded, developing countries had demanded that Europe and the United States demolish some of their barriers to world agricultural trade, including extensive farm subsidies at home and tariffs on many imported products. The European Union (EU) and the United States both offered plans to address those issues, but in the end the various sides could not reach agreement.

On July 24, 2006, Pascal Lamy, director-general of the Geneva-based World Trade Organization (WTO)—the international agency that monitors existing trade rules and oversees trade negotiations—announced the suspension of the Doha Round. Despite efforts by some Doha participants to revive the talks, it was not clear in late 2006 when or even if they would resume.

Bilateral deals. The Doha Round's collapse left nations scrambling for the best trading deals they could get outside of a global framework. China, for instance, closed a series of trade deals with African leaders at a November trade conference in Beijing, the Chinese capital. The agreements gave China access to African oil and minerals in return for increased Chinese aid to countries of the region and investment in a variety of manufacturing and infrastructure projects.

The United States signed a trade pact with small but oil-rich Oman in July that was the latest in a series of targeted, individual deals. The U.S. government also attempted to build on the 2005 Central American Free Trade Agreement with a broader proposed trade zone called the Free Trade Area of the Americas. However, that project stalled as it encountered strong opposition from a number of adversarial Latin American leaders led by Venezuela's President Hugo Chávez.

Trade growth. The International Monetary Fund (IMF), in its September 2006 "World Economic Outlook," projected that world trade would grow by 9 percent during 2006—up from 7.4-percent growth in 2005 but slower than the 10.6-percent rate of growth seen in 2004. The IMF is a United Nations-affiliated organization that provides short-term credit to member nations and performs analyses of world economies.

Trade imbalances continued to be a prominent feature of world trade in 2006, prompting some economists to warn of threats to future world economic stability if such trends continued. The United States, with the world's largest economy and the richest consumer market, increased its already enormous trade deficit. This trend resulted from importing goods of greater volume and total value than the U.S. goods sent abroad. Economists in late 2006 estimated that the U.S. trade deficit would top out at $780 billion for 2006, compared with $726 billion for 2005. A quarter or more of the deficit was expected to accrue from trade with China.

China, despite surging domestic demand from its huge population—the world's largest—continued to export more goods than it took in. Despite China's need to buy oil and other commodities from abroad, the country's manufacturing sector continued to expand feverishly, sending more and more products into the international marketplace.

Oil-producing countries—including Russia, many nations in the Middle East, and some in Latin America and Africa—raked in huge profits at the expense of energy-hungry and resource-poor

regions as energy prices soared in mid-2006. Some countries with modest energy resources had other highly valuable commodities that they traded profitably in 2006. Chile, for example, ran up trade surpluses on the strength of its production and export of copper.

Antitrade nationalism. Tensions between erstwhile trading partners occasionally flared in 2006 due to factors as wide-ranging as fears of terrorism and concerns about the loss of jobs to overseas competitors. In February, a sudden furor erupted in the United States when media outlets revealed that DP World, a company owned by the government of Dubayy in the United Arab Emirates, had been cleared by the U.S. government to take over operations of six major U.S. seaport terminals. With commentators raising fears of Middle East-based terrorists infiltrating the ports to attack sensitive U.S. facilities or bring in bombs, Congress threatened to block the deal. Under the pressure of U.S. public opinion, DP World withdrew from the ports deal. The episode reminded some analysts of the public furor in 2005 over a Chinese energy company's attempt to buy a U.S. firm and its oil reserves, and led some to wonder if public opinion in the United States was turning decisively against free trade. ■ John Boyd

See also **Bank; Economics, United States; Economics, World; Energy supply.**

Internet. The number of United States residents who used the Internet at home grew from nearly 143 million in November 2005 to more than 150 million in November 2006, according to Nielsen//NetRatings, a New York City-based Internet market research firm. In June 2006, the firm reported that about three-fourths of the country's home Internet users had broadband connections.

Social networking sites on the World Wide Web drew media attention in 2006 as their popularity skyrocketed. Such sites allow users to create detailed online profiles, link to other users' profiles, and communicate with other users. A user's profile may include photographs, lists of interests, other personal details, journal entries, creative writing, artwork, songs, or video clips. The leading social networking site, MySpace.com, was among the 10 most visited Web sites in the United States during much of 2006, according to firms tracking Internet usage. Nielsen//NetRatings reported that the number of U.S. Internet users visiting MySpace grew from 16.2 million during July 2005 to 46 million during July 2006—an increase of 183 percent. MySpace, based in Santa Monica, California, is owned by News Corporation of New York City.

MySpace and such similar Web sites as Facebook.com and Xanga.com became places where teens and young adults would post personal information. Many adults became concerned about predators possibly using the sites to track and target young people. These concerns led the U.S. House of Representatives to pass a bill in July that would have required many schools and libraries to bar minors from accessing social networking sites. Critics of the legislation said that the benefits of such sites outweighed the risks and that the bill would inadvertently ban many news sites and other sites that allowed user profiles and interaction. The bill did not become law because the U.S. Senate failed to act on it before the end of 2006.

Video-sharing sites, especially YouTube.com, also became tremendously popular in 2006. Such sites allow users to upload self-created video clips for public viewing. The YouTube site, officially launched in December 2005, attracted one of the fastest-growing audiences in Internet history. Nielsen//NetRatings reported that the number of U.S. Internet users visiting YouTube rose from 4.9 million in January 2006 to 19.6 million in June 2006—a 297-percent increase. By July, users were viewing, on average, more than 100 million videos per day at the site. In a major deal in November, YouTube, Inc., based in San Bruno, California, was purchased by Google Inc.—the Mountain View, California, firm best known for its market-leading Web search engine—for $1.65 billion in stock.

Television transformed. As video content became easier to transmit and download over the Internet, traditional television companies—worried about losing viewers to Web-based digital competitors—scrambled to offer full shows, clips, and other TV content over the Web in 2005 and 2006. In October 2005, Apple Computer, Inc., of Cupertino, California, introduced a video-capable version of its iPod digital music player and began offering digital video through its iTunes Store on the Web. The Walt Disney Company of Burbank, California—which owns the New York City-based ABC, Inc., TV network—became the first traditional TV firm to offer popular network shows, including "Lost" and "Desperate Housewives," through iTunes. Other major TV network owners followed suit, offering shows on iTunes and elsewhere. In January 2006, Google launched a Web video store that offered TV shows from New York City-based CBS Corporation, including "CSI: Crime Scene Investigation" and "I Love Lucy." Viewers had to pay a fee to download TV shows from Apple's and Google's services. However, in April, ABC startled the industry when it announced that it would offer some of its network shows, with nonskippable commercials, for free on ABC.com. Also that year, many traditional and cable TV firms began to offer made-for-the-Web shows and rebroadcasts of past TV shows on special broadband Web channels, such as CBS.com's Innertube.

Net neutrality. In 2006, a major public debate erupted in the United States over whether regulation was needed to guarantee "network neutrality"—that is, to ensure that the owners of phone and cable lines and other Internet traffic "pipes" remain neutral and refrain from giving better network access to some content and application providers but not others. Proponents of net neutrality regulation—including Google and other large Web providers as well as the Consumers Union and other public interest groups—argued that it would keep phone and cable firms from having too much power over the Web. Regulation, proponents said, would keep the network owners from giving priority delivery to some Web sites over others based on the site providers' payment of an access fee, their ties to the network owners, or any other factor. However, opponents of regulation—including such network owners as AT&T Inc. of San Antonio—said that because of technological limitations, phone and cable firms might need to give priority to such high-bandwidth services as movies or phone calls to ensure quality delivery of those services, and they might need to impose access fees to raise funds for technology upgrades. Several proposals that addressed net neutrality were introduced in Congress, but none became law in 2006.

■ Dave Wilson

See also **Computer; Electronics; Popular music; Radio; Telecommunications.**

In 2006, social networking Web sites—especially MySpace.com—skyrocketed in popularity. Such sites allow their users to create and view detailed personal profiles, which may include lists of interests, journal entries, photos, songs, or video clips. MySpace was among the 10 most visited Web sites in the United States during much of 2006.

Iranian artists hold aloft containers of uranium during a parade in the town of Mashad in April 2006 to celebrate a reported advancement in Iran's uranium enrichment program. Iranian officials maintained that the enrichment program was only for the peaceful use of nuclear energy.

Iran. In an unprecedented gesture, Iran's President Mahmoud Ahmadinejad sent a letter in May 2006 to United States President George W. Bush in which the Iranian leader called for bringing together the followers of Islam, Christianity, and Judaism because they all believe in a single God. According to many experts in Middle East affairs, the real objective of the letter was to criticize U.S. policies toward less developed countries and to declare that "Liberalism and Western-style democracy ... have failed." In August, President Ahmadinejad said that he wanted to have a televised public debate with President Bush.

Nuclear program. Iran defied an August 31 deadline set by the United Nations (UN) Security Council to halt its uranium enrichment program. Uranium enrichment could produce fuel for civilian nuclear reactors or for nuclear weapons. President Ahmadinejad denied that Iran was pursuing a nuclear weapons program and maintained that Iran had a legal right to exploit peaceful nuclear energy.

In late December, the UN Security Council voted to impose sanctions on Iran that banned the import and export of materials that could be used for uranium enrichment and ballistic missiles. The approval of the sanctions package had been delayed for several months because Russia and China were opposed to certain provisions.

Terrorism. In November, a judge in Argentina issued an arrest warrant for former Iranian President Ali Akbar Hashemi Rafsanjani and eight other Iranians for their role in the July 1994 bombing of a Jewish cultural center in Buenos Aires, the capital of Argentina. The attack killed 85 people and injured 300 others. The bombing was carried out by the Lebanon-based group Hezbollah, which, according to terrorism experts, is armed and financed by Iran.

Iran's Supreme Leader Ayatollah Ali Khamenei praised Hezbollah for its 34-day war against Israel in July and August 2006. Before a UN resolution ended the fighting on August 14, the conflict led to the deaths of about 100 Israelis and about 1,000 Lebanese.

Opposition to theocracy. Iranian authorities arrested Ayatollah Muhammad Kazemini Borujerdi in October for calling for the separation of religion and politics, a move that would threaten Iran's *theocracy* (a government in which God is recognized as supreme ruler). Borujerdi's arrest was prompted by his growing popularity, which was often represented in 2006 by large crowds near his home praying and chanting slogans against the rulers of the Islamic republic.

■ Mary-Jane Deeb

See also **Israel; Lebanon; Middle East; United Nations.**

Iraq. United States President George W. Bush met in November 2006 with Iraqi Prime Minister Nouri Kamel al-Maliki in Amman, the capital of Jordan. At a press conference following the meeting, President Bush reiterated that he would not pull U.S. forces out of Iraq "until the job is complete." President Bush said the United States would continue to support Prime Minister al-Maliki's government and accelerate the transfer of security authority to the Iraqis. The prime minister spoke out against the breakup of Iraq, stressing that he wanted to cooperate with all parties in Iraq that were willing to maintain national unity. He also argued that Iran's role in destabilizing Iraq had been vastly exaggerated, noting that although there had been "interventions" by Iran, his government would never allow any outside force to dominate Iraq.

Iraq Study Group Report. In December, a *bipartisan* (two-party) team led by former Secretary of State James A. Baker III (a Republican) and former U.S. Representative Lee H. Hamilton (a Democrat from Indiana) reported its assessment of the ongoing violence in Iraq. The violence began after the U.S.-led invasion of Iraq in March 2003 toppled Iraqi President Saddam Hussein from power. The Iraq Study Group Report stated, "The situation in Iraq is grave and deteriorating. There is no path that can guarantee success, but the prospects can be improved."

The study group recommended that the United States launch a diplomatic initiative that would include Iraq's neighbors (particularly Iran and Syria), as well as key states outside the region, in efforts to stabilize Iraq. The report also suggested that the United States take a more active role in addressing the Arab-Israeli conflict, noting that resolving this long-standing problem would bring greater overall stability to the Middle East.

The Iraq Study Group Report advised the Bush administration to encourage the Iraqis "to take control of their own destiny" and to allow the U.S. military to transfer more responsibilities to the Iraqi army and security forces. The report concluded that a substantial "redeployment" of U.S. forces out of Iraq should occur by 2008. President Bush promised to consider the recommendations in the report and announce a new Iraq policy by early 2007.

United Nations mandates. In November 2006, the United Nations (UN) Security Council voted to extend the presence of the multinational force in Iraq through the end of 2007. The extension came at the request of the Iraqi government and in accordance with UN Resolution 1546, which created the multinational force in 2004 to contribute to "the maintenance of security and stability in Iraq." The Security Council also decided to extend through 2007 the requirements of UN Resolution 1483, which called for revenues from the sales of Iraqi natural gas, petroleum, and petroleum products to be deposited in the Development Fund for Iraq. This fund was monitored by the International Advisory and Monitoring Board, an audit oversight body established by the UN.

War-related deaths. Violence in Iraq increased throughout 2006, with Sunnis and Shiites settling accounts with bombings, killings, and kidnappings. Sectarian violence became more widespread after Sunnis bombed the al-Åskari Shrine, or Golden Mosque, in Samarra, one of the most revered Shi`ah shrines, in February.

In December, the Iraq Body Count (IBC) project, consisting of an independent group of scholars in the United Kingdom, issued a report on the number of Iraqis killed since the war began. The IBC project recorded between 50,096 and 55,576 civilian deaths in the war. A survey titled "The Human Cost of the War in Iraq," which was published online in October by the British medical journal *The Lancet,* reported that the war had caused 655,000 Iraqi deaths. According to this report, "Since March 2003, an additional 2.5 percent of Iraq's population have died above what would have occurred without conflict."

Experts explained that the difference in fatality figures between the two reports might have been related to the different ways in which the numbers were computed. The IBC figures were based on reported deaths of civilians caused directly by bombings, shootings, and other killings. The *Lancet* report, on the other hand, focused on the overall Iraqi death toll caused directly or indirectly by the war situation, including such factors as disease and malnutrition.

U.S. troops. On Dec. 31, 2006, two U.S. soldiers were killed in an explosion in Diyala province Iraq. Their deaths raised the total number of U.S. military deaths since the war began in March 2003 to at least 3,002, according to the U.S. Department of Defense. The casualties also pushed the death count in Iraq over the number of people killed in the Sept. 11, 2001, terrorist attacks on the United States.

December 2006, with the deaths of at least 111 U.S. troops, was the deadliest month of the year for American forces in Iraq. Most of the American deaths resulted from bombings. The Pentagon attributed the increasing death toll in late 2006 to the larger number and greater visibility of U.S. troops in Baghdad, the Iraqi capital, as well as to the increased intensity of the Sunni insurgency in the western province of Anbar.

At the end of 2006, more than 140,000 U.S. troops were on the ground in Iraq. Many of

Smoke billows from a burning truck that was assaulted by gunmen in Baghdad on February 1. Such attacks and roadside bombings with improvised explosive devices (IED's) became nearly daily occurrences in Baghdad and other areas of Iraq in 2006, making travel extremely difficult.

As the insurgency in Iraq continued to rage in 2006, secular violence between Shi`ah and Sunni Muslims spiraled out of control.

Iraqis clear rubble from the ruins of the al-Àskari Mosque in Samarra after the shrine was bombed in February. The destruction of one of the most revered Shi`ah shrines proved to be the tipping point that ignited all-out sectarian violence in Iraq.

FOCUS ON IRAQ

A solidarity poster of American journalist Jill Carroll, who was kidnapped in Iraq and held hostage for three months, is removed from Rome's city hall after Carroll was set free on March 30. The kidnappers killed her Iraqi translator, Alan Enwiyah, during the initial ambush in Baghdad, the scene of hundreds of kidnappings in 2006.

Iraqi soldiers survey the scene of a suicide car bombing on a Baghdad street on February 28. On the same day, four separate explosions in the city left 36 people dead and scores of others injured. Hundreds of Iraqi civilians died in similar attacks in 2006.

these troops were engaged in the fighting in Baghdad and Anbar province.

Saddam execution. In November—after a year-long trial—a five-judge panel in Baghdad found deposed former President Saddam Hussein guilty of crimes against humanity and sentenced him to death by hanging. The charges against Hussein stemmed from the executions of 148 Shiite men and boys in the town of Dujail during the 1980's. Six codefendants, including Hussein's half-brother, were also found guilty of charges related to the crimes.

The lengthy trial was interrupted several times by outbursts from Hussein, as well as by the assassinations of three of his lawyers and the resignations of two judges. Hussein's appeal of his death sentence was denied in late December 2006, requiring—according to Iraqi law—that the former dictator be executed within 30 days. On December 30, Iraqi authorities hanged Hussein, shortly after U.S. military officials transferred the former dictator to their custody. At the time of the execution, Hussein was being tried a second time for his role in the killing of tens of thousands of Shiites and Kurds in the 1980's and 1990's.

■ Mary-Jane Deeb

See also **Armed forces; Iran; Middle East; United Nations; Year in brief.**

Ireland. Taoiseach (Prime Minister) Bertie Ahern's Fianna Fáil party remained in power in 2006 as part of a coalition with the Progressive Democrats, despite calls by opposition parties Fine Gael and Labour for early elections. The opposition charged the governing coalition with failing to deal effectively with problems in education, crime, health, and government spending. In July, Fianna Fáil indicated that parliamentary elections would probably take place in May 2007.

In September 2006, Ahern was accused of accepting unrecorded payments from wealthy donors while he served as minister of finance in 1993 and 1994. However, his popularity remained undiminished. After he apologized, his personal approval rating rose by a point, to 53 percent.

Also in September 2006, Mary Harney, the tanaiste (deputy prime minister) and leader of the Progressive Democrats, announced her resignation as tanaiste and party leader. Harney, who helped found the Progressive Democrats in 1985 and, in 1993, became the first woman to lead an Irish political party, stated that a new leader should run in the 2007 election. Michael McDowell was elected in 2006 as party leader and tanaiste. Harney remained in her post as minister for health.

Economy. The Finance Ministry reported that the Irish economy continued to perform well in 2006 and would end the year with an estimated budget surplus of 4.4 billion euros ($5.6 billion). In July, the private Economic and Social Research Institute projected that the economy would grow by 5.6 percent in 2006 with an average inflation rate of 3.8 percent. Economists warned, however, that growth was likely to slow after 2007. Also in July 2006, Bank of Ireland economists estimated that the nation had the second wealthiest population in the world (after Japan), with an average wealth of 150,000 euros ($192,000) per person.

Easter parade. In 2006, for the first time in 35 years, a military parade was held on April 16 to commemorate the anniversary of the Easter Rising (1916), the event that led to the founding of the Republic of Ireland. Commemorations of the event had ended in the early 1970's following an outbreak of violence in Northern Ireland. Political analysts claimed the move was an attempt by Ahern to attract nationalist support before the 2007 parliamentary elections. Such support usually went to nationalist party Sinn Féin, which had ties with Northern Ireland's Irish Republican Army.

Former Taoiseach Charles Haughey died on June 13, 2006. Haughey led Fianna Fáil from 1979 to 1992 and served as prime minister in three administrations. However, his reputation was damaged by allegations of corruption in 1997.

■ Rohan McWilliam

See also **Europe; Northern Ireland.**

Islam. In February, cartoons satirizing the Prophet Muhammad, which had been published in a conservative Danish newspaper in September 2005, led to protests throughout the Islamic world. Several Muslim governments boycotted Danish imports, putting financial stress on some consumer goods companies in Denmark. Protesters attacked Danish embassies in Iran, Lebanon, and Syria.

Some Muslims noted that many European nations had bans on anti-Semitic cartoons and blasphemy laws against certain comments about Christianity. Such nations had few restrictions on what was perceived as anti-Muslim hate speech.

**Shi`ah Islam** rose in prestige among many Arab and non-Arab Muslims in 2006. (The Shi`ah are one of two major divisions of Islam; the Sunnis are the other.) In Iraq, the Shi`ite-led legislature elected in late 2005, which replaced the Sunni government of Saddam Hussein, approved Shiite Nouri Kamel al-Maliki as prime minister in April 2006. Experts noted that, as a result, Shi`ah Islam gained legitimacy in Iraq and across the Middle East. Shiite militias continued to fight the United States-led coalition forces in Iraq, which further enhanced their standing with militant Muslims.

In Lebanon, the militant Shiite group Hezbollah gained prestige among some Muslims by battling much larger Israeli forces to a standstill. Israel had attacked Hezbollah's forces in response

A Muslim cleric attempts to restore order in February 2006 after protesters set fire to the Danish embassy in Beirut, the capital of Lebanon. Thousands of people had gathered to protest cartoons satirizing the Muslim Prophet Muhammad that were first published in a Danish newspaper in September 2005. Muslim clerics helped to convince the protesters to disperse.

to the killing of eight Israeli soldiers and the capture of two others. After 34 days of fighting, a United Nations (UN)-brokered cease-fire went into effect in August. Some analysts noted that Hezbollah's claim of success caused alarm within al-Qa`ida, which adheres to the smaller Wahhabi sect of Islam, with some members regarding the Shi`ah group as more of a threat than the United States.

Hamas. In January, Palestinian voters gave the Islamist party Hamas a parliamentary majority. Hamas, which refused to recognize Israel or to renounce violence, subsequently received little financial aid as many governments suspended funding to the Palestinian Authority (PA). As a result, the PA could not govern effectively. Many Palestinians grew increasingly dependent on UN food aid.

Somalia, which had been ruled by warlords since the early 1990's, developed a new order in 2006 under the Islamic Courts Union, an organization of religious courts and a militia alliance led by Muslim Sheik Sharif Sheik Ahmed. In June, the group took control of Mogadishu, the capital.

Later that month, the union changed its name to the Conservative Council of Islamic Courts in Somalia and replaced Ahmed with Sheik Hassan Dahir Aweys. The U.S. government previously had alleged that Aweys had links to al-Qa`ida. In December, troops from Ethiopia and from Somalia's transitional government retook Mogadishu.

Morocco continued to develop a moderate form of national Islam in 2006. In May, the Dar al-Hadith al-Hassania seminary in Rabat graduated 50 women in its first class of female *murchidates,* Muslim religious guides. The country also decided in 2006 to revise the institution's curriculum. Under the direction of Kambiz Ghanea Bassiri, an American Muslim and professor of religious studies at Reed College in Portland, Oregon, the seminary began teaching courses on other world religions.

The Vatican. Pope Benedict XVI sparked controversy on Sept. 12, 2006, with a theology lecture he delivered in Bavaria, Germany, on the role of Greek reason in religion. He quoted a dialogue from the 1300's between a Muslim intellectual and a Byzantine prince, later an emperor, who said that Islam contained nothing new except such negative qualities as an orientation toward violence. Some scholars said the pope was suggesting that reason played no part in an inherently violent Islam.

On Sept. 17, 2006, the pope issued a statement of regret. However, some observers noted that the speech seemed consistent with his stance, as a cardinal, that predominantly Muslim Turkey did not belong in the European Union.

In November, the pope visited Turkey and met with the head of the Religious Affairs Directorate, Ali Bardakoglu. There, the pontiff declared that Turkey is "a bridge between Asia and Europe."

United Kingdom. Police in the United Kingdom (U.K.) in August 2006 seized 24 suspects allegedly involved in a radical Islamist plot to use liquid explosives to blow up planes destined for the United States. Some of the British Muslim suspects had ties to Pakistan, whose authorities made arrests in coordination with U.K. police, and others were European converts to Islam.

In October, Member of Parliament Jack Straw ignited controversy when he stated that, while he supported the right of British Muslim women to wear a full facial veil, he had asked his constituents to unveil their faces when visiting him. Straw said that the veil impeded face-to-face conversation and represented "a visible statement of separation and of difference."

United States. Louis Farrakhan, who had led the Nation of Islam since the late 1970's, moved away from his leadership role in the organization in 2006. Farrakhan, who was reportedly ill, had in the late 1990's moved closer to traditional Sunni Islam.

In November 2006, Keith Ellison of Minnesota became the first Muslim elected to the U.S. Congress, winning a seat in the House of Representatives. Some conservatives objected to Ellison's plan to take the oath of office with his hand on the Qur`an instead of the Bible. ■ A. Kevin Reinhart

See also **Africa; Denmark; Iraq; Israel; Roman Catholic Church; Terrorism; United Kingdom.**

Israel. On Jan. 4, 2006, Prime Minister Ariel Sharon suffered a massive stroke, which left him in a coma for the rest of the year. His deputy, Ehud Olmert, assumed duties as acting prime minister and leader of the centrist Kadima Party. Sharon had formed Kadima in November 2005 as a splinter group from the right-wing Likud Party.

Parliamentary elections. Kadima fared less well than expected in parliamentary elections that were held in March 2006. Kadima won 29 seats in the Israeli Knesset (parliament), followed by the Labor Party, which won 20 seats. The Likud Party and the ultra-Orthodox Shas Party each won 12 seats.

In May, Prime Minister Olmert formed a coalition Cabinet composed of Kadima, Labor, Shas, and the Gil Pensioners' parties, giving him a slender majority of 67 seats in the 120-member Knesset. Olmert appointed Labor leader Amir Peretz as defense minister and former Labor leader Shimon Peres as minister for the development of Negev and Galilee. Peres's position was important because of the government's plan to remove Israeli settlers from isolated settlements in the Arab-dominated West Bank and relocate them to the thinly populated regions of Negev and Galilee.

In October, Prime Minister Olmert convinced the leader of Yisrael Beitenu (Israel My Home), a Russian immigrant party, to join his coalition Cabinet. The prime minister's parliamentary majority thus increased to 78 members.

Conflict in Gaza. On June 25, militants belonging to Hamas, the governing party of the Palestinian government, conducted a well-organized raid into Israel from the Gaza Strip. The raid resulted in the kidnapping of an Israeli soldier and the killing of two others. The military wing of Hamas had ended a 16-month truce with Israel on June 9, after Israeli airstrikes on Gaza killed seven Palestinian civilians. On June 8, Israeli airstrikes had killed a prominent Hamas leader and three other Palestinian militants in Gaza.

As the fighting between Palestinian militants and Israeli forces escalated, the United Nations (UN) estimated that 114 Palestinians had been killed as a result of Israeli airstrikes on Gaza by July 19, and only one Israeli had been killed by Palestinian rockets. All attempts to obtain the release of the captured Israeli soldier failed because Hamas demanded in exchange the release of Palestinian prisoners, a condition that was unacceptable to Israel.

Conflict with Hezbollah. Lebanese fighters with Hezbollah—a militant Shiite Muslim group backed by Syria and Iran—provoked a war with Israel on July 12, after they crossed the "blue line" marking the Israeli-Lebanese border. The fighters kidnapped two Israeli soldiers and killed eight others. The massive Israeli retaliation against Hezbollah positions in Lebanon, consisting mainly of aerial bombardments, did not deter Hezbollah from firing more than 4,000 Katyusha rockets into northern Israel. The conflict lasted for 34 days, resulting in at least 140 Israeli civilians and soldiers killed and more than 1,000 others wounded.

Before UN Security Council Resolution 1701—which ended the fighting—was implemented on August 14, Israel launched a large-scale ground campaign but was unable to dislodge Hezbollah from most of its fortified bunkers in southern Lebanon. Critics of Prime Minister Olmert charged that Israel was not able to win decisively against Hezbollah because the government waited too long to launch the ground offensive.

Resolution 1701 called for 15,000 Lebanese army soldiers and another 15,000 soldiers from an expanded UN Interim Force in Lebanon to be deployed to the region between Israel's border and Lebanon's Litani River. This deployment removed Hezbollah fighters from the Israeli-Lebanese border region, pacifying the area for the first time in approximately 40 years. Thus, the deployment was expected to eliminate the military threat that Hezbollah had long posed to residents of northern Israel.

Nuclear "slip of the lip." In an interview on German television in December, Prime Minister Olmert created an international controversy when he seemed to include Israel among those nations in possession of nuclear weapons. The interviewer asked Olmert to comment on calls by the Iranian government for the destruction of Israel. Iran was believed by many military experts to be developing technology for nuclear weapons in 2006. In response to the question, Olmert said, "Iran openly, explicitly, and publicly threatens to wipe Israel off the map. Can you say that this is the same level, when you are aspiring to have nuclear weapons, as America, France, Israel, Russia?" (The United States, France, and Russia are all nuclear powers.)

Military experts in the United States and other countries had long believed that Israel had nuclear weapons. However, the Israeli government had never officially confirmed or denied these beliefs. According to international affairs experts, this "policy of ambiguity" was intended mainly to avoid fueling a Middle East arms race.

Although Prime Minister Olmert later denied that he had listed Israel as a nuclear power, many Israeli politicians condemned his remarks for undermining Israeli's long-time policy of secrecy regarding nuclear weapons. One Israeli newspaper referred to the prime minister's remarks as a "nuclear slip of the lip." ■ Marius Deeb

See also **Iran; Judaism; Lebanon; Middle East; People in the news** (Ehud Olmert); **Syria.**

Italy. Romano Prodi became prime minister of Italy in 2006, after his center-left Union coalition narrowly defeated the center-right House of Freedom government led by flamboyant media baron and incumbent Prime Minister Silvio Berlusconi in national elections held in April. Berlusconi challenged the razor-thin victory, though he resigned from office on May 2. The Union coalition, made up of nearly a dozen center and left parties, provided Prodi with a solid majority in Italy's lower house. However, in the Senate, a margin of two seats that later dropped to one significantly weakened the government's power to effect change.

Berlusconi's government, elected in May 2001, lasted nearly four years—making it the longest-serving Italian government since World War II (1939-1945). (Berlusconi was forced to resign briefly in 2005, after two of the parties in his governing coalition withdrew from the government; however, he quickly formed a new coalition that governed until May 2006.) The Prodi government was the first to be elected under a proportional representation system that had been reinstated under Berlusconi. (From 1993 to 2004, a system based primarily on majority had been in effect.) On May 10, 2006, an electoral college made up of both houses of Parliament and regional representatives elected Giorgio Napolitano president. Napolitano then appointed Prodi prime minister.

Israeli soldiers rest along the Israeli-Lebanese border on August 14 after Israel halted its offensive against Lebanese guerrillas belonging to the militant group Hezbollah. More than a month of fighting was stopped by United Nations Security Council Resolution 1701.

A campaign poster of Italian Prime Minister Silvio Berlusconi looms over Rome's Piazza Navona in anticipation of national elections in April. In the elections, Romano Prodi's Union coalition narrowly defeated Berlusconi's Forza Italia and other members of his center-right coalition, bringing down Italy's longest-serving government since World War II (1939-1945).

In June, Italian voters overwhelmingly rejected a referendum to revise the Constitution to significantly increase the powers of the prime minister and Italy's regional governments. The measure had been drafted by the Berlusconi government.

New policies. Italy's new government confronted an economy that had been performing poorly for several years. In particular, the country's budget deficit exceeded 4 percent of its *gross domestic product* (GDP—the total value of goods and services produced in a country in a year). The high deficit caused Italy to violate the Stability and Growth Pact for the fourth straight year. According to the terms of the pact, members of the European Union (EU) that use the euro must limit their deficits to 3 percent of GDP.

Prodi initially called for cutting governmental outlays and increasing revenue by clamping down on tax evasion. However, the instability of his coalition forced him to increase income taxes on the upper middle class and reduce spending cuts in his first budget bill, submitted in September. The measures proved so unpopular that in early December, some 700,000 people demonstrated against them in Rome. Berlusconi renewed calls for a recount of election votes. Nevertheless, the Senate passed the budget bill on December 15.

Intelligence shakeup. In November, the Prodi government announced without explanation the removal of Italy's head of military intelligence, Nicolo Pollari, and three top civilian intelligence directors. Analysts attributed the move to a scandal involving the participation of Italy's intelligence services in the kidnapping and deportation to Egypt in 2003 of a militant Islamic cleric known as Abu Omar at the request of the United States Central Intelligence Agency (CIA). Omar claimed to have been tortured in Egypt, and in December 2006, Italian prosecutors asked for the indictment of 26 Americans as well as Pollari because of his alleged participation.

Foreign policy. In August, Italy played an important role in bringing the conflict between Israel and the Lebanese Islamist militia Hezbollah to an end. Eager to showcase Italy's role on the international stage, Prodi called for a conference in Rome after the outbreak of hostilities. This began the process that led to United Nations Security Council Resolution (1701), which formed the basis of the cease-fire. After the French hesitated to contribute peacekeeping troops, Italy offered to take the lead role among EU participants, providing as many as 3,000 soldiers for deployment on the ground. Both Israel and Lebanon were pleased to have Italy take the lead instead of France, as both considered Italy to be more impartial and to have less at stake in the final political and military correlation of forces in Lebanon.

Also in August, the death of as many as 50 emigrants as they tried to cross the Mediterranean Sea from North Africa to land on an island off Sicily highlighted the problem of illegal immigration to Italy and to Europe. During the first half of 2006, more than 10,000 people from Africa landed on the Italian island of Lampedusa. The Italian government suspected that Libyan leader Mu'ammar Muhammad al-Qadhafi was behind the increase in illegal maritime immigration. However, several attempts by Berlusconi to negotiate with Qadhafi were met by demands for restitution for Libyan suffering under Italy's colonial regime.

The Italian economy was one of the slowest-growing in Europe in 2006, with a growth rate of 1.7 percent, according to EU economists. Nevertheless, the growth was an improvement over 2005, during which growth rate was estimated at 0 percent. Unemployment continued to decline, from 8 percent in 2004 to 7.7 percent in 2005 and 7.1 percent in 2006. Although Italy's budget deficit in 2006 remained well above EU-imposed limits for countries that use the euro, Finance Minister Tommaso Padoa-Schioppa remained optimistic that Prodi's austerity budget would bring the deficit down to 2.8 percent in 2007.   ■ Jeffrey Kopstein

See also **Europe; Soccer: A Special Report.**

Ivory Coast. See Côte d'Ivoire in **Africa.**

Jamaica. See **West Indies.**

Japan. Junichiro Koizumi, who became Japan's prime minister in 2001, stepped down in 2006. Koizumi was replaced by his chief Cabinet secretary, Shinzo Abe.

Koizumi made major changes in Japanese political and economic affairs during his tenure. With the economy improving after a long stagnation, Koizumi continued to be popular. By the rules of the governing Liberal Democratic Party (LDP), however, his term ended as party president, and the LDP named its president as prime minister. Abe was elected LDP president on September 20. The LDP majority in parliament then elected him prime minister. He took office on September 26.

Abe, at 52, was the youngest Japanese prime minister since World War II (1939-1945). Abe's grandfather, Nobusuke Kishi, was a Cabinet minister who signed Japan's declaration of war on the United States in 1941. Although Kishi had been jailed by the allies after Japan's defeat, he became prime minister from 1957 to 1960. Kishi's brother was prime minister in the 1960's. Abe's father was foreign minister.

Abe came into office with a tough reputation on nationalism issues. He had risen to public prominence in 2002 by successfully pressing North Korea to return Japanese citizens it had kidnapped in the 1970's. For his Cabinet, Abe chose a number of social conservatives. He told

parliament on September 29 that he wanted to make education more patriotic and to rewrite Japan's post-World War II Constitution. The Constitution, which had been dictated by American officials during the U.S. postwar occupation of Japan, banned military forces. Although gradually reinterpreted to permit large and well-equipped "self-defense" forces, the Constitution still limited their deployment outside Japan's home islands. Abe wanted to end the restrictions.

The new prime minister faced economic problems, despite the gradual recovery from an economic depression that began in 1990. The gap between rich and poor had widened, but Abe addressed the need to cut health and social security spending. He emphasized self-help ideas rather than government handouts for the poor.

Koizumi's legacy. Koizumi was credited by political observers with having made three major changes. A flamboyant, even charismatic figure, Koizumi became prime minister in 2001 by appealing to ordinary LDP members over the heads of party leaders, who had passed power around between LDP factions in backroom agreements. Koizumi's blunt attack on problems, a break with decades of rule by leaders with vested interests, opened up the political process to a more public view.

Koizumi also made economic reforms. Some of these began to break links between big business—mainly public works contractors—government bureaucrats and LDP leaders. Although all three profited, this had led to questionable projects and a huge public debt. Koizumi also tried to raise Japan's assertiveness in foreign affairs.

Koizumi's foreign affairs role was shadowed, however, by his periodic visits to Yasukuni, a shrine commemorating Japanese war dead, including some who were judged war criminals after World War II. These visits particularly angered two neighbors that had suffered from Japanese occupation, China and South Korea.

Foreign relations were tense in 2006 between Japan and several of its neighbors. Before becoming prime minister, Abe had regularly visited Yasukuni. He indicated that he expected to continue to make such visits, perhaps more privately than Koizumi had done. Despite this, Abe visited China on October 8 for diplomatic talks. He then went to South Korea for similar talks.

On June 23, Japan agreed to increase the joint production of antimissile defenses with the United States. After North Korea tested a nuclear device on October 9, Japan imposed sanctions on the Communist nation, banning all imports from North Korea and barring North Korean ships from Japanese waters.

On August 16, Russian border guards killed a Japanese fisherman and captured three others.

Prime Minister Junichiro Koizumi of Japan, wearing a pair of Elvis Presley's sunglasses, impersonates the "King of Rock 'n' Roll" for Priscilla and Lisa-Marie Presley and U.S. President George W. Bush during a tour of Graceland, Presley's mansion in Memphis in June. The tour was arranged for Koizumi, an Elvis fan, during his final official visit to the United States.

The incident occurred near islands in the Kuril chain that were seized by the Soviet Union at the end of World War II. In 2006, Russia and Japan both claimed several of the islands, near which Japanese fishing had long gone unchallenged. On August 30, two of the fishermen were released. Their boat was confiscated, and the captain was held until he paid Russia a large fine.

Democratic Party. The main opposition to the LDP in parliament, the Democratic Party (DPJ), struggled in 2006. Seiji Maehara, who became the party's leader in 2005, resigned on March 31, 2006, amid a scandal in which the DPJ attempted to discredit the LDP. A DPJ official claimed in February to have an e-mail that tied the LDP to the head of an Internet company who was under investigation for breaking securities laws. The e-mail was shown to be fake, and Maehara resigned. He was succeeded on April 7 by Ichiro Ozawa.

Ozawa had been secretary-general of the LDP until he resigned amid party turmoil and scandals in 1993 to become the key backroom figure in a shifting group of politicians who took power from the LDP for nearly 10 months. The period of 10 months was the only time the LDP had not governed Japan since the 1950's.

A prince is born. On Sept. 6, 2006, the wife of the Japanese emperor's younger son, Prince Akishino, gave birth to a son, calming a politically explosive debate over the succession to Japan's Chrysanthemum Throne. The prince was named Hisahito, which means "virtuous, calm, and everlasting." In Japan, the emperor has no direct political power, but he has a semireligious status as the symbol of the nation.

Emperor Akihito's elder son, Crown Prince Naruhito, had a daughter, Aiko, in 2001. Akishino and his wife, Princess Kiko, already had daughters in 1991 and 1994. With no male in line to continue a monarchy claimed to be 2,600 years old, Koizumi in 2006 prepared a bill for parliament to allow a woman on the throne. The proposed legislation stirred fierce opposition to having the monarchy passed down through Aiko rather than through the male line. When Kiko's pregnancy was announced, the parliamentary bill was put aside.

Economy. Japan's economy reached a turning point in 2006 after it had become the world's first major industrial power since the 1930's to suffer *deflation* (falling prices). From 1997 to 2004, Japan's domestic output fell by 5 percent. In 2006, it showed signs of recovery. By May, unemployment rates had fallen to 4 percent, the lowest since 1998. On July 14, 2006, Japan's central bank raised its interest rate, which had been at zero for more than six years, to 0.25 percent. ■ Henry S. Bradsher

See also **Asia; Korea, North; People in the news** (Shinzo Abe).

Jordan. Jordanian authorities in July 2006 suspended a charity group affiliated with the Muslim Brotherhood, an organization dedicated to establishing a government under Islamic law. Authorities accused the Muslim Brotherhood of using private donations to increase its political clout in Jordan.

In June, four members of Jordan's parliament who belonged to the Muslim Brotherhood were arrested in Zarqa, Jordan, for attending the funeral of Jordanian-born Qa`ida terrorist leader Abu Musab al-Zarqawi. Al-Zarqawi had been killed in Iraq by a United States air strike.

Jordan's King Abdullah II held several summits with Arab leaders in 2006 to try to revive the peace process between Palestinians and Israelis and to support the Lebanese government in its efforts to end the July-August war between Hezbollah and Israel. (Hezbollah is a radical Islamist group in Lebanon.) King Abdullah met Egyptian President Hosni Mubarak in March, July, and October. In August, the Jordanian monarch visited Saudi Arabia's King Abdullah to discuss the conflict in Lebanon. The Jordanian king also continued to be in contact on a regular basis with Palestinian President Mahmoud Abbas.

■ Marius Deeb

See also **Iraq; Israel; Lebanon; Middle East; Terrorism.**

Judaism. Israel's Jewish population overtook that of the United States in 2006, according to the Jerusalem-based Jewish People Policy Planning Institute. With more than 5.3 million Jews, Israel became the world's largest Jewish community.

In January, Israeli Prime Minister Ariel Sharon suffered a massive stroke and fell into a coma. Deputy Prime Minister Ehud Olmert replaced him. Olmert pledged to proceed with unilateral withdrawals from the West Bank as part of a plan to separate Israel from the Palestinians. Olmert's Kadima party—formed in November 2005 by Sharon—won a March 2006 election and formed a coalition with the Labor Party as the key partner.

In January Palestinian Authority elections, Hamas won control of the government from Fatah, one of the largest groups within the Palestine Liberation Organization. Hamas refused to renounce violence or to recognize Israel's right to exist. As a result, many governments suspended funding to the Palestinian Authority.

The June kidnapping of Israeli soldier Gilad Shalit near the Gaza Strip triggered intense fighting with Hamas and other Palestinian militants. On November 26, a cease-fire took effect.

The killing of eight soldiers and the kidnapping of two others in July near Israel's border with Lebanon sparked a summer conflict with Hezbollah, a radical Islamist group in Lebanon. Hezbollah struck Israel's northern cities, including Haifa, with Katyusha missiles. Israel bombed areas in southern Lebanon and in Beirut, the capital. In August, after 34 days of warfare, the United Nations expanded its peacekeeping force in southern Lebanon to prevent further hostilities. Israel suspended its plans to withdraw from the West Bank.

United States. The U.S. Commission on Civil Rights, based in Washington, D.C., in April declared anti-Semitism on college campuses a "serious problem." The commission called for university leaders to defend their students and to ask Middle Eastern studies programs to present a balanced view of debates related to Israel.

Jewish organizations tightened security in July after a Muslim gunman attacked the Jewish Federation of Greater Seattle, killing one woman and injuring five others. The shooter said that he was "angry with Israel."

In a move to win unconnected Jews to declining Conservative Judaism, the Jewish Theological Seminary, the movement's flagship institution, in April named a new chancellor: Arnold Eisen, a former religious studies professor at Stanford University in California. On the issue of homosexual rabbis, Eisen said that he would "like to see it possible for gay and lesbian students to be ordained."

In December, the movement's Committee on Jewish Law and Standards of the Rabbinical Assembly voted to permit the ordination of gay rabbis and to recognize same-sex unions. Some Conservative Jews claimed that the movement had disregarded its pledge to adhere to Jewish law.

Jews played an active role in efforts to raise public awareness of the genocide in the Darfur region of Sudan, recalling the plight of European Jews during the Holocaust. Many Jews participated in an April rally in Washington, D.C., raised money to stop the suffering, and encouraged government action to end the atrocities.

World. Anti-Semitism continued to be a major concern of Jews around the world. In Paris, a gang tortured and murdered a 23-year-old Jew named Ilan Halimi in February. In Poland, the country's chief rabbi was attacked in May as he left Warsaw's main synagogue. In Iran, a prominent newspaper held a Holocaust cartoon contest to protest Danish cartoons that had depicted the Prophet Muhammad in ways offensive to many Muslims.

In November, an Argentine judge issued arrest warrants in connection with the 1994 bombing of a Jewish community center in Buenos Aires. The warrants named nine former Iranian officials, including former President Akbar Hashemi Rafsanjani.

■ Jonathan D. Sarna and Jonathan J. Golden

See also **Islam; Israel; Lebanon; Middle East; People in the news** (Ehud Olmert).

Kampuchea. See Cambodia.

Kazakhstan. Kazakhstan's political opposition suffered setbacks in 2006 after President Nursultan Nazarbayev won a third seven-year term in elections in December 2005. Western observers widely criticized the elections, in which Nazarbayev took 91 percent of the vote. In February 2006, top opposition leader Altynbek Sarsenbayev was murdered in what appeared to be a contract killing. In August, courts sentenced former Interior Ministry employee Rustam Ibragimov to death for the murder, but his sentence was commuted to life in prison. In addition, former presidential administration head Erzhan Utembayev was sentenced to 20 years in prison for paying Ibragimov for the murder. Ibragimov alleged that Sarsenbayev was involved with a plot to overthrow Nazarbayev.

On July 4, Nazarbayev's ruling Otan Party further consolidated its power by approving a merger with the Asar Party, headed by Nazarbayev's daughter Dariga Nazarbayeva. On September 10, regime opponents gathered to found a new party, the Pan-National Social Democratic Party. Delegates elected Zharmakhan Tuyakbai, a former presidential candidate of For a Just Kazakhstan, to lead the party. The party immediately announced that it would join forces with For a Just Kazakhstan to oppose the Nazarbayev government.

■ Juliet Johnson

See also **Asia; Disasters.**

Kenya. Scandals and party realignments dominated Kenyan politics in 2006. President Mwai Kibaki, who had won election in 2002, pledged to end government corruption and to reform the nation's constitution. However, Kibaki-backed constitutional reforms went down in defeat in a November 2005 referendum, and new scandals involving high-level officials broke in 2006.

Scandals. Three ministers resigned from Kibaki's Cabinet in February, all implicated in a scam exposed by John Githongo, President Kibaki's former anticorruption adviser who went into exile in London in 2005. Githongo described how Kenyan officials had steered government contracts to a phony corporation and pocketed the funds. An investigation ordered by Kibaki produced no high-level indictments, and the president reappointed two of the discredited ministers in November 2006.

New scandals brought to light in 2006 and revelations from ongoing scandals raised serious concerns among international aid donors. During 2006, two United Nations-affiliated monetary institutions—the International Monetary Fund (IMF) and the World Bank (WB)—suspended aid to Kenya amounting to nearly $600 million.

The National Rainbow Coalition (NARC), which had brought President Kibaki to power, and the Kenya African National Union (KANU), the country's chief opposition party, both fractured in 2006. The troubles in NARC were the legacy of the 2005 referendum, when coalition partner Raila Odinga, leader of the Liberal Democratic Party (LDP), broke with President Kibaki and campaigned against the constitutional reforms. With LDP out of NARC, Kibaki allies assembled a new progovernment coalition in 2006, which they named NARC-Kenya.

In November, former President Daniel arap Moi ousted Uhuru Kenyatta, KANU's most recent presidential nominee, from KANU party leadership. Kenyatta's determination to lay claim to party leadership raised the prospect of two competing KANU parties. These political developments created a fluid political landscape leading up to December 2007 elections, analysts said.

Sensitive court case. In May 2006, Thomas Cholmondeley, a white landowner with huge holdings in Kenya, was charged with murder for the second time in slightly more than a year. In both cases, he shot and killed a black man whom Cholmondeley claimed had been trespassing. Cholmondeley was acquitted of the first shooting. The case threatened to enflame race relations in Kenya, where residents of European descent are a small minority. ■ Pieter Esterhuysen

See also **Africa.**

Kiribati. See **Pacific Islands.**

Korea, North. Defying repeated warnings by many countries, Communist North Korea conducted its first nuclear test, exploding a small nuclear device on Oct. 9, 2006. The test drew strong international criticism, and the United Nations (UN) took steps to penalize the North Korean government.

North Korea had long accused the United States of aggressive intentions. North Korean officials stated that the explosion proved its nuclear capability to "protect its sovereignty and right to existence" from a U.S. threat. Experts believed that the comparatively small size of the explosion suggested a misfiring.

The explosion came after North Korea test-launched seven missiles on July 5, including a long-range ballistic missile that quickly self-destructed. North Korean officials called the tests "routine military exercises" for self-defense. North Korea had tested a long-range missile that flew over Japan in 1998.

Reaction. Japan urged the UN to condemn the missile tests and to call on member nations to prevent North Korea from acquiring further missile technology. The North declared that it would continue developing weapons.

The UN Security Council called upon North Korea to resume talks with China, Japan, Russia, South Korea, and the United States. Since 2003,

Residents of Sariwon, North Korea, participate in one of many nationwide government-sponsored rallies on Oct. 27, 2006, to celebrate the country's first nuclear test. The test, which took place on October 9, drew international condemnation.

the five nations had attempted to convince North Korea to abandon its nuclear weapons program in return for security guarantees and economic aid. The talks stalled in November 2005, and briefly resumed in December 2006, but no agreements were reached.

Economic moves. United States-led efforts to restrict North Korea's weapons program had by 2006 effectively knocked the country out of the international banking system. The crackdown followed accusations by U.S. officials of North Korean counterfeiting of U.S. currency, money laundering, and other illegal activities. Banks in China, Mongolia, Singapore, and Vietnam in 2006 also began restricting transactions with North Korea.

Disaster. In July, Typhoon Ewiniar battered North Korea. The country was drenched by roughly 20 inches (50 centimeters) of rain, which triggered landslides. The government, following its usual policy of trying to hide mistakes and disasters, admitted that "hundreds" of people had died. Foreign aid organizations were skeptical of a South Korean charity's report that nearly 55,000 people had died but said that damage was widespread. South Korea had halted food aid to the North because of the July missile tests.

The World Food Program (WFP), a United Nations affiliate, reported that the floods had destroyed crops, worsening an already existing shortfall between North Korean farm output and consumer needs. In August, WFP officials announced that North Korea had agreed to accept an additional 160 tons (150 metric tons) of food aid. The North had been forced to rely on foreign food aid since the mid-1990's as a result of drought, floods, and farm mismanagement. However, the government limited the ability of aid organization representatives to supervise food distribution. The organizations feared that ordinary people might be left hungry while food supplies were stockpiled for North Korea's armed forces.

■ Henry S. Bradsher

See also **Asia; Korea, South; United Nations.**

Korea, South. South Korean President Roh Moo-hyun's foreign policy in 2006 reflected the country's strained relations with North Korea, with the United States, and with neighboring Japan. Roh's government had for years followed a "sunshine policy" of trying to engage the North in friendly relations, through trade and providing aid.

The policy was largely based on fear of what might happen if the North unleashed its large military forces or if its regime collapsed. The policy did little to slow the North's antagonism, however. In July, North Korea tested a ballistic missile, and Roh halted food aid to the country. On October 9, North Korea exploded a nuclear device, and South Korea instituted sanctions against the North. Under the new sanctions, some North Korean government officials were not allowed into the South, and trade between the two countries was to be heavily monitored by the South's government.

The United States, in an effort to halt North Korea's nuclear weapons program, followed a sterner policy toward the North, which caused tensions between U.S. and South Korean leaders. In September 2006, Roh received a cool welcome in Washington, D.C., from U.S. President George W. Bush. The two agreed on trying to lure the North back to multilateral weapons talks but did not reach agreement in other areas.

Politics. On April 19, Han Myung-sook became South Korea's first woman prime minister. She replaced Lee Hae-chan, who was forced out in a scandal after he was caught playing golf instead of dealing with a railway strike.

In local elections on May 31, Roh's Uri Party suffered the worst defeat of a governing party in national history, winning only 1 of 16 contests for big-city mayoral offices and provincial governorships. Roh, who had almost two years left in his term, saw his popularity plummet over his failure to achieve a breakthrough in relations with North Korea or to reinvigorate the South Korean economy. The opposition Grand National Party (GNP) won 12 of these races. GNP officials had asked voters to use the contests as a referendum on Roh's administration. The Millennium Democratic Party won two posts, and an independent candidate won one.

Corruption. A man who symbolized South Korea's rapid economic growth since the 1960's, 69-year-old Kim Woo Choong of the Daewoo Group, was sentenced on May 30, 2006, to 10 years in prison for accounting fraud and embezzlement. He was also ordered to forfeit $23 billion. After Daewoo, an industrial conglomerate, collapsed in 1999, Kim fled the country. He surrendered to Korean authorities in 2005.   ■ Henry S. Bradsher

See also **Asia; Korea, North.**

Kuwait. See **Middle East.**

Kyrgyzstan. See **Asia.**

Labor and employment. The employment expansion that began in the United States in 2004 continued in 2006. In October, the U.S. unemployment rate among workers 16 years and older fell to 4.4 percent—the lowest rate in more than five years. According to the U.S. Bureau of Labor Statistics (BLS), 6.7 million workers were unemployed out of a civilian work force of more than 151 million people.

Despite the improved economic news, there remained much uneasiness about job security among both white-collar and blue-collar employees. Workers in some historically high-paying industries made wage and benefit concessions as their employers struggled to avoid or emerge from bankruptcy. Other companies announced restructuring plans costing thousands of U.S. jobs.

In November 2006, the seasonally adjusted unemployment rate in the United States was 4.5 percent among all workers 16 years and older—compared with 5.0 percent a year earlier. Unemployment rates were 3.9 percent among men, 4.0 percent among women, 15.1 percent among teen-agers, 3.9 percent among white workers, 8.6 percent among African American workers, and 4.9 percent among Hispanic workers.

Compensation (wages, salaries, and benefits) for civilian workers increased by 3.3 percent in the 12 months that ended in September 2006, according to the Employment Cost Index of the BLS. Wages and salaries alone rose by 3.2 percent. Productivity (output per hour) of production and nonsupervisory workers was 1.3 percent greater in the third quarter of 2006 than in the same quarter a year earlier. Average weekly earnings (seasonally adjusted) of these same workers increased 4.0 percent from September 2005 to September 2006. Adjusted for inflation, earnings rose 2.2 percent.

Airline industry. After the terrorist attacks on the United States on Sept. 11, 2001, airlines lost billions of dollars as many people avoided air travel and security costs increased. Over the next five years, many airlines were forced to seek bankruptcy protection despite "givebacks" of agreed wage and benefit increases by unions.

In January 2006, United Airlines of Elk Grove Village, Illinois, and the Association of Flight Attendants (AFA) reached a tentative agreement establishing a *deferred pension plan* to replace the airline's *defined pension plans.* Under a deferred plan, pension payouts after retirement depend on the size and duration of deferred compensation; defined pension plans state specific benefits to be paid to retirees based on such factors as pay and employment longevity. In 2005, United had transferred its four defined plans, with a total funding shortfall of $9.8 billion, to the government's Pension Benefit Guaranty Corporation in the largest pension default in U.S. history.

Also in January 2006, the Air Line Pilots Association, International (ALPA) approved a package of concessions to Comair, a subsidiary of Delta Air Lines based in Cincinnati, Ohio. The approval helped Atlanta-based Delta in its bankruptcy restructuring, saving it an estimated $17.3 million annually. In May, the ALPA ratified an agreement that cut Delta pilots' pay by 14 percent and changed work rules and benefits to save the airline $280 million annually.

The International Association of Machinists (IAM) approved a four-year agreement in January covering 8,600 flight attendants working for Continental Airlines Inc. of Houston. The agreement froze the attendants' pay to save Continental some $72 million annually.

To help Northwest Airlines of Eagan, Minnesota, emerge from bankruptcy, the ALPA approved pay and cost cuts in May for 5,000 pilots. The cuts were expected to save the airline $358 million annually.

Negotiations between Northwest and its flight attendants were difficult. After the independent Professional Flight Attendants Association agreed in March to cost savings of $195 million annually, the rank-and-file at Northwest overwhelmingly rejected the agreement. The flight attendants voted in July to select the Association of Flight Attendants (AFA), an affiliate of the American Federation of Labor Congress of Industrial Organizations (AFL-CIO), as their new bargaining agent. When the AFA agreed to $195 million in annual savings, the members again rejected the agreement.

Northwest sought to impose the cost savings without an agreement, but the AFA threatened sporadic job actions, including work stoppages. In August, a federal bankruptcy court in New York rejected Northwest's bid to prevent union job actions. In September, a federal district court in New York overturned the bankruptcy court's decision after the U.S. Justice Department intervened on the airline's side.

In November, the Aircraft Mechanics Fraternal Association voted to end its 15-month strike against Northwest by accepting a tentative agreement under which not all strikers' jobs would be protected. In addition, striking mechanics who volunteered not to return would receive as much as 10 weeks of separation pay.

In stark contrast to the preceding bargaining agreements, FedEx Corporation of Memphis and the APA agreed in September on a tentative four-year contract that increased pay for the company's 4,700 pilots by 18 percent. Each pilot would also receive a signing bonus of as much as $30,000.

Automobile industry. The Ford Motor Company of Dearborn, Michigan, announced in January that it would eliminate between 25,000 and 30,000 hourly and salaried jobs by 2012. The company also said it would close 14 manufacturing plants in North America as part of a cost-cutting and restructuring program.

In February 2006, Ford announced it would extend its voluntary incentive severance proposal to employees at the 14 plants scheduled for closing. Workers with one year of service were eligible for a $10,000 lump sum payment or half pay and cash stipends for four years to pursue educational opportunities. Workers with 30 years of service or more would get a $30,000 payment and full retirement benefits.

In January, the U.S. division of Daimler-Chrysler AG of Germany announced plans to eliminate 6,000 administrative and management positions—approximately 20 percent of its white-collar workers—worldwide by 2009. In March 2006, the company revealed plans to change health care payments for 13,800 current and 3,200 retired salaried employees. Beginning in 2007, the company and retirees were to share higher health premium costs based on the exit salary of the retiree.

In February 2006, General Motors Corporation (GM) of Detroit proposed freezing contributions to salaried retirees' health plans at 2006 levels. The company also proposed to restructure current salaried employees' health plans. In March, GM and the United Automobile Workers reached agreement on buyouts for employees of the troubled auto parts supplier Delphi Corporation of Troy, Michigan, as part of GM's drive to cut 30,000 jobs by 2008. Delphi filed for bankruptcy in April 2006.

Communications industry. In January, the Communications Workers of America (CWA)—a union with 11,000 workers—and the International Brotherhood of Electrical Workers—with 1,000 workers—each ratified 40-month contracts with AT&T Inc. of San Antonio. The contracts provided wage increases of 10.75 percent over the term, improved job security and pensions, and maintained previous health care benefits for AT&T employees.

Also in January, the New York City-based telecommunications company Verizon Communications Inc. announced plans to cut 7,000 jobs over three years. The company said the cuts were made necessary by its purchase earlier in the month of MCI, Inc., of Ashburn, Virginia.

In March, the CWA and Cingular Wireless LLC of Atlanta, Georgia, agreed on a four-year contract covering 11,000 workers in nine Southeastern states. The pact provided signing bonuses of $500 and wage increases of 11.25 percent over the term of the contract. The union members ratified the agreement in May.

Aerospace industry. In February, IAM members ratified a revised contract offer from the Boeing Company of Chicago, ending a strike that began in November 2005. The contract, which covered 1,500 workers in Alabama, California, and Florida, provided wage increases of 2 percent in the first and second year and 2.5 percent in the third year. The workers were scheduled to receive bonuses of either $2,000 or $3,000, depending on their location and the contract year.

In April, the IAM ratified a three-year contract with Lockheed Martin Corporation of Bethesda, Maryland, covering 3,700 workers at a Texas plant that assembled fighter jets. Wages would were to rise by 4 percent in the first year and 3 percent in the second and third years. As was often the case in agreements in 2006, workers received a ratification bonus, which was $2,000 in this case.

Hospitality industry. In September, UNITE HERE (formerly the Union of Needletrades, Industrial, and Textile Employees, and Hotel Employees and Restaurant Employees) reached agreement with 13 San Francisco hotels on a five-year agreement. The pact covered 4,200 workers and called for wage increases totaling $3 an hour and the maintenance of current health care plans. In October, UNITE HERE members ratified a four-year agreement covering 2,500 workers at four Sheraton hotels on Waikiki Beach in Hawaii. The contract provided wage and benefit increases, with wages rising $2.40 an hour for non-tipped workers and $1.20 an hour for tipped workers. The union also approved a similar pact at the Hilton Hawaiian Village covering over 1,500 workers.

Unions. The BLS reported in January that 12.5 percent of U.S. workers belonged to labor unions in 2005. Union membership increased by 213,000 during that year to a total of 15.7 million. Of these members, 36.5 percent worked in local, state, or federal government, and 7.8 percent worked in private industry. The highest proportion of union workers in the public sector were in local government—41.9 percent—and the lowest in the federal government—27.8 percent.

In May 2006, the Laborers' International Union of North America notified the AFL-CIO that it would complete disaffiliation from the federation effective June 1. The union was one of the seven founding members of the Change To Win Labor Federation (CTW) that was formed in 2005. Four of the other founding unions had previously disaffiliated and discontinued paying per capita dues to the AFL-CIO.

In March 2006, the Service Employees International Union (SEIU) agreed to pay the AFL-CIO $4 million to settle a lawsuit filed by the AFL-CIO over withheld per capita dues. The suit had stemmed from the SEIU's July 2005 disaffiliation from the AFL-CIO.

Federal government. Addressing the growing problem of large pension defaults, President George W. Bush signed the Pension Protection Act into law in August 2006. The act required most employers to fully fund defined benefit pension plans by 2013. It also required employers who file for bankruptcy and terminate their pension plans to pay $1,250 per participant before exiting from bankruptcy. Most airlines, which experienced some of the greatest pension problems of the 2000's, were given 10 years to meet their pension obligations.

International unemployment, as measured in the 30 nations of the Organisation for Economic Co-operation and Development (OECD), stood at 6.1 percent in August 2006—compared with 6.5 percent in August 2005. Among the major industrial OECD nations, the jobless rates were lowest in Japan (4.2 percent) and the United States (4.7 percent). Among major nations, rates were highest in France (9.0 percent) and Germany (8.5 percent). Among all OECD nations, the lowest unemployment rates were in Norway (3.3 percent) and New Zealand and South Korea (each 3.4 percent). The highest rates were in Poland (14.2 percent) and Slovakia (13.1 percent). ■ Robert W. Fisher

See also **Automobile; Aviation; Economics, U.S.; Telecommunications; Transportation.**

Labrador. See Canadian provinces.

Laos. See Asia.

CHANGES IN THE UNITED STATES LABOR FORCE

	2005	2006*
Civilian labor force	149,266,000	151,137,000
Total employment	141,674,000	144,104,000
Unemployment	7,592,000	7,032,000
Unemployment rate	5.1%	4.7%
Change in weekly earnings of production and nonsupervisory workers (nonfarm business sector)		
Current dollars	3.2%	4.0%
Constant (1982) dollars	-0.2%	2.2%
Change in output per employee hour (nonfarm business sector)	2.7%	1.3%

*All 2006 data are through the third quarter of 2006 (preliminary data).
Source: *World Book* estimates based on data from the U.S. Bureau of Labor Statistics.

LATIN AMERICA

Voters in 13 Latin American countries either went to the polls for presidential elections in 2006 or had new leaders installed as a result of elections in late 2005. The countries included Bolivia, Brazil, Chile, Colombia, Costa Rica, Ecuador, Guyana, Haiti, Jamaica, Mexico, Nicaragua, Peru, and Venezuela. Elections in most of these countries proceeded smoothly and delivered a widely accepted verdict. In Mexico, however, the presidential election of July 2, 2006—the closest in Mexican history—resulted in the bitter polarization of people along class lines. A widespread belief among supporters of the defeated candidate, Andrés Manuel López Obrador, that the election was fraudulent fueled months-long protests in the streets of Mexico City, the capital. López Obrador and his supporters rejected the legitimacy of incoming President Felipe Calderón, when he was inaugurated on December 1.

In Cuba, change at the top occurred when an ailing Fidel Castro relinquished power provisionally to his younger brother, Raúl, in July 2006.

Fidel underwent treatment for an undisclosed intestinal ailment and remained out of public view for the rest of the year. Raúl Castro had long been groomed to succeed Fidel, and with Cuba's economy growing, Cubans seemed disposed to accept the prescribed transition of power within the Communist regime, observers noted—at least in the short term.

Regionwide election themes. Political analysts identified several factors that apparently influenced how Latin Americans voted in 2006. Among them was outrage over official corruption—fueled, as in Brazil and Peru, by videotapes showing government officials accepting cash bribes. The high incidence of crime in such cities as São Paulo, Brazil's industrial powerhouse and largest city—where a wave of gang warfare left 200 dead in May—proved to be another factor.

Jamaica's first woman prime minister, Portia Simpson Miller, took her oath of office in Kingston, the capital, on March 30. Simpson Miller, who represented one of the most violence-prone districts of Kingston, vowed to "break the power of the criminals."

In another Latin American country, Chile, voters elected Michelle Bachelet president, making

her that nation's first female leader. Bachelet, who took office in March, signaled her commitment to equality by appointing equal numbers of male and female Cabinet ministers.

Pocketbook issues. In 2006, the economies in Latin America underwent significant changes, with many of them experiencing strong growth. Economic gains, however, were uneven and did not benefit everyone. According to the Center for Economic and Policy Research, a Washington, D.C.-based think tank, Latin America experienced an increase in *per capita* (per person) income of only 14 percent in the quarter century from 1980 through 2005. The figure for the 20-year period spanning the years 1960 to 1980 was, in sharp contrast, 82 percent.

Nevertheless, many economists recognized that the pace of economic growth had quickened since 2000. The 2006 Regional Economic Outlook of the International Monetary Fund (IMF)—a United Nations-affiliated organization that provides short-term credit to member nations—projected a regionwide rate of growth of nearly 5 percent. The report also indicated that unemployment and the rate of inflation were declining in Latin America as a whole.

Meanwhile, many Latin American consumers were angry about increased costs for water, elec-

tric power, and telephone service, which had resulted from the privatization of previously state-owned utilities, a strategy strongly urged on regional governments by officials of the United States government. This pocketbook issue played an important role in elections in many countries, most notably in the Andean nations of Bolivia, Ecuador, and Peru, where hikes in utility rates sparked intermittent violence.

State-owned companies, such as the petroleum companies of Brazil, Mexico, and Venezuela, and companies that exported minerals produced record profits in 2006. To meet the growing demand for raw materials in Asia, where India and China were undergoing headlong

In years of normal precipitation, Iguaçu Falls (opposite), on the border between Brazil and Argentina, consists of some 275 cascades, some of which plunge 237 feet (72 meters). Low rainfall in central South America in 2006 reduced one of the world's greatest waterfalls (below) to a mere trickle of its normal flow.

FACTS IN BRIEF ON LATIN AMERICA

Country	Population	Government	Monetary unit*	Foreign trade (million U.S.$) Exports[†]	Imports[†]
Antigua and Barbuda	79,000	Governor General James B. Carlisle; Prime Minister Baldwin Spencer	dollar (2.70 = $1)	214	735
Argentina	38,223,000	President Néstor Kirchner	peso (3.11 = $1)	40,000	28,800
Bahamas	325,000	Governor General Arthur Hanna; Prime Minister Perry Christie	dollar (1.00 = $1)	469	1,820
Barbados	273,000	Governor General Sir Clifford Husbands; Prime Minister Owen Arthur	dollar (2.00 = $1)	209	1,476
Belize	267,000	Governor General Sir Colville Young, Sr.; Prime Minister Said Wilbert Musa	dollar (1.96 = $1)	350	622
Bolivia	9,301,000	President Evo Morales	boliviano (8.00 = $1)	2,371	1,845
Brazil	180,996,000	President Luiz Inácio Lula da Silva	real (2.16 = $1)	115,100	78,020
Chile	16,366,000	President Michelle Bachelet	peso (537.15= $1)	38,030	30,090
Colombia	46,248,000	President Álvaro Uribe Vélez	peso (2,390.00 = $1)	19,300	18,000
Costa Rica	4,399,000	President Óscar Arias Sánchez	colón (522.09 = $1)	7,005	9,690
Cuba	11,373,000	President Fidel Castro	peso (1.00 = $1)	2,388	6,916
Dominica	79,000	President Nicholas J. O. Liverpool; Prime Minister Roosevelt Skerrit	dollar (2.70 = $1)	74	234
Dominican Republic	8,660,000	President Leonel Fernández Reyna	peso (33.60 = $1)	5,818	9,747
Ecuador	13,553,000	President Rafael Correa**	U.S. dollar	9,224	8,436
El Salvador	6,795,000	President Elías Antonio Saca	U.S. dollar	3,586	6,678
Grenada	102,000	Governor General Daniel Williams; Prime Minister Keith Mitchell	dollar (2.70 = $1)	40	276
Guatemala	13,280,000	President Oscar Berger	quetzal (7.63 = $1)	3,940	7,744
Guyana	768,000	President Bharrat Jagdeo	dollar (200.69 = $1)	587	682
Haiti	8,662,000	President René Préval; Prime Minister Jacques-Èdouard Alexis	gourde (38.10 = $1)	391	1,471
Honduras	6,970,000	President Manuel Zelaya	lempira (18.90 = $1)	1,726	4,161
Jamaica	2,725,000	Governor General Kenneth Hall; Prime Minister Portia Simpson Miller	dollar (66.03= $1)	1,608	4,093
Mexico	107,725,000	President Felipe Calderón Hinojosa	peso (11.08 = $1)	213,700	223,700
Nicaragua	5,850,000	President Daniel Ortega**	gold cordoba (17.80 = $1)	1,550	2,865
Panama	3,140,000	President Martín Torrijos Espino	balboa (1.00 = $1)	7,481	8,734
Paraguay	5,747,000	President Nicanor Duarte Frutos	guarani (5,330.00 = $1)	3,130	3,832
Peru	28,360,000	President Alan García Pérez	new sol (3.25 = $1)	15,950	12,150
Puerto Rico	3,930,000	Governor Aníbal Acevedo Vilá	U.S. dollar	46,900	29,100
St. Kitts and Nevis	45,000	Governor General Cuthbert Montraville Sebastian; Prime Minister Denzil Douglas	dollar (2.70 = $1)	70	405
St. Lucia	168,000	Governor General Pearlette Louisy; Prime Minister Kenneth Davis Anthony	dollar (2.70 = $1)	82	410
St. Vincent and the Grenadines	122,000	Governor General Sir Frederick Nathaniel Ballantyne; Prime Minister Ralph E. Gonsalves	dollar (2.70 = $1)	37	225
Suriname	445,000	President Runaldo Ronald Venetiaan	dollar (2.75 = $1)	881	750
Trinidad and Tobago	1,315,000	President George Maxwell Richards; Prime Minister Patrick Manning	dollar (6.27 = $1)	9,161	6,011
Uruguay	3,486,000	President Tabaré Ramón Vázquez Rosas	peso (23.83 = $1)	3,550	3,540
Venezuela	25,045,000	President Hugo Chávez Frías	bolivar (2,147.30 = $1)	52,730	24,630

*Exchange rates as of Oct. 9, 2006.   **Inaugurated January 2007.   [†]Latest available data.

industrialization, both Brazil and Peru dramatically expanded cargo-handling facilities at their major ports of Santos and Callao, respectively.

Skepticism about foreign companies. Residents of many regions of Latin America had experienced environmental degradation first-hand as a result of industrial exploitation, especially by mining companies. According to polls conducted in 2006, many Latin Americans believed that their state-owned companies were more likely to adhere to environmental standards than foreign-owned companies. This attitude resulted in many Latin Americans casting a skeptical eye on investments by firms from abroad.

In the Patagonian region of southern Chile, for example, people mobilized to fight the plans of Endesa, S.A., a corporation headquartered in Madrid, Spain, to build six hydroelectric dams on ecologically sensitive streams. Similarly, strong resistance developed in northern Chile and Argentina to the plans of the Barrick Gold Corporation of Toronto, Canada, to establish a gold mine near the high Andean border between the two countries. Local residents expressed concerns that water supplies would be contaminated by the mining, which produces toxic by-products.

Resource nationalism. In light of these concerns, it was scarcely surprising that in 2006 Latin Americans favored politicians who promised to defend local and national resources against reckless exploitation by international corporations. Sociologists dubbed this growing trend of protecting national resources "resource nationalism." Public opinion in most Latin American countries also favored maximizing revenues from the foreign companies and reinvesting them in such human needs as feeding the hungry, creating jobs, and improving education.

One of the most controversial practitioners of resource nationalism in Latin America was President Hugo Chávez Frías of Venezuela, who used revenues from his country's vast oil reserves to raise Venezuelans' standard of living and also to cultivate clients among the nations of Latin America. To the dismay of officials of the administration of U.S. President George W. Bush, Chávez—one of Bush's most outspoken international critics—easily won reelection to Venezuela's presidential office in December.

Chávez's policies. In 2006, Chávez's government mandated that foreign oil companies allot a 60-percent stake in their operations in Venezuela to the state-run oil company. It also collected more than $300 million from foreign companies for 2005 back taxes and fines. Venezuelan authorities were able to enforce these policies for one overwhelming reason: geologists confirmed that the country had huge untapped

petroleum reserves just at a time when world demand for oil was exploding. In mid-2006, geologists announced that the layer of oil-rich sand deep under the Orinoco Basin of eastern Venezuela was three times thicker than previously believed. According to some experts, this deposit might hold 1.3 trillion barrels of oil.

Challenges to the United States. President Chávez challenged U.S. dominance in world affairs, whenever and wherever possible. On travels abroad, Chávez condemned U.S. policies he described as imperialistic and courted close relations with leaders of countries unfriendly to the United States, including Iran, North Korea, and Syria. Chávez achieved maximum global name recognition in September, when, in a speech to the United Nations (UN) General Assembly, he referred to U.S. President Bush as "the devil."

In an ongoing political shift to the left in Latin America, Daniel Ortega Saavedra, a leftist and close Chávez ally, won election to Nicaragua's presidency in November, replacing a centrist predecessor. While Ortega had headed the Sandinista (Marxist) government in Nicaragua during the 1980's, the administration of United States President Ronald Reagan had financed an armed rebel group that opposed the Sandinista regime. Analysts expected that this background would complicate relations between the United States and the new Nicaraguan government.

Benefits of oil wealth. In Venezuela, President Chávez's policy of reinvesting proceeds from the country's oil wealth in public programs was paying off, economists noted in 2006. Some economists corroborated claims of Venezuelan authorities that Chávez's administration had reduced poverty in the country by 25 percent.

Chávez also mounted an unprecedented regional foreign aid program. Following the March 2005 inauguration of Uruguay's leftist President Tabaré Vázquez, Venezuela made a series of large grants to Uruguay. The biggest Venezuelan-sponsored project in the country in 2006 was a major upgrade of the principal public hospital in Montevideo, the capital, fitting it with a state-of-the-art organ transplant unit.

Venezuela also sponsored a number of public works projects in Caribbean countries, including a major highway in Jamaica and airport expansion projects in the Dominican Republic and the island country of Antigua and Barbuda. Venezuela's most ambitious foreign aid outreach was a program that supplied oil to 17 energy-poor Latin American nations on deeply discounted terms.

■ Nathan A. Haverstock

See also various Latin American countries;
Latin America: A Special Report.

Bolivians of American Indian descent (above), angered by plans to exploit their nation's natural gas, demonstrated in La Paz, the capital, in June 2005, paralyzing the economy and forcing President Carlos Mesa to resign. In December, the people elected one of the protest leaders, leftist Evo Morales (at right in inset, with Venezuelan President Hugo Chávez, left, and Cuban President Fidel Castro, center). An Aymara Indian, Morales became Bolivia's first indigenous president.

**Latin America chooses
new leaders in a dramatic,
continent-wide shift toward
liberal policies.**

LATIN AMERICA
SWINGS LEFT

By Nathan A. Haverstock

"T he looting by the foreign companies has ended!" declared President Evo Morales, as he ordered Bolivian troops to occupy foreign-owned oil and natural gas installations on May 1, 2006. "The time has come, the awaited day, an historic day in which Bolivia retakes absolute control of our natural resources."

With this bold move, Morales fulfilled a campaign promise to the people who had elected him, the overwhelming majority of whom were Indians who make up more than 60 percent of Bolivia's population. The new president was one of them, an Aymara Indian and a coca grower by profession. (In Bolivia, chewing the plant's bitter leaves or drinking coca tea to ward off hunger, cold, and altitude sickness is a legal and common practice among Indians.) Morales had achieved prominence as the head of Bolivia's coca-growers federation, defending the legality of coca consumption in defiance of the United States government. (The United States has spent billions of dollars in Andean nations such as Bolivia to eradicate coca plants—from which the illegal drug cocaine is also made—as part of the war on drugs.)

Upon Morales's inauguration in January 2006, he joined the ranks of strong-willed leftist presidents who came to power in Latin America during the late 1990's and early 2000's as part of a political renewal inspired by liberal goals. The newly elected leaders appealed, in particular, to lower- and middle-class voters disappointed by their governments' failure to create opportunities for advancement for the more than 40 percent of the region's population that remained mired in poverty. Those at the bottom of the economic ladder in Latin America, angry at the growing disparity between rich and poor, had taken to the streets in peaceful demonstrations of unprecedented size to protest social injustice, electoral fraud, corruption, and crime. In record numbers, they turned out on election day to support candidates who promised to put the people's interests first.

By 2006, Latin America had clearly shifted to the left on the political spectrum. The region's new leaders established strong economic ties with China, Cuba, India, and Russia to the consternation of some officials in Washington, D.C. Their concern came as no surprise, because while Latin America embraced more liberal ideals, the U.S. government was controlled by conservative Republican policy-makers. The conservatives were unsympathetic to hemispheric leaders who expressed skepticism about the value of free trade, the U.S. trade embargo against Communist Cuba, and the morality of the U.S.-led war in Iraq. This divergence between the political direction of the U.S. government and Latin America's new left-leaning leaders became particularly noticeable during the second term of U.S. President George W. Bush.

Chávez—the first of a new breed

The lightning rod in this crucial issue was Hugo Chávez Frias. Chávez was inaugurated president of Venezuela in 1999 and thus became the first of the new breed of South American leftist leaders. After coming to power, Chávez made a reputation as a master of what was commonly called "petroleum politics"—the use of oil revenues to enhance national standing in the world and influence the course of events. (With its vast reserves, Venezuela was the world's fifth-largest oil exporter in 2006.)

A former army lieutenant colonel, Chávez attained prominence for his leadership role in a failed—but popular—1992 military *coup* (overthrow) against a government that was removed for corruption one year later. His promise, once in power, to remove the cancer of corruption from the body politic resonated throughout Latin America, where more than a dozen former presidents were under indictment for having accepted bribes or for looting the national treasury while in office. Latin Americans also hailed his success in increasing Venezuela's share of the profits from petroleum produced within its borders by foreign companies from 34 to 50 percent.

Chávez's strategy for achieving his objectives was aided by unsettled conditions in the Middle East and the war in Iraq. The uncertainty over the outcome of events in that area—together with high levels of global consumption and demand—pushed up the world price for a barrel of oil more than eight-fold, from $9 when Chávez took office to more than $75 a barrel by mid-2006. The meteoric rise in price enabled foreign oil companies to continue operating very profitably in Venezuela, despite the increased income taxes Chávez imposed on them.

At the same time, the windfall revenues accruing to Venezuela from this surge in oil prices allowed Chávez to spend freely both at home and abroad to win allies and influence other national leaders. He invested billions of dollars to provide the poor of Venezuela with heavily subsidized food from state-run supermarkets. He also oversaw the construction of schools and health clinics for the dwellers of the shantytowns that ringed the capital, Caracas. Previous administrations had largely ignored these areas, and Chávez's popularity among the urban poor soared.

By 2004, after only five years in office, Chávez's approval rating among Venezuelans topped 70 percent. Most Venezuelans also supported Chávez when he overhauled the institutions of what he called "the rancid

The author:
Nathan A. Haverstock is an affiliate scholar at Oberlin College in Oberlin, Ohio.

LATIN AMERICA POLITICAL MAP

NORTH AMERICA

United States

Gulf of Mexico

North Atlantic Ocean

Mexico

Bahamas

Cuba

Dominican Republic

Puerto Rico (United States)

St. Kitts and Nevis

Jamaica

Haiti

Antigua and Barbuda

Belize

Honduras

Caribbean Sea

Dominica

Saint Lucia

Guatemala

Barbados

El Salvador

Nicaragua

Grenada

St. Vincent and the Grenadines

Trinidad and Tobago

North Pacific Ocean

Costa Rica

Venezuela

Guyana

Panama

Suriname

French Guiana (France)

Colombia

Galapagos Islands (Ecuador)

Equator

Ecuador

Peru

Brazil

SOUTH AMERICA

Bolivia

South Pacific Ocean

Paraguay

Chile

Uruguay

Argentina

South Atlantic Ocean

Latin American countries featured in special report

Other Latin American countries

Falkland Islands (United Kingdom)

oligarchy"—the courts, the legislature, and the press. The people who lived in the gated communities and luxury condominiums of Caracas may have feared a possible dictatorship, but they were too weak and divided to block him. In December 2006, Chávez was reelected to another six-year term.

Chávez spread some of his country's oil wealth among the poor abroad as well as those at home. By 2005, Venezuela was providing more than twice as much financial aid to Latin America as the United States. (The difference was even greater if U.S. military assistance for the war on drugs was subtracted from the total.) Chávez provided discounted oil through deferred payment plans to such poor nations in the Caribbean as Dominica and Grenada. To the consternation of the U.S. government, one of the largest recipients of this aid was Communist Cuba, led by Chávez's mentor and friend President Fidel Castro Ruz. Castro, in turn, sent some 20,000 Cuban nurses and physicians to work in the health clinics and hospitals

Brazil's first left-wing president, Luiz Inácio Lula da Silva (left), greets farmers during his *Fome Zero* (Zero Hunger) campaign. At his inauguration in 2003, Lula promised that by the end of his four-year-term in office, no Brazilian would be "going to bed hungry."

Chávez had established in Venezuela's poor neighborhoods.

Even more galling to the administration of President Bush was Chávez's provision of nearly 40 million gallons (151 million liters) of heating oil at a 40-percent discount to more than 180,000 low-income households in the United States during the winter of 2005-2006. Chávez worked through local nonprofit groups in such places as New York City's Harlem neighborhood and an Indian reservation in Maine. The fuel was provided by Citgo, Venezuela's wholly owned U.S. subsidiary headquartered in Houston. Nevertheless, Chávez made himself unpopular with great numbers of Americans when he referred to President Bush as "the devil" in a speech before the United Nations (UN) General Assembly in September 2006. Thousands of Native Alaskan villagers responded by choosing to forgo the offer of discounted oil for the winter of 2006-2007 as a result. Still, by December 2006, low-income residents of 16 other states had agreed to accept the oil.

While Chávez was taking steps to improve his image among the world's developing nations, forceful leftist leaders in Brazil and Argentina joined him on the political scene in South America. The two new presidents, like Chávez, believed in the strong central role of government in addressing the problem of poverty.

Brazil elects its first leftist president

In Brazil in 2003, Luiz Inácio Lula da Silva of the Workers Party became his country's first left-wing president. Lula, as he was popularly known, was born into a poor family and left school to begin working at the age of 14. He was a machinist by profession and had attained political prominence as a union leader.

During his inaugural address, he announced a program called *Fome Zero* (Zero Hunger). The purpose of the program, according to Lula, was to ensure by the end of his four-year term in office that no Brazilian was "going to bed hungry." As both critics and supporters pointed out, meeting such a goal was virtually impossible. According to government estimates, about 46 million Brazilians—one-fourth of the population—were malnourished when Lula took office. Nevertheless, his initiative prompted a warm response across Brazil's political spectrum, as well as from abroad. Political opponents, celebrities, and business leaders all contributed generously, eager to be associated with a good cause.

In time, the Zero Hunger program evolved into a broader attack on poverty called *Bolsa Familia* ("the family wallet" or "family grant"). Under this system, monthly payments of about $15 were distributed to the heads of low-income families. The payments were conditional upon proof that children between the ages of 6 and 15 were regularly attending school (instead of working); undergoing periodic health examinations; and receiving inoculations against preventable diseases. By mid-2006, 9 million Brazilian families were enrolled in the program.

Despite a vote-buying and illegal campaign-financing scandal that rocked his Workers Party, Lula won a landslide victory in a run-off election on October 29. Tens of millions of poor voters reelected Brazil's working-class leader, who had increased social spending without a corresponding increase in taxes. His campaign was aided by the fact that during his presidency, Brazil—Latin America's largest economy— regularly chalked up record surpluses from its overseas trade. Brazil's favorable trade balance was based on the country's self-sufficiency in petroleum, a result of its global leadership in the use of alternative, environmentally friendly fuels.

Kirchner settles Argentine debt

In neighboring Argentina, an equally unexpected transformation unfolded after President Néstor Carlos Kirchner of the old-line Peronist, or Justicialist, party took office in May 2003. Of German-Swiss-Croatian ancestry, Kirchner, who had governed the southernmost province of Santa Cruz for 12 years, assumed his new job at a moment when Argentina was struggling with the worst depression in its history. More than half of all Argentines lived below the poverty line, a surprising number for a country that had once been one of the richest in the world. Unemployment had reached a high of 18 percent.

To resolve their plight, Argentines voted for the candidate who pledged to stand up for them in their country's long-running dispute with the International Monetary Fund (IMF), a Washington, D.C.-based UN affiliate. The dispute stemmed from the repayment of Argentina's foreign debt, which was in default. The failure of previous administrations to resolve this matter led to the rapid devaluation of Argentina's currency— which lost 70 percent of its value in the first six months of 2002—and the collapse of the economy. The IMF's demand that Argentina repay its foreign debt in full, Kirchner argued, would only worsen the situation and prolong the depression.

In March 2005, Kirchner, without help from the IMF, reached an agreement with creditors to settle Argentina's past-due debts for just thirty cents on the dollar. His victory was applauded throughout Latin America, where the poor of other nations had borne the brunt of IMF-mandated austerity programs similar to the one the agency had wanted to impose on Argentina. The plans often required cutbacks in spending on public health, education, and aid programs in the interest of paying debts often incurred by corrupt, outgoing regimes.

Kirchner prevailed, with solid public support—including frequent anti-IMF demonstrations in Buenos Aires during the drawn-out negotiations—and made himself highly popular. With his authority

GROSS NATIONAL INCOME FOR SELECTED COUNTRIES*

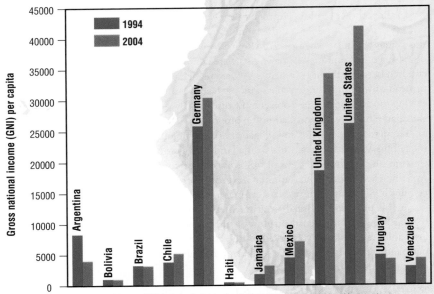

*Gross national income (GNI) includes the total value of all goods and services produced in a country in a year, as well as income earned from other countries, minus income earned by non-residents.

Source: World Development Reports for 1996 and 2006, World Bank.

enhanced, he was able to persuade owners of markets, restaurants, and businesses to voluntarily comply with government-mandated price controls aimed at making life affordable for those emerging from poverty. Freed of the debt problem, the Argentine economy improved quickly, growing by more than 8 percent in the first six months of 2006.

Regional solidarity on trade issues

With their respective national economies stronger, Kirchner, Lula, and Chávez were able to undertake several ambitious regional enterprises. In January 2006, they agreed to build a $20-billion natural gas pipeline that was 5,000 miles (8,000 kilometers) long and linked their three nations. Together, they worked to reinvigorate the South American common market. Through the World Trade Organization, based in Geneva, Switzerland, Brazil took the lead in fighting for the removal of the subsidies that the U.S. and European governments paid their farmers. These subsidies, which totaled more than $100 billion annually, placed Latin American growers at a competitive disadvantage.

To offset U.S. dominance in hemispheric trade, the new leaders forged stronger ties with commercial partners in other areas of the world— particularly China, India, Japan, and Russia—where there was sharply increased demand for their region's raw materials and commodities. By June 2006, Chávez had increased the sale of Venezuelan crude oil to China by 40 percent in a single year. Also in 2006, China became the fourth-largest trading partner for both Brazil and Argentina. China both purchased tons of raw materials—such as ore and soybeans—from a number of Latin American nations and sold an ever-increasing assortment of its manufactured goods in the region. Russia sold $3 billion in arms, including

DISTRIBUTION OF WEALTH IN SELECTED COUNTRIES*

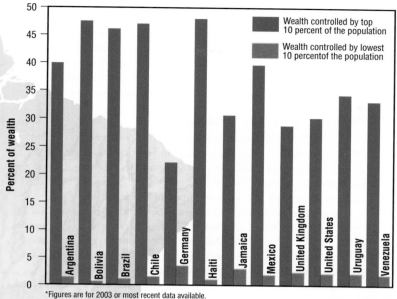

Percent of wealth

Wealth controlled by top 10 percent of the population

Wealth controlled by lowest 10 percent of the population

Argentina, Bolivia, Brazil, Chile, Germany, Haiti, Jamaica, Mexico, United Kingdom, United States, Uruguay, Venezuela

*Figures are for 2003 or most recent data available.
Source: 2006 World Development Indicators, World Bank.

A shantytown grows in the shadow of Buenos Aires, the capital of Argentina. In Argentina, as in many Latin American nations, a tremendous gap exists between the rich and poor. The richest 10 percent of the people control 40 percent of the wealth, while 39 percent of Argentines live in poverty.

automatic rifles and helicopters, to Venezuela in 2006 and began negotiations with Argentina to sell that country helicopters as well.

The three leaders also collaborated on cultural matters. With Uruguay, they established *Nueva Television del Sur* (New Television of the South), or Telesur. The Spanish-language network began broadcasting from Caracas in 2005. Brazil developed a comparable network for Portuguese speakers in 2005. The new networks presented the news from a Latin American perspective, in an attempt to counter the perceived bias of existing international networks and what many Latin Americans viewed as cultural imperialism by U.S. broadcast outlets. Both networks highlighted the music and art of native peoples and carried extensive coverage of such regionally popular sports as soccer.

The leaders also consulted one another whenever a mis-understanding arose, as it did immediately after Bolivian President Morales's May Day nationalization declaration. Brazil's state-controlled oil company was the biggest investor in the properties that were nationalized. And Brazil and Argentina were both dependent on the Bolivian fields for a large percentage of their natural gas.

Kirchner, Lula, and Chávez met with Morales and agreed that the nationalization must be accomplished to their mutual satisfaction, though the process was delayed because Bolivia lacked both the funds and the technical expertise to carry it out according to the announced timetable. Chávez offered Bolivia Venezuela's help in creating a national energy company to overcome the obstacle of managing its natural gas resources. Moreover, the three leaders invited Morales to join them in building the proposed continental pipeline. Later in the year, Kirchner agreed to a 47-percent increase in the amount Argentina was paying for natural gas imports from Bolivia. Lula negotiated a smaller increase for Brazil that would take into account its large investment in developing this resource.

Uruguayan president joins ranks

In March 2005, the leaders of Argentina, Brazil, and Venezuela welcomed to their ranks the first left-wing president in Uruguayan history, Tabaré Vazquez, an *oncologist* (physician specializing in cancer). Vazquez had served previously as the mayor of Montevideo, the capital, a post that is considered Uruguay's second-most-important elected office.

To win the election, Vazquez forged a coalition designed to appeal to as broad a group of voters as possible. The membership of his Progressive Encounter-Broad Front-New Majority coalition ran the gamut from the center to the radical left. The latter included former rebels called Tupamaros who had terrorized Uruguay in the late 1960's and early 1970's. The Tupamaros had laid down their arms, accepted amnesty, and become participants in the political process.

After taking office, Vazquez immediately restored diplomatic relations with Cuba and aligned his administration with the left-wing regimes of Argentina, Brazil, and Venezuela. He also announced a $100-million investment in education and antipoverty programs. Much of the money was earmarked to rehabilitate a nationwide network of hospitals and clinics that had long provided universal care.

First woman president in Chile

In 2006, Chilean voters elected their first woman president, Veronica Michelle Bachelet Jeria. Bachelet was the head of Chile's Socialist Party and a pediatrician by profession. Like Vazquez in Uruguay, she had triumphed as the candidate of a left-wing coalition forged by the popular, outgoing president in whose Cabinet she had served as health minister and minister for defense. Bachelet was the daughter of an air force general who died in jail in 1974 under the dictatorship of Augusto Pinochet Ugarte. She herself was tortured, and later exiled, by the Pinochet regime.

Bachelet's election marked a historic transition in Chilean attitudes on social issues. She was a single (separated) mother of three children in a nation that was traditionally very conservative on family issues and the last in the Americas to permit divorce in

Bolivian soldiers guard the entrance to a foreign-owned oil refinery in Santa Cruz, Bolivia. On May 1, 2006, Bolivia's new President Evo Morales nationalized the country's oil and gas industry.

2004. In defiance of heated opposition from the Roman Catholic Church, Bachelet, a self-described *agnostic* (a nonbeliever in organized religion), had public secondary schools provide free morning-after birth control pills to girls as young as 14 years old in mid-2006. The step was necessary, according to Bachelet, to curtail the high incidence of unwanted teen-age pregnancies.

Bachelet was also an ardent spokeswoman for women's rights in a nation known for its typically *macho* (male-oriented) culture. Bachelet set aside half of the positions in her Cabinet for women. To accelerate the rate at which women entered the job market, her administration opened more than 200 day care centers during its first 100 days in office and proposed a bill that would guarantee the care of all children until they reached eight years of age. The reforms were aimed at helping single mothers—who head nearly one-third of Chile's families—to escape poverty by seeking gainful employment outside the home.

Change in smaller nations

The willingness of Latin America's new leaders to adopt novel approaches to solving old problems—even at the risk of alienating members of the establishment—was evident in Jamaica as well. In February 2006, members of the left-wing People's National Party elected Portia Simpson Miller their new leader. When the incumbent prime minister stepped down, Simpson Miller became Jamaica's first woman chief executive. Like the leftist leaders of Bolivia and Brazil, Simpson Miller was raised in humble circumstances. Her election, said a local commentator, reflected the desire of poor Jamaicans for a prime minister "who had walked in their shoes."

Simpson Miller began her political career as the representative to Jamaica's Parliament for South West St. Andrew, a poor and violence-prone neighborhood of Kingston, the capital, and served in the cabinet for several years. Beginning in 2002, Simpson Miller oversaw social service programs in neighborhoods as tough as the one that she represented. She earned a reputation—as well as sharp criticism—for working with the criminal gangs that, in effect, controlled many ghettos.

The UN peacekeeping mission in Haiti adopted a somewhat similar strategy in respecting the turf controlled by lawless groups to create stability for an election in 2006, following the U.S.-led intervention that forced former President Jean-Bertrand Aristide from office in 2004. The 2006 election marked the return to power of Aristide's estranged protégé, leftist President René Préval, the only democratically elected Haitian head of state to have completed his constitutionally mandated term in office (1996-2000). Préval drew wide support from among the poverty-stricken in the hemisphere's poorest nation.

Venezuela, with its vast oil resources, was the world's fifth largest exporter of oil in 2006. Venezuelan President Chávez in 2006 demanded that private multinational oil firms operating in Venezuela agree to convert their contracts to joint ventures with the state oil company, Petróleos de Venezuela SA (PDVSA).

In Nicaragua, leftist Sandinista leader and former President Daniel Ortega (1984-1990) returned to power after winning that country's presidential election in November 2006. (The Sandinistas were a rebel group that formed in the mid-1970's in response to the dictatorial rule of the Somoza family, who received support from the U.S. government. Ortega was voted out of office in 1990, at the end of a civil war in which the United States backed rebels called contras.) Although some foreign investors expressed concern over Ortega's winning the election (his government had seized private assets in the 1980's), Ortega asserted that he had changed and that his top priorities were to help the 80 percent of Nicaraguans who live on less than $2 a day and to attract foreign investors.

In Ecuador, leftist leader Rafael Correa, a U.S.-trained economist, won a run-off presidential election in November 2006 over Alvaro Noboa, a conservative banana tycoon and the richest man in Ecuador. Both candidates had promised to double the monthly government stipend to the poor and to create jobs and fight poverty and corruption. However, Correa had stated he would refuse to pay back all of Ecuador's foreign debt, which he considered "illegitimate," and opposed a free-trade agreement with the United States. Noboa vowed to attract foreign investment to Ecuador. Correa, in the campaign before the first round of the election, had touted his close connection to Venezuela's Chávez. However, he toned down his rhetoric after he came in in second place, after Noboa.

Turmoil follows Mexican election

The 2006 presidential campaign in Mexico resulted in a polarization of the country's electorate along class lines. The left-wing Democratic Revolutionary Party chose as its candidate Andrés Manuel López Obrador, a charismatic former mayor of Mexico City. To win office, López Obrador exploited potentially volatile differences between the country's rich and poor at rallies that attracted millions of mostly poor Mexicans. The unprecedented size of the crowds at such events caused alarm among wealthy Mexicans, who supported Felipe Calderón Hinojosa of the ruling National Action Party. A former energy minister and lackluster campaigner, Calderón had been hand-picked by his party's incumbent president, Vicente Fox. Calderón lagged in the polls until the final days. Then a blitz of television advertising, paid for by anonymous big business donors, turned the tide. The ads alleged that once López Obrador was in office, he would become a dictator in the mold of Venezuelan President Chávez.

Mexico's election officials found the accusation unfair and the involvement in financing Calderón's campaign by outgoing President Vicente Fox's administration unethical, if not unlawful. Nevertheless, Calderón was declared the winner by the narrowest margin in Mexican history—less than 1 percent. López Obrador declared the results fraudulent. To support his demand for a total recount of the votes, his supporters constructed a makeshift tent village in the heart of downtown Mexico City, paralyzing commerce for six weeks. On September 5, Mexico's electoral tribunal denied his demand and certified Calderón

XXX REUNION DEL CONSEJO
DEL MERCADO COMÚN, CUMBRE
DE JEFES DE ESTADO DEL MERCOSUR
Y ESTADOS ASOCIADOS

Argentina - Córdoba 2006

MERCOSUR   MERCOSUL

the winner. Nevertheless, on November 21, López Obrador had himself sworn in as president of a "parallel government" before 100,000 supporters in Mexico City and vowed to disrupt Calderón's government.

Ordinary people flex their political muscle

Throughout Latin America, as in Mexico, the common people— whether candidates won or lost in 2006—were politically on the move. This was especially true of those who had been largely marginalized because of their poverty or ethnicity. Their outrage over government corruption, as expressed through massive and economically paralyzing—but peaceful—demonstrations, led to the ouster of governments in Bolivia, Ecuador, and Peru. Similarly, their demands for justice and revenge caused more than a dozen presidents or former presidents to be removed from office or indicted in Argentina, Brazil, Chile, Nicaragua, and elsewhere on charges of human rights abuses or corruption while in office.

To a considerable extent, the swing to the left in Latin America reflected a sense of empowerment born of these succeses. Exercising their constitutional right to seek redress for their grievances, irate ordinary citizens turned out of office dozens of elected state officials, including governors and the mayors of many municipalities.

By 2006, millions of people who had understandably exhibited little interest in systems of governance from which they were largely excluded were no longer content to be bystanders in the political process. In an earlier era, such disaffected people had resorted to violence and armed insurrection to vent their frustration. With leaders on the scene with whom ordinary citizens could identify, there was the hope that by peacefully working together, the people of Latin America could achieve more equitable and inclusive societies.

The leaders of several Latin American nations gather at a meeting of Mercosur, the Latin American trade bloc, in Cordoba, Argentina, in July 2006. They include, from left to right in the front row, Cuban President Fidel Castro, Uruguayan President Tabaré Vazquez, Brazilian President Luiz Inácio Lula da Silva, Argentine President Néstor Kirchner, Paraguayan President Nicanor Duarte, Venezuelan President Hugo Chávez, Chilean President Michelle Bachelet Jeria, and Foreign Minister of Mexico Luis Enersto Derbez.

A Lebanese man navigates a rubble-strewn street in Beirut in the wake of Israeli airstrikes on the Lebanese capital in July. The 34-day conflict between Israel and Hezbollah—a Lebanon-based Shiite militant group with connections to Syria and Iran—was triggered by Hezbollah's kidnapping of two Israeli soldiers. At least 1,000 Lebanese died in the conflict.

Lebanon. On July 12, 2006, Lebanese fighters with the pro-Syria Hezbollah organization crossed the "blue line" marking the Lebanese-Israeli border. The fighters kidnapped two Israeli soldiers and killed three others in a raid. An additional five Israeli soldiers were killed in the initial Israeli response to the raid. A devastating 34-day conflict then ensued between Hezbollah and Israel.

During the conflict, Israeli forces attacked the strongholds of Hezbollah in southern Lebanon and in the Shi`ah-dominated southern suburbs of the capital, Beirut, as well as bridges throughout Lebanon. The Israelis targeted a total of 350 Lebanese villages, towns, and cities in retaliation for thousands of rockets fired by Hezbollah into northern Israel. More than 1,000 Lebanese civilians were killed in the fighting. The conflict cost the Lebanese economy more than $15 billion.

The fighting stopped on August 14, after United Nations (UN) Security Council Resolution 1701 was implemented. The resolution called for 15,000 soldiers of the Lebanese Army to maintain order in southern Lebanon. These troops were to be assisted by as many as 15,000 peacekeeping members of an expanded United Nations Interim Force in Lebanon (UNIFIL). Most of the UNIFIL soldiers were from European Union countries, particularly France and Italy. The deployment of these forces—between Lebanon's Litani River and the Lebanese-Israeli border—prevented Hezbollah fighters from launching rockets into Israel.

Pierre Gemayel assassination. On November 21, Pierre Gemayel, the minister of industry and a son of former Lebanese president Amin Gemayel, was assassinated in a hail of gunfire as he drove down a highway through Beirut. Gemayel was a prominent Christian politician who opposed Syria's years of domination of Lebanon. Christian, Sunni, and Druze leaders of the Cedar Revolution blamed the killing on Syria. The Cedar Revolution was a series of civic actions that led to the withdrawal of Syrian troops from Lebanon in April 2005. According to these leaders, Hezbollah and its two masters—Syria and Iran—were seeking to topple the democratically elected government of Lebanon. Parties associated with Lebanese opposition to Syria had won a parliamentary majority in elections in 2005.

Hundreds of thousands of Lebanese—many condemning Syria and Hezbollah—gathered in Beirut for Gemayel's funeral. The slaying of Gemayel raised fears that the Syrian government planned to assassinate other leaders of the Cedar Revolution.

International tribunal. Gemayel was among the Cabinet ministers who had voted on Nov. 13, 2006, to approve the UN blueprint for an international tribunal to prosecute the perpetrators of the assassination in February 2005 of former Prime Minister Rafik Hariri, an event that some experts have suggested helped spark the Cedar Revolution. Earlier UN investigative reports implicated Syrian officials and Hezbollah in the assassination of Hariri.

The November 2006 government vote in favor of the UN tribunal came just two days after five ministers belonging to Hezbollah and Amal, another pro-Syria party, resigned from the Cabinet. These ministers, together with one Christian ally, quit when their demands for increased government representation were not met. The ministers also objected to the UN investigation of the Hariri assassination and other terrorist operations in Lebanon, including the December 2005 slaying of Jubran Tueni. Tueni was a member of Lebanon's parliament and publisher of Lebanon's most prestigious newspaper.

Experts in Lebanese affairs noted that the objections to the international tribunal were related to the fact that the Syrian regime of Bashar al-Assad, who controlled Hezbollah and Amal, was the primary target of the UN investigation. ■ Marius Deeb

See also **Israel; Middle East; Syria.**

Lesotho. See Africa.
Liberia. See Africa.

Library. Rebuilding efforts continued in 2006 to restore libraries in Gulf Coast communities devastated by hurricanes Katrina and Rita in August and September 2005, respectively. Because local governments in the region had few tax dollars to spare, nonprofit groups and large corporations that sell products to libraries donated cash, reading materials, furniture, and computer equipment to towns in Alabama, Louisiana, Mississippi, and Texas. In addition, some communities in other parts of the country "adopted" damaged Gulf Coast libraries, sending used bookmobiles, building materials, and various items collected from book drives.

In June 2006, the American Library Association (ALA) became the first national organization to hold a major conference in New Orleans, Louisiana, since Hurricane Katrina had flooded 80 percent of the Crescent City 10 months earlier. During the conference, public and private funders announced $20 million in donations to storm-ravaged libraries in four states.

Financial woes continued for many libraries in 2006. Some local and state governments received more sales-tax dollars than they had expected because consumers were buying more goods and services, and rising home values increased the amount of property taxes collected. However, many government officials hesitated to give libraries any of the extra money because they feared the public would resent increased government spending.

Two notable exceptions involved the District of Columbia Public Library, for which a mayoral task force recommended a multimillion-dollar overhaul in January, and the public libraries in Pennsylvania, which were granted a 23-percent funding increase in September.

Citizens in several areas of the United States where library services were threatened organized protests and fund-raising drives in 2006. Such efforts led to libraries remaining open or reopening in a number of cities, including Providence, Rhode Island, and Hampden, Massachusetts.

Federal support. In 2006, for the second year in a row, the administration of U.S. President George W. Bush proposed to increase federal support for public libraries. The administration's fiscal year 2007 proposal called for $220.9 million in federal funds, which was $10.3 million more than the amount spent in 2006. The added funds were designed to help libraries pay for Internet access and such community programming as homework help and adult-literacy classes. However, the administration also asked Congress to slash funding for the library network of the Environmental Protection Agency.

Internet. Online access to information at libraries continued to expand in 2006, as proved by a September report from Florida State University in Tallahassee. According to the report, 99 percent of public libraries in the United States offered free Internet service, compared with 25 percent 10 years earlier. The Online Computer Library Center, the world's largest library cooperative, debuted a public Web site in August on which visitors can find nearby libraries that own some of the more than 70 million titles listed.

Libraries also sought to place the unabridged versions of more of their holdings on the World Wide Web. The University of California campuses, the University of Wisconsin at Madison, and the Complutense University of Madrid all signed agreements with the search-engine firm Google Inc. in 2006 to allow that company to digitize the contents of their shelves. The libraries agreed to the deal even though Google was defending itself in an ongoing lawsuit brought by several publishing firms that claimed the book-scanning project violated U.S. copyright law.

Patriot Act. President Bush signed a reauthorized USA PATRIOT Act on March 9 that retained Section 215—the "Library Provision." This section allowed law enforcement agencies to secretly review the reading and Internet records of patrons. Many libraries questioned the constitutionality of this provision.   ■ Beverly Goldberg

Libya. United States Secretary of State Condoleezza Rice announced in May 2006 that the United States was restoring full diplomatic relations with Libya. Those relations were broken off in 1980 after Libyans set fire to the U.S. embassy in the capital, Tripoli. The U.S. government partially restored relations with Libya in 2004 after Libyan leader Mu'ammar Muhammad al-Qadhafi renounced the use of weapons of mass destruction. In June 2006, the U.S. Department of State rescinded Libya's designation as a state sponsor of terrorism.

Oil and gas. The Western Libyan Gas Project (WLGP) entered its third year of operation in 2006. The WLGP transmits natural gas from Libya to Europe via the Green Stream, an underwater pipeline about 320 miles (520 kilometers) long. Italy's Ente Nazionale Idrocarburi holds a 75-percent interest in WLGP, and Libya's National Oil Company (NOC) holds the remaining 25 percent. According to WLGP administrators, the project produced 353 billion cubic feet (10 billion cubic meters) of natural gas in 2005—up from 247 billion cubic feet (7 billion cubic meters) in 2004. Libya consumed 71 billion cubic feet (2 billion cubic meters) of the gas, while selling 282 billion cubic feet (8 billion cubic meters) to Europe.

In 2006, Marathon Oil Corporation of Houston and its partners in the former Oasis Group (Amerada Hess and ConocoPhillips) returned to their former oil and gas exploration and production operations in Libya's Sirte Basin. The U.S. firms, which had suspended their work in Libya in 1986, announced in December 2005 that they would pay $1.3 billion to the NOC to conduct exploration and production activities in the Sirte Basin for the next 25 years.

Bulgarian nurse retrial. In December 2006, a court in Tripoli convicted and sentenced to death five Bulgarian nurses and a Palestinian physician for purposely infecting more than 400 children with HIV, the virus that causes AIDS, in a hospital in northeastern Libya. A Libyan court previously had convicted the defendants in 2004 for the same offenses and condemned them to death, but—after the verdict was criticized by many international observers—Libya's Supreme Court reversed the verdict and called for a retrial. Defense attorneys argued that Libyan authorities had used torture to extract confessions from the accused individuals.

Press freedom. According to a November 2006 report by Reporters Without Borders, an international journalists' advocacy group based in France, Libya remained a "press freedom predator" in 2006. However, the group noted approvingly that Libya had relaxed its policies on Web site censorship.   ■ Mary-Jane Deeb

See also **Energy supply; Middle East.**

Liechtenstein. See Europe.

Literature. In 2006, the Pulitzer Prize for fiction was awarded to Geraldine Brooks for her novel *March.* The book, set during the American Civil War (1861-1865), follows the travels of a Union chaplain and abolitionist, March, whose character is based on the absent father of the sisters in Louisa May Alcott's *Little Women.* The other finalists for the fiction Pulitzer were another Civil War novel, E. L. Doctorow's *The March*—about General William Tecumseh Sherman's march through Georgia and the Carolinas—and Lee Martin's *The Bright Forever,* which tells the story of the disappearance of a young girl in a small Indiana town in the 1970's.

Kiran Desai, daughter of the novelist Anita Desai, won the 2006 Man Booker Prize for her novel *The Inheritance of Loss.* The novel depicts the struggle for cultural identity by a retired judge, his granddaughter, and his cook, all of whom live in northern India, and the cook's son, an illegal alien living in New York City. Hermione Lee, head of the prize committee, praised *The Inheritance of Loss* for its "humane breadth and wisdom, comic tenderness, and powerful political acuteness." The Man Booker Prize, the United Kingdom's most prestigious literary award, was sponsored in 2006 by the Man Group, a British securities fund.

Philip Roth. The third volume of the collected works of Philip Roth was released by the Library of America in 2006. In 2005, Roth became only the third living writer—after Saul Bellow and Eudora Welty—to be honored by the nonprofit publisher of classic American literature. Volume 3 of this eight-volume series of Roth's works, *Novels 1973-1977,* includes *The Great American Novel* (1973), *My Life as a Man* (1974), and *The Professor of Desire* (1977). In addition, Roth was awarded in 2006 the PEN/Nabokov Award, a prize given to an author whose body of work "represents achievement in a variety of literary genres and is of endearing originality and consummate craftsmanship." The award is given by the New York City-based PEN American Center.

Not content to rest on his laurels, in 2006 Roth published a new novella, *Everyman,* which takes its title from an anonymous 1485 morality play in which a man is visited by the figure of Death and must answer for his life. Roth updates this story, beginning with the funeral of a New Jersey advertising man in his seventies and then retracing the steps of the man's long and unhealthy life. Critical reaction to *Everyman* was mixed. London's *Daily Telegraph* called it a "brilliantly compressed account of a life," while *The New York Times* noted that "harrowing evocations of age and infirmity do not a novel make."

American literature. Roth was not the only elder statesman of American literature to publish a new work in 2006. John Updike released *Terrorist,* the story of Ahmad Ashmawy, an American Muslim teen-ager who becomes involved in a terrorist plot. The book was praised by many as an attempt to look at the human face of extremism in a serious and thoughtful way. Others found the book unworthy of its subject and too reliant upon stereotypes and clichés to make a valuable comment.

In 2006, Cormac McCarthy followed his 2005 novel *No Country for Old Men* with a similarly violent and disturbing effort, *The Road.* In a gray, post-apocalyptic United States, the heroes of *The Road,* an unnamed father and son, make their way south in hopes of survival. The book returns to some of McCarthy's common themes of perseverance and humanity in a dangerous and unpredictable world. It is written more as a universal fable than as a novel, and its characters are sketched out with few distinguishing details.

Richard Ford delighted his fans in 2006 with the publication of *The Lay of the Land,* the third work in a trilogy that began with *The Sportswriter* (1986) and continued with *Independence Day* (1995), which won both the 1996 Pulitzer Prize for fiction and the PEN/Faulkner Award. The books constitute the history of a man named Frank Bascombe, who works in successive careers as a sportswriter and a New Jersey real estate agent.

The reclusive Thomas Pynchon, author of the 1974 National Book Award-winning *Gravity's Rainbow,* created a stir in the literary world in 2006 after he posted a description of his own as-yet-unreleased novel *Against the Day* on the Amazon.com Web site. "Spanning the period between the Chicago World's Fair of 1893 and the years just after World War I," he wrote, "this novel moves from the labor troubles in Colorado to turn-of-the-century New York, to London and Gottingen, Venice and Vienna, the Balkans, Central Asia, Siberia at the time of the mysterious Tunguska Event, Mexico during the Revolution, postwar Paris, silent-era Hollywood, and one or two places not strictly speaking on the map at all." The book was released in November 2006.

George Saunders published *In Persuasion Nation,* a collection of short stories marked by a satirical approach to consumerism and other aspects of modern American life. Saunders was also one of 2006's recipients of a highly prestigious $500,000 MacArthur Fellowship. The fellowships, popularly called "genius grants," are awarded to talented individuals thought to possess "exceptional creativity, promise for important future advances based on a track record of significant accomplishment, and potential for the fellowship to facilitate subsequent creative work." The fellowships are awarded annually by the John D. and Catherine T. MacArthur Foundation, a private grantmaking program in Chicago.

Claire Messud's *The Emperor's Children,* her fourth book, was consistently praised by critics in the United States and the United Kingdom. In the book, the author examines themes of ambition and entitlement as they affect the family, friends, and enemies of a New York intellectual named Murray Thwaite. Richard Powers's ninth novel, *The Echo Maker,* examines identity and memory through its portrait of a man who develops Capgras syndrome, a rare neurological disorder, after a car accident.

In 2006, Dave Eggers released *What is the What,* a fictionalized biography of a Sudanese refugee, Valentino Achak Deng, who lives in the United States. Novelist and short story writer T. C. Boyle took the crime of identity theft as the subject of his new thriller, *Talk Talk.* The book pits a deaf woman wrongfully accused of a felony against the criminal responsible for framing her.

National Book Festival. On September 30, the 2006 National Book Festival was held in Washington, D.C. The festival, which is organized by the Library of Congress and which has been hosted by First Lady Laura Bush each year since 2001, is meant to promote lifelong literacy and features readings by more than 70 writers in a number of categories. "Fiction & Fantasy" included such notables as Geraldine Brooks, Christopher Buckley, Khaled Hosseini, and Alice McDermott; readings in "Mysteries & Thrillers" included George Pelecanos, Alexander McCall Smith, and Scott Turow.

New classics. A number of English-language authors were honored in 2006 by publication in Alfred A. Knopf's esteemed Everyman's Library series of reprinted classics. Additions to the series included Indian writer R. K. Narayan's collected novels, in two volumes; a volume of short stories for adults by Roald Dahl, the renowned British author known best for his children's books; Toni Morrison's Pulitzer Prize-winning novel *Beloved* (1987); the Canadian writer Margaret Atwood's *The Handmaid's Tale* (1985); and *Carried Away,* a selection of 17 stories by Canadian writer Alice Munro. Munro also published a new book of stories in 2006, *The View From Castle Rock.*

In May, Morrison's *Beloved* was voted "the single best work of American fiction published in the last 25 years" in a survey of "prominent writers, critics, editors and other literary sages" conducted by Sam Tanenhaus, the editor of *The New York Times Book Review.* The runners-up in this contest included Don DeLillo's *Underworld* (1997), Cormac McCarthy's *Blood Meridian* (1985), John Updike's "Rabbit" novels (1960-1990, published in an omnibus edition in 1995), and Philip Roth's *American Pastoral* (1997). Tanenhaus was criticized for the survey's ambi-

guity. It was unclear, for instance, if short story collections published after 1980 but containing previously uncollected work written prior to 1980 were eligible. He was also criticized for the survey's scope, as the last *Times* survey of this type was conducted in 1965, leaving a 15-year gap of books not eligible for either survey.

The mystery genre enjoyed a boom in 2006. Renowned British espionage writer John Le Carré released *The Mission Song,* about a British-Congolese interpreter who becomes involved with a shadowy organization called The Syndicate, which claims to be capable of bringing peace to Congo. George Pelecanos released *The Night Gardener,* in which two former detectives revisit an unsolved series of murders from 20 years earlier after it appears that the killer has struck again.

Walter Mosley added *Fear of the Dark* to his series of Fearless Jones mystery novels, which includes *Fearless Jones* (2001) and *Fear Itself* (2003). The novels, set in Los Angeles in the 1950's, follow the adventures of Fearless Jones as told through the eyes of his friend, mild-mannered bookstore owner Paris Minton. In 2006, Mosley also published *Fortunate Son,* a novel exploring racial tension and destiny in the United States.

Alexander McCall Smith published *Blue Shoes and Happiness,* the seventh installment of his humorous "No. 1 Ladies' Detective Agency" series. Set in Botswana, the series chronicles the cases of self-taught private investigator Precious Ramotswe and her assistant, Grace Makutsi. Carl Hiassen, whose amusing treatments of the seedy underside of Florida are generally classified as crime fiction, added *Nature Girl* to his long list of novels.

British novels. Several popular and preeminent novelists in the United Kingdom published new works in 2006. Martin Amis's book *The House of Meetings* featured a novella (also titled "The House of Meetings") about slave labor camps in the Soviet Union and two short stories inspired by the terrorist attacks on the United States in 2001 and the invasion of Iraq. In 2006, Peter Carey released *Theft: A Love Story,* a comic novel about a failed Australian painter.

The Irish writer Roddy Doyle's *Paula Spencer,* a follow-up to his 1996 novel, *The Woman Who Walked Into Doors,* offered an exacting portrait of a woman struggling with alcoholism and family problems. Other noteworthy releases in 2006 included the Scottish novelist Irvine Welsh's *The Bedroom Secrets of the Master Chefs* and Will Self's *The Book of Dave,* in which a London cab driver's journal is discovered in the far future and becomes the basis of a religion.   ■ Stefan Beck

See also **Literature for children; Nobel Prizes; Poetry; Pulitzer Prizes; Theater.**

Literature for children.

Fiction—realistic, historical, and fantasy—continued to spark strong interest among elementary school and middle school readers. Some of the outstanding books of 2006 included the following:

Picture books. *So Sleepy Story* by Uri Shulevitz (Farrar, Straus and Giroux). Sometimes a "sleepy sleepy house" doesn't stay that way. As music wafts in through the window, objects that glowed a quiet blue grow golden, and even the dishes dance—briefly—before the peaceful blue of sleep returns. Ages 2 to 5.

I'm Dirty by Kate McMullan, illustrated by Jim McMullan (Joanna Cotler). A backhoe loader, energetically cleaning up a junk-littered vacant lot, loves his job, which he calls "Easy as pie. Make that a MUD pie." Ages 3 to 5.

Lilly's Big Day by Kevin Henkes (Greenwillow). Lilly's teacher does not choose her as the flower girl, but Lilly manages, finally, to enjoy the wedding as "first assistant." Ages 4 to 7.

Pancakes for Supper by Anne Isaacs, illustrated by Mark Teague (Scholastic). Toby's all dressed up to go to town, but a bump sends her out of the wagon and into a tall tale. She fends off the forest animals with clever trades and comes out with maple syrup to share. Ages 5 to 7.

Edwina, The Dinosaur Who Didn't Know She Was Extinct by Mo Willems (Hyperion). Edwina does odd jobs and bakes delicious cookies for her neighbors, so no one wants her to become extinct. Reginald's school report, however, reveals the ugly truth. Both Reginald and Edwina get over the bad news. Ages 5 to 7.

Olivia Forms a Band by Ian Falconer (Atheneum). Olivia's family plans to attend the fireworks. When she learns there will be no band, the piglet plans to become one herself. Ages 4 to 8.

Chowder by Peter Brown (Little, Brown). "Chowder has always been different." The Wubbingtons' bulldog uses the toilet and plays with the computer. He would like to find some animal friends, though, and finally succeeds at a mall petting zoo, with a wild game of kickball. Ages 6 to 8.

I Am Not a Baby by Jill McElmurry (Schwartz & Wade). Leo Leotardi's family treats him—and dresses him—as "the baby," even after he starts school, graduates, goes to work, and gets married. They finally stop when his own baby calls him "Dada." Ages 6 to 8.

Probuditi! by Chris Van Allsburg (Houghton Mifflin). Calvin and his friend watch a hypnotist's act and try out the technique themselves by making Calvin's little sister, Trudy, think she's a dog. What *was* that word to bring her out of the trance? Van Allsburg's warm browns make the retro world seem as real as Trudy's secret trick. Ages 6 to 8.

The Runaway Dinner by Allan Ahlberg, illustrated by Bruce Ingman (Candlewick). A little boy's dinner jumps off the table and leads the family on a silly chase. Ages 4 to 8.

Fiction. *The Wright 3* by Blue Balliett, illustrated by Brett Helquist (Scholastic). A teacher draws the attention of three sixth-graders to Frank Lloyd Wright's Robie House, which is near their school in Chicago and is in danger of being destroyed. Is it truly haunted? Petra, Calder, and Tommy learn to use their different strengths to solve the mystery. Ages 9 to 14.

Crispin: At the Edge of the World, by Avi (Hyperion). In the second book of a planned trilogy set in England in the late 1300's, Crispin flees with Bear, the juggler who befriended him. When Bear is wounded, they are taken in by an old woman and a disfigured girl, whom Crispin fears are witches. He learns to judge people by their actions. Ages 10 to 13.

The End by Lemony Snicket (HarperCollins). In Book 13 of "A Series of Unfortunate Events," the Baudelaire orphans are still having trouble with Count Olaf, and the author is still having fun with words and plots that twist and turn. The Baudelaires discover an island full of secrets, and readers find a chapter even after the last chapter and have some—but not all—of their questions answered. Ages 9 to 14.

Things Hoped For by Andrew Clement (Philomel). Gwen has come from West Virginia to live with her grandfather in New York City and pursue her dream of admission to a music conservatory. Robert is in town for his own audition. By the time they meet, Gwen's grandfather has mysteriously disappeared. The book is a portrait of young people who love their art and are in the process of shaping their future. Ages 11 to 15.

The Book Thief by Markus Zuzak (Knopf). The narrator—Death—has much to occupy him in World War II (1939-1945) Germany. He tells the story of Liesel, a 9-year-old foster child who steals books, and of her foster family and the young Jewish man that they hide. Ages 12 to 16.

The Astonishing Life of Octavian Nothing, Traitor to the Nation. Volume I: The Pox Party by M. T. Anderson (Candlewick). Octavian, a young African boy living at the time of the Revolutionary War in America (1775-1783), recounts his life as an experiment at the hands of a group of men who consider themselves scientists. Ages 12 to 17.

This Is All: The Pillow Book of Cordelia Kenn by Aidan Chambers (Bodley Head). Chambers, a prize-winning British young-adult author, narrates the story as Cordelia Kenn, a young woman who, as she nears age 20, wants to record her life story from the age of 16 for the daughter she is expecting. Cordelia uses frank and explicit language to explain her path to finding love and her true vocation as a poet. Ages 15 to 17.

Fantasy. *The Miraculous Journey of Edward Tulane* by Kate DiCamillo, illustrated by Bagram Ibatoulline (Candlewick). Although he is owned by a loving child, Edward Tulane is an arrogant and self-satisfied china rabbit. As he passes through many hands during a long journey, he learns much, including the joys and sorrows of love. Ages 7 to 10.

Horns and Wrinkles by Joseph Helgerson, illustrated by Nicoletta Ceccoli (Houghton Mifflin). Mysterious happenings frequently occur along the Mississippi River, where Claire and her cousin Duke live. Duke's parents have been turned to stone. Claire tries to save them, with the help of Duke—who has grown a rhino horn for showing a lack of kindness—and a trio of bumbling, good-hearted trolls. Ages 9 to 13.

Wintersmith by Terry Pratchett (HarperTeen). In the third volume of a trilogy, young witch-in-training Tiffany Aching attracts the attention of the Wintersmith, the natural force who controls winter. If he succeeds in keeping her in his castle, the balance of the seasons will be upset. The Wee Free Men—blue pixies—struggle to protect her, as does Roland, her boyfriend-in-training. Tiffany learns that there are consequences, even to actions as seemingly innocent as learning new steps at a dance. Ages 10 to 14.

Informational books. *Something Out of Nothing: Marie Curie and Radium* by Carla Killough McClafferty (Farrar, Straus and Giroux). Curie was the first woman to win a Nobel Prize and the first person to win it twice. McClafferty's detailed biography explores Curie's studies, her research, and her marriage to fellow scientist Pierre, as well as her determination and the difficult conditions of her work. Ages 10 to 14.

Team Moon: How 400,000 People Landed Apollo 11 on the Moon by Catherine Thimmesh (Houghton Mifflin). Many people remember the three astronauts involved in the 1969 moon landing, but Thimmesh shows just how many others worked in the background to achieve a successful landing. Personal interviews and period photographs bring the project to life. Ages 10 to 14.

Awards. The 2005 Newbery Medal was awarded to Lynne Rae Perkins for *Criss Cross*. The award is given by the American Library Association (ALA) for "the most distinguished contribution to children's literature" published during the previous year. The ALA's Caldecott Medal for "the most distinguished American picture book" was awarded to Chris Raschka, the illustrator of *The Hello Goodbye Window*, written by Norton Juster. The Michael L. Printz Award, for excellence in literature for young adults, went to John Green, for *Looking for Alaska*.   ■ Mary Harris Russell

See also **Literature.**

Lithuania. See **Baltic states; Europe.**

Los Angeles. Democrat Antonio Villaraigosa entered his second year as mayor of Los Angeles in 2006, amid controversy over his efforts to control the city's public school system and to address the problem of homelessness.

Villaraigosa urged the state legislature to increase mayoral involvement in the operations of the Los Angeles Unified School District, the second largest school district in the nation. In August, the legislature agreed to shift the budget and contracting authority over the district from the seven-member school board to the district superintendent. It also gave the mayor direct control over a number of low-performing schools. Opponents called the reform a power grab by the mayor and threatened lawsuits. However, on September 18, Governor Arnold Schwarzenegger, a Republican, signed the legislation. He believed the reform could help schools that were afflicted by poor academic achievement and an overloaded bureaucracy. The reform was scheduled to take effect in January 2007 and have a five-year lifespan.

The mayor's policies on homelessness included a plan to reduce the concentration of homeless services in downtown skid row and to better distribute such services throughout the county. The $100-million plan—approved by the county board of supervisors in April 2006—established five centers across the county to provide temporary shelter and social services for transients. However, many people criticized the plan, claiming that it would worsen the problem of homelessness in suburban areas.

The Getty. The J. Paul Getty Trust—the world's wealthiest nonprofit arts institution—continued to rebuild its organization following investigations into both its financial practices and its acquisition of ancient artifacts. The Italian and Greek governments claimed that a number of objects held by the Getty had been taken illegally from archaeological sites in their countries. By late 2006, the Getty had reached tentative agreements with both countries to return several disputed antiquities, with arrangements for the Getty to display other objects from the countries in the future.

The Getty Villa in Malibu—where J. Paul Getty housed his first collection of art and artifacts—reopened in January after extensive renovation.

Construction. The effort to revitalize downtown Los Angeles continued in 2006, the year of the city's 225th birthday. In April, architect Frank Gehry announced plans to build a major condominium and office tower complex behind his landmark Walt Disney Concert Hall. In June, developers unveiled plans to build a 54-story, 1,000-room hotel complex near the city's Convention Center.

Local architecture firm Jeffrey M. Kalban & Associates designed a state-of-the-art information

Supporters of the Democratic Union for Integration (DUI), an ethnic Albanian political party, rally before Macedonia's July 5, 2006, parliamentary elections, in which the DUI and its coalition partners, the Social Democrats, were voted out of office.

and advanced computer technology facility as part of a project to expand the east campus of the University of Southern California. In addition, a $175-million outdoor shopping mall, the Gateway, was scheduled to be built in South Gate, south of Los Angeles, by 2008.

Transportation. Security remained a major concern at the Los Angeles and Long Beach port complex, the nation's busiest container port complex. Officials projected that some 15.6 million 20-foot (6-meter) containers would move through the ports in 2006—a nearly 11 percent increase from 2005. In September 2006, the U.S. Congress designated millions of dollars to upgrade port security.

The Chicago-based Boeing Company—which employed about 5,500 workers in the Los Angeles area in 2006—announced in August that it would close its C-17 military jet assembly plant in Long Beach by 2009.

Growth. The United States Census Bureau reported in April that Riverside and San Bernardino counties—known locally as the Inland Empire—were among the fastest-growing urban areas in the nation. Experts attributed much of the growth to housing affordability and jobs.

■ Margaret A. Kilgore

See also **Art; City.**

Luxembourg. See Europe.

Macedonia. In July 2006 parliamentary elections, candidates of the Internal Macedonian Revolutionary Organization (IMRO) outpolled the ruling Social Democrats and were able in August to form a government in partnership with the Democratic Albanian Party and with IMRO leader Nikola Gruevski as prime minister. Although the majority of Macedonians are Slavs, ethnic Albanians account for about one-quarter of the population. Macedonia's political arrangements dated from the signing in 2001 of the Ohrid agreement, a peace pact that ended an armed insurgency led by ethnic Albanian guerrillas.

Prime Minister Gruevski, embracing the goal of eventual membership in the European Union (EU), advanced a reform agenda endorsed by EU leaders. Prominent on this agenda were proposed reforms of the judiciary and the police as well as market-oriented economic reforms. In September 2006, Gruevski unveiled a proposal for tax reform designed to simplify the tax system and create incentives for foreign investment.

Macedonia's economy continued to be burdened by high unemployment in 2006. According to economists, the midyear jobless rate in the country stood at about 36 percent.

■ Sharon L. Wolchik

See also **Europe.**

Madagascar. See Africa.

Magazine publishers struggled with falling subscription and newsstand sales during 2006. The Audit Bureau of Circulations (ABC)—an industry trade group based in Schaumburg, Illinois—reported that 348, or 54 percent, of the 654 consumer magazines it tracked reported circulation decreases during the first six months of the year. The newsstand sales of the newsweeklies *Time* and *Newsweek* declined by 19 percent.

Industry experts blamed the slump largely on the amount of information and entertainment available on the Internet and on the large number of magazines covering such similar topics as celebrity news. A number of print magazines were discontinued, as publishers increased their emphasis on online publications. In April, the print magazines *Elle Girl,* which was launched in 2001, and *Celebrity Living,* which was less than a year old, ceased publication.

Changes at Time Inc. Time Inc., a division of New York City-based Time Warner Inc., underwent a number of changes in 2006. In July, the company announced that it was shutting down the six-year-old *Teen People,* with the final print edition in September. The magazine's Web site continued to operate.

Time magazine announced in August that, beginning in 2007, the magazine would be available on newsstands on Friday mornings. *Time* began as a Friday magazine in 1923 but switched to Monday publication in 1960. The shift back to Fridays was an attempt to increase newsstand sales, especially among shoppers in supermarkets.

In September 2006, Time Inc. announced plans to divest itself of a number of consumer magazines, including such well-known titles as *Popular Science, Field & Stream,* and *Outdoor Life,* as well as such hobbyist titles as *Ride BMX* and *Yachting.*

Magazines identified with a celebrity showed mixed results in the first half of 2006, according to the ABC. Circulation of *O: The Oprah Magazine*—cofounded by television talk show host Oprah Winfrey—declined by 10.9 percent from the previous year, down to 2.3 million. *Martha Stewart Living* increased its circulation by 3.9 percent, up to 2 million. The homemaking expert's company, Martha Stewart Living Omnimedia, launched a new lifestyle magazine, *Blueprint,* in May.

Subscription cards. In an unusual promotion, Royal Philips Electronics of the Netherlands paid Hearst Corporation of New York City $2 million to eliminate subscription cards from the September issues of four magazines. In the issues, Philips ran advertisements promoting the company's efforts to make life easier. The ads read, "Simplicity is not having subscription cards fall out of your magazine."   ■ Mark Fitzgerald

Malawi. See **Africa.**

Malaysia. Prime Minister Abdullah bin Ahmad Badawi introduced on March 31, 2006, a five-year economic plan that emphasized improving education and helping rural development. One-fifth of the $54-billion plan was to be devoted to education. This emphasis reflected the fear that Malaysia's educational system was producing too many graduates without the technical skills needed to compete in the global economy. The plan also aimed to continue to reduce poverty. The number of poor Malaysians had been cut from 22.8 percent of the population in 1990 to 5.7 percent of Malaysia's 26 million people in 2006.

In 2006, Abdullah came under attack from two sides. An opposition politician, Anwar Ibrahim, attacked Abdullah's lack of specific action against corruption. He also called for ending policies favoring the ethnic Malay majority over citizens of Chinese and Indian origin. Abdullah's ruling United Malays National Organization had used those policies to consolidate its power. Abdullah also came under fire from Mahathir bin Mohamad, who had served as prime minister from 1981 to 2003 and picked Abdullah as his successor. Mahathir criticized Abdullah for reversing policies Mahathir had established as prime minister.
          ■ Henry S. Bradsher

See also **Asia.**

Manitoba. See **Canadian provinces.**

Mauritius. In July 2006, the Parliament of Mauritius passed Prime Minister Navin Ramgoolam's budget, the first by his ruling Social Alliance coalition since coming to power in July 2005. The budget encompassed an economic reform program intended to turn around the island nation's faltering economy. Among the proposed reforms were measures to make Mauritius a more attractive climate for foreign investment, to reduce the nation's large budget deficit, and to encourage the development of the computer technology and telecommunications industries.

Economists explained that the country's economic troubles stemmed from declines in its two chief industries, textile manufacturing and sugar cultivation. Both industries had been affected by changes in international trading patterns.

The sugar industry had long been boosted by purchases at subsidized prices by the European Union (EU). However, the EU sharply reduced the subsidies in 2006. In the textile industry, intense competition from low-cost producers in Asia rendered some Mauritian factories unprofitable, resulting in their closure. As a result, some 20,000 textile workers had lost their jobs since 2001. In 2006, overall unemployment in the island nation peaked at 9.5 percent, the Mauritian government reported.   ■ Pieter Esterhuysen

See also **Africa; International trade.**

Medicine. The first successful transplant of laboratory-grown organs into human beings was reported in April 2006. Doctors at the Institute for Regenerative Medicine at Wake Forest University School of Medicine in Winston-Salem, North Carolina, described how they had used patients' own cells to grow new bladders in a laboratory and then transplanted the bladders into the patients.

The study involved seven patients ages 4 to 19 with spina bifida, a birth defect that often involves damage to nerves that control the bladder. Standard treatment for the condition involves repairing the nonfunctioning bladder tissue with the patient's intestinal tissue. However, patients who undergo such treatment often develop serious problems, including cancer. The Wake Forest researchers instead removed muscle and bladder cells from the patients, placed them onto a bladder-shaped *scaffold* (mold), and allowed them to grow for several weeks. They then sewed the laboratory-grown bladders onto the patients' natural bladders, where the organs fused and the scaffolds decomposed. The new bladders continued to function well seven years later.

Breast cancer drop. The number of women in the United States diagnosed with the most common form of breast cancer dropped dramatically from August 2002 to December 2003 (the latest years for which statistics were available), according to a study reported in December 2006. The authors of the study—researchers from the M. D. Anderson Cancer Center in Houston—attributed the drop, the first in breast cancer rates since 1945, to a significant decrease in the number of women using hormone replacement therapy (HRT) to treat the symptoms of menopause. Many women abandoned HRT after a 2002 study by the National Women's Health Initiative as well as a number of other clinical trials found that women who used estrogen and progestin therapy were more likely to develop breast cancer than those who did not.

The Anderson researchers found that the rates of all forms of breast cancer dropped by 7 percent during the period studied. However, rates of estrogen-positive breast cancer, which accounts for 70 percent of all cases of breast cancer in the United States, dropped by 15 percent. The researchers cautioned that additional data from other countries were needed to confirm their results.

Drug errors. At least 1.5 million Americans are sickened, injured, or killed annually by preventable mistakes involving medications. That was the conclusion of a report issued in July by the Institute of Medicine, an advisory organization that is part of the National Academy of Sciences. According to the report, a hospitalized patient in the United States can expect at least one medication error every day, made by physicians, nurses, pharmacists, or patients themselves, and caused by such factors as confusion over drug names and incorrect dosages. Insulin, morphine, potassium chloride, heparin, and warfarin were most commonly linked with errors.

The institute recommended several changes to minimize the risks of medication errors, including the regular use by hospitals of detailed computer records on patient drug use. The institute also recommended that, by 2010, all physicians use electronic prescriptions (e-prescriptions) to prevent errors caused by illegible handwriting. To avoid mistakes made by patients, the report called on the U.S. Food and Drug Administration to improve drug information provided to consumers.

Dementia risk. The leading risk factors for developing dementia are similar to those for cardiovascular disease—obesity, high blood pressure, and elevated cholesterol levels. Investigators at the Aging Research Center at the Karolinska Institute in Stockholm, Sweden, reported in August that having any one of these conditions doubles the risk of developing dementia. Having all three conditions increases the risk six fold. The researchers developed a "risk score" that predicted the occurrence of dementia in a 20-year-study of more than 1,400 people.

■ Alfred J. Smuskiewicz

See also **AIDS; Drugs; Health care issues; Mental health; Public health.**

Mental health. The controversy over whether antidepressant drugs cause suicidal feelings and behavior—particularly in adolescents—continued in 2006. The United States Food and Drug Administration (FDA) had issued such a warning about antidepressants—particularly about 10 newer drugs—in 2004. However, studies of the issue varied in their findings.

Researchers at the FDA analyzed 24 drug trials in which antidepressant drugs were used to treat depression and other psychiatric conditions in 4,582 children and adolescents. Their results, published in March 2006, revealed that the use of antidepressants might have decreased the number of suicides. Researchers at Harvard Medical School and Brigham and Women's Hospital, both in Boston, studied 65,103 patients who had been treated with antidepressants at various times from 1992 to 2003. They reported in January 2006 that the risk of suicide was highest in the month before patients started treatment with antidepressants and that newer antidepressants did not significantly increase the risk of suicide.

However, researchers at the British-based drug company GlaxoSmithKline found an increase in the risk of suicide among 9,000 people who had taken the company's antidepressant drug paroxetine (sold under the brand name Paxil) for a variety of psychiatric conditions. Of some 3,500 people from ages 18 through 30 who took paroxetine for depression, 11 reported attempting suicide.

In December, the FDA published one of the most comprehensive studies to date—a review of 372 studies that examined about 100,000 patients and a dozen antidepressants. It indicated that though suicidal behavior by people taking antidepressants was rare, young adults ages 18 through 24 who took the drugs were more than twice as likely to report a suicide attempt as those who did not take such medications. The FDA proposed adding a warning label to antidepressants for the young adult age group, as well as for adolescents.

Also in 2006, a landmark study conducted by researchers at the University of Texas in Dallas reported in October that two-thirds of people with depression can be helped. However, trying as many as four different antidepressant medications may be necessary.

Social isolation. People in the United States are becoming more socially isolated, according to a June report by sociologists at Duke University in Durham, North Carolina. The team compared the responses of some 1,400 people to questions on the General Social Survey in 2004 with responses from a similar number of people in 1985. The survey, conducted since 1972 by the National Opinion Research Center at the University of Chicago, evaluates social attitudes. The results showed that in 2004, Americans had nearly one-third fewer "close" friends— that is, friends with whom they felt comfortable discussing "important matters"—than they had in 1985. The percentage of Americans saying they had no one with whom to discuss important matters rose from 10 in 1985 to 25 in 2004.

Girls and ADHD. Many teen-age girls with attention-deficit hyperactivity disorder (ADHD) experience serious academic, emotional, and social problems even after the hyperactivity symptoms common in childhood disappear, according to the results of a study published in June 2006. The study was conducted by psychologists at the University of California at Berkeley. ADHD is a behavioral condition in which people—usually boys and young men—have difficulty paying attention or controlling impulses. Few studies had focused on girls with ADHD, however.

Researchers monitored and administered psychological tests to 140 girls between the ages of 6 to 12 with ADHD and 88 without the condition during a summer camp session. When they repeated the process five years later, they found that about two-thirds of the girls with ADHD continued to have learning and social problems with psychiatric symptoms, but only about half still had problems with hyperactivity and impulsiveness. Just as in boys, hyperactivity had decreased and inattention increased with age.   ■ Alfred J. Smuskiewicz

See also **Drugs; Medicine.**

Mexico. Felipe Calderón Hinojosa of the National Action Party (PAN) was sworn in for a six-year term as president of Mexico on Dec. 1, 2006. Calderón succeeded Vicente Fox, also of PAN. Calderón's inauguration was conducted under tight security, with some 100,000 hostile demonstrators filling the streets of Mexico City, the capital, and with tensions running high inside the hall of Congress, where legislators and government officials were assembled for the ceremony. Calderón won the presidency on July 2 in the closest presidential election in Mexican history. According to results certified by the nation's Federal Electoral Tribunal, Calderón carried the election with a plurality of 234,000 votes out of 41.6 million ballots cast.

The election and its contested outcome left Mexicans deeply polarized along class lines. Many supporters of the defeated candidate, Andrés Manuel López Obrador of the Party of the Democratic Revolution (PRD)—a charismatic and popular former mayor of Mexico City, who drew strong support from the lower middle and poorer classes—believed the election was fraudulent.

While officials of the Federal Electoral Tribunal debated through August about allowing recounts, thousands of López Obrador's supporters constructed a makeshift tent city 5 miles (8 kilometers) long in downtown Mexico City, disrupting commerce in the capital. On September 5, the Federal Electoral Tribunal declared Calderón the winner and rejected demands for a full recount. The PRD leaders subsequently formed a shadow government headed by López Obrador. López Obrador's parallel "government," which selected Cabinet members and drew up a budget, ignored Calderón's December inauguration, rejecting its legitimacy.

Oaxaca rebellion. On October 29, President Fox ordered 4,000 federal riot police into the heart of Oaxaca, a picturesque historic city 230 miles (370 kilometers) southeast of Mexico City. The action was in response to a five-month siege of the city's center by protesters with various political agendas, all united in their demand that the Oaxaca state governor be removed.

The crisis began in May with a teacher's strike for better pay and working conditions in the school system of the state of Oaxaca. The situation escalated in June when Oaxaca State Governor Ulises Ruiz Ortiz of the Institutional Revolutionary Party (PRI) deployed police in an unsuccessful attempt to remove the strikers, who had occupied the central plaza in Oaxaca. The strikers' cause soon drew supporters, including leftist political activists, to the city. The protesters formed an alternate government called the People's Assembly of Oaxaca, which seized media and government buildings and demanded the governor's removal from office. The resulting stalemate disrupted commerce and Oaxaca's tourist industry.

The federal forces deployed by President Fox cleared Oaxaca's city center and reinstalled Governor Ruiz who, despite the urging of federal officials, refused to resign. At the end of 2006, the city remained tense and under occupation by federal troops.

Mine disaster. On February 19, 65 miners were killed by an underground gas explosion and the collapse of a tunnel in a coal mine at San Juan de las Sabinas in northern Mexico. Their deaths sparked angry protests over safety regulations at the mine, which critics claimed were inadequate and poorly enforced.

In early March, 250,000 workers carried out wildcat strikes at 70 mining operations in central and northern Mexico. The strikes brought Mexico's mining industry to a standstill for days. Industry observers said that striking workers were protesting government intervention in union affairs as well as the conditions that had led to the February coal mine disaster at San Juan de las Sabinas.

Violence at steel plant. In April, hundreds of federal riot police converged on 2,300 steelworkers, who for three weeks had shut down operations at the Sicartsa steel mill in Lázaro Cárdenas, about 215 miles (346 kilometers) southeast of Mexico City. Three workers were killed in the ensuing violence and dozens more wounded, but the strikers held their ground and the police eventually withdrew.

The strike began with worker demands for the reinstatement of a union leader whom they claimed had been illegally deposed by the federal government. The strike lasted until mid-August, when owners of the steel plant made various concessions to workers, including a 6-percent pay increase.

Antitrust laws. Mexico's Congress voted in April to strengthen the nation's antitrust laws to cope with unprecedented concentrations of economic power. A prime example was the telecommunications conglomerate controlled by Mexico's Carlos Slim Helu—the world's third-richest person according to the March 2006 issue of *Forbes* magazine—who had unsuccessfully lobbied the Mexican Congress to reject the antitrust overhaul.

Through his company Teléfonos de México (TELMEX), Slim controlled 95 percent of all local telephone lines in Mexico. In April, he added to his communications empire telephone companies in the Dominican Republic, Puerto Rico, and Venezuela. After the acquisition, Slim's subsidiary company, América Móvil, provided cellular phone service to 120 million subscribers in 16 countries.

■ Nathan A. Haverstock

See also **Latin America: A Special Report.**

Micronesia, Federated States of.

See **Pacific Islands.**

Supporters of presidential candidate Andrés Manuel López Obrador mass in Mexico City's central plaza in July 2006 to demand a recount of votes cast in Mexico's July 2 presidential election. A court later rejected a recount.

MIDDLE EAST

Four major conflicts raged in the Middle East in 2006. Two of the conflicts continued at year's end—the war in Iraq and the conflict between government forces and rebels in Sudan's Darfur region. Fighting also erupted in the Gaza Strip between Palestinian militants and Israeli forces, and along the Lebanese-Israeli border between Israel and Hezbollah.

War in Iraq. In the war in Iraq, which began when United States-led forces invaded the country in March 2003 to topple Iraqi President Saddam Hussein, insurgency attacks against coalition troops increased in 2006, with sectarian violence between Sunni and Shi`ah Muslims intensifying. These two rival Islamic sects settled scores with bombings in markets and crowded streets and even attacks on each other's mosques.

On June 7, a U.S. airstrike killed Abu Musab al-Zarqawi, the leader of the Iraqi branch of the Islamic terrorist network al-Qa`ida. The killing, however, had little impact on reducing the violence in Iraq. Experts on Iraqi affairs agreed that the vast majority of Iraqi insurgents were not led by al-Qa`ida but by the military and intelligence network of deposed President Hussein's Baath Party. By December 31, the number of U.S. troops killed in Iraq since the beginning of the war totaled at least 3,002. Civilian deaths among Iraqis were estimated at as many as 56,000 by the Iraq Body Count project, an independent group of scholars in the United Kingdom.

Meeting in Amman. United States President George W. Bush met with Iraqi Prime Minister Nouri Kamel al-Maliki on November 30 in Amman, the capital of Jordan. President Bush reassured the prime minister that he would not pull U.S. troops out of Iraq "until the job is complete." Also during November, the United Nations (UN) Security Council extended the presence of the multinational force in Iraq until the end of 2007.

The Iraq Study Group Report was published in December 2006 after nine months of work by a *bipartisan* (both parties) team headed by former U.S. Secretary of State James A. Baker III (a Republican) and former Congressman Lee H. Hamilton (a Democrat from Indiana). "The situation in Iraq is grave and deteriorating," concluded the authors of the report, which included a number of recommendations on how the United States should handle the growing Iraqi insurgency. The recommendations included launching a diplomatic initiative to involve Iraq's neighbors and key states outside the region in achieving stability in Iraq. The report called for constructive engagement with Iran and Syria because of the ability of these nations "to influence events within Iraq."

The Iraq Study Group Report advised the Bush administration to promote the transfer of more power to the Iraqi army and security forces by speeding up their training. The report's recommendations set a number of landmark goals for Iraq to achieve with respect to national reconciliation, security, and governance. It concluded with a proposal for a substantial "redeployment" of U.S. troops out of Iraq by 2008.

Leadership change in Israel. After Israeli Prime Minister Ariel Sharon suffered a massive stroke in January 2006, Ehud Olmert, his deputy, became acting prime minister and led the centrist Kadima Party in parliamentary elections in March. In the elections, Kadima won 29 seats in the Israeli Knesset (parliament)—more than any other political party—putting Olmert in a position to become prime minister in his own right.

On May 1, Olmert formed a coalition Cabinet composed of ministers from Kadima and three other political parties—Labor, the ultra-Orthodox Shas, and the Pensioner's Party. In October, Prime Minister Olmert added the Russian immigrant party Yisrael Beitenu to his coalition, thereby increasing his majority in the Knesset to 78 out of a total of 120 members.

Gaza conflict. A truce reached in February 2005 between the Palestinians and Israelis broke down in June 2006, when renewed conflict erupted in the Gaza Strip between Palestinian militants and Israeli forces. The conflict intensified after the military wing of Hamas, the governing party in the Palestinian government, conducted a well-organized raid into Israel from Gaza on June 25. During the raid, an Israeli soldier was kidnapped and two others were killed.

The conflict continued unabated until the two sides reached a truce on November 26. However, all attempts to obtain the release of the captured Israeli soldier failed. Hamas demanded in exchange the release of Palestinian prisoners, a condition unacceptable to Israel.

Hamas-Fatah rivalry. On December 14, a gun battle between Hamas militants and guards loyal to the Fatah movement, a rival of Hamas, claimed a bodyguard of Ismail Haniyeh, the prime minister of the Hamas-led government. The battle erupted as a convoy carrying Haniyeh entered Gaza from Egypt. Israeli Defense Minister Amir Peretz had ordered that the convoy be stopped to prevent Prime Minister Haniyeh from bringing in millions of dollars of donations he had collected in Muslim countries.

This incident highlighted the intensifying rivalry between Hamas and Fatah, which escalated throughout the year. Fatah continued to vie for power after Hamas won parliamentary elections in January, thus ending Fatah's rule of the Palestinian government. Palestinian President Mahmoud Abbas, a member of Fatah, was seen by most observers as more willing to negotiate with Israel than the hard-line Hamas leaders. Unlike Hamas, Fatah recognized Israel's right to exist.

On December 16—in what was seen by most political observers as a daring challenge to Hamas—President Abbas called for new parliamentary elections. The elections would be held as early as June 2007. According to many observers, Abbas made the call because of mounting frustration at the political deadlock that characterized the power-sharing arrangement between Fatah and Hamas.

Hezbollah-Israel conflict. Lebanese fighters with Hezbollah, a militant group backed by Syria and Iran, provoked a war with Israel when they crossed the "blue line" marking the Lebanese-Israeli border on July 12, 2006. The Hezbollah militants kidnapped two Israeli soldiers and killed eight others. In retaliation, Israel attacked the strongholds of Hezbollah in southern Lebanon and the southern suburbs of Beirut, the Lebanese capital, as well as bridges throughout Lebanon. Israeli aerial bombardments hit a total of 350 villages, towns, and cities in Lebanon. However, the massive Israeli offensive did not deter Hezbollah from firing more than 4,000 Katyusha rockets into northern Israel.

The war, which lasted 34 days, resulted in the deaths of approximately 140 Israelis and the wounding of more than 1,000 others. The estimated casualties among the Lebanese were more than 1,100 killed and at least 8,000 others wounded. The conflict cost the Lebanese economy more than $15 billion.

The war stopped on August 14 with the implementation of UN Security Council Resolution 1701. The resolution called for the deployment of 15,000 soldiers of the Lebanese army to maintain order in southern Lebanon. These soldiers were to be assisted by an expanded UN Interim Force in Lebanon consisting of approximately 15,000 soldiers.

The deployment of these forces between the Litani River in Lebanon and the Lebanese-Israeli border cleared the region of Hezbollah fighters, pacifying the Lebanon-Israel border for the first time in four decades. The deployment also eliminated the military threat posed by Hezbollah to residents of northern Israel.

Syrian influence in Lebanon. In November, Hezbollah (with its pro-Syria allies) unsuccessfully attempted to enlarge its proportion of seats in the Lebanese Cabinet to more than one-third of the 24 members required to have veto power. Following this defeat, Hezbollah ministers and their allies resigned from the Cabinet in protest.

This move did not prevent Prime Minister Fouad Siniora from holding a Cabinet meeting on November 13 to approve the blueprint for a UN-established international tribunal to prosecute the perpetrators of the February 2005 assassination of former Lebanese Prime Minister Rafik Hariri. The UN tribunal was also charged with investigating many other terrorist operations in Lebanon. The Syrian regime of Bashar al-Assad was the main target of the UN investigation.

On Nov. 21, 2006, Pierre Gemayel, a Lebanese Cabinet minister and son of former Lebanese President Amin Gemayel, was assassinated in Beirut. Pierre Gemayel was a prominent opponent of Syria's domination of Lebanon. Many Lebanese politicians and Middle East analysts accused Syria of ordering the assassination.

In December, Hezbollah and its allies staged huge rallies in downtown Beirut to call for the toppling of the democratically elected government of Lebanon. According to many Middle East analysts, however, the government retained the support of many Lebanese.

Conflict in Darfur. In May 2006, representatives of Sudan's government and the Sudan Liberation Movement (SLM), the largest rebel group in Darfur, signed the Darfur Peace Agreement in Abuja, the capital of Nigeria. Olusegun Obasanjo, the president of Nigeria and chairman of the African Union—an organization working for cooperation among African nations—mediated the agreement. Darfur is a region in western Sudan where fighting between government forces and various rebel groups began in 2003.

Other rebel organizations, including a breakaway faction of the SLM and the Justice and Equality Movement, refused to sign the agreement. They claimed that the agreement did not recognize the political, economic, and cultural rights of the people of Darfur.

In July, an Israeli police officer stands guard as firefighters put out a blaze in northern Israel caused by the strike of a missile launched by Lebanese fighters with Hezbollah. Renewed fighting between Israel and Hezbollah began on July 12, when Hezbollah fighters crossed into Israel from Lebanon, kidnapping two Israeli soldiers and killing a number of others.

A 34-day conflict between Israel and Hezbollah militants in July and August 2006 ended in a stalemate.

A Lebanese woman mourns the destruction on August 1 of her home in a suburb south of Beirut, the capital. Israeli aerial bombardments pounded the area in an attempt to root out Hezbollah militants. The month-long war between Israel and Hezbollah ended with United Nations peacekeeping troops stationed in southern Lebanon.

Hezbollah militants in Tyre, Lebanon, launch a Katyusha rocket aimed for northern Israel. Hezbollah launched thousands of Katyusha and other rockets on northern Israel during the 34-day conflict, killing at least 40 civilians. Israeli air attacks killed more than 1,000 Lebanese civilians.

FACTS IN BRIEF ON MIDDLE EASTERN COUNTRIES

Country	Population	Government	Monetary unit*	Foreign trade (million U.S.$) Exports[†]	Imports[†]
Bahrain	714,000	King Hamad bin Isa Al-Khalifa; Prime Minister Khalifa bin Salman Al-Khalifa	dinar (0.38 = $1)	11,170	8,830
Cyprus	806,000	President Tassos Papadopoulos; (Turkish Republic of Northern Cyprus: President Mehmet Ali Talat)	pound (0.46 = $1)	1,927	5,967
Egypt	76,346,000	President Mohammed Hosni Mubarak; Prime Minister Ahmed Nazif	pound (5.74 = $1)	14,330	24,100
Iran	68,899,000	Supreme Leader Ayatollah Ali Khamenei; President Mahmoud Ahmadinejad	rial (9,159.00 = $1)	55,420	42,500
Iraq	27,253,000	President Jalal Talabani; Prime Minister Nouri Kamel al-Maliki	new dinar (1,471.63 = $1)	17,780	19,570
Israel	6,797,000	President Moshe Katzav; Prime Minister Ehud Olmert	new shekel (4.26 = $1)	40,140	43,190
Jordan	5,870,000	King Abdullah II; Prime Minister Marouf al-Bakhit	dinar (0.71 = $1)	4,226	8,681
Kuwait	2,740,000	Emir Sabah al-Ahmad al-Jabir al-Sabah; Prime Minister Nasser Muhammad al-Ahmad al-Sabah	dinar (0.29 = $1)	44,430	12,230
Lebanon	3,808,000	President Emile Lahoud; Prime Minister Fouad Siniora	pound (1,512.25 = $1)	1,782	8,855
Oman	2,826,000	Sultan and Prime Minister Qaboos bin Said	rial (0.39 = $1)	19,010	8,709
Qatar	636,000	Emir Hamad bin Khalifa al-Thani; Prime Minister Abdallah bin Khalifa al-Thani	riyal (3.64 = $1)	24,900	6,706
Saudi Arabia	26,292,000	King and Prime Minister Abdullah ibn Abd al-Aziz Al Saud	riyal (3.75 = $1)	165,000	44,930
Sudan	35,667,000	President Umar Hassan Ahmad al-Bashir	dinar (207.87 = $1)	6,989	5,028
Syria	19,064,000	President Bashar al-Assad; Prime Minister Mohammed Naji al-Otari	pound (52.21 = $1)	6,344	5,973
Turkey	74,204,000	President Ahmet Necdet Sezer; Prime Minister Recep Tayyip Erdogan	new lira (1.49 = $1)	72,490	101,200
United Arab Emirates	4,318,000	President Khalifa bin Zayed al-Nahyan; Prime Minister Mohammad bin Rashid al-Maktum	dirham (3.67 = $1)	103,100	60,150
Yemen	21,426,000	President Ali Abdullah Saleh; Prime Minister Abd al-Qadir Ba Jamal	rial (197.78 = $1)	6,387	4,190

*Exchange rates as of Oct. 9, 2006.   [†]Latest available data.

Iran's nuclear ambitions. The Iranian government ignored a deadline of Aug. 31, 2006, established by the UN Security Council, to halt its uranium enrichment program. Uranium enrichment is a process that can be used to produce fuel for civilian nuclear reactors or for nuclear weapons. Iran's President Mahmoud Ahmadinejad denied that Iran was pursuing a nuclear weapons program. At the same time, he maintained that Iran had a right to develop nuclear energy for peaceful purposes.

In late December, France, Germany, the United Kingdom, and the United States reached an agreement with Russia and China on a UN Security Council resolution to impose sanctions on Iran. The resolution banned any effort to supply Iran with materials and technology that could contribute to its nuclear program.   ■ Marius Deeb

See also **Africa; Armed forces; Iran; Iraq; Israel; Lebanon; People in the news** (Nouri Kamel al-Maliki); **Sudan; Syria; Terrorism; United Nations; United States, Government of the;** various Middle East country articles.

Mining. See **Energy supply.**

Moldova. Leaders of Moldova's separatist, pro-Russia Trans-Dniester region held an independence referendum on Sept. 17, 2006. Election officials reported that an overwhelming 97.1 percent of Trans-Dniestrian voters favored the region's independence and eventual unification with Russia, and 94.6 percent of voters disapproved of reuniting with Moldova. Moldovan President Vladimir Voronin rejected the referendum results, but the Russian government called for the results to be respected.

The referendum followed increasing tensions between the Moldovan government and the Trans-Dniestrian leadership. On March 3, the government of Ukraine introduced new customs rules requiring that goods shipped from Trans-Dniester be cleared by Moldovan customs authorities. Russia's government then banned wine imports from Moldova and Georgia on March 27, dealing a significant blow to the Moldovan economy. Moldova and Georgia have stronger ties with the West than with Russia.

On March 30, the Organisation for Security and Co-operation in Europe indefinitely suspended reconciliation talks between Trans-Dniester and Moldova. The following day, Trans-Dniestrian leaders announced plans for the controversial referendum. ◼ Juliet Johnson

See also **Europe**.

Monaco. See Europe.

Mongolia. See Asia.

Montenegro. In a May 2006 referendum endorsed by the European Union (EU), a majority of Montenegrins voted for independence. On June 3, Montenegro's parliament formally declared independence, dissolving the country's union with Serbia. The Serbian government promptly endorsed Montenegro's independence, and on June 28, the United Nations admitted Montenegro to the world body as the 192nd member nation.

Independence was the culmination of a movement that began in the 1990's, when Yugoslavia began breaking apart. By 1995, Yugoslavia was comprised only of Serbia and Montenegro. Montenegro's leaders sought to distance themselves from the controversial policies of Serbian leaders but remained in the Serbian-dominated union. Under EU pressure, Montenegro agreed in 2003 to remain in a unified state renamed Serbia and Montenegro until 2006. When that agreement expired, Montenegrin leaders acted quickly to end the union.

Economists rated Montenegro as one of the poorest parts of the former Yugoslavia. Unemployment in 2006 hovered around 28 percent. At the same time, the country experienced a boom in property values, as developers rushed to invest in Montenegro's scenic Adriatic coast for resort development. ◼ Sharon L. Wolchik

See also **Europe; Serbia**.

Montenegrins celebrate national independence from Serbia in Podgorica, Montenegro's capital, upon receiving news that the number of "yes" votes counted in the May 21, 2006, referendum exceeded the 55-percent threshold requirement.

Montreal in 2006 staged the First World Outgames from July 29 to August 5, the city's biggest sporting event and gathering of athletes since the 1976 Summer Olympics. The Outgames took place one week after the Gay Games VII, held in Chicago. The $17-million (all amounts are in Canadian dollars) event attracted more than half a million people to the sport competitions and cultural activities, which included an international conference on lesbian, gay, bisexual, and transgender human rights. Nearly 19,000 people from 111 countries took part as competitors, delegates, or volunteers. Montreal had originally won the right to host the 2006 Gay Games, but a disagreement in 2003 between the local organizers and the Federation of Gay Games resulted in the event being moved to Chicago. Organizers then formed the Gay and Lesbian International Sporting Association to stage the alternative competition in Montreal. The Outgames were to move to Copenhagen, Denmark, in 2009.

Loto-Québec complex. A nearly $1.2-billion project to build a casino and entertainment complex along the St. Lawrence River—announced jointly in 2005 by Loto-Québec, the provincial government agency responsible for lotteries and gaming, and international entertainment giant Cirque du Soleil, Inc.—was abandoned in March 2006. The March 9 release of a government-commissioned feasibility report raised many questions that led Cirque to back out of the deal. Loto-Québec dropped out shortly thereafter, explaining that it needed the presence of the performance empire to make the project work.

New sports facility. Another project originally destined for the same south-central area of the city—a $15-million, 13,500-seat stadium—had a change of venue, to Olympic Park, in the shadow of Olympic Stadium. Montreal's family-owned Saputo Inc., Canada's largest dairy processor and one of North America's biggest cheese producers, promised to donate half the cost, with the remainder coming from the private sector. The project, to be called Complexe Place du Public, will serve as home field for the Montreal Impact of the United Soccer League First Division. It will include the stadium, which will be capable of expanding to 18,000 seats; practice fields; and two indoor soccer facilities. The project was expected to open in 2007.

1976 Olympics paid off. On June 30, 2006, the $1.5-billion bill for the Montreal Olympics was finally paid off through a special tax on tobacco instituted in 1976. The final price tag for the facilities reached almost $2.3 billion, including interest (all amounts in Canadian dollars). Instead of abolishing the tax, the provincial finance minister said in presenting the 2006-2007 budget on March 23, 2006, that the tax would

continue. The additional income will be used to create a new fund with a $30-million annual budget to build and maintain such sports facilities as swimming pools, soccer fields, and gymnasiums.

Crime. Montreal's third fatal post-secondary school shooting in 17 years occurred on Sept. 13, 2006, when a lone gunman, Kimveer Gill, opened fire on the Dawson College campus. An 18-year-old female student was killed and 20 others were injured before the gunman took his own life. Gill had no apparent affiliation with the community college—the largest community college in Québec—or with any of its 10,000 students.

Vito Rizzuto, reputed godfather of the most powerful Mafia organization in Canada, was extradited to New York City on August 17. Rizzuto had fought the move since his January 2004 arrest at the request of the United States government on charges of racketeering. He was wanted in connection with the 1981 gangland slaying of three Mafia captains linked to the Bonnano crime family of New York City. Rizzuto lost his final appeal when the Supreme Court of Canada refused to hear his challenges of decisions by lower-court judges, and the federal justice minister ordered him to be removed to New York City.

■ Mike King

See also **Canada; Canadian provinces.**

Morocco. See **Middle East.**

Motion pictures. Film fare for 2006 began with a whimper but went out with a bang. One of the year's most anticipated films, Martin Scorsese's *The Departed,* released in the fall, generally lived up to its hype. A bloody yet perversely funny portrait of Boston gangland warfare, the film earned the director his best reviews since 1990's *GoodFellas.* Scorsese's excursions into such period films as 1997's *Kundun,* 2002's *Gangs of New York,* and 2004's *The Aviator* had drawn measured praise, but some critics placed *The Departed* near the level of the Scorsese classic *Raging Bull* (1980). *The Departed* also earned kudos for Matt Damon and Leonardo DiCaprio as two gang infiltrators on opposing sides of the law. Jack Nicholson, as a vicious gang boss, gave a bravado "mad dog" performance, and Mark Wahlberg showed unexpected flair as a snarling, sarcastic law enforcer.

Fall release causes sensation. *Borat: Cultural Learnings of America for Make Benefit Glorious Nation of Kazakhstan,* a satirical "mockumentary," follows the adventures of naive, vulgar, and overzealous (but fictitious) Kazakhstani TV reporter Borat Sagdiyev (British comedian Sacha Baron Cohen), who is dispatched to the United States to report on a country he knows about only through television. The 2006 film, which includes interviews with real people who are not in on the joke, caused an uproar for its depiction of Americans.

Big acclaim for two "little" films. *Little Miss Sunshine* was foremost among smaller films winning endorsements from critics and audiences in 2006. Codirected by husband-and-wife team Jonathan Dayton and Valerie Faris, the film featured Greg Kinnear, Toni Collette, Steve Carell, and Alan Arkin in a wryly observant comedy about a dysfunctional family whose preteen daughter becomes an unlikely talent-show contestant.

Little Children, released later in the year, was acclaimed for its satiric examination of suburban life. Directed by Todd Field, the film focuses on a group of adulterous young married couples who fear for their children's safety when a pedophile moves into the neighborhood.

Raising the flag. Another widely anticipated film, Clint Eastwood's *Flags of Our Fathers,* which re-creates World War II's (1939-1945) climactic battle of Iwo Jima, also drew largely solid endorsements. The film looks at the story behind the famous photo of the six men who raised the American flag at Iwo Jima, emphasizing the youthfulness of the men and the tragic toll the fierce combat took even on its survivors. The 76-year-old Eastwood also filmed *Letters from Iwo Jima,* a Japanese-language film that re-creates the battle from a Japanese perspective and was scheduled for release early in 2007.

Kings, queens, and superheroes. Helen Mirren and Forest Whitaker won praise in 2006 for their portrayals of contemporary historical figures. *The Queen*, featuring Mirren as Queen Elizabeth II, focuses on the monarch's conflicts with British Prime Minister Tony Blair in the days following the automobile accident that killed her ex-daughter-in-law, Diana, Princess of Wales. Whitaker's performance as Ugandan dictator Idi Amin in *The Last King of Scotland* was noted for the way the actor captured the dictator's ferocity as well as his sense of showmanship. Ben Affleck earned strong reviews as George Reeves, TV's "Superman," in *Hollywoodland*, which questions Reeves's alleged 1959 suicide.

Other treatments of real-life personalities and historical figures had less positive receptions in 2006. Sofia Coppola's lavish film biography of *Marie Antoinette* received wildly mixed reactions from critics and audiences. With a rock music score, the film concentrates on the doomed queen's early years as a frivolous society figure, with few hints of her eventual demise at the guillotine. Kirsten Dunst's performance in the title role earned both mild praise and critical indignation, particularly in France. The title of Steven Shainberg's *Fur: An Imaginary Portrait of Diane Arbus* more than suggested that the film would not present a realistic portrait of the iconic, suicidal photographer. Public response was largely indifferent to both the film and Nicole Kidman's performance as the troubled artist.

On a commercial level, *Pirates of the Caribbean 2: Dead Man's Chest* became the third film in history to reach a $1-billion worldwide gross, trailing 1997's *Titanic* and 2003's *The Lord of the Rings: The Return of the King*. The 2006 pirate sequel, in which Johnny Depp reprised his wildly popular role as Captain Jack Sparrow, benefited from residual fervor from the initial installment, 2003's *Pirates of the Caribbean: The Curse of the*

ACADEMY AWARD WINNERS IN 2006

The following winners of the 2005 Academy Awards were announced in March 2006:

Best Picture, *Crash*

Best Actor, Philip Seymour Hoffman, *Capote*

Best Actress, Reese Witherspoon, *Walk the Line*

Best Supporting Actor, George Clooney, *Syriana*

Best Supporting Actress, Rachel Weisz, *The Constant Gardener*

Best Director, Ang Lee, *Brokeback Mountain*

Best Original Screenplay, Paul Haggis and Bobby Moresco, *Crash*

Best Screenplay Adaptation, Larry McMurtry and Diana Ossana, *Brokeback Mountain*

Best Animated Feature, Nick Park and Steve Box, *Wallace & Gromit in the Curse of the Were-Rabbit*

Best Cinematography, Dion Beebe, *Memoirs of a Geisha*

Best Film Editing, Hughes Winborne, *Crash*

Best Original Score, Gustavo Santaolalla, *Brokeback Mountain*

Best Original Song, Jordan Houston, Cedric Coleman, and Paul Beauregard, "It's Hard Out Here for a Pimp" from *Hustle & Flow*

Best Foreign-Language Film, *Tsotsi* (South Africa)

Best Art Direction, John Myhre and Gretchen Rau, *Memoirs of a Geisha*

Best Costume Design, Colleen Atwood, *Memoirs of a Geisha*

Best Sound Mixing, Christopher Boyes, Michael Semanick, Michael Hedges, and Hammond Peek, *King Kong*

Best Sound Editing, Mike Hopkins and Ethan Van der Ryn, *King Kong*

Best Makeup, Howard Berger and Tami Lane, *The Chronicles of Narnia: The Lion, the Witch and the Wardrobe*

Best Visual Effects, *King Kong*

Best Animated Short Film, *The Moon and the Son: An Imagined Conversation*

Best Live-Action Short Film, *Six Shooter*

Best Feature Documentary, *March of the Penguins*

Best Short Subject Documentary, *A Note of Triumph: The Golden Age of Norman Corwin*

Joaquin Phoenix and Reese Witherspoon portray country music stars Johnny and June Carter Cash in James Mangold's *Walk the Line.* Witherspoon received the Academy Award for best actress for her performance.

Biographical films again won Academy Awards in 2006. A film about a deep love between two cowboys garnered praise and Oscars.

Philip Seymour Hoffman won the Academy Award for best actor for his uncanny portrayal of author Truman Capote in Bennett Miller's *Capote*. The film traces Capote's self-destruction as he researched and wrote the true-crime classic *In Cold Blood (1966)*, as well as his relationship with one of the condemned killers.

Thandie Newton and Matt Dillon starred in *Crash*, which examines the impact of racism in the interconnected stories of people from different racial, social, and economic backgrounds living in Los Angeles. The film won three Oscars, including one for best picture.

Jake Gyllenhaal (left) and Heath Ledger (right) starred as two cowboys whose love for each other endures through several decades in Ang Lee's *Brokeback Mountain*. The film won three Academy Awards, including best director for Lee.

Black Pearl. Critics and many moviegoers felt the sequel lacked the novelty of the original, but its spectacular visual effects lured ticket buyers.

The effects-laden seafaring adventure helped push the 2006 summer box-office tally to $3.4 billion, an improvement over 2005's $3.2-billion haul. Other buoyant 2006 summer box-office winners included *The Da Vinci Code*, starring Tom Hanks in a critically snubbed adaptation of Dan Brown's controversial best-selling novel, and *X-Men: The Last Stand*, allegedly the final installment in the successful franchise. TV's "Friends" star Jennifer Aniston enjoyed her first genuine box-office success with *The Break-Up*, and Meryl Streep had a substantial hit playing a comic villainess in *The Devil Wears Prada*. Streep also gave a tour-de-force performance in 2006 as half of a country-singing sister act with Lily Tomlin in Robert Altman's *A Prairie Home Companion*. Based on the long-running radio show hosted by Garrison Keillor, the film is a whimsical, reflective piece that the outspoken director described as "about death." Just months after the film's summer release, Altman died of cancer in November at 81.

Following the commercial success of 2004's biblical drama *The Passion of the Christ*, Mel Gibson in 2006 directed another controversial film, the highly violent *Apocalypto*. A critical and popular success, *Apocalypto* depicts the ancient Maya empire in decline. As dialogue in *The Passion of the Christ* was notable for being in Aramaic and Latin, the dialogue in *Apocalypto* is in a Maya dialect. Before the film's fall release, the director faced public scrutiny after making anti-Semitic remarks to a police officer following an arrest for drunken driving in Malibu, California.

Remakes and flops. Among the year's flops were two needless remakes of earlier successes, *All the King's Men* and *The Poseidon Adventure*. The former was a particularly glaring failure, considering its pedigreed cast headed by Sean Penn, Anthony Hopkins, Kate Winslet, and Jude Law. *Miami Vice*, a reimagining of the popular 1980's television series, and *The Black Dahlia*, a reinvestigation of the notorious 1947 Hollywood murder of an aspiring starlet, also proved disappointing.

007 in 2006. Much interest centered on the casting of Daniel Craig as the sixth actor to play Agent 007 James Bond in the year-end release of *Casino Royale*. Based on Ian Fleming's first Bond novel, the film introduces Bond before he holds his license to kill. The Fleming novel is given a contemporary twist in the new film as Agent 007, in his first mission, must stop a banker from winning a casino tournament in Montenegro and using the prize money to fund terrorist activities. Unlike such suave predecessors in the Agent 007 role as Sean Connery, Roger Moore, and Pierce Brosnan, Craig was noted for his wiry appearance and edgy

screen persona. The "blond Bond" won over critics and proved highly popular with audiences.

9/11: Five years later. Filmmakers in 2006 took note of the fifth anniversary of the Sept. 11, 2001, terrorist attacks on the United States. The often-controversial Oliver Stone directed in 2006 the reverent *World Trade Center*, which salutes efforts to rescue two New York City police officers buried beneath the Twin Towers' rubble. British director Paul Greengrass's *United 93* received favorable reviews for its documentary-style account of the hijacked flight that crashed in a field near Shanksville, Pennsylvania. Danny Leiner's *The Great New Wonderful* also won praise for its interlocking stories of various New Yorkers in the aftermath of the 9/11 attacks.

Documentaries. The recent popularity of documentaries continued in 2006 with *An Inconvenient Truth*, former U.S. Vice President Al Gore's investigation into global warming; *Shut Up & Sing*, which focuses on the repercussions of the popular American country singing group the Dixie Chicks in the wake of the lead singer's statements critical of U.S. President George W. Bush; *Sketches of Frank Gehry,* Sydney Pollack's take on the unconventional American architect; and *Who Killed the Electric Car?,* a timely pondering on the role of politics and big business in the fate of this once-promising mode of transportation.

Foreign films. Spain's Pedro Almodóvar remained a fixture in U.S. art houses. The director's *Volver*, starring Penélope Cruz and Carmen Maura in a tale of a dead mother's reappearance to help solve her daughters' problems, was one of the year's most eagerly awaited imports. The German thriller *Perfume: The Story of a Murderer*, starring Dustin Hoffman and Alan Rickman and based on an international best seller, proved to be a huge hit in its native land and was expected to be an art-house magnet in the United States.

Local hits. American films continued to post strong overseas grosses in 2006, with both *Superman Returns* and *World Trade Center* winning larger audiences in countries outside the United States. However, locally produced efforts found increasing favor in their native lands. For the first time in 21 years, Japanese films accounted for more than half of that country's box-office tally, with the thriller *Limit of Love: Umizaru* among the champions. *Tied Hands*, an Israeli film about the effect of AIDS on one family, earned favor with Israeli audiences and critics.

The Yacoubian Building, with a $4-million budget that made it the most expensive feature in the history of Egyptian filmmaking, became a local smash. It focuses on the experiences of an eclectic group of individuals living on the same block in contemporary Cairo.

In Australia, several films earned strong box-office status. *Kokoda* relates the experiences of Australian soldiers in New Guinea during World War II (1939-1945), and *Ten Canoes*, a comedy of Aboriginal life, was widely praised by critics and audiences. *Ten Canoes* also seemed destined for wide release outside Australia. *Kenny*, a comedy about a naïve man who runs a portable toilet company, was a surprise smash hit in Australia.

Cruise control. In August, actor Tom Cruise was dropped from his 14-year contract with Paramount Pictures, where executives cited Cruise's bizarre public conduct as the reason. In November, Cruise and his producing partner, Paula Wagner, took over United Artists, a studio founded in 1919 by Charlie Chaplin, Douglas Fairbanks, Sr., Mary Pickford, and D. W. Griffith. ◼ Philip Wuntch

See also **People in the news** (George Clooney; Philip Seymour Hoffman; Reese Witherspoon).

Mozambique. See Africa.

Myanmar.
On Oct. 10, 2006, the army generals who had ruled Myanmar without a constitution since 1988, reconvened the convention charged with writing an organizing statement for the country. They refused, however, to release from house arrest the leader of the National League for Democracy (NLD), Aung San Suu Kyi, who won the 1991 Nobel Peace Prize for her struggle to achieve democracy in Myanmar. The NLD swept the last free elections in 1990, but the generals refused to turn over power until the constitutional convention that had been sitting sporadically since 1993 prepared a document guaranteeing continued military control. The NLD

boycotted the 2006 convention because of Suu Kyi's detention.

Razali Ismail, a Malaysian diplomat assigned by the United Nations (UN) to implement Myanmar's move toward constitutional democracy, resigned in frustration on Jan. 8, 2006. In May and November, UN Undersecretary General for Political Affairs Ibrahim Gambari met with Myanmar's top leaders to discuss the country's political situation, but no major breakthroughs were forthcoming. Myanmar continued throughout 2006 to refuse to allow UN human rights envoys to enter the country. ◼ Henry S. Bradsher

See also **Asia**.

Namibia. See Africa.
Nauru. See Pacific Islands.

Military personnel parade through Myanmar's new administrative capital, Naypyidaw Myodaw, in March 2006. The parade was the first official ceremony in the new capital after military rulers began moving ministries from the previous capital, Yangon, in 2005.

Nepal. In April 2006, after 19 days of demonstrations during which police killed at least 19 people, King Gyanendra Bir Bikram Shah Dev of Nepal gave up the absolute power that he had seized 15 months earlier. Political parties and Maoist rebels began discussions toward establishing a new form of government in the Himalayan nation. When he declared a state of emergency on Feb. 1, 2005, Gyanendra had accused the government of not dealing effectively with the rebels. In November 2006, the rebels and government officials signed a peace deal, ending the civil war that had resulted in the deaths of some 13,000 people since 1996.

Unrest. Seeking public endorsement of his control, the king held municipal elections on Feb. 8, 2006. Both the Maoists and an alliance of seven opposition parties urged people not to vote, and fewer than 20 percent of voters turned out. As sporadic clashes between the army and the Maoists continued in the countryside, the alliance and Maoists launched urban demonstrations demanding an end to absolute monarchy.

As the demonstrations became increasingly violent, the army decided it was unwilling to support police in crushing the protests. It asked the political parties to form a new government. Left powerless, Gyanendra on April 24 restored the parliament that he had dissolved in 2002.

New government. In early May 2006, the Maoists announced a cease-fire in the civil war, and in June they joined an interim government with the seven-party alliance. The head of the Nepali Congress Party, 84-year-old Girija Prasad Koirala, became prime minister of the new government.

In mid-May, parliament voted unanimously to end the king's command of the army, his legal immunity, and his exemption from taxes. Parliament also ended the status of Nepal as the world's only officially Hindu country. The contentious issue of whether Nepal should become a republic without a king, as the Maoists wanted, or remain a constitutional monarchy was pushed into the future. Plans were made to elect an assembly to draft a new constitution that would decide such questions.

On November 16, Maoist leaders and government officials signed an agreement under which an estimated 30,000 Maoist soldiers were to be confined to *cantonments* (temporary quarters for troops), with an equal number of army troops confined to barracks. On November 21, Maoist leaders and government officials signed a peace deal, which ended the civil war, put Maoist weapons under United Nations control, and brought the Maoists into Nepal's political system.

Economics. Nepal struggled economically during 2006, partially due to political upheaval. The World Bank, a United Nations affiliate, threatened in September to withhold some aid unless reforms were adopted. ■ Henry S. Bradsher

See also **Asia.**

Prodemocracy protesters flee from police in Kathmandu, Nepal's capital, on April 22, 2006. After 19 days of demonstrations, King Gyanendra Bir Bikram Shah Dev restored the parliament he had dissolved in 2002. A new government was formed in May 2006.

Netherlands. The government of Prime Minister Jan Peter Balkenende's center-right Christian Democratic Alliance (CDA) collapsed in June 2006. The coalition—made up of Balkenende's Christian Democratic Party, the Liberal Party, and Democracy 66 (D66)—broke apart when the three D66 members resigned on June 29, following a disagreement over immigration policy. On July 7, Queen Beatrix installed a temporary minority government—consisting of the remaining two parties under the leadership of Balkenende—to govern until early elections in November.

Although the opposition center-left Labor Party had made gains in local elections in March, the country's improved economic performance and gaffes by Labor Party leader Wouter Bos during the campaign caused the Christian Democrats to emerge again as the strongest party and to gain the responsibility of forming a new government. Balkenende led a caretaker government as he attempted to form a new governing coalition.

Immigration and Islam. The Dutch continued in 2006 to struggle with issues surrounding Muslim immigration. Such issues had risen to the forefront in 2004, after Theo van Gogh, the maker of a film critical of the treatment of women in Muslim communities, was murdered by an Islamic radical with dual Dutch-Moroccan citizenship. In May 2006, popular Muslim parliamentarian Ayaan Hirsi Ali resigned from her post after Immigration Minister Rita Verdonk threatened to revoke Hirsi Ali's passport for lying on an application for asylum in 1992. Hirsi Ali, a Somali immigrant who wrote the screenplay for van Gogh's film, had been living under police protection because of threats to her life from Islamic radicals. Members of D66 resigned their government posts to protest Verdonk's handling of the matter. Hirsi Ali moved to the United States.

In November 2006, the newly elected parliament ordered the Dutch Cabinet to pardon thousands of asylum seekers who had remained in the Netherlands—some for as many as ten years—after their asylum appeal had failed. The Balkenende government had ordered the deportation of 26,000 such failed asylum seekers. Verdonk refused to comply with the parliament's decision, and her Liberal Party threatened to quit the government if the parliament censured her. In December, Balkenende stripped Verdonk of her immigration portfolio and froze the deportations to avert another government crisis.

The Dutch economy grew by 3 percent in 2006, according to estimates by European Union economists, much better than expected. Unemployment fell to 3.9 percent from 4.7 percent in 2005. ■ Jeffrey Kopstein

See also **Europe.**

New Brunswick. See Canadian provinces.

New York City. New Yorkers were reminded of the Sept. 11, 2001, terrorist attacks on the city when a small airplane slammed into a high-rise apartment building on Manhattan's East Side on Oct. 11, 2006. Cory Lidle—a pitcher for the New York Yankees and a recently licensed pilot—and a flight instructor were on the plane. Both were killed in the crash. No one in the building or on the ground was killed.

Authorities determined that the crash was most likely the result of winds and pilot inexperience. However, in the moments immediately following the crash, many people feared that it was a terrorist act. The scare prompted the United States government to send fighter jets to protect major U.S. cities, and counterterrorism squads to visit the crash scene. On October 13, the Federal Aviation Administration—an agency in the U.S. Department of Transportation—announced new restrictions on flights by small planes over New York City's East River corridor.

Ground Zero developments. On April 27, the city began construction of the 1,776-foot (541-meter) Freedom Tower, which was to be a central part of the redevelopment of the former World Trade Center site. However, like other Ground Zero issues, the project was controversial. The construction agreement called for federal and state offices to occupy a number of floors in 2011, when the skyscraper was scheduled to open, but many workers—especially those who lost colleagues in the Sept. 11, 2001, attacks—did not want to move into the tower.

In September 2006, as the city observed the fifth anniversary of the attacks, the remains of about 1,150 victims still had not been recovered. On October 19, however, utility workers excavating part of the disaster site discovered bone fragments and other human remains in a paved-over manhole. Medical experts were hopeful that the remains could be linked to specific victims through DNA testing. Many critics charged that the authorities had been too hasty in concluding the search for remains in 2002. Following the discovery, officials renewed the search for remains at a number of nearby sites.

Housing complex sold. Stuyvesant Town and Peter Cooper Village—a Manhattan housing complex with more than 11,200 apartments—was sold in October 2006 to a joint venture between two real estate companies. Tishman Speyer Properties, L.P., based in New York City, and Black-Rock Realty Advisors, Inc., based in Florham Park, New Jersey, bought the 80-acre (30-hectare) complex from MetLife, Inc., a New York City-based insurance company, for more than $5 billion.

MetLife established the complex in 1947 for returning World War II (1939-1945) veterans, and over the years the complex has housed teachers, police officers, and other middle-class New Yorkers. Many people feared that the sale of the complex would result in individual units being sold as condominiums at market prices.

Trans fats. New York City's Board of Health voted in December 2006 to ban restaurants from serving food that contains *trans fats.* Scientists believe that trans fats, which are derived from hydrogenated oils and are found in many processed foods, increase the risk of heart disease. Another measure approved by the Board of Health required many restaurants to post the caloric content of menu items.

Fashion Week, a twice-yearly fashion industry showcase, wore out its welcome in 2006 at Bryant Park, where the event has been held since 1993. The park's management claimed that the event had become too disruptive. Mayor Michael R. Bloomberg said that the February 2007 event would go on as scheduled, but that the city would work with the fashion industry to find a suitable new site.

Population. The United States Census Bureau in October 2006 revised its estimate of New York City's mid-2005 population. The bureau changed the figure to 8,213,839—an increase of more than 70,600 from a previous estimate. City officials had claimed that the original estimate was too low.   ■ Owen Moritz

See also **City.**

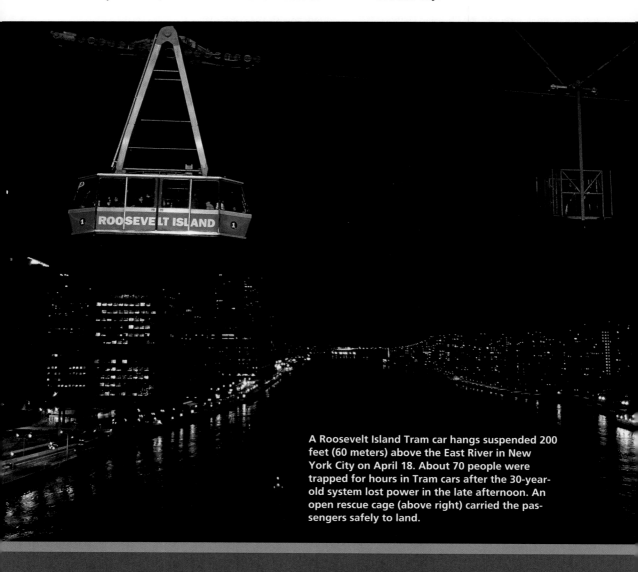

A Roosevelt Island Tram car hangs suspended 200 feet (60 meters) above the East River in New York City on April 18. About 70 people were trapped for hours in Tram cars after the 30-year-old system lost power in the late afternoon. An open rescue cage (above right) carried the passengers safely to land.

New Zealand. Controversies over campaign spending by New Zealand political parties, the conduct of senior politicians, and unprecedented intrusion into the private lives of party leaders created political storms in 2006. The effects included falling support for the governing Labour Party and a leadership change in the major opposition party.

Electoral spending. In April 2006, Auditor General Kevin Brady announced that he would investigate spending by all parties in the 2005 election campaign. In October 2006, he released a report showing that parties had unlawfully spent a total of $1.1 million, of which $825,000 had been wrongly spent by the Labour Party. (All amounts in New Zealand dollars.) Labour insisted that it had acted under a previously accepted interpretation of spending rules. It agreed to repay the funds, and on October 18, Parliament passed special legislation making past election spending lawful. Although the National Party was only a minor transgressor, it faced a different election-spending issue when it failed to allow for $112,000 in consumer taxes on its television campaign advertising and so breached the broadcasting-spending cap. The party was embarrassed to find that it could not legally reimburse television companies forced to pay the tax.

Ministers under investigation. In March, the government's senior legal officer, Attorney General David Parker, resigned all of his portfolios after being accused of filing false legal documents. He was cleared after an investigation but did not resume his post. An investigation by a senior lawyer cleared an associate minister, Taito Philip Field, of charges that he had expedited a man's immigration application in return for work on his house. However, the investigation raised other issues that led police to launch their own investigation. Amid ongoing accusations from opposition politicians, Field stood down from Parliament in August. In October, police searched his office in Parliament, his electorate office, and his residence, seizing documents and copies of computer files.

Political "sleaze." A country that had generally allowed politicians a degree of privacy in their family lives was regaled by the media in September with rumors involving Labour and National party leaders. Questions were raised over the sexual orientation of the prime minister's husband, Peter Davis. Davis strongly refuted the claims. In addition, National leader Donald Brash, who had faced accusations of an extramarital affair, resigned from both the leadership and Parliament following publication of a book that revealed internal National Party e-mails said to show him in a bad light. On November 27, National elected member of Parliament John Key to succeed Brash.　■ Gavin Ellis

See also **Pacific Islands.**

Newfoundland and Labrador. See Canadian provinces.

Selected news from 2006:

Adios, flamingos. After making about 20 million pink plastic flamingos, Union Products Inc., the Leominster, Massachusetts-based company whose ornaments became staples of lawns across the United States, closed on Nov. 1, 2006. In the 1950's, Don Featherstone created the original pink flamingo mold from clay, using a National Geographic photograph as a guide. The iconic—and, to some, hideously tacky—ornaments made their debut in a 1957 Sears catalog, selling for $2.76 per pair. By the 1990's, they had become a gay pride symbol, a kitsch art object, and a birthday gag—Leominster Mayor Dean Mazzarella awoke on the morning of his 40th birthday to find 40 of the fake birds on his lawn.

An engineer inspects the 17-foot (5-meter) statue of Lord Nelson atop Nelson's Column, which towers nearly 170 feet (50 meters) above London's Trafalgar Square. The monument honors Admiral Horatio Nelson, who led the British fleet to victory in the 1805 Battle of Trafalgar. Restorers in 2006 performed the first scientific measurement of the 160-year-old monument and discovered that it was nearly 17 feet (5 meters) shorter than previously believed.

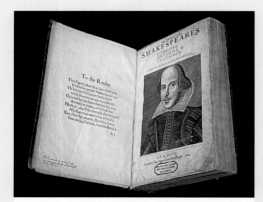

This First Folio edition of William Shakespeare's plays, containing 36 of his works, was sold by Sotheby's auction house in London for £2.8 million ($5.2 million) in July. One of about 140 known copies of the First Folio, the book is still encased in its original binding from the 1600's.

Company executives cited increased plastic costs and energy prices as the final nails in the flamingos' coffin. Although other companies continued to produce their own versions of the pink flamingo ornament, kitsch lovers mourned the passing of Featherstone's original.

Are you going to eat that? A construction crew working in the structural foundations of New York City's Brooklyn Bridge in March 2006 discovered a cache of Cold War-era food and supplies. An official from the New York Department of Transportation believed the medical supplies, paper blankets, water drums, and 350,000 packaged crackers must have been stored in the bridge foundation by the Office of Civilian Defense in the early 1960's. The Office of Civilian Defense was a government organization that in

1961 began establishing fallout shelters, public buildings and underground areas where people might be protected from the fallout from a nuclear explosion. Most fallout shelters have since been dismantled, making the forgotten Brooklyn Bridge shelter of great interest to historians.

First Folio sale. In July 2006, the London auction house Sotheby's sold a rare complete copy of Shakespeare's First Folio, intact in its original binding, for $5.2 million to a London book dealer. In 1623, seven years after Shakespeare's death, two former members of his theater company collected 36 of Shakespeare's plays and had them printed in one volume. Scholars believe that a number of Shakespeare's plays could have been lost forever had the First Folio not been printed. The collection was the first printing for 18 of his plays, including *Julius Caesar*, *Macbeth*, and *Twelfth Night*.

Of the approximately 750 original copies of the First Folio, only about 140 still exist, and most are incomplete. Of great interest to Shakespeare scholars was the fact that this copy contains handwritten notes that experts believe were made by contemporary scholars and could provide insight into how readers in the 1600's understood the playwright's work.

The world's highest field test. British mountaineer Graham Hoyland conducted a unique experiment in 2006 that provided evidence that climbers George Mallory and Andrew Irvine might have reached the summit of Mount Everest in 1924, nearly 30 years before Tenzing Norgay and Sir Edmund Hillary did so in 1953. Irvine and Mallory disappeared on Mount Everest in June 1924, and scientists have debated whether they could have reached the summit. In 1999, climbers discovered Mallory's body on the mountain's north face, and forensic textile experts replicated his clothes based on samples that had been preserved in ice.

The replica clothing, which was made from

The original pink flamingo lawn ornament, designed by Don Featherstone, went extinct in 2006 with the closing of Leominster, Massachusetts-based Union Products Inc. The ornaments debuted in 1957 at $2.76 per pair.

cotton, silk, wool, and wool gabardine, took three years to create and was found to be significantly lighter than modern cold-weather climbing gear. In June 2006, Hoyland completed a series of field tests of the clothing in hopes of proving that the climbers were not, as some people believed, too ill-equipped to reach the summit. For comparison, an associate wore modern cold-weather gear made of down.

Hoyland discovered that Mallory's clothing was more than adequate to keep him warm and gave him an excellent range of movement, which can be critical when working at high altitudes. Hoyland did discover, however, that the buttons on the replica clothing were difficult to fasten in the cold and deduced that Mallory and Irvine probably donned the gear at a base camp partway up the mountain and left it on for the remainder of their fateful journey.

A presidential overhaul. In 2006, Mount Vernon, the estate of the first U.S. president, George Washington, unveiled two new buildings as part of a $110-million effort to enhance visitors' understanding of Washington's life and world. In the past, Mount Vernon's exhibits concentrated on Washington's life at the plantation; the new expansions provide a more fully-rounded portrait. A centerpiece of the first building, the Ford Orientation Center, is the 20-minute film *We Fight to Be Free,* which provides an introduction to Washington's military career and features reenactments of his participation in the French and Indian War (1754-1763) and his famed 1776 crossing of the Delaware River during the Revolutionary War in America (1775-1783).

The second building, the Donald W. Reynolds Museum and Education Center, is an exhibit gallery featuring artifacts from Washington's life. Among the artifacts on display in the Reynolds Museum are the shoe buckles Washington wore to his inauguration, his ivory dentures, his will, his military sword, and a reproduction of Martha Washington's gold wedding dress. One gallery contains a re-creation of a soldier's hut in Valley Forge, Pennsylvania, where Washington and his troops spent the winter of 1777-1778. In addition, the Reynolds Museum offers three newly commissioned life-sized wax figures of Washington as he may have appeared at ages 19 (prior to the French and Indian War), 45 (as a general in the Revolutionary War), and 57 (as president). The sculptures are the result of two years of forensic and historical research, coupled with computer artistry.

Space shot. On Nov. 23, 2006, Russian cosmonaut Mikhail Tyurin made sports history when he hit a golf ball from a tee positioned outside the International Space Station (ISS). The stunt was funded by Element 21 Golf of Toronto, Canada, who filmed the shot for an advertisement for a new type of golf club. Element 21 paid the Russian Space Agency an undisclosed sum to supervise the stunt, which used clubs made of the same scandium alloy that was used in the construction of the ISS. Scandium is lighter than titanium, which is extremely popular for golf clubs. Officials with Element 21 estimated that the ball Tyurin hit would orbit Earth for three years before burning up in Earth's atmosphere.

Rewriting history. A team of researchers led by archaeologist Julie Schablitsky of the University of Oregon Museum of Natural and Cultural History in Eugene and anthropologist Kelly Dixon of the University of Montana in Missoula reported in January 2006 that a new examination of remains from the Donner Party showed no proof of cannibalism. The Donner Party was a group of settlers who became snowbound in the Sierra Nevada mountain range in eastern California in the severe winter of 1846-1847. Of the 81 members of the party, only 45 survived. Accounts from the era suggest that the group resorted to cannibalism to survive.

From 2003 to 2006, Schablitsky and Dixon's team studied remains found at the Adler Creek Camp, including thousands of human bone fragments. The bones showed no evidence of "pot polish," which would mean that they had been cooked. The team concluded that the Donner Party had eaten both wild and domesticated animals. If any of the party resorted to cannibalism, the researchers concluded, it was a last-resort measure taken during the last few weeks of their ordeal by fewer than 12 members of the party.

Return to sender. On Aug. 28, 2006, the son of a U.S. veteran of World War II (1939-1945) returned a collection of 17 letters dating from the 1200's to Poland. The letters were written in Latin on *vellum* (animal-skin parchment)

by Pope Alexander IV (who reigned 1254-1261), Pope Gregory X (who reigned 1271-1276), and other high-ranking Roman Catholic officials.

An American engineer, George Gavin, discovered the letters in the mud near a destroyed train in Austria during the war and brought them home as souvenirs. Upon his death, his son, Philip Gavin, entrusted the letters to the Milwaukee archdiocese of the Roman Catholic Church, which had the letters authenticated in 2003. Philip Gavin decided that the letters should be returned to Poland and enlisted the help of Neal Pease, a history professor from the University of Wisconsin at Milwaukee. Pease flew to Warsaw, where he handed the letters over to the deputy director of the Polish national archives.

Although the full contents of the letters were not disclosed because they are still being studied, the professor who authenticated the documents revealed that they primarily detailed real estate transactions. Historians believed that the documents, however mundane, would improve researchers' understanding of the economics and government of Poland in the 1200's.

Adwaita of India dies. Adwaita, an Aldabra tortoise that once belonged to British colonial administrator Robert Clive (1725-1774), died on March 22, 2006. Adwaita, which means "the only one" in Bengali, was believed to have been about 250 years old. Clive, known as Clive of India, joined the English East India Company, Britain's (now the United Kingdom) trading company in India, in 1743 and played a crucial role in establishing Britain's colonial rule there. He left India in 1760 only to return several years later to serve as governor. He left India for good in 1767. Historians believe Clive received Adwaita as a gift at some point in the mid-1760's, and that Adwaita lived at Clive's former estate until 1875, when the tortoise was moved to the Alipore Zoological Garden in Calcutta (now Kolkata).   ■ S. Thomas Richardson

A giant tortoise that once belonged to Robert Clive, who established British colonial rule in India in the late 1700's, receives care at the Alipore Zoological Garden in Kolkata, India. The tortoise, believed to have been about 250 years old, died on March 22, 2006.

Devotees of Jain Dharm, an ancient religion and philosophy, pour milk over a statue of the sage Gomateswara in Shravanabelagola, India, in February 2006, during the Mahamastak Abhisheka ceremony. The ceremony, which took place from February 8 to 19, drew nearly 3 million people. The statue is the world's largest *batholithic* (carved from a single mass of granite or other volcanic rock) structure.

Newspaper. The second largest newspaper chain in the United States, San Jose-based Knight Ridder Inc., went out of existence on June 27, 2006, when it was purchased by the McClatchy Company of Sacramento, California. McClatchy bought Knight Ridder for $4.5 billion and assumed a $2-billion debt. After reselling 12 of Knight Ridder's 32 daily newspapers, McClatchy became the nation's second largest daily newspaper publisher measured by circulation, with 32 dailies and a combined circulation of 3.3 million. Knight Ridder had offered itself for sale under pressure from several large shareholders who were dissatisfied with the declining stock price. Before its dissolution, Knight Ridder sold *The Philadelphia Inquirer* and its tabloid sister, the *Philadelphia Daily News,* to a group of Philadelphia investors for $562 million.

On August 2, two newspaper companies acquired four former Knight Ridder dailies from McClatchy for $1 billion. New York City's Hearst Corporation bought *The Herald* of Monterey, California, and the *St. Paul* (Minnesota) *Pioneer Press* and transferred them to Denver's MediaNews Group Inc., in exchange for an equity in the chain. MediaNews also purchased the *San Jose Mercury News* and the *Contra Costa* (California) *Times*.

Circulation. Daily newspaper circulation at midyear stood at 45,414,979, a 2.5-percent decrease compared with the same period in 2005, according to the Audit Bureau of Circulations in Schaumburg, Illinois. Sunday circulation dropped by 3.1 percent. Newspaper publishers responded with a variety of cost-cutting measures. *The New York Times* announced in July 2006 plans to narrow its broadsheet width by 1.5 inches (3.8 centimeters). *The Boston Globe* revealed in August that it was cutting an unspecified number of news pages. The Dallas-based Belo Corp. announced in September that 111 staff members at *The Dallas Morning News* had accepted "voluntary severance" packages.

Tribune Company of Chicago, under pressure to boost its stock price, announced in May a $2-billion program to buy back as much as 25 percent of company shares. The company's flagship daily, the *Chicago Tribune,* announced in July that it was cutting 120 jobs. In October, Jeffrey M. Johnson, publisher of the Tribune-owned *Los Angeles Times,* was forced to resign after he refused to comply with demands by the owners that he make staff cuts he considered damaging to the paper.

Advertising revenues for the second quarter of 2006 stood at $12.4 billion, up 1.1 percent compared with the same period in 2005, reported the Newspaper Association of America in Vienna, Virginia. Advertising on newspaper Web sites increased by 33.2 percent to $667 million.

■ Mark Fitzgerald

Nicaragua. On Nov. 5, 2006, Nicaraguans elected Daniel Ortega Saavedra of the left-wing political party Sandinista National Liberation Front as president. A self-described Marxist, Ortega served previously as a member of the *junta* (ruling group) that governed Nicaragua following the 1979 overthrow of dictator Anastasio Samoza Debayle. From 1985 to 1990, Ortega served as the country's elected president.

During the period of Sandinista rule, the United States government financed the *contras,* an armed rebel group that opposed the Sandinista regime, which was eventually replaced through the democratic process. Ortega lost presidential elections in 1996 and 2001, but he remained a force in politics as the Sandinista party leader.

To win office in 2006, Ortega softened his anti-U.S. rhetoric and sought the support of Nicaragua's Roman Catholic hierarchy by supporting legislation to ban abortions, which the Nicaraguan Congress approved in October. As president-elect, Ortega declared that he would promote proposals to build hydroelectric power plants with funding from Brazil and Venezuela and seek an agreement with the Venezuelan government of Hugo Chávez to receive subsidized oil shipments.   ■ Nathan A. Haverstock

See also **Latin America: A Special Report.**

Niger. See **Africa.**

Nigeria.

Nigeria. With presidential and legislative elections looming in April 2007, preelection politicking dominated political life in Nigeria in 2006. President Olusegun Obasanjo, in office since 1999, gave up hopes of running for a third presidential term when, in May 2006, Nigeria's parliament rejected a constitutional amendment to remove the presidential two-term limit.

Pipeline explosion. On May 12, as many as 200 people were burned to death in the explosion of a gasoline pipeline 30 miles (48 kilometers) east of Lagos, Nigeria's largest city. On December 26, more than 280 people were killed in a Lagos suburb when an oil pipeline exploded. In both cases, investigators reported finding evidence that activities of thieves cutting into the pipeline had set off the explosions.

Coastal regions of Nigeria are crisscrossed by pipelines, a result of oil drilling and refining activities centered in the Niger Delta. The pipelines have repeatedly been tapped by thieves, often with catastrophic results. Pipeline explosions in the delta region killed 1,000 people in 1998 and 60 others in a 2005 incident.

Delta violence. Insurgent groups continued to carry out numerous kidnappings and acts of violence and sabotage in the Niger Delta in 2006. At Port Harcourt, Nigeria's chief oil port, gunmen on January 24 stormed the offices of the Italian oil company Eni S.p.A., killing nine people. On February 18, nine foreign workers for the oil infrastructure firm Willbros Group, Inc., were abducted but eventually released unharmed. On June 2, gunmen using speedboats invaded an oil rig in the Atlantic Ocean off the delta coast, kidnapping eight workers. The workers were released two days later. On October 2, armed men in speedboats raided a convoy of barges supplying facilities of the Anglo-Dutch company Royal Dutch Shell plc. As many as 14 Nigerian soldiers were killed.

Several insurgent groups operating in the Niger Delta obtained support, analysts said, from disaffected residents who claimed they received little benefit from Nigeria's oil wealth. Violence directed against foreign oil companies reduced Nigeria's oil production by 20 percent in 2006.

Religious strife. Publication in European newspapers of a cartoon that many Muslims judged blasphemous to the Prophet Muhammad sparked outbreaks of violence across Nigeria in February. The violence began with attacks by Muslims on Christians in the predominantly Muslim north, which prompted reprisals by Christians. In the southern city of Onitsha, Christian mobs went on a rampage in mid-February, killing more than 100 Muslims and driving thousands into the countryside. ■ Pieter Esterhuysen

See also **Africa; Disasters.**

Masked militants patrol waterways of the Niger Delta in February 2006. The militants, members of an armed rebel group known as Movement for the Emancipation of the Niger Delta, kidnapped nine foreign workers at oil-production facilities on February 18 but had released all nine by late March.

Nobel Prizes in literature, peace, economics, and the sciences were awarded in October 2006 by the Norwegian Storting (parliament) in Oslo and by the Karolinska Institute, the Royal Swedish Academy of Sciences, and the Swedish Academy of Literature, all in Stockholm. Each prize was worth about $1.4 million.

The 2006 Nobel Prize in literature went to novelist Orhan Pamuk, the first Turkish citizen to win a Nobel Prize in any field. Pamuk gained international popularity for his novels about the conflicts of cultures within Turkey and his native city of Istanbul—clashes between the past and the present, East and West, and secularism and Islam, Turkey's dominant religion.

Pamuk's first novel, *Cevdet Bey* (1976), is a portrait of the modern Turkish ruling class and the development of capitalism in Turkey. *The White Castle* (1985), Pamuk's fourth novel, was his first to be translated into English. It tells of a young Italian scholar who is captured by Turkish pirates and given to a scientist. Gradually, the identities of the scholar and scientist become interchangeable. The ideas that identities are uncertain and reality is ambiguous appear as common themes throughout Pamuk's fiction. His other works include *The Black Book* (1990), *My Name Is Red* (2001), and *Istanbul: Memories of a City* (2003).

The 2006 Peace Prize was awarded to economist Muhammad Yunus of Bangladesh, known as the "world's banker to the poor," and the Grameen Bank, which Yunus founded in 1976. Yunus has been a pioneer in the development of the microcredit movement for economic development, the practice of lending small amounts of money to poor people to start their own businesses. Such people generally lack the financial resources that qualify them for loans from conventional banking institutions.

By 2006, the Grameen Bank had extended credit to an estimated 7 million people, nearly all of them women. "Microcredit has proved to be an important liberating force in societies where women in particular have to struggle against repressive social and economic conditions," the Nobel Committee said. "Economic growth and political democracy cannot achieve their full potential unless the female half of humanity participates on an equal footing with the male."

The 2006 Nobel Prize in physiology or medicine went to Andrew Z. Fire of Stanford University in Stanford, California, and Craig C. Mello of the University of Massachusetts Medical School in Worcester for their 1989 discovery of a fundamental biological process used in cells to "silence" genes. The process, called *RNA interference*, destroys the ability of a molecule called ribonucleic acid (RNA) to help produce the proteins essential to the structure and functioning of cells. RNA interference plays a crucial role in controlling the actions of certain unstable genes and defending the body against viruses. The process has become an important tool for studying how genes function and for developing treatments for a wide range of illnesses and conditions, including viral infections, cardiovascular disease, and cancer.

The 2006 Nobel Prize in economic science was awarded to economist Edmund S. Phelps of Columbia University in New York City for his work on the relationship between the short-term and long-term effects of economic policy. In particular, Phelps explored the trade-offs between two important goals of economic stabilization—low employment and low *inflation* (a continual increase in prices throughout a nation's economy). In the late 1960's, Phelps theorized that inflation depends not only on unemployment but also the expectations that companies and employees hold about future increases in wages and prices. According to this theory, by maintaining a low rate of inflation, governments can dampen public expectations of rising inflation rates in the future and so help keep unemployment rates low.

The 2006 Nobel Prize in chemistry went to biologist Roger D. Kornberg of Stanford for creating highly detailed images of the process cells use to copy and transport the genetic information needed to maintain life. Kornberg produced images of this process on the molecular level using crystallography, a technique for visualizing the arrangement of atoms. The Swedish Academy noted that alterations in the transcription process contribute to the development of cancer, heart disease, and various kinds of inflammation. Understanding the transcription process also is important for scientists attempting to use stem cells to replace cells in diseased or damaged organs.

The 2006 Nobel Prize in physics went to American scientists John C. Mather of the Goddard Space Flight Center in Greenbelt, Maryland, and George F. Smoot of the Lawrence Berkeley National Laboratory in Berkeley, California, for their findings about energy that formed soon after the origin of the universe 14 billion years ago. Mather and Smoot used temperature measurements of the cosmic background radiation (CMB radiation) made by the Cosmic Background Explorer satellite, which was launched in 1989. CMB radiation formed in the heat of the early universe and cooled as the universe expanded. Mather found a pattern and Smoot found variations in the radiation that provided strong support for the big bang theory, the most widely held theory about the origin of the universe. Their work "marked the inception of *cosmology* (the study of the origin of the universe) as a precise science," the Nobel Committee said. ■ Barbara A. Mayes

See also **Literature; Physics.**

Northern Ireland. Attempts to restore the province's assembly dominated events in Northern Ireland in 2006. The assembly had been established after the signing of the 1998 Good Friday Agreement, brokered by Tony Blair and Bertie Ahern—prime ministers of the United Kingdom (U.K.) and the Irish Republic, respectively—with the Northern Irish parties. The agreement sought to end the violence between Roman Catholic and Protestant segments of the population that had erupted in 1969. The nationalist Catholic party Sinn Fein (which means "Ourselves Alone" in Gaelic) demanded the reabsorption of Northern Ireland into the Republic of Ireland (Ireland had been partitioned in 1922). The Unionist parties, supported primarily by the Protestant majority, wanted Northern Ireland to remain a province of the U.K. The agreement led to a cease-fire and to the formation of the assembly in which Catholic and Protestant groups were to share power. However, continued allegations that the military wing of Sinn Fein—the Irish Republican Army (IRA)—had not abandoned violence led the British government to suspend the assembly in 2002.

In the U.K. election of 2005 and the 2003 Northern Ireland assembly election, moderate parties on both sides were eclipsed by more extreme groups. The Ulster Unionist Party, a Protestant group, lost to Ian Paisley's Democratic Unionist Party, and the Catholic Social Democratic and Labour Party lost to Sinn Fein, led by Gerry Adams. Paisley refused to sit in a government with Sinn Fein because he was not convinced that the IRA had abandoned terrorism, despite the IRA's formal renunciation of violence in July 2005 and the confirmation of the Independent International Commission on Decommissioning (IICD) in 2006 that the IRA had destroyed its weapons.

Peace talks. Multiparty talks to restore the assembly and restart the peace process began in February 2006. The Independent Monitoring Commission (IMC) reported that the IRA was no longer involved in terrorist acts. However, the IMC disagreed with the IICD's determination about the destruction of IRA weapons and asserted that some IRA members were involved in criminal activities. As a result, Ian Paisley continued to refuse to share power with Sinn Fein. The IRA later disowned former members who had been involved in organized crime activities.

In April 2006, Blair and Ahern issued an ultimatum to the Northern Irish parties that, unless an agreement on power sharing was reached by November 24, the forthcoming election would be cancelled and assembly members' salaries would not be paid. Northern Ireland would then continue to be ruled from London, though this time in cooperation with the Republic of Ireland.

Assembly reconvenes. On May 15, the Northern Ireland Assembly reconvened at Stormont Castle in Belfast—without power—as a first stage in the construction of a power-sharing executive. Adams nominated Paisley as first (prime) minister, with Martin McGuinness of Sinn Fein as his deputy. Paisley refused the nomination, maintaining that the IRA remained a terrorist organization. Adams, in turn, threatened to withdraw Sinn Fein from the assembly. In June, Blair and Ahern repeated their ultimatum to close the assembly if the two sides could not work together.

The St. Andrews Agreement. In October, Blair and Ahern met with Northern Ireland politicians at St. Andrews in Scotland. After three days of talks, the prime ministers issued an agreement, which included plans for the creation of a power-sharing executive and for elections to take place in March 2007, when power would be restored to the assembly. All parties had to agree to support the police service of Northern Ireland, which Sinn Fein had claimed was biased against Catholics. It was understood that failure to establish an executive would lead to the dissolution of the assembly. Although party members favored restoring the executive, they only conditionally supported the agreement. ■ Rohan McWilliam

See also **Ireland; United Kingdom.**

Northwest Territories. See **Canadian territories.**

Norway. Norway's governing coalition—made up of the Labor Party, the Socialist Left Party, and the Center Party—remained stable in 2006. The coalition came to power in 2005 with Jens Stoltenberg as prime minister.

In 2006, the government again allocated a portion of the country's windfall profits from offshore oil and natural gas reserves to the Government Pension Fund. The fund, which grew to 207 billion euros ($276 billion) in 2006, was to be used in the future, when oil and gas revenues dropped off. In November, the United Nations ranked Norway first on its Human Development Index, an annual analysis of quality of life. Nevertheless, the right-wing Progress Party urged the government to spend part of the oil and gas revenue on road construction and on increased funding for the health and education systems.

EU relations. Public opinion surveys in 2006 indicated that as many as 48 percent of Norwegians continued to oppose their country's becoming a full-fledged member of the European Union (EU). Although Norway shared many of the advantages of membership and bore some of the costs, many Norwegians feared that full membership would infringe on Norwegian sovereignty and divert a larger share of the country's oil profits to the poorer regions of Europe.

In February 2006, Norway filed a complaint

with the World Trade Organization stating that the EU had imposed measures to limit the amount of Norwegian salmon on the European market. In response to pressure from Scottish and Irish salmon farmers, the EU had set a minimum import price for Norwegian farmed salmon.

Foreign loans. In October 2006, the Norwegian government announced the cancellation of debt incurred by poorer countries—including Ecuador, Egypt, Jamaica, and Peru. Those countries purchased Norwegian ships with government credits between 1976 and 1980 but later defaulted on the loans. Critics charged that the loans were a self-serving means of supporting Norway's shipbuilding industry. Norway acknowledged that the loans were extended without a proper needs assessment and risk analysis.

Norway's economy performed well in 2006. Government economists projected that the country's *gross domestic product* (the value of all goods and services produced in a year) would grow by 2.4 percent in 2006. The unemployment rate was 2 percent in November, down from 3 percent a year earlier.   ■ Jeffrey Kopstein

See also **Europe**.

Nova Scotia. See Canadian provinces.
Nuclear energy. See Energy supply.
Nunavut. See Canadian territories.
Nutrition. See Food.

Ocean. The world's largest marine reserve was designated in June 2006, when United States President George W. Bush established the Northwest Hawaiian Islands Marine National Monument. The reserve, stretching some 1,200 miles (1,900 kilometers) across the Pacific Ocean from northwest of the island of Kauai to beyond the Midway Atoll, protects more than 7,000 species of birds, marine mammals, sea turtles, and fish. Approximately one-fourth of these species, many endangered, are found only in the Hawaiian Islands.

The monument preserves the largest intact coral reef ecosystem under U.S. jurisdiction. Restrictions on human activities were put in place to help protect sensitive corals and other animals that live on the reserve's reefs, *atolls* (rings of coral), *seamounts* (volcanoes on the seafloor), and islands. Plans called for the phase-out of all fishing there by 2011. Removing corals and the mining of minerals and petroleum were also banned. Access to the reserve was to be limited to certain zones, with all visitors required to obtain permits. Jean-Michel Cousteau, son of the late ocean explorer Jacques Cousteau, helped persuade President Bush to establish the monument by showing him an underwater video of the area in April 2006.

Commercial whaling. At the annual meeting of the International Whaling Commission (IWC) in June, pro-whaling nations led by Japan narrowly won a vote calling for the eventual resumption of commercial whaling. Other nations immediately challenged the vote. The threat that commercial whaling might resume prompted activists to begin a "Save the Whales Again!" campaign. Lending support to this campaign, several U.S. senators drafted a resolution supporting the long-standing U.S. opposition to whaling.

The Cambridge, England-based IWC, an international organization responsible for conserving whales, banned commercial whaling in 1986 to protect many threatened and endangered species, including blue, sperm, fin, and right whales. Norway, however, ignored the ban, while Japan and Iceland continued to kill the relatively abundant minke whales under controversial "scientific research" programs.

The government of Iceland announced in October 2006 that it would issue commercial licenses to hunt 40 minke and fin whales during the season. Japan planned to kill 850 minke, humpback, and fin whales in the internationally protected waters of the Southern Ocean Whale Sanctuary during the 2006–2007 whaling season. Japanese officials said the whales eat too many fish and compete with their fishing fleet.

Do dolphins recognize "names"? A study released in May 2006 suggested that bottlenose dolphins give each other "names" that they use to identify individuals. Scientists had never before documented the ability of a nonhuman animal to transmit and recognize such identity information.

Scientists had long known that dolphins and other whales often whistle and click to signal their locations—important information in the sea, where there are few visual cues to help animals remain in contact with one another. Marine biologist Vincent Janik of the Sea Mammal Research Unit at the University of St. Andrews in Scotland discovered that the whistles made by bottlenose dolphins signify more than just location.

Experimenting with bottlenose dolphins in Sarasota Bay, Florida, Janik's team of researchers recorded what they believed to be the "signature whistles" (names) of several dolphins. They then electronically altered these recordings to remove any voice features that would provide clues about the callers' identities. The researchers next played the whistles to dolphins through underwater speakers. In 9 out of 14 cases, a listening dolphin turned most often toward the speakers if the calls were the signature whistles of its relatives or close members of its pod (group). These results indicated to the scientists that the dolphins recognized the called names of animals with which they were familiar —even when the dolphins did not recognize the voices of the individuals making the calls.   ■ Christina S. Johnson

See also **Biology**.

THE 2006 OLYMPICS

The 20th Winter Olympic Games took place in Turin, Italy, at the base of the Alps

ALPINE SKIING

Men's Combined
GOLD	Ted Ligety	United States
SILVER	Ivica Kostelic	Croatia
BRONZE	Rainer Schoenfelder	Austria

Men's Downhill
GOLD	Antoine Deneriaz	France
SILVER	Michael Walchhofer	Austria
BRONZE	Bruno Kernen	Switzerland

Men's Giant Slalom
GOLD	Benjamin Raich	Austria
SILVER	Joel Chenal	France
BRONZE	Hermann Maier	Austria

Men's Slalom
GOLD	Benjamin Raich	Austria
SILVER	Reinfried Herbst	Austria
BRONZE	Rainer Schoenfelder	Austria

Men's Super-G
GOLD	Kjetil Andre Aamodt	Norway
SILVER	Hermann Maier	Austria
BRONZE	Ambrosi Hoffmann	Switzerland

Women's Combined
GOLD	Janica Kostelic	Croatia
SILVER	Marlies Schild	Austria
BRONZE	Anja Paerson	Sweden

Women's Downhill
GOLD	Michaela Dorfmeister	Austria
SILVER	Martina Schild	Switzerland
BRONZE	Anja Paerson	Sweden

Women's Giant Slalom
GOLD	Julia Mancuso	United States
SILVER	Tanja Poutiainen	Finland
BRONZE	Anna Ottosson	Sweden

Women's Slalom
GOLD	Anja Paerson	Sweden
SILVER	Nicole Hosp	Austria
BRONZE	Marlies Schild	Austria

Women's Super-G
GOLD	Michaela Dorfmeister	Austria
SILVER	Janica Kostelic	Croatia
BRONZE	Alexandra Meissnitzer	Austria

Slalom skiier Anja Paerson of Sweden

Biathlete Michael Roesch of Germany

BIATHLON

Men's 10-K Sprint
GOLD	Sven Fischer	Germany
SILVER	Halvard Hanevold	Norway
BRONZE	Frode Andresen	Norway

Men's 12.5-K Pursuit
GOLD	Vincent Defrasne	France
SILVER	Ole Einar Bjoerndalen	Norway
BRONZE	Sven Fischer	Germany

Men's 15-K Mass Start
GOLD	Michael Greis	Germany
SILVER	Tomasz Sikora	Poland
BRONZE	Ole Einar Bjoerndalen	Norway

Men's 20-K Individual
GOLD	Michael Greis	Germany
SILVER	Ole Einar Bjoerndalen	Norway
BRONZE	Halvard Hanevold	Norway

Men's 4 x 7.5-K Relay
GOLD	Ricco Gross	Germany
	Michael Roesch	
	Sven Fischer	
	Michael Greis	
SILVER	Ivan Tcherezov	Russia
	Sergei Tchepikov	
	Pavel Rostovtsev	
	Nikolay Kruglov	
BRONZE	Julien Robert	France
	Vincent Defrasne	
	Ferreol Cannard	
	Raphael Poiree	

Women's 10-K Pursuit
GOLD	Kati Wilhelm	Germany
SILVER	Martina Glagow	Germany
BRONZE	Albina Akhatova	Russia

Women's 12.5-K Mass Start
GOLD	Anna Carin Olofsson	Sweden
SILVER	Kati Wilhelm	Germany
BRONZE	Uschi Disl	Germany

Women's 15-K Individual
GOLD	Svetlana Ishmouratova	Russia
SILVER	Martina Glagow	Germany
BRONZE	Albina Akhatova	Russia

Women's 4 x 6-K Relay
GOLD	Anna Bogaliy	Russia
	Svetlana Ishmouratova	
	Olga Zaitseva	
	Albina Akhatova	
SILVER	Martina Glagow	Germany
	Andrea Henkel	
	Katrin Apel	
	Kati Wilhelm	
BRONZE	Delphyne Peretto	France
	Florence Baverel-Robert	
	Sylvie Becaert	
	Sandrine Bailly	

Women's 7.5-K Sprint
GOLD	Florence Baverel-Robert	France
SILVER	Anna Carin Olofsson	Sweden
BRONZE	Lilia Efremova	Ukraine

Bobsledders Andre Lange (right) and
Kevin Kuske of Germany

BOBSLED

Four-Man

GOLD	Rene Hoppe Martin Putze Andre Lange Kevin Kuske	Germany
SILVER	Alexey Voevoda Filipp Egorov Alexandre Zoubkov Alexej Seliverstov	Russia
BRONZE	Cedric Grand Beat Hefti Martin Annen Thomas Lamparter	Switzerland

Two-Man

GOLD	Andre Lange Kevin Kuske	Germany
SILVER	Lascelles Brown Pierre Lueders	Canada
BRONZE	Martin Annen Beat Hefti	Switzerland

Women's

GOLD	Sandra Kiriasis Anja Schneiderheinze	Germany
SILVER	Valerie Fleming Shauna Rohbock	United States
BRONZE	Jennifer Isacco Gerda Weissensteiner	Italy

CROSS-COUNTRY SKIING

Men's 15-K Classical

GOLD	Andrus Veerpalu	Estonia
SILVER	Lukas Bauer	Czech Republic
BRONZE	Tobias Angerer	Germany

Men's 30-K Pursuit (15+15)

GOLD	Eugeni Dementiev	Russia
SILVER	Frode Estil	Norway
BRONZE	Pietro Piller Cottrer	Italy

Men's 4 x 10-K Relay

GOLD	Fulvio Valbusa Giorgio di Centa Pietro Piller Cottrer Cristian Zorzi	Italy
SILVER	Andreas Schluetter Jens Filbrich Rene Sommerfeldt Tobias Angerer	Germany
BRONZE	Mats Larsson Johan Olsson Anders Soedergren Mathias Fredriksson	Sweden

Men's 50-K Free, Mass Start

GOLD	Giorgio di Centa	Italy
SILVER	Eugeni Dementiev	Russia
BRONZE	Mikhail Botwinov	Austria

Men's Sprint

GOLD	Bjoern Lind	Sweden
SILVER	Roddy Darragon	France
BRONZE	Thobias Fredriksson	Sweden

Men's Team Sprint

GOLD	Fredriksson / Lind	Sweden
SILVER	Svartedal / Hetland	Norway
BRONZE	Alypov / Rotchev	Russia

Women's 10-K Classical

GOLD	Kristina Smigun	Estonia
SILVER	Marit Bjorgen	Norway
BRONZE	Hilde G. Pedersen	Norway

Women's 15-K Pursuit (7.5+7.5)

GOLD	Kristina Smigun	Estonia
SILVER	Katerina Neumannova	Czech Republic
BRONZE	Evgenia Medvedeva-Abruzova	Russia

Women's 30-K Free, Mass Start

GOLD	Katerina Neumannova	Czech Republic
SILVER	Julija Tchepalova	Russia
BRONZE	Justyna Kowalczyk	Poland

...ss-country skiers Alena Sidko of Russia (left, in blue), Chandra Crawford of Canada (center),
...Claudia Kuenzel of Germany (right)

Women's 4 x 5-K Relay

GOLD	Natalia Baranova-Masolkina Larisa Kurkina Julija Tchepalova Evgenia Medvedeva-Abruzova	Russia
SILVER	Stefanie Boehler Viola Bauer Evi Sachenbacher Stehle Claudia Kuenzel	Germany
BRONZE	Arianna Follis Gabriella Paruzzi Antonella Confortola Sabina Valbusa	Italy

Women's Sprint

GOLD	Chandra Crawford	Canada
SILVER	Claudia Kuenzel	Germany
BRONZE	Alena Sidko	Russia

Women's Team Sprint

GOLD	Dahlberg / Andersson	Sweden
SILVER	Renner / Scott	Canada
BRONZE	Saarinen / Kuitunen	Finland

CURLING

Men's

GOLD	Canada
SILVER	Finland
BRONZE	United States

Women's

GOLD	Sweden
SILVER	Switzerland
BRONZE	Canada

Figure skater Shizuka Arakawa
of Japan

FIGURE SKATING

Ice Dancing

GOLD	Tatiana Navka Roman Kostomarov	Russia
SILVER	Tanith Belbin Benjamin Agosto	United States
BRONZE	Elena Grushina Ruslan Goncharov	Ukraine

Men's Free Skating

GOLD	Evgeni Plushenko	Russia
SILVER	Stephane Lambiel	Switzerland
BRONZE	Jeffrey Buttle	Canada

Women's Free Skating

GOLD	Shizuka Arakawa	Japan
SILVER	Sasha Cohen	United States
BRONZE	Irina Slutskaya	Russia

Pairs Figure Skating

GOLD	Tatiana Totmianina Maxim Marinin	Russia
GOLD	Zhang Dan Zhang Hao	China
BRONZE	Shen Xue Zhao Hongbo	China

FREESTYLE SKIING

Men's Aerials

GOLD	Han Xiaopeng	China
SILVER	Dmitri Dashinski	Belarus
BRONZE	Vladimir Lebedev	Russia

Men's Moguls

GOLD	Dale Begg-Smith	Australia
SILVER	Mikko Ronkainen	Finland
BRONZE	Toby Dawson	United States

Women's Aerials

GOLD	Evelyne Leu	Switzerland
SILVER	Li Nina	China
BRONZE	Alisa Camplin	Australia

Women's Moguls

GOLD	Jennifer Heil	Canada
SILVER	Kari Traa	Norway
BRONZE	Sandra Laoura	France

ICE HOCKEY

Men's

GOLD	Sweden
SILVER	Finland
BRONZE	Czech Republic

Women's

GOLD	Canada
SILVER	Sweden
BRONZE	United States

Freestyle skiier Dale Begg-Smith
of Australia

Luge team Wolfgang Linger (left) and
Andreas Linger of Austria

LUGE

Doubles

GOLD	Andreas Linger	Austria
	Wolfgang Linger	
SILVER	Andre Florschuetz	Germany
	Torsten Wustlich	
BRONZE	Gerhard Plankensteiner	Italy
	Oswald Haselrieder	

Men's Singles

GOLD	Armin Zoeggeler	Italy
SILVER	Albert Demtschenko	Russia
BRONZE	Martins Rubenis	Latvia

Women's Singles

GOLD	Sylke Otto	Germany
SILVER	Silke Kraushaar	Germany
BRONZE	Tatjana Huefner	Germany

NORDIC COMBINED

Men's Individual Gundersen 15-K

GOLD	Georg Hettich	Germany
SILVER	Felix Gottwald	Austria
BRONZE	Magnus-H. Moan	Norway

Men's Sprint 7.5-K

GOLD	Felix Gottwald	Austria
SILVER	Magnus-H. Moan	Norway
BRONZE	Georg Hettich	Germany

Men's Team 4 x 5-K Relay

GOLD	Michael Gruber	Austria
	Christoph Bieler	
	Felix Gottwald	
	Mario Stecher	
SILVER	Bjoern Kircheisen	Germany
	Georg Hettich	
	Ronny Ackermann	
	Jens Gaiser	
BRONZE	Antti Kuisma	Finland
	Anssi Koivuranta	
	Jaakko Tallus	
	Hannu Manninen	

Short track speed skater Sun-Yu Jin
of South Korea

SHORT TRACK SPEED SKATING

Men's 1,000-Meter

GOLD	Hyun-Soo Ahn	South Korea
SILVER	Ho-Suk Lee	South Korea
BRONZE	Apolo Anton Ohno	United States

Men's 1,500-Meter

GOLD	Hyun-Soo Ahn	South Korea
SILVER	Ho-Suk Lee	South Korea
BRONZE	Li JiaJun	China

Men's 500-Meter

GOLD	Apolo Anton Ohno	United States
SILVER	Francois-Louis Tremblay	Canada
BRONZE	Hyun-Soo Ahn	South Korea

Men's 5,000-Meter Relay

GOLD	Hyun-Soo Ahn	South Korea
	Ho-Suk Lee	
	Se-Jong Oh	
	Ho-Jin Seo	
	Suk-Woo Song	
SILVER	Eric Bedard	Canada
	Jonathan Guilmette	
	Charles Hamelin	
	Francois-Louis Tremblay	
	Mathieu Turcotte	
BRONZE	Alex Izykowski	United States
	J.P. Kepka	
	Apolo Anton Ohno	
	Rusty Smith	

Women's 1,000-Meter

GOLD	Sun-Yu Jin	South Korea
SILVER	Wang Meng	China
BRONZE	Yang (A) Yang	China

Women's 1,500-Meter

GOLD	Sun-Yu Jin	South Korea
SILVER	Eun-Kyung Choi	South Korea
BRONZE	Wang Meng	China

Women's 3,000-Meter Relay

GOLD	Chun-Sa Byun	South Korea
	Eun-Kyung Choi	
	Da-Hye Jeon	
	Sun-Yu Jin	
	Yun-Mi Kang	
SILVER	Alanna Kraus	Canada
	Anouk Leblanc-Boucher	
	Amanda Overland	
	Kalyna Roberge	
	Tania Vicent	
BRONZE	Marta Capurso	Italy
	Arianna Fontana	
	Katia Zini	
	Mara Zini	

Women's 500-Meter

GOLD	Wang Meng	China
SILVER	Evgenia Radanova	Bulgaria
BRONZE	Anouk Leblanc-Boucher	Canada

Skeleton athelete Maya Pedersen of Switzerland

SKELETON

Men's

GOLD	Duff Gibson	Canada
SILVER	Jeff Pain	Canada
BRONZE	Gregor Staehli	Switzerland

Women's

GOLD	Maya Pedersen	Switzerland
SILVER	Shelley Rudman	Great Britain
BRONZE	Mellisa Hollingsworth-Richards	Canada

SKI JUMPING

NH Individual

GOLD	Lars Bystoel	Norway
SILVER	Matti Hautamaeki	Finland
BRONZE	Roar Ljoekelsoey	Norway

LH Individual

GOLD	Thomas Morgenstern	Austria
SILVER	Andreas Kofler	Austria
BRONZE	Lars Bystoel	Norway

LH Team

GOLD	Martin Koch Andreas Kofler Thomas Morgenstern Andreas Widhoelzl	Austria
SILVER	Janne Ahonen Janne Happonen Matti Hautamaeki Tami Kiuru	Finland
BRONZE	Lars Bystoel Tommy Ingebrigtsen Roar Ljoekelsoey Bjoern Einar Romoeren	Norway

Ski jumper Lars Bystoel of Norway

Snowboarder
Shaun White of
the United States

SNOWBOARD

Men's Halfpipe
GOLD	Shaun White	United States
SILVER	Daniel Kass	United States
BRONZE	Markku Koski	Finland

Men's Parallel Giant Slalom
GOLD	Philipp Schoch	Switzerland
SILVER	Simon Schoch	Switzerland
BRONZE	Siegfried Grabner	Austria

Men's Snowboard Cross
GOLD	Seth Wescott	United States
SILVER	Radoslav Zidek	Slovakia
BRONZE	Paul-Henri Delerue	France

Women's Halfpipe
GOLD	Hannah Teter	United States
SILVER	Gretchen Bleiler	United States
BRONZE	Kjersti Buaas	Norway

Women's Parallel Giant Slalom
GOLD	Daniela Meuli	Switzerland
SILVER	Amelie Kober	Germany
BRONZE	Rosey Fletcher	United States

Women's Snowboard Cross
GOLD	Tanja Frieden	Switzerland
SILVER	Lindsey Jacobellis	United States
BRONZE	Dominique Maltais	Canada

SPEED SKATING

Men's 1,000-Meter
GOLD	Shani Davis	United States
SILVER	Joey Cheek	United States
BRONZE	Erben Wennemars	Netherlands

Men's 10,000-Meter
GOLD	Bob de Jong	Netherlands
SILVER	Chad Hedrick	United States
BRONZE	Carl Verheijen	Netherlands

Men's 1,500-Meter
GOLD	Enrico Fabris	Italy
SILVER	Shani Davis	United States
BRONZE	Chad Hedrick	United States

Men's 500-Meter
GOLD	Joey Cheek	United States
SILVER	Dmitry Dorofeyev	Russia
BRONZE	Kang Seok Lee	South Korea

Men's 5,000-Meter
GOLD	Chad Hedrick	United States
SILVER	Sven Kramer	Netherlands
BRONZE	Enrico Fabris	Italy

Men's Team Pursuit
GOLD	Matteo Anesi	Italy
	Stefano Donagrandi	
	Enrico Fabris	
	Ippolito Sanfratello	
SILVER	Arne Dankers	Canada
	Steven Elm	
	Denny Morrison	
	Jason Parker	
	Justin Warsylewicz	
BRONZE	Sven Kramer	Netherlands
	Rintje Ritsma	
	Mark Tuitert	
	Carl Verheijen	
	Erben Wennemars	

Women's 1,000-Meter
GOLD	Marianne Timmer	Netherlands
SILVER	Cindy Klassen	Canada
BRONZE	Anni Friesinger	Germany

Women's 1,500-Meter
GOLD	Cindy Klassen	Canada
SILVER	Kristina Groves	Canada
BRONZE	Ireen Wust	Netherlands

Women's 3,000-Meter
GOLD	Ireen Wust	Netherlands
SILVER	Renate Groenewold	Netherlands
BRONZE	Cindy Klassen	Canada

Women's 500-Meter
GOLD	Svetlana Zhurova	Russia
SILVER	Wang Manli	China
BRONZE	Ren Hui	China

Women's 5,000-Meter
GOLD	Clara Hughes	Canada
SILVER	Claudia Pechstein	Germany
BRONZE	Cindy Klassen	Canada

Women's Team Pursuit
GOLD	Daniela Anschuetz Thoms	Germany
	Anni Friesinger	
	Lucille Opitz	
	Claudia Pechstein	
	Sabine Voelker	
SILVER	Kristina Groves	Canada
	Clara Hughes	
	Cindy Klassen	
	Christine Nesbitt	
	Shannon Rempel	
BRONZE	Yekaterina Abramova	Russia
	Varvara Barysheva	
	Galina Likhachova	
	Yekaterina Lobysheva	
	Svetlana Vysokova	

Speed skater Marianne Timmer
of the Netherlands

FACTS IN BRIEF ON PACIFIC ISLAND COUNTRIES

Country	Population	Government	Monetary unit*	Foreign trade (million U.S.$)	
---	---	---	---	Exports[†]	Imports[†]
Fiji	866,000	President Ratu Josefa Iloilovatu Uluivuda (suspended) Prime Minister Laisenia Qarase (ousted)**	dollar (1.72 = $1)	682	1,235
Kiribati	91,000	President Anote Tong	Australian dollar (1.34 = $1)	17	62
Marshall Islands	60,000	President Kessai Hesa Note	U.S. dollar	9	54
Micronesia, Federated States of	112,000	President Joseph J. Urusemal	U.S. dollar	22	149
Nauru	13,000	President Ludwig Scotty	Australian dollar (1.34 = $1)	0.06	20
New Zealand	4,087,000	Governor General Anand Satyanand; Prime Minister Helen Clark	dollar (1.52 = $1)	22,210	24,570
Palau	21,000	President Tommy Esang Remengesau, Jr.	U.S. dollar	18	99
Papua New Guinea	5,757,000	Governor General Sir Paulius Matane; Prime Minister Sir Michael Somare	kina (3.02 = $1)	2,833	1,651
Samoa	184,000	Head of State Malietoa Tanumafili II; Prime Minister Tuila'epa Sailele Malielegaoi	tala (2.76 = $1)	94	285
Solomon Islands	517,000	Governor General Nathaniel Waena; Prime Minister Manasseh Sogavare	dollar (7.62 = $1)	171	159
Tonga	107,000	King George Tupou V	pa'anga (2.01 = $1)	34	122
Tuvalu	11,000	Governor General Filoimea Telito; Prime Minister Apisai Ielemia	Australian dollar (1.34= $1)	1	31
Vanuatu	218,000	President Kalkot Mataskelekele; Prime Minister Ham Lini	vatu (111.95 = $1)	205	233

*Exchange rates as of Oct. 9, 2006.
[†]Latest available data.
**In December 2006, Frank Bainimarama, Fiji's military chief, seized control of the government.

Pacific Islands.

In 2006, voters in the Solomon Islands and Samoa cast ballots in national elections. A new king took the throne in Tonga, and the military chief of Fiji overthrew that country's elected government.

Fiji. The Commonwealth of Nations suspended Fiji following a bloodless coup in December. The Commonwealth of Nations is an association of independent countries and other political units that have lived under British law. On December 5, Frank Bainimarama, Fiji's military chief, seized control of the country, accusing Prime Minister Laisenia Qarase of corruption and of not dealing effectively with the perpetrators of a 2000 coup attempt.

Bainimarama admitted that his coup was illegal, but argued that Fiji's government was indecisive and had been unable "to save our people from destruction." He appointed physician Jona Senilagakali as caretaker prime minister and scheduled a meeting with Fiji's Great Council of Chiefs (GCC), which appoints the president and vice president. Bainimarama intended to reappoint President Ratu Josefa Iloilovatu Uluivuda, whom he had deposed. However, the GCC refused to recognize Bainimarama's authority.

Papua New Guinea. Researchers in May 2006 began a three-year geophysical survey of Papua New Guinea aimed at providing the country's mining department with scientific data to identify potential mineral deposits. Mining continues to be the country's major source of export income. The $20-million project was funded by a grant from the European Union.

The Asian Development Bank, a United Nations affiliate based in Tokyo, announced in July that it would give Papua New Guinea more than $2 million for a survey to help officials monitor public knowledge of and attitudes toward HIV and AIDS, among other goals. Major contributors to this grant included Australia, Japan, and New Zealand. Papua New Guinea was to provide about $1 million in funding.

Solomon Islands. In April 2006, the people of the Solomon Islands elected a new Parliament, which in turn held a secret-ballot election to choose a new prime minister. Initial results showed Snyder Rini, the deputy prime minister, with enough support to form a coalition government. However, Rini was immediately faced with a no-confidence vote. People accusing Rini of corruption rioted in Honiara, the capital, causing millions of dollars in damage. In early May, after order had been restored, Manasseh Sogavare, the leader of the Social Credit Party, was elected prime minister by the House of Representatives.

Tonga. King Taufa'ahau Tupou IV of Tonga died on September 10 in Auckland, New Zealand, at the age of 88. He was one of the world's longest-reigning monarchs, having ascended to the throne at the death of his mother, Queen Salote Tupou III, in 1965. His son became King George Tupou V on his father's death. In July 2006, Tupou IV's nephew Prince Tu'ipelehake, his wife, and their Tongan driver were killed in an auto accident in California.

Samoa. Prime Minister Tuila'epa Sailele Malielegaoi of Samoa ran unopposed in an April election for his seat in Parliament. His Human Rights Protection Party was a decisive victor in the election, winning 31 of 49 seats. The main opposition party, the Samoa Democratic United Party, took only 10 seats, and independents took 8.

Palau. In October, Palau's government moved from Koror to a newly built capital in Melekeok. The new capital lies on the eastern coast of Babeldaob, the main island of Palau. Much of the money for the construction came in the form of loans from Taiwan. Since Palau first officially recognized Taiwan as an independent nation in 1999, Taiwanese loans have helped Palau develop its infrastructure of roads, as well as construct a senior citizen center and a community center in Koror. ■ Eugene Ogan

See also **Australia; New Zealand.**

Painting. See Art.

Pakistan struggled in 2006 to deal with Islamic militants along its border with Afghanistan; separatist guerrilla warfare in the southwest; internal strife between its Sunni Muslim majority and Shi`ite Muslim minority; and political challenges to President Pervez Musharraf's military government.

Border tension. Taliban extremists and members of the al-Qa`ida terrorist organization sought refuge along Pakistan's border with Afghanistan after United States-led forces drove the Taliban from power in Afghanistan in 2001. In 2003, Pakistan's army, working with U.S. intelligence agents, unsuccessfully attempted to regain control over border areas where tribes had traditionally fought off central-government control.

A Pakistani soldier supervises rescuers searching the site of a collapsed bridge in Mardan, Pakistan, on August 6. A crowd gathered to watch the river rise during torrential monsoon rains, and the bridge, undermined by flood waters, collapsed, killing at least 40 people.

On Sept. 5, 2006, Pakistan's government signed a peace agreement with tribal elders of the North Waziristan region. The elders agreed to stop militant attacks into Afghanistan; in return, the government would end major military operations in the region. International observers described this as a face-saving way to get the army out of the area. In late September, a U.S. intelligence officer announced that Taliban attacks in adjacent areas of Afghanistan had increased by 300 percent since the signing of the agreement.

During a visit to Afghanistan on September 7, Musharraf admitted that militants were crossing from Pakistan to detonate bombs in Afghanistan. He denied that his government supported the militants, though both British and American sources noted that Pakistani military intelligence maintained ties with the Taliban. Relations between Musharraf and Afghan President Hamid Karzai remained tense, despite an effort by U.S. President George W. Bush to resolve differences at a White House dinner in their honor on September 27.

Religious tensions. On July 14, a suicide bombing in Karachi killed Allama Hassan Turabi, a leader of Pakistan's Shi`ite clerics, touching off riots by hundreds of his supporters. Turabi had complained earlier that Shi`ite Muslims were being systematically murdered while police focused on Taliban and al-Qa`ida problems.

Baluchistan, Pakistan's largest and poorest province, was torn by strife in 2006—as it had been much of the time since Pakistan was founded in 1947. Its traditional tribal leaders resisted encroachment by other Pakistanis and sought a larger share of money from the province's gas and other natural resources for the 5 million people of the region. After attacks on railways, gas pipelines, and the police spread, the army began hunting former Interior Minister Nawab Akbar Khan Bugti, one of the leaders of the uprising. On Aug. 26, 2006, the 79-year-old Bugti and others were killed in a mountain cave, setting off days of protests and rioting.

Politics. A no-confidence motion in Pakistan's Parliament against Prime Minister Shaukat Aziz, who was accused of employing corrupt senior officials, failed to pass on August 29. With parliamentary elections due by the end of 2007, political maneuvering intensified in 2006.

Benazir Bhutto and Nawaz Sharif, two former prime ministers who had left Pakistan in 1999 and 2000, respectively, after being accused of corruption, formed a political alliance in 2006 in hopes of defeating Musharraf. Bhutto and Sharif, who had alternated terms as prime minister before Musharraf seized power in 1999, announced in May 2006 that they would return to Pakistan despite the possibility that one or both might be jailed. Musharraf contended on May 16 that Pakistan had no future for what he called "rejected, corrupt" politicians.

At a conference in Havana, Cuba, on September 17, Musharraf and Prime Minister Manmohan Singh of India agreed to resume high-level talks. Efforts to resolve tension, including the status of the disputed Jammu and Kashmir state, had been stalled since July 11 terrorist bombings in Mumbai, India. India's police officials accused Pakistan's military of involvement in the attacks.

■ Henry S. Bradsher

See also **Asia; Disasters; India; Terrorism.**

Palau. See **Pacific Islands.**

Paleontology. The discovery of the fossilized bones of an animal that was evolving from a marine animal to a land animal was reported in April 2006 by a team of United States paleontologists. The 375-million-years-old fossils, found on a remote Arctic island, represent one of the most spectacular examples of a transitional species ever found. The fossils clearly show a nearly even blend of characteristics found in fish and in the first four-legged land animals. The species was named *Tiktaalik (tihk TAH lihk),* an Inuit word meaning *long, flattened fish* by discoverers Edward B. Daeschler of the Academy of Sciences in Philadelphia; Neil H. Shubin of the University of Chicago; and Farish A. Jenkins, Jr., of Harvard University in Cambridge, Massachusetts.

The remarkably well-preserved fossils reveal significant details about the transition of gill-respiring fish to air-breathing amphibians. Specifically, the fossils show lobe-finned fish (the group that includes lungfish and coelacanths) evolved into *tetrapods* (four-legged, land-dwelling, air-breathing animals). The oldest known true tetrapods date from about 365 million years ago.

Tiktaalik, which was about 10 feet (3 meters) long, had fishlike jaws as well as evidence of gills, fins with webbing, and scales. It also had features common to amphibians, including a neck and upward-facing eyes. In addition, what had been the simple fins of fish had started to develop into the fingers and swiveling wrist of a tetrapod. Scientists believe that *Tiktaalik* spent most of its life in the water but used its short, leglike fins to crawl onto land to find food, escape predators, or lay eggs.

Fossilized embryos. Two studies published in 2006 provided insights into the relationship between modern *metazoans* (multicellular animals) and ancient animals known from fossilized *embryos* (early stage of cell division following an egg's fertilization). The tiny, well-preserved embryos consist of several dozen to several hundred cells. Scientists found them in deposits near Doushantuo, China, were dated to more than 580 million years ago, during the late Proterozoic Era.

In June, paleontologists Jun-Yuan Chen of the Nanjing Institute of Geology and Paleontology in China, David J. Bottjer of the University of Southern California in Los Angeles, and colleagues described *lobes* on the embryos (groups of cells that develop into specialized adult structures). This kind of developmental pattern is seen mainly in such metazoans as *mollusks* (including clams, snails, and squids) and *annelids* (segmented worms). The discovery indicated that complex, multicellular organisms existed at least 40 million years earlier than believed.

In October, paleontologist James W. Hagadorn of Amherst College in Massachusetts and colleagues reported on images they made of the embryos using microscopes and *computed tomography* (an X-ray system that produces three-dimensional images). The pictures allowed the scientists to see internal structures and as many as 1,000 cells in some of the embryos. The researchers also discovered evidence of *asymmetrical* (unequal-sided) cell division in some embryos. This feature is typical of modern multicellular species, suggesting that the embryos belonged to animals that were closely related to the first modern metazoans.

Ancient spider web and prey. The discovery of a chunk of amber containing remnants of spider web silk—along with attached prey—was reported in June by *entomologists* (insect experts) Enriqué Peñalver and David Grimaldi of the American Museum of Natural History in New York City and paleontologist Xavier Delclos of the University of Barcelona in Spain. The amber formed when resin from a *conifer* (evergreen) tree fell on the web and then hardened. The scientists collected the specimen from sediments dated to approximately 110 million years ago, during the Early Cretaceous Period. Although the spider was not present in the amber, a beetle, a fly, and a wasp's leg were stuck to the silk. The unusual fossil proved that more than 100 million years ago, some spiders made vertical cobwebs to trap their prey—just as their relatives do today.

Dwarf dinosaurs. Animals that are isolated on small islands may undergo a rapid evolutionary change to a smaller size. Paleontologist P. Martin Sander of the University of Bonn in Germany and colleagues described this process, called dwarfism, in a sauropod dinosaur dating from about 150 million years ago, during the Late Jurassic Period.

Sauropods, including such giants as *Apatosaurus* and *Brachiosaurus* were the largest animals to ever walk on land. Many of these dinosaurs were more than 80 feet (24 meters) long and weighed more than 100 tons (91 metric tons). Sander's group described a sauropod, called *Europasaurus holgeri,* based on 11 well-preserved

A reconstruction of *Tiktaalik roseae* (left) lies next to the fossil of the animal described in April by paleontologists at the Academy of Natural Sciences in Philadelphia and other institutions. The scientists said the 375-million-year-old fossil, found in an ancient river delta in Arctic Canada, represented a "missing link" between fish and land animals. Its front fins have an armlike bone structure.

skeletons found in marine sediments in Germany. The paleontologists determined that the dinosaurs, which were only about 20 feet (6.2 meters) long as adults, were dwarf sauropods. They also concluded that the animals lived on a small island in an ancient seaway. The island would not have had enough plant food to support gigantic sauropods. Thus, large dinosaurs adapted to the limited food resources by becoming smaller, the scientists concluded.

Dinosaur neighbor. Large, fish-eating beaverlike animals lived alongside dinosaurs 164 million years ago, during the Jurassic Period, in what is now China, according to a February report describing a fossil found by Chinese paleontologists. Scientists found impressions of fur, webbed feet, and a scaly broadened tail on the fossil, which is larger than any other known Jurassic mammal. Scientists had previously believed that mammals did not begin to thrive until dinosaurs became extinct.   ■ Carlton E. Brett

Panama. In a referendum on Oct. 22, 2006, Panamanian voters approved, by a margin of greater than 3-to-1, a plan to expand and modernize the Panama Canal. The proposal called for a $5.2-billion investment in new three-step locks on either end of the existing canal to accommodate the increasingly larger vessels being used to transport products and commodities in international trade. The new locks were projected to be completed in 2014, the 100th anniversary of the opening of the Panama Canal. Panama also moved ahead in 2006 with a $600-million construction project to create a state-of-the-art port facility on the Pacific side of the canal. The port was designed to accommodate a rapidly expanding volume of trade with Asia.

Economists reported a 7.7-percent rate of growth in Panama's economy during the period of January through August 2006. A major contributor to the increase, they noted, was a significant expansion in foreign trade, especially trade with Singapore. For the first five months of 2006, Panama's trade with Singapore was valued at $1.7 billion, a 64-percent increase over the comparable period in 2005.

■ Nathan A. Haverstock
See also **Latin America.**

Papua New Guinea. See Pacific Islands.

Paraguay. See Latin America.

PEOPLE IN THE NEWS

in 2006 included those listed below, who were all from the United States unless otherwise indicated.

Abe, Shinzo (1954–), became prime minister of Japan in September 2006. He was made premier shortly after being elected leader of the ruling Liberal Democratic Party (LDP). Abe succeeded Junichiro Koizumi, who remained popular but stepped down because LDP rules set limits on leadership positions. Abe became the first Japanese prime minister born after World War II (1939-1945).

Abe was born on Sept. 21, 1954, in Nagato, in the southwestern part of the island of Honshu. In 1977, he graduated from the Faculty of Law at Seikei University in Tokyo. In 1982, he became an assistant to his father, Foreign Minister Shintaro Abe.

Shinzo Abe was elected to Japan's legislature, the Diet, first in 1993. Japan is divided into political units called prefectures, and Abe represented his home prefecture, Yamaguchi. In 2000, he became deputy chief Cabinet secretary to Prime Minister Yoshiro Mori. Abe retained his position when Koizumi succeeded Mori in April 2001. In October 2005, Koizumi appointed Abe to the post of chief Cabinet secretary.

See also **Japan.**

Alito, Samuel A., Jr. (1950–), a judge on the U.S. Court of Appeals for the Third Circuit, was sworn in as an associate justice on the United States Supreme Court on Jan. 31, 2006. In October 2005, President George W. Bush nominated Alito to fill the seat being vacated by Associate Justice Sandra Day O'Connor. President Bush had previously nominated John. G. Roberts, Jr., for the position. Following the death of Chief Justice William Rehnquist in September 2005, President Bush nominated Roberts for the post of chief justice. He then nominated Alito to succeed Justice O'Connor.

Samuel Anthony Alito, Jr., was born on April 1, 1950, in Trenton, New Jersey. He graduated from Princeton University in New Jersey, in 1972 and from Yale Law School in New Haven, Connecticut, in 1975. He served as a law clerk from 1976 to 1977. From 1977 to 1981, he served as assistant U.S. attorney for the District of New Jersey. In 1981, he became assistant to the U.S. solicitor general in the administration of President Ronald Reagan. In this position, Alito argued 12 cases before the Supreme Court. In 1985, he became deputy assistant attorney general in the U.S. Department of Justice. From 1987 to 1990, he served as U.S. attorney for the New Jersey District. He was appointed to the Court of Appeals in 1990.

See also **Supreme Court of the United States.**

Bachelet, Michelle (1951–), became president of Chile in March 2006 following her victory in a presidential runoff election in January. Bachelet, a physician, is Chile's first female president. She leads the center-left *Concertación* coalition, which has governed Chile since 1990.

In her election campaign, Bachelet pledged to continue fiscal policies favoring strong economic growth, but she also advocated creating greater economic opportunity for women, *indigenous* (native) peoples, and Chile's poorest citizens. In 2006, economists rated Chile's economy as one of the strongest in Latin America.

Ben Bernanke

Verónica Michelle Bachelet Jeria was born in Santiago, Chile, on Sept. 29, 1951. In the early 1970's, she attended the University of Chile and joined the Socialist Party. In September 1973, military forces under the command of Augusto Pinochet Ugarte mounted a successful *coup d'état* (overthrow) against the government of democratically elected President Salvador Allende and cracked down on Allende supporters. Bachelet's father, General Alberto Bachelet Martínez of the Chilean Air Force, was arrested and later died in prison. In January 1975, Michelle Bachelet, who had been active in Socialist Party politics, and her mother were arrested, tortured, and then allowed to flee the country.

Bachelet returned to Chile in 1979. After completing her medical studies, she worked as a physician and public health consultant. Democratic rule returned to Chile in 1990. In 2000, President Ricardo Lagos Escobar appointed Bachelet as minister of health in his Cabinet, and in 2002 he moved her to the position of defense minister. Bachelet left the Cabinet in 2004 to campaign for the presidency.

See also **Chile; Latin America: A Special Report.**

Bernanke, Ben Shalom (1953–), an

economist, was sworn in on Feb. 1, 2006, as chairman of the Board of Governors of the Federal Reserve System for a four-year term. The Federal Reserve System, commonly called the Fed, is an independent federal agency that directs the U.S. banking system and helps control the nation's interest rates and money supply. President George W. Bush appointed Bernanke to succeed Alan Greenspan, who retired after serving 18 years as the Fed chairman.

Ben S. Bernanke was born in Augusta, Georgia, on Dec. 13, 1953. He graduated from Harvard University in Cambridge, Massachusetts, in 1975 and in

1979 received a Ph.D. degree in economics from the Massachusetts Institute of Technology (MIT), also in Cambridge. From 1979 to 1983, Bernanke served on the economics faculty of Stanford University in California. From 1983 to 2002, he taught economics at Princeton University in New Jersey. His teaching career also included visiting professorships at MIT and New York University in New York City.

In 2002, Bernanke became a member of the Fed's Board of Governors, the executive body that administers the system. He also served as chairman of the president's Council of Economic Advisers from June 2005 until his appointment as Fed chairman in early 2006. During much of 2006, the Fed, under Bernanke's leadership, continued policies established under Greenspan.

See also **Bank; Economics, United States.**

Bolten, Josh (1954–), was selected by U.S.

President George W. Bush in March 2006 to serve as White House chief of staff. Bolten replaced Andrew H. Card, Jr., who resigned after more than five years on the job. The White House chief of staff manages the president's schedule, controls access to the president, and oversees other staff working for the president. Previously, Bolten had served as deputy chief of staff (2001–2003) and director of the Office of Management and Budget (2003–2006) in the Bush administration. According to political analysts, he has been an influential policy adviser to the president on such domestic issues as tax cuts and creation of the Department of Homeland Security.

Joshua Brewster Bolten was born on Aug. 16, 1954, in Washington, D.C., where he also grew up. His father was an agent with the Central Intelligence Agency (CIA) and his mother, a professor of history at Washington's George Washington University. He attended college at Princeton University in New Jerey and earned a law degree from Stanford University in California.

Bolten served in the administration of President George Herbert Walker Bush in the early 1990's as congressional liaison. In the mid-1990's, he worked for the New York City-based investment banking firm Goldman Sachs Group, Inc., at its London office. Bolten began working for George W. Bush in 1998 as policy director for the then-Texas governor's presidential campaign.

See also **United States, Government of the.**

Warren Buffett (right) with Bill Gates

investment company. During this period, Buffett married his first wife, Susan Thompson, with whom he had three children. (Following the 2004 death of Susan Buffett, Warren Buffett in August 2006 married Astrid Menks.)

In 1955, Buffett returned to Omaha and started his own investment firm, which would eventually become the core of the immensely profitable Berkshire Hathaway holding company. Among investors, Warren Buffett's views on stock market trading are so influential that he is popularly known as "the oracle of Omaha," and his holdings are so valuable that rumors of his ill health (unfounded, for the most part) have caused brief downturns in the stock market.

Buffett, Warren (1930–), pledged 85 percent of his Berkshire Hathaway stock, the basis of his multibillion-dollar fortune, to the Bill & Melinda Gates Foundation in June 2006. At the time of the announcement, the pledged stock was worth more than $30 billion, making it the largest philanthropic gift in U.S. history. Buffett is the chief executive officer of, and largest stockholder in, Berkshire Hathaway Inc., an Omaha, Nebraska-based *holding company* (umbrella corporation that owns a number of individual companies). Bill Gates is the chairman of Microsoft Corporation, based in Redmond, Washington, and the Bill & Melinda Gates Foundation is a charitable foundation established by Gates and his wife. Various financial publications in 2006 rated Bill Gates as the richest person in the world and Buffett, the second richest. (The two men are friends and have partnered in bridge tournaments.)

Warren Edward Buffett was born on Aug. 30, 1930, in Omaha. His father, Howard Buffett, was a stockbroker who represented an Omaha congressional district as a Republican in the U.S. House of Representatives for several terms in the 1940's. Warren made his first stock investment (from the proceeds of his paper route) at age 11. At age 16, he enrolled in the Wharton School of Business of the University of Pennsylvania in Philadelphia. After two years, he transferred to the University of Nebraska in Lincoln, where he earned a bachelor's degree in 1950.

Warren Buffett lived in New York City in the early 1950's, obtaining a master's degree from the Columbia University Graduate School of Business and working for an

Clooney, George (1961–), received Academy Award nominations in 2006 in three categories, and on March 5 won the Academy Award for best supporting actor for his performance in *Syriana* (2005). In that film, Clooney portrayed a discredited CIA agent caught in a web of high-stakes Middle East intrigue. The other two nominations were for best director for *Good Night, and Good Luck* (2005) and for best original screenplay as co-author of the same film, which investigated aspects of the career of journalist Edward R. Murrow.

George Timothy Clooney was born on May 6, 1961, in Lexington, Kentucky. Clooney's father, Nick Clooney, worked as a television newscaster and radio talk show host in Cincinnati, Ohio, and the family lived in a small town in nearby northern Kentucky. George Clooney's aunt was the singer Rosemary Clooney.

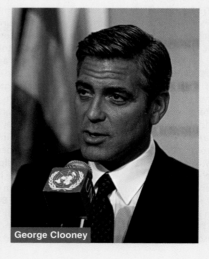
George Clooney

George Clooney began his acting career in television, starting with the comedy series "E/R" in 1984. From 1994 to 1999, he starred in the hit dramatic series "ER." In 1999, Clooney left television to concentrate on motion-picture roles, which have included *From Dusk till Dawn* (1996), *Out of Sight* (1998), *The Perfect Storm* (2000), *O Brother, Where Art Thou?* (2000), *Ocean's Eleven* (2001), and its sequel, *Ocean's Twelve* (2004). Clooney made his directing debut with *Confessions of a Dangerous Mind* (2002).

See also **Motion pictures.**

Couric, Katie (1957–),

became anchor of "CBS Evening News" in September 2006. She is the first woman selected as the solo host of a television nightly newscast for a major network. In May, Couric left the NBC "Today" show after a 15-year run as coanchor of the highly rated morning news show.

Katherine Anne Couric was born on Jan. 7, 1957, in Arlington, Virginia. She attended the University of Virginia in Charlottesville, earning a bachelor's degree in American studies in 1979. After graduation, Couric landed a job as news desk assistant at ABC's Washington, D.C., bureau. Later, she worked as an associate producer and as a reporter for CNN. In the mid-1980's, she worked as a reporter for local television stations in Washington, D.C., and in Miami, Florida.

Katie Couric

Couric went to NBC in 1989, to become the deputy Pentagon correspondent. In 1990, she joined the "Today" show as a correspondent. In 1991, she replaced Deborah Norville as the cohost.

Couric's husband of eight years, John Paul Monahan III, died of colon cancer in January 1998. (The couple had two daughters.) After a month's absence, Couric resumed duties at the "Today" show, and she became an active spokeswoman for early detection of colon cancer.

See also **Television.**

Dobbs, Lou (1945–),

in 2006 became the leading media spokesperson for tightening U.S. border controls to stem the tide of illegal immigration. Experts estimated that at least 12 million illegal immigrants were living in the United States during 2006. Dobbs hosted the influential television business news show "Lou Dobbs Tonight" on Cable News Network (CNN). In his commentaries, Dobbs routinely criticized the administration of President George W. Bush and politicians of both major parties for their alleged ineffectiveness at curbing illegal immigration. His comments helped publicize the problem until it became a major political issue in 2006. Dobbs also lambasted U.S. business executives whose corporations were *outsourcing jobs* (relocating U.S. factories to countries where labor costs were cheaper). Illegal immigration and job outsourcing, Dobbs asserted, were eroding the economic position of the U.S. middle class.

Lou Dobbs was born on Sept. 24, 1945, in Childress, Texas. He grew up in the Texas Panhandle and in Idaho and, as a youth, worked on farms. Dobbs graduated from Harvard University in Cam-

bridge, Massachusetts, in 1967 with a bachelor's degree in economics. In the late 1960's and the 1970's, Dobbs worked as a reporter and broadcast journalist in Arizona and Washington state. In 1980, he joined broadcasting magnate Ted Turner in launching CNN. Dobbs cocreated and hosted the business news show "Moneyline," which became the number-one draw for advertising revenue for CNN. He left in 1999 to help launch space.com, a Web site about space and space travel, but returned to CNN in 2001.

See also **Television; United States, Government of the: A Special Report.**

García, Alan (1949–),

became president of Peru in July 2006 following his victory over opponent Ollanta Humala in a June runoff election. García had previously served as president of Peru from 1985 to 1990. His first administration had ended in economic and political chaos with annual inflation of greater than 7,000 percent and a surging insurrection by the Shining Path, a Maoist revolutionary group. Political analysts explained that, in 2006, García appealed to a new generation of voters with no personal memory of his earlier presidency and that many older middle-class voters feared that Humala, a nationalist candidate with strong support from Venezuela's President Hugo Chávez,

Lou Dobbs

would discourage foreign investment by nationalizing industries and thereby depress economic growth.

Alan García Pérez was born on May 23, 1949, in Lima, Peru's capital. He earned a law degree in Peru in 1973 and spent the following years studying in universities in Spain and France. García returned to Peru in 1977 and became active in the American Popular Revolutionary Alliance (APRA), a left-of-center political party. He rose quickly in party ranks and won election to the presidency in 1985. Alberto Fujimori, who succeeded García as president in 1990, suspended Congress in 1992 and issued arrest warrants for political opponents, including García. By then, García had fled to Colombia. He spent nearly 10 years in exile, in Colombia and in France. García returned to Peru in 2001.

See also **Latin America: A Special Report; Peru.**

Harper, Stephen Joseph (1959–),

became prime minister of Canada in February 2006, after leading the Conservative Party of Canada to victory in a January election. He succeeded Paul Martin of the Liberal Party.

Stephen Joseph Harper was born on April 30, 1959, in Toronto, Ontario. Harper enrolled in the University of Toronto but did not complete a degree program there. He later attended the University of Calgary in Alberta, eventually earning a master's degree in economics in 1991.

Harper had moved to Alberta in 1978 to work in the oil industry. He had earlier identified himself as a political liberal, but in the 1980's he aligned himself with the Progressive Conservative Party. He began criticizing the energy policies of Prime Minister Pierre Elliot Trudeau of Canada's Liberal Party as too regulatory and harmful to Alberta's oil industry.

Harper ran unsuccessfully for the House of Commons in 1988. However, he eventually won election to that body from a Calgary district in 1993 and served in the House of Commons until 1997.

Harper continued to advocate conservative causes, particularly limiting the role of Canada's federal government. In 2001, he collaborated with other leading conservatives in writing *The Alberta Agenda,* a document that

advocated erecting a political "firewall" around Alberta to drastically reduce the federal government's role in the province. The document, published in a Toronto newspaper, became known as the "firewall letter."

In 2002, Harper won a special election to the House of Commons from Alberta. He became the leader of the conservative opposition in Parliament and eventually head of the Conservative Party of Canada. As prime minister, Harper supported free-market reforms and government downsizing. He also strengthened ties with the administration of U.S. President George W. Bush.

See also **Canada; Canada, Prime Minister of.**

Hoffman, Philip Seymour (1967–),

won the Academy Award for best actor on March 5, 2006, for his portrayal of writer Truman Capote in the biographical film *Capote.* Hoffman's performance in *Capote* also netted him Golden Globe and Screen Actors Guild awards for best actor.

Philip Seymour Hoffman was born on July 23, 1967, in suburban Rochester, New York. He became interested in drama as a high school student. He attended the Tisch School of the Arts of New York University in New York City and graduated in 1989 with a Bachelor of Fine Arts degree. Hoffman made his feature film debut in *Triple Bogey on a Par Five Hole* in 1991. Other films followed, including *My New Gun* (1992), *Boogie Nights* (1997), *The Talented Mr. Ripley* (1999), *Magnolia* (1999), and *Cold Mountain* (2003).

Hoffman also has appeared in a number of theatrical roles. He received a Tony nomination for best actor in 2000 for his performance in a Broadway revival of Sam Shepard's *True West.* He won another Tony nomination for best actor in 2003 for his performance as Jamie Tyrone in a Broadway revival of Eugene O'Neill's *Long Day's Journey into Night.*

See also **Motion pictures.**

Jefferts Schori, Katharine (1954–), was

elected presiding bishop of the Episcopal Church in June 2006. Her nine-year term officially began November 1. Previously, she had served as the Episcopal Church's bishop of Nevada. The presiding bishop is the spiritual leader of the U.S.-based Episcopal Church, a member

Katharine Jefferts Schori

of the Anglican Communion. The Anglican Communion is an international organization of more than 30 self-governing churches descended from the Anglican Church of the United Kingdom. Jefferts Schori is the first woman ever elected to head a church in the Anglican Communion.

Katharine Jefferts was born in Pensacola, Florida, on March 26, 1954. She attended Stanford University in California, from which she received a Bachelor of Science degree in biology in 1974. She subsequently earned master's and doctoral degrees in oceanography from Oregon State University in Corvallis. In 1979, Katharine Jefferts married Richard Miles Schori. In the 1980's and early 1990's, Jefferts Schori worked in the U.S. Marine Fisheries Service in Seattle.

Jefferts Schori received a Master of Divinity degree in 1994 from Church Divinity School of the Pacific in Berkeley, California, and was *ordained* (made a priest) in the Episcopal Church. She later earned a Doctor of Divinity degree from the same institution. Jefferts Schori served a church in Corvallis, Oregon, for several years before being elected bishop of Nevada in 2001.

See also **Protestantism.**

Ellen Johnson-Sirleaf

Johnson-Sirleaf, Ellen (1938–),

was sworn in as president of Liberia on Jan. 18, 2006. She was elected to the office in a November 2005 presidential runoff election. The 2005 election was Liberia's first presidential poll since the beginning of a civil war that ravaged the country for most of the 1990's and ended in 2003. Johnson-Sirleaf, an economist, became the first woman to be elected president of an African country.

Ellen Johnson was born on Oct. 29, 1938, in Monrovia, the capital of Liberia. She married James Sirleaf, also Liberian, in 1957. In 1971, Johnson-Sirleaf received a master's degree in public administration from Harvard University in Cambridge, Massachusetts. Later in the 1970's, she served as Liberia's minister of finance in the administration of President William R. Tolbert, Jr.

In 1980, a group of military leaders led a successful *coup* (overthrow) of Tolbert's government and installed Samuel K. Doe as president. Ellen Johnson-Sirleaf opposed Doe and was imprisoned for a time in 1985. She supported a rebellion led by Charles Taylor in 1989 to overthrow the Doe regime but later broke with Taylor, who was widely regarded as the chief instigator of Liberia's 14-year civil war. In 2003, domestic and international pressure forced Taylor out of office and into exile. An internationally brokered transitional administration took control of the country pending the installation of an elected government.

See also **Africa.**

Kaczynski, Jaroslaw, and Kaczynski, Lech, (1949–), are twin

brothers who in 2006 held positions in the Polish government as prime minister and president, respectively. Lech Kaczynski, elected president of Poland in 2005, appointed Jaroslaw Kaczynski as the nation's prime minister in July 2006. The appointment was occasioned by the resignation of Prime Minister Kazimierz Marcinkiewicz. Jaroslaw had previously been the official party leader of the governing right-of-center Law and Justice Party.

The twin Kaczynski brothers were born on June 18, 1949, in Warsaw, the capital, at a time when the city still lay largely in ruins from World War II (1939–1945). Members of the Kaczynski family had participated in the anti-German resistance during the war, and the Kaczynskis opposed the Soviet-sponsored Communist regime that took control of Poland in the late 1940's. Like many Poles, the Kaczynski family was Roman Catholic.

When Lech and Jaroslaw were 12 years old, they starred in a 1961 Polish film based on the popular children's story *Two Who Stole the Moon.* The film was named one of the best Polish movies of the 1900's, and the brothers won instant fame. Both brothers attended college in Poland and obtained law degrees. They were active in the Solidarity union movement that challenged Communist rule in 1980, and Lech was imprisoned for a time during the Polish regime's crackdown in the early 1980's. Jaroslaw played an

Lech Kaczynski and Jaroslaw Kaczynski

important part in negotiations in 1989 that led to the end of Communist one-party rule in Poland.

In 2000, Lech Kaczynski was offered the position of justice minister in the center-right government led by Jerzy Buzek. The Buzek government was defeated in parliamentary elections in 2001. However, Lech Kaczynski campaigned for and won the presidency in 2005 elections.

See also **Poland.**

Maliki, Nouri Kamel al- (1950–),

became prime minister of Iraq in May 2006. Maliki is a leader of the conservative religious party Dawa, which is associated with the Shi`ah branch of Islam. Dawa is part of the United Iraq Alliance (UIA), the largest political group in Iraq.

In early 2003, U.S.-led coalition forces overthrew Saddam Hussein, then dictator of Iraq, and occupied the country. Iraqis in January 2005 elected a National Assembly to draft a constitution for a new government. Maliki was elected among a block of UIA members, who made up the largest political grouping in the assembly. In October 2005, Iraqi voters approved the draft constitution submitted by the National Assembly.

Iraqi voters in December 2005 elected a new permanent Council of Representatives to replace the National Assembly. The UIA, which again won the largest bloc of seats, nominated interim Prime Minister Ibrahim al-Jafari to continue as prime minister, but Jafari withdrew his candidacy in April 2006. The UIA then nominated Maliki, who was subsequently approved by the council. Maliki's government faced

Nouri Kamel al-Maliki

increasing threats from violent sectarian conflict between Shi`ites and Sunnis, members of the two major branches of Islam.

Nouri Kamel al-Maliki was born on July 1, 1950, at Al Hindiyah in southern Iraq. Following a crackdown on Dawa in the late 1970's by Hussein, Maliki fled the country, residing first in Iran and later in Damascus, Syria. Maliki returned to Iraq around the time of the U.S.-led invasion in 2003.

In late October 2006, Maliki announced that he represented the interests of Iraqis—not the United States—and refused to agree to demands laid down by the administration of U.S. President George W. Bush. He also ordered U.S. troops out of Sadr City, a Baghdad neighborhood believed to harbor various Shi`ite militia members.

See also **Iraq; Middle East.**

Morales, Evo (1959–), an Aymara Indian,

became the first *indigenous* (native) president of Bolivia on Jan. 22, 2006. Morales, the leader of the leftist Movement Toward Socialism (MAS) and head of the coca growers' federation, was elected president in December 2005. Because coca is the plant from which the illegal drug cocaine is made, Morales's rise to the presidency proved controversial outside Bolivia. However, chewing coca leaves or brewing them into tea is legal in Bolivia.

Juan Evo Morales Ayma was born on Oct. 26, 1959, in an impoverished region of the Andes Mountains. In the early 1980's, the Morales family moved to a lowland region in the province of Cochabamba. There, Morales became a coca grower and, in time, emerged as a leader of regional and national coca growers.

Morales helped found MAS and in 1997 was elected to the Bolivian Congress. In 2002, he lost a presidential election to Gonzalo Sánchez de Lozada. In 2003, Morales participated in public protests against Sánchez de Lozada's plan to export natural gas to North America. The protests ended with Sánchez de Lozada's resignation in October 2003. Further protests resulted in the resignation of Sánchez de Lozada's successor, President Carlos Mesa, in June 2005 and the installation of a caretaker government that held power until Morales's inauguration.

As president, Morales placed all Bolivian natural gas fields under government control, in fulfillment of demands by the protesters who had brought down his presidential predecessors. He also sponsored a constitutional convention for which elections were held in July 2006, with MAS winning a majority of convention delegates.

See also **Bolivia; Latin America: A Special Report.**

Nasrallah, Sheik Hassan (1960–),

a Muslim cleric, led the Lebanon-based radical Islamic group Hezbollah in a monthlong conflict with Israel in July and August 2006. Hezbollah, a terrorist organization, in 2006 was funded by and received arms from the governments of Iran and Syria.

In July, Hezbollah fighters crossed into northern Israel and captured two Israeli soldiers, prompting military reprisals by Israel on Lebanon. Hezbollah responded by firing missiles on population centers in northern Israel. Over 1,000 people in Lebanon and Israel died as a result of the conflict, and Israeli air attacks inflicted serious damage on parts of Lebanon.

Hassan Nasrallah was born in a poor Shi`ite neighborhood of Beirut, Lebanon, on Aug. 31, 1960. When Lebanon's civil war broke out in 1975, Nasrallah's family fled Beirut and settled in their ancestral Shi`ah village in south Lebanon. In 1982, Nasrallah helped to form Hezbollah to fight Israeli forces, which subsequently occupied southern Lebanon. Along with other Hezbollah leaders, Nasrallah has advocated the extermination of Israel.

In 1992, Nasrallah was chosen secretary-general of Hezbollah after Israeli forces assassinated the movement's leader, Sheik Abbas al-Musawi. Nasrallah's own son became a Hezbollah fighter and was killed by Israeli soldiers in 1997. A charismatic leader who quotes classical Arabic texts, Nasrallah emerged from the conflict with Israel with greatly enhanced prestige in predominantly Muslim countries of the Middle East, according to Middle East experts.

See also **Israel; Lebanon; Middle East.**

Olmert, Ehud (1945–), became prime min-

ister of Israel in May 2006. He had served as acting prime minister after Prime Minister Ariel Sharon suffered a major stroke in January 2006.

In 1973, Olmert was elected to the Knesset, the Israeli parliament, as a member of Israel's conservative Likud party. He served under Prime Minister Yitzhak Shamir as minister without portfolio responsible for minority affairs from 1988 to 1990 and as health minister from 1990 to 1992. He was elected mayor of Jerusalem in 1993 and held the office untill 2003.

In 2003, Prime Minister Ariel Sharon appointed Olmert deputy prime minister, communications minister, and finance minister. Olmert was one of the first Israeli Cabinet members to suggest that Israel withdraw troops and settlers from the Gaza Strip, which Israel had fully or partially occupied since 1967.

In November 2005, Olmert joined Sharon in quitting the Likud party to form a new party, Kadima. Sharon formed Kadima as a means to carry out his plan for withdrawal from the Gaza Strip, which was accomplished in 2005.

Ehud Olmert was born in Binyamina, Israel, on Sept. 30, 1945. His father served in the Knesset. The younger Olmert graduated from Hebrew University in Jerusalem with a bachelor's degree in psychology and philosophy after serving in the Israeli Army. He also received a law degree from Hebrew University.

See also **Israel; Lebanon; Middle East.**

Paulson, Henry M., Jr. (1946–), was

sworn in as the 74th secretary of the U.S. Department of the Treasury on July 10, 2006. President George W. Bush nominated Paulson, and the U.S. Senate confirmed him in June to replace outgoing Secretary John W. Snow. Paulson had previously headed Goldman Sachs Group, Inc., a New York City-based investment banking firm.

Henry Merritt Paulson, Jr., was born on March 28, 1946, in Palm Beach, Florida, but grew up in Barrington, Illinois, near Chicago. Paulson attended Dartmouth College in Hanover, New Hampshire, graduating with a bachelor's degree in 1968. He received a Master's Degree in business administration from Harvard University in Cambridge, Massachusetts, in 1970.

Paulson served as staff assistant to the U.S. assistant secretary of defense from 1970 to 1972 and as staff assistant to President Richard M. Nixon from 1972 to 1973. In 1974, he began working in the Chicago office of Goldman Sachs. Paulson became a partner in the firm in 1982 and eventually moved to New York City. In 1994, he became the firm's chief operating officer, and in 1999, chairman and chief executive officer. Paulson also served as chairman of the board of directors for the Nature Conservancy, an environmental conservation group.

See also **Cabinet, U.S.; United States, Government of the.**

Snow, Tony (1955–), became the White

House press secretary in April 2006. Snow had previously worked as a conservative columnist and a news commentator for the Fox television network. Snow's appointment marked the first time that a professional journalist had been tapped for the White House press position since

Tony Snow

President Gerald Ford chose NBC commentator Ron Nesson in 1974.

Tony Snow was born on June 1, 1955, in Berea, Kentucky. He grew up in Cincinnati, Ohio. Snow earned a bachelor's degree in philosophy from Davidson College in Davidson, North Carolina, in 1977. During his career, Snow worked as an editor or editorial writer for a number of U.S. newspapers, including the *Greensboro* (North Carolina) *Record, The* (Norfolk) *Virginian-Pilot; The Washington Times,* and *The Detroit News.* In the early 1990's, he worked in the administration of President George H. W. Bush as a speechwriter. Snow went to Fox in 1996 and became a broadcast news celebrity as the host of "Fox News Sunday" and "Weekend Live with Tony Snow."

Witherspoon, Reese (1976–), won the Academy Award for best actress on March 5, 2006, for *Walk the Line.* The film is a biography of country music star Johnny Cash. Witherspoon played Cash's second wife, singer June Carter Cash.

Laura Jean Reese Witherspoon was born in Baton Rouge, Louisiana, on March 22, 1976. In the early 1980's, the family settled in Nashville, Tennessee, where Reese grew up. As a child, she appeared in local television commercials and began to take acting classes.

At age 14, Witherspoon was chosen for the lead in the feature film *The Man in the Moon* (1991). While still in high school, she also appeared in made-for-TV movies and mini-series as well as the feature film *A Far Off Place* (1993). Witherspoon enrolled in Stanford University in California in 1994. However, she interrupted her education in 1996 to make more films. In addition to *Walk the Line,* Witherspoon has appeared in many major films, including *Pleasantville* (1998), *Cruel Intentions* (1999), the hit comedy *Legally Blonde* (2001), and *Sweet Home Alabama* (2002).

See also **Motion pictures.**

■ Robert Knight

Peru. On July 28, 2006, Alan García Pérez of the American Popular Revolutionary Alliance (APRA) was sworn in as president of Peru. García had previously served as the country's president from 1985 to 1990, when runaway inflation had crippled the Peruvian economy. At the outset of his new term, García pledged to fight corruption, trim government bureaucracy, and increase revenues from the exploitation of Peru's mineral and energy wealth.

García had narrowly defeated Ollanta Humala in a runoff election in June 2006. In August, Humala was charged with human rights violations stemming from his participation in a 1992 military campaign against members of the Shining Path guerrilla movement. Despite this legal complication, Humala continued to exert political influence through his leftist Union for Peru, which controlled 45 seats in Peru's 120-seat *unicameral* (single-chamber) congress—compared with 36 for APRA.

Drug trafficking. In mid-July 2006, an assassin shot and killed Judge Hernán Saturno Vergara in a downtown restaurant in Lima, the capital. The judge had been hearing a court case against Mexican nationals accused of participation in the Tijuana cartel, an organization that ships the illegal stimulant drug cocaine from South America to the United States. Peruvian authorities in 2006 estimated that $400 million in laundered illegal drug profits had entered Peru since 2003.

Mine protest. In August 2006, farmers and environmental activists blocked roads serving the Yanacocha Gold Mine to protest the alleged pollution of local water resources by mining operations involving the use of highly toxic cyanide. Yanacocha, Latin America's largest gold mine, is situated on an intensively farmed, high plateau 350 miles (560 kilometers) north of Lima. In 2006, the majority owner of the mine was the Newmont Mining Company of Denver.

Company managers responded to the protest by shutting down operations. The impasse was broken on August 29, when the mine owners and demonstrators agreed to settle their differences under the auspices of a specially appointed government commission.

As part of the settlement, more than 30 companies with mining operations in Peru agreed to pay the Peruvian government $774 million to be invested in building roads and other infrastructure and reducing poverty in rural areas. Political pundits noted the claims of APRA supporters that the government-brokered settlement fulfilled an election campaign pledge by President García to use profits from Peru's mining industry to better the lives of Peruvians. ■ Nathan A. Haverstock

See also **Latin America: A Special Report; People in the news (Alan García).**

Petroleum and gas. See Energy supply.

Philadelphia. A rapidly increasing homicide rate became a major concern for Philadelphia in 2006. Although homicides declined in many United States cities during the course of the year, Philadelphia experienced an increase of about 15 percent compared with 2005. A number of young children and teen-agers were among Philadelphia's murder victims in 2006. In one especially violent 36-hour span in early October, there were six homicide-related deaths, including a 17-year-old shooting victim and an infant who had been severely beaten.

Philadelphia's homicide rate became a major news story in 2006 and the subject of numerous community meetings and government discussions. Police stated that a flood of illegal guns into the city—in addition to a street mentality that made guns attractive—contributed to the increased violence. The violence was most prevalent in poor neighborhoods outside Center City, Philadelphia's downtown area.

Slot machines. The Philadelphia Park racetrack in October received a shipment of 100 slot machines—the first slot machines permitted under a 2004 state law that expanded legalized gambling. The law made licenses available to several racetrack casinos throughout the state. New slot parlors were also planned for Philadelphia and other Pennsylvania cities.

Pennsylvania Governor Ed Rendell and many state lawmakers predicted that the slot machines would eventually generate about $1 billion per year to fund cuts in property taxes and wage taxes. In October 2006, the state legislature approved a bill that would give $5 million annually in gambling proceeds to the Philadelphia school district, which was grappling with a deficit of about $73 million. Philadelphia officials expected to receive a total of about $24 million per year from slot revenues.

Convicted councilman. Rick Mariano, an electrician who became a city councilman, was convicted of corruption and fraud following a two-week trial in March. Jurors found him guilty of accepting nearly $30,000 in bribes in exchange for granting businesses inexpensive city-owned land, tax breaks, and other favors. Federal prosecutors claimed that the crimes cost taxpayers about $700,000. Mariano became the first Philadelphia elected official to be convicted of a crime in 15 years. He began serving a 6 ½-year sentence in August at a federal prison camp in suburban Philadelphia.

Newspaper sale. Philadelphia's two major daily newspapers—the *Philadelphia Daily News* and *The Philadelphia Inquirer*—returned to local ownership in 2006, when a group of Philadelphia investors purchased the papers from the Sacramento, California-based McClatchy Company. The

$562-million sale, which was completed in June, also included the newspapers' online services, as well as other publications distributed in and around Philadelphia. The investors formed a new company, Philadelphia Media Holdings LLC, committed to locally owned journalism.

Prior to the sale, McClatchy had acquired the two Philadelphia papers—in addition to 30 other dailies—through a merger with Knight Ridder Inc., a San Jose-based communications company.

Rocky statue. A statue of Rocky Balboa—the fictional Philadelphia boxer featured in the 1976 Academy Award-winning motion picture *Rocky* and its sequels—was unveiled in September 2006 outside the Philadelphia Museum of Art. Actor Sylvester Stallone, who portrayed the Rocky Balboa character in the movie series, was on hand for the statue's unveiling.

The *Rocky* films had long been associated with the Philadelphia Museum of Art because of a famous scene in which Balboa runs up the museum's steps while training. The statue, which was originally used as a prop for *Rocky III* (1982), previously stood outside the Spectrum, a concert and sports venue in South Philadelphia. Stallone filmed the sixth movie in the *Rocky* series—shot largely in Philadelphia—in 2006.

◼ Howard S. Shapiro

See also **City; Newspaper.**

Philippines. President Gloria Macapagal-Arroyo declared a state of emergency in the Philippines on Feb. 24, 2006. She acted hours after senior military officials said that they had blocked the 12th attempt in 20 years to overthrow the government. Critics questioned whether it was a significant attempt, suggesting that the incident consisted of marines who had objected to their commander's being relieved of duty.

Following the declaration, thousands of demonstrators marched through the financial district of the country's capital, Manila. Led by former President Corazon Aquino, the demonstrators called for Macapagal-Arroyo's resignation on renewed charges that the president had rigged her election in 2004. Macapagal-Arroyo survived an impeachment attempt in 2005 over the allegations, which were paired with charges of administration corruption. The demonstrations ended peacefully, and upon lifting the state of emergency on March 3, 2006, Macapagal-Arroyo declared, "the conspiracy has been broken up."

Insurgents. In June, Macapagal-Arroyo set a two-year deadline for security forces to wipe out the New People's Army (NPA), the Communist group that began a guerrilla war in 1969 to overthrow the government. Some 40,000 people died during the NPA's peak period in the 1970's and 1980's, but the group began to fade in the 1990's.

A rescue helicopter surveys the damage after a mudslide on Leyte Island in the Philippines buried the village of Guinsaugon on Feb. 17, 2006. Disaster workers recovered only 139 of the more than 1,000 people who were killed in the mudslide.

The NPA revived in recent years, spreading its operations to 69 of the country's 79 provinces. The Philippine Army redeployed troops from fighting the Moro Islamic Liberation Front (MILF) on the southern island of Mindanao to opposing the Communist guerrillas.

Diplomatic talks held in Malaysia between Philippine government officials and the MILF on ending a separate, sporadic MILF rebellion broke down on Sept. 7, 2006. The MILF sought more autonomy for Muslims in the southern islands of the predominantly Roman Catholic nation.

On September 28, the director of the government's Anti-Terrorism Task Force, Ric Blancaflor, announced that the most dangerous threat to national stability was a small group of Filipino converts to Islam, the Rajah Solaiman Revolutionary Movement. He accused the group of urban bombings and other terrorist acts.

Leftist killings. In August, Macapagal-Arroyo announced the formation of a commission to investigate a wave of killings of leftist political activists. Amnesty International, a London-based human rights group, reported on August 15 that 66 leftists had been murdered in 2005 and an additional 51 died in the first 6 months of 2006. The group concluded that the government was implicated in some of the murders. Leftist activists denied any connection with the Communist NPA.

They claimed that their aim was to resist domination of the Philippines by a small elite that had for generations controlled politics to exploit the poor.

The economy of the Philippines improved in 2006. Taxes approved in 2005 raised government revenue, enabling Macapagal-Arroyo to announce during her State of the Nation address on July 24, 2006, plans to create more jobs and boost economic growth. According to the plan, growth will focus on four economic areas: agribusiness, mining, export-oriented manufacturing, and tourism.

Many Filipinos continued in 2006 to seek jobs abroad, and remittances from overseas workers were an important element in many families' income. Nurses from the Philippines had been in high demand abroad for many years, with several thousand going to the United States annually. The revelation in August that nursing board examinations had been leaked in advance to applicants created an uproar. On September 27, Macapagal-Arroyo ordered that applicants be reexamined to restore the integrity and respect of the profession.

Typhoon Durian struck the Philippines on November 30 with 165-mile- (265-kilometer-) per-hour winds that loosened debris on the slopes of the Mayon volcano on Luzon. Ensuing mudslides killed an estimated 1,000 people and destroyed several villages. ■ Henry S. Bradsher

See also **Asia; Disasters.**

Physics. Physicists have long wondered whether the fundamental constants of nature are truly constant or whether they change over billions of years. According to a study published in April 2006, the constant known as *mu*—the ratio of the mass of the proton to that of the electron—may have decreased by 0.002 percent during the past 12 billion years. The study was carried out by an international team of physicists headed by Wim Ubachs of the Free University of Amsterdam in the Netherlands.

Hydrogen atoms consist of a positively charged proton and a negatively charged electron. Hydrogen atoms emit and absorb light at specific wavelengths. These wavelengths are related to the proton-electron mass ratio—the proton being roughly 1,836 times as massive as the electron. The researchers performed precision laboratory measurements of the wavelengths emitted by hydrogen today. They then compared these results with the wavelengths given off by *interstellar* (between stars) hydrogen at a distance of 12 billion light-years. In effect, the scientists measured mu as it was 12 billion years ago.

The wavelength analysis uncovered the tiny—yet statistically significant—change in mu over time. If verified by other researchers, this finding would indicate that the constants of the universe change—and that the laws of physics hold deeper secrets than physicists had expected.

Gravity in the microworld. In August 2006, an extremely precise measurement of acceleration caused by gravity on a scale of micrometers (millionths of a meter) was published by a team of physicists led by Guglielmo Tino at the University of Florence in Italy. Using a recently developed technique called optical trapping, the researchers studied an effect of *quantum mechanics* (the behavior of atoms and subatomic particles) called Bloch oscillation. When a group of supercold atoms of strontium was trapped in a mesh of crisscrossing laser beams, the atoms were subjected to the steady force of gravity. However, the atoms were not free to move in the direction of the force. Instead, they *oscillated* (moved back and forth). The frequency of this oscillation provided a measure of the strength of gravity.

The investigators obtained a measurement with a tiny uncertainty—of only one part in a million. The experimenters hoped to increase the precision of this measurement by as much as a factor of 10. The increase would allow them to detect possible deviations from accepted theories of gravity, including the existence of such phenomena as unseen, extra dimensions of space. Some ideas in particle physics indicate the existence of such phenomena.

Cosmic inflation supported. Researchers analyzing data collected by the Wilkinson Micro-wave Anisotropy Probe (WMAP) satellite revealed in March the best evidence to date for cosmic inflation—the theory that, in the first instants of its existence, the universe went through a period of extremely rapid expansion. It then settled down into the slower, fairly steady expansion we see today.

WMAP, launched by the National Aeronautics and Space Administration (NASA) in 2001, scans the entire sky for cosmic microwave background (CMB) radiation, energy and light that was emitted when the universe was approximately 300,000 years old. This radiation is nearly uniform in all directions, but small deviations of about one part in 100,000 provide a gold mine of information about conditions in the early universe.

The bright spots in the CMB radiation reveal the presence of "seeds" of energy, around which the earliest stars and galaxies formed. Many physicists believe that such seeds originated from quantum fluctuations that occurred during the inflationary era. If this idea is true, the deviations in CMB radiation should increase as parts of the sky that are farther and farther apart are compared. The WMAP researchers reported clear evidence that this is indeed the case.

■ Robert H. March

See also **Nobel Prizes.**

Poetry. Readers' continued interest in poetry as an aural art form—that is, an art form to be heard—as opposed to one appreciated primarily or exclusively through reading, has led poets and poetry organizations to utilize a relatively new technology to disseminate poetry: the podcast. Podcasts, which have become increasingly popular in recent years, are computer audio files that can be downloaded and listened to on a computer or a media-content player, such as Apple Computer's iPod. In April 2006, the Academy of American Poets, a national organization for the promotion of poetry based in New York City, began using this technology for what it calls "poetcasts," files of poets reading from their work that can be downloaded free of charge over the Internet at the academy's Web site.

According to the academy, the poetcasts "are like online radio shows, except that you don't have to tune in at a given time. Instead, users 'subscribe' to podcasts . . . and episodes download directly onto your computer as they are released." Poets who read from their work in this format in 2006 included two former poets laureate of the United States, Robert Pinsky and Louise Glück. The Academy of American Poets, in addition to maintaining an extensive Web site devoted to poets and poetry, is the sponsor each April of National Poetry Month, a celebration that draws attention to poetry around the United States through a series of readings and events.

A new poet laureate. The librarian of Congress, James H. Billington, announced in 2006 that Donald Hall would succeed Ted Kooser as poet laureate for the United States. Hall lives at Eagle Pond Farm in Wilmot, New Hampshire. Over the course of his long career as a writer, he has produced poems, plays, essays, and children's books, as well as celebrated memoirs of his life at the farm.

Perhaps Hall's best-known book of poems, *Without* (1998), recounts the illness of his wife—the poet Jane Kenyon, who died of leukemia in 1995—and his struggle with loss and grief at her death. Despite their painful subject matter, the poems in *Without* and in *The Old Life* (1996) constitute one of the great portraits of a marriage in contemporary letters: "The hour/ we lived in, two decades/ by the pond, has transformed/ into a single unstoppable day. . . ."

In April 2006, Hall published *White Apples and the Taste of Stone: Selected Poems 1946-2006,* a career retrospective that also includes new poems. His plain-spoken verses display a fondness for storytelling and wit. Hall's down-home subjects, from farm life to baseball, are explored in poems that wear their artfulness lightly yet deliver a strong emotional punch.

Remembering Emma Lazarus. In October 2006, Charles Martin, the poet in residence at the Cathedral Church of St. John the Divine in New York City, oversaw the induction of Emma Lazarus into the cathedral's American Poets' Corner. Lazarus, born in New York City in 1849, was honored beside such other esteemed American poets as Emily Dickinson, Walt Whitman, Robert Frost, and Langston Hughes. The Poets' Corner at St. John the Divine recalls a similar site at Westminster Abbey in London. Because of his connection with Westminster, Geoffrey Chaucer was buried in the abbey upon his death in 1400. Eventually, other poets and writers came to be buried or memorialized in the area where Chaucer was laid to rest, and it became known as Poets' Corner. The American Poets' Corner where Lazarus was inducted was created in 1984.

Lazarus's best-known poem, "The New Colossus" (1883), appears on a plaque within the pedestal upon which stands the Statue of Liberty. The poem concludes, "Give me your tired, your poor,/ Your huddled masses yearning to breathe free,/ The wretched refuse of your teeming shore./ Send these, the homeless, tempest-tost to me,/ I lift my lamp beside the golden door!" A new edition of her work, *Emma Lazarus: Selected Poems,* edited by the poet John Hollander, was published in 2005. ■ David Yezzi

See also **Literature.**

Poland. During 2006, Poland's conservative governing coalition, led by the Law and Justice party, narrowly held onto power through several government crises. In July, Prime Minister Kazimierz Marcinkiewicz resigned. President Lech Kaczynski then nominated as prime minister his twin brother, Jaroslaw Kaczynski, who went on to win approval from the Polish parliament. Critics suggested that Jaroslaw Kaczynski had always been the behind-the-scenes power in the governing coalition and that Marcinkiewicz was pushed out when he asserted too much independence from the Kaczynski brothers.

In September, the Kaczynski brothers—president and prime minister—ousted Deputy Prime Minister Andrzej Lepper from the Cabinet, stripping him of his posts of deputy prime minister and agriculture minister. Prime Minister Jaroslaw Kaczynski stated that the action was in response to Lepper's alleged corruption, but some political analysts speculated that policy disagreements lay behind the minister's removal.

Following a turbulent three-week period in which the prime minister scrambled to assemble a new governing coalition, President Lech Kaczynski in mid-October reappointed Lepper as deputy prime minister, restoring him to the Cabinet. Analysts speculated that the Kaczynskis backpedaled on Lepper to avoid a no-confidence vote in parliament, which would force early elections.

Poland's economy continued to expand in 2006. The gross domestic product (GDP)—the value of all goods and services produced in a given year—grew at an annual rate of from 5 to 6 percent in the first half of 2006, compared with 4.3 percent in 2005. Inflation remained low, running at under 1 percent. Unemployment also showed improvement, declining from 17.4 percent in 2005 to 14.9 percent in late 2006.

According to a survey published in June 2006, Poland was rated the most attractive location in Europe for foreign investors. Economists projected that foreign investment would reach a record $8.7 billion in 2006.

Foreign policy. In June, Polish leaders announced that 500 Polish soldiers would join NATO-led peacekeepers in Afghanistan in 2007. Approximately 100 Poles were serving with coalition troops there in 2006. In September, Prime Minister Jaroslaw Kaczynski visited United States President George W. Bush in Washington, D.C., and reaffirmed Poland's support for U.S. policies in Iraq. In November, President Lech Kaczynski announced that Poland would keep 900 troops in Iraq as part of coalition forces until at least mid-2007. ■ Sharon L. Wolchik

See also **Europe; People in the news** (Jaroslaw and Lech Kaczynski).

Pollution. See **Environmental pollution.**

Popular music. The business of popular music in the United States remained in a state of flux in 2006. Sales of CD's declined by about 14 percent in the first half of the year, according to the Recording Industry Association of America (RIAA), continuing a trend that began in 1999. Consumers continued to move toward digital downloads as the music medium of choice, and the major labels struggled to find a viable business model in the new marketplace.

In a record industry turnabout, in December 2006, the London-based EMI Group PLC began experimenting with selling copy-protection-free MP3's of the music of some of its artists—including Grammy-winning jazz-pop singer Norah Jones. Available through Yahoo.com, the service was an effort to satisfy consumer demand and to provide access to Apple Computer Media Inc.'s iPod. In February 2006, iTunes—Apple's online music store—hit the 1-billion mark in downloads. Competitor eMusic announced in November that it was closing in on iTunes with some 100 million downloads.

MySpace.com, the social networking Web site, sponsored a series of concerts and solidified its reputation as a force in pop music. The grassroots power of MySpace music communities was credited with the success of the debut album of the Florida hard-rock Christian band Underoath. *Define the Great Line* shot to number two on *Billboard* magazine's top 200 chart of bestselling U.S. albums immediately after release.

Country music goes pop. Country music remained a powerful force in popular music in 2006. No popular music act sold more new albums during the year than the Ohio trio Rascal Flatts. Featuring burnished, pop-leaning harmonies, the group's *Me and My Gang* sold 3 million copies in the United States with such hits as "What Hurts Most" and "My Wish." Carrie Underwood, the fourth-season winner of TV's "American Idol," sold nearly 4 million copies of her debut album, *Some Hearts,* by late 2006 in the United States alone. She was named female vocalist of the year at the Country Music Association (CMA) Awards in November.

Veteran duo Brooks & Dunn won three CMA awards for their hit "Believe" in addition to the award for best vocal duo. Kenny Chesney was named CMA entertainer of the year. Brad Paisley's *Time Well Wasted* was named country album of the year, selling more than 1.5 million copies by year's end. Husband-and-wife country superstars Tim McGraw and Faith Hill launched their "Soul2Soul II" tour in April. The tour grossed nearly $90 million, making it the highest-grossing country music tour of all time.

Political rhythms. The polarization in U.S. politics was reflected in a number of high-pro-

GRAMMY AWARD WINNERS IN 2006

Record of the Year, "Boulevard of Broken Dreams," Green Day

Album of the Year, *How to Dismantle an Atomic Bomb,* U2

Song of the Year, "Sometimes You Can't Make It on Your Own," U2

New Artist, John Legend

Pop Vocal Performance, Female, "Since U Been Gone," Kelly Clarkson

Pop Vocal Performance, Male, "From the Bottom of My Heart," Stevie Wonder

Pop Performance by a Duo or Group with Vocal, "This Love," Maroon 5

Traditional Pop Vocal Album, *The Art of Romance,* Tony Bennett

Solo Rock Vocal Performance, "Devils & Dust," Bruce Springsteen

Rock Performance by a Duo or Group with Vocal, "Sometimes You Can't Make It on Your Own," U2

Hard Rock Performance, "B.Y.O.B.," System of a Down

Metal Performance, "Before I Forget," Slipknot

Rock Song, "City of Blinding Lights," U2

Rock Album, *How to Dismantle an Atomic Bomb,* U2

Alternative Music Album, *Get Behind Me Satan,* The White Stripes

Rhythm-and-Blues Vocal Performance, Female, "We Belong Together," Mariah Carey

Rhythm-and-Blues Vocal Performance, Male, "Ordinary People," John Legend

Rhythm-and-Blues Performance by a Duo or Group with Vocal, "So Amazing," Beyoncé and Stevie Wonder

Rhythm-and-Blues Song, "We Belong Together," Johnta Austin, Mariah Carey, Jermaine Dupri, and Manuel Seal, Jr.

Rhythm-and-Blues Album, *Get Lifted,* John Legend

Contemporary Rhythm-and-Blues Album, *The Emancipation of Mimi,* Mariah Carey

Rap Solo Performance, "Gold Digger," Kanye West

Rap Performance by a Duo or Group, "Don't Phunk with My Heart," The Black Eyed Peas

Rap Album, *Late Registration,* Kanye West

Rap Song, "Diamonds from Sierra Leone," DeVon Harris and Kanye West

Contemporary Jazz Album, *The Way Up,* Pat Metheny Group

Jazz Vocal Album, *Good Night, and Good Luck,* Dianne Reeves

Jazz Instrumental, Solo, "Why Was I Born?" Sonny Rollins

Jazz Instrumental Album, Individual or Group, *Beyond the Sound Barrier,* Wayne Shorter Quartet

Large Jazz Ensemble Album, *Overtime,* Dave Holland Big Band

Country Album, *Lonely Runs Both Ways,* Alison Krauss and Union Station

Country Song, "Bless the Broken Road," Bobby Boyd, Jeff Hanna, and Marcus Hummon

Country Vocal Performance, Female, "The Connection," Emmylou Harris

Country Vocal Performance, Male, "You'll Think of Me," Keith Urban

Country Performance by a Duo or Group with Vocal, "Restless," Alison Krauss and Union Station

Country Vocal Collaboration, "Like We Never Loved at All," Faith Hill and Tim McGraw

Country Instrumental Performance, "Unionhouse Branch," Alison Krauss and Union Station

file releases in 2006. In May, Neil Young released *Living With War,* with caustic lyrics about the administration of U.S. President George W. Bush in such songs as "Let's Impeach the President" and "Lookin' For a Leader." Also in May, Paul Simon, another 1960's music icon, released *Surprise,* his first album in six years, which features the forlorn "Wartime Prayers." Pearl Jam scored its biggest radio hit in years in May 2006 with the geopolitical rant "World Wide Suicide," which reached number one on *Billboard*'s U.S. modern rock chart.

The Flaming Lips had the best sales week of their 23-year career in April with the album *At War With the Mystics,* a surreal commentary on modern U.S. politics and religion. In July, Michael Franti and his band Spearhead released *Yell Fire!,* an album that was informed by Franti's travels to Iraq, Israel, and the Palestinian territories. The singer's travels were filmed for the politically charged documentary *I Know I'm Not Alone,* released in December.

The Dixie Chicks remained a controversial force in pop culture in 2006 because of the ongoing fallout from a 2003 incident in which lead singer Natalie Maines made a disparaging comment about President Bush from the stage at a concert in England. In May 2006, the Chicks released their sixth studio album, *Taking the Long Way,* which is laced with political content on such songs as "Lubbock or Leave It" and "Not Ready to Make Nice." The album debuted at number one on the *Billboard* 200, making the trio the first female group in music history to produce three albums that debuted at number one. In September, *Shut Up & Sing,* a documentary film focusing on the Dixie Chicks in the aftermath of Maines's remarks, premiered at the Toronto International Film Festival and earned favorable reviews.

Jay-Z returns. New York hip-hop kingpin Jay-Z came out of his short retirement—he walked away from the microphone in 2003 to become a full-time record executive and entrepreneur—with the highly anticipated release of *Kingdom Come* in November 2006. The album debuted at number one on the *Billboard* 200 with 680,000 copies sold in its first week, the strongest single week of sales all year. The album features an impressive supporting cast of top rap artists, including Kanye West, Dr. Dre, and Pharrell Williams. In December, Jay-Z's famous girlfriend, Beyoncé

Knowles, also had a number-one album with *B'Day,* released in September. It sold more than 1.4 million copies in the United States by year's end.

The surprise pop sensation of the year was *High School Musical,* the soundtrack to the Disney Channel's original 2006 movie of that name. The album became one of the year's best-selling CD's, with 3.1 million copies sold. The musical, which premiered in January, tells the story of two teenagers from different social groups who overcome challenges to star in a campus production. The soundtrack, released 10 days before the movie aired on the Disney Channel, debuted at number 143 on the *Billboard* 200, with fewer than 7,000 copies sold. After the movie aired, however, the CD shot up the chart, hitting number one in March.

The success of *High School Musical* led a banner year for the Disney Channel as a force in pop music. The soundtrack to the Disney Channel original movie *Cheetah Girls 2* debuted at number five on the *Billboard* 200 in August. The soundtrack to the hit Disney Channel series *Hannah Montana* debuted at number one in stores in October.

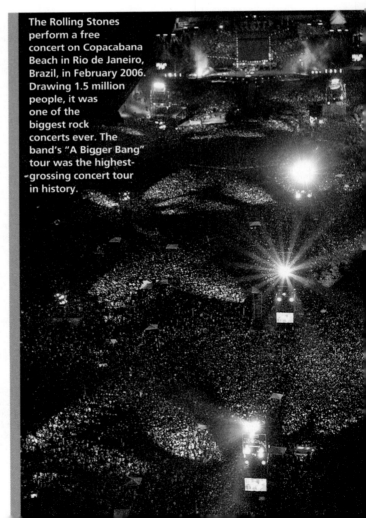

The Rolling Stones perform a free concert on Copacabana Beach in Rio de Janeiro, Brazil, in February 2006. Drawing 1.5 million people, it was one of the biggest rock concerts ever. The band's "A Bigger Bang" tour was the highest-grossing concert tour in history.

Justin Timberlake, formerly of 'N Sync, released *FutureSex/LoveSounds* in September. The album sold 684,000 copies in its first week, debuting at number one on the *Billboard* 200, and set a record for the most pre-orders and most digital copies sold in a week by iTunes. The album was hailed as a sophisticated hybrid of pop, dance, hip-hop, and rock.

Other top sellers. The Red Hot Chili Peppers scored in May with their two-CD release, *Stadium Arcadium,* the first number-one album of their career. It included one of their biggest radio hits, "Dani California." Nelly Furtado scored a hit with the album *Loose,* which took the singer in a dance-pop direction. Colombian singer Shakira continued her crossover to the U.S. market with the hit single "Hips Don't Lie." Christina Aguilera, John Mayer, and Jack Johnson all had brisk-selling new releases.

The Beatles hit the charts in 2006—36 years after the band's split. An ambitious reimagining of the band's recordings was released in November as *Love,* the soundtrack to a new production by Cirque du Soleil, the surreal, Canadian-based circus troupe best known for its elaborate productions in Las Vegas. *Love* was produced by Sir George Martin, the Beatles' esteemed producer, who worked with his son, Giles, to interpolate and weave shared drum cadences and other musical common points to create a smooth collage of the band's seminal songbook.

Madonna's "Confessions" tour began in Los Angeles in May. Buoyed by pricey tickets and intense fan interest, "Confessions" became the most lucrative tour by a female artist in music history, grossing nearly $195 million. The tour generated controversy for a segment during which Madonna hung from a mirrored crucifix, wearing a crown of thorns.

Out with a "Bang." The Rolling Stones' "A Bigger Bang" world music tour had become the highest-grossing music tour in history by November, with $437 million in earnings. The band expected to continue the tour in 2007.

Death. Ahmet Ertegun, 83, music magnate and founder of Atlantic Records, died in December 2006 from complications from a fall suffered at a Rolling Stones concert in October. Ertegun helped shape the careers of John Coltrane, Ray Charles, Aretha Franklin, Otis Redding, the Rolling Stones, Led Zeppelin, and many other top jazz, rock, soul, and pop performers.

Soul singer James Brown died on Christmas morning 2006 after being hospitalized for pneumonia in Atlanta, Georgia. Nicknamed "the Godfather of Soul" and described as the "hardest working man in show business," Brown ranked among the most influential artists in popular music. He was 73. ■ Geoff Boucher

Population. On Sept. 14 and 15, 2006, the United Nations (UN) General Assembly discussed, for the first time, the growing trend known as international migration. In 2005, an estimated 191 million people—about half of them women—worked in countries other than their own, often for long periods. Such workers, who often endure hardship, make significant contributions to the economies of both their destination country and their country of origin. According to the World Bank, a UN agency, the money international migrants sent home totaled an estimated $232 billion in 2005, up from $102 billion in 1995.

In 2005, 28 countries were host to 75 percent of the total number of migrants. The United States hosted the largest number of long-term migrants in the world—38 million—an increase from 23 million in 1990. Other countries that experienced an increase of migrants from 1990 to 2005 included Russia, where the number rose from 11.5 million to 12.1 million; Germany, with an increase from 5.9 million to 10.1 million; France, from 5.9 million to 6.5 million; Canada, from 4.3 million to 6.1 million; the United Kingdom, from 3.8 million to 5.4 million; and Australia, from 4 million to 4.1 million.

Young people. World Population Day, celebrated on July 11, 2006, and sponsored by the UN Population Fund (UNFPA), focused on the lives of people in the world under 25 years of age. The group—the largest youth generation in history—faces difficulties in finding jobs and gaining access to education and health services. By mid-2006, young people constituted nearly half of the world population of 6.54 billion. According to the UNFPA, about 500 million young people lived on less than $2 a day in 2006. About 57 million young men and 96 million young women lived in developing countries and could not write or read. Some 14 million girls ages 15 to 19 became mothers in 2006, and every day 6,000 young people became infected with HIV—a figure that represented half of all new infections of the virus that causes AIDS.

India to overtake China in population. According to the German Foundation for World Population, an aid group headquartered in Hanover, India was expected to become the world's most populous nation by 2035. The group's report was issued in August. In 2005, India had a population of 1.1 billion and China, 1.3 billion. The study also revealed that Africa and developing countries worldwide would have the fastest population growth, while populations in some developed countries would continue to decline. Germany's population of 82 million was projected to drop by 7 million people by 2050. Ethiopia's population of 82 million was expected to double by the same time. ■ J. Tuyet Nguyen

See also **U.S., Government: A Special Report.**

Portugal. In January 2006, Portugese voters elected a new president, Anibal Cavaco Silva. Cavaco Silva was the first president to come from a center-right party since the return of democracy in 1974. The government, under the leadership of Prime Minister José Sócrates and his Socialist Party, came to power in 2005 with a mandate to radically reform the economy. Both the president and the center-left prime minister expressed their commitment to this goal.

Economic reform. In 2006, the Socialist government announced significant spending cuts. According to European Union (EU) economists, Portugal's budget deficit in 2005 amounted to 6 percent of the country's *gross domestic product* (GDP—the total amount of goods and services produced in a year), the highest among countries that use the euro. Portugal's deficit violated the EU's Stability and Growth Pact—an agreement stipulating that all countries using the euro keep their budget deficits under 3 percent of GDP—and opened the possibility of financial sanctions.

The Sócrates government began reforms of the social security system and public administration as part of a broader agreement with the EU. According to the terms of the agreement, the budget deficit was to be reduced to 4.6 percent of GDP in 2006 and 3.7 percent of GDP in 2007 before being brought under the 3 percent mark in 2008. In 2006, the government began raising the age of retirement for public sector workers from 60 to 65 years. The judiciary increased its working hours. In addition, a program to teach English was implemented in primary schools, to improve the competitiveness of the work force. Tax increases for such goods as automobiles and cigarettes were introduced to generate additional revenue.

The drastic reductions led to strikes and demonstrations. In October, most of the country's 138,000 primary and high school teachers participated in a strike. Nevertheless, Sócrates was overwhelmingly reelected as Socialist Party leader on October 30. In early November, some 80 percent of the country's more than 700,000 public sector workers went on strike, affecting schools, hospitals, courts, and other services nationwide. On November 30, Parliament approved a budget for 2007 that included further cuts, including a 5.1-percent wage cut for public sector workers.

Portugal's economy, according to EU economists, grew at a rate of 1.25 percent in 2006, up from 0.4 percent in 2005. The unemployment rate remained at 7.6 percent for a second straight year.   ■ Jeffrey Kopstein

See also **Europe.**

President of the United States.
See **United States, President of the.**

Prince Edward Island. See Canadian provinces.

Prisons. Statistics issued by the United States Department of Justice (DOJ) in November 2006 revealed that in 2005, for the first time, the number of adults in prison or in jail or on probation or parole in the United States exceeded 7 million. Department of Justice officials noted that this number represented approximately 3 percent of the entire U.S. adult population, or 1 in every 32 adults. The total figure included 4.2 million adults on probation, 780,000 on parole, and 2.2 million incarcerated in federal and state prisons and local jails.

The DOJ reported that the number of adult prisoners under federal or state jurisdiction at the end of 2005 was more than 1.5 million. During 2005, the population of federal and state prisons rose 1.9 percent—the same growth rate as in 2004. Fourteen states experienced prison-population increases of at least 5 percent during 2005, led by South Dakota (up 11.9 percent), Montana (up 10.9 percent), and Kentucky (up 10.4 percent). Eleven states had prison population decreases, led by Georgia (down 4.6 percent), Maryland (down 2.4 percent), and Louisiana (down 2.3 percent).

Female prisoners. More than half a million women and girls were being held in prisons and other detention facilities worldwide in 2006, according to a first-of-its-kind report on female inmates published in August by the International Centre for Prison Studies at King's College London in the United Kingdom. The report noted that about a third of the female inmates—more than 183,000—were in the United States. China held more than 71,000, Russia more than 55,000, and Thailand more than 28,000.

Sexual violence in prisons. Federal, state, and local corrections officials in the United States reported 6,241 allegations of sexual violence in prisons and jails in 2005, according to a July 2006 DOJ report. This figure, the report noted, was the equivalent of 2.8 allegations per 1,000 inmates—an increase from the 2.5 allegations per 1,000 inmates reported during 2004. The largest share of the allegations (38 percent) involved staff-initiated sexual misconduct against inmates, including consensual and nonconsensual acts. Other allegations involved inmate-on-inmate nonconsensual sexual acts (35 percent); staff-initiated comments, gestures, or other sexual harassment toward inmates (17 percent); or inmate-on-inmate nonconsensual, abusive sexual touching (10 percent).

Death row. At the end of 2005, there were 3,254 U.S. prisoners, including 52 women, awaiting execution, the DOJ reported in December 2006. Fifty-nine men and one woman were executed in 2005.   ■ Alfred J. Smuskiewicz

See also **Courts; Crime; Human rights; State government.**

Prizes. See Nobel Prizes; Pulitzer Prizes.

Protestantism. The Anglican Communion struggled in 2006 to resolve a fierce internal dispute over homosexuality in the church. In March, Archbishop of Canterbury Rowan Williams warned that the 77-million-member Communion, which consists of churches that developed from the Church of England, was on the verge of a "rupture." The debate centered on the Episcopal Church in the United States and its election of Gene Robinson, an openly gay bishop, in 2003.

Since then, some Episcopal dioceses have openly disagreed with this policy. In December 2006, a number of parishes in Virginia left the Episcopal Church to join African dioceses or a North American offshoot of the Anglican Church in Nigeria, whose leaders strongly oppose the ordination of gay clergy. In June 2006, Archbishop Williams had proposed a "two-tiered" membership in the Communion. This plan allowed "churches in association" to remain in the Communion and follow chosen policies but withdrew decision-making power. However, the presiding bishop of the Episcopal Church opposed the plan.

The Communion came under additional stress in June when the Episcopal Church elected Katharine Jefferts Schori as its first female presiding bishop. The act disturbed African churches and conservative American Episcopalians who held traditional views of gender roles. Bishop Schori sought to maintain the church's policies on homosexuality and called for common ground.

Evangelicals. Although most evangelicals remained distinctively more conservative than mainline Protestants in 2006, some expressed more moderate views on certain issues. Increasing numbers of evangelicals favored stem-cell research, according to an August survey by the Pew Forum on Religion and Public Life, a research organization in Washington, D.C. The survey revealed that supporters favor conducting this research for its potentially healing measures and do not seeing it as a violation of the right to life.

Environmental concerns promised to become a new point of controversy within the Protestant community. In February, the World Council of Churches (WCC) appealed to denominations around the world to rally their resources to face the threat of global warming and climate change. In the same month, 86 evangelical leaders began a similar campaign called the Evangelical Climate Initiative. A 2006 movie on global warming, titled *The Great Warming*, was intended to appeal to evangelicals. However, a conservative group called the Interfaith Stewardship Alliance denounced the plans. The National Association of Evangelicals, the largest American evangelical organization, remained neutral.

Ecumenism. The WCC promoted *ecumenism* (the movement for Christian unity) at its February assembly in Pôrto Alegre, Brazil. The WCC, which some observers perceived as foundering, reached out to evangelical and Roman Catholics.

In the United States, 34 churches and organizations meeting in Atlanta, Georgia, announced the formation of the Christian Churches Together in the USA. The initiative—the first national ecumenical group to include Catholics—had an estimated total constituency of 100 million Christians.

African American churches remained politically active in 2006 but not always predictably so. In June, many conservative black ministers endorsed two African American Republican candidates for governor—Ken Blackwell, Ohio's secretary of state, and Lynn Swann, a former football star who ran for office in Pennsylvania. However, many other African American church leaders continued to identify with the Democratic Party.

Israel. Protestants worked in 2006 to improve their relationship with Israel. In June, the Presbyterian Church (U.S.A.) rejected a resolution requiring the church to sell off its investments in firms that operate in Israel. The church adopted the measure in 2005 to protest what it considered Israeli human rights violations against Palestinians. Some American Jews and Presbyterians had strongly protested the measure. ■ Martin E. Marty

See also **People in the news (Katharine Jefferts Schori).**

Public health. Concerns about a possible global *pandemic* (simultaneous epidemics) of *avian influenza* (bird flu) continued in 2006. Public health officials worried that the highly *pathogenic* (disease-causing) H5N1 strain of bird flu might *mutate* (change genetically) and become more easily transmissible from person to person. The H5N1 strain normally spreads to people from close contact with infected poultry or wild birds, though transmission among family members—and between patients and health care providers—has also been reported.

As of late 2006, most reported human cases of avian influenza had occurred in China, Indonesia, Thailand, and Vietnam. Since the first reported cases in 2003, at least 258 people had been infected worldwide, and 154 people had died, according to the World Health Organization (WHO), a specialized agency of the United Nations.

In June 2006, WHO scientists reported the first laboratory-confirmed evidence of H5N1 virus transmission from person to person. The cases occurred in a family in Indonesia, causing the deaths of seven family members. Scientists noted that all seven people were blood relatives—rather than spouses—raising the possibility that some individuals might be genetically predisposed to the ill effects of H5N1 infection. There were far more avian influenza infections in Indonesia in 2006 than in any other country—55 cases, with 45 deaths by November 29.

Chinese officials reported 12 new cases of H5N1 infection, including 8 deaths, as of October 31. However, the Chinese government provided few details on these cases, making it difficult for international health organizations to evaluate the state of avian influenza in the Communist nation.

In 2006, Chinese Ministry of Health and WHO officials confirmed that a man whose death in Beijing, the capital, in November 2003 was attributed to severe acute respiratory syndrome (SARS) actually died of avian influenza. The man's death became the first official laboratory-confirmed H5N1 case. Previously, the first case of human H5N1 infection was thought to have occurred in China in October 2005.

Childhood influenza. Physicians often fail to diagnose influenza in children, researchers led by pediatrician Katherine Poehling of Vanderbilt University Medical Center in Nashville, Tennessee, reported in February 2006. Such errors increase the risk that the disease will spread.

Poehling's team examined data from three U.S. counties and found that influenza was correctly diagnosed only 28 percent of the time in children who were hospitalized with the disease. A correct diagnosis was made only 17 percent of the time for pediatric outpatients. The Advisory Committee on Immunization Practices, a group of immunization experts that advises federal health care officials, used Poehling's results to revise its guidelines on childhood vaccinations. According to the new guidelines, all children ages 6 months to 5 years (instead of the previous 6 to 23 months) should be vaccinated against influenza every year.

E. coli outbreak. On October 26, California health authorities announced that an outbreak of illness caused by the microbe *Escherichia coli* had ended. By October 6, 199 people in 26 states had become ill—and 3 people had died—after eating fresh spinach tainted with a particularly lethal strain of a microbe called O157:H7. The intestinal bacterium can cause severe food poisoning, including kidney failure. Authorities traced the tainted spinach to an area of California's Salinas Valley, where O157:H7 was found in cattle manure in pastures near the spinach fields.

Secondhand smoke—smoke inhaled unintentionally by nonsmokers—is unsafe to breathe in any quantity, according to a June report by the U.S. surgeon general. Even small amounts of secondhand smoke cause health problems in nonsmokers and increase the risk of lung cancer by 20 to 30 percent and of heart disease by 25 to 30 percent. The report also noted that secondhand smoke puts children at risk for asthma, ear infections, and respiratory infections.   ∎ Alfred J. Smuskiewicz

See also **AIDS; Drugs; Indonesia; Medicine.**

Puerto Rico. On May 1, 2006, Governor Aníbal Acevedo Vilá ordered a partial shutdown of the commonwealth government. Puerto Rico is a self-governing commonwealth of the United States, and its government is the island's largest employer. The governor acted in response to the failure of Puerto Rico's legislature, which was controlled by his political opponents, to approve a budget that would address a deficit estimated at $740 million for 2006.

The shutdown, which lasted for nearly two weeks, closed 43 out of 118 governmental agencies and put nearly 100,000 Puerto Ricans out of work. It also led to the temporary closure of 1,000 schools throughout Puerto Rico, affecting 500,000 students.

The government crisis was eventually resolved by a nonpartisan commission suggested by Roberto Gonzáles Nieves, the Roman Catholic archbishop of Puerto Rico. He and other religious leaders mediated between the major political parties involved—Governor Acevedo Vilá's Popular Democratic Party and the opposition New Progressive Party. The impasse ended on May 13, when leaders of both political parties accepted the commission's recommendations. These included provisions for a bank loan to close the budget gap, a package of austerity measures, and the implementation of a sales tax.

Local political observers traced the crisis back to the 2004 gubernatorial election, which was the closest in Puerto Rican history and was eventually was decided by the courts. At issue then and later between Puerto Rico's two major political parties was the island's governmental status. Acevedo Vilá's Popular Democratic Party favored making improvements to the existing commonwealth arrangement with the United States, but the opposition New Progressive Party favored U.S. statehood. The parties' inability to compromise on the all-important status issue made it difficult for the government to function effectively, said political experts.

Mainland police recruitment. Recruiters from the police department of Baltimore, Maryland, visited Puerto Rico in July 2006 to recruit Spanish-speaking police officers. At a university campus in San Juan, the capital, and in the town of Arecibo, about 60 miles (97 kilometers) west of San Juan, the recruiters received 1,000 applications for 130 positions.

Other mainland U.S. cities, including Atlanta, Georgia, and Washington, D.C., had recruited law enforcement officers in Puerto Rico to serve their growing Hispanic communities. Puerto Ricans are U.S. citizens and can move to the mainland without any immigration restrictions.   ∎ Nathan A. Haverstock

See also **Latin America.**

Pulitzer Prizes in journalism, letters, and music were announced on April 17, 2006, by Columbia University in New York City on the recommendation of the Pulitzer Prize Board.

Journalism. Two public service prizes were awarded—to *The Sun Herald* of Biloxi-Gulfport (Mississippi) and *The Times-Picayune* of New Orleans, Louisiana. Both prizes recognized coverage of Hurricane Katrina, which ravaged the region in August 2005. The prize for breaking news went in 2005 to *The Times-Picayune* for Katrina reporting. *The Dallas Morning News* won the breaking news photography award for images of Katrina's aftermath.

Susan Schmidt, James V. Grimaldi, and R. Jeffrey Smith of *The Washington Post* won the investigative reporting award for their probe of lobbyist Jack Abramoff, the key figure in a congressional corruption scandal. *The Washington Post*'s David Finkel won the explanatory reporting prize for his study of the United States government's efforts to bring democracy to Yemen. The beat reporting prize went to Dana Priest of *The Washington Post* for her reports on secret prisons where the United States detained terror suspects.

There were two national reporting awards. One went to James Risen and Eric Lichtblau of *The New York Times* for stories on U.S. domestic counterterrorism eavesdropping activities. The other went to *The San Diego Union-Tribune* and Copley News Service for reports on bribe taking by former Representative Randy "Duke" Cunningham (R., California). Joseph Kahn and Jim Yardley of *The New York Times* won the international reporting prize for stories on China's legal system.

Nicholas D. Kristof of *The New York Times* won the commentary award. Rick Attig and Doug Bates of *The Oregonian* in Portland were honored for editorial writing. Jim Sheeler of the *Rocky Mountain News* in Denver won for feature writing. The feature photography prize went to Todd Heisler of the *Rocky Mountain News*. The criticism prize went to Robin Givhan of *The Washington Post*. Mike Luckovich of *The Atlanta* (Georgia) *Journal-Constitution* won for editorial cartooning.

Letters and music. Geraldine Brooks won the fiction prize for her novel *March*. David M. Oshinsky's *Polio: An American Story* won the history award. Kai Bird and Martin J. Sherwin won for the biography *American Prometheus: The Triumph and Tragedy of J. Robert Oppenheimer*. Claudia Emerson's *Late Wife* won for poetry. Caroline Elkins won the nonfiction prize for *Imperial Reckoning: The Untold Story of Britain's Gulag in Kenya*. Yehudi Wyner's *Piano Concerto: Chiavi in Mano* won for music.   ■ Alfred J. Smuskiewicz

See also **Theater.**

Qatar. See **Middle East.**

Quebec. See **Canadian provinces.**

Radio. In the face of rapidly growing competition from Internet radio, satellite radio, and downloadable music, a coalition of major radio station operators in the United States launched an effort in 2006 to promote HD Radio—a technology that transmits programs digitally over existing AM and FM frequency bands. In February, the HD Digital Radio Alliance kicked off a $200-million advertising campaign to boost sales of the digital radio receivers. Alliance members included such industry titans as Clear Channel Communications, Inc., of San Antonio and CBS Corporation of New York. HD Radio allows one or more digital channels to be broadcast along with its existing analog channel over the same AM or FM band. There were 11,003 commercial radio stations (4,751 AM and 6,252 FM) in the United States as of September 30, according to the Federal Communications Commission. By late 2006, more than 1,000 stations—reaching over three-fourths of the U.S. population—had begun HD Radio transmissions.

In its campaign, the alliance stressed the high-quality sound of HD Radio, as well as the fact that, unlike satellite radio, listeners could tune in to HD Radio for free. However, the alliance found a major obstacle in the much higher cost of a digital radio compared with a regular AM-FM radio.

Industry deals. Clear Channel—the largest U.S. radio station owner—agreed in November to be bought by a group of private-equity firms led by Bain Capital, LLC, and Thomas H. Lee Partners L.P., both based in Boston. The $26.7-billion transaction ranked as one of the largest media buyouts in U.S. history. Analysts said Clear Channel's owners likely believed that going private would be a wise move for themselves and their shareholders, given Wall Street investors' declining faith in traditional radio. The company's stock value had been in decline since 2000.

Clear Channel also announced on Nov. 16, 2006, that it would sell its small-market radio stations—448 of its more than 1,100 stations—and all 42 of its television stations. CBS also found buyers for about 40 of its small-market radio stations in 2006. Earlier, on February 6, the Walt Disney Company of Burbank, California, announced that it would spin off the ABC Radio Network, Inc.—a Dallas-based subsidiary with 22 radio stations—and merge it with Citadel Broadcasting Corporation of Las Vegas, Nevada, to form a new radio company called Citadel Communications.

Satellite radio. The country's two satellite radio companies—XM Satellite Radio Holdings Inc. of Washington, D.C., and Sirius Satellite Radio Inc. of New York City—continued to chip away at traditional radio's dominance. As of September 30, XM had more than 7.1 million subscribers, an increase of 43 percent in one year, and Sirius had more than 5.1 million subscribers, a 135-percent increase since September 2005. However, both firms were far from profitable in 2006, reporting millions of dollars in net losses.

On January 9, the controversial Howard Stern provided satellite radio's highest-profile debut of 2006 and the most disappointing when he failed to attract as large an audience as anticipated. Both XM and Sirius also introduced new channels for niche audiences. Sirius debuted its Metropolitan Opera Radio channel and its Catholic Channel, a joint venture with the Archdiocese of New York, in September. XM countered with the September launch of its Oprah & Friends channel, which aired programs produced by Harpo, Inc., Oprah Winfrey's Chicago-based company.

Air America money woes. The parent company of Air America Radio—the liberal talk radio network launched in 2004 to counter the perceived dominance of such conservative radio hosts as Rush Limbaugh—filed for bankruptcy protection on Oct. 13, 2006. The filing by Piquant, LLC, of New York City allowed Air America to continue to broadcast while reorganizing its finances. According to bankruptcy court documents, the company had assets of about $4.3 million and liabilities of about $20.3 million. ■ Gregory Paeth

See also **Telecommunications.**

Religion. See Eastern Orthodox; Islam; Judaism; Protestantism; Roman Catholic Church.

Republican Party. The Republican Party (or GOP, for Grand Old Party) suffered a major reversal in midterm elections on Nov. 7, 2006, losing control of both the United States House of Representatives and U.S. Senate. Republicans also saw their edge in governor's offices turn into a deficit as Democratic candidates across the country rode a wave of voter dissatisfaction to victory. Exit polls revealed that voters were unhappy with the war in Iraq, weary of congressional scandals, and ready for a change in leadership.

Republican response. Republican National Committee (RNC) Chairman Ken Mehlman nevertheless sought to put a positive spin on the election results. He noted that party members knew the 2006 elections would be difficult and went on to say that, historically, the party in power six years into a presidency typically loses many congressional seats as voters grow restive for change.

The scope of the Democratic victory, however, resonated with Mehlman. Appearing on NBC's "Today" show, Mehlman said voters "sent a message we, as Republicans, need to spend time making sure we understand." He suggested that to recover, Republicans would need to recommit themselves to conservative principles, work on a bipartisan basis with Democrats, and root out corruption among their ranks.

Mehlman announced his resignation as chair-

Arnold Schwarzenegger and his family celebrate his reelection as governor of California on November 7. Nationally, however, Schwarzenegger's fellow Republicans fared poorly, losing control of the U.S. House and Senate as well as a number of state governorships.

man the week after the election. Senator Mel Martinez of Florida was selected to replace him.

House of Representatives. Republicans lost 30 seats in the House as Democrats ousted 22 incumbents. At the same time, Democrats retained all of their House seats plus one seat held by a Democratic-leaning independent—gaining a 233-202 majority. In a sign of the difficulties faced by Republicans nationally, Representative Jim Leach (R., Iowa), a moderate, 30-year House veteran who voted against the Iraq War, lost to Democrat Dave Loebsack.

Senate. A number of incumbent Republican senators were defeated on November 7. Senators Richard J. Santorum of Pennsylvania, Michael DeWine of Ohio, James M. Talent of Missouri, and Lincoln D. Chafee of Rhode Island all lost bids for reelection.

Republican hopes of retaining control of the Senate hinged on two races that went down to the wire. In Virginia, Democrat James H. Webb, Jr., beat incumbent Republican Senator George F. Allen. Allen's reelection hopes were damaged when he used a derogatory ethnic term in describing a man who was taping an Allen rally. In Montana, Democrat Jon Tester defeated three-term Republican Senator Conrad R. Burns. Burns was hurt by revelations that he had received campaign contributions from Jack Abramoff, a lobbyist and Republican fund-raiser who in January pleaded guilty to bribing public officials.

Scandals rocked the GOP throughout 2006, and the party paid for them at the ballot box. In the House, Representatives Bob Ney (R., Ohio), Mark Foley (R., Florida), Don Sherwood (R., Pennsylvania), and Curt Weldon (R., Pennsylvania) were accused of unethical or morally questionable behavior, and all four of their usually "safe" Republican seats were lost to Democrats.

Republican gubernatorial bulwarks. Election news was not all bad for Republicans. California Governor Arnold Schwarzenegger won his first full term by defeating Democrat Phil Angelides. Incumbent Rick Perry prevailed over three other candidates to hold the governor's office in Texas. Florida's governor's mansion remained in Republican control as State Attorney General Charlie Crist beat Democratic Representative Jim Davis in a bid to succeed retiring Governor Jeb Bush.

Other GOP incumbents who won reelection included Governors Bob Riley of Alabama; M. Jodi Rell of Connecticut; Sonny Perdue of Georgia; Dave Heineman of Nebraska; Linda Lingle of Hawaii; Donald Carcieri of Rhode Island; Mark Sanford of South Carolina; Mike Rounds of South Dakota; and Jim Douglas of Vermont.

New Republican governors included Jim Gibbons of Nevada, C. L. "Butch" Otter of Idaho,

and Sarah Palin of Alaska.

Nevertheless, Republicans were outpaced in gubernatorial races by Democrats. Prior to the election, Republicans held 28 governorships compared with 22 for the Democrats. The election neatly reversed the ratio.

Rumsfeld out at Defense. President George W. Bush accepted the resignation of Defense Secretary Donald H. Rumsfeld on November 8, one day after the Republicans were routed. Bush nominated former Central Intelligence Agency Director Robert M. Gates to succeed Rumsfeld. Bush pledged to work with Democrats on the war in Iraq and said Gates would bring a fresh perspective to the conduct of the war.

Fund-raising. The Republican National Committee, Republican Senatorial Committee, and National Republican Congressional Committee raised a total of $435.4 million through mid-October, according to the Federal Election Commission. The Democratic National Committee, Democratic Senatorial Campaign Committee, and Democratic Congressional Campaign Committee raised a total of $332.7 million over the same period. ■ Geoffrey A. Campbell

See also **Cabinet, U.S.; Congress of the United States; Democratic Party; Elections; State government; United States, Government of the; United States, President of the.**

Roman Catholic Church. Pope Benedict XVI completed a quiet first year of his papacy in April 2006. The new pope softened the spotlight on the Vatican, in contrast to his high-profile and at times combative predecessor, John Paul II. Benedict, who was labeled "the enforcer" as a cardinal and whose election to the papacy led many Catholics to predict crackdowns on dissidents and a rollback of liberal reforms, proved surprisingly moderate in his approach.

In January, Benedict issued an encyclical called *Deus Caritas Est* (God Is Love), a positive and well-received treatise about the church's teaching on erotic love and the Christian's obligation to social justice. In April, in his first Easter address, Benedict called for the international community to seek peaceful solutions to conflicts over nuclear arms.

The new pope traveled abroad throughout 2006. In May, he went to Poland, where he honored the Polish-born John Paul and visited the Auschwitz Nazi death camp . In July, Benedict traveled to Spain to speak at a conference promoting the traditional family. During his visits, Benedict emerged as an effective teacher who, despite years as a scholar, could express complex ideas to ordinary Catholics and even to children.

Islam controversy. The quiet of the new papacy was shattered on Sept. 12, 2006, when a passage of an address that Benedict delivered in

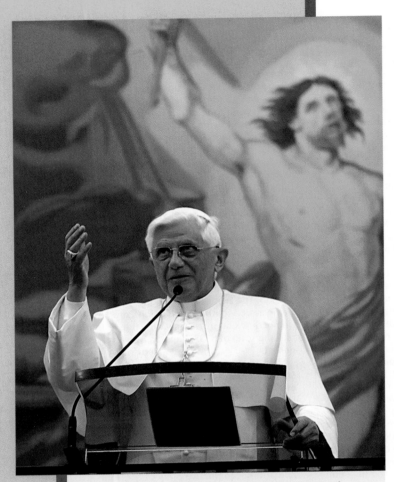

Pope Benedict XVI delivers his Sunday prayer in Castel Gandolfo, Italy, on September 17, expressing his regrets to Muslims who were offended by a September 12 lecture he had given in Bavaria, Germany. The pontiff said he was "deeply sorry for the reaction in some countries to a few passages of my address."

September 25 at his summer residence in Castel Gandolfo, Italy. There, he expressed "total and profound respect for all Muslims." Following the meeting, the Iraqi representative to the Vatican announced that it was time to move on from the crisis.

Benedict also took the opportunity to call for reciprocity in the relationship between Islam and Christianity in response to some Muslim nations' prohibitions on open worship by non-Muslims. The Vatican asked for such nations to extend non-Muslims the same religious freedom that Muslims enjoy in the West.

Clergy sex abuse. Benedict broke with John Paul in 2006 by reopening the case against Father Marcial Maciel Degollado, founder of the Legionaries of Christ, a conservative religious order with United States headquarters in Orange, Connecticut. For years, John Paul had ignored a growing list of sex abuse accusations against Degollado, whom the former pope had long praised. However, in April, based on evidence collected from former seminarians and priests of the order, Benedict prohibited Degollado from publicly saying Mass and giving lectures and interviews.

United States. Catholics became increasingly involved in 2006 in the fight against embryonic stem cell research, some calling it the destruction of human life. Embryonic stem cell research involves using cells grown from a human embryo in a laboratory. Such cells can be used to replace damaged tissues and treat diseases.

The clergy sex-abuse scandal remained a problem in 2006. In March, cardinals of the Washington, D.C., and Baltimore, Maryland, archdioceses fought lawmakers' attempts to extend statutes of limitation to allow more victims to file suits. The scandal had cost the church more than $1.5 billion by late 2006, the Associated Press reported.

In November, the U.S. Conference of Catholic Bishops approved a document for bishops called "Ministry to Persons with a Homosexual Inclination." The statement frustrated many gay Catholics by calling for acceptance of gay people while condemning homosexual acts. ■ Thomas W. Roberts

See also **Islam.**

Bavaria, Germany, offended many Muslims around the world. The pope's talk, a theology lecture on the relationship between reason and faith, quoted a dialogue from the 1300's between a Christian prince, later an emperor, and a Muslim intellectual. Benedict quoted the prince as saying, "Show me just what Muhammad brought that was new, and there you will find things only evil and inhuman, such as his command to spread by the sword the faith he preached." The quotation sparked outrage and protest throughout the Islamic world.

On Sept. 17, 2006, the pope said he was "deeply sorry for the reaction in some countries to a few passages of my address" and stated that the quotation did not reflect his personal beliefs. Benedict met with representatives from Muslim nations on

Romania. European Union (EU) officials announced in September 2006 that Romania would be admitted to the association of 25 European countries in January 2007. Along with Bulgaria, which was scheduled for EU admission at the same time, Romania was to be subjected to continued monitoring by EU officials in the areas of combating crime and corruption, food safety, proper use of EU funds, and aviation safety.

Romania's economy continued to expand in 2006. Foreign direct investment increased by over 50 percent in the first quarter of the year. According to a survey published in June 2006, Romania ranked fifth in Europe in terms of foreign investment and job creation. Romania's gross domestic product, the value of all goods and services produced in a country in a year, increased by a robust 7 percent in the first half of 2006. Unemployment declined from 5.8 percent in 2005 to 5.1 percent in August 2006.

In September, Romania sent 190 additional troops to Afghanistan in response to an appeal from the North Atlantic Treaty Organization command for extra troops to use in offensive operations against the resurgent Taliban. The reinforcements brought Romania's troop total in Afghanistan to nearly 800.   ■ Sharon L. Wolchik

See also **Afghanistan; Europe.**

Rowing. See **Sports.**

Russia. Buoyed by strong oil and gas revenues, Russian President Vladimir Putin's government increased its control over key Russian industries and pursued a more nationalistic foreign policy in 2006. Assertive Russian energy policies, two high-profile political assassinations, an escalating diplomatic conflict with neighboring Georgia, and Russian assistance to Iran all heightened tensions between Russia and the West. Politically, the Russian government battled a wave of *xenophobia* (hatred of foreigners) and achieved significant victories over Chechen separatists.

Economy. The Russian economy grew by nearly 7 percent in 2006, supported by high international prices for oil and natural gas. The strong economy encouraged the Russian government to lift its remaining currency controls on July 1, making it easier for foreign and Russian investors to move money into and out of the country. In August, the Russian government used its windfall profits to finish repaying in full the $22.5 billion it owed the Paris Club, an informal group of 19 wealthy creditor countries. As of November 1, Russia held more than $187 billion in foreign currency reserves and over $272 billion in total reserves, the third highest in the world after China and Japan.

Russia's bid to join the World Trade Organization (WTO) achieved a significant breakthrough in November when the Russian and United States governments approved a bilateral agreement on the terms for Russian entry. Russia is the largest economy outside the 149-member WTO, which promotes international trade and acts as a neutral judge in trade disputes. United States concerns over agricultural quotas, intellectual property rights protections, and opening the Russian financial services market had long blocked the deal. Both sides had tried but failed to resolve their differences in time to sign an agreement at the July Group of Eight summit in St. Petersburg, Russia. Russian Economic Development and Trade Minister German Gref and U.S. Trade Representative Susan Schwab signed the agreement on November 20 at the Asia-Pacific Economic Cooperation summit in Hanoi, Vietnam.

Russia's government suffered setbacks in its efforts to battle economic corruption and organized crime. Contract killers shot Central Bank of Russia Deputy Chairman Andrei Kozlov in Moscow on September 13. Kozlov died the following day. Kozlov had spearheaded the Central Bank's efforts to combat money laundering and to revoke the licenses of problem banks in Russia.

State-business relations. The Russian government further asserted state influence over its oil and gas industries in 2006 as an integral part of its economic development strategy. In a speech in June, President Putin noted, "the advantage of our country is natural resources. …The only question is the mechanism of control." On August 1, a Moscow court declared Yukos oil company, once Russia's largest, bankrupt, clearing the way for the sale of its remaining assets. On July 19, the state-owned gas monopoly Gazprom had offered to buy Yukos's 20-percent stake in Gazpromneft (formerly known as Sibneft and renamed in May), the most valuable remaining Yukos asset. Yukos President Steven Theede resigned his position the following day, declaring that he could no longer expect to recover any value for the company.

In a blow to foreign investors, Gazprom announced on October 9 that it would develop the Shtokman natural gas field in the Barents Sea on its own. Foreign companies had hoped to participate in developing the estimated 131 trillion cubic feet (3.7 trillion cubic meters) of gas. The Russian government also refused European Union demands to open access to Russia's Gazprom-owned gas pipeline system. In January, the Russian government briefly cut gas supplies to Europe to influence a price dispute with Ukraine.

In September, the Russian government called into question the Production Sharing Agreements (PSA's) reached with foreign oil companies in the 1990's. The Russian government increasingly viewed the foreign-controlled PSA's as undesirable, because they do not yield profits for Russia until the partner companies recoup their invest-

World leaders attend the Group of Eight (G8) Summit in St. Petersburg, Russia, on July 16, 2006. Russian President Vladimir Putin (top, center) hosted the meeting.

ments. The government accused the Exxon Mobil Corporation of the United States and Royal Dutch Shell PLC of the Netherlands of amassing unacceptable cost overruns on the offshore Sakhalin-1 and Sakhalin-2 oil and gas projects. Russian officials withdrew environmental approval for the Sakhalin-2 liquefied natural gas project on September 18. On September 22, the Russian government awarded an oil field near the Exxon Mobil-run Sakhalin-1 project to the state-owned oil company Rosneft rather than to Exxon Mobil.

Political assassinations. Assassins killed two high-profile opponents of the Putin government in 2006. On October 7, outspoken journalist Anna Politkovskaya was murdered in the entryway of

her Moscow apartment building. Politkovskaya wrote extensively and critically about the war in Chechnya for the independent newspaper *Novaya Gazeta.* Although Putin denounced the murder, he also angered Politkovskaya's supporters by calling her influence on Russian politics "insignificant." By the end of 2006, police had made no arrests in connection with the killing.

On November 23, Alexander Litvinenko, a former Russian spy turned Putin critic, died of radiation poisoning in a London hospital. Physicians determined that he had ingested polonium-210, a radioactive isotope. Further investigations revealed trace amounts of polonium-210 in numerous public locations where Litvinenko or his associates had been, including on several airplanes. Litvinenko had fled Russia in October 2000 after accusing the Federal Security Service (FSB) of corruption. He had also claimed that the FSB ordered him in 1998 to kill Boris Berezovsky, one of Russia's wealthiest men. In addition, Litvinenko wrote a book accusing the FSB of planning the deadly August 1999 apartment-block bombings that preceded Russia's invasion of Chechnya in September of that year. On his deathbed, Litvinenko accused Putin of orchestrating his murder, but Putin and the Russian government denied any involvement.

Conflict with Georgia. The Georgian and Russian governments clashed throughout 2006 over the status of two Russian-supported breakaway regions of Georgia on the Georgian-Russian border. Georgian president Mikheil Saakashvili wanted to bring the regions back under Georgian control. Tensions flared in September when the Georgian government detained four Russian military officers and accused them of spying. Georgia later released the officers, but Russia cut off trade, mail, and transport links with Georgia. In October, Russian officials raided numerous Georgian businesses in Moscow and deported hundreds of Georgians suspected of being illegal immigrants. Russian gas giant Gazprom then escalated the conflict by announcing on November 2 that it intended to double the price of gas for Georgia in 2007.

Conflict over Iran. The Russian government in 2006 defied U.S. and European calls to restrict Iran's nuclear energy program and reiterated its intention to supply nuclear fuel to Iran's Bushehr nuclear plant. On August 4, the U.S. State Department announced sanctions against Russian arms exporter Rosoboronexport and aircraft manufacturer Sukhoi for violating the 2000 Iran Nonproliferation Act. The sanctions forbade U.S. companies from dealing with the Russian firms. In November, U.S. officials lifted the sanctions on Sukhoi.

Politics. On April 17, a controversial new law requiring foreign nongovernmental organizations (NGO's) to reregister with the government went into effect. NGO representatives claimed that the complicated new measures were intended to exhaust their resources and dissuade them from challenging governmental authority. Numerous foreign NGO's were forced to suspend their operations when they failed to reregister by the October 18 deadline, including Amnesty International and Human Rights Watch.

On October 28, three Russian political parties merged to form one new party, A Just Russia. The Russian government had encouraged the Party of Life, Rodina (Motherland), and the Russian Party of Pensioners to join forces to create an alternative progovernmental party to work alongside the current pro-Kremlin party United Russia.

Anti-immigrant extremists in Russia carried out marches, bombings, and murders throughout 2006. On August 21, a bomb killed 11 people and injured more than 40 others at a Moscow market popular with Central Asians and Caucasians. Thousands of nationalists participated in "Russia Marches" on November 4, People's Unity Day, despite government efforts in several cities to ban them. Amnesty International criticized Russia for the country's growing number of hate crimes, which claimed almost 40 lives in 2006. The Russian government denounced the extremists, and President Putin signed legislation in July intended to combat violent xenophobia in Russia.

Chechnya. Russian efforts to stamp out Chechen separatism scored a significant victory on July 10, when the Russian government announced the death of resistance leader and vice president of the Chechen shadow government Shamil Basayev. Basayev had organized numerous deadly terrorist attacks in southern Russia, including the 2004 attack on a school in Beslan and the 1995 hostage-taking in Budyonnovsk. The shadow government's president, Abdul-Khalim Sadulayev, was killed in a June 17 raid in Chechnya. Sadulayev's successor Doku Umarov vowed to fight on.

■ Juliet Johnson

See also **Eastern Orthodox Churches; Europe; Georgia; Moldova; Terrorism; United Kingdom.**

Safety. In 2006, 90 percent of parents and legal guardians of children ages 8 to 18 in the United States believed that they should be responsible for ensuring that their children have safe experiences using the Internet. However, only 34 percent of these parents and guardians considered themselves knowledgeable enough to carry out this responsibility. These findings, based on a survey of 374 parents and guardians in the United States, were reported in August by Cable in the Classroom, an education organization headquartered in Washington, D.C.

Cable in the Classroom noted that parents are increasingly concerned about their children's online activities, including meeting strangers on social networking Web sites and divulging private information in personal blogs. The researchers concluded that coordinated action among parents, teachers, and children was needed to protect against online dangers.

Young drivers. Laws restricting 16-year-old drivers from carrying teen-age passengers and driving at night help reduce the occurrence of fatal accidents, reported researchers at the Johns Hopkins Bloomberg School of Public Health in Baltimore, Maryland, in July. The researchers found that the number of 16-year-old drivers involved in fatal traffic accidents was 20 percent lower in states that had Graduated Driver Licens-

Crosses topped with coal miners' helmets serve as a memorial to 12 miners killed following a January 2006 explosion at the Sago Mine near Buckhannon, West Virginia. A December report blamed a lightning strike for igniting methane gas deep within the mine.

ing programs. In such programs, new drivers receive probationary licenses with several restrictions. The restrictions are phased out as the drivers gain experience behind the wheel. At the time of the study, 19 states had some elements of Graduated Driver Licensing.

School bus injuries send 17,000 U.S. children to hospital emergency rooms each year, according to a study released in November. The total includes crash-related injuries, as well as injuries associated with roughhousing, slipping and falling, and being jostled during stops and turns. The researchers, led by Jennifer McGeehan of Columbus Children's Hospital in Ohio, said that the increased use of safety belts on school buses could significantly reduce the number of injuries.

■ Alfred J. Smuskiewicz

See also **Disasters; Public health.**

Sailing. See Boating.

Saint Kitts & Nevis. See Latin America; West Indies.

Saint Lucie. See Latin America; West Indies.

Saint Vincent & the Grenadines. See Latin America; West Indies.

Samoa. See Pacific Islands.

San Marino. See Europe.

São Tomé and Principe. See Africa.

Saskatchewan. See Canadian provinces.

Saudi Arabia instituted a number of reforms in 2006 to comply with requirements of the World Trade Organization (WTO), which it joined in December 2005. The WTO oversees global trade agreements and arbitrates disputes among member states. The Saudi reforms included removing trade barriers, lowering tariffs, and eliminating the use of Saudi agents as representatives of foreign companies. The kingdom also liberalized its markets and restructured its legal system.

Looking east. Saudi reforms paved the way for increased trade with both China and India in 2006. King Abdullah ibn Abd al-Aziz Al Saud visited both of these nations in January.

The king's visit to China was the first by a Saudi monarch since China and Saudi Arabia established diplomatic relations in 1990. The king sought to strengthen political and economic ties between the two countries. China imported about 450,000 barrels of oil a day—14 percent of its total oil imports—from Saudi Arabia in 2006. The value of trade between China and Saudi Arabia was expected to grow beyond the high of $15 billion reached in 2005. The Saudis hoped to attract many new Chinese firms to invest in large projects involving petrochemicals, *desalinization* (removing salt from seawater), and telecommunications.

King Abdullah's visit to India was the first by a

Saudi monarch to that country since 1955. The king hoped to improve relations that had long been strained over Kashmir, a mostly Muslim region in Asia claimed by India, a mostly Hindu nation.

Experts in Saudi affairs noted that by looking east to export its oil and import technical expertise, Saudi Arabia was weaning itself from its dependence on the United States, which had been its main economic partner and political ally for nearly a century. Many Saudis resented growing U.S. criticism of Saudi Arabia regarding human rights issues and alleged links to terrorism. Neither Chinese nor Indian officials showed any desire to interfere in Saudi internal political affairs or press for social reform in the kingdom.

Antiterrorism campaign. In May 2006, the state-owned Saudi TV1 launched an antiterrorism campaign, broadcasting television ads to mobilize public opinion against violence and terrorist acts. The Gulf Cooperation Council, an organization of six Arab nations in the Arabian Peninsula, produced the ads. The Riyadh Al-Ikhbariyah satellite television channel continued broadcasting a serial, begun in 2005, aimed at rallying people against terrorism.   ■ Mary-Jane Deeb

See also **Energy; Middle East; Terrorism.**

School. See Education.

Senegal. See Africa.

Serbia. Issues related to the physical composition of the nation dominated politics in Serbia in 2006. In May, the majority of citizens of Montenegro, a region along the Adriatic coast southwest of Serbia, voted for independence. In June, Serbian leaders recognized Montenegro as an independent nation. Recognition also came from the European Union (EU) and the United Nations (UN). Serbia and Montenegro had formed a single nation since the breakup of greater Yugoslavia in the early 1990's.

The status of Kosovo, nominally a province of Serbia, posed a far greater challenge to the international community than Montenegro's independence; UN officials backed by North Atlantic Treaty Organization (NATO) peacekeepers continued in 2006 to administer Kosovo, home to an ethnic Albanian majority and a small ethnic Serb minority. The NATO force went in 1999, after Serbian President Slobodan Milosevic's army carried out a policy of ethnic cleansing in Kosovo—that is, forcibly evicting ethnic Albanians to make way for Serbs. Under pressure of NATO air-strikes, Serbia withdrew its troops from Kosovo a few months later, making way for NATO peacekeepers.

Slobodan Milosevic, who was replaced by Vojislav Kostunica as president of Serbia in 2000, died in custody at the International War Crimes

Onlookers view the coffin of ex-president Slobodan Milosevic in a hearse in Belgrade, Serbia, on March 15, 2006. The Serbian leader had died in the custody of the International War Crimes Tribunal in The Hague, Netherlands, where he was on trial for war crimes.

Tribunal in The Hague, Netherlands, in March 2006. Serbian authorities had delivered Milosevic to the tribunal in 2001 for trial on war crimes. Milosevic's trial was in progress when he died.

The removal of Milosevic from power did not, however, resolve the question of Kosovo's status. Kostunica and Serbian Prime Minister Boris Tadic in 2006 continued to insist on Serbian possession of the province, and in October, Serbian voters approved a new national constitution declaring Kosovo to be an "inalienable" part of Serbia.

At UN-sponsored negotiations between Serbian and Kosovar representatives in Vienna in mid-2006, the Albanian-majority Kosovars pressed for a timetable for independence. After the negotiations deadlocked in September 2006, international sponsors persuaded the parties to postpone a final settlement until 2007.

EU relations. Serbian hopes in 2006 for progress on eventual EU membership faltered when EU officials suspended preliminary talks in May, admonishing Serbian officials to deliver Ratko Mladic to the War Crimes Tribunal. Mladic, a Bosnian Serb allegedly responsible for the massacre of 7,500 Muslim men and boys at Srebrenica, Bosnia, in 1995, was rumored to be hiding somewhere in Serbia.   ■ Sharon L. Wolchik
See also **Europe.**

Seychelles. See Africa.

Sierra Leone. In 2006, war-devastated Sierra Leone began to prepare for national elections scheduled for July 2007. Sierra Leone's 10-year civil war ended in an internationally brokered peace agreement in 2002. President Ahmad Tejan Kabbah had won reelection that year in nationwide democratic elections but was ineligible to run for a third term in 2007. His successor as leader of the ruling Sierra Leone People's Party (SLPP), Vice President Solomon Berewa, was the likely presidential front-runner.

Political analysts expected that Berewa's chief rivals would be Ernest Koroma, leader of the All People's Congress (APC), the country's main opposition party, and Charles Margai, who in late 2005 left the SLPP to form a new party, the People's Movement for Democratic Change (PMDC).

Sierra Leone's political life in 2006 was dominated by charges and countercharges between Berewa and his political opponents. Charles Margai was under indictment throughout 2006 on charges of having colluded in an assassination attempt on Berewa in November 2005. Margai denied the charges. In June 2006, the vice president alleged that Koroma was using armed bodyguards to intimidate him.

Security. Following the December 2005 withdrawal of the United Nations peacekeeping force deployed in 1999 in Sierra Leone, local security forces generally kept the peace in 2006, analysts observed. However, human rights groups alleged that former soldiers were being recruited with cash to join militias elsewhere in Africa. The payments offered a powerful incentive, economists noted, in an economy hobbled by 80-percent unemployment.

Regional association. Leaders of the governments of Sierra Leone, Liberia, and Guinea gathered in Monrovia, Liberia's capital, in October 2006 for a summit of the Mano River Union (MRU), a customs union formed in 1973 that had ceased functioning during the civil wars of the 1990's. The ministers pledged to revive the association to promote common economic interests.

Trial moved. Liberia's former President, Charles Taylor was arrested and returned to Liberia from exile in Nigeria in March 2006. Taylor, charged with numerous war crimes, was expected to be tried at the United Nations Special Court in Freetown, Sierra Leone's capital. Officials of the International War Crimes Tribunal in The Hague, Netherlands, however, moved Taylor's trial to that court, to the apparent relief of Sierra Leonean political leaders, who feared the destabilizing effect of a Taylor trial. During Liberia's civil war, Taylor's partisans had operated for a time in Sierra Leone.   ■ Pieter Esterhuysen
See also **Africa.**

Singapore. The People's Action Party (PAP), which had ruled Singapore since it gained its independence in 1965, won a 10th straight parliamentary election on May 6, 2006. The election was the first polling victory for Lee Hsien Loong, who became prime minister in 2004.

Three opposition parties, which had contested only 29 out of 84 parliamentary seats in the 2001 election, cooperated to run candidates in more than half the constituencies in 2006. This helped the opposition raise its share of the vote from 25 percent in 2001 to 33 percent in 2006. The opposition won only two seats, however.

Part of PAP's electoral appeal was a continuation of the prosperity that it had brought to the small island-nation. On the eve of the election, Lee announced that the economy in 2006 might grow faster than the 4- to 6-percent goal set by the government. With space for additional industrial expansion limited, Singapore sought new investment opportunities throughout Asia.

The International Monetary Fund and the World Bank, affiliates of the United Nations, held their annual meeting in Singapore on September 19 and 20. Strict government controls prevented the kind of violent protests that had marked the group's recent meetings.   ■ Henry S. Bradsher
See also **Asia.**

Skating. See Hockey; Ice skating; Sports.

Benjamin Raich of Austria skirts a gate on March 5, 2006, during the first run of the giant slalom in the FIS Alpine World Cup competition. Raich dominated the men's 2006 skiing season, easily winning the Alpine World Cup overall title and taking the giant slalom title for the second consecutive year.

Skiing. Benjamin Raich of Austria and Janica Kostelic of Croatia dominated the 2006 skiing season, easily sliding into Alpine World Cup overall titles. Kostelic's victory in the season-ending giant slalom on March 18 in Åre, Sweden, set a new record for World Cup points earned in a season, with 1,970. She broke the record of 1,960 points set in 1997 by Sweden's Pernilla Wiberg.

Men. Raich's strong performance contrasted starkly with Bode Miller's poor season. Miller emerged as a star in 2005 after becoming the first American to win the overall title in 22 years. Miller struggled on and off the slopes, due partly to a series of embarrassing interviews—including one in which he admitted to skiing while intoxicated. After the interview, Miller apologized and received warnings from United States skiing officials. At the Winter Olympics in Turin, Italy, Miller failed to win a medal.

Raich clinched his first World Cup overall title with fourth place in the slalom on March 11, 2006, in Shiga-kogen, Japan. He ended the season with 1,410 points, well ahead of second-place finisher Aksel Lund Svindal of Norway, who had 1,006 points. Despite his difficulties, Miller finished third with 928 points. Raich also captured the giant slalom title for the second straight year. Svindal captured his first title—in the super-giant slalom (super-G)—finishing just two points ahead of Austrian Hermann Maier. Austria's Michael Walchhofer won the downhill title, and Italian Giorgio Rocca captured the slalom title despite failing to finish his final four races.

Women. Kostelic, who also won the slalom, clinched the overall title on March 16, with a fourth-place finish in the season's final super-G. Sweden's Anja Paerson, who won the giant slalom with a seventh-place finish in the season's final race, finished second in the overall chase with 1,662 points. Paerson had arthroscopic surgery on her left knee immediately after the season. Austria's Michaela Dorfmeister, who finished third with 1,364 points, captured the downhill and super-G. She retired after her final race.

Cross-country. On March 19, Germany's Tobias Angerer won his first World Cup overall title, leading Jens Arne Svartedal by a commanding 252 points (829 points to 577). Marit Bjoergen of Norway won her second straight women's overall title in the World Cup.

Nordic combined. Finland's Hannu Manninen captured his third straight combined World Cup title. He won 12 events during the season.

Ski jumping. Jakub Janda of the Czech Republic won the World Cup overall title, clinching the championship at the second-to-last meet on March 18 in Planica, Slovenia. ■ Michael Kates

See also **Olympics: A Special Report.**

Slovakia. A new government came to power in Slovakia in 2006, ending the eight-year tenure of centrist Prime Minister Mikulas Dzurinda. Dzurinda's ruling coalition had fallen apart in February, necessitating the calling of early elections. In the resulting parliamentary elections in June, the left-of-center Smer Party led by Robert Fico outpolled Dzurinda's Slovak Democratic and Christian Union.

In early July, Fico formed a governing coalition consisting of his Smer Party; the nationalist Movement for a Democratic Slovakia, led by former Prime Minister Vladimir Meciar; and the extreme nationalist Slovak National Party. The latter was led by Jan Slota, a politician who had acquired a reputation for making highly provocative remarks about the Hungarian and Roma (sometimes called Gypsy) minorities in Slovakia.

The inclusion of Slota's party in the governing coalition raised alarms in various member nations of the European Union (EU)—of which Slovakia is a member—and fears in neighboring Hungary that Hungarian antidiscrimination policies embraced by the Dzurinda government would be reversed. Relations between Slovakia and Hungary deteriorated even further in August, after a series of scattered anti-Hungarian incidents in Slovakia involving mainly young people made headlines. In September, the foreign ministers of Slovakia and Hungary issued a joint statement rejecting extremism and calling for calm.

Prime Minister Fico's agenda focused on reversing some of the promarket reforms adopted by the Dzurinda government. Chief among them was the flat, 19-percent national tax enacted by Dzurinda, to be replaced by a progressive tax code that would shift more of the tax burden to the wealthy and to corporations. Fico also pledged to reduce unemployment, increase social welfare benefits, and improve health care.

Meanwhile, Slovakia's economy continued to boom. In the second quarter of 2006, gross domestic product—the value of all goods and services produced in a country in a year—surged ahead at an annual rate of 6.7 percent. Some economists warned, however, that the Fico government would have to move slowly on its economic program—particularly if it were to consider raising tax rates on foreign companies—to avoid discouraging foreign investment.

Foreign policy. Fico's government moved to fulfill a campaign promise to bring home Slovak soldiers participating in the United States-led coalition in Iraq. In October, the foreign minister announced that the contingent of about 100 soldiers would be withdrawn before mid-2007.

■ Sharon L. Wolchik

See also **Europe.**

Slovenia. See Europe.

Soccer. Italy won the 2006 FIFA World Cup, the biggest prize in international soccer, beating France 5-3 on penalties after extra time in the final in Berlin on July 9. (FIFA is the Fédération Internationale de Football Association, the governing body for international soccer.)

International soccer. Qualification matches for the 2008 European Championships began on Aug. 16, 2006, and were scheduled to finish on Nov. 21, 2007. The Confederation of North, Central American and Caribbean Association Football (CONCACAF) halted the practice of inviting guest countries to take part in the Gold Cup. The 2007 competition will be limited to regional teams.

International club competition. The CONCACAF Champions Cup final was contested by two Mexican clubs. América defeated Toluca 2-1 on *aggregate* (total goals), drawing 0-0 in the away leg on April 12, 2006, and winning the home leg 2-1 on April 19.

Barcelona (Spain) won the Union of European Football Associations Champions League. The team defeated Arsenal of England 2-1 in the final at the Stade de France in Paris on May 17.

For the second time in the history of South America's major club competition—and for the second consecutive year—two teams from the same country—Brazil—met in the final of the Copa Libertadores. In the competition, Internacional won its first trophy. The team beat defending champion São Paulo 4-3 on aggregate, after winning the away leg 2-1 on August 9 and drawing 2-2 at home on August 16.

The FIFA Club World Cup took place from December 10 through 17 in Japan. The competing teams comprised the champions of Africa (Al Ahly, Egypt); Asia (Chonbuk, or Jeonbuk, Motors, South Korea); Europe (Barcelona, Spain); North and Central America (América, Mexico); South America (Internacional, Brazil); and Oceania (Auckland City, New Zealand).

In the final, Internacional defeated Barcelona, the favorite, 1-0 with a goal scored by substitute striker Adriano in the 82nd minute. In the match for third place, Al Ahly beat América 2-1. Both its goals were scored by Mohamed Aboutrika.

Major League Soccer (MLS). The Houston Dynamo won the MLS Cup, defeating the New England Revolution on penalties after a 1-1 tie at Pizza Hut Park in Frisco, Texas, on November 12. The scores were level at 0-0 after the regulation 90 minutes. During extra time, Taylor Twellman put New England ahead, but Brian Ching equalized 71 seconds later. With no more scoring, the match went to penalties, and Houston edged the shootout 4-3. Ching was voted the competition's Most Valuable Player award.

The 2006 competition was the first MLS Cup final in which both teams failed to win their respective conferences in regular-season games. D.C. United won the Eastern Conference, seven points ahead of New England, but lost to New England 1-0 in the play-off final. FC Dallas won the Western Conference, six points ahead of Houston, but lost in the play-off semifinals 5-4 to the Colorado Rapids on penalties after a 4-4 tie.

Reaching the semifinals in the Eastern Conference were the New York Red Bulls, who lost 2-1 to D.C. United, and the Chicago Fire, who lost 4-2 on penalties to New England after a 2-2 tie. In the Western Conference, the Colorado Rapids lost 3-1 to Houston in the final. In the semifinals, CD Chivas U.S.A. (Los Angeles) lost 3-2 to Houston.

The Chicago Fire won the Lamar Hunt US Open Cup for the fourth time, defeating the Los Angeles Galaxy 3-1 in the final at Toyota Park, the Fire's new home in Bridgeview, Illinois.

The MLS will implement the Designated Player Rule for the 2007 season, allowing each club to sign one player who would normally be considered outside its salary cap. Clubs may trade Designated Player slots, but no team will be allowed to have more than two. Toronto FC was scheduled to join the Eastern Conference of the MLS in 2007. The structure of the MLS will feature a 30-game regular season. One of the 13 clubs will have a bye each week. In addition, all MLS matches will be broadcast live on television for the first time.

Italy's bribery scandal. While Italy's international stars were winning the World Cup in Germany, back home a match-fixing scandal was unfolding that had serious repercussions for some of the leading clubs and many individuals. Juventus was relegated from Serie A (first division) to Serie B (second division) and received a 30-point penalty (reduced to 9 points after two appeals) for the 2006-07 season. The club was also stripped of its 2004-05 and 2005-06 league titles. Other leading Serie A clubs, including AC Milan, Fiorentina, and Lazio, were docked points for the 2006-07 season. Juventus soon made up its deficit, however, and was atop of Serie B by December.

Several individuals were also punished, including Juventus Director General Luciano Moggi and Italian Soccer Federation Vice President Innocenzo Mazzini. Both were suspended from all soccer activities for five years. Some administrators and referees also received suspensions.

Women's soccer. The United States women's team defeated Canada 2-1 in extra time to win its third consecutive CONCACAF Women's Gold Cup championship. The final was held on Nov. 26, 2006, at The Home Depot Center in Carson, California. The women's team had won the cup in 2000 and 2002. Defensive midfielder Leslie Osborne gave the United States the lead in the sixth minute with a 15-yard shot, but Randee Her-

mus equalized for Canada just before halftime. Although the United States dominated the game, the team did not clinch a victory until the last minute of extra time. With the seconds running down, Kristine Lilly completed a successful penalty conversion after Carli Lloyd was fouled in the box.

On Nov. 22, 2006, the U.S. women's team had beaten Mexico 2-0 in Carson to clinch a place in the 2007 FIFA Women's World Cup, to be staged from September 10 through 30 in China. The wins in California stretched the team's record unbeaten run to 32 games, dating back to the final match of 2004. Under head coach Greg Ryan, the United States closed out 2006 with an 18-0-4 record.

Other qualifiers for the Women's World Cup include Argentina and Brazil (South America); Canada (North America); host China, Australia, and North Korea (Asia); Ghana and Nigeria (Africa); and Denmark, England, Germany, Norway, and Sweden (Europe). The remaining place will go to the winner of the Oceania qualification tournament to be held in June 2007.

U.S. striker Kristine Lilly became the first soccer player, male or female, to make 300 appearances when she played against Norway on Jan. 18, 2006.

The FIFA Under-20 Women's World Championships were staged in Russia from August 17 through September 3. The United States won its three group matches and defeated archrival Germany 4-1 in the quarter-finals. However, the U.S. team lost in the semifinals to China and in the third-place match to Brazil, both on penalties. North Korea defeated Brazil 1-0 in the semifinals and went on to beat China 5-0 in the final at Lokomotiv Stadium in Moscow.

Technology. A landmark breakthrough in the use of video technology to help soccer referees will be implemented in 2007. FIFA planned to use goal-line video equipment in junior competitions in 2007. If the technology is successful, FIFA plans to use it at the 2007 Club World Cup in Tokyo and, possibly, other FIFA competitions.

Awards. FIFA announced the World Players of the Year on Dec. 18, 2006. Central defender Fabio Cannavaro of Italy and Real Madrid (Spain) won the men's award, while the women's award went to striker Marta (she uses only her first name) of Brazil and Umea (Sweden).

Death. Ferenc Puskás, of Hungary, Honved (Hungary), and Real Madrid, died on Nov. 17, 2006, at the age of 79. Arguably among the half dozen greatest soccer players of all time, he scored 83 goals in 84 appearances for his country, 357 goals in 354 games for Honved, and 512 in 528 for Real Madrid. Puskás helped Real win the European Cup in 1960, the high point being its 7-3 victory over Eintracht Frankfurt (Germany) in the final, in which he scored four goals.   ■ Norman Barrett

See also **Soccer: A Special Report.**

Italy defeated France 5-3 on penalties to win its fourth World Cup title.

THE 2006 WORLD CUP

By Norman Barrett

Italy took their fourth World Cup title when they defeated France 5-3 on penalties after extra time, the scores having been level 1-1 at the end of 90 minutes. Only Brazil, with five, has won more World Cup championships. The finals of soccer's world championship, run by FIFA (Fédération Internationale de Football Association) and staged every four years, took place in Germany from June 9 through July 9, 2006. Zonal competitions involving 198 countries led 32 teams to compete in the finals.

The final will be remembered for an extraordinary incident in extra time, when a moment of sheer madness marked the end of the career of one of the greatest footballers of all time. French captain Zinedine Zidane, who had announced his retirement before the tournament, suddenly turned and head-butted Italian defender Marco Materazzi in the chest after Materazzi made a disparaging remark about Zidane's sister. Despite the incident, for which Zidane received a red card, he won the Golden Ball award for outstanding player of the tournament. So ended the career of the three-time winner of FIFA's World Footballer of the Year award (1998, 2000, and 2003), a midfielder of outstanding dribbling, passing, and shooting skills, great vision, and inspiring leadership.

Group stage

The first round of the finals was marked by several surprises, as Ecuador edged Poland out of second place in group A, and Ghana did the same to the Czech Republic in group E. Australia, in group F, tied Croatia 2-2 and reached the second round for the first time. Several tournament favorites, including Argentina, Brazil, the Netherlands, and France also moved to the next round.

Knockout stages

Fans witnessed no real surprises in the round of 16, though it took a controversial last-minute penalty converted by Francesco Totti for Italy to defeat Australia and a stunning volley from Maxi Rodriguez in extra time for Argentina to beat Mexico. Ronaldo scored Brazil's first goal in their defeat of Ghana, which took his goal tally in World Cup finals to 15 (4 in 1998, 8 in 2002, and 3 in 2006), beating the 14-goal record set by German striker Gerd Müller in 1970 and 1974.

Two of the four quarterfinals went to penalties; the Germans again showed their mastery of the spot kick with a 4-2 verdict over Argentina, and England once more demonstrated their aversion to the

2006 WORLD CUP (GROUP STAGE)

W Win **T** Tie **L** Loss **GF** Goals (For) **GA** Goals (Against)
Pts Points   • Advanced to second round

Group A	W	T	L	GF	GA	Pts
•Germany	3	0	0	8	2	9
•Ecuador	2	0	1	5	3	6
Poland	1	0	2	2	4	3
Costa Rica	0	0	3	3	9	0

Group B	W	T	L	GF	GA	Pts
•England	2	1	0	5	2	7
•Sweden	1	2	0	3	2	5
Paraguay	1	0	2	2	2	3
Trinidad and Tobago	0	1	2	0	4	1

Group C	W	T	L	GF	GA	Pts
•Argentina	2	1	0	8	1	7
•Netherlands	2	1	0	3	1	7
Côte d'Ivoire	1	0	2	5	6	3
Serbia and Montenegro	0	0	3	2	10	0

Group D	W	T	L	GF	GA	Pts
•Portugal	3	0	0	5	1	9
•Mexico	1	1	1	4	3	4
Angola	0	2	1	1	2	2
Iran	0	1	2	2	6	1

Germany's Miroslav Klose (below, in white jersey) and Jorge Guagua of Ecuador vie for the ball during a Group A match.

Australia's Lucas Neill (above, in yellow jersey) and Japan's Naohiro Takahara fight for the ball during a Group F game.

Group E	W	T	L	GF	GA	Pts
•Italy	2	1	0	5	1	7
•Ghana	2	0	1	4	3	6
Czech Republic	1	0	2	3	4	3
USA	0	1	2	2	6	1

Group F	W	T	L	GF	GA	Pts
•Brazil	3	0	0	7	1	9
•Australia	1	1	1	5	5	4
Croatia	0	2	1	2	3	2
Japan	0	1	2	2	7	1

Group G	W	T	L	GF	GA	Pts
•Switzerland	2	1	0	4	0	7
•France	1	2	0	3	1	5
South Korea	1	1	1	3	4	4
Togo	0	0	3	1	6	0

Group H	W	T	L	GF	GA	Pts
•Spain	3	0	0	8	1	9
•Ukraine	2	0	1	5	4	6
Tunisia	0	1	2	3	6	1
Saudi Arabia	0	1	2	2	7	1

shootout, losing out 3-1 to Portugal. Italy defeated Ukraine 3-0, and World Cup champions Brazil lost 1-0 to France in the last quarterfinal and were eliminated.

In the first semifinal, Germany, with the score 0-0 in extra time, were two minutes away from a penalty shootout, when Italy scored twice through left back Fabio Grosso and substitute Alessandro del Piero. In the other semifinal, a Zidane penalty in the 33rd minute against Portugal carried France through to the final. The Germans took third place in the tournament by defeating Portugal 3-1 at Stuttgart on July 8 and finished as tournament top scorers with 14 goals. Germany striker Miroslav Klose won the Golden Shoe award (also known as the Golden Boot) as the tournament's top individual scorer with five goals.

Carlos Tevez of Argentina (in striped jersey) avoids a tackle while fighting Mario Mendez of Mexico for the ball in a round of 16 match.

The final

The 2006 World Cup final, held at the Olympic Stadium in Berlin, was played against the background of a game-fixing scandal in Italy in which several leading clubs were implicated. This, however, did not appear to have an adverse effect on the Italian national side, though they went one down after only six minutes. French striker Thierry Henry headed the ball to Florent Malouda, who was clumsily fouled by Materazzi in the box. Up against Gianluigi Buffon, one of the world's best goalkeepers, Zidane daringly forsook power and chipped his spot kick in off the bar,

Wayne Rooney of England (second from right) is given a red card by referee Horacio Elizondo of Argentina during England's quarter-final match against Portugal.

The author:
Norman Barrett, a former World Book editor, is the author of numerous books on soccer and other sports.

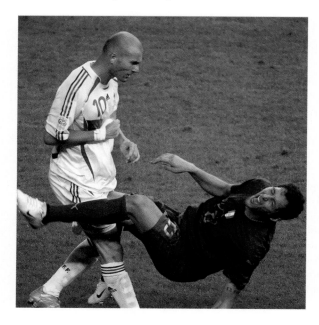

Marco Materazzi of Italy (in blue) falls to the ground after being head-butted by Zinedine Zidane of France during the 2006 World Cup final. Despite the incident, Zidane won the Golden Ball award for player of the tournament.

French goalkeeper Fabien Barthez attempts to block a penalty kick from Fabio Grosso of Italy during the 2006 World Cup final. Grosso made the shot, winning the game for Italy.

having sent the keeper the wrong way. Italy was not behind for long, and it was Materazzi who atoned for his earlier transgression, going upfield to head home a corner from Andrea Pirlo in the 19th minute. The Italians faded physically in the second half and France dominated the game without being able to score. In extra time Buffon brilliantly tipped a Zidane header over the bar. Then came Zidane's headbutting of Materazzi. France's 10 remaining men held out for the final minutes of extra time and so the match went to penalties.

The Italians did not have a good record for shootouts in major competitions, but this time they put all five away. French striker David Trezeguet, a 100th-minute substitute, missed the team's second penalty when the ball struck the bar and bounced down the wrong side of the line. The winning spot kick was scored by Italy's left back Fabio Grosso.

And so the World Cup was decided on penalty kicks, 5-3 to Italy. The final certainly was not a good advertisement for international soccer, but the tournament as a whole, superbly organized by the German hosts and watched on television by millions in virtually every country in the world, held viewers enthralled for four weeks, encompassing as it does all the drama and artistry—and skulduggery—of the world's favorite sport.

ROUND OF 16		QUARTERFINALS		SEMIFINALS	
Germany	**2**				
Sweden	0	**Germany**	**1 (4)**		
Argentina	**2***	Argentina	1 (2)		
Mexico	1*			Germany	0*
Italy	**1**			**Italy**	**2***
Australia	0	**Italy**	**3**		
Switzerland	0 (0)	Ukraine	0		
Ukraine	**0 (3)**				
England	**1**				
Ecuador	0	England	0 (1)		
Portugal	**1**	**Portugal**	**0 (3)**		
Netherlands	0			**Portugal**	0
Brazil	**3**			**France**	**1**
Ghana	0	Brazil	0		
Spain	1	**France**	**1**		
France	**3**				

Results with asterisk indicate score after extra time.

Results in parentheses indicate goals scored in penalty shootouts.

FINAL

Italy	**1 (5)**
France	1 (3)

Team captain Fabio Cannavaro of Italy holds the World Cup trophy after Italy defeated France 5-3 on penalties on July 9, 2006. The victory gave Italy its fourth World Cup title.

THIRD PLACE

Germany	**3**
Portugal	1

Social Security. In its 2006 report to the United States Congress, the Social Security Board of Trustees projected that, without reforms, the Old-Age and Survivors Insurance Trust Fund would be exhausted by 2040—a year earlier than the board had projected in 2005. The 2006 report, issued on May 1, also projected that benefit payments would grow rapidly between 2010 and 2030 and would begin to exceed tax revenues in 2017. This rise in payments was expected because of the retirement of *baby boomers*—the large group of people born from 1946 to 1964. According to the report, meeting Social Security obligations through 2080 would require additional revenue of $4.6 trillion in 2006 dollars.

The trustees' report also noted that in 2005, the Social Security program took in $702 billion in revenue and paid $521 billion in benefits to about 48 million people. This surplus caused the program's assets to grow to $1.86 trillion.

On Oct. 18, 2006, the Social Security Administration announced that monthly Social Security and Supplemental Security Income benefits would increase by 3.3 percent in 2007. This cost-of-living adjustment was smaller than the 4.1-percent increase in 2006. ■ Geoffrey A. Campbell

See also **United States, Government of the.**
Solomon Islands. See Pacific Islands.
Somalia. See Africa.

South Africa. Elections for local governing councils took place across South Africa on March 1, 2006. Such elections are held in a nationwide poll every five years. The African National Congress (ANC), the country's governing party, swept more than three-quarters of all local councils, including five of the six largest city governments. The ANC suffered its only setback in Cape Town (the country's seat of parliament), where it lost control of the city government to a coalition of parties led by the Democratic Alliance (DA).

Despite ANC victories, the voting revealed some potential weaknesses in the ANC's mandate. Voter turnout was only about 47 percent, and millions of potential voters refrained even from registering to vote. Moreover, some 4 million voters who had supported the ANC in the 2004 national and provincial elections failed to do so in the 2006 local council elections. Commentators ascribed the ANC's weaker performance to a failure of ANC-dominated governments, both at the local and national level, to fulfill promises to relieve the country's serious housing shortage and improve water supplies and sanitary services.

Jacob Zuma, the embattled former deputy president of South Africa who had been groomed as President Thabo Mbeki's successor until the president dismissed him from government in June 2005, stayed in the public spotlight in 2006 as sev-

eral court cases in which he was involved produced favorable outcomes for him. In May, a South African court acquitted Zuma of a rape charge. Zuma admitted having had sex with his accuser but insisted that she had given her consent. Then in September, a judge in another court refused the state's request for a postponement of a corruption case against Zuma, effectively halting legal proceedings. The corruption charges involved allegations of soliciting bribes from a French arms company in return for defense contracts with the South African government. Legal analysts pointed out that Zuma could be recharged at a later time if prosecutors built a credible case against him.

Following the favorable verdict in the rape trial, Zuma was reinstated as deputy leader of the ANC, making him a leading contender for ANC party leader, slated to be chosen by the ANC party congress in December 2007. The party leader would likely succeed Mbeki as president after the end of his second and final term in 2009. The ANC commanded an overwhelming majority in the South African parliament, which elects the country's president.

ANC divisions. The "Zuma affair," as Jacob Zuma's several legal entanglements came to be known, caused a division within the ANC alliance, which comprised the ANC ruling party, the Congress of South African Trade Unions (COSATU), and the South African Communist Party (SACP). Leaders of COSATU and SACP accused President Mbeki's administration of neglecting grievances of South Africa's black workers while favoring business interests. They demonstrated broad support for a Zuma presidency, which they believed would give priority to the interests of the black working class. Some ANC members, however, regarded Zuma as an unsuitable presidential candidate. Women's groups were particularly hostile to his candidacy. Meanwhile, no credible Zuma opponent emerged on the ANC political scene in 2006.

Crime statistics released by the South African Police Service for the year ending on March 31, 2006, revealed marginal declines in the numbers of murders and rapes. However, car hijackings and armored-car robberies increased by 74 percent.

One of South Africa's most spectacular robberies occurred in March 2006 at Johannesburg International Airport (now OR Tambo International Airport). An armed gang stole more than $16 million being transferred from a passenger airplane to an armored truck in a high-security area. Analysts said that the sophistication of this and various other crimes suggested that crime syndicates were flourishing in the country.

Transfrontier game park. In June 2006, environmental ministers representing South Africa, Botswana, and Zimbabwe signed an agreement creating a new *transfrontier* (multiple-country) park, the Limpopo-Shashe Transfrontier Conservation Area (TFCA). Transfrontier conservation areas are based on existing national parks in the participating countries to which lands are added to create a single, contiguous conservation area straddling international borders. South Africa and neighboring countries had previously established five other TFCA's. In addition to expanding wildlife habitats, TFCA's remove artificial obstacles associated with borders so that wildlife migration routes can be reestablished. Wildlife preservation advocates also pointed out that wildlife populations can be better managed through an integrated approach. In addition, government officials of the three countries anticipated that the park would attract tourists and create jobs to benefit local populations.

P. W. Botha, leader of South Africa from 1978 to 1989, died on October 31. Botha was the last presidential defender of *apartheid,* the system of racial segregation that had once been enshrined in law in South Africa but was dismantled in the early 1990's.   ■ Pieter Esterhuysen

See also **Africa.**

South America. See **Latin America** and the various country articles.

South Carolina. See **State government.**

South Dakota. See **State government.**

Space exploration. Assembly of the International Space Station (ISS) resumed in 2006 after a delay of nearly four years. During that time, the United States National Aeronautics and Space Administration (NASA) made several design changes to its shuttle fleet to try to prevent a recurrence of the problems that led to the fatal Columbia accident in 2003. Following the shuttle's return to flight in July 2006, NASA advanced its plans to send human explorers out into the solar system after construction of the ISS was completed and the shuttle was retired in 2010.

Also in 2006, robotic space probes produced exciting results and opened up opportunities for further discovery. New orbiters reached Mars and Venus to study the surface of those planets. The fastest rocket ever launched sent a small spacecraft hurtling toward an encounter with Pluto in 2015. A European orbiter sent back close-up pictures of the moon before plowing into the lunar surface in a planned crash, and a NASA spacecraft delivered samples of comet dust to scientists waiting in the Utah desert. Finally, Spirit and Opportunity, NASA's Mars Exploration Rovers, continued to crawl across the surface of the red planet, long after their mission was to have ended in mid-2004.

Space shuttle. By 2006, the space shuttle was nearing the end of its service life. In the wake of the Columbia disaster, NASA had redesigned the spacecraft's large propellant tank so that its foam insulation, which prevents ice from forming on the tank's sides, would not fall off and damage the shuttle orbiter in which the crew rides. Seven astronauts died aboard Columbia when a piece of foam fell off the tank and cracked the shield that protects the orbiter from the heat caused by the friction of reentry into Earth's atmosphere.

After the first post-accident test flight in 2005 showed the problem had not been completely solved, engineers spent another year working on it. In July 2006, the crew of the shuttle Discovery proved that the work had been a success. Their in-flight inspection of the orbiter's protective ceramic tiles and panels of high-temperature plastics revealed no significant damage.

Discovery carried supplies and parts to the space station, as well as German astronaut Thomas Reiter. Reiter joined U.S. astronaut Jeff Williams and Russian cosmonaut Pavel Vinogradov to form the first three-member ISS crew since shortly after the accident. The crew had been cut to two to conserve water, which is normally delivered to the station by the shuttle.

With the shuttle cleared to fly again, NASA resumed work on the station. On September 11, the shuttle Atlantis arrived with a section 45 feet (14 meters) long that included two solar array wings with a span of 240 feet (73 meters). A big rotary joint was to keep the flat part of the arrays pointed at the sun so they could generate the maximum amount of electric power possible. Astronauts used the orbiter's robot arm to pull the 17-ton (15-metric ton) part from the cargo bay and hand it over to the station's arm, which positioned it so mechanical bolts could attach it to the station. Two teams of spacewalkers took turns connecting the arrays to the space station power, data, and cooling systems. The work continued in December, when Discovery brought more station hardware and spacewalkers to finish the wiring.

After Atlantis departed, a Russian Soyuz capsule arrived at the space station on September 20 with two new crew members—NASA's Michael Lopez-Alegria and Mikhail Tyurin of Russia. Riding in the third seat was Anousheh Ansari, the first female space tourist and the first space traveler born in Iran. Ansari returned to Earth on September 28 with Williams and Vinogradov, who had completed their six-month tour of duty.

Astronomers cheered on October 31, when NASA administrator Michael Griffin announced that Discovery would be sent in 2008 to service the Hubble Space Telescope. Plans called for shuttle crew members to add two new cameras to the orbiting observatory, as well as repair its batteries and stabilizing equipment. Without such repairs, the telescope was not expected to remain operational for more than two or three years.

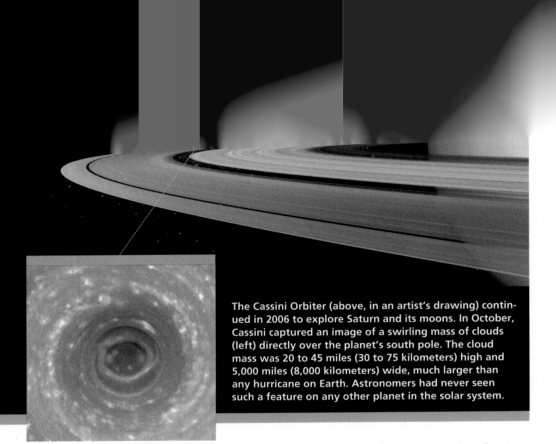

The Cassini Orbiter (above, in an artist's drawing) continued in 2006 to explore Saturn and its moons. In October, Cassini captured an image of a swirling mass of clouds (left) directly over the planet's south pole. The cloud mass was 20 to 45 miles (30 to 75 kilometers) high and 5,000 miles (8,000 kilometers) wide, much larger than any hurricane on Earth. Astronomers had never seen such a feature on any other planet in the solar system.

Next generation spacecraft. NASA engineers continued in 2006 to develop spacecraft for carrying human explorers back to the moon and eventually to Mars and other destinations. NASA teams tested the engines that were to power a family of launch vehicles named Ares and worked on developing a four-to-six-seat crew exploration vehicle called Orion. Orion was to be launched into space atop the Ares I. The spacecraft's first orbital test flight was planned for as early as 2012.

Robotic probes collected data during 2006 from various destinations in the solar system. The European Space Agency's (ESA's) Venus Express and NASA's Mars Reconnaissance Orbiter reached their target planets in April and March, respectively. In January, NASA launched its New Horizons probe to Pluto. With a record departure speed of 36,250 miles (58,339 kilometers) per hour, New Horizons was set to fly by Pluto on July 14, 2015.

Meanwhile, the Stardust spacecraft returned from its trip to comet Wild-2, named for the Swiss astronomer who discovered it. The probe landed in the Utah desert on Jan. 15, 2006. Launched in 1999, Stardust flew through the comet's tail and trapped bits of comet dust, the first available for direct study. An initial analysis of the dust, published in December 2006, revealed a variety of minerals, rather than the one or two primary minerals that scientists had expected. This finding suggests that the dust formed in a number of environments and that before the formation of the planets in the solar system, the universe was more turbulent than scientists had believed.

Smart-1, a small orbiter that the ESA sent to Earth's moon to test advanced instruments and solar-electric propulsion techniques, also ended its mission in 2006. It crashed into the surface of the moon on September 3 as planned. The Swedish-built spacecraft produced valuable scientific data to the end, including low-angle images of the thin layer of dust that floats above the moon's surface.

On the surface of Mars, NASA's two rovers continued to defy the odds. Spirit parked on a sunlit slope to continue returning data on its surroundings despite the lower solar power available to its instruments from reduced winter sunlight. Opportunity, which was better positioned to generate power, finally reached Victoria Crater—its destination since late 2004 and the largest crater on Mars visited by a rover. Controllers used Opportunity's cameras to create a full-color mosaic image of the crater, which is 2,625 feet (800 meters) wide, for studying the geology of the crater walls.

In early November 2006, NASA engineers lost contact with the Mars Global Surveyor (MGS) spacecraft. Since it entered orbit in 1997, MGS had returned more data on Mars than all previous missions combined. ■ Frank Morring, Jr.

See also **Astronomy.**

Spain. The governing Spanish Socialist Workers' Party, under the leadership of Prime Minister José Luis Rodríguez Zapatero, spent much of 2006 negotiating with the leaders of the country's regions over greater autonomy and a larger share of the national budget. Parliament passed several pieces of legislation—including one allowing gay marriage and another, fast-track divorce—that were vigorously opposed by the conservative opposition Popular Party. Both measures enjoyed broad support in opinion surveys.

Catalonia. Negotiations with Catalonia over a new constitutional arrangement that would give the wealthy northeastern region more autonomy generated controversy in early 2006. An army general was fired in January after he warned of "serious consequences" if too much autonomy was conceded to Catalonia and stated that the situation might require military intervention. The negotiations remained on track, despite fears expressed by conservatives and nationalists that Spain's other regions would also ask for the powers granted to Catalonia. In June, 49 percent of Catalonians voted in a referendum on autonomy, passing it with 74 percent of the vote. The document used the word "nation" to describe Catalonia but stopped short of permitting separatist "self-determination."

Basque country. In March, the Basque terrorist organization ETA (whose initials stand for Basque Homeland and Freedom in the Basque language) announced an unprecedented "permanent" cease-fire. The ETA, which advocates creating a country for Basques in an area that includes parts of Spain and France, has been blamed for more than 800 deaths since the 1960's. In response, Rodríguez Zapatero promised to begin negotiations with the group's leaders over their demands, a decision denounced by many Spaniards as capitulation to terrorism. On Dec. 30, 2006, the ETA blew up a parking garage at Barajas International Airport in Madrid, the capital, after warning authorities that a blast was imminent. The attack left 19 people injured and 2 missing. Rodríguez Zapatero immediately suspended all efforts to organize peace talks with the ETA, though he did not abandon the peace process. A spokesman for the separatist group, however, said that peace talks were "more necessary than ever."

Economy. European Union (EU) economists praised Spain's economy as one of the best performing in the EU in 2006, with a growth rate of 3.8 percent. The country's unemployment rate dropped to 8.1 percent, down from 9.2 percent in 2005. Nevertheless, some economic analysts warned of a possible slowdown beginning in 2007, because of the economy's dependence on rising housing prices and consumer demand as its main sources of growth. ■ Jeffrey Kopstein

See also **Europe.**

Sports. The alleged use of illegal performance-enhancing drugs and questions about the reliability of drug testing cast a pall over the sporting world—from baseball to cycling to track and field—in 2006. A doping scandal in Spain knocked nine riders—including two favorites—out of the Tour de France even before it began. Cyclist Floyd Landis of the United States was in danger of becoming the first rider in the 103-year history of the world's most famous and important bicycle race to have his title revoked, after he allegedly tested positive for an unacceptably high ratio of the male hormone testosterone and synthetic testosterone.

American sprinter Justin Gatlin, co-holder of the 100-meter world record, tested positive for a high ratio of synthetic testosterone and other steroids after running in a relay race on April 22. He was banned from track and field for eight years. He avoided a lifetime ban by agreeing not to challenge the test results.

American sprinter Marion Jones initially tested positive for the blood-doping drug erythropoietin (EPO) at the U.S. Championships on June 23. But her "B" sample (the second half of an original sample, held for confirmation testing) came up negative, clearing her name.

Both the National Football League (NFL) and Major League Baseball resisted calls to add human growth hormone (HGH)—which some experts considered fairly common in professional sports—to their drug-testing programs. NFL and baseball officials stated that HGH tests used to test Olympic athletes were questionable and said they were awaiting a "reliable" urine test.

Baseball's Barry Bonds, under the microscope as part of the federal investigation into illegal steroid distribution, passed Babe Ruth for the number-two spot on the all-time home run list in Major League Baseball. But his achievement received little fanfare and no celebration because Bonds was under a cloud—a potential indictment for perjury in the Bay Area Laboratory Co-operative (BALCO) steroid distribution investigation case. In addition, he faced potential tax-evasion charges for allegedly not reporting income from the sale of memorabilia.

In professional team sports in 2006, the Miami Heat captured its first title in the National Basketball Association. The Hurricanes became the first professional team from North Carolina to win a title, taking the Stanley Cup in the National Hockey League. The Pittsburgh Steelers captured the Super Bowl in the NFL, and the St. Louis Cardinals won baseball's World Series.

In the Professional Golfers' Association of America (PGA), Tiger Woods rebounded after missing his first cut at a major event as a professional to win the final two major titles of the year—the British Open and the PGA Championship. Woods ranked second in overall major titles, with 12, trailing only Jack Nicklaus, who won 18. Woods became the youngest player to win 50 PGA events, doing so at age 30.

In tennis, Switzerland's Roger Federer posted a 27-1 record in the four majors, winning three—the Australian Open, Wimbledon, and the U.S. Open. With his loss in the finals of the French Open, he just missed becoming the first man since Australian Rod Laver in 1969 to win the Grand Slam. Amelie Mauresmo captured two majors in 2006, her victory at Wimbledon being the first by a French woman since Suzanne Lenglen in 1925.

Tour de France. Spanish authorities set the 2006 Tour de France on its ear the evening before the race began. On June 30, they sent race organizers a lengthy summary of police investigations into a doping ring that allegedly supplied cyclists—and other athletes—with blood transfusions and banned performance enhancers. The report named nine riders—including favorites Ivan Basso of Italy and Jan Ullrich of Germany. Thirteen riders were immediately banned from the event by race organizers—with many suspended by their racing teams. Although four riders were cleared, the reduced field improved Landis's chances.

The 30-year-old Landis competed in the Tour while suffering from a painful degenerative hip that would require surgery. He nearly cost himself a chance to win with a horrible performance in Stage 16, the second of three stages in the Alps. Landis fell to what looked like an insurmountable 8 minutes, 8 seconds behind. Written off as finished, Landis, in 11th place, erased all but 30 seconds of that deficit in Stage 17. He secured a 59-second victory in the 2,270-mile (3,653.5-kilometer) race on the final time trial, the second-to-last stage on July 22. His victory on July 23 marked the 11th by an American in 21 years.

Stage 17 became the focus of the doping controversy after Landis's team announced on July 27 that Landis's "A" urine sample had tested positive for a high ratio of testosterone. The team suspended him. A test of the "B" sample on August 15 offered the same results.

Landis appealed on several grounds, including alleged problems with the accuracy of the test itself and whether the identifying number on the sample matched the identifying number assigned to the cyclist. If he loses the appeal, which was scheduled for 2007, he would face a two-year ban from cycling as well as the loss of his title.

Duke lacrosse scandal. Duke University in Durham, North Carolina, canceled the season of its highly ranked men's lacrosse team after a woman hired to dance at an off-campus team party in March 2006 told police that three of the team's players raped her. The accusation—made by an African American woman against three white players—stoked racial tensions in Durham. The lacrosse coach resigned on April 5 after a sexually graphic e-mail from another player sent to team members came to light shortly after the alleged rape occurred.

In April and May, a grand jury indicted the three accused players on charges of rape, kidnapping, and sexual assault. Defense attorneys contended that genetic samples taken from 46 players on the team (the lone African American player did not have to submit to a test) and other evidence proved their clients' innocence. The rape charges were dropped in December after the woman altered her version of the event. On December 28, the North Carolina Bar Association filed ethics charges against the prosecutor in the case, District Attorney Mike Nifong, accusing him of making inflammatory statements about the case, including "improper commentary about the character, credibility and reputation of the accused."

Land-speed record. The United Kingdom's Andy Green broke a land-speed record for a diesel-powered car on August 22 in Utah's Bonneville Salt Flats, smashing the old mark set in 1973 by about 93 miles (150 kilometers) per hour. Green averaged 328.767 miles (529 kilometers) per hour in his two passes. On Aug. 23, 2006, Green broke his record with an average speed of 350.092 miles (563.418 kilometers) per hour.

Award. Duke University's J. J. Redick won the 76th annual James E. Sullivan Award, presented by the Amateur Athletic Union to the best U.S. amateur athlete of 2006. He was the first men's basketball player selected since Bill Walton in 1973.

Equestrian. Marcus Ehning of Germany won the 2006 World Cup individual show jumping championship in July in Kuala Lumpur, Malaysia. Anky van Grunsven of the Netherlands won the dressage championship in April in Amsterdam, the Netherlands.

Gymnastics. Russian-born U.S. gymnast Nastia Liukin won her second straight U.S. national title on August 19 in St. Paul, Minnesota. Her victory came a day after Alexander Artemev, who was born in Belarus, captured the men's title.

Marathon running. At the Boston Marathon on April 17, Kenyan Robert Cheruiyot set a course record with a time of 2 hours, 7 minutes, and 14 seconds—one second faster than the mark set in 1994. In 2006, Rita Jeptoo became the sixth Kenyan woman in seven years to win. Her time was 2 hours, 23 minutes, and 38 seconds. At the London Marathon on April 23, Felix Limo of Kenya won the men's race with a time of 2 hours, 6 minutes, and 39 seconds. Deena Kastor of the United States won the women's race with a time of 2 hours, 19 minutes, and 36 seconds. At the New

York Marathon on November 5, Marilson Gomes dos Santos of Brazil won the men's race in 2 hours, 9 minutes, and 58 seconds. Jelena Prokopcuka of Latvia won the women's race with a time of 2 hours, 25 minutes, and 5 seconds. At the Chicago Marathon on October 22, Cheruiyot won the men's race in 2 hours, 7 minutes, and 35 seconds. Ethiopia's Berhane Adere won the women's race in 2 hours, 20 minutes, and 42 seconds.

Rodeo. Trevor Brazile of Decatur, Texas, won the All-Around World Champion Cowboy title in the National Finals Rodeo on December 9 in Las Vegas, Nevada.

Rowing. The Dutch club Hollandia Roeiclub captured the Grand Challenge Cup on July 2 at the Henley Royal Regatta in Henley-on-Thames, England, beating the United Kingdom's Leander Club and Oxford Brookes University by a length. Princeton University captured the Ladies' Challenge Plate, beating the Leander Club and Britain's Molesey Boat Club by half a length. The U.S. women's eight broke its own world record by more than a second on August 27 at the world championships in Eton, England, finishing in 5 minutes, 55.50 seconds.

Sled dog racing. Jeff King of Alaska won his fourth Iditarod Trail Sled Dog Race on March 15, finishing the trip of more than 1,100 miles (1,770 kilometers) across Alaska from Anchorage to Nome in 9 days, 11 hours, and 11 minutes. The 50-year-old, who also won in 1993, 1996, and 1998, was the oldest winner in the history of the race. Susan Butcher, who in 1986 became the race's second female winner, died at age 51 of leukemia on Aug. 5, 2006.

Soap Box Derby. Fourteen-year-old Garrett Kysar of Charles Town, West Virginia, won the Masters Division of the 69th All-American Soap Box Derby on July 22 in Akron, Ohio.

Speed skating. Shani Davis, the first African American to win an individual gold medal at the Winter Olympic Games, won his second straight men's overall title at the World All-Around Speed Skating Championships on March 19 in Calgary, Canada, edging past rival Chad Hedrick, who was disqualified in the final race. Davis set a record for points with 145.742 and a world record in the 1,500-meter race, finishing in 1 minute and 42.68 seconds. Canada's Cindy Klassen won her second overall title in three years by sweeping all four events—the 500-, 1,500-, 3,000-, and 5,000-meter. She also set a record for points with 154.580 and beat her own world record in the 3,000-meter at 3 minutes and 53.34 seconds.

Triathlon. Australian Emma Snowsill became the first woman to win three world championship titles in the same year by capturing the women's elite race at Lausanne, Switzerland, on September 3. Her time of 2 hours, 4 minutes, and 3 seconds was 45 seconds better than that of the second-place finisher. In 2006, Snowsill also won World Cup races in South Africa in June and in Canada in July. The United Kingdom's Tim Don captured the men's elite race in 1 hour, 51 minutes, and 32 seconds.

Tour de France winner Floyd Landis of the United States ponders a question during a news conference on July 28, 2006, after he was suspended for failing a drug test taken during a crucial leg of the race. Maintaining his innocence, Landis accused the testing laboratory of inaccuracy and appealed the decision.

Other champions:

Archery. World Field Championships in September in Göteborg, Sweden: men's compound, Morgan Lundin, Sweden; women's compound, Silke Hoettecke, Germany; men's recurve, Michele Frangilli, Italy; women's recurve, Dolores Cekada, Slovenia; men's barebow, Giuseppe Seimandi, Italy; women's barebow, Luciana Pennacchi, Italy; men's team, United States; women's team, Sweden.

Badminton. Men's singles: Lin Dan, China; men's doubles: Fu Haifeng and Cai Yun, China; women's singles, Xie Xingfang, China; women's doubles: Gao Ling and Huang Sui, China; mixed doubles: Nathan Robertson and Gail Emm, United Kingdom.

Biathlon. Norway's Ole Einar Bjoerndalen won a record-tying fourth overall World Cup title with his 62nd win, on March 25 in Oslo, Norway. Germany's Kati Wilhelm won the women's overall title.

Curling. Men's world champion: Scotland; women's world champion: Sweden.

Fencing. Team world champion: France.

Field hockey. Champions Trophy gold medal: men, the Netherlands; women, Germany.

Lacrosse. Men's National Collegiate Athletic Association champion: University of Virginia (Charlottesville) in May in Philadelphia. Women's NCAA champion: Northwestern University in Boston in May.

Motorcycle racing. FIM Grand Prix MotoGP champion: Nicky Hayden, United States.

Shooting. China captured the most gold medals—32—at the 49th World Shooting Championships, held from July 21 to August 5 in Zagreb, Croatia. Russia topped the total medal count with 59 (24 gold), five more than China.

Softball. Women's world championship: the United States defeated Japan 3-0 on September 5 in Beijing.

Volleyball. Men's world championships: Brazil defeated Poland 3 games to 0. Women's world championships: Russia defeated Brazil 3 games to 2.

Water polo. World Cup champions: men, Serbia and Montenegro on June 18 in Budapest, Hungary; women, Australia on August 3 in Tianjing, China.

Weightlifting. Women's 165-pound (75 kilogram) champion: Mi-Ran Jang, South Korea; Men's 231-pound (105-kilogram) champion: Hossein Reza Zadeh, Iran.   ■ Michael Kates

See also **Australian rules football; Automobile racing; Baseball; Basketball; Boating; Bowling; Boxing; Cricket; Football; Golf; Hockey; Horse racing; Ice skating; Olympics: A Special Report; Skiing; Soccer: A Special Report; Swimming; Tennis; Track and field.**

Sri Lanka in 2006 sank back into civil war between its Sinhalese Buddhist ethnic majority and its Tamil Hindu ethnic minority. In 1983, the Liberation Tigers of Tamil Eelam (LTTE) began a guerrilla war to win independence for the Tamils. After more than 64,000 people had died in fighting and LTTE suicide attacks, Norwegian mediators arranged a cease-fire in February 2002. LTTE leaders in 2006 announced an end to the cease-fire.

Bombings. The government and LTTE blamed each other for fighting that began to increase in late 2005. On June 15, 2006, more than 60 civilians were killed by a rebel land mine. A motorcycle bomber killed the country's third highest-ranking military official on June 26. A bomb on August 14 targeted the ambassador from Pakistan, one of the Sri Lankan army's major suppliers. He survived, but seven others died.

Battles erupted in northern and eastern areas of the country as the Sri Lankan air force and navy retaliated against LTTE bombings. In late July, the army launched its first major ground offensive since 2002. The navy sank 11 LTTE vessels on Sept. 25, 2006, in its largest naval battle since 2002.

Civilians caught in the middle. In August 2006, LTTE leaders accused the air force of killing 61 children in the bombing of an orphanage. Government officials said the building was a training center for LTTE, which is known to use children as soldiers. International aid monitors were unable to verify the body count but said that at least 19 people, mostly young girls, died in the bombing. By November, more than 1,000 civilians had been killed in the conflict.

LTTE and Europe. Officials from the European Union (EU) on May 29 declared LTTE a terrorist organization, banning monetary support to the organization from EU countries. The LTTE then demanded that monitors of the 2002 cease-fire representing the EU leave. In early October 2006, the government and the LTTE agreed with a Norwegian envoy to hold talks on stopping the violence. A meeting in Geneva on October 28 and 29 not only failed to achieve results, but also ended without an agreement to meet again. Velupillai Prabhakaran, the leader of the LTTE, announced in November that the 2002 cease-fire was "defunct," and the LTTE's only option was to push for independence.

Economy. In a September 2006 report issued by the World Bank, a United Nations affiliate, officials estimated that the civil conflict lowered by 2 or 3 percent the economic growth that Sri Lanka needed to reduce poverty. Although the west and south of the country kept overall growth at a healthy level, budget deficits and public debt strained nonmilitary resources.

■ Henry S. Bradsher

See also **Asia.**

State government.

Democrats made huge gains in state governorships and legislatures in the midterm elections on Nov. 7, 2006. In a year in which states had their best economic growth in decades, legislative activity focused on boosting school funding and delivering tax cuts.

Election results. Democrats won 20 out of 36 governors' races in November to hold 28 governorships—the most since 1994. Democrats also won a majority of the 6,119 state legislative seats. Democrats were poised to control both houses in 23 states, with Republicans the majority in both houses in 15 states. Nebraska was nonpartisan, and the rest of the states were split. Republicans lost control of legislatures in Colorado, Indiana, Iowa, Michigan, Minnesota, New Hampshire, Oregon, Pennsylvania, and Wisconsin.

Democratic gains included winning the New Hampshire House of Representatives for the first time since 1922, while also gaining the state Senate and governorship there. Democrats also took the governorship, House of Representatives, and Senate in Iowa for the first time in 40 years and in Colorado for the first time in 48 years.

Governor's races. In the November 2006 elections, Democrats picked up six governor's seats from Republicans while retaining all Democratic seats. In Maryland, Baltimore Mayor Martin O'Malley, a Democrat, ousted Republican Governor Robert Ehrlich, Jr., the only sitting governor to lose in November. Democrat Deval L. Patrick became Massachusetts's first African American governor and the second to be elected in the United States. The first was Virginia's L. Douglas Wilder in 1990. Patrick defeated Republican Lieutenant Governor Kerry Healey. In Ohio, Democratic U.S. Representative Ted Strickland beat Republican Secretary of State J. Kenneth Blackwell, who had cochaired President George W. Bush's reelection campaign in Ohio in 2004. New York Attorney General Eliot Spitzer, who has sued big business for consumers, replaced Republican Governor George E. Pataki, who stepped down after 12 years in office. Democratic Attorney General Mike Beebe in Arkansas and former Denver district attorney Bill Ritter in Colorado also won formerly Republican seats.

Iowa remained Democratic, with Secretary of State Chet Culver replacing Governor Tom Vilsack. Democratic governors who won reelection were Janet Napolitano of Arizona, Rod Blagojevich of Illinois, Kathleen Sebelius of Kansas, John Baldacci of Maine, Jennifer Granholm of Michigan, John Lynch of New Hampshire, Bill Richardson of New Mexico, Brad Henry of Oklahoma, Ted Kulongoski of Oregon, Ed Rendell of Pennsylvania, Phil Bredesen of Tennessee, Jim Doyle of Wisconsin, and Dave Freudenthal of Wyoming.

Republican Governor Frank H. Murkowski of Alaska was the only governor to lose his own primary, falling to challenger Sarah Palin, the former mayor of Wasilla. Palin became the state's first woman governor by defeating the Democratic candidate, former Governor Tony Knowles.

Republicans retained 15 governorships. In Florida, Republican Attorney General Charlie Crist defeated Democratic Representative Jim Davis in the contest to replace Governor Jeb Bush, barred from serving a third term. Idaho voters gave a narrow victory to Republican U.S. Representative C. L. "Butch" Otter over Democrat Jerry Brady. In Nevada, Republican U.S. Representative Jim Gibbons won the race to replace Governor Kenny Guinn, also barred from serving a third term.

In Nebraska, Republican Governor Dave Heineman won election to the post he took over when Governor Mike Johanns became President Bush's secretary of agriculture in 2005. Republican governors reelected were Bob Riley of Alabama, Arnold Schwarzenegger of California, M. Jodi Rell of Connecticut, Sonny Perdue of Georgia, Linda Lingle of Hawaii, Tim Pawlenty of Minnesota, Donald Carcieri of Rhode Island, Mark Sanford of South Carolina, Mike Rounds of South Dakota, Rick Perry of Texas, and James Douglas of Vermont.

Ballot measures. Seven states approved bans on same-sex marriages—Colorado, Idaho, South Carolina, South Dakota, Tennessee, Virginia, and Wisconsin. Only Arizona defeated a constitutional provision to limit marriage to a man and a woman. In December, the governor of New Jersey signed into law a bill giving gay couples all the rights and responsibilities of marriage, though not the right to call such unions "marriages."

South Dakota voters repealed a law passed earlier in 2006 that would have severely restricted abortions. Measures limiting abortions for minors lost in California and Oregon. Missouri voters narrowly approved a measure endorsing access to stem cell research, therapies, and cures. Voters in Michigan approved Proposal 2, which banned racial, gender, and ethnicity preferences in public college admissions and government hiring.

Efforts to put a cap on state and local government spending lost in Maine, Nebraska, and Oregon. However, voters limited government power to seize private property in Arizona, Georgia, Florida, Michigan, Nevada, New Hampshire, North Dakota, Oregon, and South Carolina.

State revenues. Overall, states ended the fiscal year with $57 billion in surpluses, according to the bipartisan National Conference of State Legislatures. The most popular uses for the money included increasing education funding (24 states), health spending (14 states), and *capital projects*—that is, construction of income-producing facilities (14 states).

Eighteen states voted to boost "rainy day funds." These funds, also called *budget stabiliza-*

SELECTED STATISTICS ON STATE GOVERNMENTS

State	Resident population*	Governor†	Legislature† House (D)	(R)	Senate (D)	(R)	State tax revenue‡	Tax revenue per capita‡	Public school expenditure per pupil§
Alabama	4,557,808	Bob Riley (R)	62	43	23	12	$ 7,800,000,000	$1,710	$ 7,300
Alaska	663,661	Sarah Palin (R)	17	23	9	11	1,858,000,000	2,800	10,170
Arizona	5,939,292	Janet Napolitano (D)	28	32	12	18	11,008,000,000	1,850	5,590
Arkansas	2,799,154	Mike Beebe (D)	75	25	27	8	6,552,000,000	2,360	6,310
California	36,132,147	Arnold Schwarzenegger (R)	48	32	25	15	98,435,000,000	2,720	8,210
Colorado	4,665,177	Bill Ritter (D)	39	26	20	15	7,648,000,000	1,640	8,280
Connecticut	3,510,297	M. Jodi Rell (R)	106	45	24	12	11,585,000,000	3,300	12,440
Delaware	843,524	Ruth Ann Minner (D)	18	23	13	8	2,725,000,000	3,230	11,420
Florida	17,789,864	Charlie Crist (R)	41	79	14	26	33,895,000,000	1,910	7,650
Georgia	9,072,576	Sonny Perdue (R)	74	106	22	34	15,676,000,000	1,730	9,150
Hawaii	1,275,194	Linda Lingle (R)	43	8	20	5	4,434,000,000	3,480	8,750
Idaho	1,429,096	C.L. "Butch" Otter (R)	19	51	7	28	2,934,000,000	2,050	6,970
Illinois	12,763,371	Rod Blagojevich (D)	66	52	37	22	26,412,000,000	2,070	10,270
Indiana	6,271,973	Mitch Daniels (R)	51	49	17	33	12,854,000,000	2,050	8,980
Iowa	2,966,334	Chet Culver (D)	54	45	30	20	5,751,000,000	1,940	7,810
Kansas	2,744,687	Kathleen Sebelius (D)	47	78	10	30	5,599,000,000	2,040	8,180
Kentucky	4,173,405	Ernie Fletcher (R)	61	39	#16	21	9,091,000,000	2,180	8,200
Louisiana	4,523,628	Kathleen Blanco (D)	#62	41	24	15	8,639,000,000	1,910	8,810
Maine	1,321,505	John Baldacci (D)	**89	60	18	17	3,071,000,000	2,320	11,290
Maryland	5,600,388	Martin O'Malley (D)	106	35	33	14	13,497,000,000	2,410	9,620
Massachusetts	6,398,743	Deval L. Patrick (D)	141	19	35	5	18,015,000,000	2,820	12,280
Michigan	10,120,860	Jennifer Granholm (D)	58	52	17	21	23,525,000,000	2,320	10,070
Minnesota	5,132,799	Tim Pawlenty (R)	85	49	44	23	15,881,000,000	3,090	9,680
Mississippi	2,921,088	Haley Barbour (R)	74	46	27	23	5,432,000,000	1,860	6,760
Missouri	5,800,310	Matt Blunt (R)	71	92	13	21	9,544,000,000	1,650	7,680
Montana	935,670	Brian Schweitzer (D)	††49	50	26	24	1,876,000,000	2,000	8,360
Nebraska	1,758,787	Dave Heineman (R)	unicameral (49 nonpartisan)				3,797,000,000	2,160	7,980
Nevada	2,414,807	Jim Gibbons (R)	27	15	10	11	5,010,000,000	2,070	7,090
New Hampshire	1,309,940	John Lynch (D)	239	161	14	10	2,022,000,000	1,540	10,210
New Jersey	8,717,925	Jon Corzine (D)	49	31	22	18	22,934,000,000	2,630	13,780
New Mexico	1,928,384	Bill Richardson (D)	42	28	24	18	4,471,000,000	2,320	8,630
New York	19,254,630	Eliot Spitzer (D)	105	45	28	34	50,190,000,000	2,610	13,550
North Carolina	8,683,242	Mike Easley (D)	68	52	31	19	18,640,000,000	2,150	7,470
North Dakota	636,677	John Hoeven (R)	33	61	21	26	1,403,000,000	2,200	7,760
Ohio	11,464,042	Ted Strickland (D)	46	53	12	21	24,007,000,000	2,090	10,030
Oklahoma	3,547,884	Brad Henry (D)	44	57	24	24	6,859,000,000	1,930	6,750
Oregon	3,641,056	Ted Kulongoski (D)	31	29	**17	11	6,523,000,000	1,790	8,140
Pennsylvania	12,429,616	Ed Rendell (D)	102	101	21	29	27,263,000,000	2,190	10,050
Rhode Island	1,076,189	Donald Carcieri (R)	60	15	33	5	2,629,000,000	2,440	11,090
South Carolina	4,255,083	Mark Sanford (R)	51	73	20	26	7,318,000,000	1,720	8,530
South Dakota	775,933	Mike Rounds (R)	20	50	15	20	1,110,000,000	1,430	7,910
Tennessee	5,962,959	Phil Bredesen (D)	53	46	16	17	10,007,000,000	1,680	7,080
Texas	22,859,968	Rick Perry (R)	69	81	11	20	32,785,000,000	1,430	7,400
Utah	2,469,585	Jon Huntsman, Jr. (R)	20	55	8	21	4,686,000,000	1,900	5,350
Vermont	623,050	James Douglas (R)	‡‡93	49	23	7	2,243,000,000	3,600	12,330
Virginia	7,567,465	Tim Kaine (D)	§§40	57	17	23	15,919,000,000	2,100	9,280
Washington	6,287,759	Christine Gregoire (D)	63	35	32	17	14,840,000,000	2,360	8,170
West Virginia	1,816,856	Joe Manchin III (D)	72	28	23	11	4,301,000,000	2,370	9,790
Wisconsin	5,536,201	Jim Doyle (D)	46	53	18	15	13,452,000,000	2,430	10,070
Wyoming	509,294	Dave Freudenthal (D)	17	43	7	23	1,740,000,000	3,420	11,970

*July 1, 2005, estimates. Source: U.S. Census Bureau.
†As of January 2007. Source: National Governors' Association; National Conference of State Legislatures; state government officials.
‡2005 figures. Source: U.S. Census Bureau.
§2005-2006 estimates for elementary and secondary students in fall enrollment. Source: National Education Association.

#One independent.
**Two independents.
††One Constitutional Party.
‡‡Six Progressive Party; two independents.
§§Three independents.

tion funds, are mandatory savings that state governments can use to maintain critical state services during economic downturns.

States also returned money to residents in the form of tax breaks. Twenty states cut personal income taxes, 21 states reduced business taxes, and at least 8 states lowered property taxes.

New Jersey's government shut down for three days in July when the Legislature and Democratic Governor Jon S. Corzine could not agree on a budget. The governor and lawmakers finally agreed to raise sales tax and to lower property taxes.

Workplace issues. Voters in six states approved increases in the minimum wage, including cost-of-living adjustments tied to inflation: Arizona, Colorado, Missouri, Montana, Nevada, and Ohio. In 2005, four states—Florida, Oregon, Vermont, and Washington—had enacted cost-of-living provisions. By 2006, nearly half the states had set their minimum wages higher than the federal floor of $5.15 an hour. Twelve states in 2006 passed new laws requiring a boost for the lowest-paid wage earners: Arkansas, California, Delaware, Illinois, Maine, Maryland, Massachusetts, Michigan, North Carolina, Pennsylvania, Rhode Island, and West Virginia.

Capital punishment. On December 15, Florida Governor Bush suspended executions after what was described as a "botched" execution was carried out in Florida on December 13. He appointed a commission to study the humanity and constitutionality of lethal injections. The execution had taken more than 30 minutes and required two lethal injections. In California, a federal judge ruled on December 15 that lethal injection constituted cruel and unusual punishment and was, therefore, unconstitutional.

Health and environmental issues. Massachusetts and Vermont took steps to provide health care insurance for all their residents. Massachusetts required people to buy health insurance and companies to offer insurance. Vermont required private insurers to offer health plans overseen by a state commission. Tennessee extended health insurance to uninsured workers, families, and people with chronic illnesses who were cut off by state plan changes in 2005.

Smoking bans in public places passed in Arizona, Nevada, and Ohio. Voters raised tobacco or cigarette taxes in Arizona, New Jersey, South Dakota, Texas, and Vermont and defeated higher tobacco taxes in California and Missouri. California moved to curb global warming. Governor Schwarzenegger signed a law to require the state's major manufacturers, utilities, and refineries to reduce emissions of greenhouse gases by 25 percent by 2020. ■ Elaine Stuart McDonald

See also **Courts; Democratic Party; Elections; Republican Party.**

Stocks and bonds.
Stock markets worldwide found traction in 2006 as economic growth and moderate inflation inspired investor confidence. Major stock markets in Asia, Europe, Latin America, and the United States posted double-digit percentage gains. The rally was especially welcome in U.S. markets, whose stocks had barely budged in 2005.

U.S. markets. There were two main contributors to the upbeat year in U.S. stocks. First, in August 2006, the Federal Reserve System (the Fed), the central bank of the United States, suspended its two-year campaign of steadily increasing short-term interest rates. Second, corporate profits showed unexpected strength throughout 2006. In the third quarter of the year alone, the major companies in the Standard & Poor's (S&P's) 500 Index, a benchmark of 500 large-company U.S. stocks, posted record-high profits totaling more than $200 billion.

A third element boosting stock market optimism was a decline in oil prices, which began to fall in August after more than five years of steady advance. Oil prices peaked at more than $77 a barrel in futures-market trading in August, but prices were quoted at $62 a barrel by mid-December. Gasoline prices eased as well, providing a benefit to consumers at the pump.

The Dow Jones Industrial Average, an index of 30 major companies, was up by 10 percent for the year through mid-December—after being virtually unchanged during 2005. On Oct. 3, 2006, the Dow set its first record-high daily close (11,727) in nearly seven years. The S&P's 500 Index rose 13 percent in 2006, and the Russell 2000 Index of small-company U.S. stocks was up by 18 percent.

Bonds steady. The Fed held short-term interest rates steady at 5.25 percent through the end of 2006, after 17 consecutive increases that took rates from 1.00 percent in May 2004 to 5.25 percent in June 2006. Fed officials continued to express fear of *inflation* (a continual increase in prices throughout a nation's economy), warning that they might hike rates again if the economy showed signs of heating up. However, long-term interest rates declined in the second half of the year after bonds rallied because of weaker economic reports, especially in the housing sector.

The yield on 10-year U.S. Treasury notes—which represents a benchmark interest rate for many home mortgages—started the year at 4.4 percent. Yields then climbed to nearly 5.2 percent in June only to retreat to 4.5 percent by mid-December.

Conservative mutual funds that invested in government debt securities returned approximately 4 percent in 2006. Riskier funds that were invested in so-called high-yield corporate debt securities were up 9.6 percent for the year.

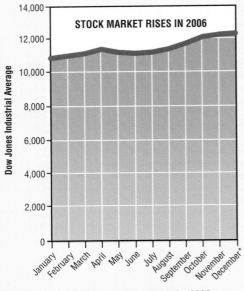

STOCK MARKET RISES IN 2006

Dow Jones Industrial Average

14,000
12,000
10,000
8,000
6,000
4,000
2,000
0

January February March April May June July August September October November December*

Closing month averages for 2006
* December figure is as of the 16th.

The Dow Jones Industrial Average climbed above 12,000 for the first time in 2006 and closed the year at yet another all-time high.

Winners and losers. Stocks of manufacturers of basic materials, especially steelmakers, were the top performers in 2006. Higher prices for industrial commodities, as well as mergers and rumors of mergers among commodity producers, kept this sector in play throughout the year. Share values of stainless-steelmaker Allegheny Technologies, Incorporated of Pittsburgh, Pennsylvania, nearly tripled, and those of steelmaker Nucor Corporation of Charlotte, North Carolina, nearly doubled.

Energy stocks fell out of their long-held position as the top-performing sector of the U.S. stock market in 2006. In their place, telecommunications companies rebounded, with shares of BellSouth Corporation of Atlanta increasing in value by nearly 70 percent through mid-December.

Technology stocks, which were favored by many active investors, showed mixed results in 2006. Shares of Research in Motion Limited of Waterloo, Ontario—manufacturer of the popular BlackBerry handheld communication devices—advanced by more than 90 percent.

The Internet search engine company Google Inc., of Mountain View, California, continued to astound investors. Google issued its first public shares in August 2004 at $85. The value of these shares had reached more than $500 by November

2006. By contrast, shares of Yahoo! Inc., a well-known Internet service company based in Sunnyvale, California, lost about a third of their value in 2006.

Shares of semiconductor maker Intel Corporation of Santa Clara, California, declined in value by 17 percent—making this stock the worst performer in the Dow Jones Industrial Average. The best-performing stock in the Dow was General Motors Corporation of Detroit, which was up 52 percent, despite the automobile manufacturer's widely reported financial problems.

International markets. Investors in the United States continued in 2006 to pour money into overseas stocks and mutual funds specializing in non-U.S. investments. The U.S. dollar weakened against major currencies for much of the year, boosting returns to U.S. investors.

Among the best-performing stock markets in 2006, based on the performance of principal stock indexes, were those of Shanghai, China (up 86 percent in U.S. dollar terms); India (up nearly 50 percent); Brazil and Mexico (each up more than 40 percent); and Germany (up 32 percent).

Despite signs that Japan's long-running economic slump was ending, Japanese stocks continued to lag in world markets in 2006. The Nikkei 225 Index of major stocks traded on the Tokyo Stock Exchange was up by only 3 percent in U.S. dollar terms. A rally in the second half of the year failed to make up for a sharp drop in May and early June. ■ Bill Barnhart

See also **Economics, United States; Economics, world; Energy supply; International trade.**

Sudan. The continuing conflict in the Darfur region dominated news about Sudan in 2006, affecting that nation's relations with countries both inside and outside of Africa. Darfur is a western region in Sudan where fighting between government forces and rebel groups began in 2003. The fighting had led to the deaths of hundreds of thousands of people and left 2 million others homeless. Many international groups accused the government and government-backed militias of massive human rights abuses in Darfur.

The regional impact of the Darfur conflict was evident in January 2006, when officials in Khartoum, the Sudanese capital, hosted the African Union (AU) summit. The AU is an organization working to achieve cooperation among African states. Leaders of the nations at the summit—citing human rights violations by the Sudanese government—balked at allowing Sudan to take over the rotating chair of the AU. Sudan withdrew its bid to lead the AU in 2006 after the African leaders agreed it could chair the group in 2007.

Darfur Peace Agreement. In May 2006, the Darfur Peace Agreement was signed in Abuja,

A Sudanese girl stands amid the makeshift shelters of the Zam Zam refugee camp in the Darfur region of Sudan in June. The camp was home to about 40,000 people displaced by the fighting between government forces and rebel groups.

capital of Nigeria, by representatives of the Sudanese government and the Sudan Liberation Movement (SLM), the largest rebel group in Darfur. Leaders of the AU, including President Olusegun Obasanjo of Nigeria and President (and AU Chairman) Denis Sassou-Nguesso of Congo (Brazzaville), helped broker the agreement.

Khalil Ibrahim, leader of the Justice and Equality Movement, and Abdul Wahid Nur, head of a SLM faction, refused to sign the agreement. These two rebel leaders from Darfur claimed that the agreement did not recognize the political, economic, and cultural rights of the people of Darfur.

United States and United Nations. In September, United States Senators Edward M. Kennedy (D., Massachusetts) and Gordon H. Smith (R., Oregon) expressed their support for the Darfur Peace Agreement. They introduced bipartisan legislation calling for the Sudanese government to allow a United Nations (UN) peacekeeping force to enter Darfur to implement the peace treaty. The UN Security Council had approved a 17,000-member peacekeeping force for Darfur in August, but the Sudanese government refused to allow the force into the region.

The Kennedy-Smith bill also called for the North Atlantic Treaty Organization to enforce a no-fly zone over Darfur. In December, Sudan approved a phased deployment of a limited UN-AU peacekeeping force in Darfur.

Global Day for Darfur. Amnesty International and Human Rights Watch—human rights organizations based in London and New York City, respectively—were among a number of organizations that sponsored a "Global Day for Darfur" on September 17. Meetings and rallies took place in an estimated 50 cities in more than 30 countries. Speakers at the gatherings demanded that the Sudanese government allow UN peacekeepers in Darfur to protect civilians.

Conflict with Chad. In February, President Umar al-Bashir of Sudan and President Idriss Deby of Chad signed the so-called Tripoli Agreement, a peace treaty ending a border war that had devastated towns in eastern Chad and Darfur since December 2005. Mu`ammar al-Qadhafi, the leader of Libya, was party to the agreement.

Just two months later, in April 2006, Chad severed diplomatic relations with Sudan. Chadian officials accused the Sudanese government of aiding rebels from the United Front for Change, a coalition of armed groups that tried to overthrow the government of Chad in April. The *coup* (overthrow) attempt led to the deaths of approximately 350 people, including government troops, rebels, and civilians.

Despite Sudan's denial of involvement in the coup attempt, President Deby threatened to expel some 200,000 Sudanese refugees from Chad. Many of these refugees had fled the conflict in Darfur. ■ Mary-Jane Deeb

See also **Africa; Middle East; United Nations.**

Supreme Court of the United States.

During its 2005-2006 term, which ended on June 29, 2006, the Supreme Court of the United States issued a major ruling on the president's authority to prosecute suspected terrorists. The court also decided cases involving assisted suicide, military recruiters at colleges, the drawing of congressional voting districts, and limits on political campaign donations and spending. The court delivered signed opinions in 69 cases during the term.

The court started the term on Oct. 3, 2005, with one new member, Chief Justice John G. Roberts, Jr., who succeeded the late Chief Justice William H. Rehnquist. A second new member, Justice Samuel A. Alito, Jr., joined the court on Jan. 31, 2006, midway through the term, replacing Justice Sandra Day O'Connor, who retired. The Senate Judiciary Committee voted 10 to 8 to approve Alito on January 24, and the full Senate confirmed him on January 31 by a vote of 58 to 42. Alito's nomination generated the most Senate opposition since Justice Clarence Thomas barely won confirmation in 1991 by a vote of 52 to 48. Alito had spent 15 years as a judge on the Third U.S. Circuit Court of Appeals. Some Democrats and liberal advocacy groups warned that he would be more conservative than O'Connor, who had become a moderate swing vote in many cases involving such social issues as abortion and gender discrimination.

Prosecuting terrorists. In a 5-to-3 ruling on June 29, 2006, the Supreme Court ruled that military commissions set up by the president to try terrorism suspects violated federal law and international treaties. Roberts did not participate because he formerly sat on a federal appeals court that had ruled in the case. President George W. Bush had authorized the commissions to prosecute suspects who had been captured during fighting in Afghanistan and Iraq and who were held at a U.S. military base at Guantánamo Bay, Cuba. The procedures followed by the commissions did not include several key protections required for defendants who are tried by courts-martial under the Uniform Code of Military Justice. Congress adopted the Uniform Code to cover prosecutions for all branches of the U.S. military. The court said that the administration had not justified setting up a significantly different system for terrorism suspects. The court also said the commissions did not comply with a provision of the Geneva Conventions of 1949, international treaties signed by the United States that govern the treatment of prisoners of war.

Assisted suicide. On Jan. 17, 2006, the court stopped efforts by the U.S. Department of Justice to prevent physicians in Oregon from prescribing lethal doses of drugs to terminally ill patients who want to end their lives. Under an Oregon law passed in 1994, the Death with Dignity Act,

patients who are dying can, under some circumstances, ask their doctors to prescribe drugs that will enable them to commit suicide. Oregon is the only state with such a law. In 2001, U.S. Attorney General John Ashcroft had said that physicians who helped their patients under the Oregon law would lose their licenses to write prescriptions. Ashcroft contended that he had that power from the federal Controlled Substances Act of 1970, under which the federal government regulates drugs. However, the justices, by a 6-to-3 vote, said that the act does not allow the attorney general to punish physicians who follow state law allowing assisted suicide.

Military recruiting. On March 6, 2006, the court ruled 8 to 0 that universities receiving federal funding for research, scholarships, and other purposes must give recruiters for the U.S. military the same access to students as other prospective employers have. Under a federal law known as the Solomon Amendment, universities can lose their federal funds if one part, such as a school of law or business, tries to exclude military recruiters or give them reduced access to job-seeking students. A group of law schools challenged the law, saying that having to accommodate the military recruiters violated the schools' rights of free speech and free association under the First Amendment. The schools said that accommodating recruiters, in effect, forced them to endorse the military's policy of excluding openly homosexual men and women. The justices said the schools were free to criticize the policy but could not discriminate against the military recruiters.

Congressional redistricting. In a complicated case from Texas, the court on June 28 issued two decisions about how states may draw the boundaries of the districts used for electing members of Congress. Traditionally, state legislatures have redrawn congressional district maps after U.S. census figures are released so that the districts take into account population growth and shifts. Texas redistricted after the 2000 Census. In 2003, the Republican-controlled Legislature, in a controversial move, adopted another new map to elect more Republicans to Congress. Although citizen groups challenged the new map, the court ruled that it did not amount to unconstitutional gerrymandering. Gerrymandering is the drawing of voting boundaries to influence the outcome of an election. The court left open the possibility that a redistricting plan could be so skewed toward one party that it would be unconstitutional, but the justices did not specify conditions extreme enough to be violations.

On a second issue, the court ruled that the boundaries of one district in far west Texas violated the federal Voting Rights Act of 1965. That act bars governments from taking actions that reduce the voting power of racial and ethnic minority groups that have historically faced discrimination. The court said that Texas had intentionally split an area with a large population of Latino voters who often voted together.

Campaign finance. The court on June 26, 2006, struck down Vermont's law limiting how much political candidates could spend on their campaigns and how much they could accept as donations from individuals. Vermont's restrictions on individual contributions ranged from a low of $200 to candidates for state representative to a maximum of $400 for candidates running for governor or other statewide office. Candidates could spend only $2,000 to run for state representative and up to $300,000 to run for governor. The court ruled that campaign spending limits violate First Amendment free speech guarantees. The justices also said that some contribution limits can be imposed without violating the First Amendment but that Vermont's were too low.

Employment law. In a Tennessee case decided on June 22, the court gave greater protection to workers who suffer retaliation for complaining about discrimination on the job. The case revolved around the Civil Rights Act of 1964, which forbids employment discrimination based on race, color, religion, sex, or national origin and bars retaliation against employees or job applicants for taking part in a discrimination investigation. The court, by a 9-to-0 vote, upheld a jury verdict favoring a woman forklift operator who had been reassigned to a less desirable job after she complained about sexual harassment by her supervisor. The court said the reassignment could be considered illegal retaliation.

Death penalty. In a 9-to-0 ruling on June 12, 2006, the court said that a death row inmate in Florida could challenge the three-drug sequence the state planned to use to execute him. Clarence E. Hill had been convicted of killing a police officer and sentenced to death in 1983. He argued that Florida's execution method violated the Eighth Amendment ban on cruel and unusual punishment. Under Florida's lethal injection method, one drug is administered as a painkiller, a second drug then paralyzes the muscles so that the inmate cannot move or cry out, and a third causes a fatal heart attack. Hill's appeal said that the first drug would not be strong enough to prevent him from feeling needless pain while the other two drugs were given. The justices said he could raise those claims in lower courts. However, a district court in Florida and an appeals court in Georgia refused to hear Hill's challenges, ruling that he should have filed earlier. He was executed on Sept. 20, 2006.

■ Geoffrey A. Campbell
See also **Courts; People in the news** (Samuel Alito).

Sweden. The Alliance for Sweden defeated the Social Democratic Party—which had governed the country since 1994 and for 65 of the past 74 years—in elections held in September 2006. The center-right Alliance coalition—made up of the Moderate, Center, Liberal, and Christian Democratic parties—under the leadership of Prime Minister Fredrik Reinfeldt took 48 percent of the vote, compared with 46 percent for the Social Democrats and their allies, the Left and Green parties. The new government took office on October 6.

The campaign. Political observers noted that though the country's economy was performing well in 2006, Swedes had grown tired of former Prime Minister Goran Persson, who had governed since 1996, was perceived by many voters as overly dominant. A series of minor scandals involving nepotism and petty corruption further ate away at the Social Democratic Party's popularity. In addition, though government statistics appeared to show that unemployment was low—about 5 percent—critics claimed that unemployment was actually about 17 percent after government work programs, early retirement, and sick leave were factored in. Unemployment among youth and Muslim immigrants was even higher.

During the campaign, Reinfeldt assured voters that he would continue Sweden's "cradle to grave" welfare state. He promised to maintain funding for education and for health, child, and elderly care while lowering taxes. However, he vowed that his main focus would be to address high unemployment and job creation. Reinfeldt advocated cutting unemployment benefits from their current level of 80 percent of an employee's last paycheck to about 65 percent in an effort to encourage people back to work. These policies, combined with Reinfeldt's relatively young age— 41 years compared with Persson's 58 years— helped him attract younger and immigrant voters.

Although Reinfeldt won the campaign, his government quickly ran into difficulty. Two Cabinet ministers resigned, and several others came under investigation for failing to pay unpopular fees and service taxes. In addition, legislation introduced in Parliament to cut employment subsidies angered workers and labor unions, who called for nationwide demonstrations in December 2006. The results of a poll published on November 24 showed that public support for the government had fallen to 45 percent, and support for the Social Democrats had risen to 51 percent.

Sweden's economy grew at the rate of 4 percent in 2006, according to European Union (EU) economists; EU economists estimated the unemployment rate at 7.3 percent, rather than the 5 percent claimed by the government.

■ Jeffrey Kopstein

See also **Europe.**

Swimming. Brendan Hansen of the United States rolled through the U.S. National Championships held in August 2006 in Irvine, California. He broke his own world records in the 100-meter breaststroke with a time of 59.13 seconds and in the 200-meter breaststroke with a swim of 2 minutes, 08.74 seconds. American swimmer Michael Phelps captured the 200-meter and 400-meter individual medley, 100-meter and 200-meter butterfly, and 200-meter freestyle.

Pan Pacific Championships. American men set five world records at the Pan Pacific Championships in Victoria, Canada, in August. Phelps broke his own records in the 200-meter butterfly (1:53.80) and the 200-meter individual medley (1:55.84). Phelps and teammates Cullen Jones, Neil Walker, and Jason Lezak set a world record of 3:12.46 in the 400-meter freestyle relay. Aaron Peirsol broke his own 200-meter backstroke record in 1:54.44, and Hansen broke his world record in the 200-meter breaststroke with a time of 2:08.50. One women's world record fell at the championships. Jessicah Schipper of Australia won the 200-meter butterfly in 2:05.40.

European Championships. Britta Steffen of Germany captured four golds at the European Championships in Budapest in August. She set a record of 53.30 in the 100-meter freestyle, breaking the mark set by Australia's Libby Lenton earlier in 2006 at the Commonwealth Games in Melbourne, Australia. Steffen and teammates Petra Dallman, Daniela Samulski, and Annika Liebs also won the 800-meter freestyle relay with a new record of 7:50.82. Laure Manaudou of France won her fourth gold of the championships by shaving nearly a second from her own record in the 400-meter freestyle (4:02.13). Leisel Jones of Australia set two world records at the Games: at the trials, she beat her own mark in the 200-meter breaststroke in 2:20.54; at the Games, she shaved more than a half-second off the 100-meter breaststroke record she set earlier in 2006, with a posting of 1:05.09.

Short-course world championships. Aaron Lochte of the United States set records in the 200-meter individual medley (1:53.31) and 200-meter backstroke (1:49.05), also winning gold in the 400-meter individual medley. Australian women set a world record in the 400-meter medley (3:51.84). Women from the Netherlands set a record in the 400-meter freestyle relay (3:33.32).

Lenton captured the gold medal as the anchor on the Australian women's team, plus three individual golds—50-meter freestyle, 100-meter freestyle, 100-meter butterfly—and was named top female swimmer. Australian Matt Welsh won four titles—in the 50-meter backstroke, 100-meter backstroke, 50-meter butterfly, and 100-meter individual medley.   ■ Michael Kates

Switzerland. Although Switzerland's policy of strict neutrality kept it out of most international institutions, the nation continued in 2006 to strengthen trade and economic ties with the European Union (EU). In November, Swiss voters narrowly approved an $800-million aid package for the 10 nations admitted to the EU in 2004. The money was to be used by the EU's cohesion fund, which promotes economic development. Nearly half of the package, which was to be paid out over 10 years, was designated for Poland. Much of the rest will earmarked for Hungary and the Czech Republic. The Swiss People's Party opposed the aid because the party believed it set a precedent that would require Switzerland to provide the same for Romania and Bulgaria, which were slated to join the EU in 2007. Proponents of the package maintained that the aid package strengthened Switzerland's trading relationship with EU member nations.

National referenda. In September 2006, voters rejected a proposal to divert profits from the Swiss Central Bank to prop up the country's pension system. The Swiss Central Bank made windfall profits in the mid-2000's from the sale of gold at high market prices. Also in September, a majority of voters approved a new set of immigration laws designed to reduce what lawmakers saw as "abuses" of asylum laws. Under the new law, refugees are required to show authorities valid identity papers within 48 hours of entering Switzerland. Opponents of the law noted that many oppressive regimes destroy identification documents and that to expect victims fleeing torture or war to have valid identification was unrealistic. The new law also restricts most immigration from non-European countries to highly skilled workers only.

In November, voters approved a unified monthly child allowance. Previously, the amount parents received had been determined by individual *cantons* (states), but the new measure standardized the payment nationwide. On the same slate of referenda, voters rejected a proposal to make English the only foreign language taught in primary schools in Zurich, Switzerland's largest city. German, one of the country's four national languages, is the primary language in the Zurich canton. The referendum, if approved, would have put English before the other three national languages—French, Italian, and Romansh.

Economy. Economists with the Organisation for Economic Co-operation and Development, a 30-nation association headquartered in Paris, forecast that the Swiss economy would grow by about 3 percent in 2006. The country's unemployment rate was estimated to fall from 4.3 percent in 2005 to 3.9 percent in 2006.   ■ Jeffrey Kopstein

See also **Europe.**

Syria. The arrest in May 2006 of Syrian intellectual and prodemocracy activist Michel Kilo led 22 Syrian and Lebanese writers and journalists to sign a petition demanding his release. As of late 2006, Kilo remained under arrest.

Public support for Kilo was one of several signs that opposition to the regime of President Bashar al-Assad had gained strength in 2006. In June, opposition leaders meeting in London called for peaceful resistance and civil disobedience so that the Syrian people could "gradually tear down the barrier of fear." Abdul Halim Khaddam, a former vice president of Syria, and Ali Sadr al-Din al-Bayanouni, leader of the banned Syrian Muslim Brotherhood, chaired the conference.

Hariri investigation. The United Nations commission investigating the suicide bombing that killed former Lebanese Prime Minister Rafik Hariri and 22 others in February 2005 finalized a draft resolution in November 2006. The resolution authorized an international tribunal to investigate the incident. Earlier commission reports had implicated Syrian officials in the assassination of Hariri, an opponent of Syria's domination of Lebanon.

Alliance with Iran. During his visit to Syria in January 2006, President Mahmoud Ahmadinejad of Iran endorsed Syria's support of Hezbollah, a radical Islamist group in Lebanon, and Hamas, a radical Islamist group that won Palestinian elections in January. According to many experts on Middle East affairs, Syria and Iran used Hezbollah to provoke a brief conflict between Israel and Hezbollah in July and August, partly to overthrow the Lebanese government.

After a cease-fire took effect in August—with the Lebanese government still intact—President Assad praised "the heroic battles" fought by Hezbollah. In November, Hezbollah ministers and pro-Syrian allies resigned from the Lebanese government when their demands for increased government representation were not met.

Attack on U.S. embassy. Syrian security forces repelled an attack by four gunmen on the United States embassy in Damascus, the capital of Syria, on September 12. The attack resulted in the death of a Syrian guard and injuries to 11 other people, none of them American. United States Secretary of State Condoleezza Rice thanked the Syrians for securing the embassy. However, some experts on terrorism believed that Syrian authorities staged the attack to persuade U.S. officials that Syria was fighting terrorism and should be included in talks on regional issues. Since Hariri's assassination, the administration of U.S. President George W. Bush had shunned any dialogue with Syria.   ■ Marius Deeb

See also **Iran; Israel; Lebanon; Middle East.**

Taiwan. Prosecutors in Taiwan indicted Wu Shu-Chen, the wife of President Chen Shui-bian, on Nov. 3, 2006, on charges of embezzlement, forgery, and perjury. They said Wu and Chen had "jointly used the opportunity provided by [his] office to swindle" the equivalent of $450,000 from a special presidential budget for secret diplomacy. By law, Chen could not be prosecuted while he was president. In a televised speech on November 5, Chen denied the charges. He declared that he had nothing to hide and was prepared to face investigation. In addition, he announced that he would resign if Wu was convicted of corruption.

Political turmoil. The scandal followed months of political turmoil as the opposition Kuomintang (KMT) party accused Chen of corruption. Auditors discovered in July that almost the entire $48-million special budget for state affairs in 2006 had already been spent. The auditors called $36 million of the expenditures "questionable." Prosecutors also investigated whether Wu had wrongly received $8,000 worth of gift certificates, but they said there was insufficient evidence to indict her on that charge. In addition, Chen's son-in-law was convicted in December on charges of insider trading. The various charges invigorated efforts by the KMT and independent activists to force Chen from office. The opposition had sought to oust him since he narrowly won reelection in 2004.

Demonstrators began massing in the center of Taipei, Taiwan's capital, on Sept. 9, 2006, to demand Chen's resignation. Over the course of several days, hundreds of thousands of protesters took to the streets, led by Shih Ming-teh, a founder and former chairman of the DPP, which Chen now headed.

Frank Hsieh resigned as prime minister on January 17. Su Tseng-chang then became the fifth person to hold the position since Chen became president in 2000. Su had stepped down as DPP chairman after the party lost badly to the KMT and its allies in December 2005 local elections. Chen announced on May 31, 2006, that he was delegating many of his domestic policy powers to the prime minister.

Relations with China. Chen announced in February that the National Unification Council had "ceased to function." Both Taiwan and China officially say they are one country, but their joint council had done no work for years. China has repeatedly said it would invade Taiwan if Taiwan abandoned the one-country theory and declared itself independent. China called abandoning the council "a grave provocation." Under pressure from the United States, which is pledged to defend Taiwan, Chen backed away in June from steps toward independence.

■ Henry S. Bradsher

See also **Asia; China.**

Tajikistan. Emomali Rahmonov won a third seven-year term as president of Tajikistan in elections on Nov. 6, 2006. Rahmonov became head of state in 1992 and was first elected president in 1994. Changes to the Tajik Constitution made in 2003 allowed Rahmonov to serve up to four terms.

Official results gave Rahmonov 79.3 percent of the 2006 vote. His closest competitor, Olimzon Boboyev of the Economic Reform Party, received 6.2 percent. Three major opposition parties (the Democratic Party of Tajikistan, the Social Democratic Party, and the Islamic Renaissance Party) boycotted the election. The Organisation for Security and Co-operation in Europe (OSCE) criticized the election as falling short of international standards, citing a lack of competition, media bias, and widespread voting irregularities. The OSCE found, however, that the 2006 election represented an improvement over the 1999 presidential poll, in which Rahmonov received 96 percent of the vote.

Many potential challengers to Rahmonov had been jailed in recent years. Ghaffor Mirzoev, the former commander of the Presidential Guard and head of the Drug Control Agency, was arrested in August 2004 and was sentenced in August 2006 to life in prison for a *coup* (overthrow) attempt, abuse of office, and murder. ■ Juliet Johnson

See also **Asia.**

Tanzania. See Africa.

Taxation. United States President George W. Bush on May 17, 2006, signed into law the Tax Increase Prevention and Reconciliation Act of 2005. The law extended reduced tax rates on capital gains and dividends and increased the exemption levels for the *alternative minimum tax* (AMT). The AMT is a tax that people with higher incomes must pay in addition to regular income tax. The original intention of the AMT was to prevent people with very high incomes from using special tax benefits to pay little or no tax. Over the years, however, the AMT has had a substantial impact on upper-middle-class taxpayers.

The Tax Increase Prevention and Reconciliation Act also included provisions to raise revenue for the government. The law placed restrictions on the tax-free treatment of some corporate spin-off transactions and extended penalties for people involved in prohibited *tax shelters*—that is, methods to avoid income tax liability.

On December 20, President Bush signed a bill that extended a number of tax breaks that had expired at the end of 2005. The extended breaks included deductions for higher education costs and for research and development initiatives.

IRA benefit for soldiers. President Bush on May 29, 2006, signed into law an amendment to federal tax law designed to benefit members of the armed forces. The measure enabled military personnel serving in combat zones to make contributions to individual retirement accounts (IRA's), even if the wages on which the contributions are based are not taxed. In general, taxpayers are not allowed to make IRA contributions based on income that is not taxable.

State taxation of retirement income. Congress in 2006 approved two measures designed to clarify rules regarding the state taxation of retirement income. One measure, signed into law by President Bush on August 3, prohibited state taxation of certain payments made by partnerships to retired partners who live out of state. Another measure, also signed by President Bush on August 3, clarified the treatment of self-employment under laws limiting state taxation.

Pension reform. On August 17, President Bush signed the Pension Protection Act of 2006, a law designed to protect retirees who depend on employer pensions. The measure made permanent the pension provisions introduced in the 2001 tax law reforms. The provisions—which include higher limits on pension contributions—had been set to expire in 2010. The new pension law also established incentives for charitable giving by taxpayers and gave employers more flexibility in giving investment advice to participants in retirement plans. ■ Geoffrey A. Campbell

See also **Congress of the United States.**

Telecommunications. Wireless technology advanced on several fronts in 2006. In addition, mergers and take-overs continued to reshape the telecommunications industry.

Municipal Wi-Fi. The development of municipal wireless networks progressed rapidly in 2006. By September, about 300 cities, towns, and other localities in the United States either had set up such networks or were in the process of doing so. Some networks were designed to allow anyone with a properly equipped computer to access the Internet wirelessly, for little or no cost, in most or all areas of the community. Other networks were intended only for police officers, firefighters, or other municipal employees.

Most municipal networks in 2006 relied on Wi-Fi technology, which allows high-speed wireless data transfer by radio waves over distances of a few hundred feet. Most of the networks were at least partially owned or operated by private firms. Cities that launched wireless networks in 2006 included Philadelphia; Anaheim, California; Toronto, Canada; and Taipei, Taiwan. Cities working to establish networks included Chicago, Houston, Paris, Phoenix, and San Francisco.

Wireless spectrum auction. The Federal Communications Commission (FCC), which regulates broadcast communication in the United States, auctioned off more than 1,000 Advanced

Wireless Services (AWS) radio spectrum licenses in 2006. The AWS spectrum consists of bands of radio frequencies that are designated for such broadband wireless services as Internet access or video transmission. Over 100 firms bid a total of nearly $14 billion for pieces of the AWS spectrum. The top bidders included T-Mobile USA, Inc., of Bellevue, Washington; Verizon Wireless of Bedminster, New Jersey; and a consortium consisting of Sprint Nextel Corporation of Reston, Virginia, and four cable television providers: Comcast Cable Communications, Inc., of Philadelphia; Time Warner Cable Inc. of Stamford, Connecticut; Cox Communications, Inc., of Atlanta, Georgia; and Bright House Networks LLC of St. Petersburg, Florida.

WiMAX network. Meanwhile, Sprint Nextel announced in August that it would use its existing spectrum holdings to develop a nationwide broadband mobile network based on WiMAX technology. WiMAX allows high-speed wireless data transfers of up to 30 miles (48 kilometers).

Merger mania continues. AT&T Inc. of San Antonio acquired BellSouth Corporation of Atlanta, Georgia, in 2006. The deal—finalized in December shortly after its approval by the FCC—created a telecommunications giant larger than AT&T's nearest competitor, Verizon Communications Inc. of New York City. Once the take-over was complete, AT&T offered landline phone service in 22 states and became the sole owner of Atlanta-based Cingular Wireless LLC, the country's largest cellular phone company. Cingular was a joint venture of AT&T and BellSouth. Also in 2006, two major manufacturers of telecommunications network equipment—Alcatel, based in Paris, and Lucent Technologies Inc., based in Murray Hill, New Jersey—merged to form a new company, Alcatel-Lucent, based in Paris.

Call database. A May 11 article in *USA Today* alleged that AT&T, Verizon, and BellSouth had agreed to provide the U.S. National Security Agency (NSA) with phone call records for millions of U.S. residents. The newspaper said the NSA was compiling a call database for use in detecting patterns of terrorist activity. AT&T neither confirmed nor denied the allegation, but Verizon and BellSouth denied it. In a partial retraction on June 30, *USA Today* said it could not confirm that Verizon or BellSouth had cooperated with the NSA.

News reports in December 2005 had revealed a secret NSA antiterrorism wiretapping program that allowed the agency to intercept calls and e-mails between people in the United States and overseas without a court warrant. In 2006, several lawsuits challenged the program's legality. On August 17, a U.S. district judge in Detroit ruled the program unconstitutional. Federal officials appealed the ruling. ■ Jon Van

See also **Computer; Electronics; Internet.**

Television. In a risky move designed to attract younger viewers, two decade-old television networks combined to form a new network for the 2006 fall season. Another new network also was launched for the 2006 fall season; a major shuffling of programs, news anchors, and talk-show personalities between networks also took place in 2006; and several long-running, highly popular, and critically acclaimed series had their finales.

Networking. In January, the struggling UPN and WB networks announced they would merge to form a new network, the CW Television Network. UPN and WB—which were both launched in 1996—had reportedly lost almost $2 billion in their respective bids to attract younger viewers, and executives believed that by joining forces they could deliver a more profitable product. The new network was launched on Sept. 20, 2006, with "America's Next Top Model."

In addition to "America's Next Top Model," the CW featured five other series inherited from UPN during its first fall season: "Everybody Hates

EMMY AWARD WINNERS IN 2006

COMEDY

Best Series: "The Office"
Lead Actress: Julia Louis-Dreyfus, "The New Adventures of Old Christine"
Lead Actor: Tony Shalhoub, "Monk"
Supporting Actress: Megan Mullally, "Will & Grace"
Supporting Actor: Jeremy Piven, "Entourage"

DRAMA

Best Series: "24"
Lead Actress: Mariska Hargitay, "Law & Order: Special Victims Unit"
Lead Actor: Kiefer Sutherland, "24"
Supporting Actress: Blythe Danner, "Huff"
Supporting Actor: Alan Alda, "The West Wing"

OTHER AWARDS

Miniseries: "Elizabeth I"

Reality/Competition Series: "The Amazing Race"

Variety, Music, or Comedy Series: "The Daily Show with Jon Stewart"

Made for Television Movie: "The Girl in the Café"

Lead Actress in a Miniseries or Movie: Helen Mirren, "Elizabeth I"

Lead Actor in a Miniseries or Movie: Andre Braugher, "Thief"

Supporting Actress in a Miniseries or Movie: Kelly Macdonald, "The Girl in the Café"

Supporting Actor in a Miniseries or Movie: Jeremy Irons, "Elizabeth I"

TOP-RATED U.S. TELEVISION SERIES

The following were among the most-watched television series for the 2005-2006 regular season, which ran from Sept. 18, 2005, to May 24, 2006.

1. "American Idol" (Tuesday) (FOX)
2. "American Idol" (Wednesday) (FOX)
3. "CSI" (CBS)
4. "Desperate Housewives" (ABC)
5. "Grey's Anatomy" (ABC)
6. "Without a Trace" (CBS)
7. "Dancing with the Stars" (ABC)
8. "CSI: Miami" (CBS)
9. "Survivor: Guatemala" (CBS)
10. "NFL Monday Night Football" (ABC)
11. "House" (FOX)
12. (tie) "NCIS" (CBS)
    "Survivor: Panama-Exile Island" (CBS)
    "The Unit" (CBS)
15. "Two and a Half Men" (CBS)
16. (tie) "Dancing with the Stars Results" (ABC)
    "Deal or No Deal" (Monday) (NBC)
18. "Cold Case" (CBS)
19. "Lost" (ABC)
20. (tie) "CSI: New York" (CBS)
    "Law and Order: SVU" (NBC)

Copyright – Nielsen Media Research, 2006.

Chris," "Veronica Mars," "All of Us," "Girlfriends," and "WWE Friday Night SmackDown!" It also had five series from the WB: "7th Heaven," "Small-ville," "Supernatural," "One Tree Hill," and "Gilmore Girls."

The CW also added two new series. "The Game," a spin-off of "Girlfriends," revolved around the significant others of professional football players. "Runaway," which told the story of a family that became fugitives after the father was framed for murder, was canceled in October. WB's "Reba" debuted on the CW in November.

The Fox Television Stations Group, which owned several UPN affiliates, also created a new network. Called My Network TV, the new network offered English soap operas in the style of Spanish-language telenovelas. For its September launch, My Network TV offered two shows, "Desire" and "Fashion House." The latter featured popular 1980's actresses Morgan Fairchild and Bo Derek.

Anchors away. In 2006, two networks tapped morning news programs to find new anchors for their evening news broadcasts. In April, CBS announced that Katie Couric would anchor "CBS Evening News" after 15 years as the co-host of NBC's "Today." After a heavy promotional cam-paign, Couric began her stint on September 5, drawing 13.6 million viewers in her first appear-ance and outperforming the competition. How-ever, "CBS Evening News" fell into third place in October. By November, its average audience had declined to 7.3 million viewers—1.1 million behind ABC's "World News" and 1.6 million behind NBC's "Nightly News." Couric's ratings matched those of her predecessor, Bob Schieffer, during the same period of 2005.

ABC initially assigned the duo of Bob Woodruff and former "20/20" co-anchor Elizabeth Vargas to replace Peter Jennings, who died of lung cancer in August 2005. However, Woodruff was seriously injured by the explosion of a roadside bomb while reporting in Iraq in January 2006. Vargas announced she was pregnant in February. In May, ABC named Charles Gibson, a co-anchor of its "Good Morning America" program, to replace Woodruff and Vargas as lone anchor of "World News Tonight." In July, the program was renamed "World News with Charles Gibson."

In November, award-winning veteran broad-cast journalist Ed Bradley died of leukemia at age 65. One of the first African American reporters on national television, Bradley joined the staff of CBS's "60 Minutes" as a correspondent in 1981.

Daytime talk shows. Meredith Vieira, one of four co-hosts of the ABC daytime program "The View," took Couric's old post at "Today" in September 2006. In turn, the outspoken Rosie O'Donnell then replaced Vieira at "The View" amid some controversy.

Star Jones Reynolds, who had been with "The View" for its entire nine years, also stirred con-troversy when she abruptly announced on the air in June 2006 that she would be leaving the show. ABC had decided not to renew Jones Reynolds's contract, but she was to stay with the show until July. The network had conducted research show-ing that viewers increasingly disapproved of Jones Reynolds, according to co-host and execu-tive producer Barbara Walters.

"Monday Night Football," a staple of ABC for 36 years, switched to ESPN in fall 2006. NBC launched "Football Night in America," a roundup of Sunday's football action, and "NBC Sunday Night Football." The changes were accompanied by an arrangement with the National Football League (NFL) that allowed NBC leeway in scheduling to ensure compelling match-ups for their Sunday night broadcasts.

A winning "Deal" for NBC. In October, NBC Universal announced it would lay off 700 employ-ees and would rely on "nonscripted" program-ming during the 8 p.m. EST hour in a bid to cut $750 million from its budget.

One of these nonscripted NBC programs was the game show "Deal or No Deal," hosted by actor-comedian Howie Mandel. The show, which premiered in December 2005, became a television phenomenon in 2006. In the game, contestants make a series of choices from among 26 cases, each associated with a cash amount, to win from 1 cent to $1 million.

Other notable new shows. In March, CBS launched "The Unit," a drama about U.S. Special Forces soldiers and their wives. "Ugly Betty," **based on a popular Colombian telenovela,** launched in fall 2006 to strong ratings. The ABC dramatic comedy revolves around an intelligent but plain, socially awkward woman who works as a secretary at a fashion magazine.

NBC's "Heroes," about a group of people who develop superhuman abilities, also premiered in the fall and attracted a sizable audience.

Series finales. Several popular and critically acclaimed series were canceled during the 2005-2006 television season.

The Sci Fi Channel announced in August 2006 that it would not renew "Stargate SG-1" for an 11th season. The series, about adventurers who travel to distant worlds and protect Earth from alien threats, was the longest-running science-fiction series on American television. It aired its 200th episode in August 2006.

NBC's popular "Will & Grace" was canceled after eight seasons. The award-winning situation comedy about the relationship between a gay lawyer and his best friend, a woman who runs an interior design firm, closed with the two characters becoming estranged but then reuniting years later.

Another award-winning NBC series, "The West Wing" was canceled after seven critically acclaimed seasons. The political drama concluded with the election of Matt Santos (Jimmy Smits) as president, succeeding Jed Bartlet (Martin Sheen) after two terms.

The ABC series "Alias" was canceled after five seasons. The thriller, which launched the career of actress Jennifer Garner, ended with her character, Cen-

tral Intelligence Agency (CIA) agent Sydney Bristow, settling into a relatively normal life with her husband, Michael Vaughn, and child, yet ready to spring into action when needed.

Two quirky comedies that generated high praise from critics but low ratings from audiences also were canceled. Fox's Emmy Award-winning "Arrested Development," narrated and coproduced by Ron Howard, was canceled after three seasons, and Showtime's dramatic comedy "Huff" ended after two seasons.

Barker bows out. In October, Emmy Award-winning game show host Bob Barker announced his retirement after 50 years in television. The 82-year-old Barker had hosted the popular game show "The Price is Right" for 35 years. The daytime game show is the longest-running in television history. Barker was scheduled to retire in June 2007.   ■ Raoul Mowatt

See also **Internet; People in the news** (Katie Couric; Lou Dobbs; Tony Snow).

America Ferrera stars in "Ugly Betty" as Betty Suarez, an intelligent but plain, socially awkward young woman who works as a secretary at a fashion magazine. The series is based on the popular Colombian telenovela "Yo soy Betty, la fea."

Popular United States tennis star Andre Agassi waves an emotional good-bye to a cheering crowd at the U.S. Open after losing in the third round of the men's singles competition on Sept. 3, 2006. Agassi announced in June that the U.S. Open would be his final tournament.

Tennis. Switzerland's Roger Federer dominated the men's tour again in 2006, capturing three majors—including his fourth straight Wimbledon—while finishing as the runner-up in the French Open. He became the only man to win both Wimbledon and the U.S. Open in the same year for three years in a row.

Popular tennis star Andre Agassi of the United States retired from the sport on September 3 after losing in the third round of the U.S. Open to qualifier Benjamin Becker. Agassi won eight majors in his career.

In women's tennis, Amelie Mauresmo of France enjoyed a breakout year. She won two Grand Slam titles after failing in her first 32 efforts.

Australian Open. Mauresmo won her first Grand Slam title in Melbourne, beating Belgium's Justine Henin-Hardenne on January 28. Henin-Hardenne retired with stomach pains, trailing 6-1, 2-0. Federer captured his second Australian Open, rallying from a set down to beat unseeded Marcos Baghdatis of Cyprus 5-7, 7-5, 6-0, 6-2 on January 29. American twins Bob and Mike Bryan won the men's doubles title; China's Zi Yan and Jie Zheng won the women's doubles; and India's Mahesh Bhupathi and Switzerland's Martina Hingis won the mixed doubles.

French Open. Henin-Hardenne became the first woman since 1994 to win the title without dropping a set, topping Russian Svetlana Kuznetsova 6-4, 6-4 on June 10 in Paris. It was Henin-Hardenne's third French Open title in four years and her second in a row.

Spain's Rafael Nadal stopped Federer's march to a noncalendar Grand Slam (winning all four events in a row stretching from one year to the next) in a final billed as the match of the year. Nadal defended his French Open title on June 11 and won a record 60th straight on clay, rallying from a disastrous first set to beat Federer 1-6, 6-1, 6-4, 7-6 (4). Sweden's Jonas Bjorkman and Belarus's Max Mirnyi won the men's doubles title; American Lisa Raymond and Australian Samantha Stosur won the women's doubles; and Slovenia's Katarina Srebotnik and Serbia's Nenad Zimonjic won in mixed doubles.

Wimbledon. Unlike in the Australian Open, Mauresmo's final against Henin-Hardenne went the maximum three sets on July 8. Mauresmo rallied from a set down to beat the Belgian 2-6, 6-3, 6-4. On July 9, Federer avenged his French defeat to Nadal with a 6-0, 7-6 (5), 6-7 (2), 6-3 victory. Nadal was the only player to take a set off Federer at Wimbledon.

Mark Knowles of the Bahamas and Canada's Daniel Nestor beat Sweden's Simon Aspelin and Australia's Todd Perry 5-7, 6-3, 6-7 (5), 6-3, 23-21 in 6 hours, 9 minutes—the longest match of any kind in Wimbledon history and the longest doubles match in Grand Slam history. The Bryan brothers won the men's doubles title; Yan and Zheng won the women's doubles; and Israel's Andy Ram and Russia's Vera Zvonareva won in mixed doubles.

U.S. Open. Top-seeded Federer toppled resurgent American Andy Roddick, the 2003 Open champ, to capture the men's title on Sept. 10, 2006, in New York City. Federer had too much firepower for the ninth-seeded Roddick, rolling to a 6-2, 4-6, 7-5, 6-1 victory. Federer dropped just two sets during the tournament.

Russia's Maria Sharapova, the third seed, toppled the number one and two seeds in back-to-back matches to capture her second major and her first U.S. Open. After beating top-seeded Mauresmo in the semifinals in three sets—6-0 in the final set—Sharapova swept away Henin-Hardenne on September 9, 6-4, 6-4.

Martin Damm of the Czech Republic and Leander Paes of India captured the men's doubles title. Nathalie Dechy of France and Zvonareva won the women's doubles. Americans Martina Navratilova and Bob Bryan won in mixed doubles.

The Davis Cup. Russia defeated Argentina 3 matches to 2 in Moscow on December 3 to win its second Davis Cup. Russia also won in 2002.

■ Michael Kates

Terrorism. Terrorist incidents continued to affect every region of the globe in 2006. While terrorism declined in some parts of the world—including East and Central Asia, Europe, and North America—the Middle East and South Asia suffered from alarming levels of death and destruction. The use of terrorism as a political tactic showed few signs of slowing, and many experts feared that individual attacks were becoming even more deadly and destructive.

The Middle East. Intensifying violence in Iraq accounted for the vast majority of terrorism-related deaths in the Middle East in 2006. Militant groups continued to carry out attacks against both military and nonmilitary targets. Many of the militants opposed Iraq's new government, which was backed by the United States. Abu Musab al-Zarqawi, a Jordanian linked to the al-Qa`ida terrorist organization, led a major campaign of violence before he was killed by a United States airstrike on June 7.

Israel, Lebanon, and Turkey remained major terrorist targets in 2006. The radical Islamic Jihad of Palestine was among the most active groups in carrying out attacks. It claimed responsibility for an April 17 bombing outside a restaurant in Tel Aviv, Israel, which killed nine people and injured many more. The same site had been bombed just months earlier.

A series of political assassinations—which began in 2005 with the assassination of former Prime Minister Rafiq Hariri—continued to shake Lebanon in 2006. On November 21, Pierre Gemayel, a leader of Lebanon's Maronite Christian community, was gunned down by unknown assailants. Turkey, meanwhile, faced numerous acts of terrorism against government and police targets. Kurdish nationalist groups claimed responsibility for many of them.

South Asia. Heavy terrorist activity in Afghanistan, India, Nepal, Pakistan, Sri Lanka, and Thailand combined to make South Asia one of the most dangerous regions of the world in 2006. Afghanistan experienced an especially large number of attacks and fatalities, due in part to the resurgence of the Taliban, the militant Islamic group that controlled most of Afghanistan from the mid-1990's to 2001.

The region's most devastating attack in 2006 occurred in Mumbai (formerly Bombay), India's largest city. On July 11, a series of seven bombs exploded on the city's commuter train system. The explosions, which took place during the evening rush hour, killed at least 200 people and injured hundreds more. The Indian government accused militants based in Pakistan of playing a role in the attack.

Africa. A terrorist bombing shook the resort town of Dahab, Egypt, on April 24. The attack involved the coordinated detonation of three bombs in busy areas favored by vacationers and pedestrians. The explosions resulted in 23 deaths and numerous injuries. Nasser Khamis al-Mallahi, the Egyptian extremist suspected of planning the attack, was later killed by Egyptian police. Other terrorist acts in Africa involved the Salafist Group for Call and Combat, a militant group responsible for a number of attacks on government and civilian targets in Algeria.

Russia. A wave of attacks against political and religious targets in Russia continued in 2006. The October 7 assassination of outspoken journalist Anna Politkovskaya heightened already-rising concerns about lawlessness and organized crime in that country. In November, Alexander Litvinenko, a former Russian spy who had been investigating the journalist's death, mysteriously fell ill in London and died from radiation poisoning. Traces of polonium-210, a radioactive isotope, were later found in numerous public locations where Litvinenko or his associates had been.

Latin America. Most terrorist activity in Latin America took place in Colombia. Fighting continued there between the Revolutionary Armed Forces of Colombia, other militant groups, and the government.   ■ Richard E. Rubenstein

See also **Afghanistan; Aviation; Colombia; Egypt; India; Iraq; Israel; Lebanon; Russia; Turkey.**

Thailand. After months of political turmoil, Thailand's armed forces seized power in a bloodless *coup* (overthrow) on Sept. 19, 2006. Prime Minister Thaksin Shinawatra was in New York City at the time, for a meeting of the United Nations.

Unrest. In January, members of Thaksin's family sold their stake in a telecommunications empire that Thaksin built before entering politics, to investors in Singapore. The $1.9-billion sale led to accusations of insider trading and tax-dodging. After massive demonstrations in February and March in the capital, Bangkok, calling for his resignation, Thaksin sought public support by calling a parliamentary election for April 2. The opposition boycotted the election, however, and a full parliament was not elected. In May, a Thai court annulled the election results, accusing several election commissioners of mismanagement. Thaksin resigned the prime minister's job on April 4, but he later resumed the position. New elections were scheduled for October but political instability and uncertainty continued, and many military officers felt Thaksin was interfering with senior military assignments to promote his supporters.

Junta. General Sondhi Boonyaratkalin, as head of the *junta* (military government), a self-appointed six-member group called the Council of Democratic Reform, became acting prime minister. King Bhumibol Adulyadej, who had earlier cautiously indicated his displeasure with the political situation, endorsed their move the next day. Many observers believed that the military had acted with advance approval from the king.

Surayud Chulanont, a respected former army commander, was sworn in as interim prime minister on October 1. The six generals, with the new title of Council for National Security, said a new constitution would be drafted within nine months and parliamentary elections would then be held. Thaksin announced from London in October that he was resigning as head of the governing Thai Rak Thai party. Many of the members also quit.

Separatists. Thaksin had been accused of bungling a response to a Muslim separatist movement in southern Thailand, a predominately Buddhist country. More than 1,700 people had died in the south since 2004. In 2006, a human rights group accused authorities of using excessive force, torture, and arbitrary detentions on the rebels. In November, Surayud apologized for Thaksin's policies. Sondhi, the first Muslim to head the army, initiated talks with the rebels. In a speech in the south in November, Surayud advocated Shari`ah, Muslim law, for the south. He expressed interest in "a constructive dialogue with all concerned parties" as long as they did not ask for independence.

■ Henry S. Bradsher

See also **Asia.**

Thousands of candles light Thailand's royal palace in Bangkok, the capital, on June 9, 2006, in celebration of the 60th anniversary of the ascension to the throne of King Bhumibol Adulyadej. He was crowned in 1946 at the age of 18.

Theater. New hit Broadway musicals—typically big-budget extravaganzas of spectacle, song, and dance that command equally big sales at the box office—were in short supply in 2006. Whereas previous seasons had given rise to such successful Broadway musicals as *The Producers* (2001), *Mamma Mia!* (2001), *Rent* and *Chicago* (both 1996), and others, the recent lackluster season failed to produce a single smash hit to rival these time-honored crowd pleasers. According to the League of American Theaters and Producers, such musicals as *Wicked* (2003), *Jersey Boys* (2005), and the long-running *The Lion King* (1997) continued to lead the field in terms of weekly sales. Such 2006 Broadway newcomers as *Mary Poppins*, based on P. L. Travers's 1934 book and the 1964 Walt Disney film, and the revival of *A Chorus Line,* the 1975 hit musical about aspiring theater performers, lagged far behind, however.

One big-budget musical that fared well financially was *The Color Purple,* despite initial skepticism by Broadway power brokers, lukewarm reviews, and no big-name stars. It is based on the Pulitzer Prize-winning novel by Alice Walker and the Oscar-nominated 1985 motion picture directed by Steven Spielberg and starring Oprah Winfrey. Produced by Winfrey, the $11-million musical had recouped its investment and ticket sales remained strong one year after opening on Broadway in December 2005. By the end of 2006, over $7 million in tickets had already been sold for a Chicago production of the show set to open in April 2007.

Pop musicals. As a number of new musicals met with lukewarm sales and mixed reviews, one new musical stood out in 2006 as a critical flop. *The Times They Are A-Changin'*, which opened at the Brooks Atkinson Theater in October 2006, conceived and directed and choreographed by Twyla Tharp, was a theatrical adaptation of songs by the singer-songwriter Bob Dylan. The elements of the show appeared promising: Tharp had successfully adapted the songs of pop musician Billy Joel for *Movin' Out* in 2002, and Dylan was widely held to be one of America's greatest and most popular songwriters. But the pairing of Tharp's imagery with Dylan's lyrics failed to win enthusiastic reviews. As Ben Brantley wrote in *The New York Times,* "If the choreography at times defies gravity, the show itself may be the most earthbound work Ms. Tharp has produced. Even as the dancers seem to fly, Mr. Dylan's lyrics are hammered, one by one, into the ground."

In general, recent Broadway musicals based on pop music have not done as well as earlier shows in the same vein—such as *Mamma Mia!,* based on the music of the Scandinavian pop group ABBA—or more recently, last season's Tony Award winner for best musical, *Jersey Boys,* which tells the story of the pop group the Four Seasons. Recent shows that faded quickly included *Good Vibrations* (2005, with the music of the Beach Boys); *Lennon* (2005, with the music of John Lennon); and *Ring of Fire* (2006, with the music of Johnny Cash).

No Pulitzer in drama. A certain amount of controversy surrounded the decision of the

The Drowsy Chaperone, a zany 1920's-style Broadway musical, won five Tony Awards in 2006, including Best Featured Actress in a Musical for Beth Leavel and Best Original Score for Lisa Lambert and Greg Morrison.

Pulitzer Prize Board in April not to award a prize in drama in 2006. In declining to award a Pulitzer in drama, the board turned down the recommendations of a panel of jurors chaired by *Newsday* theater critic Linda Winer and made up of other theater critics, an academic, and a playwright.

The plays recommended as finalists by the jury were *Red Light Winter,* by Adam Rapp; *Miss Witherspoon,* by Christopher Durang; and *The Intelligent Design of Jenny Chow,* by Rolin Jones. The Pulitzer Board—which comprised 19 journalists and academics in 2006—declined to award the prize for drama 15 times since the prizes were established in 1917, most recently in 1997. There was no clear frontrunner among the nominees, leading many observers in the theater community to predict that 2006 would not see a Pulitzer Prize in drama. Even so, critics such as Christopher Rawson of the *Pittsburgh* (Pennsylvania) *Post-Gazette* called the board's refusal to award the drama prize an "insult."

Hare in America. The British playwright David Hare chose to open his latest play, *The Vertical Hour,* not in London but at the Music Box Theatre in New York City. Speculation in the United Kingdom as to why Hare chose to open his play abroad focused on his discontent with the way the National Theatre in London handled the production of his last play, *Stuff Happens* (2004). Despite sold-out houses, no more dates could be added to the play's run after its 60 scheduled performances. *The Vertical Hour* was directed by Sam Mendes,

the Oscar-winning director of the 1999 film *American Beauty,* and featured the actress Julianne Moore, best known for her work in such films as *Vanya on 42nd Street* (1994) and *The Hours* (2002, for which Hare wrote the screenplay).

Both *The Vertical Hour,* Hare's 24th play and his 10th on Broadway, and *Stuff Happens,* which portrayed such real-life politicians as U.S. President George W. Bush, British Prime Minister Tony Blair, U.S. Secretary of State Condoleezza Rice, and former U.S. Secretary of Defense Donald Rumsfeld, are about the Iraq War. *Stuff Happens* examines the political machinations behind the war, sometimes incorporating politicians' actual words into the script. *The Vertical Hour* examines the opinions of an American woman, Nadia Blye, a former war correspondent turned Yale political science professor, and those of her British husband and her father-in-law.

Mendes has spoken about Hare's plays falling into two major categories: roughly the "Brechtian," influenced by the presentational and often political style of the German playwright Bertolt Brecht; and the "Chekhovian," reminiscent of the Russian playwright Anton Chekhov, whose character-driven works include the delicate and melancholy masterpieces *The Sea Gull* (1896) and *The Cherry Orchard* (1904). Mendes sees *Stuff Happens* as among Hare's Brechtian-type plays, and *The Vertical Hour, Skylight* (1995), and *The Secret Rapture* (1988) as Chekhovian. In 2007, Hare was scheduled to direct Vanessa Redgrave on Broadway in Joan Didion's play *The Year of Magical Thinking,* based on Didion's 2005 memoir. His adaptation for television of Jonathan Franzen's 2001 novel *The Corrections* will also be seen in 2007.

The Humana Festival of New Plays at the Actors Theatre of Louisville in Kentucky was founded in 1976 by Jon Jory, Actors Theatre's producing director from 1969 to 2000. During the Actors Theatre's 1979-1980 season, the Humana Foundation first sponsored the festival of new plays and, beginning with the 1981-1982 season, the festival was renamed the Humana Festival of New American Plays in honor of the Louisville-based company's ongoing support.

Over the course of its 30-year history, the Humana Festival has produced over 300 plays—from short pieces and 10-minute plays to one-acts and full-lengths—by more than 200 playwrights. As many as 3,000 scripts are submitted each year for consideration in the Actors Theatre's New Play Program, and nearly 75,000 scripts have been submitted since 1976. In addition to producing new plays, the festival also sponsors the publication of many of them in annual anthologies.

The Humana Festival has over the years developed a reputation for identifying important new work, and three plays chosen by the festival have won the Pulitzer Prize: *The Gin Game* (1977), by D.L. Coburn; *Crimes of the Heart* (1979), by Beth Henley; and *Dinner with Friends* (2000), by Donald Margulies.

The 2006 festival included *Act a Lady,* by Jordan Harrison, about a group of Midwestern men in the 1920's who dress as women in a French farce to raise money for the local Elks Lodge; *Natural Selection,* by Eric Coble, a science-fiction end-of-the-world satire set in a world's fair-style theme park; *Hotel Cassiopeia,* by Charles L. Mee, a rumination on the work of the reclusive artist Joseph Cornell, who populated delicate shadowbox sculptures with evocative everyday objects; and *Six Years,* by Sharr White, about the aftermath of war and its effect on the lives of a married couple from 1949 to 1973. ■ David Yezzi

Toronto. Mayor David Miller swept to an easy reelection in the November 2006 elections, earning 57 percent of the total vote. His closest rival, city councilor Jane Pitfield, received about 32 percent. Miller will have a longer term and more power than any previous Toronto mayor as a result of two changes enacted in 2006 by Ontario's provincial government.

In May, the Ontario government extended the term of office for municipal officials from three years to four years. The following month, it passed the City of Toronto Act, which gave city officials new authority to undertake initiatives and to raise taxes without having to get provincial approval. The City of Toronto Act also greatly increased the mayor's control over what issues come before the city council. It enabled the mayor to appoint chairs of municipal committees and to select members of a new executive committee that sets priorities for the council.

Heading into his second term, Miller committed himself to easing the city's traffic congestion by extending bus and streetcar service. He also led a number of other Canadian city mayors in demanding a larger municipal share of federal and provincial tax revenues.

Cultural buildings. In June, the Canadian Opera Company opened the Four Seasons Centre for the Performing Arts—a $181-million theater built specifically for opera and ballet—in central Toronto. A. J. Diamond, a well-known Toronto-based architect, led the team that designed the theater, which boasts state-of-the-art acoustics.

Other major projects under construction in 2006 included the new Art Gallery of Ontario, designed by the famous Toronto-born architect Frank Gehry, and an ambitious addition to the Royal Ontario Museum, by the Polish-born American architect Daniel Libeskind. Work was also underway on the Festival Centre, a permanent home for the Toronto International Film Festival.

Many Torontonians expressed hope that the cultural buildings would bring new life to the city in the same way that Gehry's Guggenheim Museum brought worldwide attention to the city of Bilbao, Spain, in 1997. A number of observers "talked up" the projects as an attempt to create a "Bilbao effect" for Toronto.

Nuit Blanche. All through the night of Sept. 30, 2006, and into the early hours of the next morning, Torontonians tramped the downtown streets in a celebration of the visual arts—the Toronto Nuit Blanche (white night), an all-night contemporary arts festival. The Nuit Blanche concept began in Paris in 2002 and spread to Rome, Madrid, and a number of other cities. The 2006 festival, Toronto's first, was part of a 16-month "Live with Culture" project, which was designed to showcase the city's artistic and cultural offerings.

Reduced gun violence. Following an alarming increase in gun violence in 2005—a year in which Toronto had 52 firearm-related murders—many people feared that the problem would worsen in 2006. In response, the Ontario government in March committed $30 million to help troubled young people in 13 Toronto neighborhoods. Toronto police also carried out aggressive campaigns to break up gangs and to reduce gang violence. The efforts appeared to have a positive impact, as gun-related homicides in 2006 fell by about 40 percent from 2005.

The 905. The Ontario government in April 2006 established the Greater Toronto Transit Authority to better coordinate the transportation operations between Toronto and nearby cities and towns. The move highlighted the importance of the rapidly growing suburban area outside Toronto, nicknamed "the 905 region" after its telephone area code. The 905 region drew additional attention in 2006 when work began on a 50-story residential tower in Mississauga, a small city on Toronto's western border. Some observers called the structure "the Marilyn Monroe building" because of the graceful curves of its design. ■ David Lewis Stein

See also **Architecture: A Special Report; City.**

Toys and games. Contrary to common belief, more Americans shopped for Christmas gifts on the day before Christmas Eve in 2006 than on "black Friday," the day after Thanksgiving, according to surveys by MasterCard Worldwide of Purchase, New York. Sales made between these two days account for more than half of all toys sold in the United States in a given year—and Wal-Mart Stores, Inc. of Bentonville, Arkansas, and Target Corporation of Minneapolis, Minnesota, engaged in an all-out price war to corner that market in 2006. Wal-Mart started discounting toys in mid-October with the company's "most aggres-sive pricing strategy ever," which Target an-nounced it would match. Wal-Mart enjoys more than $5.85 billion in toy sales annually, while Tar-get sells more than $3.5 billion each year out of the total $22-billion U.S. toy market.

Another retailer, KB Toys Incorporated of Pitts-field, Massachusetts, sought in 2006 to appeal to the growing grandparent generation, which accounts for more than 40 percent of sales at the mall-based, specialty toy chain. The company cre-ated the Grandparents' Rewards Club, which offers savings on their toy purchases one day a week all year long. Grandparents purchase about 25 percent of all toys for children under the age of 18, according to the 2006 Survey of the American Consumer by Mediamark Research Inc., of New York City.

Mall madness. It was "hurry up and wait" as thousands of consumers queued up at retail stores —in some cases overnight or longer—awaiting the arrival of two of the next generation of video game platforms, the PlayStation 3 from Sony Corporation and the Wii (pronounced *wee*) from the Nintendo Company Limited, both of Japan. In some instances, after these two products went on sale in November 2006 in limited supply, scuffles broke out as con-sumers jockeyed to snap up the items from store shelves. Some retail locations were forced to close temporarily until order was restored.

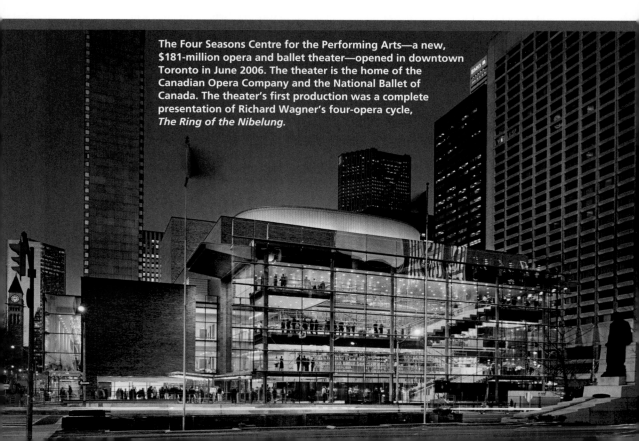

The Four Seasons Centre for the Performing Arts—a new, $181-million opera and ballet theater—opened in downtown Toronto in June 2006. The theater is the home of the Canadian Opera Company and the National Ballet of Canada. The theater's first production was a complete presentation of Richard Wagner's four-opera cycle, *The Ring of the Nibelung.*

T.M.X. Elmo—the 10th anniversary edition of Tickle Me Elmo by Mattel. Inc.— proved to be one of the hottest toys of 2006. Elmo responded to tickling by slapping his knee, kicking his feet, and rolling on his belly.

Tickled to be 10. Video games were not the only new-generation toy products unveiled in 2006. Celebrating the 10th anniversary of its debut in the toy industry, Tickle Me Elmo reemerged in 2006 as T.M.X. Elmo. Manufactured by the Fisher-Price division of Mattel, Inc. of El Segundo, California, T.M.X. Elmo responded to tickling by slapping his knee and sitting on the floor laughing hysterically. He then rocked himself back up, asking for more, and further responded by falling to the ground, kicking his feet, and scooting across the floor on his back. In his third, and most "extreme" response, the plush toy rolled on his belly and slapped the floor.

An immediate sellout at stores soon after its introduction in September, T.M.X. Elmo quickly appeared on the auction Web site eBay, where in addition to online bids for the toy, postings offered leads to the names of retail stores that were expecting shipments of the product. One Web site even offered to scour the Internet for the availability of the toy and e-mail the results to consumers.

Web pets. Combining youngsters' interest in the Internet and love of collecting stuffed toys, Webkinz online "adoptions" on the product's Web site surpassed 1.5 million by November, according to Canadian manufacturer Ganz Incorporated of Woodbridge, Ontario. Each Webkinz or Lil' Kinz plush animal came with a unique access code that allowed its owner to officially "adopt" the toy on the Webkinz Web site. There, a digital version of the toy was created and "lived" on the site. The child could customize this virtual playground and share adventures with the online digital pet.

Penguin polka. The 2006 plush parade in toyland also featured one fleet-footed penguin. Tap Dancing Mumble, a character from the animated box-office hit movie *Happy Feet* (2006), two-stepped his way into success as a dancing, electronic stuffed toy from Thinkway Toys of Markham, Ontario. Mumble flapped his wings, danced to the beat of any music played, and responded to voices with sayings of his own.

■ Diane P. Cardinale

See also **Electronics**.

Track and field. The illegal use of performance-enhancing drugs dominated track and field in 2006. A notable false-positive drug test for a record-setting Olympic medalist from the United States also made headlines.

Gatlin's troubles. Justin Gatlin of the United States, the defending Olympic champion for and co-holder of the 100-meter record, was banned from the sport for eight years after testing positive for synthetic testosterone and other steroids at the Kansas Relays in Lawrence in April 2006. Gatlin also tested positive for a banned stimulant in 2001 and received a one-year suspension.

Gatlin did not challenge the accuracy of the April 2006 test but appealed the length of his suspension. He also fought the decision by the International Association of Athletics Federations (IAAF), which governs track and field, to strip him of his 100-meter record.

In August, the U.S. Anti-Doping Agency, an independent agency that is responsible for managing the testing for U.S. Olympic, Pan American, and Paralympic athletes, offered to reduce Gatlin's suspension if he cooperated with its inquiry into American track coach Trevor Graham. Gatlin was one of several athletes coached by Graham who had received drug suspensions. In November, Graham was indicted for lying to federal agents, allegedly for denying that he had provided athletes with performance-enhancing drugs.

Gatlin's run tying the 100-meter record also stirred controversy though, in this case, Gatlin was not at fault. At the Qatar Grand Prix in Doha on May 12, Gatlin seemed to break Jamaican Asafa Powell's 2005 record of 9.77 seconds by 0.01 second. However, five days later, the IAAF announced that Gatlin's time had been recorded incorrectly. He was clocked at 9.766, which should have been rounded to 9.77 seconds. Powell matched his 2005 record in the 100-meter event twice in 2006—on June 11 in Gateshead in the United Kingdom and on August 8 in Zurich, Switzerland.

Other drug suspensions. American sprinter John Capel was suspended for two years for testing positive for marijuana at an English meet in February, his second positive test for the substance. LaTasha Jenkins, the 2001 world indoor silver medalist and U.S. indoor champion in the 200-meter sprint, tested positive for the steroid nandrolone in July 2006. She faced a minimum two-year ban from competition.

Jones cleared. Marion Jones of the United States, a five-time Olympic medalist, initially tested positive for the blood-doping drug erythropoietin (EPO) on June 23 after winning the 100-meter dash—her 14th national title—at the U.S. Outdoor Track and Field Championships in Indianapolis. However, Jones was cleared by a negative test on her second, or "B," sample.

European championships. Portugal's Francis Obikwelu swept the 100- and 200-meter sprints at the 2006 European Championships in Göteborg, Sweden, in August. He was the first man to pull off the double victory since 1978.

Hitting the jackpot. Powell and U.S. runners Jeremy Wariner (400 meters) and Sanya Richards (400 meters) swept their events in the six IAAF Golden League races, which ended on Sept. 3, 2006, in Berlin. They each received nearly $250,000 in bonus money. In addition, the $1-million Golden League Jackpot was split into two purses. Half went to six-meet winners Powell, Wariner, and Richards. The other half was split between the six-time winners and three athletes who won their events at five meets.

World records. Ethiopian Meseret Defar broke the women's 5,000-meter record on June 3 in New York City with a time of 14 minutes, 24.53 seconds. China's Liu Xiang's 12:88 seconds in the 110-meter hurdles on July 11 in Lausanne, Switzerland, broke a record he co-held with Colin Jackson of the United Kingdom by .03 seconds.

Russian pole vaulter Yelena Isinbayeva broke her own indoor record with a leap of 16 feet, 1 ¼ inch (4.91 meters). She set the record on February 12 in Donetsk, Ukraine. ■ Michael Kates
See also **Sports.**

Transit. See Transportation.

WORLD TRACK AND FIELD RECORDS ESTABLISHED IN 2006

Event	Holder	Country	Where set	Date	Record
WOMEN INDOOR					
1,500 meters	Yelena Soboleva	Russia	Moscow	February 18	3:58.28
High jump	Kajsa Bergqvist	Sweden	Arnstadt, Germany	February 4	2.08m
Pole vault	Yelena Isinbayeva	Russia	Donetsk, Ukraine	February 12	4.91m
4X400 meters relay	Russia	Russia	Glasgow, Scotland	January 28	3:23.37
MEN OUTDOOR					
20 kilometers	Haile Gebrselassie	Ethiopia	Phoenix	January 15	55:48
Half marathon	Haile Gebrselassie	Ethiopia	Phoenix	January 15	58:55
110 meters hurdles	Liu Xiang	China	Lausanne, Switzerland	July 11	12.88
4X800 meters relay	Kenya	Kenya	Brussels, Belgium	August 25	*7:02.43
WOMEN OUTDOOR					
5,000 meters	Meseret Defar	Ethiopia	New York City	June 3	14:24.53
15 kilometers	Kayoko Fukushi	Japan	Marugame, Japan	February 5	46:55
20 kilometers	Lornah Kiplagat	Netherlands	Debrecen, Hungary	October 8	1:03.21
25 kilometers	Constantina Tomescu	Romania	Chicago	October 22	*1:21.31
30 kilometers	Constantina Tomescu	Romania	Chicago	October 22	*1:38.30
Hammer throw	Tatyana Lysenko	Russia	Tallinn, Estonia	August 15	77.80m

m = meters
* = not yet ratified.   Source: International Association of Athletics Federations (IAAF).

Transportation. A political controversy erupted in February 2006 when it became widely known that Dubayy Ports (DP) World, a company based in the United Arab Emirates, had agreed to purchase London-based Peninsular and Oriental Steam Navigation Company (P&O). A small part of P&O's global business involved the management and operation of a number of terminals at six busy ports in the United States.

Although the sale had been common knowledge among transportation professionals for months, the news took the U.S. Congress by surprise. Members of both the Republican and Democratic parties argued that Arabic control of U.S. port operations would increase the chances of terrorists smuggling bombs into the United States in shipping containers. The administration of U.S. President George W. Bush sought in vain to lessen these concerns by pointing out that port security would remain under the control of the U.S. Department of Homeland Security.

Faced with the prospect of the Congress passing resolutions blocking the sale, DP World agreed in March to transfer its newly acquired U.S. operations to a U.S.-based firm. In December, DP World sold the U.S. operations to American International Group Inc., of New York City.

Record oil prices. Political uncertainties in the Middle East and elsewhere—coupled with operational problems at drilling sites and refineries—drove the price of oil to nearly $80 a barrel in August. The resulting increases in the prices of gasoline and diesel fuel increased costs for trucking, shipping, and bus firms, which passed their costs on to their customers. The average retail price of gasoline in the United States rose to more than $3 a gallon during the summer. By October, oil prices had fallen to below $60 a barrel, with associated falls in gasoline prices.

Train bombings in India. On July 11, seven bombs exploded on crowded commuter trains in Mumbai (formerly known as Bombay), the financial center of India. The blasts killed more than 200 people and injured more than 700 others. Arrests following the attacks pointed to the involvement of Lashkar-e-Taiba, a radical Islamic group based in Pakistan. The Mumbai attacks followed fatal bombings by Islamic radicals on commuter trains in Madrid, Spain, in March 2004, and in London, in July 2005.

Indiana toll road. In April 2006, government officials in Indiana signed a deal to lease the state's 157-mile (253-kilometer) toll road to a joint venture of Cintra SA of Spain and Macquarie Infrastructure Group of Australia. The foreign partnership paid the state $3.8 billion at the start of the lease in June, agreeing to operate and maintain the road—and retain all tolls paid—for the next 75 years.

Leases of public infrastructure became increasingly common in many nations in the 2000's, bringing cash infusions to local governments. However, critics argued that governments making such deals sacrificed future steady streams of toll revenues for one-time cash boosts.

Accidents. During an overnight voyage from Saudi Arabia to Egypt on Feb. 3, 2006, the Egyptian ferry *Al Salam* sank in the Red Sea after catching fire. Authorities believed that approximately 1,000 people died in the accident.

The Canadian ferry *Queen of the North* sank off the northern coast of British Columbia on March 22, after striking a rock. Two of the 101 passengers and crew aboard were missing and presumed dead.

On April 18, 69 passengers became stranded hundreds of feet above the East River in New York City when electric power was lost to the aerial tramway that links Manhattan to Roosevelt Island. The tramway consists of cable cars similar to those used on ski lifts. Workers spent almost 12 hours rescuing the passengers.

Norman Y. Mineta, the longest-serving U.S. secretary of transportation, stepped down in July. Mineta had been the only Democrat in President Bush's Cabinet since Bush took office in January 2001. Mineta had previously served as secretary of commerce under President Bill Clinton.

50th anniversaries. The transportation industry in 2006 marked the 50th anniversary of two events that radically changed transportation in the United States. On June 29, 1956, President Dwight D. Eisenhower signed into law the Federal-Aid Highway Act, which provided federal money to construct a system of interstate highways. The 47,000-mile (76,000-kilometer) system of multilane highways—combined with developments in aviation—led to the elimination of most rail passenger service in the United States and profoundly affected U.S. cities and towns.

Earlier in 1956, North Carolina entrepreneur Malcom McLean inaugurated freight service using shipping containers. On April 26 of that year, a converted tanker departed Newark, New Jersey, for Houston, loaded with 58 containers filled with manufactured products. McLean's seemingly simple idea was a vast improvement over previous practices, in which goods were loaded onto ships piece by piece in time-consuming operations. The widespread adoption of shipping containers contributed to the development of global trade.

■ Ian Savage

See also **Cabinet, U.S.; Disasters; Energy supply: A Special Report; Middle East; New York City; Terrorism.**

Trinidad and Tobago. See Latin America; West Indies.

Tunisia. See Africa.

Turkey. Prime Minister Recep Tayyip Erdogan met with United States President George W. Bush at the White House in Washington, D.C., in October 2006. The two leaders discussed a number of issues, including Turkey's bid to join the European Union, which the United States supported; and the global war on terrorism, which the prime minister and president pledged to combat jointly.

Terrorism. Legislation containing sweeping provisions to fight terrorism was submitted to the Grand National Assembly (Turkey's parliament) in April. Amnesty International, a human rights organization based in London, condemned the legislation for its potential to violate international human rights laws.

August was an especially violent month for terrorist attacks in Turkey. A bomb on August 12 exploded outside an Internet cafe in Istanbul, and another bomb exploded on August 15 near Istanbul's Blue Mosque. A small number of injuries were reported from the blasts. On August 27, four bombs—in the resort city of Marmaris and the Bagcilar area of Istanbul—wounded 28 people, including 10 British. On August 28, a bomb in a shopping area in Antalya killed three people and injured dozens of others.

The Kurdistan Freedom Falcons claimed responsibility for several bombings. Terrorism experts believed that this group was an affiliate of the Kurdistan Workers Party, a group fighting for a separate homeland in southeastern Turkey.

Hijacking. In October, a Turkish man hijacked a plane to Italy. Authorities arrested him after the plane landed. The hijacker, who claimed he was a Christian convert in need of political *asylum* (shelter and protection), said he wanted to deliver a message to Pope Benedict XVI.

Freedom of speech. Journalist Perihan Magden was acquitted in July on charges that she had attempted to turn the Turkish people against military service, which is compulsory in Turkey. In a magazine column, Magden had defended the right of a young man to refuse to perform his military service.

Writer Elif Shafak was acquitted in September on charges of "insulting Turkishness." The charges stemmed from her novel *The Bastard of Istanbul,* in which one of the fictional characters discussed the 1915 Armenian *genocide* (systematic extermination of a cultural or racial group).

In October 2006, Turkish novelist Orhan Pamuk won the Nobel Prize in literature. Pamuk had previously faced prosecution in Turkey for his writings on the Armenian genocide.

■ Mary-Jane Deeb

See also **Europe; Nobel Prizes; Terrorism.**

Turkmenistan. See Asia.

Tuvalu. See Pacific Islands.

Uganda. In February 2006, Uganda held its first multiparty elections since 1980. In the presidential polling, Ugandans reelected President Yoweri Museveni of the National Resistance Movement (NRM) over his nearest rival, Kizza Besigye of the Forum for Democratic Change (FDC), for a third presidential term. Museveni received 59 percent of the vote, and Besigye, 37 percent. Besigye contested the outcome, but Uganda's Supreme Court on April 6, 2006, rejected his challenge. Museveni's NRM also won a parliamentary majority in the February elections, with the FDC emerging as the strongest opposition party in Parliament.

Between 1986, when Museveni seized power in a military *coup* (government overthrow), and 2005, Uganda had functioned politically as a one-party state. Although political parties were allowed to organize, they could not run candidates in elections. Technically, candidates for Parliament were elected as nonpartisan, but in actuality, the NRM controlled Parliament and all the country's high offices. In 2005, however, President Museveni yielded to demands for greater democracy, permitting voters to choose between a continuation of the one-party status quo or the implementation of a multiparty electoral system. In a July 28, 2005, referendum, Ugandans voted overwhelmingly for the multiparty system.

Peace talks. In July 2006, representatives of the Ugandan government and the Lord's Resistance Army (LRA), a rebel group based in northern Uganda, met in Juba, Sudan, for peace talks sponsored by the Sudanese government. The talks produced a temporary truce in late August and an extension of the truce on November 1.

The Juba peace talks raised hopes of ending 20 years of guerrilla warfare in Uganda. Since the mid-1980's, the LRA, a quasi-religious cult led by self-styled "prophet" Joseph Kony, had operated in northern Uganda, battling government troops and terrorizing the local population. International human rights groups had documented a number of LRA atrocities, including a 2004 massacre of more than 200 people at a refugee camp and the enslavement of thousands of children for use as soldiers, servants, or sex slaves.

A demand for amnesty by Kony and his associates became the chief impediment to reaching a comprehensive peace settlement. President Museveni agreed in 2006 to a blanket amnesty. However, United Nations officials insisted that arrest warrants issued by the International Criminal Court in The Hague, Netherlands, for LRA leaders on charges of war crimes must not be invalidated. The Juba negotiators continued to grapple with this dilemma late in 2006.

■ Pieter Esterhuysen

See also **Africa.**

Ukraine. Disputes over Ukraine's relationships with Russia and the West caused political turmoil throughout 2006.

Crisis. Trouble first arose in early January, after President Viktor Yushchenko concluded a controversial natural gas deal with Russia. The Russian government had demanded that Ukraine pay higher tariffs for Russian gas and briefly cut off supplies to pressure the nation to comply. Yushchenko defended the resulting agreement as the best possible under the circumstances. However, opposition parliamentarian and former Yushchenko Prime Minister Yulia Tymoshenko blasted the deal as too expensive. On January 10, the Verkhovna Rada (parliament) voted to dismiss Prime Minister Yuri Yekhanurov's Cabinet.

The crisis deepened after parliamentary elections on March 26 failed to produce a stable coalition government. The pro-Russian Party of Regions, led by former Prime Minister Viktor Yanukovich, won 32 percent of the vote and 186 seats in the 450-seat Verkhovna Rada. The Yulia Tymoshenko Bloc came in second with 22 percent and 129 seats, followed by Yushchenko's Our Ukraine (14 percent and 81 seats), the Socialist Party (6 percent and 33 seats), and the Communist Party (4 percent and 21 seats). The Organisation for Security and Co-operation in Europe judged the election free and fair.

After the elections, the Yulia Tymoshenko Bloc, Our Ukraine, and the Socialist Party attempted to form a coalition government. Tymoshenko announced a coalition agreement on June 22, but it quickly collapsed. The Socialist Party broke away from its Orange Revolution partners to form a new "anti-crisis" coalition with the Party of Regions and the Communist Party on July 7, and the Verkhovna Rada elected Socialist Party leader Oleksandr Moroz as its speaker. The election threw the Verkhovna Rada into chaos.

On August 3, Yushchenko, Our Ukraine, the Party of Regions, the Socialist Party, and the Communist Party signed a declaration of national unity pledging their commitment to move Ukraine toward NATO and World Trade Organization membership, as well as toward a closer economic relationship with Europe. Yushchenko then nominated Yanukovich as prime minister, a move approved by the Verkhovna Rada on August 4. The Yulia Tymoshenko Bloc remained in opposition.

Yushchenko and Yanukovich clashed almost immediately, especially after Yanukovich declared in September that Ukraine would slow any move toward NATO membership. In October, Our Ukraine went into opposition and forced its ministers in the Yanukovich Cabinet to tender their resignations. ■ Juliet Johnson

See also **Disasters; Europe; Moldova.**

Unemployment. See Economics, United States; Economics, World; Labor and employment.

United Arab Emirates. See Middle East.

Left without heat by a Russian shut-off of gas supplies, a Ukrainian woman carries firewood to her stove in Kiev, Ukraine's capital, in January 2006. Russia halted gas supplies for several days to persuade Ukraine to sign a deal accepting higher gas prices.

UNITED KINGDOM

Prime Minister Tony Blair's Labour Party government retained power in the United Kingdom (U.K.) throughout 2006 after winning election to an unprecedented third term in 2005. However, David Cameron's Conservatives emerged as a strong opposition party that increasingly led in opinion polls. Bowing to considerable pressure, Blair announced in 2006 that he would leave office in 2007.

The Labour government, which had been in office since 1997, lost popularity among voters over criticism that it had become divided and corrupt. Although many British citizens were concerned about terrorism and national security, support for the deployment of British troops in Iraq and Afghanistan as part of the United States-led war on terror remained low. The economy enjoyed strong growth and low inflation in 2006. Labour's Chancellor of the Exchequer (treasurer) Gordon Brown— regarded as the most likely person to succeed Blair — was credited with the stability of the economy.

Liberal Democrats. On January 7, Charles Kennedy, the leader of the centrist Liberal Democratic party, resigned after admitting that he had a problem with alcohol, a charge he had long denied. Further scandal overtook the party later in the month when a leading candidate to replace Kennedy, Mark Oaten (the party's home affairs spokesman and a married man), abandoned his bid for the post after a newspaper revealed his association with male prostitutes. In March, party members elected Deputy Leader and Foreign Affairs Spokesman Sir Menzies Campbell as party leader.

Labour Party. Several senior members of the government experienced personal or political difficulties in 2006. Culture, Media, and Sport Secretary Tessa Jowell was embarrassed by allegations that her husband, lawyer David Mills, had received, under suspicious circumstances, money linked to Italian Prime Minister Silvio Berlusconi. On March 5, Jowell announced that she and her husband were separating. She retained her seat in the Cabinet.

On April 26, the government was rocked by what the press called a "triple whammy." Home Secretary Charles Clarke was embarrassed by revelations that government procedures for deporting foreign nationals who had been imprisoned were not being followed. The government had failed to deport nearly 300 foreign nationals following their release, even after the problem had been revealed in 2005. Clarke faced calls for his resignation. Also on April 26, 2006, the press revealed that Deputy Prime Minister John Prescott had been having an affair with a secretary in his office. On the same day, Health Secretary Patricia Hewitt was heckled at a conference of the Royal College of Nursing in Bournemouth after claiming that the National Health Service was enjoying its "best year ever." Delegates complained about cuts in service and difficult working conditions.

The Conservative Party, led by Cameron, enjoyed a considerable recovery in 2006. Cameron, who was 39 when he became leader in December 2005 following the party's defeat in the general election, immediately targeted his appeal to voters, such as centrists and young people, who had deserted the Conservatives in the late 1990's. He modernized his appeal by asking musician and poverty activist Bob Geldof to advise the party on Third World debt and by obtaining the support of leading environmentalist Zac Goldsmith on green issues. Cameron further insisted that teen-agers (particularly young people wearing hooded tops, who are often feared) should be understood rather than demonized. George Osborne, Cameron's *shadow chancellor* (opposition party member who monitors treasury issues), rejected calls from the party's right wing for tax cuts by a future Conservative government. Instead, Osborne insisted that public services and the health of the economy would be a priority. By the end of 2006, the Conservatives were regularly leading in opinion polls.

British National Party (B.N.P.). Nick Griffin, the leader of the far-right B.N.P., and fellow party member Mark Collett were acquitted twice in 2006 —in February and again in November—of stirring up racial hatred. A party meeting during which Griffin referred to Islam as a "vicious, wicked faith" and Collett called asylum seekers "cockroaches" was secretly filmed by a television journalist. Griffin and Collett argued successfully that the remarks had been made at a private event for like-minded party members.

Elections. Labour fared badly in local elections in May and in by-elections. The poor results increased pressure on Blair to leave office. In February, Labour lost its "safe" seat of Dunfermline and West Fife in Scotland to the Liberal Democrats. The loss was particularly embarrassing for Chancellor of the Exchequer Brown, who held the seat for the neighboring constituency.

In June, Labour failed to regain what had once been the safe Labour seat of Blaenau Gwent in Wales. Labour lost the seat in the 2005 general election to former Labour member Peter Law. Law ran as an independent because he objected to the imposition of an all-female short list of Labour candidates for the constituency. Following Law's death in April 2006, another independent and former

Labour Party member, Dai Davis, won the seat. Patricia Law, Peter Law's widow, was elected to the Welsh Assembly seat for the area as an independent. Political observers considered the results a sign of disaffection among the government's supporters, in particular with Blair's "New Labour" approach, a strategy that involved moving what had previously been a strongly left-wing party to the center.

Also in April, the Conservatives beat back a Liberal Democrat challenge for the safe seat of Bromley and Chislehurst. Labour ranked fourth in the voting. The by-election was called because of the death of Member of Parliament (MP) Eric Forth in May.

In the May 4 local elections, the Conservatives came out on top with 40 percent of the vote, gaining 11 new councils. Labour was pushed into third place with 26 percent, just behind the Liberal Democrats, who received 27 percent. Shortly before the election, Minister of State for Work Margaret Hodge was criticized for reporting publicly that large numbers of her white, working-class constituents in Barking, East London, were considering voting for the B.N.P. to protest the number of people of color moving into the area. According to the B.N.P., such people were putting pressure on local social services. The B.N.P.

Queen Elizabeth II accepts cards from children (top) gathered in Windsor in honor of her 80th birthday on April 21, 2006. Postage stamps featuring the queen at various stages of her life (above) were released on April 18. Elizabeth, the longest-reigning monarch in Europe, ascended the throne in 1952.

An installation of masks celebrates the reopening of the Kelvingrove Art Gallery and Museum in Glasgow, Scotland, on July 11, 2006. A three-year renovation increased the museum's exhibition space and restored the structure's Victorian interior.

gained 11 seats on the Barking and Dagenham Council in the local election, and Hodge was blamed for giving the B.N.P. publicity.

Cabinet reshuffle. The day after Labour's poor showing in the May local elections, Blair reshuffled his Cabinet. Home Secretary Clarke was replaced by former Defence Secretary John Reid. Prescott remained deputy prime minister, but many of his responsibilities for local government were transferred to former Education Secretary Ruth Kelly, who became secretary of state for communities and local government. Prescott was criticized for retaining a full Cabinet salary and the use of Dorneywood, a publicly owned country house. Prescott gave up the use of Dorneywood in late May. Foreign Secretary Jack Straw was replaced by Margaret Beckett, who became the first woman to run the Foreign Office, a major government post. Straw became leader of the House of Commons. New appointments to the Cabinet included Hazel Blears, who became chair of the Labour Party and minister without portfolio; Stephen Timms, who became chief secretary to the treasury; and Douglas Alexander, who combined the roles of Scottish secretary and secretary for transport.

Loans for peerages scandal. In March, Scotland Yard began investigating claims that both the Labour and the Conservative parties had accepted loans from wealthy donors to finance the 2005 election campaign in exchange for the promise of a seat in the House of Lords. (Under current law, loans to political parties do not have to be publicly declared if they are made at commercial rates of interest.) The Lords Appointments Commission rejected four Labour appointments after learning of the loans. In July, senior Labour fund-raiser Lord Levy was briefly arrested and questioned about his involvement in securing improper loans. In October and November, Scotland Yard interviewed former Conservative Party leader Michael Howard and wrote formal requests for information to a number of Cabinet members. Blair was questioned in December. All denied any wrongdoing.

The Liberal Democrats were also scrutinized for allegedly taking money from a foreign donor (a violation of the law). Some critics argued that the loan issue demonstrated the need for state funding of political parties to eliminate possible corruption. In March, Blair called for greater transparency in party funding and appointed civil servant Sir Hayden Phillips to review the issue.

Leadership succession. Pressure on Blair to resign as prime minister increased during the summer of 2006. His obvious successor was Chancellor of the Exchequer Brown, who was known to be anxious to take over. However, in July, John McDonnell, an MP in the left wing of the Labour Party, announced that he would challenge Brown for the leadership.

Relations between Blair and Brown supporters within the party and in the government worsened throughout the year. On September 6, Tom Watson, a defense minister and a Brown supporter, quit the government after signing a letter calling on Blair to resign for the good of the party and the country. The letter was leaked to the press. Another six junior members of the government also quit, leading Blair's allies to suggest that the resignations were signs of a *coup* (overthrow of the government)—possibly orchestrated by Brown. Blair refused to resign but confirmed publicly that he would depart within a year, though he refused to set an exact date.

At the Labour Party conference later in September, Brown apologized to the prime minister for the difficulties between them. Brown was widely expected to win any leadership contest, and so attention then focused on who would replace Prescott in the posts of deputy party leader and deputy prime minister. Cabinet members Alan Johnson, Peter Hain, and Hilary Benn as well as junior minister Harriet Harman announced they would run for the positions.

National security. Following the July 7, 2005, bombing of a bus and several trains in London, the government introduced a new antiterrorism bill. One of the bill's provisions would have allowed the police to hold suspected terrorists for up to 90 days without charge. However, opposition to the provision in both houses of Parliament forced Home Secretary Clarke in January 2006 to reduce the imprisonment provision to 28 days. The bill, which also included a controversial clause making the glorification of terrorism a criminal offense, became law on March 22.

In February, the controversial Muslim cleric Abu Hamza was convicted of encouraging the murder of non-Muslims and inciting racial hatred. In March, the trial of seven British Muslims who were arrested in 2004 and accused of planning terrorist attacks in the U.K. began. In May 2006, reports by the Home Office and Parliament's Intelligence and Security Committee about the July 2005 bombings concluded that the security service MI5 could not have prevented the attacks, though two of the bombers were known to MI5. The report found that the al-Qa'ida terrorist group was not involved. However, the revelation that two bombers had visited Pakistan and that one had said he wanted to visit an al-Qa'ida training camp led to criticisms of the report and demands for an independent inquiry.

On August 10, air services were disrupted when police announced that they had uncovered a plot to blow up planes flying from the U.K. to the United States. Twenty-four people in the U.K. were arrested that day in connection with the alleged plot and other terrorist activities.

On November 7, al-Qa'ida operative Dhiren Barot was sentenced to life in prison (with a minimum of 40 years served) for planning terrorist attacks. Barot was arrested in 2004. Evidence showed that he had been involved in devising plans for terrorist attacks in both the U.K. and the United States but had been arrested before any of the plots had been implemented. Barot pleaded guilty.

British Islam. Debate continued during 2006 about the relationship of British Muslims to the wider British community. In February, Muslims in London demonstrated over the publication of cartoons in Denmark that they believed mocked the Prophet Muhammad, even though newspapers in the U.K. refused to publish the cartoons.

In October, House of Commons Leader Straw created controversy when he revealed in a newspaper article that he routinely asked Muslim women in his constituency who wear the *niqab* (a full-face veil) to remove it when they come to his office to speak with him. He noted that the use of the niqab was not required by the Qu'ran, Islam's holy book, and argued that it was useful to see a person's face during conversation. The article created heated debate about the use of the full veil and about the integration of Muslims into British society. Members of the Muslim community held varying views about the niqab. Straw was later forced to defend himself from suggestions that he was insensitive and that his remarks had caused an increase in attacks on Muslims.

Death of a Russian agent. On November 23, Alexander Litvinenko, a former member of the Russian secret service, died after apparently being poisoned with the radioactive element polonium-210. Litvinenko had moved to the U.K. after allegedly refusing to assist the Russian intelligence agency assassinate wealthy Russian businessman Boris Berezovsky. Before he died, Litvinenko blamed the Russian government for his murder. However, Russian President Vladimir Putin denied any involvement in the agent's death. By November 30, investigators had found traces of polonium-210 at a dozen sites in the U.K. Several people were later found to have been exposed to the element.

Ken Livingstone. The Standards Board of England, a body that regulates the conduct of officials in local government, determined in February that the mayor of London, Ken Livingstone, should be suspended from office for four weeks. The decision followed a complaint that Livingstone had been offensive to journalist Oliver Finegold of London's *Evening Standard*. Finegold had asked him a question as the mayor left a party in February 2005. Livingstone compared the journalist, who is Jewish, with a concentration camp attendant and a German war criminal and refused to apologize because of his longstanding hostile relationship with the newspaper. The mayor appealed the verdict. In October 2006, a high court judge overturned the suspension, ruling that Livingstone's comments did not breach the Greater London Authority code of conduct.

Pensions. In May, John Hutton, the work and pensions secretary, reported a radical revision to the British pension system. Hutton announced that the link between state pensions and average earnings would be restored in 2012 (as long as the government could afford to do so) and that the age of retirement would rise from 65 to 66 by 2026 and to 68 by 2046. The government would continue to provide assistance to people who lost their pension when an employer went out of business. The proposals were detailed in a *white paper* (government policy document) on pension reform based on recommendations in a report by Lord Adair Turner. Turner's report had called for more generous state pensions to prevent poverty among the elderly.

Smoking ban. MP's voted overwhelmingly in February 2006 to ban smoking from all English workplaces, including private clubs and pubs, beginning in 2007. A smoking ban was already set to go into effect in Scotland and Northern Ireland over the next 13 months. ■ Rohan McWilliam

See also **Europe; Iraq; Northern Ireland; Russia; Terrorism; United Kingdom, Prime Minister of.**

United Kingdom, Prime Minister of.

Tony Blair had a difficult year in 2006, despite having won a third election for the Labour Party in 2005. In January 2006, retired General Sir Michael Rose, former commander of United Nations (UN) forces in Bosnia, declared that Blair should be impeached because the grounds for deploying British troops in Iraq—Iraq's possession of weapons of mass destruction—had been proven false. That same month, British lawyer Philippe Sands claimed in his book *Lawless World* to have uncovered a memorandum proving that Blair had agreed to support the United States even if the UN withheld approval for the Iraqi invasion and UN weapons inspectors failed to uncover evidence that Iraq possessed weapons of mass destruction. The claim contradicted statements Blair made at the time.

In 2005, Blair promised that, if elected, he would not run for a fourth term. He came under increasing pressure in 2006 to announce when he would leave office. Blair's relationship with Chancellor of the Exchequer (treasurer) Gordon Brown became increasingly difficult. It was widely believed that Blair and Brown had agreed in 1994 that Brown would not run for the post of prime minister but that Blair would, in time, step aside and allow Brown to take over. In September 2006, Blair announced that he would step down within a year. ■ Rohan McWilliam

See also **United Kingdom.**

United Nations. A dispute over the development of nuclear capability by North Korea and Iran occupied the United Nations (UN) Security Council in 2006. On July 15, the Council voted unanimously to demand that North Korea suspend its ballistic missile program, abandon nuclear development, and return to negotiations over its attempts to build nuclear weapons. The Council asked that governments take measures to prevent North Korea from acquiring ballistic missile-related technology. On October 9, North Korea conducted a nuclear test, triggering condemnation by the governments of many nations. The Council reacted by adopting sanctions against North Korea on October 14. The Council ordered a ban on direct or indirect supply, sale, or transfer of weapons, military equipment, warships, aircraft, and missiles to North Korea. Any traffic of materials related to weapons of mass destruction to that country was also banned. The North Korean government rejected the sanctions.

Similarly, the Security Council ordered Iran to stop its uranium enrichment activities—a first step in the development of nuclear technology—by August 31. However, the International Atomic Energy Agency in Vienna reported that Iran had defied the deadline and increased its work on uranium conversion. On December 23, the Council unanimously voted to impose sanctions on Iraq.

Middle East. Israel launched airstrikes against targets in Lebanon in July, after two of its soldiers were abducted by Shiite Hezbollah militants operating out of Lebanon. Hezbollah fired rockets into Israel in return. The fighting spread through Lebanon, causing extensive destruction and the deaths of hundreds of civilians. On August 11, the Security Council voted unanimously to call for a "full cessation of hostilities" in Lebanon, and the two sides agreed to stop the fighting on August 14. The UN Interim Force in Lebanon was assigned to monitor the cease-fire, and the group's military strength was increased to 15,000 troops. The Lebanese government also deployed 15,000 soldiers to southern Lebanon to establish its authority over its territory. At the same time, Israeli forces began to withdraw from Lebanon.

Africa. For several years, the Security Council had tried unsuccessfully to end the ethnic conflict between government-backed Arab militias and African rebel factions in the Darfur region of western Sudan. Fighting began in 2003 and, by 2006, more than 200,000 people had died and more than 2 million others had been displaced. On August 31, the Council voted to send as many as 20,000 peacekeepers to Darfur to replace the 7,000 African Union (AU) troops who had failed to restore peace. But the Sudanese government rejected the UN troops, saying it preferred that AU forces monitor the May 5 peace accords signed by the government and the largest African rebel group, the Sudan Liberation Army. As soon as the accords were signed, fighting escalated as government forces attacked rebel factions that had not signed the peace agreement.

Human rights. On March 15, the UN General Assembly created the Human Rights Council to replace the UN Commission on Human Rights. The commission had been discredited for allowing such rights-abusive nations as Sudan and Zimbabwe to become members and for failing to act against several cases of human rights abuse. Israel, the Marshall Islands, Palau, and the United States opposed the new council, on the grounds that it, like the former commission, lacked any real power to prevent human rights abuses. On May 9, the Assembly elected 47 members to the new council. The group began its work in June in Geneva, Switzerland.

General Assembly. Bahrain's Haya Rashid al-Khalifa was elected president of the General Assembly in July 2006. She opened the body's 61st session on September 12. Al-Khalifa urged the 192-member group to try to achieve the reforms begun by her predecessor, Jan Eliasson of Sweden.

On September 19, UN Secretary-General Kofi Annan delivered his last address to the Assembly, as he prepared to step down on December 31 after 10 years at the helm of the organization. Annan said three major problems plagued the world when he began his term—an unjust world economy, world disorder, and widespread contempt for human rights and the rule of law. Those problems remained 10 years later, but Annan continued to believe that "the only answer to this divided world must be a truly United Nations."

New secretary-general. On October 13, the General Assembly appointed South Korean Foreign Minister Ban Ki-moon as the successor to Annan for a five-year term beginning on Jan. 1, 2007. Ban pledged, "The true measure of success for the UN is not how much we promise, but how much we deliver for those who need us most."

UN Security Council. On Oct. 16, 2006, the General Assembly elected four new members to the Security Council—Belgium, Indonesia, Italy, and South Africa. Those nations were to begin a two-year term in January 2007, joining five nonpermanent members elected in 2005—Congo (Brazzaville), Ghana, Peru, Qatar, and Slovakia—and the five permanent council members, China, France, Russia, the United Kingdom, and the United States. On Nov. 7, 2006, the General Assembly elected Panama to the Latin American seat on the Council. Neither of the two original candidates for the seat—Guatemala and Venezuela—was able to reach the necessary number of votes to win the position. ■ J. Tuyet Nguyen

See also **Korea, North; Middle East; Sudan.**

United States, Government of the.

The United States-led war in Iraq continued to dominate headlines in 2006, and the government's handling of the conflict drew international attention and criticism. Public frustration over the war played a major role in the November 2006 elections, in which the Republican Party lost control of both houses of Congress to the Democrats. The election was a major setback for President George W. Bush, a Republican, who was set to face stronger political opposition in Congress in the remaining years of his presidency.

War in Iraq. In September 2006, the Senate Intelligence Committee released a report stating that the Central Intelligence Agency (CIA) had found no link between the Iraqi government of Saddam Hussein and al-Qa`ida, the terrorist organization held responsible for the attacks on the United States on Sept. 11, 2001. The Bush administration, prior to the 2003 invasion of Iraq, had claimed that such a link existed and used it as a justification for going to war.

Later in September 2006, President Bush released parts of a previously classified report on terrorism, called a National Intelligence Estimate. The report, prepared by U.S. intelligence agencies, stated that the Iraq War had unified Muslim jihadists and thereby increased terrorism globally. It found that counterterrorism efforts had disrupted the operations of al-Qa`ida, but that terrorist groups were "increasing in both number and geographic dispersion" as a result of anger over the U.S. invasion and occupation of Iraq.

As casualties in Iraq rose throughout 2006, U.S. Secretary of Defense Donald H. Rumsfeld faced heavy criticism over his handling of the war. Critics included a number of retired generals who viewed Rumsfeld's management of the conflict as a failure. Although President Bush supported Rumsfeld through most of 2006, he announced Rumsfeld's resignation the day after Republicans lost control of Congress in the midterm elections. Saying he wanted "a fresh perspective" on the war, President Bush nominated Robert Gates, a former head of the CIA, to succeed Rumsfeld.

In November, a special Iraqi court convicted Saddam Hussein of crimes against humanity and sentenced him to death by hanging. The U.S. government provided funding for the trial, and many people within the government applauded the ruling. President Bush called the decision "a major achievement for Iraq's young democracy and its constitutional government."

In December, a report by the Iraq Study Group—an independent commission devoted to the analysis of the Iraq War—described the situation in Iraq as "grave and deteriorating" and recommended a number of changes in diplomatic and military strategy. The report called for U.S. troops to be pulled out of Iraq by early 2008.

Treatment of prisoners. The U.S. government continued in 2006 to face criticism over the treatment of prisoners in the country's stated war against terrorism. An annual report from the London-based human rights organization Amnesty International, released in May, detailed alleged prisoner mistreatment both in Iraq and at the U.S. military facility at Guantánamo Bay in Cuba.

Following the 2001 terrorist attacks, the Bush administration held terrorism suspects at the Guantánamo Bay facility and established military commissions to prosecute them. However, in June, the Supreme Court of the United States, in a 5-3 decision, ruled that the commissions violated U.S. and international law. The commissions, the court decided, did not provide the protections for defendants required under the Uniform Code of Military Justice. The court ruled that they also violated provisions of the Geneva Conventions, which provide for the humane treatment of civilians, prisoners, and wounded people during wartime.

Following the ruling, the Bush administration acknowledged for the first time that the protections of the Geneva Conventions applied to prisoners held by the United States under suspicion of terrorism. In late September, Congress passed legislation that overhauled the U.S. system of military commissions. The legislation, signed by President Bush in October, cleared the way for the prosecution of terrorism suspects and included measures that prohibited certain forms of prisoner abuse.

President Bush announced in September that 14 terrorism suspects who had previously been held in secret CIA facilities around the world had been moved to Guantánamo Bay, where they would be tried by military commissions. Among the suspects was Khalid Sheikh Mohammed, allegedly a key planner of the 2001 terrorist attacks.

In October 2006, the prisoner abuse issue again came to the forefront after Vice President Dick Cheney expressed support for the use of a "dunk in water" during interrogations. Critics charged that the vice president's comment was an endorsement of *waterboarding,* an interrogation technique in which a suspect is made to believe that he or she is drowning. The Bush administration claimed that the vice president was not referring to waterboarding, a practice internationally condemned as torture.

Katrina aftermath. A Bush administration report in February 2006 evaluated the government's response to Hurricane Katrina, the 2005 storm that devastated the Gulf Coast and resulted in the deaths of more than 1,800 people. The report identified failures in the government's performance and stressed the need for reform. Much criticism targeted the Federal Emergency Management Agency (FEMA), the agency responsible for

SELECTED AGENCIES AND BUREAUS OF THE U.S. GOVERNMENT*

Executive Office of the President
President, George W. Bush
Vice President, Richard B. Cheney
White House Chief of Staff, Joshua B. Bolten
Presidential Press Secretary, Tony Snow
Assistant to the President for Domestic Policy,
  Karl Zinsmeister
Assistant to the President for National Security Affairs,
  Stephen J. Hadley
Director, Office of Science and Technology Policy,
  John H. Marburger III
Council of Economic Advisers—Edward P. Lazear, chairman
Office of Management and Budget—
  Robert J. Portman, Director
Office of National Drug Control Policy—
  John P. Walters, Director
U.S. Trade Representative, Susan Schwab

Department of Agriculture
Secretary of Agriculture, Michael O. Johanns

Department of Commerce
Secretary of Commerce, Carlos M. Gutierrez
  Bureau of Economic Analysis—J. Steven Landefeld, Director
  Bureau of the Census—Charles Louis Kincannon, Director

Department of Defense
Secretary of Defense, Robert M. Gates
  Secretary of the Air Force, Michael W. Wynne
  Secretary of the Army, Francis J. Harvey
  Secretary of the Navy, Donald C. Winter
  Joint Chiefs of Staff—
    General Peter Pace, Chairman
    General Teed Michael Moseley, Chief of Staff, Air Force
    General Peter J. Schoomaker, Chief of Staff, Army
    Admiral Michael G. Mullen, Chief of Naval Operations
    General Michael W. Hagee, Commandant, Marine Corps

Department of Education
Secretary of Education, Margaret Spellings

Department of Energy
Secretary of Energy, Samuel Wright Bodman

Department of Health and Human Services
Secretary of Health and Human Services,
  Michael O. Leavitt
  Office of Public Health and Science—John O. Agwunobi,
    Assistant Secretary
  Centers for Disease Control and Prevention—
    Julie Louise Gerberding, Director
  Food and Drug Administration—Andrew C. von Eschenbach,
    Acting Commissioner
  National Institutes of Health—Elias A. Zerhouni, Director
  Acting Surgeon General of the United States,
    Rear Admiral Kenneth P. Moritsugu

Department of Homeland Security
Secretary of Homeland Security, Michael Chertoff
  Bureau of Citizenship and Immigration Services—
    Emilio T. Gonzales, Director
  U.S. Coast Guard—Vice Admiral Thad W. Allen, Commandant
  U.S. Secret Service—Mark Sullivan, Director
  Federal Emergency Management Agency—R. David Paulison,
    Under Secretary

Department of Housing and Urban Development
Secretary of Housing and Urban Development,
  Alphonso R. Jackson

Department of the Interior
Secretary of the Interior, Dirk Kempthorne

Department of Justice
Attorney General, Alberto R. Gonzales
  Federal Bureau of Prisons—Harley G. Lappin, Director
  Drug Enforcement Administration—
    Karen P. Tandy, Administrator
  Federal Bureau of Investigation—
    Robert S. Mueller III, Director
  Solicitor General, Paul D. Clement

Department of Labor
Secretary of Labor, Elaine L. Chao

Department of State
Secretary of State, Condoleezza Rice
  Acting U.S. Ambassador to the United Nations,
    Alejandro D. Wolff

Department of Transportation
Secretary of Transportation, Mary E. Peters
  Federal Aviation Administration—
    Marion C. Blakey, Administrator

Department of the Treasury
Secretary of the Treasury, Henry M. Paulson, Jr.
  Internal Revenue Service—Mark W. Everson, Commissioner
  Treasurer of the United States, Anna Escobedo Cabral
  Office of Thrift Supervision—John M. Reich, Director

Department of Veterans Affairs
Secretary of Veterans Affairs, R. James Nicholson

Supreme Court of the United States
Chief Justice of the United States, John G. Roberts, Jr.
  Associate Justices—
    John Paul Stevens   Clarence Thomas
    Antonin Scalia   Ruth Bader Ginsburg
    Anthony M. Kennedy   Stephen G. Breyer
    David Hackett Souter   Samuel Anthony Alito, Jr.

Congressional officials†
  President of the Senate pro tempore, Ted Stevens
  Senate Majority Leader, William H. Frist
  Senate Minority Leader, Harry Reid
  Speaker of the House, J. Dennis Hastert
  House Majority Leader, John Boehner
  House Minority Leader, Nancy Pelosi
  Congressional Budget Office—Donald Marron, Acting Director
  Government Accountability Office—David M. Walker, Comptroller
    General of the United States
  Library of Congress—James H. Billington, Librarian of Congress

Independent agencies
Central Intelligence Agency—Michael V. Hayden, Director
Commission of Fine Arts—Earl A. Powell III, Chairperson
Commission on Civil Rights—Gerald A. Reynolds, Chairperson
Consumer Product Safety Commission—
  Nancy A. Nord, Acting Chairperson
Corporation for National and Community Service—
  Stephen Goldsmith, Chairperson
Environmental Protection Agency—Stephen L. Johnson, Administrator
Equal Employment Opportunity Commission—
  Naomi Churchill Earp, Chairperson
Federal Communications Commission—Kevin J. Martin, Chairman
Federal Deposit Insurance Corporation—
  Sheila C. Bair, Chairperson
Federal Election Commission—Michael E. Toner, Chairperson
Federal Reserve System Board of Governors—
  Ben S. Bernanke, Chairperson
Federal Trade Commission—Deborah Platt Majoras, Chairperson
General Services Administration—Lurita Alexis Doan, Administrator
National Aeronautics and Space Administration—Michael D. Griffin,
  Administrator
National Endowment for the Arts—Michael Dana Gioia, Chairperson
National Endowment for the Humanities—Bruce M. Cole, Chairperson
National Labor Relations Board—Robert J. Battista, Chairperson
National Railroad Passenger Corporation (Amtrak)—
  Alexander Kummant, President and CEO
National Science Foundation—Arden L. Bement, Jr., Director
National Transportation Safety Board—
  Mark V. Rosenker, Chairperson
Nuclear Regulatory Commission—Dale E. Klein, Chairperson
Peace Corps—Ronald A. Tschetter, Director
Securities and Exchange Commission—
  Christopher Cox, Chairperson
Selective Service System—William A. Chatfield, Director
Small Business Administration—Steven C. Preston, Administrator
Smithsonian Institution—Lawrence M. Small, Secretary
Social Security Administration—Jo Anne Barnhart, Commissioner
U.S. Postal Service—John E. Potter, Postmaster General

*As of Dec. 31, 2006.
†For the 109th Congress, which ended on Dec. 9, 2006.

helping communities prepare for and recover from disasters. In April 2006, a Senate panel recommended that FEMA be abolished and replaced with a new agency to handle emergencies.

In a June report, the U.S. Army Corps of Engineers acknowledged that the levees it had built in New Orleans were flawed and inadequate. The Corps took responsibility for the levee failures that caused most of the flooding that overwhelmed New Orleans in Katrina's aftermath.

Abramoff fallout. In January 2006, lobbyist Jack Abramoff pleaded guilty to charges of fraud, conspiracy, and tax evasion. He began serving a six-year prison sentence in November. A report by the House Committee on Government Reform—an investigative committee of the House of Representatives—found that Abramoff had purchased expensive gifts and dinners for Bush administration officials and other Republicans in an effort to gain political favors for his clients. Several public officials resigned or were charged with crimes in the wake of the scandal.

Valerie Plame leak. A special prosecutor investigating the leak of a CIA agent's identity decided in June 2006 not to bring charges against Karl Rove, a senior adviser to President Bush. The prosecutor, Patrick J. Fitzgerald, had been investigating whether Rove and other White House officials had in 2003 leaked the identify of Valerie Plame, then a CIA officer, in an effort to discredit or intimidate her husband, who was a critic of the administration. In September 2006, Richard Armitage, a former deputy secretary of state, stated that he was the primary source of the leak. He claimed he unintentionally disclosed Plame's identity to a newspaper columnist.

Privacy concerns. In May, *USA Today* reported that the National Security Agency/Central Security Service—an agency within the Department of Defense—had collected the phone records of millions of Americans as part of its campaign against terrorism. Many critics charged that the program was an invasion of privacy. President Bush claimed that the program was aimed only at people who had connections with terrorist groups.

Privacy concerns were again raised in late May after top U.S. law enforcement officials asked a number of Internet companies to keep records of the Web-surfing activities of their customers. The officials maintained that the records could be used to fight terrorism and child pornography.

Energy. As gasoline prices in parts of the

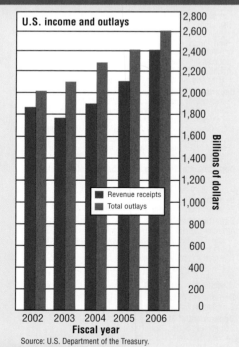

FEDERAL SPENDING　United States budget for fiscal 2006*

Billions of dollars

National defense	528.8
International affairs	29.0
General science, space, technology	20.2
Energy	0.8
Natural resources and environment	52.1
Agriculture	8.8
Commerce and housing credit	6.1
Transportation	70.8
Community and regional development	53.9
Education, training, employment, and social services	116.5
Health	252.6
Social security	548.6
Medicare	329.9
Income security	353.7
Veterans' benefits and services	69.8
Administration of justice	35.5
General government	18.9
Interest	226.6
Undistributed offsetting receipts	−68.2
Total budget outlays	**2,654.4**

*Oct. 1, 2005, to Sept. 30, 2006.
Source: U.S. Department of the Treasury.

U.S. income and outlays

■ Revenue receipts
■ Total outlays

Billions of dollars

Fiscal year
Source: U.S. Department of the Treasury.

Georgetown University students display a banner quoting Benjamin Franklin at a speech by Attorney General Alberto R. Gonzales on Jan. 24, 2006, in Washington, D.C. The students charged that security policies implemented by the U.S. government violated civil liberties.

country soared to more than $3 per gallon, President Bush in April 2006 announced a number of steps to stem the rise of energy prices. The president said the government would temporarily halt deposits to the nation's Strategic Petroleum Reserve, an emergency supply of government-owned oil. He also stressed the need for conservation, domestic energy production, and alternative fuel sources. In addition, the president said the government would investigate the possibility of price gouging in the gasoline markets.

Cheney hunting accident. During a hunting trip in southern Texas on Feb. 11, 2006, Vice President Cheney accidentally shot Harry Whittington, a Republican lawyer. The vice president did not acknowledge the incident publicly for nearly a day, a delay he attributed to his concern for Whittington and his desire to ensure that Whittington's family could be notified. Whittington, who later had a small heart attack due to a bird-shot pellet in his heart, recovered fully.

CIA changes. Porter J. Goss, director of the CIA, stepped down in May 2006, after repeated clashes with other government officials. Goss had assumed control of the CIA in September 2004, at a time when the agency faced heavy criticism over intelligence shortcomings related to the 2001 terrorist attacks and the Iraq War. President Bush selected General Michael V. Hayden, former director of the National Security Agency/Central Security Service, as the next CIA director.

Reclassification of documents. *The New York Times* in February 2006 reported that U.S. intelligence agencies had reclassified thousands of documents at the National Archives and Records Administration, a federal agency that preserves the records of the U.S. government. Many historians opposed the action, which removed from public access numerous materials that had previously been available to researchers.

Drug safety. The Institute of Medicine, a unit of the National Academy of Sciences, in September called for changes in the U.S. government's system for ensuring drug safety. A report from the institute harshly criticized the Food and Drug Administration, the government agency responsible for ensuring the safety and effectiveness of drugs. It charged that the agency did little to remove dangerous drugs from the market.

Secondhand smoke. In June, Surgeon General Richard H. Carmona reported that secondhand smoke posed an "alarming" public health problem and that only complete indoor smoking bans could protect nonsmokers. Carmona cited research showing that exposure to secondhand smoke increased risks of cancer and heart disease for nonsmokers. ■ Geoffrey A. Campbell

See also **Armed forces; Cabinet, U.S.; Congress of the United States; Elections; People in the news** (Samuel Alito; Ben Bernanke; Josh Bolten, Henry Paulson, Jr.; Tony Snow) **Supreme Court of the United States; United States, President of the.**

IMMIGRATION
POLITICS
2006

By Thomas M. DeFrank

As concerns over illegal immigration mounted, a divided Congress struggled to fix a broken system.

With the exception of the Iraq War, no issue was more volatile or divisive for the United States in 2006 than immigration. The nation's long-standing tradition of welcoming people from foreign shores was shaken by a bitter debate over the growing number of immigrants entering the country illegally. As tensions escalated, the issue prompted fierce political battles in Congress, heightened security along the border with Mexico, and massive immigrant rallies in cities across the United States.

President George W. Bush and members of Congress faced pressure to control new illegal immigration and to deal with unauthorized residents already in the country. President Bush's hope of attracting Hispanic voters to the Republican Party was threatened by a growing national backlash over the economic and cultural impact of illegal immigrants. The president's own party was deeply split over the issue. President Bush proposed a guest worker program that would allow new immigrants to enter the country and many illegal immigrants to remain in the country under temporary work arrangements. Many other Republicans, however, argued that immigration reform should emphasize stronger law enforcement, and not the liberalization of existing laws. Some critics claimed that any plan that allowed illegal immigrants to gain legal status amounted to "amnesty" for lawbreakers.

The urgency of finding a political solution to the problem was linked to a new demographic reality: Immigration has fueled an explosion in U.S. population growth. According to the United States Census Bureau, the foreign-born population in the United States grew from 19.8 million in 1990 to 31.1 million in 2000. In 2006, the Office of Immigration Statistics, an agency of the U.S. Department of Homeland Security, estimated that 10.5 million illegal immigrants lived in the United States at the start of 2005 and that the number would grow by an average of 408,000 per year.

> "We are a nation of laws, and we must enforce our laws. We are also a nation of immigrants, and we must uphold that tradition, which has strengthened our country in so many ways. These are not contradictory goals. America can be a lawful society and a welcoming society at the same time."
>
> ~President George W. Bush

> "This debate shouldn't be about making criminals out of hard-working families ... but rather about strengthening our national security and enacting a law that reflects our best values and our humanity."
>
> ~Senator Edward M. Kennedy

Initial legislative action

President Bush had pressed for a comprehensive overhaul of immigration law as far back as 2001, the first year of his presidency. However, Congress took little legislative action on the issue until late 2005. On Dec. 16, 2005, the House of Representatives passed a controversial immigration measure that identified illegal immigration as a felony punishable by one year in prison. As passed by the House, the bill made it a crime for a person to help illegal immigrants enter or remain in the United States; increased fines for businesses that hired undocumented workers; and allowed for the deportation of noncitizens who belonged to criminal street gangs or who had been convicted of driving while intoxicated. The legislation also specified building 700 miles (1,100 kilometers) of fencing along the border with Mexico.

Country of birth	Number of unauthorized immigrants in the United States (in thousands)	Percentage of total unauthorized immigrant population*
All countries	10,500	100
Mexico	5,970	57
El Salvador	470	4
Guatemala	370	4
India	280	3
China	230	2
Korea	210	2
Philippines	210	2
Honduras	180	2
Brazil	170	2
Vietnam	160	2
Other countries	2,250	21

Figures reflect population estimates for January 2005.
*Numbers do not add up to 100 percent due to rounding.
Source: U.S. Department of Homeland Security.

More than half of all unauthorized immigrants in the United States were born in Mexico. Other leading countries of origin include El Salvador, Guatemala, India, China, and Korea.

Many political experts regarded the House bill—sponsored by Representative F. James Sensenbrenner, Jr., (R., Wisconsin)—as a rejection of President Bush's position on immigration. It abandoned the president's guest worker program and placed a stronger emphasis on border security and law enforcement. The Senate, meanwhile, debated its own immigration measure, which was designed to increase border security but also allow many illegal immigrants to pursue legal status. Many House Republicans vowed to thwart any legislation that granted "amnesty" to illegal immigrants.

The House effort to make felons of illegal immigrants triggered a strong reaction from the nation's immigrant population. On April 10, 2006, hundreds of thousands of demonstrators participated in peaceful "Day of Action" protests in Chicago, Los Angeles, Phoenix, Washington, D.C., and numerous other cities across the United States. Although the majority of illegal immigrants in the United States in 2006 were Hispanic, the rallies also attracted significant numbers of immigrants from Africa, Asia, Europe, and other parts of the world.

Seeking a "middle ground"

Hoping to generate momentum for a solution less severe than the House bill, President Bush addressed the nation on the evening of May 15. In his speech, the president tried to promote what he called "a rational middle ground" between the House and Senate positions. He announced plans to deploy up to 6,000 National Guard troops to Southwestern States to assist the U.S. Border Patrol, an enforcement agency within the U.S. Customs and Border Protection agency. The president also argued that attempts to make criminals of undocumented immigrants were unrealistic and needlessly punitive. He urged Congress to adopt his guest worker plan and endorsed the idea of allowing some illegal immigrants to remain in the country and eventually apply for citizenship. "America can be a lawful society and a welcoming society at the same time," the president declared.

On June 6, a construction support company from Utah became the first National Guard unit to deploy to the border with Mexico. Members of the company took up positions near San Luis, Arizona, about 25 miles (40 kilometers) south of Yuma, the nation's busiest Border Patrol station. Many state governors—who have control over the National Guard units from their states during peacetime—opposed the plan, because they did not want to divert Guard resources from other

The author:
Thomas M. DeFrank is a political journalist and author. He is the Washington bureau chief of the *New York Daily News*.

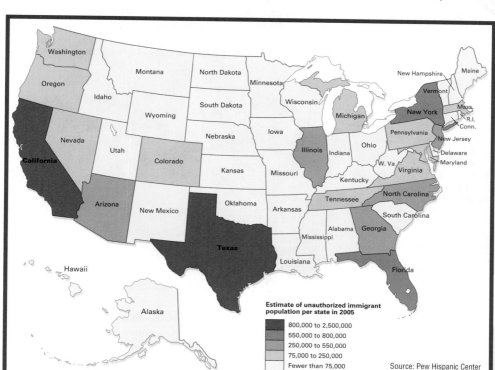

Estimate of unauthorized immigrant population per state in 2005

- 800,000 to 2,500,000
- 550,000 to 800,000
- 250,000 to 550,000
- 75,000 to 250,000
- Fewer than 75,000

Source: Pew Hispanic Center

responsibilities. California Governor Arnold Schwarzenegger turned down a request from the Bush administration to increase California's commitment of Guard troops to make up for shortages of troops in Arizona and New Mexico. Nevertheless, on August 5, President Bush announced that 6,000 Guard troops had been deployed to Southwestern States and that his border security promise had been fulfilled.

The Senate passed its own sweeping reform of immigration law on May 25. Developed primarily by Senator Edward M. Kennedy (D., Massachusetts) and Senator John S. McCain (R., Arizona), the bill was considerably more moderate than the House bill. It included a guest worker provision that would annually allow 200,000 immigrants to obtain temporary visas to enter the country and start on a path toward citizenship. The bill allowed about 7 million illegal immigrants who have lived in the United States for more than five years to seek U.S. citizenship, but only after holding a job, passing background checks, paying fines and back income taxes, and learning English. An additional 3 million illegal immigrants who have lived in the country between two and five years could also become citizens, but they would first have to

About 25 percent of the unauthorized immigrants in the United States in 2006 lived in California. Other states with large numbers of illegal immigrants included Texas, Florida, New York, and Illinois.

"The new policies as provided for under this legislation will increase border security and provide for a new, temporary worker program to enable foreign workers to work legally in this country when there are jobs that American workers won't fill. And, it will acknowledge and address in a humanitarian and compassionate way the current undocumented population."

~Senator John S. McCain

"We come to this country not to take from America, but to make America strong. And we do not deserve to be treated the way we have been treated."

~Jaime Contreras, president of the National Capital Immigration Coalition

Many agricultural businesses, which rely on foreign workers to harvest their crops, favor plans that would allow illegal immigrants to remain in the United States under temporary work arrangements.

leave the country and return as guest workers with temporary visas. Illegal immigrants who have lived in the country for fewer than two years would be required to leave. The Senate bill included measures to double the size of the Border Patrol by 2011 and to construct 370 miles (600 kilometers) of fencing and 500 miles (800 kilometers) of vehicle barriers along the border with Mexico. The bill also declared English the national language of the United States.

Senator Kennedy described the bill as "a comprehensive and realistic attempt to solve the real-world problems that have festered for too long in our broken immigration system." President Bush commended the Senate for its bipartisan approach to the issue. The Congressional Budget Office, an agency that supplies members of Congress with information related to the economy, estimated in May that the Senate bill would increase the U.S. population by 8 million people by 2016 and expand the costs of federal benefits by more than $50 billion. Critics of the bill claimed that the actual numbers would be significantly higher.

A congressional conference committee was expected to meet during the summer of 2006 to resolve the differences between the House and Senate immigration bills. However, hopes for a legislative compromise faced a setback in June, when House Republican leaders announced that members would hold summer hearings in districts across the country to gauge public sentiment at the local level. Many observers viewed the hearings as an attempt by House Republicans to sidestep a politically volatile vote on immigration until after the congressional elections in November. In July, President Bush indicated that, although he remained committed to a comprehensive reform package, he was willing to consider a compromise that emphasized law enforcement and border security and delayed other proposals. According to political experts, the president's advisers hoped that an "enforcement-first" posture would persuade Republican members of Congress to reach an agreement.

As the national government struggled to reach a consensus, state and local jurisdictions grew tired of waiting and passed their own legislation on a number of issues related to immigration. Many states enacted laws that curbed illegal workers' entitlements to education, unemployment payments, and other government benefits.

On October 26, President Bush signed into law a bill authorizing the construction of a 700-mile (1,100-kilometer) fence along the border. However, the measure did not include any funds to build the fence, and critics denounced it as an election-year ploy designed to placate Republican voters and lawmakers.

Many immigrants work in such areas as construction and lawn care. Although economists disagree on the impact of immigrant labor on wages, most believe that the U.S. economy as a whole would suffer without the input of foreign workers.

A history of immigration

The political furor over immigration in 2006 obscured the historical legacy of the United States as a "nation of immigrants" that welcomes those who seek a better life in the New World. That lofty tradition is reflected in the lines of a poem inscribed on the pedestal of the Statue of Liberty in New York Harbor. "The New Colossus" (1883), by the American poet Emma Lazarus, reads:

> "Give me your tired, your poor,
> Your huddled masses yearning to breathe free,
> The wretched refuse of your teeming shore.
> Send these, the homeless, tempest-tost to me.
> I lift my lamp beside the golden door!"

After the United States declared its independence in 1776, the fledgling country welcomed immigrants without restriction. After the War of 1812 (1812-1815), immigration from western Europe—particularly the United Kingdom and Ireland—increased dramatically. By 1850, the foreign-born population of the United States was about 2 million. During the American Civil War (1861-1865), Congress passed legislation that encouraged more immigrants to come to the country.

Between 1820 and 1920—in what has been called the "Century of Immigration"—about 36 million foreigners came to the United States. More than half of that total arrived at the federal government's immigration station on Ellis Island in New York Harbor. The largest contingent of immigrants—about 6 million—were Germans, followed by large numbers of Italians, Irish, Austro-Hungarians, British, and Russians. By 1910, America's foreign-born population had expanded to about 14 million people.

Early traces of an immigration backlash appeared in the mid-1800's. A surge in Irish Catholic immigrants gave rise to the American Party, founded in 1854. The party—whose members believed that the country's political, educational, and economic values were being corrupted by immigrants—was commonly known as the Know-Nothing Party. The Know-Nothings pressed for limits on Irish immigration and briefly experienced political success in some northern cities. A number of other groups also took action against immigrants. The Ku Klux Klan, for instance, emerged in the mid-1860's and waged an often-violent campaign against people it considered un-

Heightened security along the U.S. border with Mexico (above) became a central issue in the immigration debate in 2006. Civilian volunteers called "Minutemen" (right) constructed new fences and stood watch at many crossing points.

American, including African Americans, Jews, Roman Catholics, and immigrants.

A separate backlash movement began in the western United States during the 1850's. Following the discovery of gold in California in 1848, large numbers of Chinese laborers moved into the region and began competing with American workers for jobs. As tensions escalated over several decades, many politicians, labor union officials, and newspaper editors spoke of the "Yellow Peril" and argued for restrictions on Chinese immigration. In 1882, Congress passed the Chinese Exclusion Act, which declared that "in the opinion of the government of the United States, the coming of Chinese laborers to this country endangers the good order of certain localities." The act suspended Chinese immigration for 10 years and barred citizenship for Chinese immigrants already in the United States. Anyone who helped Chinese immigrants enter the country could be fined and jailed. Anti-Chinese sentiment remained so widespread that the restrictions were later made permanent. The act was not repealed until 1943.

An 1892 cartoon depicts an immigrant stealing bread and butter from an American family's dinner table. The original caption described the theft as "the inevitable result to the American workingman of indiscriminate immigration."

The first immigration quota systems were instituted in the 1920's, as politicians began to fear that the United States could not continue to absorb increasing numbers of unskilled laborers from abroad. The Emergency Quota Act of 1921 was designed to stem the flow of immigrants from eastern and southern Europe. Three years later, another act further clamped down on European immigration. It restricted the total influx to about 150,000 annually, but allowed immigrants to bring family members without restriction. No limits were set for Western Hemisphere immigration. Many historians believe that the quota systems of the 1920's triggered the first major instances of illegal immigration to the United States.

> "**Deploying the National Guard to the border does nothing to end the economic exploitation that is driving illegal immigration. Our laws must include uniform enforcement of workplace standards to ensure a more just and level playing field.**"
> ~John J. Sweeney, **president of the AFL-CIO**

The Great Depression, a worldwide economic slump in the 1930's, prompted even greater restriction of immigration. The number of immigrants legally admitted to the country fell from about 280,000 in 1929 to about 23,000 in 1933. The number of new immigrants increased gradually during the late 1930's, but was driven down again during World War II (1939-1945). In 1952, the Immigration and Nationality Act—also called the McCarran-Walter Act—incorporated a number of previous immigration laws, established new quotas for many countries, and made citizenship available to people of all origins. In 1965, amendments to the act ended nationality-based quotas and introduced annual limits of

A woman holds a poster of a Resident Alien card at a 2006 protest calling for increased rights for unauthorized immigrants. The Resident Alien card represents legal resident status in the United States.

170,000 from the Eastern Hemisphere and 120,000 from the Western Hemisphere. By the 1960's and 1970's, legal immigration was on the upswing again, as political refugees from Cuba and Vietnam were allowed entry in large numbers. In 1978, Congress replaced the separate immigration limits for the Eastern and Western hemispheres with a single annual world quota of 290,000. According to the Population Resource Center, legal immigration totaled 4.5 million during the 1970's and increased to 6 million during the 1980's. (The Population Resource Center—based in Washington, D.C., and Princeton, New Jersey—is a nonprofit organization that provides population research findings and demographic data to government policymakers.)

The Immigration Reform and Control Act of 1986 granted legal status to about 3 million illegal immigrants and allowed additional agricultural workers into the United States during the harvest season. The act also established penalties for employers that hired illegal workers. However, critics of the law argued that it did not significantly reduce the flow of illegal immigrants into the country. In 1988, Congress approved expedited deportation proceedings for illegal immigrants who were identified as "aggravated felons," such as those convicted of drug trafficking.

In 1990, further amendments to the Immigration and Nationality Act of 1952 increased the number of immigrants legally allowed into the United States. The limit was changed to 700,000 annually from 1992 to 1994 and to 675,000 annually beginning in 1995. The government also approved visas for an unlimited number of immediate family members. By the end of the 1990's, the country had admitted about 9 million legal immigrants—more than in any other decade in the nation's history. Illegal immigration to the United States also rose during the 1990's. The government sought to address the issue by increasing the size of the Border Patrol and by improving surveillance and security measures along the border with Mexico. Nevertheless, the lure of the

American Dream continued to draw tens of thousands of undocumented immigrants to the United States.

Political stalemate

In 2006, there was little doubt that the nation's immigration policy had become a pawn in a political struggle for the Hispanic vote. Traditionally, Hispanic voters have favored Democratic candidates. However, President Bush and his chief political strategist, Karl Rove, hoped that a tolerant approach to immigration reform would help attract Hispanic voters to the Republican Party. They were aided in this effort, ironically, by many Democrats, who were anxious to retain Hispanic loyalties. Conservative Republicans, however, insisted that a more punitive policy was necessary to save the party from a growing backlash against illegal immigrants. Some lawmakers made a national security argument, saying that stricter border security was needed to keep terrorists out of the country after the attacks on the United States of Sept. 11, 2001.

The immigration debate in 2006 also had a powerful economic component. President Bush maintained that the U.S. economy would suffer without foreign workers, who tended to fill lower-paying jobs that many Americans declined to accept. Immigrants also contributed to the economies of their native countries through foreign remittances. The Inter-American Development Bank estimated that legal and illegal immigrants in the United States sent about $40 billion to their families and friends in Latin America and the Caribbean in 2005. (The Inter-American Development Bank, based in Washington, D.C., is an institution that promotes economic and social development.)

Although economists disagree over the impact of illegal immigration on wages and job opportunities in the United States, most believed in 2006 that foreign workers had a positive overall effect on the U.S. economy. Illegal immigrants "harvest our crops, tend our gardens, work in our restaurants, and clean our houses," according to Senator McCain. "Some Americans believe we must find all these millions, round them up, and send them back to the countries they came from. I don't know how you do that. And I don't know why you would want to."

Ironically, the prospects for comprehensive immigration reform improved considerably after the Republicans lost control of the Senate and the House of Representatives in the November 2006 elections. President Bush's guest worker program was popular among many Democrats, who now controlled the legislative machinery of Congress. Democrats were expected to submit a new bill in the 110th Congress, which convenes in January 2007. Even so, the issue promises to remain volatile and divisive as the flow of illegal immigrants continues.

> **"Mexico believes it will take more than just enforcement or building walls to truly solve the challenges posed by the migration phenomenon, and that comprehensive reform is in the interest of both nations."**
>
> **~Mexican President Vicente Fox Quesada**

> **"The problem in our lack of border security and illegal immigration is becoming increasingly obvious: two political parties that are beholden to corporate America, the largest employers of illegal aliens, and the leadership of both parties that are selling out American citizens in search of cheap labor and political advantage."**
>
> **~Lou Dobbs, CNN anchor**

At a White House address on September 6, President George W. Bush acknowledges the existence of previously secret, offshore Central Intelligence Agency prisons, from which 14 high-value terrorism suspects recently had been transferred to Guantánamo Bay in Cuba.

United States, President of the.

With the United States military mired in an increasingly violent war in Iraq, President George W. Bush endured low approval ratings throughout 2006. Polls indicated that a majority of citizens disapproved of his job performance. RealClearPolitics.com, a Web site that culls political articles from around the Internet, reported in December that, on average, major polls were showing an approval rate for Bush of less than 37 percent and a disapproval rate of 60 percent. According to political experts, midterm election voters registered their unhappiness with President Bush and the Republican Party by giving Democrats control of Congress.

Antiterrorism and executive power. President Bush's efforts to broaden the executive branch's power to fight terrorism suffered setbacks in 2006. On June 29, the U.S. Supreme Court rejected the military commissions he had set up in 2001 to try foreign terrorism suspects being held in a U.S. military prison at Guantánamo Bay, Cuba. The court, in *Hamdan v. Rumsfeld,* ruled that the commissions violated the international treaties known as the Geneva Conventions, which govern wartime prisoner treatment. The court also ruled that the commissions were unauthorized by current U.S. law. The Bush administration had previously declared that because Guantánamo detainees were "unlawful enemy combatants," they did not qualify for protection under the Geneva Conventions. Shortly after the Supreme Court's 2006 ruling, however, the administration announced that it would apply Geneva protections to all terrorism suspects in U.S. custody. President Bush also sought congressional authorization for the military commissions. An act passed by Congress in September and signed by the president on October 17 gave him most of the extra executive powers he had sought to interrogate and try terrorism suspects.

In December 2005, news reports revealed that President Bush had authorized a secret National Security Agency (NSA) wiretapping program for purposes of monitoring possible terrorism activity. The program allowed the NSA to intercept calls and e-mails between people in the United States and overseas without a court warrant. However, on Aug. 17, 2006, a U.S. district judge in Detroit ruled that the program was unconstitutional. The Bush administration appealed the ruling.

On September 6, President Bush acknowledged for the first time that the U.S. Central Intelligence Agency (CIA) had been holding terrorism suspects in secret prisons—nicknamed "black sites"—outside the country. Bush said the CIA had used "alternative" procedures to interrogate suspects at these prisons, but he did not reveal the procedures.

First Bush veto. On July 19, President Bush issued the first veto of his presidency. The vetoed bill would have eased restrictions on federal funding for embryonic stem cell research. Bush, who had imposed the restrictions in 2001, said he could not back the use of tax dollars to destroy living human embryos. Supporters of the bill, however, pointed to the potential of embryonic stem cells to help treat diseases and disabilities. A veto override attempt in the U.S. House of Representatives failed to secure the necessary two-thirds majority.

The stem-cell veto remained President Bush's only veto at the end of 2006. However, he issued "signing statements" challenging about 1,000 provisions in bills he was signing into law—more challenges than all previous presidents combined. In response, the American Bar Association in August adopted a resolution opposing signing statements that expressed a president's intent to ignore provisions of the law being signed.

Ford dies. Former President Gerald R. Ford, who served from 1974 to 1977, died on Dec. 26, 2006, at age 93. He had lived longer than any other president. Ford became president after Richard Nixon resigned as a result of the Watergate political scandal. ■ Geoffrey A. Campbell

See also **Cabinet, U.S.; Congress of the United States; Elections; Human rights; People in the news** (Josh Bolten, Tony Snow); **Republican Party; Supreme Court of the United States; Taxation; United States, Government of the.**

Venezuela.

President Hugo Chávez Frías won reelection as president of Venezuela on Dec. 3, 2006. Chávez was first elected president in 1998. He was reelected for a second term in 2000 and survived a *coup* (overthrow) attempt against his government in 2002. In 2004, he emerged victorious from a recall election, a special election mandated by the gathering of a required number of signatures on petitions.

Chávez's chief opponent in the December 2006 presidential election was Manuel Rosales, governor of the Venezuelan state of Zulia. Rosales rallied a splintered and dispirited opposition, political experts observed, garnering 37 percent of votes compared with Chávez's 63 percent.

Chávez had proved unbeatable, analysts suggested, due to a a sixfold increase in revenues from Venezuela's oil exports during his presidential tenure. The president, they observed, had overseen the reinvestment of a large percentage of this wealth in social programs popular with a broad section of the Venezuelan public.

Programs for the poor. By the end of 2006, the Venezuelan government had earmarked $20 billion from surging oil revenues for a special development fund created to finance the social programs that were the hallmark of the Chávez administration. Public spending, overall, increased by 40 percent in the first quarter of 2006,

according to figures from Venezuela's Central Bank. Much of the money was spent to provide free education, health care, and heavily subsidized food at 15,000 outlets patronized by nearly half of all Venezuelans.

Within Latin America, Chávez distributed surplus Venezuelan wealth—particularly in the form of steeply discounted oil supplies—earning goodwill from a number of countries. In 2006, Venezuela provided more than twice as much financial assistance to Latin American countries as did the United States.

On the international stage, Chávez seemed to seize every opportunity to denounce the policies of U.S. President George W. Bush, whom Chávez labeled "imperialistic." At the same time, Chávez cultivated close relations with nations decidedly unfriendly to the United States, including Cuba, Iran, and North Korea.

The pitch of verbal insults between the governing administrations of Venezuela and the United States reached a new high in September 2006, when President Chávez addressed the United Nations General Assembly in New York City. "The devil came here yesterday, right here," he said at the same rostrum from which President Bush had spoken the previous day. "It still smells of sulfur," Chávez added.

Economy. During the first half of 2006, the Venezuelan economy expanded by nearly 10 percent, and the value of stocks traded on the Caracas exchange increased by 70 percent. The impact of the economic boom was evident everywhere in Caracas, the capital, where three-bedroom apartments in upscale neighborhoods commanded rents as high as $6,000 a month.

Squeezing foreign investors. In April, the Venezuelan government mandated that foreign oil companies allot a 60-percent stake in their operations in Venezuela to Petróleos de Venezuela S.A., the state-run oil company. Previously, these foreign companies had paid Venezuela only production fees. Two of the foreign companies, Total S.A. of France and Eni S.p.A. of Italy, refused to accommodate the new rules of investment, and their fields were seized in April by the Venezuelan government.

Iranian investment. During 2006, Petropars, the national oil company of Iran, announced plans to invest $4 billion to produce oil and natural gas in Venezuela. In November, Khodro, an Iranian automobile manufacturer, began production of cars at a factory near Caracas. Analysts speculated that Venezuela's economic outreach to Iran was part of President Chávez's overall campaign of aligning Venezuela with nations that actively opposed the United States in foreign affairs. ■ Nathan A. Haverstock

See also **Latin America: A Special Report.**

Vietnam. The ruling Communist Party of Vietnam (CPV) held a National Party Congress from April 18 to 25, 2006. Such congresses take place every five years. A focus of this year's speeches was widespread corruption, which some delegates said threatened the legitimacy of the party's power. The CPV's secretary-general, Nong Duc Manh, was elected to a second five-year term. Having already purged some officials on corruption charges, he pledged to be tougher in fighting corruption.

The CPV dropped President Tran Duc Luong and Prime Minister Phan Van Khai from its ruling group, the Politburo. In June, the National Assembly approved Nguyen Minh Triet as president and Nguyen Tan Dung as prime minister.

Both the new president and the prime minister were known as economic reformers, and the latter had overseen economic reforms for the previous eight years. During that time, Vietnam had enjoyed impressive economic growth while reducing the number of people living in poverty. At the congress, Manh reiterated his goals of making Vietnam an industrialized nation by 2020 and further reducing the country's poverty level. The country exhibited its growing prosperity in November 2006 by hosting the annual conference of the Asia-Pacific Economic Cooperation forum.

■ Henry S. Bradsher

See also **Asia; Disasters.**

Vital statistics. See Census; Population.

Washington, D.C.

Adrian M. Fenty, a Democrat who had been a member of the District of Columbia (D.C.) Council, was elected mayor of Washington, D.C., on Nov. 7, 2006. Fenty ran against Republican David W. Kranich and won 90 percent of the vote.

Fenty won the Democratic primary on September 12 after setting a record by raising $3 million for a Washington mayoral campaign. Fenty's primary victory virtually assured him the mayor's job in Washington, where registered Democrats outnumbered Republicans by a ratio of 9 to 1.

Fenty began immediately after the primary to work with outgoing Mayor Anthony A. Williams, also a Democrat, to plan a transition. Fenty toured Baltimore, Chicago, Los Angeles, New York, and San Francisco and spoke with officials in those cities about schools, police, security, and city finances. The incoming mayor said he wanted to run a more efficient government and operate the city "like a business."

Born in 1970, Fenty grew up in Washington's Mount Pleasant neighborhood. He graduated from Oberlin College in Ohio and the law school of Howard University in Washington, D.C. Before winning his first council term in 2000, he was the lead attorney for the council's Committee on Education, Libraries, and Recreation.

The Thunderbirds, a demonstration flight team of the United States Air Force, fly over the new Air Force Memorial in Arlington, Virginia—just outside Washington, D.C.—on Oct. 12, 2006. The flight was a practice run for the memorial's opening ceremony, which took place on October 14. The memorial's soaring spires represent flight.

School reform. Fenty stated in 2006 that the improvement of public schools was a top priority. Of the city's 146 public schools, 118 failed to meet the reading and mathematics standards set by the No Child Left Behind Act, a federal law that regulated public education. Fenty considered a plan that would increase the mayor's authority over schools and change Washington's Board of Education from an elected school board to an appointed advisory group.

Crime-fighting effort. Reacting to a rise in the number of robberies and a summer spike in homicides in 2006, Mayor Williams signed an emergency crime bill into law on July 21, after it was passed by the D.C. Council. A provision of the law instituted a 10 p.m. curfew for youths ages 16 and younger. The law also allowed the city to install surveillance cameras in neighborhoods and gave police greater access to juvenile records.

The council approved a revised crime bill on October 18, with new funding for youth programs and police overtime. The revision also relaxed the youth curfew to 11 p.m. Sundays through Thursdays and to midnight on Fridays and Saturdays. City officials said the crime rate had gone down during the summer, after the initial emergency crime bill went into effect.

Military monuments. A new United States Air Force Memorial was dedicated in Arlington, Virginia—across from the Pentagon and next to Arlington Cemetery—on October 14. Designed by the German-born American architect James Ingo Freed, the memorial features three stainless steel spires, the tallest reaching 270 feet (82 meters). The spires represent flight and the three core values of the Air Force: integrity, service, and excellence. Prior to the dedication, the Air Force was the only U.S. military branch not represented by a memorial in the nation's capital. The memorial honors more than 54,000 airmen who died in combat while serving in the Air Force.

The National Museum of the Marine Corps—designed by the architectural firm Fentress Bradburn—opened in November on a 135-acre (55-hectare) site next to the Marine Corps base at Quantico, Virginia, which is about 35 miles (56 kilometers) south of Washington, D.C. The building, which features a 210-foot (64-meter) tilted mast rising through a glass atrium, contains suspended aircraft and many other exhibits.

The federal government in August approved a plan to build an underground Vietnam Veterans Memorial visitors center between the Lincoln Memorial and the Vietnam Veterans Memorial wall. Plans for the 25,000-square-foot (2,300-square-meter) center included exhibits and possibly a movie theater and three-dimensional battle scene. ■ Howard S. Shapiro

See also **City.**

Weather. Exceptionally warm weather across the United States ushered in 2006. The contiguous 48 states recorded the highest average January temperature since record keeping began in 1895—8.5 °F (4.8 °C) above normal. Every state measured above-normal temperatures, and 15 states reported their highest January temperature on record. Several cities in the Great Plains and Midwest noted their warmest January, including Minneapolis, Minnesota, where the temperature failed to fall below 0 °F (-17.7 °C) for only the second time since 1891.

The unusual warmth was caused by the retreat of the jet stream to the United States-Canada border, a pattern that also favored wet weather along parts of the West Coast. A storm that began on New Year's Eve and continued on New Year's Day brought 5 to 10 inches (13 to 25 centimeters) of rain to parts of northern California, where high waters on the Russian and Napa rivers flooded hundreds of houses and businesses. In the upper elevations of the Northwest, late January 2006 snow depths were more than 150 percent above normal.

In contrast, extreme dryness marked winter from the interior Southwest to the southern Great Plains. Arizona had its driest winter on record, and New Mexico and Oklahoma had their second driest. By the end of February, a mere 1.6 inches (4.1 centimeters) of snow had fallen in Flagstaff, Arizona, since autumn 2005, compared with a normal snowfall of 72.5 inches (184 centimeters). A record-setting streak of 143 rainless days in Phoenix ended on March 11, 2006.

The warm winter led to meager snowfalls in most of the Midwest and Northeast, where Rochester, Minnesota, registered its lowest snowfall for January. Three cities—Rapid City, South Dakota; Green Bay, Wisconsin; and Harrisburg, Pennsylvania—tied their lowest snowfall records. However, a potent *northeaster* (storm) dumped heavy snow on a small area of the Northeast seaboard on February 11 and 12. New York City set a record with a snowfall of 26.9 inches (68.3 centimeters).

Winter in Europe and Asia. Record cold and snow marked the winter across parts of Europe and Asia. Moscow shivered through its coldest winter since that of 1978-1979. On Jan. 18, 2006, the temperature fell to -22 °F (-30 °C), causing the deaths of at least 89 people. Earlier in the month, frost was observed in New Delhi, India, for the first time in 70 years. In East Asia, heavy snow smothered parts of northern Japan in January, measuring over 13 feet (4 meters) in places. More than 100 deaths were attributed to the heavy snow, the highest death toll from the effects of snow in Japan in more than 20 years. Snowfall was unusually heavy across central Europe as well, especially in the Alps, where France reported a record 47 avalanche fatalities from December 2005 to March 2006. Later in the spring, snowmelt

Asphalt melts from the heat in Givors, near Lyon, in southeastern France in late July. Most of Europe sweltered as a two-week heat wave settled over the area, with temperatures well over 86 °F (30 °C). More than 100 people died from the heat in France alone.

Children race past a torrent of water released from a pond in an effort to control flooding in the city of Tabor, Czech Republic, in March. Heavy rain and snowmelt from unusually warm weather resulted in flooding throughout Europe.

Heat waves, massive flooding, and early winter storms made 2006 another year of extreme weather.

Floodwaters reach as high as the street signs in Easton, Pennsylvania, as the Delaware River overflows its banks in June. The flooding was among the worst to hit the northeastern United States in decades.

and heavy rain led to severe flooding when Europe's second longest river, the Danube, reached its highest level in 111 years.

Warm start to spring. April 2006 was the warmest April on record in the 48 contiguous states, the second month of record warmth in 2006. It was especially hot in the southern Great Plains, where Dallas set its highest April temperature record of 101 °F (38 °C) on the 17th.

Spring brought severe weather to the Central States. On March 12, thunderstorms spawned 113 tornadoes that swept the Great Plains, killing 10 people. The tornadoes set a record for the greatest number on a single March day. On April 2, a cold front sparked thunderstorms that produced 86 tornadoes across the eastern Great Plains and Midwest. Twenty-eight people were killed, primarily in Tennessee. Days later, more than 100 tornadoes again struck Tennessee, killing 12 people.

Drought conditions expanded across much of the Great Plains and the Southern States during May. Sunny, hot weather in Florida ignited wildfires over several weeks, forcing intermittent closures of parts of Interstate 95.

Recurrent heavy rain in New England from May 10 to 15 led to widespread flooding. Thousands fled their houses, especially in the Merrimack River Valley in southeastern New Hampshire and northeastern Massachusetts, where 12 to 17 inches (30 to 43 centimeters) of rain fell, causing the worst flooding in 70 years. Three cities—Portland, Maine; Concord, New Hampshire; and Burlington, Vermont—all logged their wettest May on record.

Summer storms and record heat. More than 10 inches (25 centimeters) of rain fell in parts of the Northeast from June 22 to 28. The Susquehanna River overflowed its banks, forcing the evacuation of 200,000 people around Wilkes-Barre, Pennsylvania. Flooding was also widespread in southern New York and the Washington, D.C., area.

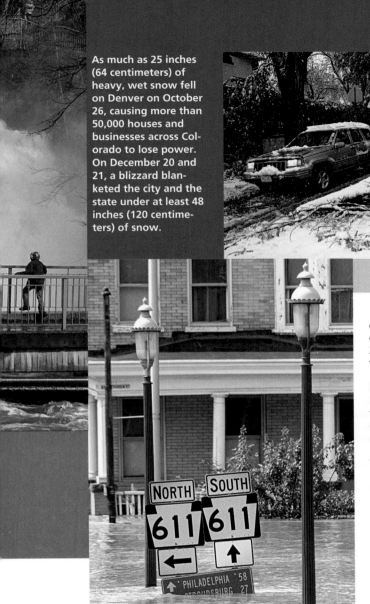

As much as 25 inches (64 centimeters) of heavy, wet snow fell on Denver on October 26, causing more than 50,000 houses and businesses across Colorado to lose power. On December 20 and 21, a blizzard blanketed the city and the state under at least 48 inches (120 centimeters) of snow.

From mid- to late June, blistering heat gripped much of the West. On June 13 and 14, Houston and Denver each tied records for the earliest reading of 100 °F (38 °C) or higher. On June 26, Portland, Oregon, reached 102 °F (39 °C), its highest June temperature on record. In Las Vegas, Nevada, the monthly average of 90.5 °F (32.5 °C) made June 2006 the hottest June on record in that city. For the nation as a whole, June 2006 was the second warmest since record keeping began.

Exceptional heat continued in most of the nation in July. More than 2,300 daily temperature records were broken, and more than 50 locations reported their hottest July day on record. Usta, South Dakota, reached 120 °F (49 °C) on July 15,

equaling the highest temperature ever measured in that state. July 2006 was the nation's second warmest July on record.

By early August, record-setting heat had enveloped the Northeast. Between August 1 and 3, temperatures reached 100 °F (38 °C) or higher on one or more days in four cities—Providence, Rhode Island; New York City; Baltimore; and Washington, D.C.

Frequent summer thunderstorms in the Southwest helped alleviate serious drought conditions that followed the second driest winter on record in the region. But heavy rain also caused local flooding. From July 28 to August 4, more than 15 inches (38 centimeters) of rain fell on El Paso, nearly twice its normal annual total.

Hurricane season. The first hurricane of the Atlantic season, Ernesto, formed south of Haiti on August 24. The storm reached hurricane strength on August 27, then weakened to a tropical storm as it moved northwest across Cuba and Florida and off the Southeast Coast into the Atlantic. Ernesto made landfall again near Long Beach, North Carolina, on August 31 and moved across eastern North Carolina and Virginia. A pressure difference between the storm center and strong high pressure over New England led to wind gusts over 70 miles (113 kilometers) per hour near the Middle Atlantic Coast.

Autumn fires and storms. On September 13, wildfires in the United States set a new record for area burned. A total of 8,694,000 acres (3,518,000 hectares) was consumed, eclipsing the record set in 2005. The 10-year average for area burned by wildfires was 4.9 million acres (2 million hectares).

Severe thunderstorms swept across the Midwest on September 22 and 23, causing at least 11 deaths. From 5 to 10 inches (13 to 25 centimeters) of rain brought flooding to parts of Kentucky, and more than 30 tornadoes struck the Mississippi Valley.

Unprecedented early season snows fell in the Great Lakes States on October 12 and 13. Buffalo, New York, had its biggest snowstorm for so early in the season. One to two feet (30 to 60 centimeters) of snow brought down thousands of tree limbs, knocking out power to nearly 400,000 homes and businesses. In the South, devastating thunderstorms that began November 15 and produced several tornadoes caused the deaths of a dozen people.

The autumn wet season began with recurrent flooding rain in parts of the Pacific Northwest. Stampede Pass in the Washington Cascades had 8.22 inches (20.9 centimeters) of rain on November 7, the wettest day on record there. November was the wettest month on record at the Seattle-Tacoma International Airport, where more than 15 inches (38 centimeters) of rain fell. On December 14, the airport recorded wind gusts of a record 69 miles (111 kilometers) per hour during the worst windstorm the Northwest had experienced in a decade. At least 14 people died in the storm, and more than 1.5 million homes and businesses lost power.

■ Fred Gadomski and Todd Miner

Welfare.
Wade F. Horn, the assistant secretary for children and families at the United States Department of Health and Human Services (HHS), announced in February 2006 that caseloads under the Temporary Assistance for Needy Families (TANF) program had declined between the first and second quarters of 2005. TANF is a program that provides cash assistance and helps with child care services for low-income workers and the unemployed.

Overall, the number of individuals and families receiving welfare payments have fallen significantly since welfare reform was signed into law in August 1996. Between August 1996 and June 2005, TANF family caseloads fell by 2,512,752 to 1,895,756—a 57-percent decline. Caseloads for individuals fell by 7,792,314 to 4,449,811—a 64-percent decline—over the same period.

TANF reauthorized. President George W. Bush in February 2006 signed into law a reauthorization of the TANF program. Prior to the reauthorization, the program had been operating under a series of temporary extensions. The reauthorization included stricter work requirements, designed to encourage recipients to get off welfare and join the nation's economic mainstream. The TANF reauthorization also included funding for "healthy marriage" and "responsible fatherhood" programs, which sought to build and strengthen families.

Fatherhood manual. The HHS Administration for Children and Families released a guide in June for helping fathers develop a strong and positive influence in the lives of their children. The guide included information and advice on such topics as how to effectively handle crying babies and how to help care for new moms.

Education program gets low marks. A study funded by the HHS Administration for Children and Families found that a pilot program designed to improve the employability of welfare recipients actually had a negative impact on earnings. The program, at Riverside Community College in California, consisted of general education coursework followed by career-directed courses. The group receiving the education earned less and stayed on TANF longer than a control group that did not receive the special schooling. The study was conducted by Abt Associates Inc. of Cambridge, Massachusetts.

New Head Start chief. Michael O. Leavitt, the HHS secretary, in March appointed Channell Wilkins to oversee the Head Start Bureau at the Administration for Children and Families. Wilkins had served as president of the board of Trenton (New Jersey) Head Start. (Head Start is a federal program designed to improve the school readiness of children from low-income families.)

■ Geoffrey A. Campbell

West Indies.
On March 30, 2006, Portia Lucretia Simpson Miller of the incumbent People's National Party became Jamaica's first woman prime minister. She had previously served in the Cabinet as minister of labor, of tourism, and of local government. In parliament, she represented one of the poorest and most violence-prone districts of Kingston, the capital.

As Simpson Miller took office, Jamaica's government was straining under a heavy public debt. Payments on the debt consumed 59 percent of budgeted revenues in 2006, the government reported. Economists noted that declining revenues from tourism and mining operations were contributing to the country's budget crunch.

Economic and social conditions on the island were difficult in 2006, with unemployment at 16 percent and inflation running at 10 percent. Armed gangs effectively controlled many urban areas, and the annual number of murders—1,670 in 2005—had increased steadily since 2000.

Simpson Miller pledged to break the power of the criminals and fight government corruption. She promised programs to assist the poor and reduce unemployment. Analysts speculated that attacking joblessness would become Simpson Miller's first priority in light of statistics showing that 85 percent of Jamaica's university graduates emigrated in 2006 to seek jobs.

Dominican Republic crime wave. In July, the administration of President Leonel Fernández Reyna deployed joint military and police patrols on the streets of Santo Domingo, the capital, and 16 other Dominican Republic cities to fight spiraling violent crime. According to statistics reported by the Dominican chief of police, the number of all types of violent crime more than doubled between mid-2005 and mid-2006. The anticrime campaign also included restrictions on the importation of firearms.

Live coverage of Parliament. In August, the government of the two-island nation of Trinidad and Tobago launched a new television channel that carried live broadcasts of sessions of Parliament. The launch of the new channel was timed to coincide with legislative deliberations over a proposed new constitution. Upon introducing the draft document on August 18, Prime Minister Patrick Manning asserted that the existing constitution, which dated from independence from the United Kingdom in 1962, no longer adequately served the country's governmental needs.

■ Nathan A. Haverstock

See also **Latin America; Latin America: A Special Report.**

Yemen. See Middle East.
Yukon. See Canadian territories.
Zambia. See Africa.

Zimbabwe. President Robert Mugabe and his ruling Zimbabwe African National Union-Patriotic Front (ZANU-PF) retained firm control in 2006 as the country's chief opposition group, the Movement for Democratic Change (MDC), splintered along factional lines. On December 17, ZANU-PF postponed presidential elections from 2008 to 2010, effectively giving Mugabe an additional two years in office. Mugabe had promised to retire at the end of his current term.

Currency revaluation. On July 31, 2006, the Reserve Bank of Zimbabwe issued new currency on which three zeroes had been slashed from banknotes, artificially strengthening the official exchange rate to 250 Zimbabwean dollars ($Z) to one United States dollar. Prior to the new issue, the $Z was officially trading at 250,000 to $1 U.S. The true exchange rate was closer to the black market rate of $Z 555,000 to $1 U.S., observed some economists.

The currency revaluation came in response to hyperinflation, which in late 2006 was running at 4 percent a day, or 1,200 percent annually. Economists blamed the inflation on the collapse of the agricultural sector since 2000 and unrestricted printing of currency by the government. They suggested that the reserve bank's 2006 revaluation would do little or nothing to address fundamental economic problems.

Zimbabwe's agricultural economy, once among the most productive in Africa, went into decline in 2000 when the Mugabe government, opting for arbitrary land confiscation rather than planned buyouts, started seizing white-owned commercial farms and awarding them to ZANU-PF associates. The cumulative result of this policy was a sharp drop in agricultural output, forcing the importation of food and dependence on food aid. The Mugabe government continued to implement the land confiscation policy in 2006, sending dozens of eviction notices to white farmers in October. The new evictions affected about 10 percent of Zimbabwe's remaining farmers, according to a spokesperson for the country's Commercial Farmers' Union.

Split in opposition party. In February, the breakaway faction of the MDC selected Arthur Mutambara, an Oxford University-educated scientist, as its leader, formalizing a rift in Zimbabwe's main opposition party. The splitup dated from a 2005 election campaign leading up to November polls for a newly created Senate in Zimbabwe's parliament. MDC party president Morgan Tsvangirai had insisted upon a boycott of the election by the party, but other MDC politicians ran for election. As a result of the disagreement, the "pro-senate" faction broke with Tsvangirai. The MDC made a poor showing in the Senate election, winning only 7 out of 50 seats.

On March 19, 2006, Tsvangirai was reelected party leader of the alternate faction of the MDC. Political analysts speculated that the splintering of the country's main opposition—strong enough in 2002 for MDC candidate Tsvangirai to seriously challenge Mugabe in a presidential election—would greatly strengthen Mugabe's hand. In local elections in March 2006, opposition candidates lost several important mayoral and council seats in some of Zimbabwe's larger cities to ZANU-PF candidates.

HIV/AIDS. According to the 2006 report of UNAIDS—the United Nations-affiliated body that coordinates the global response to HIV/AIDS—about 1.7 million adult Zimbabweans, or 20 percent of the population between ages 15 and 49, were living with HIV/AIDS by the end of 2005. The figure represented a slight infection rate decline since late 2003 but was still one of the highest in the world. The report also documented some 180,000 AIDS deaths per year in Zimbabwe and noted that life expectancy for Zimbabweans had declined to 34 years for women and 37 years for men. According to UN sources, Zimbabwe's population of about 13 million included almost 1 million orphans, most of whom were children of deceased AIDS victims.   ■ Pieter Esterhuysen

See also **Africa.**

Zoology. See Biology; Conservation; Ocean.

Zoos. A number of zoos opened exciting new exhibits in 2006 and launched new breeding programs. However, zoos also faced mounting pressure from animal rights activists critical of the confinement of animals in small enclosures. People for the Ethical Treatment of Animals (PETA)—an activist group based in Norfolk, Virginia—accused many zoos of neglecting or mistreating animals. Even many zookeepers and supporters of zoos called for changes in the methods and philosophies of exhibiting certain animals.

Elephant exhibits. Much of the controversy involved large animals, especially elephants. According to experts, many zoo exhibits are too small for such animals, which can be dangerous to care for. In July, an Asian elephant killed a keeper at the Elephant Sanctuary, a nonprofit elephant refuge in Hohenwald, Tennessee.

Zoos in Detroit, Philadelphia, San Francisco, and other cities have closed or are phasing out their elephant exhibits. In February, the Bronx Zoo in New York City announced that its three elephants would be the last exhibited there. Chicago's Lincoln Park Zoo—which received heavy criticism following the deaths of three elephants and several other animals—transformed its elephant enclosure into a camel exhibit in June. Florida's Lion Country Safari announced in September that its last two elephants would soon be moved to a new location with more room.

Some zoos took steps to expand their elephant facilities, so that they could continue breeding programs and take in animals from other zoos. In April, the Los Angeles City Council approved a $39-million expansion of the elephant exhibit at the Los Angeles Zoo. In May, the National Zoo in Washington, D.C., announced the start of a $60-million Asian elephant exhibit expansion. The Maryland Zoo in Baltimore in October described plans to increase the size of its elephant habitat and to create an "elephant trail" through wooded hillsides.

The American Zoo and Aquarium Association (AZA)—which represents most zoos and aquariums in the United States—strongly urged zoos to improve their facilities for elephants. In May, the AZA established guidelines that required outdoor elephant exhibits to have at least 1,800 square feet (167 square meters) for one elephant and an additional 900 square feet (84 square meters) for each additional elephant.

The AZA also sought to improve the public image of zoos. At the association's national conference in September, the AZA released the results of a three-year study titled "Why Zoos and Aquariums Matter: Visitor Impact Study." The results suggested that visitors leave zoos and aquariums with a heightened awareness of conservation needs.

Outdoor cats. Big Cat Falls, a $20-million outdoor exhibit, opened at the Philadelphia Zoo in May. Cold weather is no problem for the exhibit's Amur leopards, Amur tigers, and snow leopards from northern Asia. Other cats—such as American jaguars and African lions—can keep warm on heated rocks inside the enclosures.

Snow leopards also prowl Asia Trail, opened in October at the National Zoo. They share the limelight with giant pandas, plus other animals seldom seen in zoos. These include the rare clouded leopard from Southeast Asia and the Japanese giant salamander, an amphibian that can reach 5 feet (1.5 meters) in length.

Native cultures. Cultures of native peoples as well as the wildlife of their lands are featured in new exhibits in Detroit and Memphis. Australian Outback Adventure, which opened in May at the Detroit Zoo, showcases Aboriginal-style art and artifacts along with a collection of red kangaroos. Northwest Passage, unveiled in March at the Memphis Zoo, re-creates a Native American fishing village as a backdrop for its exhibits of sea lions, polar bears, black bears, and other animals of the Pacific Northwest.

Touch a shark. In May, the Newport (Kentucky) Aquarium opened the Shark Central exhibit, which allows visitors to get close to small sharks and rays in a "touch pool." The pool is modeled after a shark research facility. Chicago's Shedd Aquarium in January unveiled an exhibit of unwelcome alien species that have invaded the Great Lakes. The exhibit features zebra mussels, round gobies, snakeheads, and other species that have upset the ecological balance of the region's waters.

Notable new arrivals. An endangered snow monkey was born in April at the Minnesota Zoo, and a tiny duiker antelope arrived in March at the Binder Park Zoo in Battle Creek, Michigan. A mishmi takin, an Asian relative of the musk ox, was born in February at the Denver Zoo, and a rare Rodrigues fruit bat appeared in May at the Louisville Zoo.

The end of an era. An era ended in October when the famed Catskill Game Farm in Catskill, New York, closed. A family business for 73 years, the farm suffered from declining attendance. Its founder, Roland Lindermann, was a world-renowned expert on the large-hoofed animals that populated the farm.

New Orleans reopening. The outlook was brighter for the Audubon Aquarium of the Americas, a New Orleans, Louisiana, facility that had been shut down in the aftermath of Hurricane Katrina. The aquarium reopened in May with newly enhanced exhibits. The aquarium's IMAX Theater presented a film showing the impact of the 2005 hurricane on the region. ■ Ed Ricciuti

WORLD BOOK SUPPLEMENT

Seven new or revised articles are reprinted from the 2007 edition of *The World Book Encyclopedia.*

Consumer protection is the effort to promote the interests of buyers of goods and services. It seeks to protect consumers from unsafe products, deceptive advertising and sales methods, and unfair business practices. It also tries to provide accurate information about products so that consumers can make informed purchasing decisions. Consumer *advocates* (supporters) urge businesses and governments to deal with the concerns of consumers. They also help consumers receive compensation for damages or injuries caused by faulty products. Efforts to protect consumers are sometimes called the *consumer movement* or *consumerism.*

The actions of individual consumers play a significant role in consumer protection. However, the movement's most visible activities are carried out by consumer organizations. Such organizations include the Consumer Federation of America, the Consumers' Association of Canada, and Consumers International. These and other groups have helped bring about government regulations on the packaging and labeling of food, the marketing of cigarettes, the manufacturing of automobiles, and numerous other issues that affect consumers.

The consumer movement also includes the efforts of businesses to regulate themselves and to protect their customers. For instance, businesses in many cities operate *better business bureaus,* which protect the public from unfair business practices. Many companies also offer *warranties* and *money-back guarantees* to ensure consumer satisfaction. Most warranties are statements that promise repair, replacement, or a refund if a product fails to perform as the manufacturer said it would. A money-back guarantee promises a refund if the buyer is not completely satisfied.

The consumer's rights

Consumer advocates believe consumers have several basic rights. Such rights include (1) the right to safety, (2) the right to information, (3) the right to choose, and (4) the right to be heard. Consumers also have certain responsibilities. For example, they should use a product only for its intended purpose, and they should follow the instructions provided with the product.

The right to safety. Countries throughout the world have laws that regulate the safety of goods and services. For instance, the Consumer Product Safety Act, originally passed in 1972, seeks to protect the people of the United States against unsafe consumer products. In the United Kingdom, the General Product Safety Regulations set safety standards for many consumer products.

Government agencies may test products, inspect factories, investigate complaints, and order manufacturers to *recall* (take back) unsafe products. The United States, for instance, has a number of government agencies that promote consumer safety. They include the Food and Drug Administration, which regulates the safety of food, drugs, and cosmetics; the National Highway Traffic Safety Administration, which administers safety requirements for automobiles and related products; and the Consumer Product Safety Commission, which sets standards for many household products.

Despite the efforts to promote consumer safety, product-related accidents do occur. In such cases, many countries have systems through which consumers can receive compensation for injury or loss.

The right to information. Most people agree that consumers have a right to thorough and truthful information about the goods or services they buy. Consumers rely on information they receive through advertisements, product packaging and displays, sales presentations, Web sites, and other means.

Advertising messages. Government agencies in many countries seek to eliminate false advertising and other deceptive sales practices. In the United States, for instance, the Federal Trade Commission (FTC) monitors the truthfulness of claims made in advertisements. If a claim cannot be verified, the FTC may order the business to stop using the advertisement. In some cases, the FTC may order the business to present accurate information through *corrective advertising.*

Some nongovernment organizations also work to regulate advertising and sales practices. Advertising Standards Canada, for instance, is a regulatory organization operated by the advertising industry in Canada.

Product information. Many countries have laws that protect the consumer's access to truthful and thorough product information. In the United States, for instance, the Fair Packaging and Labeling Act of 1966 requires that the package used for a product provide certain information. This information includes the identity of the product, the manufacturer's name and address, and the net quantity of the contents.

The consumer's right to information is most widely recognized in the area of food products. Laws in many countries require food producers to provide certain information on the labels of their products. This information usually includes the name of the product and of its manufacturer, packer, or distributor; the amount of food in the package or container; a complete list of ingredients; and the name of any chemical substance added. Some countries may require additional information, such as recommended storage temperatures for frozen foods.

Many food stores use *unit pricing,* which indicates a product's price per ounce or per gram. This system helps consumers determine the best buy among several products in packages of different sizes. Food manufacturers also inform consumers by *freshness labeling,* also called *open dating.* A package is stamped with a date, which is the last day the product should be sold or used.

Consumers can also receive information from consumer organizations, such as Consumers Union in the United States; Which? in the United Kingdom; and the Australian Consumers Association. Such organizations test a wide variety of products and publish reports in magazines, newsletters, and online publications. Some groups also encourage the development of consumer education programs. Such programs emphasize the rights of consumers and provide information about managing money and making wise purchases.

The right to choose. Consumers benefit from the ability to choose from among a variety of products. To protect this ability, the consumer movement has long sought to promote free and fair competition among businesses.

The consumer's right to choose can be threatened by *mergers, collusion,* and *exclusionary practices.* A merger is the joining of multiple business firms into one company. Although some mergers have beneficial effects for consumers, others interfere with competition and reduce consumer choice. Collusion involves coordinated strategies among businesses to take advantage of consumers. *Price fixing* arrangements—in which businesses agree on a non-competitive price they will charge for products—are a common form of collusion. Exclusionary practices are actions through which one business seeks to drive out or keep out its competitors.

Many countries have antitrust laws and specialized government agencies that work to protect competition. In the United States, for instance, the Sherman Antitrust Act of 1890 forbids monopolies, price fixing, and other noncompetitive practices. Canada's main antitrust law is the Competition Act.

The right to be heard. Consumer groups, governments, and businesses have established a variety of ways in which consumers can make their voices heard. Some countries have public officials who represent consumers and assist in the development of government policies. In the United Kingdom, for instance, the National Consumer Council seeks to ensure that the interests of consumers are brought to the attention of policymakers. Many businesses have special consumer affairs offices that receive input from consumers. Better business bureaus in many communities also bring attention to consumer issues. The bureaus may offer mediation or arbitration services to settle consumer disputes.

The right to be heard also involves the ability of consumers to bring their concerns before the courts and receive fair compensation for any loss or injury. In many countries, consumers can sue by means of a *product liability suit* or a *malpractice suit.* A product liability suit is brought against a manufacturer or seller for damage or injury that is caused by a product. A malpractice suit is filed against an individual or a company in a service field, such as medicine or dentistry. In some cases, a large number of consumers can combine their claims and file a *class action* suit. Many countries have small-claims courts that handle minor consumer complaints quickly and inexpensively.

Other consumer rights. Many consumer advocates identify additional consumer rights. Such rights may include the right to satisfaction of basic needs and the right to a healthy environment. Some consumer groups have pressed for rights in particular areas of activity, such as patients' rights and travelers' rights.

History of consumer protection

Most early buyer-seller relations functioned under the principle of *caveat emptor,* a Latin phrase meaning *let the buyer beware.* People who purchased goods from shopkeepers or craftworkers were responsible for detecting faulty merchandise. Some early efforts to protect consumers emerged around the A.D. 1000's, as European craft *guilds* (associations) established standards for products created by their members. Other forms of consumer protection included laws against *usury,* the lending of money at an excessive rate of interest.

Beginnings of modern consumerism. During the late 1800's and early 1900's, the sale of many impure and unsafe products led to increased consumer interest in standards of quality. In the United States, a number of writers called *muckrakers* exposed abuses by various companies. For example, the novelist Upton Sinclair wrote *The Jungle* (1906), which described filthy conditions in the meat-packing industry. This book helped lead to the federal Food and Drugs Act of 1906.

The growth of large corporations and monopolies also contributed to an increased interest in consumer protection. These giant business companies lacked competition from other firms, and so they controlled the supply of products and charged high prices. They also marketed many low-quality products. In the late 1800's, the U.S. Congress passed the first antitrust and antimonopoly laws to protect consumers from these powerful companies. A number of other countries have also developed antitrust laws.

During the late 1800's and early 1900's, many businesses began hiring advertising agencies to carry out large-scale campaigns to promote their products. The consumer movement, in turn, increasingly emphasized the customer's need for truthful and adequate information. Consumer organizations began testing and rating products for the benefit of consumers. The first such national organization in the United States was Consumers' Research, Inc., incorporated in 1929. A group of employees from that organization formed Consumers Union in 1936.

Growth of the movement. In 1962, U.S. President John F. Kennedy proposed the idea of a consumers' bill of rights. In the following years, Congress passed consumer protection laws in a wide range of areas, including the safety of drugs and terms of product warranties.

The consumer movement gained additional attention as a result of efforts by various writers and activists of the 1950's and 1960's. The American writer Vance Packard, in *The Hidden Persuaders* (1957) and *The Waste-makers* (1960), discussed business techniques designed to increase people's desire for products. Ralph Nader, an American consumer activist, argued in *Unsafe at Any Speed* (1965) that many automobiles were unsafe. His book led to the establishment of new safety standards for motor vehicles. Nader and his group of investigators, sometimes called Nader's Raiders, also raised awareness of safety issues involving other consumer products.

During the 1970's, a period of *inflation* (rising prices), consumers became increasingly concerned with the cost and quality of products. Consumer boycotts of beef, coffee, and sugar succeeded in temporarily lowering the prices of those products in the mid-1970's. During the 1980's, increased concern for health led consumers to demand more nutrition information on food labels. In the 1990's and early 2000's, the consumer movement addressed a number of new issues. Such issues included the health risks of genetically modified foods and the financial risks of Internet fraud.

Consumer protection today. Consumer organizations today play a larger role than ever before. Various groups work to educate consumers, influence government policies, and bring lawsuits on behalf of consumers. Such efforts have had major effects on business and industry. Most companies today recognize that long-term success depends heavily on the safety and satisfaction of consumers.   Robert N. Mayer

Additional resources

The American Bar Association Guide to Consumer Law. Times Bks., 1997.
Consumer Sourcebook. Gale Research, published annually.
Miller, Fred H., and Lackey, J. D. *The ABCs of the UCC: Related and Supplementary Consumer Law.* 2nd ed. Am. Bar Assn., 2004.
Vukowich, William T. *Consumer Protection in the 21st Century: A Global Perspective.* Transnational Pub., 2002.

The Adoration of the Shepherds (1510), an oil painting on panel by Giorgione; National Gallery of Art, Washington, D.C. (© SuperStock)

The birth of Jesus is called the Nativity. According to Christian tradition, Jesus was born in a stable in Bethlehem. The version of the Nativity shown here portrays the baby Jesus lying near the mouth of a cave, attended by his parents, Joseph and Mary, and two shepherds.

Jesus Christ

Jesus Christ was one of the world's most important religious leaders. The Christian religion was founded on his life and teachings. Most Christians believe that Jesus is the son of God who was sent to earth to save humanity. Even many people who are not Christians view him as a great and wise teacher. Jesus was certainly one of the most influential people who ever lived.

The personal name of Jesus Christ was Jesus. The term *Christ* is a title that was so closely associated with Jesus that it became part of his name. It comes from the Greek word *christos*. The word is a translation of the Hebrew word *messiah* (anointed one). The Messiah was the savior God promised to send to the people of Israel. The name "Jesus Christ" means "Jesus the Messiah."

Christians make up the largest religious group in the world. The Qur'ān, the sacred scripture of Islam, presents Jesus as a great prophet. Some Jewish scholars see Jesus as a notable representative of the Judaism of his day.

Sources of information about Jesus

The New Testament Gospels. Among the earliest sources of information about Jesus are four books of the New Testament, the Gospels of Matthew, Mark, Luke, and John. The word *gospel* means *good news*. Christian tradition attributes the Gospels of Matthew and John to men who followed Jesus during his lifetime. The other two Gospels are attributed to men who became followers of Jesus after his death. Today, most scholars doubt that any of the Gospel writers knew Jesus during his lifetime. They also doubt that we know the actual names of the writers. However, most scholars think these Gospels were written between A.D. 70 and 110, about 40 to 80 years after the death of Jesus.

The Gospels of Matthew and Luke begin by describing the birth and early life of Jesus. All four of the New Testament Gospels describe the public life of Jesus in some detail, ending with his final sufferings, called his

Passion; his death; and his Resurrection. The author of the Gospel of Luke added a second volume to his story of Jesus, called the Acts of the Apostles. The Acts of the Apostles tells the story of the early Christian church up to about A.D. 62.

Other gospels. Other early Christian writings about Jesus's life and teachings, also called *gospels,* are not included in the New Testament. The most important of these writings is the Gospel of Thomas, a collection of 114 sayings of Jesus. It is written in the Coptic language and was discovered at Nag Hammadi, Egypt, in 1945. Another is the Gospel of Peter. The portion of this gospel that describes Jesus's death and Resurrection was discovered in Egypt in 1886. The Infancy Gospel of James describes the birth of Jesus, and the Infancy Gospel of Thomas describes his childhood.

Fragments of other gospels survive in quotations by writers known as the Church Fathers. These are the Gospels of the Nazarenes, Ebionites, and Hebrews. There are also fragments of a Secret Gospel of Mark in a letter of the Church Father Clement of Alexandria that was discovered in 1958.

Scholars dispute the value of the information in these non-Biblical gospels. Many experts think these writings depend on the New Testament and do not provide additional reliable information. Others think they are reliable. The dates of these writings are also disputed.

Other writings. Other New Testament writings, especially the *epistles* (letters) of Paul, include some information about Jesus and tell us about the early followers of Jesus after his death. The epistles were written from about A.D. 50 to 62, making them the earliest writings about Jesus that we possess.

Many other Christian writings provide information about Jesus that some scholars consider valuable. Non-Christian references to Jesus and the times in which he lived are found in the writings of the Jewish historian Flavius Josephus, who wrote about A.D. 90, and the Roman historian Cornelius Tacitus, who wrote about A.D. 115.

The historical Jesus

The attempt to discover the historical facts about Jesus in a disciplined way began about 1780. Since then, the effort has been revived several times, most recently in the last half of the 1900's. The attempt has not entirely succeeded for several reasons.

First, the sources of information about Jesus are not primarily intended to provide historical facts. These sources are expressions of faith in Jesus Christ. They contain factual information, but as part of an attempt to persuade people to believe in Jesus, not simply to communicate facts. Thus, it is difficult to separate the factual information from the religious and other aspects of these writings.

Second, scholars differ about the relative value of the available sources. There is general agreement that the Gospels of Matthew, Mark, and Luke are among the best sources of historical information about Jesus. However, many scholars do not consider the Gospel of John an equally good source.

There is even more disagreement about sources not included in the New Testament. Some scholars think the Gospel of Thomas is a valuable source. Others do not. Reconstructions of the historical Jesus differ when they are based on different sources.

Third, sources of information differ in what they tell us about Jesus. Some information is found only in one source, or in a few sources but not in all of them. The sources also differ in the arrangement of information. Often the order of events in one source is not the same as in others. The sources also differ in their general presentation of Jesus. All these disagreements make it difficult to identify the facts about Jesus.

Fourth, scholars disagree about what aspects of the world in which Jesus lived are the most important for understanding him. Most experts agree that Jesus needs to be understood as part of the Judaism of his time. Some argue that Jesus should be seen as a member of the Cynic school, an ancient Greek school of philosophy that valued virtue over pleasure. Others claim that Jesus was primarily a social and political activist.

The following description of the life of Jesus Christ is not a rigorous critical reconstruction of the historical Jesus. Instead, it compiles the information provided by the available sources, particularly the New Testament Gospels.

Early life

The Nativity is a term often used to mean the birth of Jesus. According to the New Testament Gospels of Matthew and Luke, Jesus was born during the lifetime of Herod the Great, who ruled Palestine. Herod died in 4 B.C., so Jesus must have been born in that year at the latest. Nobody knows what time of year Jesus was born. The day of his birth was first celebrated on December 25 in the early 300's.

The New Testament Gospels of Matthew and Luke and the Infancy Gospel of James tell of the people, places, and events connected with the birth of Jesus. All three documents record that he was born in the town of Bethlehem, in the territory of Judea. His mother was the Virgin Mary. Mary's husband was Joseph. Matthew and Luke also record that Jesus was raised in Nazareth, a town in the region of Galilee. In other details, the three accounts differ greatly.

According to Matthew, Mary and Joseph lived in Bethlehem. When Joseph discovered that Mary was pregnant, an angel appeared to him in a dream. The angel told him that the child was of the Holy Spirit. *Magi* (wise men) traveled from the east to see the newborn Messiah. The magi first asked for Jesus in Herod's court in Jerusalem. Then they followed the light of a star to Bethlehem. They found Jesus and gave him gifts of gold, frankincense, and myrrh. They had been warned not to return to Herod, so they took a different route home.

Herod became angry. He ordered the deaths of all baby boys in Bethlehem 2 years old or younger. An angel had appeared to Joseph in another dream and warned him about Herod's decree. Joseph fled with Mary and Jesus to Egypt. After Herod died, they returned and settled in Nazareth. Stories describing the first appearance of the angel to Joseph, the visit of the magi, and Herod's killing of the boys also appear in the Infancy Gospel of James.

According to Luke, Mary and Joseph originally lived

Christ Disputing with the Elders (about 1305), a fresco by Giotto in the Scrovegni, or Arena, Chapel, Padua, Italy (© SuperStock)

Jesus's childhood was probably spent in Nazareth. At the age of 12, he went to Jerusalem with Joseph and Mary to celebrate the feast of Passover. There he met with scholars in the Temple, *shown here*, and amazed them with his knowledge of religion.

in Nazareth. The angel Gabriel visited Mary and announced that her child would be the Son of God and the Messiah that was promised in the Hebrew Bible. This visit is known as the *Annunciation*. Some time before Jesus was born, Mary and Joseph went to Bethlehem to record their names in a census. They found shelter in a stable. Jesus was born there, and Mary made a cradle for him in a manger. Shepherds near Bethlehem saw angels in the sky. After Mary and Joseph had done everything commanded by Jewish law, they returned with Jesus to Nazareth. The Infancy Gospel of James also includes the stories of the Annunciation and the census.

Childhood. There is only one story in the New Testament about Jesus's childhood. Luke says that when Jesus was 12 years old, he went with Mary and Joseph to Jerusalem for the feast of Passover. He sat among the scholars in the Temple and amazed them with his wisdom. Luke ends this story by saying that "Jesus increased in wisdom and in years, and in divine and human favor" (Luke 2:52). Jesus grew up in Nazareth and probably helped Joseph in his carpentry work. Both of them may have worked in the nearby town of Sepphoris.

The Infancy Gospel of Thomas tells a number of stories about Jesus between the ages of 5 and 12. Most involve miracles worked by Jesus. The last of these stories is the one from the Gospel of Luke summarized above. Few scholars think the stories unique to the Infancy Gospel of Thomas are likely to be historical.

Public life

Baptism. All four New Testament Gospels agree that Jesus's public life began after the appearance of John

the Baptist in Judea. John preached repentance and baptized those who accepted his message with water from the Jordan River. The Gospels of Matthew and Mark describe John's baptism of Jesus, as do fragments of the Gospels of the Ebionites and Hebrews. The Gospel of Luke refers to Jesus's baptism without describing it, and the Gospel of John seems to imply it. According to Luke, Jesus was baptized when he was about 30 years old.

Ministry. The mission of Jesus was to announce that the Kingdom of God was coming, and that it had begun to arrive even as he announced it. He accomplished his mission both by words and by actions, through his miracles and his teaching. By the Kingdom of God, Jesus meant a new state of affairs on earth, which God would bring about. God would intervene in human history to eliminate every kind of evil. As a result, human beings would live in peace and justice forever.

After Jesus's Baptism, he went to Galilee to begin to spread his message. According to Matthew, Mark, and Luke, Jesus carried out the first part of his ministry in Galilee and the area around it. He chose Capernaum, near the Sea of Galilee (Lake Gennesaret) as his headquarters. At the end of his ministry in Galilee, he went to Jerusalem, where he was arrested, tried, and crucified. According to John, however, Jesus traveled be-

The Baptism of Christ (about 1450), an oil and tempera painting on wood by Piero della Francesca; the National Gallery, London

Jesus was baptized by John the Baptist with water from the Jordan River. In this painting, the three angels at the left watch the baptism while the Holy Spirit, in the form of a dove, appears above Jesus's head. A man behind John prepares to be baptized.

tween Galilee and Judea several times during his ministry.

Followers. In the course of his ministry, Jesus attracted large crowds who came to see and hear him wherever he went. Jesus also called some people to be his *disciples* (students) and to follow him as he traveled. From his disciples, Jesus chose a special group of 12 to assist him. They symbolized the reassembly of the 12 tribes of Israel at the end of time. Later, the 12 were referred to as the *apostles* (messengers). *Apostle* was also the name for a larger group of people who carried on the mission of Jesus after his death. The best-known member of this group was the apostle Paul.

The miracles. The New Testament Gospels describe many miracles that Jesus performed. In each miracle, the Kingdom of God entered into human life in a small way. The miracles brought relief from many kinds of sickness and suffering. This relief showed the meaning of the Kingdom of God.

Jesus worked four kinds of miracles: (1) *exorcisms* (casting out demons), (2) healings, (3) raising the dead, and (4) what are often called *nature* miracles. An exorcism story in the Gospels of Matthew, Mark, and Luke tells how Jesus cast an unclean spirit out of a boy with a condition resembling epilepsy. Jesus's healing miracles were responses to physical ailments, such as paralysis, blindness, and leprosy. The Gospels of Matthew, Mark, and Luke describe how Jesus healed a paralyzed man.

The New Testament Gospels include three distinct stories about Jesus's restoring a dead person to life. One of them, found in Matthew, Mark, and Luke, tells

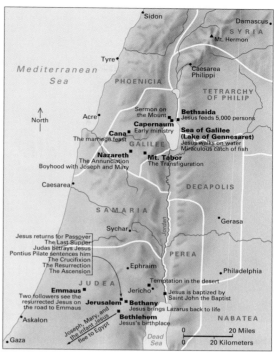

A map of ancient Palestine shows the most significant sites in Jesus's life as accepted by Christian tradition. Jesus's life centered in the regions of Judea in the south and Galilee in the north.

Jesus Heals a Blind Man (A.D. 200's), a marble relief sculpture; Roman National Museum, Terme di Diocleziano, Rome, Italy (© Erich Lessing, Art Resource)

Jesus restored a blind man's sight, one of several miracles performed by Jesus that are described in the Gospels. This carving from the A.D. 200's decorating a Christian funeral casket is one of the earliest representations of Jesus in art.

how Jesus raised from the dead the 12-year-old daughter of a synagogue leader named Jairus. Jesus's nature miracles are stories about his extraordinary power over the natural world. One nature miracle is found in all four New Testament Gospels. Jesus divided five loaves of bread and two fishes among 5,000 people so that everyone would have food.

His teaching. In addition to proclaiming the Kingdom of God by his miracles, Jesus also proclaimed it by his teaching. Jesus often used *parables* to explain the Kingdom of God. Jesus's parables are brief stories that teach lessons. Parables are widely considered to be a characteristic form of teaching used by the historical Jesus.

One parable found in the Gospels of Matthew, Mark, and Luke as well as the Gospel of Thomas is the parable of "the Mustard Seed." Jesus compared the Kingdom of God to a mustard seed. It is the smallest of all seeds but grows into a large plant in which birds can nest. The same four Gospels also include the parable of "the Sower." A farmer sowed seed that fell on different kinds of ground. Much of the seed was lost, but the seed that fell on good soil produced abundantly.

One of Jesus's best-known parables, "the Prodigal Son," is in Luke 15:11-32. It describes a father's joy at the return of his wayward son. Jesus used this story to teach God's love and forgiveness for sinners who repent.

Not all of Jesus's teaching was in parables. One of the

The Last Supper was the final meal that Jesus shared with his 12 apostles. This famous painting by the Italian Renaissance artist Leonardo da Vinci shows Jesus, seated in the center, just after he had told the apostles that one of them would betray him.

most striking examples of another kind of teaching is the Sermon on the Mount, found in Matthew 5-7. In this sermon, Jesus challenged his disciples not to fight back if they were attacked. He commanded, " If anyone strikes you on the right cheek, turn to him the other also" (Matthew 5:39). Jesus also encouraged his followers to trust that God would care for them as God cares for the birds of the air and the flowers of the field. He taught people to love God and their neighbors. Jesus stressed that each person should treat others as he or she wished to be treated. This principle is often called the *golden rule.* The Sermon on the Mount contains sayings called the *Beatitudes,* which describe certain virtues, as well as the Lord's Prayer, the most widely used Christian prayer.

The Passion

The *Passion* is a term used to indicate Jesus's suffering during the final days of his life. Christians remember these final days during Holy Week. Detailed information about the end of Jesus's life is found in the four New Testament Gospels and in the Gospel of Peter.

Jesus's proclamation of the Kingdom of God was good news for his followers. But some, especially the leaders of the Jewish community, disliked his teaching. They believed that Jesus had changed some accepted religious practices, such as the Sabbath laws. Most of all, the leaders feared that his popularity would encourage a rebellion against the Roman Empire, which would cause the Romans to destroy the Jewish nation.

Jesus probably knew that it was dangerous to carry out his ministry. But he considered his ministry to be his duty. He was determined to preach the good news of the Kingdom of God. Jesus felt that he had come to save other people by giving his own life.

Entry into Jerusalem. Jesus arrived in Jerusalem for the week of the Jewish festival of Passover. He made a triumphal entry into the city. People cheered him and covered his path with clothing and the branches of palm trees. They were grateful for his teaching and healing. Many of them believed that he would bring a better life to the Jewish nation. Jesus went into the Temple and drove out the men who were changing money and selling doves. He taught that the house of God must be for prayer, not for making money. During the next few days, Jesus spent part of his time teaching in Jerusalem. The rest of the time he spent in the nearby town of Bethany.

The Last Supper. Jesus had a final meal with his disciples in Jerusalem. This meal is often called the Last Supper. During the meal, Jesus told his disciples that one of them would betray him. According to Matthew, Mark, and Luke, the supper was the Passover meal. As Jesus gave his disciples bread, he said "This is my body." As he gave them wine, he said "This is my blood." The apostle Paul also says that on the night before he died, Jesus gave his disciples bread and wine as his body and blood (1 Corinthians 11:23-25). The ceremony of Communion is based on the Last Supper.

The trial. After the meal, Jesus and his disciples went to Gethsemane, a garden on the slope of the Mount of Olives, opposite the Temple. According to Matthew, Mark, and Luke, Jesus prayed there in agony, knowing what was about to happen to him, but he submitted himself to God's will. A band of armed men came to the garden to arrest Jesus. Judas Iscariot, one

Jesus was arrested by Roman soldiers in Gethsemane, a garden east of Jerusalem. This painting shows Jesus praying in the garden. His followers Peter, James, and John are shown sleeping in the foreground. In the background, Jesus's betrayer, Judas Iscariot, leads the soldiers to the garden.

The Agony in the Garden (about 1460), a tempera painting by Andrea Mantegna; National Gallery, London

Christ Before Pilate (1311), tempera on wood panel from *The Maestà* by Duccio di Buoninsegna; Cathedral of Siena, Italy (© Erich Lessing, Art Resource)

The trial of Jesus took place before Pontius Pilate, the Roman governor of Judea. Jewish leaders said that Jesus claimed to be king of the Jews and charged him with treason against Rome.

Christ on the Road to Calvary (about 1340), a tempera painting on wood
by Simone Martini; the Louvre, Paris (Cliché Musées Nationaux)

Jesus carried a cross to the place of his Crucifixion. The site
was a hill called Golgotha, or Calvary, located outside Jerusalem.
Many people mocked Jesus along the route to the hill.

Le Coup de Lance (1620), an oil painting on wood by Peter Paul Rubens;
Koninklijk Museum voor Schone Kunsten, Antwerp, Belgium

Jesus was crucified on a cross erected between the crosses of
two condemned thieves. This dramatic painting shows a Roman
soldier on horseback piercing Jesus's side with a lance.

of the 12, pointed him out to them. Thus, Judas was the
one who betrayed Jesus. The Gospel of Matthew says
that Judas later hanged himself.

The armed men took Jesus to the high priest's house.
There the leaders of the people questioned him. According to Matthew, Mark, and Luke, they asked him if
he was the Messiah. When he did not deny it, they said
that he had *blasphemed* (insulted God's name).

The Jewish leaders took Jesus before Pontius Pilate,
the Roman governor of Judea. They said that Jesus
claimed to be king of the Jews and charged him with
treason against Rome. According to Luke, Pilate found
out that Jesus was a Galilean and sent him to Herod An-
tipas, the ruler of Galilee. Herod mocked Jesus and sent
him back to Pilate.

It was the custom of the Roman governor to release
one Jewish prisoner at the Passover season. Pilate took
Jesus and a condemned prisoner named Barabbas onto
the steps of his headquarters and told the crowd to
choose which one should go free. The crowd turned
against Jesus and chose Barabbas. Pilate then sentenced
Jesus to die on the cross. Crucifixion was a common Roman form of execution.

The Crucifixion. According to the New Testament
Gospels of Matthew, Mark, and John and the Gospel of
Peter, the Roman soldiers mocked Jesus for claiming to

be king of the Jews. They dressed him in a robe and
placed a crown of thorns on his head. Some of the men
struck him. The Gospel of John says that Jesus carried
his own cross to the place of the Crucifixion. According
to the other New Testament Gospels, the soldiers made
a man named Simon of Cyrene carry the cross. The soldiers nailed Jesus to the cross outside the city, on a hill
called Golgotha (Calvary). On the cross, they wrote the
charge against Jesus, "The King of the Jews." They set up
his cross between the crosses of two thieves.

According to Luke, Jesus said as he hung on the
cross, "Father, forgive them; for they know not what
they do" (Luke 23:34) and later, "Father, into your hands I
commit my spirit" (Luke 23:46). According to both
Matthew and Mark, he cried out "My God, My God,
why have you forsaken me?" (Matthew 27:46; Mark
15:34). After Jesus died, a disciple named Joseph of Ari-
mathea took his body to a new tomb and sealed that
tomb with a stone.

The Resurrection. Christians believe Jesus returned
to life, an event they call his Resurrection, and celebrate
it on Easter Sunday. The New Testament Gospels and
the Gospel of Peter tell how Mary Magdalene went to
Jesus's tomb on Sunday morning. She found the stone
rolled away and the tomb empty.

The New Testament Gospels record various appearances of Jesus after the discovery of the empty tomb. He
appeared to Mary Magdalene (Matthew, Mark, and

Illuminated manuscript (early 1400's) by the Limbourg brothers from the Duc de Berry's *Très Riches Heures*; Musée Condé, Chantilly, France (Giraudon/Art Resource)

The Resurrection of Jesus, as related in the Gospels, occurred on the third day after his Crucifixion. In this picture, Jesus greets an angel standing on his tomb, while a group of Roman guards collapses on the ground around the tomb in fear and awe.

John), to Simon Peter, and to two disciples who saw Jesus on the road to Emmaus (Luke). He also appeared to the faithful disciples who met Jesus in Jerusalem (Luke, John) and in Galilee (Matthew, John). The apostle Paul listed many appearances of Jesus after his Resurrection, ending with Jesus's appearance to Paul himself (1 Corinthians 15:4-8).

According to the Acts of the Apostles, Jesus stayed on earth during the next 40 days and taught his disciples. Then he rose into heaven. This rising into heaven is called the *Ascension.*

The early Christians

Jesus's Resurrection convinced his disciples that he was not only the one who announced the coming of the Kingdom of God, but also was the Messiah, who would bring the Kingdom into being. They believed that through his death and Resurrection, Jesus had begun to free humanity from all suffering and evil. The disciples also believed that he would soon come again to complete the work he had begun.

Within a relatively short time, the disciples converted thousands of people to the new faith. The missionary activity of the apostle Paul helped to spread Christianity throughout the eastern Mediterranean area within 30 years after Jesus's death. The spread of Christianity confronted the early Christians with the question of how Gentiles should be incorporated into the Christian church. Jesus himself had not clearly answered this question, probably because he interacted mainly with other Jews. When the early Christians converted Gentiles in large numbers, it became necessary to decide whether they needed to keep the Jewish law. The early

Christians first disagreed about the answer. Finally, they decided that Gentiles could be members of the Christian church without keeping the Jewish law.

The early Christians also tried to understand Jesus more fully. They came to see that he was not only the Messiah, but also the son of God in a special sense not shared by anyone else. Eventually, they explained Jesus's relationship to God by means of the doctrine of the Trinity. This doctrine states that in one God there are three divine persons—the Father, the Son, and the Holy Spirit. According to this doctrine, Jesus, the Father, and the Holy Spirit are three persons who have one divine nature. Thus, the doctrine of the Trinity explained why Jesus had absolute authority for his teachings and absolute power to forgive sins and give eternal life.

During the A.D. 100's and 200's, the Christians suffered intermittent persecution by the Roman authorities, but the faith continued to spread. Finally, in 313, the Emperor Constantine the Great gave Christians freedom of worship by his Edict of Milan.   Terrance D. Callan

Outline

I. Sources of information about Jesus
   A. The New Testament Gospels
   B. Other gospels
   C. Other writings
II. The historical Jesus
III. Early life
   A. The Nativity
   B. Childhood
IV. Public life
   A. Baptism
   B. Ministry
   C. Followers
   D. The miracles
   E. His teaching
V. The Passion
   A. Entry into Jerusalem
   B. The Last Supper
   C. The trial
   D. The Crucifixion
   E. The Resurrection
VI. The early Christians

Questions

What does the name *Jesus Christ* mean?
Which books of the Bible tell about the life of Jesus?
Who baptized Jesus?
In what town was Jesus born? Where did he die?
What was the Nativity? the Passion?
What were two miracles that Jesus performed?
What did Jesus tell his apostles at the Last Supper?
Where was Jesus arrested?
Who was Pontius Pilate? Judas Iscariot?
Why was the Resurrection of Jesus important to his early followers?

Additional resources

Level I
Harik, Ramsay M. *Jesus of Nazareth.* Watts, 2001.
Lottridge, Celia B. *Stories from the Life of Jesus.* Groundwood Bks., 2004.
Mayer, Marianna. *Seeing Jesus in His Own Words.* Phyllis Fogelman, 2002.

Level II
Elliott, J. K., ed. *The Apocryphal New Testament.* 2nd ed. Oxford, 1993.
Meier, John P. *A Marginal Jew.* Anchor Bible, 1991-. Multivolume work.
Powell, Mark A. *Jesus as a Figure in History.* 1998. Reprint. Westminster John Knox, 2003.

Ruins of ancient civilizations dot the landscape of Latin America. Such peoples as the Olmec, Maya, Toltec, Aztec, and Inca built the region's first cities and empires. This picture shows the remains of Machu Picchu, in Peru. Constructed in the A.D. 1400's, it probably served as an estate for Inca royalty.

© Damm Fridmar, SIME/4Corners Images

Latin America

Latin America is a large region that covers all the territory in the Western Hemisphere south of the United States. It consists of Mexico, Central America, South America, and the islands of the West Indies. The region is divided into 46 political units, including 33 independent countries and 13 dependencies. Brazil is by far the largest country in Latin America, both in area and in population. It occupies more than 40 percent of the region's land area and has about a third of its population.

Before the first Europeans arrived in Latin America in the late 1400's, the region had been inhabited for thousands of years by people now called Amerindians, American Indians, or Native Americans. Such Indian groups as the Aztec, Inca, and Maya had developed the first advanced civilizations in Latin America and established the first cities and empires there.

The contributors of this article are Brian P. Owensby, Associate Professor of History at the University of Virginia, and Mary Weismantel, Professor of Anthropology at Northwestern University.

During the 1500's and 1600's, Europeans conquered most of the Indians and established colonies. Soon after the Europeans arrived, they began to bring in black Africans as slaves, especially to the West Indies and some mainland coastal areas. European rule of Latin America lasted about 300 years. The human and environmental costs of colonization were high. European governments took Latin America's natural resources, and European colonizers forced the Amerindians, and later African slaves, to work for them.

Latin America has a rich cultural heritage that blends many influences. Unlike Europe and the United States, Latin America developed from the 1400's as a mixed society of Amerindian, European, and African peoples living side by side. Despite their differences, Latin America's various peoples succeeded in living and working together for hundreds of years. Over the centuries, whites, Indians, and blacks intermarried. In the 1800's and 1900's, Arab, Asian, French, German, Italian, and Jewish immigrants contributed their own cultural traditions to Latin America. Today, most Latin Americans are of mixed ancestry. They are chiefly of Indian and white descent or of black and white descent.

The people of Latin America share many traditions and values that spring from their common colonial heritage. The majority of Latin Americans speak Spanish, Portuguese, or French, each of which developed from Latin. English or Dutch is the official language in several areas that were colonized by England or the Netherlands. Scholars disagree about whether such areas should be considered part of Latin America. This article includes these areas in its discussion of the region (see the table *Independent countries of Latin America*).

The name *Latin America* originated in the mid-1800's, when Europe and the United States were expanding their influence in other parts of the world. It was used to distinguish that part of the Americas originally settled by Europeans who spoke Romance languages, which developed from Latin, from that part of the Americas settled by Anglo-Saxon Europeans, who spoke English. Romance languages include Spanish, Portuguese, and French.

Government in Latin America has changed since the 1800's. During the early 1800's, many Latin American colonies gained their independence and became republics.

These republics endorsed democratic ideals, but, in reality, they tended to re-create the old colonial systems in new forms. The leaders of the new republics lacked the experience necessary to deal with serious social and economic problems. In some Latin American countries, military dictators seized control of the government. Other nations were ruled by a few powerful families who used their positions to increase their personal wealth. During the early and middle 1900's, anti-government protests and violent revolutions occurred throughout Latin America. Civilian and military leaders tried to bring political stability to the region. But in the process, many of these leaders restricted the civil rights of the Latin American people. By the early 2000's, however, most Latin American countries had established democratic governments.

Ways of life in Latin America have also changed. Until the mid-1900's, the majority of Latin Americans lived in rural areas. Today, about 75 percent of the people live in urban areas. The hardships of rural life as well as the hope of expanded job opportunities in urban areas have led millions of rural people to move to the cities. However, many of these people are uneducated and un-

Political units in Latin America

Independent countries				Dependencies			
Map key	Name	Capital	Official language	Map key	Name	Capital	Status
C 5	Antigua and Barbuda	St. John's	English	B 5	Anguilla	The Valley	British overseas territory; some self-government
H 4	Argentina	Buenos Aires	Spanish				
B 4	Bahamas	Nassau	English	C 4	Aruba	Oranjestad	Self-governing part of the Netherlands
C 5	Barbados	Bridgetown	English				
C 3	Belize	Belmopan	English				
F 5	Bolivia	La Paz; Sucre	Spanish; Quechua; Aymara	B 3	Cayman Islands	Georgetown	British overseas territory
				I 5	Falkland Islands	Stanley	British overseas territory
E 6	Brazil	Brasília	Portuguese				
G 4	Chile	Santiago	Spanish	D 6	French Guiana	Cayenne	Overseas department of France
D 4	Colombia	Bogotá	Spanish				
C 3	Costa Rica	San José	Spanish				
B 3	Cuba	Havana	Spanish	C 5	Guadeloupe	Basse-Terre	Overseas department of France
C 5	Dominica	Roseau	English				
C 4	Dominican Republic	Santo Domingo	Spanish	C 5	Martinique	Fort-de-France	Overseas department of France
D 3	Ecuador	Quito	Spanish				
C 3	El Salvador	San Salvador	Spanish	C 5	Montserrat	Brades Estate*	British overseas territory
C 5	Grenada	St. George's	English				
C 2	Guatemala	Guatemala City	Spanish	C 4	Netherlands Antilles	Willemstad	Self-governing part of the Netherlands
D 5	Guyana	Georgetown	English				
C 4	Haiti	Port-au-Prince	French				
C 3	Honduras	Tegucigalpa	Spanish				
C 4	Jamaica	Kingston	English	C 5	Puerto Rico	San Juan	United States commonwealth
B 2	Mexico	Mexico City	Spanish				
C 3	Nicaragua	Managua	Spanish	B 4	Turks and Caicos Islands	Grand Turk	British overseas territory
D 3	Panama	Panama City	Spanish				
G 5	Paraguay	Asunción	Spanish				
E 4	Peru	Lima	Spanish; Quechua	C 5	Virgin Islands, British	Road Town	British overseas territory; some self-government
C 5	St. Kitts and Nevis	Basseterre	English				
C 5	St. Lucia	Castries	English	C 5	Virgin Islands, United States	Charlotte Amalie	U.S. organized unincorporated territory
C 5	St. Vincent and the Grenadines	Kingstown	English				
D 6	Suriname	Paramaribo	Dutch				
C 5	Trinidad and Tobago	Port-of-Spain	English				
H 6	Uruguay	Montevideo	Spanish				
D 5	Venezuela	Caracas	Spanish				

Each independent country and each dependency has a separate article in *World Book*.   *Interim capital. Plymouth, the previous capital, was abandoned in 1996 following volcanic eruptions.

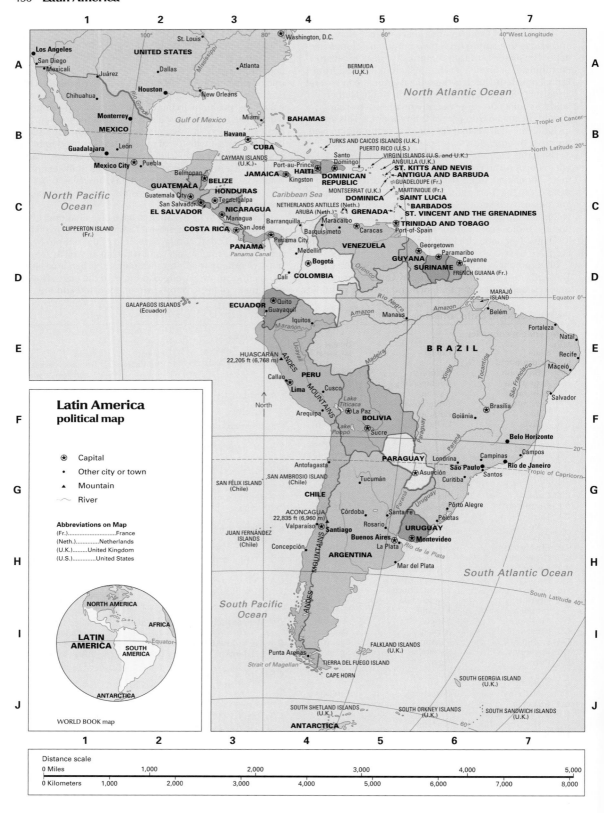

**Latin America
political map**

⊛ Capital

• Other city or town

▲ Mountain

〰 River

Abbreviations on Map
(Fr.)...........................France
(Neth.)..............Netherlands
(U.K.).........United Kingdom
(U.S.).............United States

NORTH AMERICA

AFRICA

LATIN
AMERICA   SOUTH
            AMERICA
Equator

ANTARCTICA

WORLD BOOK map

Distance scale

0 Miles		1,000		2,000		3,000		4,000		5,000
0 Kilometers	1,000	2,000	3,000	4,000	5,000	6,000	7,000	8,000

Family ties play a large role in Latin American culture. Loyalties commonly extend beyond the immediate family to grandparents, aunts and uncles, and cousins. The Mexican family shown here is preparing a meal together.

© Bob Daemmrich, PhotoEdit

skilled, and the jobs they hoped for have not been easy to find. Widespread poverty, overpopulation, and patterns of economic change contribute to political and social unrest.

People

Population. Latin America has a population of about 550 million. Since 1950, the population has more than tripled. Experts estimate that it could reach 800 million by 2050. Because of improvements in health care and a declining death rate, the rate of population growth is rising. Rapid growth has put new pressures on areas undergoing development, especially the Amazon basin.

Latin America's population is distributed unevenly over the land, which covers 8 million square miles (21 million square kilometers). Vast areas of the interior have relatively few people, while many coastal areas are densely populated. Such West Indian islands as Barbados and Puerto Rico are extremely crowded.

In South America, colonial development centered around such coastal cities as Lima, Peru, and São Paulo, Brazil, from which goods could be exported. South America's mountains and jungles served as regions of refuge for American Indians and escaped slaves. Today, highland areas in Guatemala, Mexico, and Peru support large populations, as they did before Europeans arrived.

Since about 1970, many Latin Americans have migrated to Europe and the United States. A large number of Mexican and West Indian families, in particular, have relatives in the United States. *Remittances,* money sent home by family members working abroad, are a major source of income for some people in Latin American countries.

Ancestry. The people of Latin America are predominantly of American Indian, European, African, and mixed ancestry. There are also significant populations of Asian and Arab descent.

American Indians lived in Latin America thousands of years before the first Europeans arrived. The Indians descended from people who migrated to America from Asia. The Europeans conquered most of the Indians and forced them to work in mines or on large farms called *haciendas.* Millions of Indians died of harsh treatment, in warfare, or of diseases brought by the Europeans. In some areas, such as the West Indies, the Indian population almost completely disappeared. To survive, many Indians moved to highland areas or remote forest regions.

Mesoamerica (Mexico and Central America) and the Andes region of South America have the largest American Indian populations. Indians make up a large percentage of the population in Bolivia, Ecuador, Guatemala, Mexico, and Peru. Argentina, Chile, Costa Rica, and El Salvador have smaller Amerindian populations.

Whites. Most white Latin Americans are of European descent. At first, nearly all the region's white settlers came from Spain or Portugal. The Portuguese settled primarily in Brazil. The English, French, and Dutch established colonies in the West Indies. Since the early 1800's, many people from France, Germany, Italy, and the United Kingdom have settled in Latin America. A region called the Southern Cone has the largest European American population. The Southern Cone consists of the southernmost countries of South America, including Argentina, Chile, Uruguay, Paraguay, and southern Brazil.

Blacks. European colonists established plantations in Brazil and the West Indies in the late 1500's and 1600's, creating a great demand for slave labor. From the 1500's to the 1800's, Europeans brought millions of Africans to Latin America and forced them to work as slaves. Today, descendants of African slaves live throughout Latin America. Northern Brazil and the West Indies have large black populations and strong African traditions.

People of mixed ancestry. Through the centuries, many American Indians, whites, and blacks in Latin America have intermarried. As a result, most Latin Americans are of mixed ancestry. The terms *mestizo* and *mulatto* are two of the words most commonly used to describe people of mixed race. *Mestizo* refers to people of mixed European and Indian ancestry or of mixed ancestry in general. *Mulatto* describes individuals of mixed African and European descent. Many other terms exist in various countries and languages to describe people of mixed descent. All of these terms can have a positive, neutral, or negative meaning, depending on the context in which they are used.

Mestizos make up a majority of the population in El Salvador, Honduras, Nicaragua, Colombia, Mexico, Paraguay, and Venezuela. Mulattoes are numerous in Brazil, Panama, and the West Indies.

Other groups. Latin America also has Asian and Middle Eastern populations. Parts of the West Indies and nearby coastal areas, such as Guyana, have large South Asian populations. In South America, Brazil has a large population of Japanese. Middle Easterners, including many Lebanese, live throughout Latin America. People of Jewish ancestry make up another significant population group.

Attitudes toward race. People in Latin America take pride in the region's mixed racial and cultural heritage, but racial and social prejudice are persistent problems. Racial prejudice often takes the form of preferential treatment for light-skinned individuals. People of European descent dominate the highest levels of society in many Latin American countries.

Since the early 1900's, attitudes toward race have changed. American Indian, black, and mestizo peoples have become increasingly vocal in expressing their cultural pride and demanding equal treatment for all groups. Latin American intellectuals began to celebrate their nations' mixed heritage. The upper and middle classes in such countries as Mexico and Peru began to view their countries' roots with pride after archaeologists discovered the remains of ancient civilizations. In 1925, the Mexican author José Vasconcelos discussed the complex racial and cultural makeup of the Latin American in his book *La Raza Cósmica (The Cosmic Race).* In Brazil, where about half the population had African ancestors, intellectuals credited their country's greatness to its mixture of African, Amerindian, and European races and cultures.

Many racial categories are based on social standing. For example, people of the same social class may be

Where the people of Latin America live

The population of Latin America is distributed very unevenly. This map shows that most of the people live near the coasts and in the highland regions of Mexico and the Andes Mountains of western South America. Heavily populated areas are shown in darker colors. The map also shows the location of most of Latin America's largest cities.

Major Urban Centers

● More than 5 million inhabitants

● 2 to 5 million inhabitants

○ 1 to 2 million inhabitants

Persons per mi²	Persons per km²
More than 125	More than 50
50 to 125	20 to 50
25 to 50	10 to 20
2 to 25	1 to 10
Less than 2	Less than 1

viewed as belonging to the same race, even if their ancestry differs. Likewise, individuals of different social classes may be viewed as belonging to different races, even if their ancestry is similar.

Languages. Most Latin Americans speak the language of the European country that colonized their nation. French, Portuguese, and Spanish are the three main European languages spoken in Latin America. Most Latin Americans speak Spanish. Portuguese is the official language of Brazil, and many people in the West Indies speak French. Other languages spoken in the West Indies include English, Dutch, and Creole, which combines elements of African and European languages. There are also small groups of German speakers in Brazil and Japanese speakers in Peru.

Millions of Latin Americans speak *indigenous* (native) languages. The largest indigenous language group are the Maya, who live primarily in Guatemala and southern Mexico. More than 20 distinct Maya languages and dialects exist. Other indigenous languages spoken by large populations are Quechua and Aymara. Quechua is spoken in the northern and central Andes Mountains, while Aymara is a language of the southern Andes. There are hundreds of smaller language groups in Latin America. They include the Zapotec Indians in Mexico, the Guaraní Indians in Paraguay, and the Mapuche Indians of Argentina. Latin Americans speak hundreds of indigenous languages. However, the number has decreased through the years.

Way of life

Ways of life vary widely in Latin America. About 75 percent of the population lives in large cities. Four Latin American cities and their suburbs rank among the largest urban centers in the world. They are Mexico City; São Paulo, Brazil; Rio de Janeiro, Brazil; and Buenos Aires, Argentina. About 25 percent of Latin Americans live in small towns and villages, on farms and plantations, in mining camps, or on the outskirts of archaeological sites and beach resorts where they work.

City life. Large cities in Latin America resemble those in the United States and Canada. Steel and glass skyscrapers rise in busy commercial and financial districts. Tall apartment buildings line broad boulevards. Elegant shops, restaurants, bars, and night clubs attract large numbers of customers. Cars and trucks jam wide expressways at rush hours. Modern bus and subway systems carry millions of people to and from work.

In the old sections of many Latin American cities, Spanish-style buildings stand crowded together along narrow cobblestone streets. The buildings are made of stone or adobe, and many have decorative iron grillwork over the windows.

In general, wealthy city dwellers live outside the city centers in areas that have upscale shopping malls, private clubs, and elegant restaurants. Poor migrants from rural areas have created vast new neighborhoods of improvised housing with few or no city services and high rates of theft and violence. Despite their problems, these immigrant communities brim with cultural, economic, and political vitality.

Since the 1990's, urban violence has risen sharply throughout Latin America. In Honduras and other countries, violence has become a prominent issue in election campaigns. Thousands of residents of Buenos Aires, Argentina, publicly protested rising violence in 2004. Security has become a valuable asset that only the wealthy can afford. In poorer areas, it has become increasingly common for citizens to punish criminals on their own.

Rural life. Until the late 1900's, many Latin Americans lived and worked on small family farms in isolated areas. They often operated these farms with little or no modern equipment or chemical fertilizers. Traditional methods, which depend upon hand tools and animal labor, enabled them to make a living from lands that would be too difficult to cultivate with more modern methods. Since the late 1900's, many small farmers have left rural areas, and rural traditions have faded.

Plantations, which originated in colonial times, continue to be important today. These large estates are found mainly in Brazil and the West Indies, as well as in coastal

© Jeffrey Sylvester, Alpha

Middle-class housing in Latin America consists of modern apartment buildings and comfortable single-family homes. Latin American cities have a growing middle class. The small and large apartment buildings in this picture are in a middle-class neighborhood in La Paz, Bolivia.

areas throughout Latin America. Plantations produce such crops as coffee, flowers, spices, and sugar for export. They are efficient and highly profitable.

Most rural houses in Latin America have one or two rooms. In tropical areas, the houses may have walls of wood or dried mud and sticks, dirt floors, and thatch or tin roofs. In mountain villages, most houses are built of stone or adobe and have red tile roofs. Wealthy landowners have luxurious mansions on their estates. However, many landowners hire managers to run their farms and spend most of their time in cities.

Some rural communities consist of only a few houses. Larger settlements have a church, shops, and government buildings arranged around a public square called a *plaza*. People gather in the plaza for socializing, entertainment, and ceremonies. Many villages also have an open-air market, where people gather to buy or sell food or handmade goods and to exchange news.

Some rural Latin Americans work in the mining and tourism industries. Others work on cattle ranches, catch fish, or raise llamas and other animals. Some Amerindian communities continue to follow precolonial ways of life in such remote areas as Brazil's Amazon rain forest.

Family life is extremely important in Latin America. Strong feelings of loyalty and cooperation bind not only parents and children, but also grandparents, aunts and uncles, and cousins. Such feelings may extend to people of the same ethnicity, language group, geographical region, or social class.

Family dynamics vary among different groups. For example, Roman Catholic and Protestant families tend to place authority in the male head of the household. Among many indigenous groups, such as the Aymara, Maya, and Quechua Indians, the idea that men and women should balance each other results in a more equal distribution of authority within the family.

Traditionally, in areas of Latin America with a strong European influence, only men were expected to work outside the home. Women stayed at home to care for their families. Since the mid-1900's, however, attitudes have changed, and increasing educational and career opportunities have become available to women. As a result, a growing number of women, particularly in urban areas, now work outside the home as wage laborers or professionals. Some take an active role in politics, and several women have held high government posts in Latin American countries. These women include Violeta Barrios de Chamorro, elected president of Nicaragua in 1990; Mireya Moscoso, who became Panama's first woman president in 1999; and Michelle Bachelet, elected president of Chile in 2006.

Most Latin American societies place great importance upon motherhood. Mothers provide emotional support for their families. They often handle the family finances. It is also common for adults to retain strong ties to both of their parents long after they have formed their own families. In many cases, allegiance to parents and siblings is stronger than allegiance to a spouse.

Ideas about marriage also vary in Latin America. Among wealthy families and in rural areas, marriage is considered an important social institution. But in poor urban areas, many women choose not to marry or have marriages of short duration. Since the late 1900's, gay rights movements have brought attention to individuals who choose not to marry because of their sexual orientation. However, these movements are fairly small and quite controversial in Latin American society.

Clothing styles in Latin America vary from region to region, depending on climate and custom. Many city people and young people wear clothing like that worn in the United States and Canada. International brands of clothing are widely available. However, many villagers prefer traditional styles or a combination of modern and traditional styles. On holidays and other special occasions, many Latin Americans wear traditional costumes, which commonly feature bright colors and bold patterns.

Rural Latin Americans who live in tropical climates prefer lightweight cotton clothing. Men usually wear loose-fitting shirts. The lightweight *guayabera* shirt, also known as the "Mexican wedding shirt," is especially popular in Cuba and Mexico. Popularized in the 1800's, it

© David Mangurian

Sprawling slums surround many large Latin American cities. Such areas have grown as millions of poor rural people have moved to the cities to seek a better life. This picture shows many poor families living crowded together in crude wooden shacks in a slum in São Paulo, Brazil.

has four front pockets, panels of vertical pleating and embroidery, and a straight hem. Most women dress in long skirts and blouses. People in mountain villages need heavier clothing for protection against the cold. Both men and women wear *ponchos* (blankets with a slit in the middle for the head). Women also dress in full skirts and long-sleeved blouses. They commonly drape brightly colored shawls around their shoulders. In the highlands, men wear coarse handwoven shirts and baggy pants. Farmers wear straw or felt hats for protection against the sun while working in the fields. Rural people generally go barefoot or wear sandals, many of which have soles made from old automobile tires.

Some parts of Latin America have distinctive clothing styles. For example, Indian women in the highlands of Bolivia wear felt derby hats. The *gauchos* (cowboys) of Argentina and Uruguay dress in ponchos, baggy trousers tucked into low boots, and wide-brimmed hats. Both of these styles originated in Europe, as did styles in other parts of Latin America. For example, the multilayered skirts and fringed shawls worn by women in parts of Ecuador originated in Spain. Traditional clothing styles in Brazil and other parts of Latin America came from west Africa.

Many Indian groups wear brightly colored clothing with traditional patterns. Each village has its own special colors and designs, which have been used for hundreds of years. Many Indian women and men wear woven sashes around their waists. They often use the sashes as headbands to hold bundles that they carry on their heads. Since the late 1900's, Amerindian pride and political movements for Amerindian rights have made traditional clothing styles more popular.

Food and drink. Prior to European colonization, Latin Americans had three main types of diets. In a large region centered around Mexico, the people ate mainly beans, *maize* (corn), and squash. In highland areas of South America, potatoes and other root vegetables, a high-protein grain called *quinoa,* and meat from such animals as llamas and guinea pigs were the main foods. Maize was also important in this region. People in lowland jungle areas ate a great deal of yucca, which they supplemented with wild and cultivated fruits and vegetables, as well as meat.

When European colonists met the Amerindians, an exchange of foods began. Europeans and their African slaves became accustomed to such local foods as chili peppers, maize, and tomatoes. The Europeans imported bananas and other tropical foods from Africa to Latin America and exported maize, peanuts, and yucca to Europe. The Europeans also brought rice and sugar cane, two plants from Asia, to Latin America. Today, people worldwide enjoy foods that originated in Latin America, including chocolate, corn, potatoes, tomatoes, and yucca. The cuisines we know as Central and South American, Mexican, and West Indian incorporate many foods from Africa, Asia, and Europe.

Many people in Mexico and Central America serve *tortillas* (flat bread made from corn or wheat flour) at most meals. Beans and rice form a major part of the diet of most West Indians. People in the mountainous areas of South America commonly eat potatoes. People in tropical areas eat a starchy root called *cassava.* In Argentina and Uruguay, people eat many foods made from wheat.

In the cattle-raising countries of Argentina and Uruguay, people eat a great deal of beef. In coastal areas and along rivers, fish and shellfish are popular foods. In some regions, dishes are highly seasoned with onions and hot peppers. In tropical areas, the people enjoy such fruits as bananas, mangoes, oranges, and pineapples. Latin Americans drink coffee and a variety of fruit juices. In South America, a kind of tea called *maté* is popular. Favorite alcoholic beverages include beer, rum, wine, and *aguardiente,* a brandylike drink made from sugar cane.

In highland regions of the Andes Mountains, the indigenous people commonly chew the leaves of the coca shrub. Coca contains a substance that fights off hunger, fatigue, and the harmful effects of high altitude. There is evidence that native peoples used coca as long ago as 2100 B.C. The Inca considered the plant to be sacred. Today, the Aymara and Quechua Indians use coca in religious rituals.

Coca is also used to make cocaine, an illegal drug. Since the 1980's, the United States has provided funding to South American countries, especially Colombia, to wipe out coca crops and encourage coca farmers to grow other crops. In response, indigenous *cocaleros* (coca growers) in such countries as Bolivia, Colombia, and Peru have become a significant political force.

Recreation. Soccer is the most beloved sport in Latin America. For many people, loyalty to a soccer team reflects civic or national pride and inspires great passion.

Volleyball is another popular sport in Latin America. Many West Indians play baseball, and cricket is common in countries with a British heritage, such as the Bahamas and Jamaica. Wealthy Latin Americans enjoy such activities as boating and horse racing. In many poor neighborhoods, illegal cockfighting is popular.

Fiestas (festivals) are another popular form of recreation. Latin Americans have held festivals since precolonial times. Today, many fiestas mark saints' days from the

© Jefferson Bernardes, AFP/Getty Images

Soccer, or *fútbol* in Spanish, is the most popular sport in Latin America. Many people attend professional matches, like the one shown here. Many Latin Americans also play soccer for fun.

Civic and religious festivals are a popular form of recreation in Latin America. Dancers dressed as devils, *shown here,* perform at an annual carnival in Oruro, Bolivia. Their dance, called the *diablada,* tells part of a traditional story about good and evil.

© David Mercado, Reuters/Landov

Roman Catholic calendar and such civic events as the establishment of a town. They usually include costumes, dancing, music, and elaborate floats. There may also be beauty pageants, bullfights, and other contests. Certain festivals express the identity of a region or country. For example, the annual carnival of Oruro, Bolivia, features dancers dressed as devils to represent Supay, an Amerindian god of the underworld. The dancers perform a dance called the *diablada,* which tells part of a traditional story about good and evil.

Día de los muertos (Day of the Dead) is a holiday that honors the dead. On November 2, All Souls' Day on the Roman Catholic calendar, Latin Americans visit the graves of deceased family members. In Mexico, this holiday combines a sense of playfulness with mourning. Shops sell sugar sculptures in the form of skulls and skeletons. Families build temporary altars to the dead and decorate them with candles, flowers, food, paper cutouts, and photographs. This tradition helps keep alive the memory of ancestors for future generations.

Religion. Most Latin Americans are Christians. The majority are Roman Catholics, but a growing number belong to Protestant churches. Some Latin Americans follow folk religions that combine elements of Catholicism with traditional African or indigenous beliefs. The laws of all Latin American countries guarantee freedom of worship, though some countries officially support the Catholic Church. Other religious groups in Latin America include Hindus, Jews, Muslims, and Sikhs.

Roman Catholicism. The early Spanish and Portuguese explorers brought the Roman Catholic religion to much of Latin America and converted many Indians to Catholicism. Today, more than 70 percent of the people consider themselves to be Roman Catholic. However, the percentage of Catholics who actively practice their religion varies from country to country.

During European rule, the Roman Catholic Church exercised great political power throughout Latin America. The church also dominated education and owned huge estates and other property. During the early 1800's, many Latin American colonies won their freedom. After independence, many Latin American governments took steps to decrease the Catholic Church's power. They seized much of its property and limited its control of education, hospitals, cemeteries, and public charities.

During the early 1900's, the church became closely linked to military leaders and wealthy landowners who controlled many Latin American governments. Beginning in the late 1960's, the church became increasingly active in the fight for civil and human rights and social justice. Today, the church still has considerable social and political influence, and its officials have great public visibility.

Protestantism is a small but rapidly growing segment of Latin American religion. More than 10 percent of Latin Americans consider themselves Protestant. Latin American Protestants include Baptists, Episcopalians, Lutherans, Methodists, Pentecostals, and members of the Church of Jesus Christ of Latter-day Saints (also known as Mormons). Pentecostals and Mormons are by far the fastest growing religious groups. They emphasize individual salvation through hard work and prayer.

Folk religions began to develop in Latin America during the colonial period, when African and Amerindian converts to Roman Catholicism combined elements of their new religion with traditional beliefs. For example, enslaved Africans in Brazil and the West Indies constructed altars at which they worshiped both Catholic saints and African *deities* (gods and goddesses). Missionaries sometimes built churches at the sites of Amerindian temples. By doing so, they unintentionally encouraged the Indians to associate the Catholic saints with indigenous deities.

Over time, these combinations of spiritual traditions led to the creation of new religions. Cuban *santería,* Brazilian *candomblé,* and Haitian *vodûn* (also known as *voodoo)* are three folk religions that combine Roman Catholicism with traditional African spirituality. Many folk religions include a belief in faith healing and possession by spirits.

Education in Latin America improved greatly during the middle to late 1900's. In most Latin American countries today, more than 90 percent of the people can read and write. Some exceptions are Guatemala and Haiti, where the literacy rate is lower. Every country in Latin America has a public school system.

Latin America has a number of excellent public and private universities. Five universities date from the 1500's. Autonomous Santo Domingo University, in the Dominican Republic, was founded in 1538 and ranks as the oldest institution of higher education in the Western Hemisphere. Enrollment in Latin American colleges and universities increased greatly in the 1900's. But many well-to-do families prefer to send their children to colleges and universities in Europe and the United States.

The arts

The artistic traditions of Latin America date back thousands of years to the region's Amerindian cultures. The ruins of magnificent temples and other structures still stand in such countries as Guatemala, Mexico, and Peru. Amerindian civilizations also produced beautiful ceramics, jewelry, and textiles. When Spanish and Portuguese colonists began arriving in the late 1400's, they brought European artistic traditions with them. European styles dominated Latin American art for hundreds of years. African slaves imported by the European colonists introduced African music and dance to the region. During the 1800's, the arts in Latin America began to develop a strong regional character. In the 1900's, modern Latin American artists and writers gained international recognition for their distinctive work.

Architecture. Latin America has impressive examples of precolonial architecture. These include a gracefully proportioned Maya convent at Uxmal, Mexico, and stone walls built by the Inca in Cusco, Peru. The stones of the walls fit so closely together that they required no mortar, yet could withstand earthquakes. Such Mexican sites as Teotihuacan and Tenochtitlan (present-day Mexico City) were built according to a grid plan. In contrast, the Inca constructed their cities to reflect the natural contours of the Andes. Throughout Latin America, ancient architects built enormous pyramids facing open plazas. They also combined architecture with painting and sculpture to create beautifully decorated buildings.

Coumbite (1971), an oil painting on masonite by Gerard Valcin; Flagg Tanning Corporation

Latin American painting by self-taught artists in Haiti draws upon themes from local life and folklore. This painting shows workers on a Haitian plantation.

© Guillermo Legaria, EPA/Landov

Magnificent colonial architecture can be found in many Latin American churches. The Iglesia de la Compañía de Jesús, *shown here*, is a cathedral in the Baroque style in Quito, Ecuador.

The first major European structures in Latin America were religious and government buildings. Some of the finest were Roman Catholic cathedrals and monasteries. Beginning in the late 1600's, many cathedrals, mansions, and palaces were built in the Baroque style, which featured elaborately carved columns, ornate sculptures, and a generous use of colored tile, gold, and silver. One of the most beautiful examples of Baroque style is the Iglesia de la Compañía de Jesus in Quito, Ecuador. This Catholic church was completed in the 1700's.

In the 1900's, Latin American architects were among the leading supporters of Modernist design, which featured bold geometric forms and dramatic lines. The great Mexican architect Luis Barragán combined Modernist principles with elements of traditional Mexican architecture, such as strong colors and plain, unadorned walls.

Painting. American Indian artists painted murals and pottery. In Mesoamerica, the Maya painted folding manuscripts called *codices*. The few codices that remain are written in a kind of hieroglyphics and include information about Maya beliefs and rituals. The Spaniards destroyed many codices in their effort to convert the Maya to Christianity.

From the 1500's to the 1800's, Latin American artwork was primarily religious in nature and imitated European styles. It was not until the 1900's that Latin American painting developed a distinctive character. Painters began to combine elements of Amerindian, colonial, and modern art to create works both regional and international in character. Latin American painters ranked among the most important in the world.

The Mexican painter Diego Rivera created gigantic murals depicting scenes from Mexican and world history. The paintings of Frida Kahlo, Rivera's wife, explored such subjects as folk religion, the female body, domestic violence, and infidelity. Wilfredo Lam, a Cuban painter, combined the European styles of Cubism and Surre-

Colorful Mexican murals became internationally famous during the 1900's. This mural by David Siqueiros decorates the Administration Building of the National Autonomous University of Mexico in Mexico City.

The People Go to the University—the University Goes to the People (1956), Black Star; © Estate of David Alfaro Siqueiros/SOMAAP, Mexico/VAGA, New York City

alism with Afro-Caribbean influences, including the writings of the West Indian poet Aimé Césaire and imagery from Afro-Caribbean folk religions.

Sculpture. Before the Europeans arrived, Latin American Indians created many beautiful sculptures, ranging from masks and statuettes to huge, elaborately carved panels and monuments. Indian sculptors carved a large number of their works from stone, but they also used clay, jade, gold, and wood. Many of their sculptures depicted gods and religious symbols and were used to decorate temples and religious centers.

Early colonial sculpture consisted mainly of carved decoration on churches. Much of this decoration was in the *plateresque* style, a form of stone design that resembled the delicate work of *plateros* (silversmiths). Since

the mid-1800's, much Latin American sculpture has reflected strong national pride and a growing interest in American Indian heritage. Revolutionary heroes and leaders of independence movements have also been popular subjects for sculptors.

Music. Latin America has a great diversity of musical forms and styles, and the region has given the world a wealth of musical innovation. Contemporary global music would be far different without the contributions of Latin American artists. Latin composers have also made contributions to classical and avant-garde music. But it is Latin America's popular music that has had the greatest impact. Reggae, salsa, and Latin jazz are just a few examples of Latin musical styles.

Some Latin American pop artists have gained worldwide fame. The Brazilian musicians João Gilberto and

© Günter Gräfenhain, SIME/4Corners Images

The Brazilian samba, like a number of Latin American dances, combines African and European artistic influences. These dancers are performing the samba at a nightclub in Rio de Janeiro.

Antônio Carlos (Tom) Jobim led the bossa nova movement in the 1950's and 1960's. Bob Marley, a Jamaican musician, popularized reggae in the 1960's. Ricky Martin, from Puerto Rico, became one of the leading pop singers of the late 1990's and early 2000's. Shakira, a Colombian-born singer and songwriter, has sold millions of records worldwide. Her English- and Spanish-language pop songs are influenced by rock music and by her Colombian and Lebanese background. Milton Nascimento and Caetano Veloso, two popular Brazilian musicians, have won worldwide recognition.

Archaeologists know that music was important to pre-colonial people, but they know little about how this early music sounded. Such traditional instruments as the *panpipes* (a kind of flute) have made their way into modern Latin American music. African music also influenced music in Latin America. Calypso from Trinidad and the bossa nova of Brazil are just two of the kinds of music that reflect a strong African influence.

Dance is a significant part of Latin American culture. The fusion of European and African influence has resulted in such dances as the Brazilian *samba,* the Cuban *conga,* and the Argentine *tango.* These dance forms in turn have influenced international ballroom styles, such as the *rumba* and the *cha-cha-cha.*

Today, dance takes a seemingly infinite variety of forms in Latin America. At one end of the spectrum are such formal dance companies as Mexico's Ballet Folklórico, which combines folk dances of Spanish origin with elements of ballet and modern dance. In contrast, informal dance styles are developing constantly in urban neighborhoods across Latin America.

Motion pictures. The history of motion pictures in Latin America dates back to the earliest days of the movies internationally. By the early 1900's, feature-length films were made throughout the region. Mexico has led Latin America in motion-picture production for generations. The famous Spanish director Luis Buñuel gave the Mexican film industry prestige by making movies there from 1946 to 1960. His most notable Mexican films include *Los Olvidados (The Young and the Damned,* 1950) and *The Criminal Life of Archibaldo de la Cruz* (1955). Later, the Mexican actor and director Alfonso Arau made the internationally popular film *Like Water for Chocolate* (1992) from a novel by his wife, Laura Esquivel. Mexican director Alfonso Cuarón directed some popular films in the early 2000's, including *Y tu mamá también* (2001) and *Harry Potter and the Prisoner of Azkaban* (2004).

A few prominent directors have made notable films elsewhere in Latin America. Humberto Mauro of Brazil made a classic melodrama called *Ganga bruta* (1933). More recently, the Brazilian director Fernando Meirelles directed *City of God* (2002), as well as *The Constant Gardener* (2005), which won an Academy Award. Leopoldo Torre Nilsson made several highly praised melodramas in Argentina during the 1950's and 1960's. Despite government restrictions, Cuba has produced a number of talented directors, including Santiago Alvarez, Tomás Gutiérrez Alea, and Humberto Solás.

Handicrafts. Latin Americans have a strong tradition of creating handmade objects that combine artistic beauty with practical utility. Such handicrafts include items for household use, religious objects, and textiles. This kind of art is called *arte popular* (popular art, or art

© Randy Faris, Corbis

Latin American handicrafts combine beauty and usefulness. Panama's Kuna Indians are known for their *molas*—that is, picture panels created by layering, cutting, and sewing fabric.

made by ordinary people). Today, mass-produced goods are readily available, and so Latin Americans make handicrafts mainly for the tourist market or as decorative objects for domestic consumers.

Many handicraft traditions have evolved according to the demands of buyers and new artistic influences. For example, *molas* (picture panels created by layering, cutting, and sewing fabric) made by the Kuna Indians of Panama may depict modern political slogans or images from billboard advertisements as well as traditional animals and floral motifs. Some handicrafts have crossed the line between folk art and fine art. For example, the modern *retablos* of Peruvian artist Nicario Jiménez have won international recognition. These retablos are portable boxes filled with figurines depicting everyday, historical, political, and religious events. Yarn "paintings" created by the Mexico's Huichol Indians are also highly prized by international collectors.

History

Many people have tried to understand Latin American history by comparing it to the histories of Europe and the United States. However, it is important to realize that Latin American history has developed in a way that has made Latin American countries quite different from those of Europe and North America. For example, Amerindian, European, and African cultures have existed together in Latin America, and mixed-race people have played a large role in Latin American social life, for many centuries. In contrast, in North America, the U.S. government nearly destroyed Amerindian populations in the 1800's, then forced the Indians to live on reservations apart from European society. In Latin America, Europeans, Amerindians, and Africans were also far more likely to intermarry than they were in the Anglo-American colonies that became the United States.

The Cuban writer José Marti once noted that "No Yankee or European book could furnish the key to the Hispanoamerican enigma." What he meant was that Latin American nations, like those in other regions of the world, must consider their own unique histories to discover the paths they should follow.

Stone sculpture (1300-1521), Museo Nacional de Antropología, Mexico City
(© Jean-Pierre Courau, Bridgeman Art Library)

American Indian sculpture often depicted traditional gods and goddesses. This giant statue of the Aztec goddess Coatlicue once stood in Tenochtitlan, the capital of the Aztec empire.

Early inhabitants. The first peoples of Latin America were American Indians. Scientists believe that the ancestors of these peoples came to North America from Asia between 15,000 and 30,000 years ago. Many of them crossed a land bridge that connected Asia and North America across the Bering Strait, which now separates Siberia from Alaska. By 12,500 years ago, they had spread across much of the Americas to the southern tip of South America. Some scientists believe that other early peoples may have arrived by boat and spread southward along the western coast of the Americas.

For thousands of years, the Amerindians lived in small groups, roaming widely in search of animals and edible plants. As people began to settle for longer periods in certain areas, they began to farm. Amerindians were the first people to cultivate cacao, chiles, corn, kidney and lima beans, potatoes, squash, tomatoes, and tobacco. Where agriculture became well established, small villages grew into towns and cities, and diverse civilizations arose.

The earliest of these civilizations was probably the Olmec, which thrived in what is now eastern Mexico from about 1200 to 400 B.C. Another civilization, the Maya, reached its peak from about A.D. 250 to 900 in southern Mexico, the Yucatán Peninsula, and Guatemala. The Maya produced magnificent architecture, painting, pottery, sculpture, and underground irrigation systems.

They developed an accurate calendar and a sophisticated writing system. Their mathematics recognized the concept of zero, and their astronomy was unsurpassed in its day. Scholars believe that food crises, population pressures, political turmoil, and warfare caused the Maya civilization to collapse and fragment around 900.

The Toltec controlled central Mexico from about 900 to 1200. By the early 1400's, the Aztec had replaced the Toltec as the most powerful people in the area. Both the Toltec and the Aztec built enormous pyramids for ceremonial and religious purposes. During the 1400's, the Mexica, an Aztec people, dominated Mexico's central valley, which they called Anáhuac. The Mexica created an empire of loosely joined *city-states,* each of which consisted of a city and its surrounding countryside. The Mexica demanded economic tribute from their subjects. They also believed that human sacrifice was necessary to ensure the order of the universe. They captured victims for sacrifice in ritual wars known as Flowery Wars.

In South America, the Inca emerged as the dominant group in the Andes, in what is now Peru. The Inca called their empire Tawantinsuyu. By the 1400's, the Inca capital at Cusco had a population of 200,000. It stood at the center of a far-flung communications network extending over the Andes, from Quito, Ecuador, south to Argentina. Inca farmers cut terraces into steep hillsides and used irrigation canals to carry water to their crops. The Inca had no written language. They used a sophisticated and highly accurate system of knotted strings, known as *quipus,* to keep records.

European discovery and exploration. In 1492, Christopher Columbus, an Italian navigator in the service of Spain, became the first European to reach Latin America. Columbus sailed west from Spain, hoping to find a short sea route to eastern Asia. He landed at the island of San Salvador, in the West Indies, and believed he had reached Asia.

After Columbus returned to Spain, news of his discovery created great excitement in Europe. To prevent disputes between Portugal and Spain over the newly discovered lands, Pope Alexander VI drew the Line of Demarcation in 1493. This imaginary north-south line lay about 350 miles (563 kilometers) west of two island groups in the North Atlantic Ocean—the Azores and the Cape Verde Islands. All lands west of the line belonged to Spain, and all lands to the east belonged to Portugal. However, the Portuguese soon became dissatisfied because they thought the line gave Spain too much territory. In 1494, Portugal and Spain signed the Treaty of Tordesillas, which moved the line about 1,295 miles (2,084 kilometers) west. As a result, Portugal gained the right to settle the eastern section of what is now Brazil. Portugal took possession of this area in 1500, when a Portuguese navigator named Pedro Álvares Cabral landed on the east coast of Brazil.

Columbus made four voyages to Latin America between 1492 and 1502. During these voyages, he explored many islands in the West Indies and the coasts of what are now Costa Rica, Honduras, Nicaragua, Panama, and Venezuela. Years after his voyages, Columbus continued to believe that he had happened upon outlying islands of Asia. Other explorers soon followed Columbus to Latin America. They quickly realized that the region was not Asia but a new land. Mapmakers named the land America in honor of the Italian-born explorer Amerigo Vespucci. Vespucci made several voyages to Latin America in the late 1490's and early 1500's for Spain and Portugal. Vespucci was one of the first explorers to state that the region was a "New World." Spaniards continued to refer to the region as the Indies—a term commonly used by Europeans to describe Asia. They called the native peoples Indians, even after it became clear that the continent was not part of Asia.

In 1513, the Spanish adventurer Vasco Núñez de Balboa crossed Panama and became the first European to see the eastern shore of the Pacific Ocean. His discovery provided additional proof that America was a separate continent between Europe and Asia. In 1520, the Portuguese navigator Ferdinand Magellan became the first European to discover the waterway that connects the Atlantic and Pacific oceans at the southern tip of South America. Magellan sailed down the east coast of South America and through the strait that now bears his name.

The conquest of the American Indians began soon after the Europeans arrived in Latin America. By the mid-1500's, Spanish adventurers known as *conquistadors* (conquerors, spelled *conquistadores* in Spanish) had conquered the great Indian civilizations and given Spain a secure hold on most of Latin America.

The first major conquests of the Indians occurred in Mexico and Central America. The conquistador Hernán

Important dates in Latin America

c. 10,500 B.C. Indians had spread throughout much of the Americas to the southern tip of South America.

A.D. 250-900 The civilization of the Maya Indians, in southern Mexico and northern Central America, reached its peak.

1400's-early 1500's The Aztec in Mexico and the Inca in western South America controlled large empires.

1492 Christopher Columbus became the first European to reach Latin America.

1494 Spain and Portugal agreed to the Line of Demarcation, which fixed their areas of rule in Latin America.

Early 1500's Spanish troops conquered most of Latin America's Indian civilizations.

Early 1800's Most of the Latin American colonies gained independence.

Middle to late 1900's Military regimes in several countries waged "dirty wars" of oppression against political dissidents.

1959 Fidel Castro established a Communist state in Cuba.

1980's Several Latin American countries regained civilian rule after a period of military rule.

2000's Voters in many South American countries elected left-wing leaders.

2006 Michelle Bachelet was elected president of Chile, the first woman to win a full term as president of a South American country without succeeding her husband.

© Odyssey Productions

Maya ruins include the Temple of the Giant Jaguar, *shown here,* in Guatemala. The Maya civilization reached its height in Mexico and Guatemala between about A.D. 250 and 900.

Cortés landed in Mexico in 1519. He had heard of a vast, wealthy empire inland. With only a few hundred men, Cortés knew he could not defeat an empire rumored to have 250,000 armed men. He approached cautiously, negotiating and fighting with enemies of Moctezuma II, emperor of the Aztec people (also known as the *Mexica)*.

A woman whom the Spaniards called Doña Marina, and whom the Amerindians called Malinche, accompanied Cortés. Marina had been a slave of the Maya, who had given her to Cortés as a gift. She acted as Cortés's interpreter, thus enabling him to negotiate with the peoples he encountered.

Cortés ultimately conquered the Aztec by forming alliances with their enemies, who did most of the fighting that toppled the Aztec empire by 1521. The spread of European diseases, chiefly smallpox, among the Indian population also helped Cortés.

The following year, another conquistador, known as Pedrarias, conquered the Indians of what are now Costa Rica and Nicaragua. In 1523, Pedro de Alvarado, one of Cortés's officers, conquered what are now El Salvador and Guatemala. These conquistadors, together with Balboa in Panama, secured Central America for Spain.

In 1532, the conquistador Francisco Pizarro fought his way into Peru with about 180 men. A bloody civil war had recently weakened the Inca empire there. Pizarro asked to meet the Inca ruler Atahualpa. Although he had promised to make a truce with Atahualpa, Pizarro ambushed the emperor's soldiers and captured him. Then, after promising to release Atahualpa, he forced him to choose between being burned alive as a non-Christian or being baptized as a Christian and strangled. Atahualpa chose baptism and strangulation. But his death did not seal the Spaniards' victory in Peru. Inca rebels resisted Spanish rule until the 1570's. Pizarro founded Lima in 1535. The city became Peru's capital and the center of Spanish government in South America. One of the few areas the Spanish failed to conquer was southern Chile, where the Mapuche Indians (called Araucanians by the Spanish) resisted for over 300 years.

Colonial rule. Even before the military conquest of Latin America was complete, Spanish and Portuguese settlers began pouring into the region. Many of them came in search of adventure and mineral wealth. Others established plantations to grow sugar cane, tobacco, and other crops to export to Europe. During the 1600's, the Dutch, English, and French established small colonies in Latin America, chiefly in the West Indies.

The first century of colonial rule saw a catastrophic decline in the Amerindian population. Most historians agree that by the early 1600's, Latin America's native population of over 25 million had decreased by more than 90 percent. Amerindians died in wars and of overwork, but the main cause of death was European disease, to which they had no natural immunity. Those who survived had to adapt rapidly to a new way of life.

Several groups vied for power in colonial Latin America. They included privileged colonists called *encomenderos,* Roman Catholic missionaries, representatives of the Spanish monarch known as *viceroys,* and Amerindian nobles. During the early 1500's, Spain established the *encomienda* system. Under this system, the Spanish king granted some conquistadors the right to collect tribute from native villages and force the Indians to work on

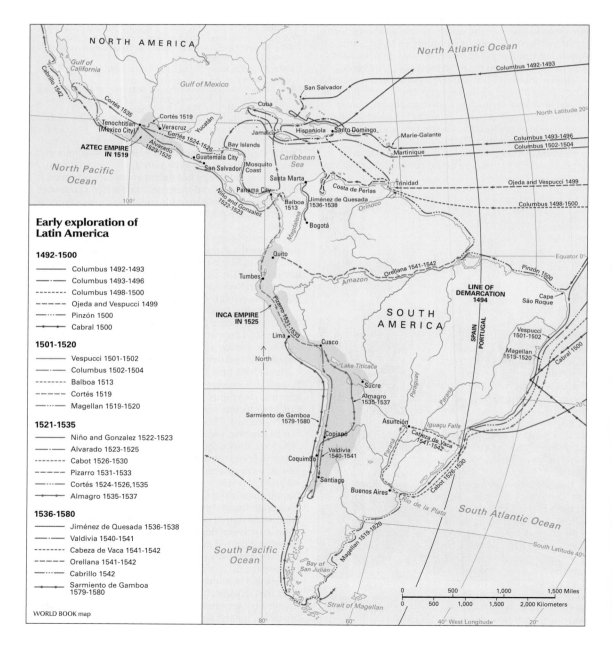

Early exploration of Latin America

1492-1500

—————— Columbus 1492-1493
——·——·— Columbus 1493-1496
- - - - - - - Columbus 1498-1500
– – – – – Ojeda and Vespucci 1499
——— · ——— Pinzón 1500
——•——•—— Cabral 1500

1501-1520

—————— Vespucci 1501-1502
——·——·— Columbus 1502-1504
- - - - - - - Balboa 1513
– – – – – Cortés 1519
—————— Magellan 1519-1520

1521-1535

—————— Niño and Gonzalez 1522-1523
——·——·— Alvarado 1523-1525
- - - - - - - Cabot 1526-1530
– – – – – Pizarro 1531-1533
——— · ——— Cortés 1524-1526,1535
——•——•—— Almagro 1535-1537

1536-1580

—————— Jiménez de Quesada 1536-1538
——·——·— Valdivia 1540-1541
- - - - - - - Cabeza de Vaca 1541-1542
– – – – – Orellana 1541-1542
—————— Cabrillo 1542
——•——•—— Sarmiento de Gamboa 1579-1580

WORLD BOOK map

Granger Collection

The Spanish conquest of the Aztec Indians of Mexico was completed in 1521. This drawing by an Aztec artist shows the Spanish and their Indian allies battling Aztec warriors.

farms or in mines. In return, these conquistadors, known as encomenderos, were supposed to protect the Indians and ensure their conversion to Christianity. In practice, the encomenderos often treated the Indians harshly and did little to Christianize them.

In contrast to the encomenderos, Spanish missionaries focused on converting the Amerindians to Christianity. Many Amerindians accepted baptism and practiced Roman Catholic rituals. However, they embraced Christianity on their own terms, often blending Catholic saints with ancestral gods and continuing to worship ancient deities secretly. This caused great frustration among missionaries, who viewed traditional religious practices as the devil's work.

The missionaries argued that overworking the Amerindians on farms and mines interfered with their efforts at conversion. Several missionaries, especially a Dominican friar named Bartolomé de Las Casas, pleaded for more humane treatment of the Indians. But millions of Indians died from overwork and harsh treatment. As the Indian population of Latin America declined, Europeans began to import black Africans as slaves. From the 1550's to the 1850's, over 10 million African slaves arrived in the Americas. Two-thirds of them, or nearly 7 million, were sent to Latin America, especially Brazil, where they worked on farms and in mines.

The chief representatives of the Spanish crown in Latin America were the viceroys. The viceroys found it difficult to impose their will upon the encomenderos, who were more concerned with their own power and wealth than with obeying orders from Spain. Nor did the viceroys have authority over the missionaries.

A fourth group, Amerindian nobles, continued to govern some native towns and cities during the 1500's. These nobles were known as caciques in Mexico and as curacas in Peru. There were too few Spaniards to rule all of the Amerindians directly. The Amerindian nobles were responsible to the encomenderos for collecting tribute from the local people, most of whom continued to live as they had before the Spaniards arrived.

Protecting the Indians. During the early and middle 1500's, religious and political leaders spent much time discussing the fate of the Amerindians. Las Casas argued that Spain must abolish the encomienda system to prevent total destruction of the American Indians. In 1542, the Spanish crown passed laws limiting the encomenderos' power. But the encomenderos largely ignored these laws. In 1550, King Charles V suspended the conquest of Latin America until lawyers and religious experts could legally and morally justify Spain's actions there. At a great debate in Valladolid, Spain, in the early 1550's, Las Casas argued that missionaries, rather than conquistadors, should carry out the conquest of America because they would do it without violence. Some historians have seen in this argument of Las Casas the first stirrings of the idea of universal human rights.

From the 1550's, the Spanish crown began to pass laws to protect Amerindians from the worst abuses of local officials. In the late 1500's, Spain created the General Indian Court in Mexico to hear cases of abuse of Amerindians and to settle disputes between Amerindians. By the late 1600's, Mexican Indians were using the Spanish legal system to defend their land, liberty, and village autonomy (self-government).

Many colonists and Amerindian nobles who depended on indigenous labor ignored the new legal protections. The Amerindians continued to work and pay tribute until the early 1800's.

Early settlers in Brazil found themselves in a sparsely populated land. Most were castaways or exiles from Portugal, and all were men. They settled in coastal areas and showed little interest in conquering the Amerindians, who lived scattered across huge tracts of rough terrain. The settlers traded with the Amerindians, especially for brazilwood, which was used for dyeing cloth.

Christian missionaries were slow to arrive in what is now Brazil. The Jesuits were among the first religious orders to convert and protect the Indians. Initially, the Indians seemed to be eager converts. Gradually, it became clear that they viewed the missions as havens from colonists who treated them like slaves. By the mid-1500's, brazilwood was no longer the only profitable product, and Portuguese colonists had begun growing sugar cane.

As elsewhere in Latin America, European diseases killed many native people of Brazil. Because growing sugar cane required many workers, the colonists began to enslave Amerindians and import slaves from Africa. As a result, African culture had an especially strong influence in Brazil.

Mestizaje. An important result of the coming together of European, Amerindian, and African peoples was the process of mestizaje, the biological and cultural mixing of people of different races and ethnicities. In the early decades after conquest, there were few European women in Latin America. European men took Amerindian and African wives and mistresses. The children born from these unions were neither fully European, fully Amerindian, nor fully African. This situation contrasted notably with the settlement of English North America, where interracial unions were exceptional and racial groups generally existed separately. Mixed-race people, known as *mestizos,* played a significant role as interpreters and mediators between different ethnic and racial groups.

Colonial discontent. During the 1700's, Spain began to enact policy changes designed to reap greater revenues from Latin America. Spain needed money to defend its large empire from European rivals, especially Britain (now the United Kingdom) and France. Some of these policy changes, known as the Bourbon Reforms, hurt the interests of *criollos* (people of Spanish ancestry born in Latin America). For example, the new rules excluded criollos from many government and church positions in favor of men born in Spain. The reforms also cracked down on the criollos' illegal trade with merchants in European countries other than Spain. Many criollo traders lost their livelihood.

The policy changes also put pressure on Amerindian communities. For example, local officials began demanding higher tribute payments from Indian villages. Such demands led to Amerindian rebellions across Spanish America. In 1780, a mestizo called Tupac Amaru launched a famous revolt against Spanish authority in Peru. The Spaniards put down the revolt over the course of three years. About 100,000 people, mostly Amerindians, died in the fighting.

By the late 1700's, criollos in Spanish America found themselves in a difficult position. They resented Spanish authority in Latin America, as did many upper-class mestizos. They were also aware of world events, including the Revolutionary War in America (1775-1783) and the French Revolution (1789-1799), and many of them supported the ideas of liberty, equality, and brotherhood.

In 1790, after about 300 years of colonial rule, five European countries controlled all of Latin America. From then on, revolutions in Latin America weakened European power in the region.

However, the criollos feared what would happen if the masses of Amerindians and lower-class mestizos took these ideas seriously.

Amerindian rebellions against colonial government had increased considerably during the second half of the 1700's. The criollos worried that without Spain's power, they might not be able to defend themselves against such rebellions. Rather than demand full independence from Spain, some criollos favored limited self-rule. Others called for representation in the Cortes, the Spanish parliament. But they were denied equal status with the representatives in Spain.

The movement toward independence in Latin America was triggered by the French General Napoleon Bonaparte's invasion of the Iberian Peninsula in 1807 and by the removal of King Ferdinand VII from the Spanish throne in 1808. These events disrupted Spanish authority in America. They sparked uprisings among Latin Americans loyal to Spain, those who favored a limited degree of autonomy, and those who desired complete independence from Europe. While the Spanish crown was preoccupied with events at home, criollos gained control of most of Latin America. Wars of independence broke out throughout the region. From Mexico to Argentina, popular leaders known as *caudillos* mobilized the peasants who fought the wars. The Spaniards also relied upon caudillos for their troops.

Mexico began its revolt against Spain in 1810. Two Roman Catholic priests, Miguel Hidalgo y Costilla and José María Morelos y Pavón, led an uprising of Amerindians and poor mestizos. The initial revolt failed, however, and Spanish troops executed both Hidalgo and Morelos. The uprisings that followed did not express the same sense of grievance from Mexican Indians and the poor. They were led chiefly by elite criollos. Mexico won its independence in 1821.

Central America also gained its independence from Spain in 1821. Central America had little economic importance, and so Spain largely ignored the area. As a result, Central Americans won their independence with little bloodshed. In 1822, Costa Rica, El Salvador, Guatemala, Honduras, and Nicaragua became part of Mexico. But in 1823 they broke away from Mexico and formed a political union called the United Provinces of Central America. Bitter regional rivalries caused this union to begin to collapse in 1838, and each of the states had become an independent republic by 1841. The territory of Panama was a Colombian province from 1821 until 1903, when it rebelled against Colombia with help from the United States and became an independent country. Belize, formerly known as British Honduras, was a British colony from 1862 to 1981, when it gained independence.

Spanish South America. The two greatest heroes in the fight for independence in Spanish South America were the Venezuelan general Simón Bolívar and the Argentine general José de San Martín. Bolívar helped win freedom for Bolivia, Colombia, Ecuador, Peru, and Venezuela. San Martín fought for the independence of Argentina, Chile, and Peru.

The Venezuelan revolutionary Francisco de Miranda led an unsuccessful revolt against the Spanish in 1806. Bolívar, who had been a follower of Miranda's, launched a new campaign in 1813. His armies fought

Detail from a mural (1931-1933) by Fernando Leal, Simón Bolívar Amphitheatre, Mexico (Dagli Orti, The Art Archive)

Simón Bolívar, a Venezuelan general, helped several Latin American colonies win their independence from Spain. This painting shows Bolívar, *seated on the horse,* and his followers fighting with Spanish troops.

against the Spanish forces for about 10 years before winning a final, great victory at Ayacucho, Peru, in 1824. The victory assured independence for the Spanish colonies in northern South America.

In the south, landowners in Chile declared their country's independence in 1810. However, Spanish forces defeated them. Armies led by San Martín and the Chilean hero Bernardo O'Higgins won lasting independence for Chile in 1818. Earlier, in 1816, San Martín had freed Argentina from Spanish rule. During the early 1820's, the forces of San Martín and Bolívar fought for Peru's independence. Peru finally became independent in 1826.

Brazil won its freedom from Portugal without a war. After Napoleon invaded Portugal in 1807, the Portuguese ruler, Prince John, fled to Brazil. John returned to Portugal 14 years later, after Napoleon's defeat. He left his son Pedro to govern Brazil, but the Brazilians no longer wanted to be ruled by Europeans. They demanded independence. In 1822, Pedro declared Brazil an empire and took the throne as Emperor Pedro I.

The West Indies. In 1791, Toussaint Louverture and others led black African slaves in Haiti in a revolt against their French rulers. In 1804, Haiti became the first independent nation in Latin America. The Dominican Republic declared its independence in 1844. A revolt broke out against Spanish rule in Cuba in 1895. The United States sided with the Cuban rebels, which led to the Spanish-American War (1898) between Spain and the United States. The United States won the war, and Cuba became a republic in 1902. Under the terms of the peace treaty, Spain also gave up its colony of Puerto Rico to the United States. Most small West Indian islands remained under British, Dutch, or French control until the mid-1900's. Since then, most of these islands have become independent. Many of the others have gained more control over their affairs.

Early years of independence. The mere fact of independence did not bring peace to Latin America. The new nations faced extraordinary difficulties. The wars had been deeply destructive across the region. Factories, farms, and mines had been destroyed, and many Latin Americans had died in the fighting. Spaniards fleeing the wars had taken their money with them, leaving the new countries with scant resources. Across Latin America, upper-class criollos struggled with one another for power. Many of them disliked new laws that abolished forced labor in mines and tribute payments from American Indians.

Political climate. Beginning in the 1820's, mostly white criollo conservatives and liberals struggled over the shape of governments. Many conservatives preferred to keep things more or less as they had been before independence. Some supported the creation of constitutional monarchies. Others supported the establishment of republics. In general, conservatives agreed that the Catholic Church should remain politically powerful.

Liberals favored policies promoting individual freedoms and equality. In practice, however, they held an unfavorable view of blacks, Indians, and mestizos, who made up majorities in many countries. Most liberals sought to reduce the political power of the church, promote private ownership of property, and educate the people. Liberal constitutions that promoted equality, however, actually stripped Amerindians of the special protections they had under Spanish law. In the 1800's, it was more difficult for Amerindians to be heard by governments than it had been prior to independence. In addition, liberal policies often disrupted Amerindian traditions. For example, they broke up collectively owned lands, forced native people to work for wages instead of living off the land, and discouraged Amerindians from allowing religion to play a large role in their daily lives.

Fidel Castro waves to crowds in Havana, Cuba, in 1959 after leading a successful revolution against the dictator Fulgencio Batista. Under Castro, Cuba became a Communist dictatorship.

Many of the new nations formed republics. However, the inexperience of the new leaders led to violent struggles. Ambitious politicians seized power in a number of countries. In other countries, wealthy landowners controlled the government.

Caudillismo. In some of the new nations, the local popular leaders known as caudillos took control of the government. The caudillos and their rural supporters, who had fought and sacrificed much in the wars for independence, were not willing simply to disarm and let urban elites and intellectuals take over their new countries. This led to a power struggle between the caudillos and liberal politicians.

In Argentina, a caudillo named Juan Manuel de Rosas assumed control of the government in 1829. Rosas ruled until 1852. Through violence, control over the land, and the granting of favors to supporters, he brought other Argentine caudillos under the authority of a central government in Buenos Aires.

Regional conflicts broke out between some Latin American nations and their neighbors during the 1800's. In Mexico, the problems of the post-independence period were compounded by a war with the United States known as the Mexican War (1846-1848). The U.S. government had proclaimed a doctrine called *manifest destiny,* which claimed that the United States should control all of North America. Under this doctrine, the United States waged an opportunistic war against Mexico, still weak from its war for independence. By the Treaty of Guadalupe Hidalgo, which officially ended the war, the United States took from Mexico the regions of California, Nevada, and Utah, most of Arizona and New Mexico, and parts of Colorado and Wyoming.

In the War of the Triple Alliance, also known as the Paraguayan War (1865-1870), Argentina, Brazil, and Uruguay attacked Paraguay. Paraguay lost at least one-fifth of its population in the war, and Argentina and Brazil won chunks of Paraguayan territory.

A dispute over Bolivian deposits of *nitrate,* a chemical used for fertilizer, led to the War of the Pacific (1879-1883), which involved Bolivia, Chile, and Peru. Chile claimed the Atacama Desert, which contained Bolivia's rich nitrate fields and provided Bolivia's only access to the Pacific Ocean. Peru sided with Bolivia.

Liberal reforms. After 1850, liberal politicians throughout Latin America began to push for government reforms. Programs varied from country to country, but most reformers promoted the liberal ideals of private property, public education, and a reduced political role for the church.

In Mexico, liberal reforms passed by justice minister Benito Juárez led to a civil war, from 1858 to 1860, between liberals and conservatives. The reforms had reduced the power of the church and the military and forced Amerindians to sell communal lands. Following Juárez's election as president in 1861, Mexican conservatives persuaded the French to oust Juárez and install Austrian Archduke Maximilian as emperor of Mexico. Juárez and his supporters reclaimed the government in 1867, and Juárez continued to push his liberal agenda. However, conservatives and Amerindians who had lost land opposed him.

International trade. After about 1870, many Latin American governments pursued policies to broaden their trade with Europe and the United States. At that time, most Latin American countries exported agricultural and mineral products to European countries and the United States, and imported manufactured goods from those countries. This economic exchange led foreign investors and Latin American governments to build railroads and improve ports to facilitate trade. In the early 1900's, foreign investors, especially from the United States, put large amounts of money into such businesses as fruit companies, mines, and public utilities. The beginning of the 1900's was also marked by considerable migration from Europe to Latin America.

United States involvement with Latin American politics increased near the end of the 1800's. During the Spanish-American War of 1898, the United States supported Cuban independence from Spain. The United States then set up a military government in Cuba. In 1903, the U.S. government insisted that the Cuban Constitution include the Platt Amendment. This amendment allowed the United States to intervene in Cuba's internal affairs when U.S. interests were threatened. As a result of the war, the United States also acquired the island of Puerto Rico from Spain.

Beginning about 1900, U.S. companies also worked to increase their trade with, and investment in, Latin America. These companies introduced new work methods to Latin America and provided products that many local people wanted to buy. At the same time, they challenged established ways of life and created resentment among farmers, landowners, and workers who felt that U.S. companies benefited at their expense.

During the 1920's and 1930's, the United States routinely dispatched naval forces to Central America in an effort to protect its business interests there. This practice became known as *gunboat diplomacy.* The presence of foreign companies, along with such policies as gunboat diplomacy, contributed to a deepening sense of nationalism within Latin America.

Political circumstances in the early to middle 1900's. As the second century of Latin American independence dawned, much had changed in the region. Leaders had established national governments, and economies had expanded. Such cities as Buenos Aires, Lima, Mexico City, and Rio de Janeiro had grown greatly. These developments added to rising social tensions among Latin Americans. Workers in mines and factories and on haciendas wanted higher wages and better working conditions. Urban, middle-class professionals demanded public education and government services. Peasants in the countryside were losing land to railroads and large landowners. And new domestic industries wanted economic protections from foreign competition.

In Mexico, such tensions came to a head in 1910, when a liberal politician named Francisco Madero declared himself in rebellion against the government of President Porfirio Díaz. In the interest of modernization, Díaz had built foreign-owned railroads, expanded the size of the government, divided Amerindian lands, and invited U.S. companies to operate in Mexico. Although these policies improved the economy, they hurt the interests of many Mexicans. Madero's rebellion set off what came to be known as the Mexican Revolution.

Two prominent revolutionaries were Emiliano Zapata and Pancho Villa. Zapata led Amerindians in southern Mexico who wanted to hold communal lands and govern their own communities. Villa led agricultural workers and miners who sought better working conditions, higher wages, and fair treatment from employers, many of which were U.S. companies.

The revolution led to many changes. The Constitution of 1917 recognized the right of Amerindian villages to hold land in common. Villages and towns received a role in government. The Constitution granted the state the power to offer public education and increase government support of domestic industry. A land reform program of the 1930's gave farms to millions of landless peasants. These policies served to level social differences to some degree. At the same time, the revolution ushered in a long period of strong centralized government.

In South America, the Great Depression of the 1930's, a worldwide economic slump, brought unemployment and poverty to many people, especially those in growing cities. In these circumstances, political leaders known as *populists* took center stage in several countries. They included Juan Perón in Argentina, Getúlio Vargas in Brazil, Victor Haya de la Torre in Peru, and Jorge Gaitán in Colombia. These leaders blended a variety of political ideas, referring to themselves as defenders, fathers, and teachers of the people. They argued that the working and middle classes should have a role in government. They also drew upon a deep sense of resentment among South Americans against foreigners, especially North Americans in the United States.

As had leaders before them, the populists sought to modernize their countries while balancing competing demands. In Argentina, Perón promised workers better wages and working conditions. But he also told employers that he would help them control workers' organizations, keep them from striking, and promote national industry. Perón encouraged workers to join government-approved labor unions and repressed Communist workers. In Brazil, Vargas followed similar policies. In Colombia and Peru, Gaitán and Haya de la Torre said they wanted to end political corruption among the wealthy, protect small-property owners, and provide workers with dignity in their jobs.

High-level politicians, conservative business people

© Daniel Munoz, Reuters/Landov

Coca farming provides a living for many people in such countries as Bolivia, Colombia, and Peru. Coca is controversial because its leaves can be used to make cocaine, an illegal drug.

and landowners, and some members of the middle class opposed the populist movement. They feared they would lose their political, financial, and social standing if the working class became too powerful. City streets became places where supporters and opponents of populism addressed the public and held protests.

Populist leaders vowed to work toward economic growth while maintaining social peace, but political and social tensions persisted. In 1948, Gaitán was shot to death in Bogotá, Colombia, just before a presidential election. Perón's support began to slip in the early 1950's, as the Argentine economy slowed. Perón then began to take unpopular measures against his critics, such as closing down a prominent Buenos Aires newspaper in 1951. In 1955, the Argentine military forced Perón to resign.

Democratic reforms. Throughout Latin America, the period immediately following World War II (1939–1945) was one of hope that democracy and economic development could solve the region's problems. Guatemala, for example, gave the right to vote to women and people who could not read and write, improved working conditions on farms, and distributed unused land belonging to the U.S.-owned United Fruit Company to landless peasants. The U.S. government, concerned about the spread of Communism and its business interests in Latin America, backed a military *coup* (take-over of the government) that ousted Guatemala's reformist President Jacobo Arbenz Guzman in 1954. This violated the United States' Good Neighbor Policy, agreed to in the 1930's, under which the U.S. government had promised to stay out of other nations' affairs.

The Cuban revolution. By the mid-1950's, there was a growing sense of frustration across Latin America. Populist leaders had achieved economic growth, but not political peace, in their countries. Reformers, such as

President Arbenz Guzman, had met conservative resistance at home and U.S. opposition. Some Latin Americans began to think that perhaps armed struggle was the only way for their countries to progress.

In Cuba, Fidel Castro and Ché Guevara led an armed rebellion against President Fulgencio Batista y Zaldívar. Batista ruled as a dictator and was widely regarded as a corrupt politician at the service of wealthy Cubans and foreign companies. Castro, a Cuban lawyer, and Guevara, an Argentine physician, led bands of guerrilla fighters against Batista's government for nearly three years, until they defeated it in 1959.

After overthrowing Batista, the Cuban rebels set up a Communist government, with Castro as its head. The Castro government passed social reforms that heavily favored the poor. It developed close ties with the Communist government of the Soviet Union, then the main rival of the United States in a struggle for international power known as the Cold War. Castro later pledged to aid Communist rebels in other Latin American countries.

In 1961, the United States created the Alliance for Progress to provide economic assistance to Latin American countries. The United States hoped the alliance would help prevent widespread revolution by alleviating financial pressures in Latin America. By the late 1960's, the alliance had failed, mainly because it spent more time and resources strengthening military forces to stand against Communism than promoting democracy and economic development.

The rise of military regimes. The Cuban revolution had an electrifying effect in Latin America. Intellectuals throughout the region began to argue for revolutionary change. By the end of the 1970's, the growth of Latin American economies slowed, and organized workers began making stronger demands on governments. All these developments caused many Latin Americans to worry that their societies were falling into disorder.

The attitudes of Roman Catholic clergy caused considerable anxiety among conservatives. In 1968, a conference of bishops held in Medellín, Colombia, encouraged governments to address the problem of poverty by giving the poor preferential treatment. In his book *A Theology of Liberation* (1971), the Peruvian priest Gustavo Gutiérrez wrote that Christian ideals demanded a commitment to creating a just society that would seek to free individuals from poverty. Many upper- and middle-class Latin Americans worried that the Catholic Church, which had long upheld conservative values, was beginning to align itself with political radicals and the poor.

In these circumstances, some military officers argued that only they could prevent their countries from becoming Communist. In Brazil, military forces overthrew President João Goulart in 1964, ushering in 20 years of military rule. Argentina experienced repeated military coups during the 1960's and 1970's. In Chile, a military coup led by General Augusto Pinochet toppled popularly elected socialist President Salvador Allende in 1973. The United States supported the coup.

The new leaders believed their countries could not progress economically until they rooted out Communist influences. They enacted conservative policies and suppressed their political opponents, even though the number of Communists in their countries was small. In a number of countries, military governments carried out campaigns of repression known as "dirty wars." Their political opponents "disappeared" or were tortured or killed in an effort to eliminate political conflict.

Not all military regimes were conservative. In Peru, military leaders seized the government in 1968 and named General Juan Velasco Alvarado president. The new government promised to end Peru's dependence on foreign investment and sought to find a middle ground between capitalism and Communism. It took over most of Peru's plantations and turned many of them into cooperatives managed by workers. In the early 1970's, it began an industrial reform program that gave workers partial control over some industries. Like other military regimes of this period, Peru's government arrested and exiled some of its political opponents.

Return to civilian government. During the late 1960's and early 1970's, armed uprisings took place in El Salvador, Guatemala, and Nicaragua. The rebels opposed military dictatorship and wanted representation in government. In Nicaragua, the Sandinista National Liberation Front, led by Daniel Ortega, overthrew the government of Anastasio Somoza Debayle in 1979. Ortega's government enacted reforms similar to those enacted by democratic reformers in the 1950's.

During this period, the United States became involved in efforts to overthrow several Latin American governments. In Nicaragua, it funded a counterrevolutionary army known as the *contras,* which aimed to overthrow the Sandinistas. In Guatemala and El Salvador, the United States provided training and equipment to armed counterrevolutionaries who opposed their nations' military rulers.

By the 1980's, military rulers faced growing opposition among ordinary citizens. Many Latin Americans disapproved of their governments' violations of human rights or were impatient with their countries' slow economic growth. Following an election in 1983, Argentina returned to civilian rule. A civilian president took office in Brazil in 1985. And in 1988, Chile held a *plebiscite* (vote of the people) on Pinochet's rule. The vote resulted in Pinochet's defeat, and he stepped down in 1990.

Neoliberalism. During the 1990's, in keeping with global trends and in response to pressures from international financial organizations, many Latin American countries adopted *neoliberal* theories of economic growth. Neoliberal theories support free-market activity over government regulation of the economy. Neoliberal policies have had mixed results. Latin American countries have strengthened their banking systems and reduced government inefficiency, but they have also cut funding for social services to help the poor. Many countries have reduced trade protections for domestic industries and *privatized* some industries—that is, sold state-controlled industries to private companies.

In 1993, Mexico, the United States, and Canada signed the North American Free Trade Agreement (NAFTA), which took effect in 1994. This agreement allowed for the freer movement of goods and money across international borders. NAFTA has had significant effects in both Mexico and the United States. Some American companies have relocated to Mexico, where wages are lower, causing many American workers to lose their jobs. In Mexico, the economy has grown and some workers have benefited. However, many Mexicans, who hoped that NAFTA would lead to higher wages and better working conditions, have been disappointed. Many have migrated to the United States seeking better employment opportunities.

Soon after NAFTA went into effect, Maya Indians took control of several towns in the Mexican state of Chiapas. The rebels' spokesperson said the adoption of NAFTA was one reason they revolted, claiming the treaty would harm them economically. The rebel group called itself the Zapatista Army of National Liberation. More than 100 people died in fighting between the Zapatistas and government troops. The government regained possession of the towns within a week and declared a cease-fire on Jan. 12, 1994. Since then, the Zapatista movement has developed as a peaceful campaign against the poverty and discrimination faced by indigenous Mexicans.

In the 2000's, Latin America faced serious economic, political, and social problems. Many people lived in poverty, the gap between rich and poor continued to widen, and rapid population growth put pressure on the region's resources. In addition, a large illegal drug trade had persisted in a number of countries since the 1970's.

Latin Americans in several countries elected leftist or reform-oriented presidents in the late 1990's and early 2000's. These leaders included Luiz Inácio Lula da Silva in Brazil, Hugo Chávez in Venezuela, Evo Morales in Bolivia, Néstor Kirchner in Argentina, and Michelle Bachelet in Chile. Such leaders have questioned the ideal of *globalization*—that is, the extension of culture and commerce across traditional national boundaries. They have also favored policies to reduce somewhat their countries' economic dependence on the United States and on international financial organizations, such as the International Monetary Fund. At times, they have argued that Latin Americans, and not foreign investors, should have control of, and profit from, natural resources and industries in their countries. They also have promised to improve the welfare of indigenous and working-class people.   Brian P. Owensby and Mary Weismantel

Additional resources

Level I
Bramwell, Martyn. *Central and South America.* Lerner, 2000.
Franklin, Sharon, and others. *Mexico and Central America.* Raintree, 2000.
Gac Artigas, Alejandro. *Yo, Alejandro: The Story of a Young Latino Boy Struggling Through Life.* 2nd ed. Ediciones Nuevo Espacio, 2001.
Tenenbaum, Barbara A., ed. *Latin America, History and Culture.* 4 vols. Scribner, 1999.

Level II
Bouvier, Virginia M., ed. *The Globalization of U.S.-Latin American Relations: Democracy, Intervention, and Human Rights.* Praeger, 2002.
Hillman, Richard S., ed. *Understanding Contemporary Latin America.* 3rd ed. Lynne Rienner, 2005.
Kapiszewski, Diana, and Kazan, Alexander, eds. *Encyclopedia of Latin American Politics.* Oryx, 2002.
Sieder, Rachel, ed. *Multiculturalism in Latin America.* Palgrave, 2002.
Vargas Llosa, Alvaro. *Liberty for Latin America: How to Undo Five Hundred Years of State Oppression.* Farrar, 2005.
Winn, Peter. *Americas: The Changing Face of Latin America and the Caribbean.* 3rd ed. Univ. of Calif. Pr., 2006.

Schmied, ZEFA

Montenegro's coastline rises sharply to the mountains at Petrovac, a town on the Adriatic Sea. Olive trees grow on the mountain slopes surrounding the town. Montenegro's name in Serbian means *black mountain,* and mountains cover most of the republic.

Montenegro, *MAHN tuh NEH groh,* is a country in southeastern Europe, bordering the Adriatic Sea. Podgorica is Montenegro's capital and largest city.

In 1918, Montenegro became part of the Kingdom of the Serbs, Croats, and Slovenes, later renamed Yugoslavia. In 1946, Yugoslavia was organized as a federal state consisting of six republics, one of which was Montenegro. Between June 1991 and March 1992, four of the republics—Bosnia-Herzegovina, Croatia, Macedonia, and Slovenia—declared their independence. In April 1992, Montenegro joined Serbia in forming a new, smaller Yugoslavia. In 2003, Yugoslavia adopted a new constitution and changed its name to Serbia and Montenegro. In 2006, Montenegro separated from Serbia and became an independent country.

Government. A president heads Montenegro's government. A 125-member assembly, led by a prime minister, makes the republic's laws. The prime minister is usually the leader of the party that controls the assembly. The voters elect the president and the assembly members to four-year terms. The Montenegrin Democratic Party of Socialists is the chief political party.

People. Most of the people are Montenegrins. The official language of the country is Montenegrin, a language related to Serbian. Minority groups in Montenegro include Albanians, Muslim Slavs, and Serbs. Children in Montenegro are required to attend school from the ages of 7 to 15. Montenegro has a university in Podgorica.

Land and climate. Mountains cover most of Montenegro, and thick forests grow over much of the republic. A narrow strip of land lies along the Adriatic Sea. Most of Montenegro has cold, snowy winters. Summers are warm in the valleys but cool in the mountains. The coast has a mild climate.

Economy. When Montenegro was part of the larger Yugoslavia, it had one of the weakest economies of the six republics. For many years, a poor network of roads and railroads held back economic development. But a railroad line opened in 1976 between Bar, Montenegro's major seaport, and Belgrade, Yugoslavia's capital. The railroad improved the transportation system and helped the economy somewhat.

Montenegro has large deposits of bauxite, coal, and lead. Factories manufacture aluminum, cement, iron and steel, and paper. The most important crops are corn, olives, potatoes, tobacco, and wheat. Farmers also grow cherries, figs, grapes, peaches, pears, and plums, and raise cattle, hogs, and sheep.

Tourism is a major source of income for Montenegro. Many vacationers come to Montenegro's coast to enjoy the warm climate and scenic beaches. People who fish, hike, hunt, and ski also visit the mountains.

Montenegro has airports in Berane, Podgorica, and Tivat. The leading daily newspaper is *Pobjeda*.

History. Present-day Montenegro became part of the Roman Empire in about 11 B.C. Slavs settled in the region in the A.D. 600's. The region became part of Serbia in the late 1100's.

The Ottoman Empire, based in modern-day Turkey, defeated the Serbs in the Battle of Kosovo Polje in 1389. Local nobles ruled Montenegro on behalf of the Ottomans until 1516, when Serbian Orthodox bishops of the monastery at Cetinje began to rule part of it. By the late 1700's, the bishops' rule extended to all of Montenegro. In 1852, Montenegro's ruler took the title of prince, and the position of bishop became a separate office.

In 1878, the Congress of Berlin, a meeting of European leaders, formally recognized Montenegro as independent. The congress granted new lands to Montenegro, about doubling its size. Prince Nicholas took the throne in 1860 and declared himself king in 1910.

In the early 1900's, a movement to unite Serbs and other Slavic peoples gathered strength in the region. Montenegro helped drive the Ottomans out of the Balkan Peninsula in the First Balkan War (1912-1913). Montenegro also aided Serbia in World War I (1914-1918). In 1918, townspeople deposed the king, and Montenegro became part of the new Kingdom of the Serbs, Croats, and Slovenes. But rural villagers organized militias to resist incorporation into the kingdom. Their resistance continued until the mid-1920's.

During World War II (1939-1945), Italian and then German troops occupied parts of Montenegro. A resistance

Montenegro

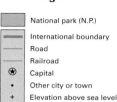

National park (N.P.)
International boundary
Road
Railroad
⊛ Capital
• Other city or town
+ Elevation above sea level

WORLD BOOK maps

movement led by a group of Communists called Partisans fought the Italian and German troops. By 1945, the Communists had gained control of all of Yugoslavia. Yugoslavia's 1946 Constitution officially organized Yugoslavia as a *federal* state—that is, a state where each of six republics, including Montenegro, largely controlled its own affairs.

In 1990, Montenegro held its first multiparty elections. Between June 1991 and March 1992, four of the Yugoslav republics—Croatia, Slovenia, Macedonia, and Bosnia-Herzegovina—declared their independence. In April 1992, the remaining two republics, Serbia and Montenegro, formed a new Yugoslavia.

In 2000, many people in Montenegro began pressing for independence from Serbia, which held most of the power in Yugoslavia. In response, the leaders of the two republics announced plans in 2002 to create a new constitution and to rename the country Serbia and Montenegro. In 2003, the plans were approved, and Yugoslavia adopted the new name.

Many people in Montenegro continued to call for independence from Serbia. Montenegro's legislative assembly ordered a referendum on independence, which was held on May 21, 2006. In the referendum, 55.5 percent of those who voted approved independence. Slightly more than 86 percent of Montenegro's eligible voters went to the polls. Shortly after the referendum, Montenegro declared its independence. Serbia then declared its own independence.   Sabrina P. Ramet

Facts in brief

Capital: Podgorica.
Principal language: Montenegrin.
Area: 5,333 mi² (13,812 km²). *Greatest distances*—north-south, 119 mi (191 km); east-west, 98 mi (158 km).
Elevation: *Highest*—Mount Durmitor, 8,274 ft (2,522 m) above sea level. *Lowest*—sea level along the Adriatic Sea.
Population: *Estimated 2006 population*—650,000; density, 122 per mi² (47 per km²).
Chief products: *Agriculture*—corn, olives, potatoes, tobacco, wheat. *Manufacturing*—aluminum, cement, iron and steel, paper. *Mining*—bauxite, coal, lead.
Flag: A red flag with a yellow border. In the center is a yellow double-headed eagle below a yellow crown. On the eagle's breast is a blue shield with a lion standing on a green field.
Money: *Basic unit*—euro. One hundred cents equal one euro.

© age fotostock/SuperStock

The historic French Quarter is one of the most famous attractions in New Orleans. Tourists on Bourbon Street, *shown here,* pass by some of the district's many restaurants and nightclubs.

New Orleans

New Orleans, *nyoo AWR lee uhnz or AWR luhnz,* is one of the world's busiest ports and, according to the 2000 census, the largest city in Louisiana. It is also a business, cultural, and industrial center of the southern United States. New Orleans lies along the Mississippi River about 100 miles (160 kilometers) north of where the river flows into the Gulf of Mexico. This location helped make the city a great shipping center.

New Orleans has long been a popular city with tourists. The largest crowds come for the annual Mardi Gras celebration, with its parades and other festivities. Tourists are also attracted by the city's historic French Quarter, much of which has the charm of an old European town. In addition, a large number of visitors come to New Orleans to hear top jazz musicians perform in the city that helped give birth to jazz in the early 1900's.

New Orleans is the South's oldest major city. It was founded in 1718 by Jean Baptiste le Moyne, Sieur de Bienville. Bienville was governor of the French colony of Louisiana. He named New Orleans after Philippe, Duke of Orleans, who ruled France for King Louis XV, then a youth. The flags of France, Spain, the Confederate States, and the United States have flown over the city.

In August 2005, Hurricane Katrina struck the Gulf Coast, causing widespread destruction. For weeks, floodwaters covered much of New Orleans. Of the more than 1,500 Louisianians who died because of the hurri-

cane, most were from New Orleans. Hundreds of thousands of people left the city in the days before and after the storm.

Months after the hurricane, most Orleanians who evacuated the city had not returned. In early 2006, experts reported that Baton Rouge, where many evacuees took shelter, ranked ahead of New Orleans in population. Only about 10 percent of the city's businesses had reopened. City officials and others debated how best to rebuild the city. Some parts of New Orleans had returned to nearly normal, but no one knew how quickly or how completely the rest of the city would recover.

The city

New Orleans covers 364 square miles (943 square kilometers), including 165 square miles (427 square kilometers) of inland water. The city occupies all of Orleans Parish and has the same boundaries as the parish. In Louisiana, counties are called *parishes.*

New Orleans is often called the *Crescent City* because its original section—the French Quarter—lay along a giant curve in the Mississippi River. Today, the main part of the city lies between the river on the south and Lake Pontchartrain on the north.

Downtown New Orleans borders the east bank of the Mississippi. Most of the city's residential districts lie west, north, and east of the downtown area. The rest occupy a finger-shaped area on the river's west bank. This area, known as Algiers, is the only part of New Orleans on the west bank.

In the late 1800's, the federal government built about 130 miles (209 kilometers) of earthen barriers, called *levees,* around the city to protect it from flooding. The longest levees lie along the Mississippi River and Lake Pontchartrain. Following the construction of these earthworks, the city installed a massive pumping system to provide drainage during rainstorms. The pumps helped dry out the soils, and much of New Orleans sank below sea level. The combination of levees and pumps transformed the local landscape and led to suburban development in low areas.

Downtown New Orleans includes the French Quarter and the main business district. This area lies on higher ground than much of the city and suffered little damage from Hurricane Katrina in 2005. The French Quarter was named after the French colonists who first settled the area. It is also called the *Vieux Carré* (pronounced *vee yoo cair RAY*), meaning *Old Square.* Most buildings in the French Quarter, however, look more Spanish than French. Fires swept through the area in 1788 and 1794. At that time, Spain ruled Louisiana, and so the rebuilding favored the Spanish style of architecture. This style can be seen in many homes and other buildings, with their landscaped patios and graceful balconies of lacy iron grillwork.

Several of New Orleans's most historic structures border Jackson Square in the heart of the French Quarter. One landmark, the St. Louis Cathedral, was completed in 1851. It stands between the Presbytere and the Cabildo. The Presbytere, built from 1794 to 1813, was used as a courthouse. The Cabildo, begun in 1795 and completed in 1799, was the seat of the Spanish government in the Louisiana Territory. The United States acquired the territory from France in the Louisiana Purchase of 1803. The official transfer of the land took place in the Cabildo. The Presbytere and the Cabildo are now museums. Fire damaged much of the Cabildo in 1988. However, the museum has been fully restored.

The Pontalba Buildings, two block-long apartment buildings, face each other across Jackson Square. They were built as luxury town houses in 1849 and are among the city's most fashionable residences. The French Quarter is also known for its nightclubs on Bourbon Street and antique shops on Royal Street. It also has a number of restaurants famous for the local cuisine, which incorporates elements of African, French, Native American, and Spanish cooking.

New Orleans's main business district lies west of the French Quarter. Large hotels, some of them converted from department stores, stand along Canal Street, the district's main thoroughfare. This broad boulevard is 171 feet (52 meters) wide. The 33-story International Trade Mart rises at the south end of Canal Street. Many firms that deal in international trade have offices in the Trade Mart. A public observation deck at the top of the building offers a spectacular view of the city and the Mississippi River.

Many modern high-rise office buildings and hotels line Poydras Street between the riverfront and the gigantic Louisiana Superdome. The 95,427-seat Superdome, the world's largest indoor stadium, is used for sports events, conventions, and trade shows. City Hall stands in the nearby Civic Center.

Residential districts. West of downtown New Orleans is a large residential area known as Uptown. It includes some of the city's oldest neighborhoods. The most famous is the Garden District, with its majestic old mansions and beautiful gardens. Americans who came to New Orleans after the Louisiana Purchase in 1803 developed the Garden District. Between the Garden District and the river lies the Irish Channel. This working-class neighborhood is filled with traditional New Orleans houses known as *shotguns* (narrow, one-room-wide houses), *shotgun doubles* (two attached shotgun houses), and *camelbacks* (shotguns with an upper level added at the rear). Also in Uptown are Tulane University, Loyola University, and 340-acre (138-hectare) Audubon Park.

City Park and a number of attractive communities along the Lake Pontchartrain shore cover much of northern New Orleans. City Park occupies 1,500 acres (607 hectares) and is one of the nation's largest city-owned parks. The New Orleans Museum of Art is in the park. Lakeview and Pontchartrain Park are among the older lakefront communities. They were built in the mid-1900's, after the former marshlands were protected by levees and pumped dry. They both suffered serious flooding when Hurricane Katrina caused floodwalls to collapse in 2005. New Orleans Lakefront Airport and the University of New Orleans also lie on the lakefront.

Most of New Orleans's newest neighborhoods have been built in the northeastern part of the city, commonly called New Orleans East. Large-scale development began there during the 1960's. New Orleans East *subsided,* or sank, after its development, and the area experienced serious flooding due to Hurricane Katrina.

The metropolitan area of New Orleans-Metairie-Kenner covers 3,155 square miles (8,171 square kilome-

ters). It extends over seven parishes—Jefferson, Orleans, Plaquemines, St. Bernard, St. Charles, St. John the Baptist, and St. Tammany. More than a million people, approximately 30 percent of Louisiana's people, lived in this area at the time of the 2000 census. Fast-growing suburbs have sprung up along the Mississippi between New Orleans and Baton Rouge with the development of large industries. Suburbs north of Lake Pontchartrain have grown rapidly. Hurricane Katrina accelerated suburban growth because many city residents moved to nearby communities.

People

Before Hurricane Katrina struck, African Americans made up more than two-thirds of New Orleans's population. Whites and a small number of Hispanics and Asians accounted for most of the rest of the population.

Facts in brief

Population: *City*—484,674. *Metropolitan statistical area*—1,316,510.
Area: *City*—364 mi² (943 km²). *Metropolitan statistical area*—3,155 mi² (8,171 km²), excluding inland water.
Climate: *Average temperature*—January, 53 °F (12 °C); July, 83 °F (28 °C). *Average annual precipitation* (rainfall, melted snow, and other forms of moisture)—64 inches (163 cm).
Government: Mayor-council. *Terms*—4 years for the mayor and the seven council members.
Founded: 1718. Incorporated as a city in 1805.

New Orleans's flag was adopted in 1918. The three stripes symbolize democracy. The fleurs-de-lis stand for the city's French heritage.

The city seal dates from 1852. The Indians honor the first inhabitants of the New Orleans area. The alligator represents the city's swamps.

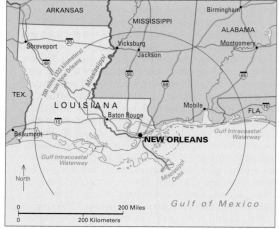

New Orleans lies in southwestern Louisiana.

WORLD BOOK map

However, hundreds of thousands of people, mainly African Americans, left the city because of the hurricane.

Many white Orleanians are descendants of European immigrants who came to the city to find opportunity and freedom during the 1800's and early 1900's. Many other Orleanians arrived from Latin American countries during the 1900's. Large numbers of blacks have lived in the city since the first slaves were brought to the area in the early 1700's. In addition, many free blacks immigrated from the West Indies, especially the Dominican Republic, from the late 1700's to the mid-1800's.

During the last half of the 1900's, the New Orleans metropolitan area experienced a shift in population common to other major urban centers in the United States. A large number of middle-class white families moved from the city to the suburbs. As a result of this population shift, wealthy whites and poor blacks formed the largest groups in New Orleans.

Ethnic groups. Nearly all the early African American residents of New Orleans came from Africa as slaves. They worked on farms and plantations near the city or in the city itself. In the early 1900's, African American musicians made New Orleans a world-famous center of jazz. Black jazz bands still follow a New Orleans custom and play as they march in funeral processions to and from cemeteries.

Downtown New Orleans

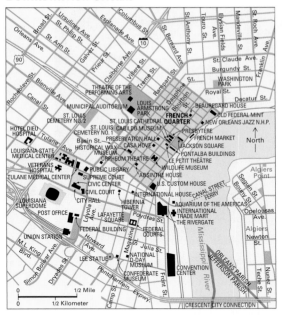

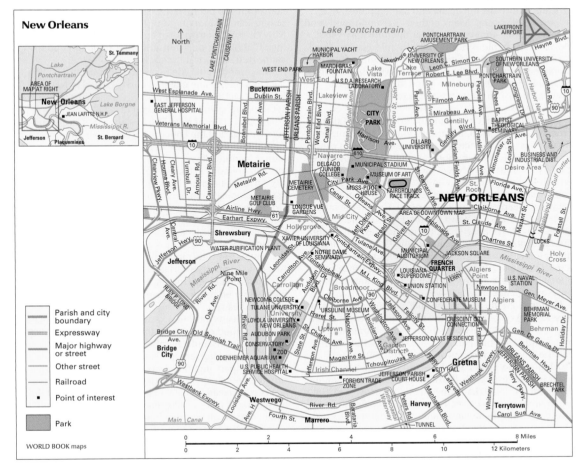

New Orleans

WORLD BOOK maps

A streetcar runs along St. Charles Avenue in the Garden District of New Orleans. The area, developed in the early 1800's, is known for its charming old homes.

Jazz musicians serenade passers-by outside a restaurant in the Garden District. New Orleans is known for its traditional brand of jazz. Musicians in the city helped give birth to jazz music in the early 1900's.

More than 325,000 African Americans lived in New Orleans before the hurricane and made up the city's largest ethnic group. Many of them were poor and lived in mainly black communities near the downtown area. However, a sizable African American middle class lived mainly in eastern New Orleans. Many neighborhoods damaged the most by the 2005 storm were largely black and poor. Some experts predicted that most African Americans displaced by the storm would not return to New Orleans.

Other groups of Orleanians include those of Cuban, French, German, Irish, Italian, Honduran, Mexican, Polish, or Vietnamese ancestry. Many residents who came from Latin America live southeast of the downtown area.

The descendants of New Orleans's early African, French, Native American, and Spanish residents are known as *Creoles.* The term *Creole* comes from a Spanish word meaning *native to the place.* The Creole influence is still strong in New Orleans. For example, on All Saints' Day (November 1), a citywide holiday that honors the dead, many Orleanians follow the Creole tradition of going to the cemetery in family groups. Creole cooking, a spicy blend of African, French, Native American, and Spanish dishes, remains popular in restaurants throughout New Orleans.

Housing. At the time of the 2000 census, nearly half of New Orleans's families owned their homes. Most of the rest rented apartments. New high-rise apartment buildings stand in various parts of New Orleans. But about half the city's housing was built before 1950. In fact, much of the housing dates from the 1800's. Many of the older homes, especially those in the French Quarter and the Garden District, have been beautifully restored. But much other housing, greatly in need of repair, is neglected because the owners cannot afford the high cost of repairs. Yet, the traditional shotguns and doubles represent a local architectural tradition and contribute to the city's unique look.

Education. Before the hurricane struck, New Orleans had about 130 public schools. About 90 percent of the public school students were African Americans. The New Orleans metropolitan area also had about 125 Roman Catholic schools and a number of other church-supported and private schools.

Nine months after the hurricane, less than one-fifth of the city's school-age children had returned to New Orleans. Fewer than half of the city's public schools were set to open again by the autumn of 2006.

The University of New Orleans, the city's largest university, is part of the Louisiana State University system. Tulane University is New Orleans's oldest institution of higher learning. It was founded in 1834. Other universities and colleges in New Orleans include Dillard University; Loyola University New Orleans; New Orleans Baptist Theological Seminary; Notre Dame Seminary Graduate School of Theology; Our Lady of Holy Cross College; Southern University of New Orleans; and Xavier University of Louisiana.

The arts. New Orleans is a leading cultural center of the South. The New Orleans Theatre of the Performing Arts houses the New Orleans Opera House Association. The Louisiana Philharmonic, a symphony orchestra completely owned by its musicians, performs in the Orpheum Theatre.

New Orleans has been known for its jazz ever since the city helped give birth to the music in the early 1900's. Black musicians and a number of white musicians helped to develop jazz in the bars and nightclubs on Basin, Rampart, and other streets both inside and outside the French Quarter. Today, old New Orleans-style jazz is still played in many places in the city. One of the most famous places is Preservation Hall, a small building where fans sit on wooden benches or stand to hear jazz.

Le Petit Théâtre du Vieux Carré is one of the city's best-known professional theater companies. The Dashiki Project Theatre is a leading African American company.

Colorful Mardi Gras parades are a highlight of the carnival season in New Orleans. Mardi Gras festivities last for about two weeks and end the day before the religious season of Lent begins. Costumed riders on a parade float, *shown here,* toss beads and other trinkets to crowds along Canal Street.

© Robyn Beck, AFP/Getty Images

Libraries and museums. The New Orleans Public Library operates a main library and several branches. Tulane University has an outstanding collection of books on Louisiana history. Tulane is also the home of the Amistad Collection, a group of books and other materials about African American life and culture. In addition to public and university libraries, the historic New Orleans Collection is one of the finest repositories of material about the development of Louisiana and the South.

The New Orleans Museum of Art has a fine display of Spanish colonial paintings and decorative art. The Louisiana State Museum operates eight historic buildings in New Orleans, including the Cabildo and Madame John's Legacy, a beautifully restored house dating from the late 1700's. Other New Orleans museums include the Moss-Pitot House, a former plantation; the Confederate Memorial Museum; the National D-Day Museum; and the Old U.S. Mint, which features jazz and Mardi Gras memorabilia.

Jean Lafitte National Historical Park and Preserve includes a large area of wetlands and the site of the Battle of New Orleans. A visitor center features displays about the battle, which was the last clash of the War of 1812.

Recreation. New Orleans has more than 100 parks. The two largest, City Park and Audubon Park, were plantations during the 1800's. City Park includes a bandstand and the 27,000-seat Municipal Stadium. Audubon Park's attractions include a large zoo. The Aquarium of the Americas, a large aquarium, stands in the French Quarter along the Mississippi River. Lake Pontchartrain and other nearby lakes are popular for boating, fishing, and sailing. The Bayou Sauvage National Wildlife Refuge in eastern New Orleans is an appealing outdoor attraction.

The city has two major league professional teams. It is the home of the New Orleans Saints of the National Football League and the New Orleans/Oklahoma City Hornets of the National Basketball Association. After the hurricane, the Hornets began to play most of their home games in Oklahoma City.

Annual events. Every year, large numbers of visitors attend New Orleans's Mardi Gras festival in February or March. The celebration climaxes the city's carnival season, which begins in January. Mardi Gras activities last about two weeks and end on Shrove Tuesday, the day before the Christian observance of Lent starts. Mardi Gras features parades and elaborate costume balls sponsored by private carnival organizations known as *krewes.* On Shrove Tuesday, also called Mardi Gras Day, the king of the Rex krewe leads a parade of several hundred floats. Brightly costumed riders on the floats toss beads, toys, and imitation gold coins called *doubloons* to the crowds.

Another popular annual event in New Orleans is the Spring Fiesta, held in April or May. It includes guided tours through charming old houses in the French Quarter and the Garden District. The Jazz and Heritage Festival is another popular spring event. New Orleans hosts the annual Sugar Bowl football game on or near New Year's Day. The game, held in the Superdome, features two of the nation's top college teams.

Social problems. The U.S. Census Bureau reported that, in the early 2000's, more than one-fourth of the city's families were poor. Most of the city's poor had little education and worked at low-paying jobs or were unemployed. Deteriorating housing in low-income areas was also a serious problem.

Economy

Months after Hurricane Katrina, most businesses in New Orleans had not reopened. The French Quarter suffered little damage, and most of its cultural and retail establishments had opened to accommodate visitors and city residents. Many workers came from across the country to help rebuild a city that suffered such great damage. Unless otherwise noted, the paragraphs below discuss the New Orleans economy before the storm.

Trade and finance. The Port of New Orleans handled millions of tons of cargo a year. About 6,000 ships from about 60 nations docked at the busy port annually. The chief exports were grain and other foods from the midwestern United States and petroleum products. The leading imports included aluminum, coffee, forest products, rubber, petroleum, and steel. The port's heaviest trading was with Latin America.

New Orleans has been a busy port for barges. The barges use the nation's two main inland waterways, the Mississippi River and the Gulf Intracoastal Waterway, which meet at New Orleans.

The New Orleans metropolitan area has been one of the South's chief centers for hotels, restaurants, and retail and wholesale trade. It had about 8,500 retail firms and over 2,000 wholesale firms.

The New Orleans area also has been a financial center. Many commercial banks and savings and loan associations have operated in the area. Their loans helped finance business expansion projects and other civic developments. The Sixth Federal Reserve District Bank operates a branch bank in New Orleans.

Industry. In the early 2000's, the New Orleans metropolitan area had about 1,000 manufacturing plants. They employed about 12 percent of the area's workers and produced more than $1 billion worth of goods yearly.

At the Michoud Assembly Facility, several companies have produced equipment for the United States space program. Michoud made the Saturn 5 rocket that launched the Apollo 11 astronauts to the moon in 1969. In the 1980's, a huge new industrial center, the Almonaster-Michoud Industrial District (now called the New Orleans Business and Industrial District), was begun. It was built around the Michoud Assembly Facility. The Avondale Shipyard, in Jefferson Parish, has been one of the nation's largest shipbuilding centers. Other leading industries in the area have included the making of food products, petrochemicals, petroleum products, and primary metals.

Transportation. Barges and oceangoing ships dock at wharves on the Mississippi River, the Inner Harbor Navigation Canal, and the Mississippi River-Gulf Outlet (MRGO). The Navigation Canal links the Mississippi and

Christopher R. Harris from Katherine Young

Shipbuilding has been one of the leading industries in the New Orleans metropolitan area. The Avondale Shipyard of Jefferson Parish, *shown here,* has been a major U.S. shipbuilding center.

Lake Pontchartrain. The 76-mile (122-kilometer) Gulf Outlet gives shippers a 44-mile (71-kilometer) short cut between New Orleans and the Gulf of Mexico.

During the 2005 hurricane, *storm surges* (rapid rises in sea level produced when winds drive ocean waters ashore) moved rapidly up these artificial waterways, knocking down levees and flooding low-lying neighborhoods. In the storm's aftermath, some government proposals have called for the closure of the MRGO. The proposals ask the federal government to pay to relocate businesses away from the waterway.

Louis Armstrong New Orleans International Airport, in the nearby city of Kenner, serves many commercial airlines. Private aircraft use New Orleans Lakefront Airport. Many trucking companies and several passenger and freight rail lines also serve the city. The Lake Pontchartrain Causeway, the world's longest bridge, extends about 29 miles (47 kilometers). It spans the lake and links New Orleans and its northern suburbs.

Communication. New Orleans has one daily newspaper, *The Times-Picayune.* It has the largest circulation of Louisiana's daily newspapers. Several television stations and a number of radio stations serve the city.

Government

The city has a mayor-council form of government. Voters elect the mayor and the seven members of the City Council to four-year terms. The mayor may serve any number of terms but not more than two in a row.

The mayor appoints a chief administrative officer to help direct the city government. The mayor also plans civic improvements. The council makes the city's laws. The mayor may veto bills passed by the council. However, any bill the mayor vetoes may still become law if at least five council members vote to repass it.

A sales tax is the city government's largest source of local revenue. But New Orleans, like other big cities, does not raise enough money from local taxes to pay for the increasing costs of services and improvements. As a result, the city has depended on the state and federal governments for about one-third of its revenue.

History

Chickasaw, Choctaw, and Natchez Indians lived in what is now the New Orleans area before Europeans arrived. In 1682, the French explorer René-Robert Cavelier, Sieur de La Salle, sailed down the Mississippi River from the Great Lakes region. He claimed the entire Mississippi Valley for France.

French and Spanish rule. Sieur de Bienville founded New Orleans in 1718. In 1722, he made it the capital of the French colony of Louisiana, which covered the central third of the present-day United States.

In 1762, King Louis XV of France gave Louisiana to his cousin, King Charles III of Spain. The French Orleanians disliked the first Spanish governor of Louisiana, Antonio de Ulloa, and drove him from the city in 1768. But in 1769, soldiers arrived from Spain and restored Spanish rule in New Orleans.

The worst urban fire in what is now Louisiana broke out in New Orleans on March 21, 1788. It started in a house on Chartres Street and destroyed over 850 buildings. Rebuilding was underway when a fire swept through 200 more structures in 1794.

In 1800, France secretly regained the Louisiana region from Spain but did not reveal the fact until March 1803. The next month, France sold Louisiana to the United States. On November 30, in preparation for the region's official transfer, the French took down the Spanish flag that still waved over New Orleans and raised the French flag. On December 20, the American flag became the third flag to fly over the city in less than a month.

The early 1800's. In 1805, New Orleans was incorporated as a city. Louisiana joined the Union in 1812, and New Orleans became the state capital. Also in 1812, the steamboat *New Orleans* arrived at New Orleans after sailing down the Ohio and Mississippi rivers from Pittsburgh. It was the first steamer to navigate the Mississippi. River trade soon boomed at New Orleans.

During the War of 1812, British troops tried to capture New Orleans. The British sought the aid of Jean Laffite, leader of a pirate band based near the city. But Laffite joined the American forces that were defending New Orleans. General Andrew Jackson commanded the U.S. troops. Jackson's army and Laffite's pirates defeated the British in the Battle of New Orleans on Jan. 8, 1815.

After the war, river trade brought increasing wealth to New Orleans. The city thrived as a cotton port and slave-trading center. The state capital was moved to Donaldsonville in 1830. But New Orleans again served as the capital from 1831 until 1849, when Baton Rouge became the capital. New Orleans held its first Mardi Gras celebration in 1838.

The Paris of America. By 1840, New Orleans had a population of 102,193 and was the nation's fourth largest city. In the mid-1800's, it attracted thousands of immigrants from Germany and Ireland. Professional opera and theater companies thrived in New Orleans during this period, and the lively and glamorous city became known as the *Paris of America.*

During the mid-1800's, New Orleans also gained a reputation as an unhealthy place. In 1832, a yellow fever epidemic swept through the city, taking about 7,700 lives. Doctors did not know that mosquitoes, which thrived in the swampy New Orleans area, were the chief carriers of the disease. The worst yellow fever epidemic in United States history hit New Orleans in 1853. It killed more than 11,000 people.

The American Civil War and Reconstruction. In 1861, Louisiana withdrew from the Union and joined the Confederate States against the North in the American Civil War (1861-1865). New Orleans's importance as a port made it a chief target of the Union forces. In April 1862, a Union fleet commanded by Captain David Farragut sailed up the Mississippi from the Gulf of Mexico. After bombarding several forts, the fleet reached New Orleans and forced it to surrender on May 1. General Benjamin F. Butler took charge of the city and made it the Union capital of Louisiana.

Union troops remained in New Orleans during the Reconstruction period after the war. African Americans and Northerners gained control of the city government. In 1866, a riot broke out between whites and blacks in New Orleans over a voting dispute. The riot resulted in the deaths of about 50 people—most of them blacks—and increased racial tension in the city. Widespread corruption in government and rising city debts also troubled New Orleans during Reconstruction. In 1877, the U.S. government withdrew its troops from the city.

During the late 1800's, New Orleans struggled to rebuild its economy. Trade at the port had slumped sharply after the Civil War, when the coming of the railroads to the Mississippi Valley caused steamboat traffic to decline. In 1878, another yellow fever epidemic killed more than 3,800 Orleanians.

Civic improvements. Port activity increased rapidly after 1879. That year, U.S. Army engineers directed by James B. Eads deepened the mouth of the Mississippi River. This project enabled oceangoing ships to reach New Orleans.

By 1900, New Orleans's population had reached about 287,000. It continued to climb steadily during the early 1900's, when thousands of Italian immigrants arrived. In 1905, New Orleans officials adopted a program to combat mosquitoes by destroying their breeding areas. This program ended the threat of yellow fever in the city.

By 1920, African American musicians had helped New Orleans win fame as a jazz center. They included Louis

Lithograph (1851) by T. H. Muller; Mariners' Museum, Newport News, Virginia (Katherine Young)

New Orleans's riverfront served as a chief port for steamboats that traveled on the Mississippi River in the mid-1800's. The booming river trade of this period brought great wealth to New Orleans, which thrived as a cotton port.

AP/Wide World

Floodwaters from Hurricane Katrina remained in low-lying New Orleans neighborhoods for weeks after the storm in 2005. The hurricane caused hundreds of deaths and great destruction.

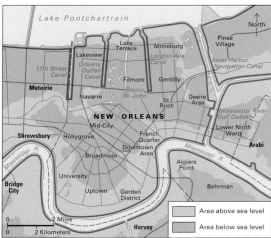

WORLD BOOK map

Much of New Orleans lies below sea level and is protected by a system of flood barriers called *levees*. The red lines on this map show the city's major levees. Areas below sea level suffered the greatest damage from Hurricane Katrina in 2005.

Armstrong, Jelly Roll Morton, and King Oliver.

During the 1920's, the development of tugboats powerful enough to push long lines of barges on the Mississippi River greatly increased trade at New Orleans's port. An annual threat of floods from the Mississippi was reduced with the completion of the Bonnet Carré Spillway in 1932. This channel connects the river to Lake Pontchartrain west of New Orleans. When floods threaten, water from the river is forced through the spillway and the lake to the Mississippi Sound.

In 1946, deLesseps S. Morrison, a Democratic reformer, was elected mayor of New Orleans. He served as mayor until 1961 and began a series of long overdue civic projects. In his first major accomplishment, Morrison combined five railroad stations into one, the Union Passenger Terminal. It opened in 1954. Other projects included the opening of the Greater New Orleans Bridge (now part of the Crescent City Connection) in 1958 and completion of the Civic Center in 1959.

Social changes. During the 1960's, far-reaching social changes occurred in New Orleans. In 1960, black students entered all-white public elementary schools in New Orleans for the first time since the Reconstruction period. The city's libraries, restaurants, and other public facilities also became integrated during the decade.

Large residential developments began in New Orleans East during the 1960's. In the mid-1960's, the production of rockets at the Michoud Assembly Facility made New Orleans a space age industrial center.

The late 1900's. The Louisiana Superdome opened in 1975. It led to the building of several hotels and motels in downtown New Orleans. A World's Fair was held in New Orleans in 1984.

Development of a 7,000-acre (2,800-hectare) business and industrial park in eastern New Orleans took place in the 1980's and 1990's. The park, reserved for business construction only, created jobs in the area.

In 1977, New Orleans voters elected Ernest N. (Dutch) Morial mayor. He was the city's first African American mayor. He was reelected in 1982 and remained in office until 1986. Marc H. Morial, Ernest's son, served as mayor from 1994 to 2002.

The early 2000's. In August 2005, New Orleans suffered one of the worst disasters in American history when Hurricane Katrina struck the Gulf Coast. The hurricane caused hundreds of deaths and widespread destruction. After the levees failed, floodwaters covered about 80 percent of New Orleans and ruined thousands of homes. Hundreds of thousands of residents evacuated the city, and many were left homeless. Some suburbs and older neighborhoods that occupy higher ground survived the storm unharmed and largely returned to normal. But many of the city's lakefront areas remained damaged. Repairs to the levees, homes, and businesses were expected to take years.   Craig E. Colten

Questions

Why is New Orleans often called the *Crescent City?*
How has the Bonnet Carré Spillway largely ended the threat of floods to New Orleans?
When was New Orleans founded? By whom?
When does Mardi Gras take place?
Who led the Americans in the Battle of New Orleans?
What kind of music is New Orleans famous for?
Why do most buildings in the French Quarter look more Spanish than French?
How do many Orleanians celebrate All Saints' Day?
What historic event took place in the Cabildo?
What two main inland U.S. waterways meet at New Orleans?

Additional resources

Cowan, Walter G., and others. *New Orleans Yesterday and Today.* 3rd ed. La. State Univ. Pr., 2001.
Fodor's New Orleans. Fodor's Travel, published annually.

Belgrade is the capital and largest city of Serbia. It lies in the northern part of the country. Belgrade stands at the junction of the Danube and Sava rivers and serves as an important river port. This picture shows a church spire rising above an older neighborhood on the Sava River.

© Slobodan Ljubisic, Shutterstock

Serbia, *SUR bee uh,* is a country on the Balkan Peninsula in southeastern Europe. Belgrade is the country's capital and largest city.

Serbia is bordered by Hungary on the north, Romania and Bulgaria on the east, Macedonia on the south, and Albania, Montenegro, Bosnia-Herzegovina, and Croatia on the west. Serbia includes the provinces of Vojvodina, in the northern part of the country, and Kosovo, in the south.

The first united Serbian state was formed in the late 1100's. The Ottoman Empire ruled the region for about 400 years, from the mid-1400's to the late 1800's. In 1918, Serbia became part of the Kingdom of the Serbs, Croats, and Slovenes. The kingdom was later renamed Yugoslavia, which means *Land of the South Slavs.*

In 1946, Yugoslavia became a Communist federal state made up of six republics, the largest of which was Serbia. In 1991 and 1992, four of the republics—Slovenia, Croatia, Macedonia, and Bosnia-Herzegovina—declared their independence. Fighting broke out between Serbs and other ethnic groups in Croatia and in Bosnia-Herzegovina. A cease-fire ended most of the fighting in Croatia in January 1992, but some fighting continued. In April 1992, Serbia and Montenegro formed a new, smaller Federal Republic of Yugoslavia.

In late 1995, the government of Croatia and the leaders of the Croatian Serbs agreed to end the war in Croatia. Also in late 1995, leaders of Bosnia-Herzegovina, Croatia, and Serbia signed a peace treaty. A number of countries then recognized the new Yugoslavia.

In 1998, fighting began between Serbian forces and ethnic Albanians in Kosovo. Serbian troops withdrew in 1999. In 2002, the leaders of Serbia, Montenegro, and Yugoslavia developed plans to craft a new constitution and to rename the country. In 2003, Yugoslavia officially became the country of Serbia and Montenegro.

In 2006, citizens of Montenegro voted in a referendum to separate from Serbia. Shortly after the referendum, Montenegro declared independence. Then Serbia declared its own independence.

Government

A president heads the government of Serbia. Voters elect the president to a four-year term. A prime minister, appointed by the president, oversees the day-to-day operations of the government. A one-house National Assembly is Serbia's legislative body. Its 250 members are elected by the people to four-year terms. All citizens who are 18 years of age and older may vote.

Serbia's major political parties are the Socialist Party of Serbia (formerly the League of Communists of Serbia), the Democratic Movement of Serbia, and the Serbian Radical Party.

The Court of the Republic of Serbia is Serbia's highest court. The National Assembly appoints judges for life.

People

Serbs make up about 85 percent of the population of what is sometimes called Serbia proper—the area excluding the provinces of Vojvodina and Kosovo. About 55 percent of the people of Vojvodina are Serbs, and nearly 20 percent are Hungarians. The province also includes large numbers of Croats, Montenegrins, Romanians, and Slovaks. In Kosovo, before the fighting that took place in the late 1990's, about 90 percent of the people were Albanians, and the rest were mainly Serbs.

Most of the people of Serbia speak Serbian. The Serbian language traditionally uses a form of the Cyrillic alphabet, the system used in writing Russian and other Slavic languages. But the Roman alphabet is also used for modern Serbian.

About half the people of Serbia live in cities. The others live in rural areas. Many rural families live in brick, stone, or wooden houses with steep roofs. Typical suburban housing consists of high-rise apartment buildings made of concrete. Most city dwellers live in older brick houses or apartment buildings.

Serbian cooking reflects both central European and Turkish influences. Serbian cooks are known for grilled, highly seasoned meats and spicy salads. *Ćevapćići,* which

Facts in brief

Capital: Belgrade.
Principal language: Serbian.
Area: 34,116 mi² (88,361 km²). *Greatest distances*—north-south, 305 mi (491 km); east-west, 210 mi (338 km).
Elevation: *Highest*—Mount Daravica, 8,714 ft (2,656 m) above sea level. *Lowest*—115 ft (35 m) above sea level on Danube River at eastern border with Romania and Bulgaria.
Population: *Estimated 2006 population*—9,860,000; density, 289 per mi² (112 per km²).
Chief products: *Agriculture*—cattle, corn, hogs, potatoes, sheep, sugar beets, wheat. *Manufacturing*—automobiles, cement, iron and steel, plastics, textiles, trucks. *Mining*—coal, copper, lead, zinc.
Money: *Basic unit*—Serbian dinar (except for Kosovo); euro (Kosovo). One hundred paras equal one dinar. One hundred cents equal one euro.

Serbia is a country on the Balkan Peninsula in southeastern Europe. It is bordered by Hungary, Romania, Bulgaria, Macedonia, Albania, Montenegro, Bosnia-Herzegovina, and Croatia.

Symbols of Serbia. The flag has red, blue, and white stripes and Serbia's coat of arms. The coat of arms has a gold crown above a red shield with a double-headed eagle on it.

consists of grilled meatballs served with raw onions on bread, is a Serbian specialty. *Ajvar* is a relish made of roasted red peppers. A favorite snack in Serbia is *burek,* a pastry layered with cheese, meat, or jam. Typical Serbian beverages include thick, sweet Turkish coffee and plum brandy.

Serbians enjoy many sports, particularly soccer. Basketball is also popular, and almost every town or village in Serbia has its own basketball team.

The traditional religion of the Serbs is Serbian Orthodoxy. Some Serbs are members of the Seventh-day Adventist Church. Hungarians and Slovaks typically belong to such ethnic churches as the Hungarian Evangelical Lutheran Church or the Slovak Evangelical Christian Church. Most Albanians in Kosovo are Muslims.

Children in Serbia must complete at least 8 years of elementary school. However, most children attend school for 12 years. Serbia has universities in Belgrade, Novi Sad, and Priština.

Most of the adults in the urban areas of Serbia are well-educated. However, in rural Serbia, especially among Albanian Muslims, families have traditionally kept girls out of school to work in the home or on the farm. This practice has kept many rural women in domestic roles.

Serbian folk music is played mainly on the accordion.

The violin and the *tamboura,* an instrument resembling a lute, are also used to accompany folk dances in certain parts of Serbia. The best-known traditional dance among the Serbs is the *kolo,* which is performed in a circle. In the late 1900's, a new, sometimes extreme, pride in Serbian culture began to sweep the republic. This movement has sparked an interest in Serbian writers of the 1900's, such as Matija Bečkovic, Miloš Crnjanski, Dobrica Ćosić, and Vuk Drašković.

Land and climate

The Pannonian Plains lie in northern Serbia. The region is mostly flat, with some low hills. The rest of Serbia is hilly or mountainous.

A number of rivers flow through Serbia. They include the Danube, one of Europe's longest waterways. The Danube enters Serbia from Hungary, forming part of the border between Serbia and Croatia. The river flows southeast across Serbia and then forms part of Serbia's border with Romania. The Iron Gate Dam on the Danube stands at Iron Gate, a gorge at the border between Serbia and Romania. The power plant of the dam supplies electric power for the two countries.

The Morava River runs north through the hills of southern and central Serbia and then empties into the Danube. The Sava River flows eastward, emptying into the Danube at Belgrade.

The Pannonian Plains have cold winters with a freezing wind called a *košava.* Summers are dry and hot, with temperatures often rising to about 100 °F (38 °C). In Belgrade, on the edge of the Pannonian Plains, the average January temperature is 32 °F (0 °C). The average July temperature is 73 °F (23 °C).

The rest of Serbia has bitterly cold winters with much snow. Heavy rains fall in early summer. Summers are warm in the mountain valleys but cool at higher elevations.

Economy

Agriculture employs a number of people in Serbia. The country's best farmland lies in Vojvodina and in Sumadija, an area south of Belgrade. Farmers grow corn, potatoes, sugar beets, and wheat. They also raise cattle, hogs, and sheep.

Factories in Serbia produce automobiles, cement, iron and steel, plastics, textiles, and trucks. Serbia has deposits of coal, copper, lead, and zinc.

A network of highways extends from Belgrade, but the rest of Serbia has fewer roads. Roads between some villages are unpaved. Railroads link Belgrade with major cities and towns in Serbia and in neighboring countries. Serbia has airports in Belgrade, Niš, and Priština. The Belgrade airport, which is the country's largest, handles international flights.

The leading daily newspapers in the country are *Večernje novosti, Politika ekspres, Politika,* and *Sport,* all published in Belgrade; and *Dnevnik,* which is published in Novi Sad.

History

Early days. During the A.D. 500's and 600's, various groups of Slavs, including the ancestors of the Serbs, settled in the Balkan Peninsula in the area of present-day Serbia. Each group had its own leader until the late 1100's, when Stefan Nemanja, a warrior and chief, formed the first united Serbian state. During the 1300's, Emperor Stefan Dušan led the country in successful wars against the Byzantine Empire. The Serbian empire began to break up after his death in 1355. The Ottoman Empire, based in what is now Turkey, defeated Serbia in the Battle of Kosovo Polje in 1389.

Ottoman rule. The Ottoman Empire conquered Serbia in the mid-1400's and ruled the region for more than 400 years, but the Serbs never lost their national pride. Djordge Petrović, a Serbian peasant who was nicknamed Black George, led an uprising against the Ottomans in 1804. Another Serbian peasant leader, Miloš Obrenović, led a second revolt in 1815. The Serbs won some liberties in these struggles. Serbia regained independence only in 1878, following the Ottoman Empire's defeat by Russia in the Russo-Turkish War of 1877-1878. In the First Balkan War (1912-1913), Serbia and the other Balkan states gained control of almost all of the Ottoman Empire's territory in Europe.

A new country. In the early 1900's, various economic and political conflicts developed between Serbia and Austria-Hungary. In June 1914, the heir to the throne of Austria-Hungary, Archduke Franz Ferdinand, was assassinated by Gavrilo Princip, a Serb from the province of Bosnia-Herzegovina in Austria-Hungary. The assassination touched off World War I, which began a month later when Austria-Hungary declared war on Serbia. After the war ended in 1918, Serbia led the way in forming the Kingdom of the Serbs, Croats, and Slovenes. Peter I of Serbia became the king. Peter died in 1921, and his son became King Alexander I.

Problems soon developed. The Slovenes and Croats believed the Serbs had too much power. They demanded greater control over their local affairs. It also proved difficult to unite the kingdom's many ethnic groups.

The country's 1921 Constitution created a constitutional monarchy. But in 1929, King Alexander abolished the Constitution and began to rule as a dictator. He renamed the country *Yugoslavia.* He created new political divisions that ignored the ethnic groups' historical borders. His actions worsened relations among the groups. He was assassinated in 1934 by a Macedonian from Bulgaria who was supported by Croatian revolutionaries.

Alexander's 11-year-old son, King Peter II, was too young to rule. Alexander's cousin, Prince Paul, ruled in the boy's place. Under Paul, an agreement was made to establish an *autonomous* (self-governing) Croatia, but not all Serbs accepted the agreement.

World War II. World War II began in 1939 as a struggle between the Axis powers, led by Germany and Italy, and the Allies, which included the United Kingdom and France. Yugoslavia was unprepared for war, so its government tried to stay on friendly terms with both sides. Under pressure from the Germans, the Yugoslav government joined the Axis on March 25, 1941. However, the Yugoslav army rebelled. The army overthrew Paul's government, and 17-year-old Peter took the throne. On April 6, Germany invaded Yugoslavia. The Yugoslav army surrendered 11 days later. Peter and other government leaders fled to London and formed a government-in-exile.

German and other Axis troops occupied Yugoslavia. A resistance movement against the Axis occupation spread among the Yugoslav peoples. Some of them joined the

© Adam Woolfitt, Corbis

A castle on the Danube River is an example of Serbia's historic architecture. Built in the early 1300's, Golubac Castle is one of the largest and most beautiful buildings along the river.

Partisans, a group led by Josip Broz Tito and the Communist Party. Other Yugoslavs joined the Chetniks, a group headed by Draža Mihajlović. The Partisans wanted to establish a Communist government. The Chetniks supported the government of King Peter. The two resistance groups fought each other, as well as the occupation forces.

Communist rule. The Partisans quickly gained the support of the Yugoslav peoples. The Communists set up a temporary government in Jajce (now in Bosnia-Herzegovina) in November 1943. Aided by Allied troops, the Partisans freed Belgrade from occupation in 1944. The Communists then began to govern Yugoslavia from the capital. By the time World War II ended in Europe in May 1945, Tito and the Communists firmly controlled Yugoslavia.

On Nov. 29, 1945, Yugoslavia became a republic called the Federal People's Republic of Yugoslavia. The monarchy was abolished, and King Peter never returned to Yugoslavia. The 1946 Constitution officially organized Yugoslavia as a *federal* state—that is, a state where each of the republics largely controlled its own affairs. The six republics were Bosnia-Herzegovina, Croatia, Macedonia, Montenegro, Serbia, and Slovenia. Vojvodina and Kosovo became autonomous provinces of Serbia.

Only one political party, the Communist Party, was permitted. The government took control of farms, factories, and other businesses. The Communists began working to develop Yugoslavia from an agricultural country into an industrial one. Opponents of the Communist government were either imprisoned or exiled.

Yugoslavia was a close Soviet ally, but Tito refused to let the Soviet Union control the country. In June 1948, the Soviet dictator Joseph Stalin broke off relations with Yugoslavia. Yugoslavia then began to develop its own style of Communist government. Yugoslavia's republics and provinces received more control over local matters. In 1955, two years after Stalin's death, Soviet and Yugoslav leaders reopened relations. But Tito refused to take sides in the Cold War, a bitter political rivalry between the

Communist nations and the Western democracies. Instead, he became a leading spokesman for uncommitted nations.

In 1971, a 23-member council called the Presidency was established to head the Yugoslav government. A new constitution in 1974 reduced the Presidency to 9 members. Tito remained the country's top leader as head of the council until he died in May 1980. Then, a system of annual rotation of the top post took effect. Eight members of the Presidency, one from each republic and province, took turns serving one-year terms as head of the council. Until 1989, the leader of Yugoslavia's Communist Party also held a seat on the Presidency but did not take a turn as its head.

Political changes and ethnic tensions. The Yugoslav economy started to decline in the late 1970's, and the country began to experience severe inflation and other economic problems. In the late 1980's, Communism was losing its grip on power across Eastern Europe, and many people in Yugoslavia called for a multiparty political system. In January 1990, Yugoslavia's Communist Party voted to end its monopoly on power in the country. Many new political parties formed. Each of Yugoslavia's republics held multiparty elections in 1990. Non-Communist parties won a majority of seats in the parliaments of Bosnia-Herzegovina, Croatia, Macedonia, and Slovenia. In Serbia and Montenegro, the Communist parties, now known as Socialist parties, won majorities.

For many years, tension had existed between ethnic groups in Yugoslavia, especially between Serbs and Croats and between Serbs and ethnic Albanians. During the 1960's, some of the Croats and Slovenes began to call for independence from Yugoslavia. These demands grew in the 1980's. Croatia and Slovenia charged that the na-

Serbia

WORLD BOOK map

▬▬	International boundary
──	Road
──	Railroad
✪	National capital
•	Other city or town
+	Elevation above sea level

Serbia map index

Cities*

Aleksinac	57,749	.C	4
Bačka Palanka	60,966	.A	2
Bečej	40,987	.A	3
Belgrade	1,576,124	.B	3
Bor	55,817	.C	4
Čačak	117,072	.C	3
Đakovica		.E	3
Gnjilane		.E	4
Jagodina	70,894	.C	4
Kikinda	67,002	.A	3
Kosovska Mitrovica		.D	3
Kragujevac	175,802	.C	3
Kraljevo	121,707	.C	3
Kruševac	131,368	.C	4
Kula	48,353	.A	2
Leskovac	126,252	.D	4
Loznica	86,413	.B	2
Negotin	43,418	.C	5
Niš	250,518	.D	4
Novi Pazar	85,996	.D	3
Novi Sad	299,294	.A	2
Orahovac		.E	3
Pančevo	127,162	.B	3
Paraćin	58,301	.C	4
Peć		.E	3
Pirot	63,791	.D	5
Požarevac	74,902	.B	4
Priština		.D	4
Prizren		.E	3
Prokuplje	48,501	.D	4
Ruma	60,006	.B	3
Šabac	122,893	.B	2
Smederevo	109,809	.B	3
Smederevska Palanka	56,011	.C	3
Sombor	97,263	.A	2
Sremska Mitrovica	85,902	.B	2
Subotica	148,401	.A	2
Stara Pazova	67,576	.B	3
Uroševac		.E	4
Valjevo	83,022	.C	2
Vranje	96,761	.C	3
Vrbas	45,852	.A	2
Vršac	54,369	.B	4
Vučitrn		.D	3
Zaječar	65,969	.C	5
Zrenjanin	132,051	.A	3

Physical features

Balkan Mountains	.D	5
Beli Drim (river)	.E	3
Danube (river)	.C	5
Daravica (peak)	.E	3
Drina (river)	.C	2
Ibar (river)	.D	3
Iron Gate Dam	.B	5
Iron Gate Reservoir	.B	4
Južna Morava (river)	.E	4
Kopaonik (mountain range)	.D	3
Midžor (peak)	.D	5
Pannonian Plains	.A	3
Sava (river)	.B	3
Timok (river)	.C	4
Tisa (river)	.A	3
Velika Morava (river)	.C	4
Zapadna Morava (river)	.C	3

*Populations of municipalities which may include rural areas as well as the urban center.
Source: 2002 census. Cities without populations are in Kosovo, which was not included in the 2002 census.

tional government took away too much of their income. They also claimed that Serbia, which had the most influence in the national government, sought to control the other republics. Demands for independence also increased among ethnic Albanians in Kosovo during the 1980's.

The breakup of Yugoslavia. In 1989, Slobodan Milošević, a strong supporter of Serbian unity and the expansion of Serbian borders, became president of Serbia. Under him, Serbia stripped Kosovo and Vojvodina of autonomy and, in 1990, dissolved the government of Kosovo.

In May 1991, Serbia blocked the election of a Croat who was scheduled to become head of the Presidency under the system of annual rotation. Partly as a result, Croatia and Slovenia declared their independence in late June. Fighting then broke out in Croatia between ethnic Serbs who claimed part of the republic and the Croat militia. In September 1991, Macedonia declared its independence. In January 1992, a cease-fire between the Serbian and Croatian forces ended most fighting. But Serbian forces still held some Croatian land.

In March 1992, a majority of Bosnian Muslims and ethnic Croats in Bosnia-Herzegovina voted for independence from Yugoslavia in a *referendum* (direct vote). Ethnic Serbs boycotted the referendum. Fighting then broke out between Serbs who claimed part of the republic and Muslims and Croats. Serbs soon gained control of about two-thirds of the republic.

In April 1992, Serbia and Montenegro formed a new Yugoslavia. In late 1995, the Croatian government and the leaders of the Croatian Serbs made peace in Croatia. They agreed to a plan that would gradually reunite the land still held by Croatian Serbs with the rest of Croatia. Also in late 1995, representatives of Bosnia, Croatia, and Serbia signed a peace plan for Bosnia. The plan called for dividing Bosnia into two parts, one to be dominated by a Muslim-Croat federation and the other by Bosnian Serbs.

Kosovo crisis. In 1997, Milošević ended his second term as Serbia's president. Yugoslavia's parliament elected him president of Yugoslavia, but some members boycotted the vote.

In early 1998, Yugoslavia received international criticism after Serbian police attacked villages in the

province of Kosovo, killing dozens of people and burning many homes. Milošević said the police attack was a crackdown on the rebel Kosovo Liberation Army, which demanded independence for the province. Fighting began between the Serbian and rebel forces. Serbian forces destroyed villages in the province and drove many of Kosovo's Albanians from their homes.

The North Atlantic Treaty Organization (NATO) sponsored peace talks in early 1999, but Serbian delegates rejected the peace plan. In March, NATO began air strikes against military targets in Yugoslavia to force the government to accept the peace plan. But Serb attacks continued, and hundreds of thousands of people fled from Kosovo. In June, however, Serbian military commanders agreed to withdraw forces from Kosovo.

NATO stopped the bombing after the withdrawal had begun and sent an international peacekeeping force to Kosovo. The United Nations (UN) sent officials to serve as a temporary regional government. The refugees returned to Kosovo, but tensions ran high between Serbs and Albanians in the province. Despite the presence of peacekeepers, the tension between Serbs and Albanians frequently erupted into violence.

The fall of Milošević. As opposition to Milošević's rule grew, the government seized or interfered with opposition newspapers and broadcasters, and protesters met stiff resistance from police forces. A series of assassinations and attempted assassinations targeted mainly foes of Milošević.

A presidential election was held in September 2000. Although some opposition groups boycotted the election, Vojislav Kostunica, leader of the Democratic Opposition party, won the majority of the votes. Milošević and his allies claimed that Kostunica had not won by a large enough majority and that a run-off election was necessary. Kostunica's supporters claimed victory, and protesters demanding Milošević's resignation filled the streets of many of Serbia's major cities. Police forces were overwhelmed by the size of the protests, and Milošević was ousted from power.

In October 2000, local elections were held in Kosovo for the first time since the end of the war. Many Serbs refused to participate in these and later elections because they believed the elections unfairly favored the Albanians. The United Nations continued to administer the region.

Independence. In 2002, the leaders of Montenegro, Serbia, and Yugoslavia formed plans to create a new constitution for Yugoslavia and to rename the country Serbia and Montenegro. The plans sought to address the concerns of Montenegro's independence movement, which demanded more self-rule for the republic. Early in 2003, the parliaments of the two republics and the national parliament of Yugoslavia approved the new constitution, and Yugoslavia officially became Serbia and Montenegro.

Many people in Montenegro continued to call for independence from Serbia. In 2006, Montenegro's legislative assembly scheduled a referendum on independence to be held in May of that year. In the referendum, citizens of Montenegro voted to separate from Serbia. Montenegro declared independence shortly after the referendum. Serbia then declared its own independence.   Sabrina P. Ramet

© Roger Lemoyne, Getty Images

Ruins of a destroyed house in Kosovo remained after Serbian forces attacked villages in the province in 1998.

© Manley Photo from Shostal

Rio de Janeiro, Brazil, on Guanabara Bay, is one of South America's most scenic cities. A famous statue of Jesus overlooks Rio from Corcovado Mountain. Most South Americans live in cities.

South America

South America is the fourth largest continent in area. Only Asia, Africa, and North America are larger. It ranks fifth among the continents in population. Asia, Europe, Africa, and North America all have more people. South America covers about 12 percent of the world's land area and has about 6 percent of the total world population. The continent is divided into 12 independent countries and 2 other political units.

South America has nearly every type of landscape and climate. The world's largest tropical rain forest grows in the Amazon River Basin, which occupies about two-fifths of the continent and contains an estimated 50 percent of Earth's plant and animal species. The Atacama Desert in northern Chile is one of the driest places on Earth. Snowy peaks and active volcanoes rise along the crest of the lofty Andes Mountains of western South America. In Argentina, Uruguay, and Venezuela, rolling grasslands stretch as far as the eye can see. South America's varied landscape also includes spectacular waterfalls, huge lakes, and rocky, windswept islands.

The continent has abundant natural resources, including rich farmlands, vast timberlands, and some of the largest deposits of valuable minerals in the world. Many

James Wiley, the contributor of this article, is Associate Professor of Geography at Hofstra University. This article was critically reviewed by Brian P. Owensby, Associate Professor of History at the University of Virginia.

South American countries, however, have not taken full advantage of their natural riches.

The countries of South America vary in their level of economic development. Most of them rely on exports of minerals and agricultural products to provide income. They must import many manufactured goods, including machinery, chemicals, and fuels. Brazil is the continent's industrial giant. It produces and exports airplanes, motor vehicles, motor-vehicle parts, and other goods.

About three-fourths of South Americans live in cities. South America's urban population has soared since the

Facts in brief

Area: 6,898,000 mi^2 (17,866,000 km^2). *Greatest distances*—north-south, 4,750 mi (7,645 km); east-west, 3,200 mi (5,150 km). *Coastline*—20,000 mi (32,000 km).

Population: *Estimated 2006 population*—368,741,000; density, 53 per mi^2 (21 per km^2).

Elevation: *Highest*—Aconcagua in Argentina, 22,835 ft (6,960 m) above sea level. *Lowest*—Valdés Peninsula in Argentina, 131 ft (40 m) below sea level.

Physical features: *Chief mountain ranges*—Andes, Brazilian Highlands, Guiana Highlands. *Chief rivers*—Amazon, Madeira, Magdalena, Orinoco, Paraguay, Paraná, Pilcomayo, Purus, São Francisco, Uruguay. *Chief gulfs*—Darién, Guayaquil, San Jorge, San Matías, Venezuela. *Chief islands*—Falkland Islands, Galapagos Islands, Marajó, Tierra del Fuego. *Chief lakes*—Maracaibo, Mirim, Poopó, Titicaca. *Largest deserts*—Atacama, Patagonia. *Highest waterfalls*—Angel, Cuquenán.

Number of countries: 12.

The **Altiplano** is a high, windswept plateau between two mountain ranges in western South America. Most of this region lies in Bolivia. These llamas are grazing on the Altiplano in southern Bolivia.

© Borchi Massimo, 4Corners Images

Dense rain forests cover most of the Amazon River Basin, an area that includes northwestern Brazil and parts of Colombia, Ecuador, Peru, and Bolivia. This photograph shows Manu National Park, part of the Manu Biosphere Reserve, in southeastern Peru.

© Gregory G. Dimijian, Photo Researchers

Independent countries of South America*

Map key	Name	Area In mi²	Area In km²	Population	Capital	Date of independence
L 5	**Argentina**	1,073,518	2,780,400	38,233,000	Buenos Aires	1816
I 5	**Bolivia**	424,164	1,098,581	9,301,000	La Paz; Sucre	1825
H 7	**Brazil**	3,300,171	8,547,403	180,996,000	Brasília	1822
K 4	**Chile**	292,135	756,626	16,366,000	Santiago	1818
F 4	**Colombia**	439,737	1,138,914	46,248,000	Bogotá	1819
G 3	**Ecuador**	109,484	283,561	13,553,000	Quito	1830
E 6	**Guyana**	83,000	214,969	768,000	Georgetown	1966
J 6	**Paraguay**	157,048	406,752	5,747,000	Asunción	1811
H 4	**Peru**	496,225	1,285,216	28,360,000	Lima	1821
E 7	**Suriname**	63,037	163,265	445,000	Paramaribo	1975
L 7	**Uruguay**	67,574	175,016	3,486,000	Montevideo	1828
E 5	**Venezuela**	352,144	912,050	25,045,000	Caracas	1830

Dependencies in South America*

Map key	Name	Area In mi²	Area In km²	Population	Status
O 6	**Falkland Islands**	4,699	12,170	3,000	British overseas territory
F 7	**French Guiana**	35,135	91,000	200,000	Overseas department of France

*Each country and dependency has a separate article in *World Book*.
Populations are 2006 estimates for independent countries and 2006 and earlier estimates for dependencies based on the latest figures from official government and United Nations sources.

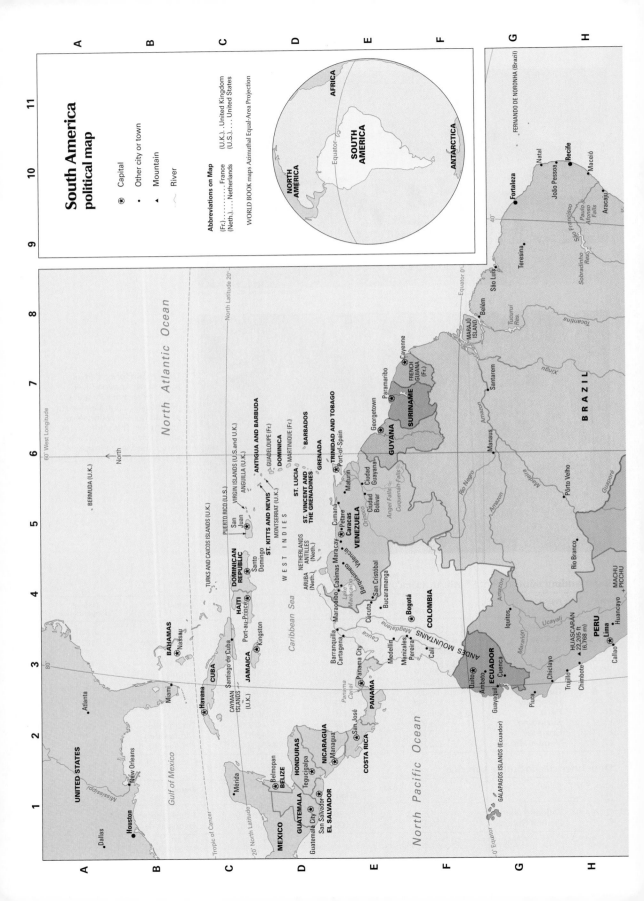

South America
political map

⊛ Capital
• Other city or town
▲ Mountain
〜 River

Abbreviations on Map

(Fr.) . . . . France   (U.K.) . . . United Kingdom
(Neth.) . . . . Netherlands   (U.S.) . . . . United States

WORLD BOOK maps Azimuthal Equal-Area Projection

NORTH AMERICA

AFRICA

SOUTH AMERICA

Equator

ANTARCTICA

FERNANDO DE NORONHA (Brazil)

North Atlantic Ocean

UNITED STATES

Dallas
Houston
New Orleans
Atlanta
Miami

Mississippi

Gulf of Mexico

Tropic of Cancer
20° North Latitude

BERMUDA (U.K.)

North
60° West Longitude
North Latitude 20°

BAHAMAS
Nassau

CUBA
Havana
Santiago de Cuba

CAYMAN
ISLANDS
(U.K.)

JAMAICA
Kingston

TURKS AND CAICOS ISLANDS (U.K.)

HAITI
Port-au-Prince

DOMINICAN
REPUBLIC
Santo
Domingo

PUERTO RICO (U.S.)
San
Juan

VIRGIN ISLANDS (U.S. and U.K.)
ANGUILLA (U.K.)

ST. KITTS AND NEVIS
MONTSERRAT (U.K.)

ANTIGUA AND BARBUDA
GUADELOUPE (Fr.)
DOMINICA
MARTINIQUE (Fr.)
ST. LUCIA
ST. VINCENT AND
THE GRENADINES
BARBADOS
GRENADA

WEST INDIES

Caribbean Sea

MEXICO
Mérida

GUATEMALA
Guatemala City

BELIZE
Belmopan

HONDURAS
Tegucigalpa

EL SALVADOR
San Salvador

NICARAGUA
Managua

COSTA RICA
San José

PANAMA
Panama City
Panama Canal

North Pacific Ocean

GALAPAGOS ISLANDS (Ecuador)
0° Equator

NETHERLANDS
ANTILLES
(Neth.)

ARUBA
(Neth.)

Maracaibo
Cabimas
Lake
Maracaibo
Barquisimeto
Valencia

Maracay
Caracas
Ciudad
Bolívar
Cumaná
Patare
Barcelona

VENEZUELA
Orinoco
Ciudad
Guayana

TRINIDAD AND TOBAGO
Port-of-Spain

Maturín

San Cristóbal
Bucaramanga
Cúcuta

COLOMBIA
Bogotá

Barranquilla
Cartagena
Medellín
Manizales
Pereira
Cali

Magdalena
Cauca

ANDES MOUNTAINS

ECUADOR
Quito
Ambato
Cuenca
Guayaquil

Angel Falls
Cuquenán Falls

Georgetown

GUYANA

Paramaribo

SURINAME

FRENCH
GUIANA
(Fr.)
Cayenne

Equator 0°

MARAJÓ
ISLAND
Belém

São Luís
Teresina

Fortaleza
Natal
João Pessoa
Recife
Maceió
Aracaju

PERU
Iquitos
Lima
Callao
Huancayo
Trujillo
Chiclayo
Chimbote
Piura

HUASCARÁN
▲ 22,205 ft
(6,768 m)

MACHU
+ PICCHU

Río Branco
Porto Velho

BRAZIL

Amazon
Río Negro
Amazon
Madeira
Guaporé
Marañón
Ucayali
Xingu
Tapajós
Tocantins
Tucuruí
Res.
Manaus
Santarem

São Francisco
Sobradinho
Res.
Paulo
Afonso
Falls

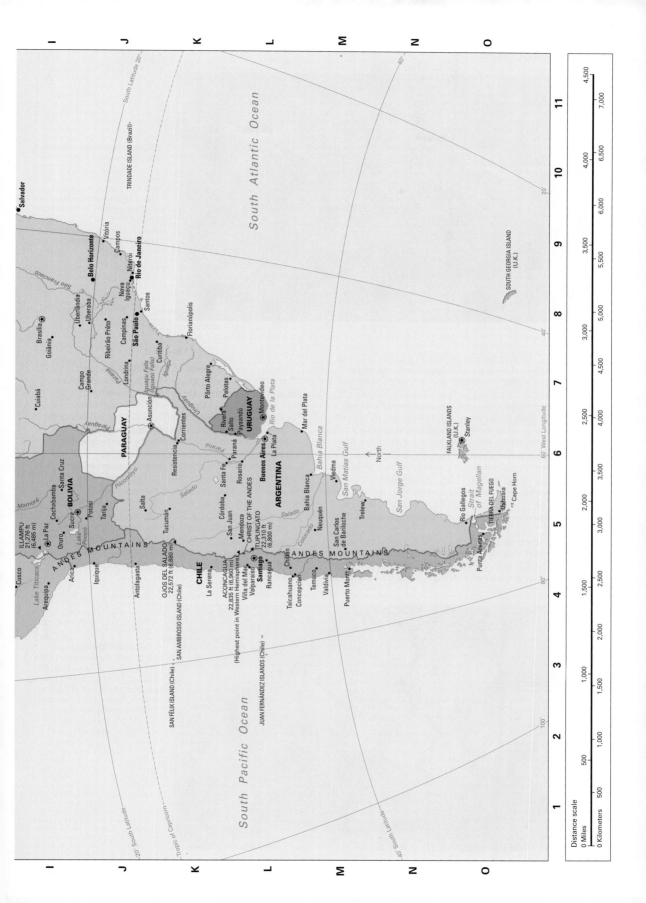

Snow-capped Aconcagua, the highest peak in the Western Hemisphere, rises 22,835 feet (6,960 meters) in the Andes Mountains in Argentina. The rugged Andes, which extend along the length of western South America, are the world's longest mountain range above sea level.

mid-1900's. This tremendous growth has occurred as millions of poor rural people have left farms and villages in search of better economic opportunities in the cities.

The standard of living in South America varies greatly. It is much higher in predominantly middle-class countries, such as Argentina and Uruguay, than in Bolivia, where most of the people struggle to earn a living. All South American countries have a small class of wealthy landowners, factory owners, and political and military leaders. But the vast majority of the people are poor. Since the mid-1900's, the gap between rich and poor has widened. But there is a growing middle class in the large cities. It consists of professional people, business people, government employees, and skilled workers.

South America is part of Latin America, a large cultural region that also includes Central America, Mexico, and the West Indies. This article discusses South America's land, climate, animal and plant life, and economy.

The land

South America covers about 6,898,000 square miles (17,866,000 square kilometers)—about one-eighth of the world's land area. The northern three-fourths of the continent lies in the tropics. The equator crosses South America about 400 miles (640 kilometers) north of the continent's widest point. Cape Horn, the southernmost tip of South America, lies only about 600 miles (970 kilometers) from Antarctica.

South America is almost totally surrounded by water. The Caribbean Sea lies to the north. The Atlantic Ocean borders South America on the northeast and east. To the south, the Drake Passage separates South America from Antarctica. The Pacific Ocean washes up against the continent's west coast. South America borders land only at the Isthmus of Panama. This narrow strip of land links Central America with Colombia, in the northwestern part of South America.

The Gran Chaco, a region of hardwood scrub forest, covers portions of Argentina, Bolivia, and Paraguay. This photograph of the Gran Chaco in Bolivia shows a tree known locally as the *toborochi*. During the dry season, the toborochi retains water in its trunk.

South America terrain map

Land region boundary
International boundary
- City
+ Elevation above sea level
▽ Depression

WORLD BOOK map

0   500   1,000   1,500   2,000   2,500 Miles
0   500   1,000   1,500   2,000   2,500   3,000   3,500   4,000 Kilometers

Physical features

Aconcagua (mountain)	F	3
Amazon River	B	4
Andes Mountains	F	3
Angel Falls	A	4
Atacama Desert	E	3
Brazilian Highlands	D	5
Cape Horn	H	4
Caribbean Sea	A	3
Cauca River	A	2
Central Plains	C	3
Chimborazo (mountain)	B	2
Cuquenán Falls	B	4
Eastern Highlands	C	5
El Misti (mountain)	D	3
Falkland Islands	H	4
Galápagos Islands	B	1
Gran Chaco (region)	E	4
Guiana Highlands	B	4
Gulf of Darién	A	2
Gulf of Guayaquil	C	1
Gulf of Venezuela	A	3
Huascarán (mountain)	C	2
Iguaçu (Iguazú) Falls	E	5
Iguaçu River	E	5
Juan Fernández Islands	F	2
La Guajira Peninsula	A	3
Lake Maracaibo	A	3
Lake Poopó	D	3
Lake Titicaca	D	3
Llanos (plains)	A	3
Magdalena River	A	3
Marajó Island	B	6
Mirim Lake	F	5
Nevado del Ruiz (volcano)	B	2
Ojos del Salado (mountain)	E	3
Orinoco River	A	4
Pampas (plain)	F	4
Paraguay River	E	4
Paraná River	E	4
Patagonia (plateau)	G	3
Pico da Bandeira (mountain)	E	6
Pilcomayo River	E	4
Point Aguja	C	2
Purus River	C	4
Rio de la Plata (estuary)	F	5
San Jorge Gulf	G	4
San Matías Gulf	G	4
São Francisco River	C	6
Selva (region)	C	3
Serra do Espinhaço (mountains)	D	6
Sertão (region)	C	7
South Georgia Island	H	6
Strait of Magellan	H	3
Tierra del Fuego (islands)	H	4
Tupungato (mountain)	F	3
Ucayali River	C	3
Uruguay River	E	5
Valdés Peninsula	G	4

© Jacques Jangoux from Peter Arnold, Inc.

The Guiana Highlands lie north of the Amazon River Basin. They consist of open grasslands with scattered trees, *shown here,* and tropical forests. Few people live in the region.

Land regions. The land surface of South America broadly resembles that of North America. Both continents have high, rugged mountain ranges in the west, vast central plains drained by mighty rivers, and older, less rugged mountains in the east. South America has three major land regions: (1) the Andes Mountains, (2) the Central Plains, and (3) the Eastern Highlands.

The Andes Mountains form a region of jagged, snow-covered peaks; broad, grassy plateaus; steep slopes; and glacier-filled valleys. The Andes stretch for about 4,500 miles (7,200 kilometers), from Venezuela in the north to Tierra del Fuego in the south. The Andes are the longest mountain range above sea level and the second highest mountain range in the world. The Mid-Atlantic Ridge, which rises from the bottom of the Atlantic Ocean, is longer, and the Himalaya in Asia are higher, than the Andes are. Many Andean peaks rise over 20,000 feet (6,100 meters) above sea level. Aconcagua, in Argentina, is the tallest mountain in the Western Hemisphere. It stands 22,835 feet (6,960 meters) above sea level.

The activity of *tectonic plates* along the western coast of South America formed the Andes over the past 10 million to 15 million years. Tectonic plates are huge, rigid pieces of Earth's crust. Their movements and interactions continue to cause volcanic eruptions and earthquakes in the Andean region.

The Andes have great economic importance for several South American countries. The mountains contain large deposits of valuable minerals, including copper, gold, lead, tin, and zinc. Farmers cultivate coffee in the rich volcanic soils on the slopes of the Andes. In the high mountain valleys and plateaus, the farmers grow thousands of distinct varieties of potatoes and such grains as barley, quinoa, rye, and wheat. Farmers also raise cattle and sheep for meat and wool.

At their widest point, the Andes divide into two mountain chains. Between these chains lies the Altiplano, a high plateau region that is cold, windswept, and nearly treeless. The Altiplano covers southeastern

Peru, western Bolivia, northeastern Chile, and northwestern Argentina. It is a difficult region to farm because few crops grow well at such high elevations.

The Central Plains extend eastward from the Andes, covering about three-fifths of South America. They are drained by huge river systems that empty into the Atlantic. Four large areas make up the Central Plains. One of these areas consists of rolling grasslands called the Llanos (pronounced *YAH nohs),* in the Orinoco River Basin of Colombia and Venezuela. These grassy plains with scattered trees provide grazing land for many large cattle ranches. Another area of the Central Plains is a lowland region called Selva, covered by tropical rain forest, in the Amazon River Basin of Bolivia, Brazil, and Peru. The third area, the Gran Chaco, consists of a hardwood scrub forest in north-central Argentina, western Paraguay, and southeastern Bolivia. The fourth area is the vast grassland of Argentina and Uruguay called the Pampas. Its fertile soil supports many farms and ranches.

The Eastern Highlands actually consist of two separate areas—the Guiana Highlands and the Brazilian Highlands. The broad Amazon River Basin separates the two areas. Mountains in the Eastern Highlands are much lower and older than the Andes.

The Guiana Highlands rise north of the Amazon basin. They lie about 3,000 to 5,000 feet (900 to 1,500 meters) above sea level. Tropical forests and open grasslands cover the region. The Guiana Highlands are thinly populated and largely undeveloped.

The Brazilian Highlands stretch south of the Amazon region to southeastern Brazil, covering nearly a fourth of the continent. The highest mountain in this region, Pico da Bandeira, rises 9,482 feet (2,890 meters) northeast of Rio de Janeiro. Most of the Brazilian Highlands, however, consist of rounded hills and flat tablelands between 1,000 and 3,000 feet (300 and 900 meters) above sea level. The southern Brazilian Highlands have fertile farms, fine cattle ranches, and rich mineral deposits.

Rivers. Five large river systems drain most of South America. These river systems are (1) the Amazon, (2) the Río de la Plata, (3) the Magdalena-Cauca, (4) the Orinoco, and (5) the São Francisco.

The Amazon River system drains about 2,700,000 square miles (7,000,000 square kilometers) of land—the world's largest drainage basin. The Amazon carries about one-fifth of the world's fresh river water. It flows some 4,000 miles (6,437 kilometers) from the Peruvian Andes to the Atlantic. Only Africa's Nile River is longer. Oceangoing ships can navigate the Amazon as far upstream as Iquitos, Peru.

The Río de la Plata system is made up of the Paraná, Paraguay, and Uruguay rivers. It provides inland water routes for Argentina, Bolivia, Brazil, Paraguay, and Uruguay. The system empties into the Río de la Plata, a bay on the southeastern coast of South America. The Itaipú Dam power plant lies on the Paraná between Paraguay and Brazil. With a generating capacity of about 12 ½ million kilowatts of electric power, the power plant is the world's largest hydroelectric plant.

The Magdalena and Cauca rivers flow northward through two fertile farming valleys in Colombia. The Cauca River flows into the Magdalena, which empties into the Caribbean Sea.

The Orinoco River runs in a broad arc through Vene-

Lake Titicaca, on the border between Bolivia and Peru, is the world's highest navigable lake at 12,507 feet (3,812 meters) above sea level. Local people use reeds growing on the lakeshore to make canoes like the one shown here.

zuela to the Atlantic. For part of its length, the Orinoco forms the border between Colombia and Venezuela. The lower Orinoco crosses the Llanos, a productive ranching area in central Venezuela. Oceangoing ships travel up the Orinoco to load iron ore at the Venezuelan river port of Ciudad Guayana.

The São Francisco River stretches for nearly 2,000 miles (3,200 kilometers) through northeastern Brazil. It flows northeastward through a large, drought-prone region and then turns toward the southeast and empties into the Atlantic. It is a broad, navigable waterway along about 900 miles (1,400 kilometers) of its middle course. Several large hydroelectric power plants generate electric power on the São Francisco.

Lakes. South America has few large lakes. Lake Maracaibo in Venezuela is the continent's largest. It covers 5,217 square miles (13,512 square kilometers). A short, narrow channel links Lake Maracaibo with the Gulf of Venezuela. Oil wells operate in the lake and along its shores.

Lake Titicaca, in the Andes, is the highest navigable lake in the world. It lies on the border between Bolivia and Peru at an elevation of 12,507 feet (3,812 meters). Crops that normally could not survive at such a high altitude grow in the area because the waters of Lake Titicaca warm the air.

Waterfalls. South America has many spectacular waterfalls. Angel Falls, in eastern Venezuela, has a longer drop than any other waterfall in the world. The water plunges 3,212 feet (979 meters) down a cliff, lands as a heavy mist, and drains into the Churún River. The world's second highest waterfall, Cuquenán Falls, also lies in southeastern Venezuela. There, the Cuquenán River drops 2,000 feet (610 meters).

Iguaçu Falls (spelled Iguazú in Argentina) are on the border between Argentina and Brazil. Many people consider these falls the most magnificent natural sight in South America. The Iguaçu River forms Iguaçu Falls when it plunges 237 feet (72 meters) along an arc about 2 miles (3.2 kilometers) wide.

Tropical rain forests cover more than a third of South America. Dense rain forests blanket most of the warm, wet Amazon River Basin and the northeast and

northwest coasts of the continent. Many valuable forest products come from the lush Amazon region.

Large areas of coastal rain forest in Brazil have been cleared for farming and ranching. In such forests, most of the soil's fertility comes from decaying leaves. As a result, the soil of the rain forest is thin and poor.

Deserts. A coastal desert extends from southern Ecuador, along the coast of Peru, to meet the Atacama Desert of northern Chile. A much smaller desert covers

Spectacular Angel Falls, in eastern Venezuela, has a longer drop than any other waterfall in the world. It plunges 3,212 feet (979 meters) down a cliff into the Churún River.

Perito Moreno Glacier, *shown here,* is in southern Patagonia, a rugged, wind-swept region of southern South America. Perito Moreno and other glaciers are major attractions at Los Glaciares National Park in Argentina.

© Damm Fridmar, 4Corners Images

WORLD BOOK map

The climate of South America

South America has a wide range of climates. Most of the continent receives ample rain. However, the Atacama Desert in northern Chile is one of the driest places on Earth. This map and legend show what the climate is like throughout the continent.

Tropical wet–Always hot and wet. Heavy precipitation well distributed throughout year.

Tropical wet and dry–Always hot, with alternate wet and dry seasons. Heavy precipitation in wet season.

Semiarid–Hot to cold. Great changes in temperature from day to night except in coastal areas. Light precipitation.

Desert–Hot to cool. Great changes in temperature from day to night except in coastal areas. Very little precipitation.

Subtropical dry summer–Hot, dry summers and mild, rainy winters. Moderate precipitation in winter.

Humid subtropical–Warm to hot summers and cool winters. Moderate precipitation in all seasons.

Humid oceanic–Moderately warm summers and generally cool winters. Moderate precipitation in all seasons.

Highland–Climate depends on altitude. Climates at various altitudes are like those found in flat terrain.

Caribbean Sea

North Atlantic Ocean

Caracas

Georgetown

Bogotá

Equator

Quito

Guayaquil

Manaus

Belém

Fortaleza

Recife

Lima

Salvador

La Paz

Brasília

Sucre

Arica, Chile
Lowest average annual rainfall
0.03 in (0.76 mm)

Rio de Janeiro

Asunción

São Paulo

Tropic of Capricorn

Córdoba

Valparaíso

Santiago

Buenos Aires

Montevideo

South Pacific Ocean

Neuquén

South Atlantic Ocean

Río Gallegos

Punta Arenas

Average January temperatures

Most of South America has hot or warm weather in January. January is a summer month south of the equator.

Degrees Fahrenheit	Degrees Celsius
Over 80	Over 27
65 to 80	18 to 27
50 to 65	10 to 18
Below 50	Below 10

Average July temperatures

July is a winter month south of the equator. South America's coldest weather occurs in the Andes and the far south.

Degrees Fahrenheit	Degrees Celsius
Over 80	Over 27
65 to 80	18 to 27
50 to 65	10 to 18
32 to 50	0 to10
Below 32	Below 0

Average yearly precipitation

Much of South America receives heavy or moderate rainfall. Drier areas are found in Argentina, Chile, and Peru.

WORLD BOOK maps

Inches	Centimeters
More than 80	More than 200
40 to 80	100 to 200
20 to 40	50 to 100
10 to 20	25 to 50
Less than 10	Less than 25

the northern part of Colombia's border with Venezuela. Patagonia, in southern Argentina, is a semidesert region. The Sertão of northeastern Brazil is a dry area covered with thorny bushes and low trees. Increasingly frequent droughts threaten to create a new desert there.

Coastline and islands. South America's long coastline has few natural harbors or bays. The best natural harbor is at Rio de Janeiro. Other bays include Todos os Santos Bay at Salvador, Brazil; the Gulf of Darién off Colombia's Caribbean coast; the mouths of the Amazon and the Río de la Plata on the Atlantic; and Ecuador's Gulf of Guayaquil on the Pacific.

South America includes several major island groups. The largest is the Tierra del Fuego group. These islands lie across the Strait of Magellan from the southernmost tip of the mainland. Argentina and Chile own them. Chile also owns the Juan Fernández Islands in the Pacific, about 400 miles (640 kilometers) off Chile's coast. The Falkland Islands, an overseas territory of the United Kingdom, lie in the South Atlantic about 320 miles (515 kilometers) east of the southern coast of Argentina. Argentina also claims these islands and calls them the *Islas Malvinas*. The Falklands and Tierra del Fuego have valuable sheep-grazing lands. The Galapagos Islands belong to Ecuador and lie in the Pacific about 600 miles (970 kilometers) off the coast of that country. They are the home of huge tortoises, sea turtles, and many other unusual animals. Marajó, an island at the mouth of the

Amazon River, belongs to Brazil. Herders raise water buffaloes on this flat, grassy island.

Climate

South America has a wide variety of climates. They range from the dry desert conditions of northern Chile to the heavy rains along the windswept southwestern coast. Steamy heat characterizes the tropical rain forest of the Amazon basin, while icy cold air surrounds the lofty, snow-capped peaks of the Andes. In general, however, most of the continent has warm weather the year around. Only in the high Andes is it always cold.

The hottest weather in South America occurs in Argentina's Gran Chaco, where the temperature reaches 110 °F (43 °C). Temperatures in the Amazon region generally range from 70 to 90 °F (21 to 32 °C) and rarely reach 100 °F (38 °C). South of the equator, summer lasts from late December to late March, and winter runs from late June to late September. In the far south of Argentina, the temperature generally ranges from 40 °F (4 °C) in July to 60 °F (16 °C) in January, but it has dropped to as low as −27 °F (−33 °C).

Most of South America receives ample rain. Rainfall averages more than 80 inches (200 centimeters) a year in four areas: (1) coastal French Guiana, Guyana, and Suriname; (2) the Amazon River Basin; (3) southwestern Chile; and (4) the coasts of Colombia and northern Ecuador. Quibdó, Colombia, the rainiest place in South America, receives more than 350 inches (890 centimeters) of rain a year. Even the wettest regions of the continent generally have a dry season, however, when there is plenty of sunshine between downpours.

In southwestern Chile, humid westerly winds blow in from the Pacific and drop most of their moisture as rain before crossing the Andes. As a result, the area east of the Andes is dry. For example, the plateaus of Patagonia, in southeastern Argentina, receive only about 10 inches (25 centimeters) of rain a year.

Coastal Peru and northern Chile are among the driest places on Earth. Arica, the northern port city of Chile, receives an average of only ³⁄₁₀₀ inch (0.76 millimeter) of rain

a year. The dry conditions in this part of the continent result from the cold Peru Current, which flows northward from Antarctica and travels along the coast. This current cools the air. Because such cool air cannot hold much moisture, little rain falls in the region.

At irregular periods, usually every two to seven years, the northward Peru Current weakens and stronger warm waters flow southward along the coast. This event is called *El Niño* (Spanish for *the child*). It usually occurs around Christmas, and its name refers to the Christ child. El Niño creates changes in the atmosphere that lead to torrential downpours in the usually dry region.

Animals of South America

This map shows some of the many kinds of mammals, birds, and reptiles that live in South America. A number of unusual and fascinating species live in the rivers, swamps, and lush tropical rain forests of the Amazon region.

WORLD BOOK map

The changes also disrupt marine life, hurting the local fishing industry.

Animal and plant life

Animals. South America has a great variety of animals, including about a fourth of all known kinds of mammals. However, it does not have such huge animals or such large herds of wild animals as are found in Africa. South America's largest wild land animal is the hoglike tapir, which lives in the Amazon region and grows about as large as a pony.

The Amazon River Basin has the greatest variety of animals on the continent. These include the capybara, the world's largest rodent, which grows up to about 4 feet (1.2 meters) long. Trees in the rain forest provide homes for many kinds of monkeys. Other unusual forest dwellers include the armadillo, the giant anteater, and the sloth. The Amazon is also the home of the green anaconda, one of the world's largest snakes. It may grow up to 30 feet (9 meters) long.

The manatee, a large water mammal, lives in the Amazon River. Amazon manatees weigh from 700 to 1,000 pounds (350 to 500 kilograms). Another large inhabitant of the river is the arapaima fish, which grows more than

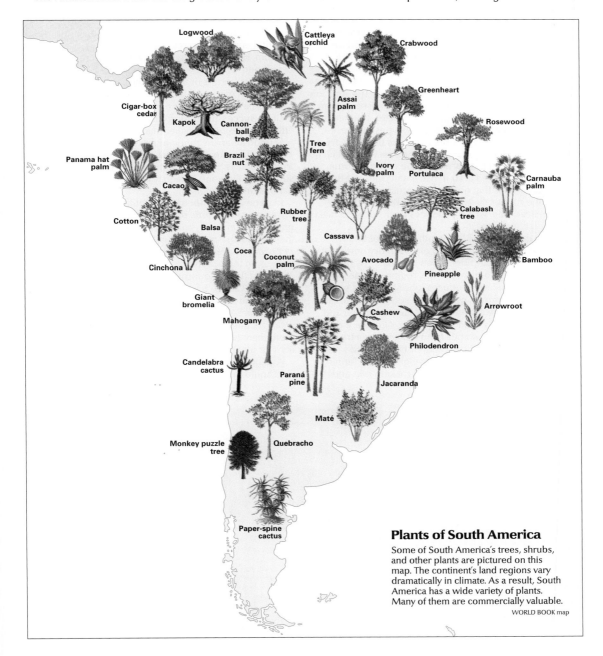

Plants of South America

Some of South America's trees, shrubs, and other plants are pictured on this map. The continent's land regions vary dramatically in climate. As a result, South America has a wide variety of plants. Many of them are commercially valuable.

WORLD BOOK map

7 feet (2.1 meters) long and commonly weighs more than 200 pounds (90 kilograms). Piranha also swim in the river. A school of these small fish may attack a much larger animal and devour its flesh, leaving only the bones.

Many kinds of birds live in South America. They include egrets, flamingos, hummingbirds, parrots, and toucans. The large, ostrichlike rhea lives in the Argentine Pampas. Ecuador's Galapagos Islands support giant tortoises, sea turtles, crabs, iguanas, and a great variety of birds. Many of these animals are *endemic* species, meaning that they live nowhere else on Earth.

The vicuña and the guanaco, two wild members of the camel family, live high in the Andes. Scientists believe the alpaca and the llama, which were *domesticated* (tamed) in South America, may be descended from the guanaco. Alpacas produce fine wool. Llamas can carry loads of as much as 130 pounds (60 kilograms). The guinea pig also was domesticated in South America.

Plants. South America has a great variety of plants, many of which grow on no other continent. The Amazon River Basin, sometimes referred to as "the green ocean," contains tens of thousands of plant species. Countless kinds of orchids and more than 2,500 types of trees grow in the Amazon rain forest. Many of the trees are hardwoods, including mahogany and rosewood, which are used in making fine furniture. The wood of some South American trees is so dense that it does not float. Other useful trees that grow in the Amazon River Basin include the rubber tree, the towering Brazil-nut tree, and the cacao tree, which produces beans used to make cocoa and chocolate.

Many valuable plants live in other parts of South America as well. The sisal plant grows in dry northeastern Brazil. It produces fibers used in making twine. The pineapple plant also grows in this region, as does the carnauba palm, which produces lubricating and polishing waxes. Coca shrubs grow in the subtropical forests. Their leaves are the source both of illegal cocaine and of other, legal drugs used in medicine. *Quinine,* a drug used to treat malaria, comes from the cinchona tree found in Ecuador and Peru. Ecuador is the world's largest producer of balsa, a lightweight wood. Tannin, a chemical used in tanning hides and making inks and dyes, comes from the quebracho tree of Argentina and Paraguay. The softwood of the Paraná pine of southern Brazil is used in the construction industry.

Several commercially valuable plants were brought to South America from other continents. These useful plants include bananas and coffee—two of South America's most important export crops. In the mid-1800's, people brought the eucalyptus tree from Australia to South America. It has become common over much of the continent and is a valuable source of firewood.

Economy

South America has abundant natural resources. These include vast stretches of fertile land; raw materials, such as hardwoods and minerals, used in manufacturing; and plentiful energy resources, such as natural gas and petroleum. However, many of these resources remain undeveloped.

All the countries of South America have developing economies. Argentina, Brazil, Chile, Uruguay, and Venezuela have the most developed economies, which include successful modern manufacturing industries. Other nations have smaller manufacturing sectors and rely upon a narrow range of agricultural and mineral exports for income. They purchase manufactured goods from overseas. Some also import food and energy resources. Bolivia and Paraguay are the least developed nations on the continent.

In general, the countries of South America have a lower *gross domestic product* (GDP)—the value of all goods and services produced in a country in a year—than do North American and European countries. The *per capita GDP*—the GDP divided by the total population—is an indication of a country's standard of living. In 2004, 5 of the 12 countries in South America had a per capita GDP above $3,000. Chile's was the highest, at $5,839. That same year, the per capita GDP of the United States was $40,245. In all of South America's countries, wealth is unevenly distributed. A few people earn far more than the per capita average, but a great majority earn far less.

Agriculture. About four-fifths of South America's land could be used for agriculture. However, only about

© Ron Giling from Peter Arnold, Inc.

Modern farming methods have become common on large farms in South America. These men in Suriname are using a combine to harvest rice. Altogether, large farms cover much more of South America's good farmland than small farms do.

one-third is actually used for agriculture, and most of that serves as pasture for grazing animals. Most land in South America is divided into large properties called *latifundios,* which are owned by a small percentage of the population. Latifundios include *haciendas* (large farms or country estates); plantations, often owned by foreign companies; and technologically sophisticated farms controlled by *agribusinesses* (companies that produce, transport, distribute, and sell farm products).

Small properties called *minifundios* greatly outnumber the latifundios. Minifundios generally provide a single family with food. They often employ traditional farming methods that rely upon human and animal labor. Minifundios cover much less of South America's good farmland than latifundios do.

Millions of rural South Americans do not own any land. They work for wages on the latifundios or as *sharecroppers,* receiving a percentage of the crops they raise as payment. Since the mid-1900's, many rural South Americans have moved to cities in search of better job opportunities. By the early 2000's, only about one-fifth of the continent's population lived in rural areas.

During the colonial period, which lasted from the 1500's to the 1800's in South America, farmers grew crops primarily for foreign markets. Each country produced just a few crops, such as cacao, coffee, cotton, and sugar. The invention of refrigerated shipping in the late 1800's made it possible to transport such perishable goods as fruits and meats over long distances.

Today, Ecuador exports more bananas than any other country in the world. Colombia is a leading banana exporter as well. Argentina, Brazil, and Colombia produce beef for European markets. Brazil and Colombia are among the world's leading exporters of coffee. Wheat and corn are the chief grains produced for consumption in South America. Farmers also cultivate potatoes and rice for domestic markets.

Since the late 1900's, many farmers have begun growing nontraditional crops. Several countries, including Colombia, cultivate flowers for sale in North America and Europe. Chile produces kiwi fruit, citrus fruits, and grapes for export during the winter months in the Northern Hemisphere. Argentina and Chile produce wine grapes, and soybeans for animal feed are a chief export of Argentina and Brazil.

Many farmers earn high profits cultivating such illegal crops as coca, used to produce cocaine; poppies, used to make heroin; and marijuana. Efforts to encourage

Agriculture and fishing in South America

This map and legend show the major uses of land in South America. The map locates the chief agricultural products. The most important crops and livestock appear in large type. The map also shows the major fishing areas and kinds of fish caught.

Commercial agriculture

Subsistence agriculture

Cereals and livestock

Grazing land

Chiefly forestland

Generally unproductive land

Fishing

growers to substitute legal crops for illegal ones often fail because the illegal crops earn high profits.

Manufacturing. Until the 1800's, Spain and Portugal hindered the development of manufacturing in South America, preferring instead to export the continent's raw materials. During the 1800's and early 1900's, newly independent countries continued this practice. At the same time, such nations as the United Kingdom and the United States discouraged the development of South American industry. In doing so, they hoped to limit local competition with their own manufactured goods. It was not until the 1930's and 1940's that South American countries began manufacturing goods for domestic use and for export to North America and Europe. Argentina, Brazil, and Chile emerged as the most industrialized nations.

In the early and mid-1900's, South American governments closely controlled their national economies. They often owned manufacturing firms, as well as airlines, banks, and utility companies. Governments tried to protect their industries from foreign competition by imposing *tariffs* (taxes) on imports and giving *subsidies* (aid payments) to domestic firms. They had to take out loans to pay these subsidies. In the 1980's, many countries could not repay their loans, which led to a debt crisis.

Following the crisis, nations began to *privatize* their industries. Privatization involves the sale of government-owned industries or portions of them to private, often foreign, companies.

Today, governments encourage the manufacture of goods for export, and South America makes a greater variety of products than ever before. Brazil, one of the world's leading industrial countries, produces airplanes, automobiles, military weapons, and televisions. São Paolo, Brazil, is South America's chief manufacturing center. In most other South American nations, manufacturing includes such consumer goods as beverages, furniture, processed foods, shoes, and textiles.

Several countries have created *export processing zones* where foreign-owned factories operate. These factories employ many South Americans. The multinational firms that own them benefit from favorable taxation policies and lower labor costs.

Mining. The mountains of South America have long been a source of mineral wealth. Deposits of gold and silver attracted the Spanish and Portuguese to the area in colonial times. Today, the Amazon River Basin is another significant source of mineral wealth.

South America's mineral resources are distributed un-

Mining and manufacturing in South America

This map locates South America's chief mineral resources and manufacturing centers. Major mineral-producing areas are indicated in large type, and lesser ones in small type. Manufacturing centers are printed in red.

Petroleum is a valuable export of several South American countries. Lake Maracaibo, in northwestern Venezuela, has many oil wells, *shown here.* Argentina, Colombia, and Ecuador also export oil.

evenly. Paraguay possesses few useful minerals. Brazil and Venezuela are leading producers of iron ore, and Brazil mines large amounts of manganese. Brazil, Guyana, Suriname, and Venezuela are among world leaders in mining bauxite, used to make aluminum. Chile is a major source of copper, mined in the Atacama Desert. Peru has copper deposits and exports zinc as well. Colombia is a leading source of emeralds, and Amazonian gold is emerging as a significant export.

Global demand for the continent's energy resources, particularly oil and natural gas, has increased since the late 1900's. Venezuela is one of the world's top exporters of oil. Argentina, Colombia, and Ecuador also export oil, while Argentina and Bolivia export large quantities of natural gas.

Mining generates great wealth for a small portion of the population and for large corporations. Because mining is highly mechanized, it creates only a few jobs. It does, however, cause substantial environmental damage. For example, mercury and other toxins used to process mineral ores pollute South America's water.

Forestry and fishing. Brazil is South America's chief producer of forestry products. All the countries in the Amazon River Basin have forestry industries that produce such hardwoods as greenheart, mahogany, and rosewood. Builders use the extremely dense greenheart, found in the Guiana Highlands, to construct ships and piers. Softwood pine trees grow in southern South America.

South American forests yield many products besides wood. These include coconuts, dates, edible nuts, oils, and ingredients used to make medicines and other pharmaceutical products. The sap of rubber trees, which grow naturally in the Amazon rain forest, is used to make rubber tires. This sap is called *latex.*

During the debt crisis of the late 1900's, many countries leased land to foreign logging firms that cut down vast areas of trees. Large-scale logging caused such environmental problems as soil erosion, water pollution, and the extinction of some species of animals, plants, and microbes. Since then, many South American countries have begun to plant trees in *afforestation* and *reforestation* programs.

Chile and Peru have South America's most valuable fishing industries. The cool Peru Current (also called the Humboldt Current), which flows along South America's west coast, is rich in *plankton* and other small organisms that many fish eat. The anchovetta, a fish used to make oil and animal feed, is one important commercial variety. Both freshwater and ocean fish provide protein in the diets of many South Americans. But decades of overfishing have reduced fish stocks worldwide and caused a decline in South America's fishing industry since the late 1900's.

Service industries employ more than half of South America's work force. They include banking, commercial sales, government services, health care, and tourism. Many service jobs, such as cleaning and food preparation, require few skills and pay low wages. Such

Boats are an important means of transportation for people and goods in South America. The cargo ships and fishing boats shown here are docked at Valparaíso, Chile's leading seaport.

industries as data processing, legal services, and telecommunications, which require high levels of education, are becoming increasingly important.

South American cities are home to many underemployed people who lack full-time jobs. They often work in the *informal economy* that exists outside of government control and taxation structures. The informal economy provides low-cost services to many South American professional people, who earn less than their counterparts in North America and Europe. The informal economy also includes such illegal activities as *prostitution* (the performance of sexual acts for payment) and the sale of illegal drugs.

International trade. The countries of North America and Europe have long ranked as South America's leading trading partners. International trade between South American countries is also important. In addition, Middle Eastern countries buy many South American products. Trade with such Pacific nations as Australia, China, Japan, and South Korea has increased since the late 1900's, as the economies of those countries have grown stronger. Major exports of South America include agricultural, forest, and mineral products. Some major imports are chemicals, foodstuffs, fuels, machinery, and transportation equipment.

All the countries of South America are members of the World Trade Organization (WTO), which sets rules for international trade and works to reduce trade barriers between countries. In 1991, Argentina, Brazil, Paraguay, and Uruguay formed a trade association called Mercosur. Mercosur strives to increase trade among members and promotes closer commercial ties with the European Union. The Andean Community, another trade association, was founded by Bolivia, Colombia, Ecuador, Peru, and Venezuela. The Andean Community has had less success increasing trade among members because several of its members produce similar goods. Venezuela withdrew from the group in 2006.

Transportation. The geography of South America presents many obstacles to transportation. Rugged mountains, dense rain forests, and harsh deserts make it difficult to construct efficient transportation systems. The continent lacks extensive rail lines. Those railroads that do exist are aging lines in need of modernization. For this reason, ships carry most of South America's imports and exports. Cargo and passenger boats travel up and down the Amazon River. Chile uses ferries to link its central region to the far south, where the irregular coastline has no paved roads.

Airlines provide passenger service within and between countries and transport some cargo. Most South Americans cannot afford to fly, nor do they own automobiles. For them, buses offer a cheap alternative. Buses travel extensively throughout the continent, on mountain roads as well as on highways. They are also the primary means of transportation in urban areas. Long-distance buses in Argentina, Brazil, Chile, and Peru provide comfortable transportation. The number of automobiles in South America is increasing, and traffic congestion and air pollution are problems in large cities. Subway systems operate in a few major cities.

Increased trade between South American nations has made it necessary to improve transportation within the continent. Countries have begun to cooperate to integrate their transportation systems and build roads to carry goods across borders and to the coast. Chile is building a huge port facility called a *megaport* on its northern coast at Mejillones. The megaport will serve as a point of access to the Pacific Ocean for Argentina, Bolivia, Brazil, and Chile.

Communication. Books, magazines, and newspapers are important means of communication in South America. In most countries, at least 90 percent of adults can read and write. Radio and television are other major means of communication.

Television has grown in significance, especially in urban areas, where it is common even in poor neighborhoods. In 2005, Venezuela launched Telesur, a TV network that broadcasts news from a Latin American point of view. Argentina, Cuba, and Uruguay also own shares of Telesur. Soccer matches and soap operas called *telenovelas* are the most popular television programs in South America.

Telephone service extends to all but the most remote communities in South America. A growing number of people use cellular phones to do their daily business. Since the mid-1990's, use of the Internet has grown.

James Wiley

Critically reviewed by Brian P. Owensby

Questions

What percentage of the world's plant species grow in the Amazon River Basin?

What are three animals domesticated in South America?

Why are ships an important means of transportation in South America?

What is Mercosur? The Andean Community?

Which countries of South America have the most developed economies?

What are South America's three major land regions, and how does the continent's land surface resemble that of North America?

What portion of the world's fresh river water does the Amazon River carry?

How does *El Niño* affect the weather in coastal Peru and northern Chile?

What are *latifundios* and *minifundios*?

How much of the land in South America is used for pasture and other agricultural purposes?

Additional resources

Level I

Petersen, David. *South America.* Children's Pr., 1998.
Sammis, Fran. *South America.* Benchmark Bks., 2000.
Sayre, April P. *South America.* 21st Century Bks., 1999. *South America, Surprise!* Millbrook, 2003.

Level II

Archer, Christon I., ed. *The Wars of Independence in Spanish America.* Scholarly Resources, 2000.
Heenan, Patrick, and Lamontagne, Monique, eds. *The South America Handbook.* Fitzroy Dearborn, 2002.
Lavallée, Danièle. *The First South Americans.* Univ. of Ut. Pr., 2000.
Parodi, Carlos A. *The Politics of South American Boundaries.* Praeger, 2002.
Santana, Gui, ed. *Tourism in South America.* Haworth Hospitality Pr., 2001.
South America, Central America, and the Caribbean. Europa. Published annually.
Wilbert, Johannes, ed. *Encyclopedia of World Cultures, Vol. 7: South America.* Macmillan, 1994.

Index

How to use the index

This index covers the contents of the 2005, 2006, and 2007 editions.

Each index entry gives the edition year and the page number or page numbers—for example, **Merkel, Angela 07:** 190, 204. This means that information on this person may be found on the pages indicated in the 2007 edition.

When there are many references to a topic, they are grouped alphabetically by clue words under the main topic. For example, the clue words under **Mexico** group the references to that topic under several subtopics.

A page number in italic type means that there is an article on this topic on the page or pages indicated. For example, there is an Update article on **Middle East** on pages 280-284 of the 2007 edition. The page numbers in roman type indicate additional references to this topic in other articles in the volumes covered.

The indications (il.) or (ils.) mean that the reference on this page is to an illustration or illustrations only, as in **Minneapolis** in the 2007 edition.

An entry followed by WBE refers to a new or revised *World Book Encyclopedia* article in the supplement section, as in **Montenegro.** This means that there is a *World Book Encyclopedia* article on pages 449-450 of the 2007 edition.

The "see" and "see also" cross-references refer the reader to other entries in the index. For example, information on music will be found under **Classical music** and **Popular music,** while additional information on museums will be found under **Art.**

Acknowledgments

The publishers acknowledge the following sources for illustrations. Credits read from top to bottom, left to right, on their respective pages. An asterisk (*) denotes illustrations and photographs created exclusively for this edition. All maps, charts, and diagrams were prepared by the staff unless otherwise noted.

8 © Chip Somodevilla, Getty
9 AP/Wide World
10 © Lucas Jackson, Landov
13-14 AP Wide World
17 © J. Emilio Flores, Getty
18 AP/Wide World
21 © Mast Irham, Corbis
22 AP/Wide World
25 © Pavel Wolberg, Corbis
26 AP/Wide World
29 © Salah Malkawi, Getty
30 © Jung Yeon-Je, Getty
33-34 AP/Wide World
39 © Jose Cendon, Getty
46 © Lealisa Westerhoff, Getty
48 AP/Wide World
49 © Marco di Lauro, Getty; © Tara Todras-Whitehill, Landov
51 AP/Wide World
52-56 © SuperStock
57 © Farrell Grehan, Alamy; © Daniel Acker, Landov
58 © SuperStock
59 © Shutterstock
60 © SuperStock
61 © Corbis; © Sarah Hadley, Alamy
62 © SuperStock
63 © John James, Alamy
64 AP/Wide World
65 © John Edward Linden, Alamy
67 © John Moore, Getty
70 AP/Wide World
71 © Chris Hondros, Getty
73 © Landov
76 NASA
77 © Chris Butler, Photo Researchers
79 © Karen Brook, Newspix
81 © Steve Holland, Landov
86 AP/Wide World
91 © Bill Greenblatt, Landov
92 AP/Wide World
95 © John Gress, Landov
96 © Lucy Nicholson, Landov
97 © Anatoly Maltsev, Corbis
104 AP/Wide World
105 © Robert Ariail, *The State*
107 © Robert McGouey, Alamy
113 © J. P. Moczulski, Landov
120 AP/Wide World
122 © Joe Chan, Landov
123 © Landov
127 AP/Wide World
129 © SuperStock; © Heinz-Peter Bader, Landov
130 Marty Sohl, Metropolitan Opera
133 © Jonathan Ernst, Landov
139 © James Watt, Ocean Stock
143 AP/Wide World
146 Shanghai City Dance Company Ltd. (www.shcitydance.com)
148 © Corbis; © Carlo Allegri, Getty
149 © Monty Brinton, Landov; © Eddie Adams, Corbis; © Landov
150 AP/Wide World; © Donna Coveney, MIT News Office
151 © Getty

152 © Bob Gomel, Getty; © Landov
153 AP/Wide World
154 © Gerald Schumann, Landov; © Alfred Eisenstaedt, Getty; © Landov
155 © Getty; AP/Wide World
156 © Bernard Gotfryd, Getty; © Getty
157 © Ed Clark, Getty; © Landov
158 White House/Gerald R. Ford Library
159 © Corbis
160 © Alex Wong, Getty
165 © John Moore, Getty
168 © Getty
169 © Roger Ressmeyer, Corbis
175 © Chip Somodevilla, Getty
178 © Shutterstock
180 © Getty; © Scott Olson, Getty
182 U.S. Fish & Wildlife Service; © Shutterstock
183 © Shutterstock; © J. Franca, Landov
185 © Shutterstock
186 © Dennis Brack, Landov
187 © Scott Olson, Getty
189 © Kimberly White, Landov
191 © Victor Tonelli, Landov
195 © Piotr Snuss, Landov
197 AP/Wide World
199 © Matt Sullivan, Landov
203 © Bay Ismoyo, Getty
206-207 © Michael Melford, Getty
209 © Gabriel Bouys, Getty
212-213 National Snow and Ice Data Center
214 © Bennett Dean, Corbis; NASA
216 © J. Johnson, Animals Animals
217 © Getty
218 © Andy Lyons, Getty
220-221 © Joe Raedle, Getty
222 © Andy Clark, Landov
224 © Paul J. Richards, Getty
226 © Arnold Michaelis, Getty
228 © J. P. Moczulski, Landov
230 AP/Wide World
232 © Zhang Jun, Landov
235 © Landov
237 AP/Wide World; © Dia Hamid, Getty
238 AP/Wide World
240 © Haitham Mussawi, Getty
242 © Chris Hondros, Getty
243 © Dario Pignatelli, Reuters
245 © Paul J. Richards, Getty
248 © Getty
252 © Shutterstock
253 AP/Wide World
256 AP/Wide World; © Adalberto Roque, Getty
260 AP/Wide World
263 © Marcos Brindicci, Landov
264 © Carlos Hugo Vaca, Landov
265 © Jorge Silva, Landov
267 © Diego Giudice, Landov
268 © Thomas Dworzak, Magnum
275 © Valdrin Xhemaj, Corbis
279 © Susana Gonzalez, Getty
282 © Uriel Sinai, Getty
283 © Samuel Aranda, Getty; © Issam Kobeisy, Landov
285 © Ivan Milutinovic, Landov

288-289 ZUMA Press
291 © Khin Maung Win, Getty
292 AP/Wide World
294 © Stephen Chernin, Getty
295-298 AP/Wide World
299 © Mario Tama, Getty
300 AP/Wide World
304 © Donald Miralle, Getty; AP/Wide World
305 © Eric Feferberg, Getty
306-307 AP/Wide World
308 © David Gray, Landov; © Joe Klamar, Getty
309-311 AP/Wide World
312 © Getty
313 © Torsten Silz, Getty
315 AP/Wide World
317 Beth Romey, University of Chicago
319 © Matthew Staver, Landov; © Ezio Petersen, Landov
320 © Andrew Gombert, Landov
321 © John Paul Filo, Landov; © Peter Morgan, Landov
322-323 AP/Wide World
324 AP/Wide World; © Thaier al-Sudani, Landov
326 © Larry Downing, Landov
328 © Michael D. Kennedy, Landov
332 © Caio Leal, Getty
338 © Robert Galbraith, Landov
340 © Dario Pignatelli, Landov
342 © Peter Macdiarmid, Getty
344 © Mark Wilson, Getty
345 © Andrija Ilic, Corbis
347 © Lee Jae-Won, Landov
350 © Wolfgang Kumm, Landov
352 © Jaime Razuri, Getty; © Thomas Lohnes, Getty
353 © Dylan Martinez, Landov; © Daniel Garcia, Getty
354-355 © Getty
358 NASA
361-375 AP/Wide World
376 © Jamie Squire, Getty
378 © Corbis
380 © Joan Marcus
382 © Steven Evans
383 AP/Wide World
387 © Sergei Supinsky, Getty
389 © Tim Graham, Getty; Landov
390 © Jeff J. Mitchell, Getty
397 AP/Wide World
398 © Lucas Jackson, Landov
402 AP/Wide World
403 © Robert W. Ginn, PhotoEdit; © David Young-Wolff, PhotoEdit
404 © Jeff Topping, Getty; © David Kadlubowski, Corbis
405 Mary Evans Picture Library
406 © Jim Ruymen, Landov
408 © Jason Reed, Landov
410 © Larry Downing, Landov
412 © Jean-Philippe Ksiazek, Getty; AP/Wide World
413 © William Thomas Cain, Getty; © Doug Pensinger, Getty